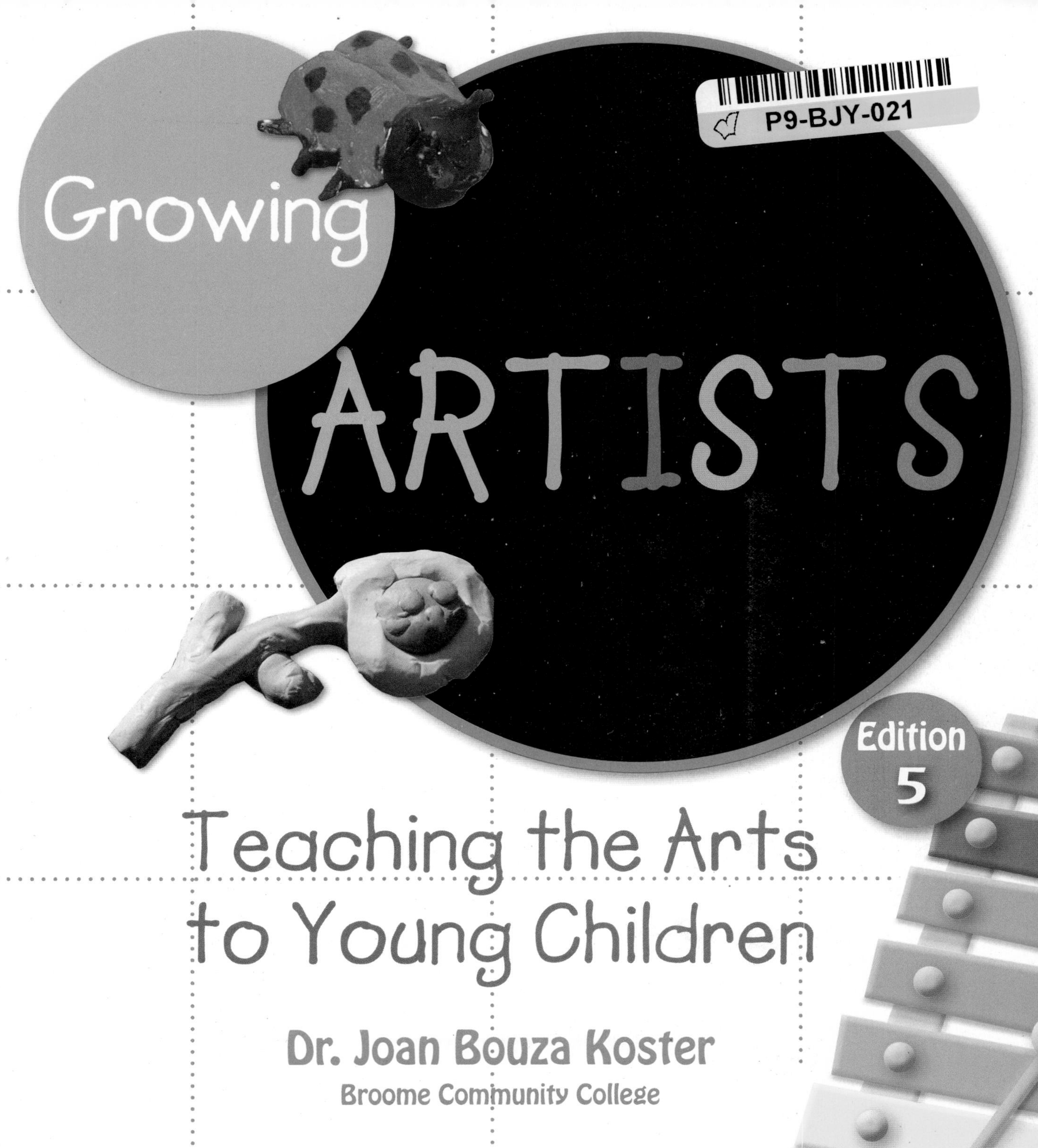

Growing ARTISTS

Teaching the Arts to Young Children

Edition 5

Dr. Joan Bouza Koster

Broome Community College

WADSWORTH
CENGAGE Learning™

Australia • Brazil • Japan • Korea • Mexico • Singapore • Spain • United Kingdom • United States

Growing Artists: Teaching the Arts to Young Children, Fifth Edition
Dr. Joan Bouza Koster

Publisher/Executive Editor: Linda Schreiber-Ganster

Acquisitions Editor: Mark Kerr

Assistant Editor: Joshua Taylor

Editorial Assistant: Genevieve Allen

Media Editor: Melanie Cregger

Marketing Manager: Kara Kindstrom

Marketing Assistant: Dimitri Hagnere

Marketing Communications Manager: Heather L. Baxley

Content Project Management: PreMediaGlobal

Art Director: Jennifer Wahi

Print Buyer: Karen Hunt

Rights Acquisition Specialist (Text, Image): Thomas McDonough

Production Service/Compositor: PreMediaGlobal

Cover Designer: Jeff Bane

Cover Image: © Dreamstime/ Dr. Joan Bozua Koster

Library of Congress Control Number: 2011920575

ISBN-13: 978-1-111-30274-0

ISBN-10: 1-111-30274-X

Wadsworth
20 Davis Drive
Belmont, CA 94002-3098
USA

Cengage Learning is a leading provider of customized learning solutions with office locations around the globe, including Singapore, the United Kingdom, Australia, Mexico, Brazil and Japan. Locate your local office at **www.cengage.com/global**

Cengage Learning products are represented in Canada by Nelson Education, Ltd.

For your course and learning solutions, visit **www.cengage.com**

Purchase any of our products at your local college store or at our preferred online store **www.cengagebrain.com**

Printed in the United States of America
1 2 3 4 5 6 7 15 14 13 12 11

Contents

Studio Page Guide

Preface

There was a time when play was king and early childhood was its domain. Fantasy was practiced leisurely and openly in a language unique to the kingdom. It is still spoken in Mrs. Ruparel-Sen's kindergarten.

Vivian Gussey Paley in A Child's Work, *University of Chicago Press, 2004*

INTRODUCTION TO THE FIFTH EDITION

Thus begins Paley's introduction to her story about a kindergarten teacher who values the creative arts and celebrates the role they play in the social, psychological, and intellectual development of children.

Teachers play a tremendous role in nurturing children's artistic and creative potential. They do so by deciding actively to provide arts experiences for their students, and by carefully planning those activities. *Growing Artists: Teaching the Arts to Young Children* provides the framework that early childhood educators need in order to design effective arts programs for children from infancy to age eight, which respect the individual pace of young artists. Throughout there is an emphasis on understanding how to foster children's development in the arts by offering open-ended arts activities and by creating a safe, sensory-appealing environment in which creativity will be nurtured. It presents an approach to arts education in which the inclusion of the visual art, music, dance, and dramatic works created by diverse peoples and cultures is valued, and where arts activities are integrated into the total curriculum in a wide variety of engaging ways.

WHAT IS THE APPROACH OF THIS BOOK?

In order that this relationship between child artists and guiding adults can be deep and meaningful, this book provides a theoretical perspective, grounded in the work of Piaget, Vygotsky, Gardner, and Kindler, and suggests effective practices drawn from the National Standards for the Arts and the National Association for the Education of Young Children's recommendations for developmentally appropriate curriculum.

WHAT IS THE PLAN OF THIS BOOK?

This book is designed to be an easy-to-use resource for both those preparing to be early childhood teachers and those currently working in the field. The ideas, methods, and suggested practices found in each chapter provide a springboard for readers to design their own curriculum. As such, this book goes beyond the presentation of isolated "projects." It provides child-tested, traditional, and innovative arts experiences that serve as both a resource and model for those creating their own repertoire of activities.

To accomplish this, the book is divided into three sections of four chapters each, which address the interrelated areas of knowledge needed in order to successfully introduce young children to the arts. The first section, "Introduction to the Arts," presents the theory and practice upon which exemplary arts education is based. It looks at learning theory, creativity, developmentally appropriate practice, and aesthetic development in young children. The second section, "Teaching the Arts," examines the components that make up a vibrant, inclusive arts program. It explains how to create an integrated arts program in a physical and social environment in which all children, including those from diverse backgrounds and those with special needs, can be successful. The third section, "Exploring the Arts," looks at the basic elements and concepts of music, creative movement, drama, and visual art, and presents ways to teach these to young children. The four chapters in this section are rich in activity ideas and present sample plans that show how to incorporate the theory, creative processing, developmentally appropriate practice, assessment methods, and inclusive teaching methods explained in the previous two sections.

Each of the 12 chapters begins with a series of guiding questions about art education for young children. These provide a guide for meaningful reading and discussion.

The first chapter sets the stage for developing a rich, integrated arts program for young children by introducing current research and educational theory as it relates to the development of young children and the teaching of art. It includes an example of how such a program would look in an early childhood program. The ensuing chapters delve into topics related to the effective teaching of art to infants, toddlers, preschoolers, kindergarteners, and primary school students.

Chapter 2 introduces the creative process as a way of understanding why children create the art they do and as a framework for structuring arts activities to allow creative growth. It addresses the role of the teacher and positive ways teachers can respond to young artists in the context of creative development.

Chapter 3 reviews what is known about the artistic development of young children and identifies the factors that influence how children approach arts activities. Authentic assessment using a variety of methods, including portfolios, is provided.

Chapter 4 examines the aesthetic experience of the arts and presents activities to develop children's sensory perception and their sensitivity to the arts elements and the environment around them.

Creating a community of caring artists is addressed in Chapter 5, which focuses on how arts activities can enhance social growth. It presents practices that increase cooperative behaviors, accommodate children with special needs, use art to deal with bias, and provide holiday art activities that are inclusive and open-ended.

How to create a setting conducive to the growth of children as artists and how to present children's work is detailed in Chapter 6. This chapter emphasizes the need to see the arts as an integral part of how teaching space is designed and arranged.

Chapter 7 provides exciting hands-on activities that open children's eyes to the varied artworks created by people from many cultures, times, and places. It provides information on organizing field trips and arranging guest artists' visits.

Integrating the arts into the curriculum is the focus of Chapter 8, which presents ways to teach an arts-rich curriculum through emergent curriculum design, integrated teaching, and the project approach. Ways to celebrate learning are shared, including creating documentation panels and holding arts celebrations.

Chapter 9 introduces the teaching of the visual arts and provides practical ways to help children express themselves through drawing, painting, modeling, constructed sculpture, collage, printmaking, computer art, and the fiber arts.

Chapter 10 focuses on the elements of music and how to introduce young children to music making and appreciation through listening to music, playing instruments, and singing.

In Chapter 11 creative movement and open-ended dance activities are explored.

Finally, Chapter 12 examines the role of the dramatic arts, including pantomime, guided imagery, narrative drama, and storytelling in the literacy development of young children and presents creative ways to foster dramatic play through puppetry, mask making, and performance.

NEW TO THIS EDITION

Topics that have been added to or updated in this new edition include:

- More in-depth coverage of the National Standards for Arts Education.

- Updated research on the importance of the arts in cognitive development, social development, and in the physical and mental health of young children. New research on artistic development is presented. More ample activity plans for one-on-one, exploration centers, and whole group arts experiences in music, dance, drama, and the visual arts with suggested assessments.
- Annotated references to in-print children's books on the arts have been updated to reflect the newest books available on the arts
- New appendix of recipes for safe, effective arts materials
- Updated appendix on Teacher Resources includes many Internet sources.

FEATURES

Within each chapter, specific information has been highlighted in order to attract attention to important ideas, present supplementary material, and provide an easy reference for the reader. Look for the following featured material.

Young Artists at Work

Short vignettes, based on the author's observations of real children in real situations, provide a vivid picture of the kind of child-art interactions most teachers can expect to find in their rooms. These vignettes lead into discussions of the philosophical basis and organizational needs of a creative and an open-ended arts program.

Quotations

Interspersed throughout the book are carefully chosen quotations from a wide variety of sources. These are designed to provoke, inspire, and introduce the wide range of thought concerning the topic of early childhood art. The quotations provide a representative survey of the researchers, educators, philosophers, and writers, both past and present, who have been involved with children and their art.

Further Reading

The books listed with annotations at the end of each chapter have been specifically selected either to expand on the ideas and concepts presented in the chapter or to further the reader's personal artistic and creative development. Readers are encouraged to read as many of these books as possible, both to become well grounded in the field and to learn more about themselves as artists. Instructors may choose to use these books as supplements to the text or as recommended reading.

Studio Pages

Each chapter includes activities designed to help readers think further about the information presented in each chapter. These include answering questions about personal beliefs and experiences, applying information from the chapter to real-life situations, and carrying out systematic observations in actual classroom settings.

Teaching in Action

These descriptions of teaching illustrate how the ideas in this book work in the reality of the classroom. They are taken directly from practicing teachers' lesson plans, teaching journals, and taped interviews.

Highlighted Information

In-text icons make the following features easier to find and use.

Arts Words. Interspersed throughout the text are relevant words important in the arts and their definitions or examples of how to use them.

Arts Tool Box. Arts tools and materials that relate to the arts activities being discussed are described in terms of age appropriateness, safety, and possible uses.

Book Box. Suggested children's books that correlate with the topics discussed in the chapter are suggested.

Classroom Museum. Ways to introduce young children to artists and their art are presented here.

Making a Connection. Activities that integrate the arts into math, science, social studies, and language activities are suggested.

Special Needs. Suggestions are given for adapting arts activities to make them accessible to all children.

Teacher Tip. This is a brief, practical idea that may prove helpful to teachers who are just starting out.

Making Plans. Throughout the book are found sample activity plans designed to help beginning teachers better picture how arts activities are organized from beginning to end. Each plan details what to do and say as well as suggests authentic ways to assess the children's progress.

Teacher to family. Sample letters to families are included in many chapters to provide examples of the ways teachers should reach out to the families of the children they teach.

*Asterisk Use

Throughout the book, whenever food items are mentioned that might be used in arts activities they are marked with an asterisk (e.g., rice*). Over the years many food items have found their way into arts activities for young children. This has become a very controversial issue in early childhood education. Although it is easy to say that such items should never be used, in actual practice educators vary greatly in how they define foods. Chapter 4 presents both sides of this debate. After reading Chapter 4, each educator must consider the implications of using such food items in arts activities and decide whether he or she feels a particular item is appropriate or not.

Appendices

The following information has been presented in the form of appendices for ease of use.

Appendix A: Safety guidelines. These guidelines detail ways to make arts activities safe for young children. It includes a table of substitutions for hazardous arts supplies.

Appendix B: Planning arts activities. This section explains the purpose of activity planning and provides guidance in writing an arts-based activity plan. Placing this information in an appendix allows readers to find it quickly and easily when writing plans, and permits instructors to introduce activity plan designs at the point they feel best fits their instruction.

Appendix C: Teacher resources. A list of sources for the special art supplies, computer software, art prints, and artifacts mentioned in the text.

Appendix D: A resource of teacher-tested recipes for arts activities.

Glossary. A listing of terms used in the text. These terms are highlighted in bold the first time they appear in the text.

Ancillary Materials

Instructor's CD-ROM. The new e-Resource component provides instructors with all the tools they need in one convenient CD-ROM. Instructors will find that this resource provides them with a turnkey solution to help them teach by making available PowerPoint® slides for each chapter, a Computerized Test Bank, and an electronic version of the Instructor's Manual.

Available with this new edition is an updated Instructor's Manual that includes invaluable information for those preparing others to teach early childhood art. The electronic instructor's manual contains

- chapter summaries
- course organizational tips
- motivating, cooperative group activities
- children's literature and questions that support the text
- authentic assessment tools
- short-answer and essay-question test bank

The Instructor's Manual is available exclusively in electronic format on the Instructor's e-Resource CD-ROM.

Online Companion™. The Online Companion™ provides much-needed access to an age-based collection of color photographs that shows the extraordinary range of arts produced by young children in exemplary art programs. In addition, it includes:

- critical thinking questions and activities related to the text and artwork

- a sample Web portfolio
- links to art-related Web sites, museums, and articles

The Online Companion™ icon appears at the end of each chapter to prompt you to go online and take advantage of the many features provided. You can find the Online Companion™ at http://www.cengagebrain.com.

WHAT DO THE TERMS MEAN?

Young Artist

In this book, young artist (or child) is used to refer to children from birth to eight years old. This age range is based on the mode of delivery for art education in our society. Most children ages eight and under are in settings such as child care, preschool, nursery school, play groups, kindergarten, primary programs, or at home, where art activities take a wide range of directions depending on the training and knowledge of the adult in charge.

In addition, these years also form an artistically and conceptually unified whole, because during this span children develop their first graphic symbol system through art. Children in the midst of this process need a nourishing environment in which to explore the arts.

Educational Settings

Programs for young children meet in many different locations, from private homes and church basements to public and private school buildings. For simplicity, classroom refers to the inside area used by the children, and outdoor area refers to any contiguous outside play area. Adaptations are included for activities in the home, as are suggestions about when to use the outdoor area.

Guiding Adults

Throughout the text, guiding adult is used interchangeably with teacher, parent, aide, and caregiver. The role of the adult in the arts is to be a guide—someone who selects and prepares the supplies, maps out the possible routes, provides encouragement along the way, takes time for side trips, and celebrates each milepost the child reaches.

ABOUT THE AUTHOR

Joan Koster is an instructor in early childhood education at Broome Community College, Binghamton, New York, and holds degrees in art education and elementary education from Adelphi University and Temple University, and a doctorate in education from Binghamton University. She also directs the Talent Development program at Homer Brink Elementary in Endwell, New York, where she works daily with prekindergarten through fifth grade students on interdisciplinary projects. Over the past 41 years, she has taught art at all levels, from preschool through college. She is the author of *Bringing Art into the Elementary School Classroom* and *Handloom Construction: A Practical Guide for the Non-Expert*. Her work in early childhood education has been published in various journals, including *Young Children,* and she has presented numerous workshops to teachers' organizations. In addition, with her husband and children, she operates a small sheep farm in upstate New York and is a professional handweaver, whose uniquely dyed work has been exhibited and marketed widely.

Acknowledgments

In addressing all the arts in this new full-color edition I have found myself drawing not only on my own expertise in the areas of music, drama, and dance, but also the knowledge and resources of others. First of all, I wish to thank my husband, not only for his patience over the many months I have worked on this book, but also for his deep knowledge and love of music of all styles. I could always count on him to answer my questions about music. Second, I want to thank my sister, with her flair for the dramatic arts, for contributing her expertise on integrating all the arts into wonderful mind-expanding experiences for children. I also appreciate the continuing kindness of my fellow teachers who have allowed me to photograph in their classrooms, helped obtain permissions, and offered wonderful suggestions.

Finally, I wish to acknowledge the critical feedback I have received over the years from my undergraduate students who have pointedly told me what they love about the book, as well as what I should improve. I also want to thank my editor, Rebecca Dashiell; Joshua Taylor; and the staff at Wadsworth for their support in producing this fifth edition. In addition, my appreciation goes to all of the members of my publishing team who have seen this work through to completion.

Last, the thoughtful and detailed advice of the following reviewers was invaluable in helping me revise this book to make it more clear and more usable.

Jane Andrews
Wartburg College

Connie Ballard
Academy of the New Church

Vincent Bates
Northwest Missouri State University

Dale Bazan
University of Nebraska-Lincoln

Audrey Beard
Jackson State University

Cynthia Benton
SUNY College at Cortland

Christian Bernhard
SUNY College at Fredonia

Allan Mcintyre
University of Texas at El Paso

Janet Cornella
Palm Beach Atlantic University

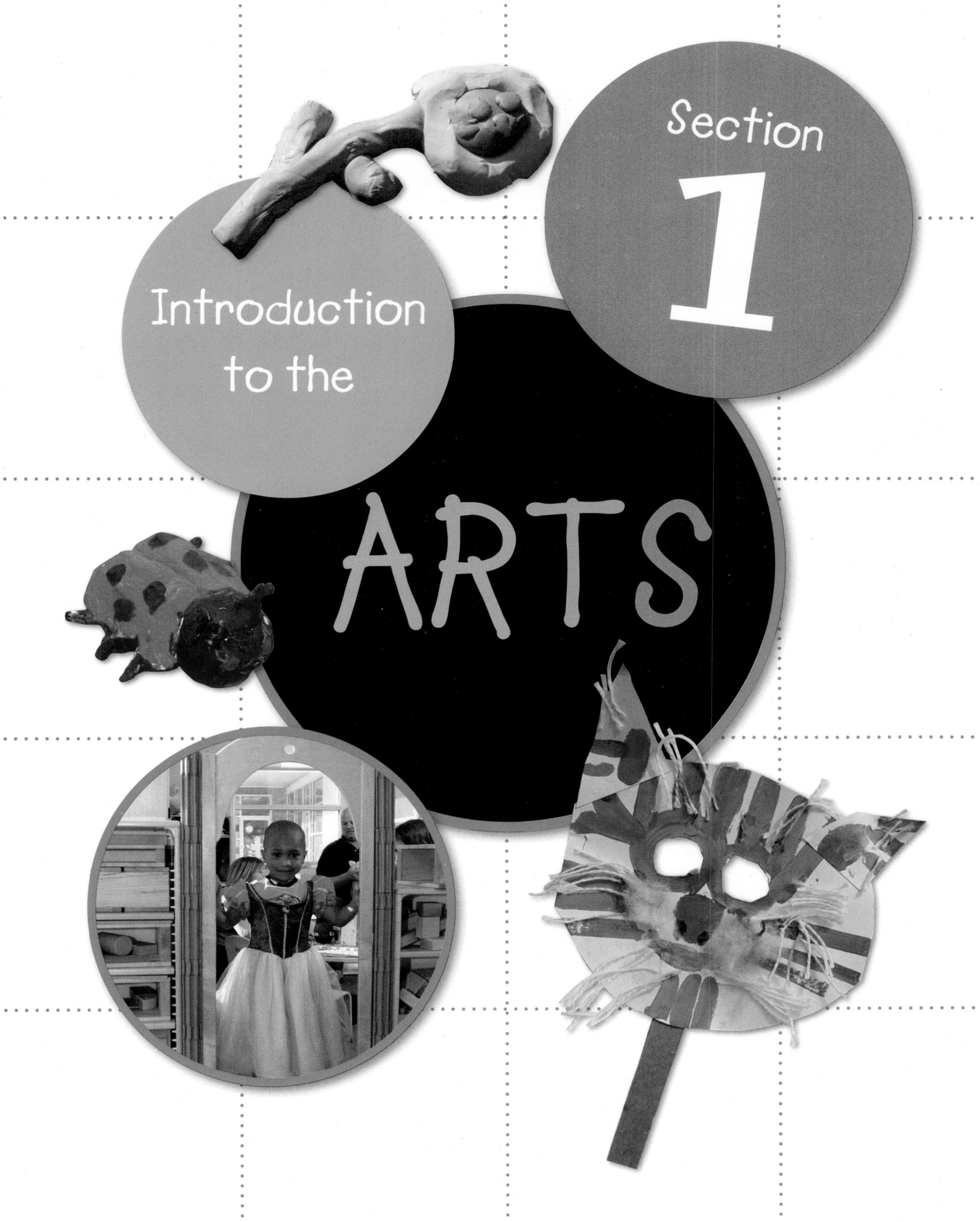
Section
1
Introduction
to the
ARTS

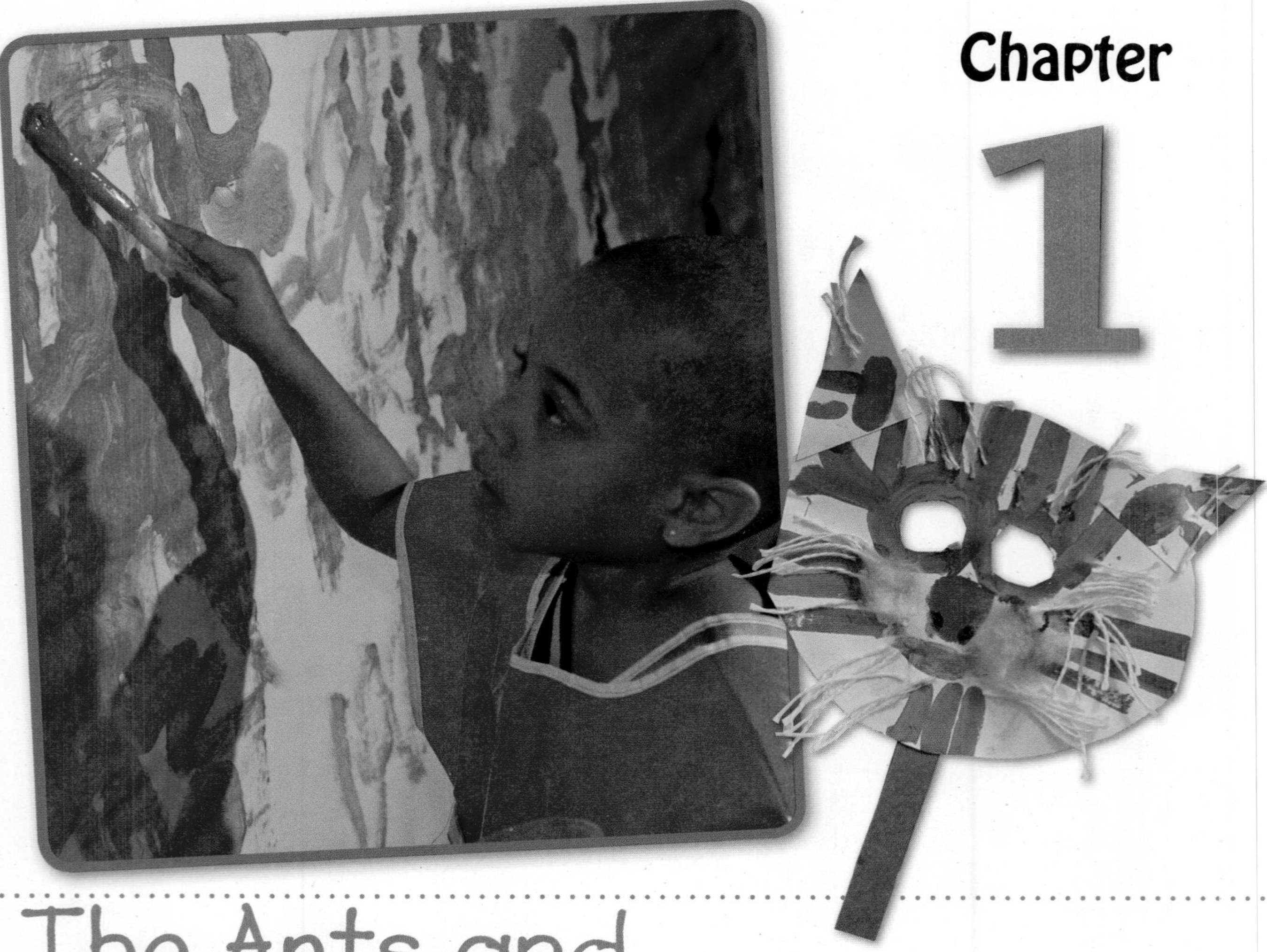

Chapter 1

The Arts and Young Children

Questions Addressed in This Chapter:

- Who are the young artists?
- What are the creative arts?
- Why should the arts be taught to young children?
- What is the relationship between the arts and learning?
- What does a well-designed arts curriculum look like?
- What is the teacher's role in early childhood arts programs?

> *"Every day everywhere in the world, young children make a fist around a pencil or crayon, or drag their fingers in earth or frosty windows, to scribble."*
>
> —*Sylvia Fein* *(1993, p. xii)*

Young Artists at Work

Maria, age one, pulls her finger through a drop of spilled cereal and then licks her finger.

Steve, age two, hums a tune as he amuses himself during his bath by decorating the tub with handfuls of bubbly white soap foam.

Lorna, age four, splashes through a puddle and then with careful deliberation makes a pattern of wet footprints on the pavement. With every step she looks back to see her "trail."

Paul, age six, spends a busy day at the beach building sand mountains and decorating them with broken shells and beach pebbles. Other children join in his fun and watch excitedly as the surf slowly creeps up and then finally washes each mountain away.

WHO ARE THE YOUNG ARTISTS?

Each of these children is a young artist, investigating elements of the arts—line, shape, color, texture, form, movement, melody, rhythm, and pattern. They are making the same artistic discoveries and decisions that all of us have made in our own lives. In doing so, they are repeating a process that has gone on as long as people have inhabited the earth. Like the circles, swirls, and lines on the walls of the caves and cliffs that were the canvasses of the earliest humans, the stone-smoothed satin black pot of a Pueblo potter, the intense sound of a jazz musician, and the flowing movement of a Chinese lotus dancer, the art of young children expresses their personal and cultural history. Their art reflects who they are at this moment in time.

Children from birth to age eight are busy discovering the nature of their world. They are not consciously artists in the way an adult is. They do not stop and say, "Now I am creating a piece of art." They are not creating a product—they are involved in a process!

They are at play. They enjoy manipulating the many materials that they find around them and expressing their creative power to change a piece of their world. In doing so they communicate their feelings and what they are learning. As they learn, they grow and develop.

In this process they gain control over their large and small muscles. Their skill in handling their bodies and artistic tools improves. Their repertoire of lines, shapes, sounds, movements, and patterns expands. They repeat their successes over and over and learn to use artistic symbols that have meaning not just to themselves but also to others around them. By the time these young artists reach age eight, they already know a great deal about the world of creative expression.

But these growing artists are also still very young. They do not yet have skillful control over their bodies and the materials they use. They make messes. They sing out of tune and bump into things. They cry if they spill paint on their shoes.

Young children have short attention spans and are infinitely curious. They get distracted by a noise and run off, leaving their paintbrush in the middle of their picture. They do not always do things in an orderly sequence. Sometimes they glue their paper to the table. Sometimes they drop clay on the floor and unintentionally step on it when trying to pick it up. Anyone working with these children soon learns that great patience is needed.

But most importantly, each child is unique. As young as they are, they each bring to the creative arts experience their own personalities as well as their family and cultural heritage. Some are timid. Others are bold. Some have listened to many folktales and others have heard none. Some have been surrounded by music from birth, and others have rarely heard a tune. One child may have been taught not to get dirty and will not touch fingerpaint, while another child revels in being as messy as possible and smears paint up to the elbows. Children grow at their own pace, but through sensitive planning of creative arts experiences, each child can find his or her personal joy and growth through the arts.

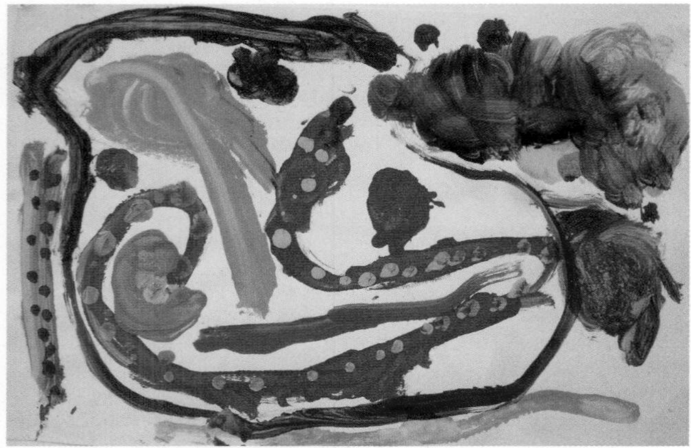

When young children create artworks, they are communicating their thoughts and feelings with the skills and knowledge that they have at that moment of time. In this tempera painting, Tyler, age four, explores ways to make lines, spots, and colors with his brush, just as artists have for thousands of years.

WHAT ARE THE CREATIVE ARTS?

The arts exist in all societies and have been part of human existence since prehistoric times. Ellen Dissanayake (1995) points out that art creation is taking ordinary things and making them special. She argues that making art is part of being human—a normal behavior in which all people participate. Jessica Davis (2008) notes that as long as people have been making tools they have also been making art. Through the creative manipulation of visual, auditory, dramatic, and spatial elements, the arts express the history, culture, and soul of the peoples of the world, both past and present.

A World Without the Arts

The arts are so much a part of our lives that we can recognize their existence only by imagining their absence. Envision our homes and clothing without patterns, textures, and colors; our books without stories; advertisements without pictures; a drive in the car without music; and our feet never dancing to the rhythm of a pop tune. Their purpose can be practical—as in the interior design of a home; communicative—as in an illustration or a television advertisement; or aesthetically and spiritually expressive—as in the swirling colors of a Van Gogh painting or the power of a Beethoven symphony.

In the same way, the creative arts are a part of every activity we offer children, through the clapped rhythms we use to catch their attention, in the box of blocks we give them to build with, and in the picture books we choose to read to them. The colors, textures, and forms of the toys we purchase, the pictures we hang on the walls, the patterns on our floors, and the sounds and rhythms they hear all form the artistic environment of the child. The arts surround us constantly. We can choose to ignore them, or we can select activities for children with an awareness of the role the arts play in our lives.

The Unique Arts

All of the arts incorporate creative problem solving, playfulness, and the expression of feelings and ideas. The term **the arts** encompasses all the different ways of doing this. In this text, the term **art form** is used to refer to the unique disciplines of creative movement or dance, drama, music, and visual art. However, these art forms should not be viewed as static, rigid categories. What makes them powerful is that they are expansive, and complementary, readily intermingled to create something new.

Creative Dance

Creative dance explores the movement and position of the body in space. Children involved in creative movement activities discover ways to physically control and coordinate the rhythmic movement of their bodies in a specific environment, alone and in cooperation with others. Specific information on creative dance and how to introduce young children to creative movement activities is provided in Chapter 11.

Drama

Drama is based on the presentation of ideas and actions through pantomime, improvisation, play acting, literature, and storytelling to create a visual and auditory performance. Dramatic activities engage children in verbal and physical communication through imitative role behavior, make believe, and social interaction with real and imaginary others. Chapter 12 presents many ways to interact with children through the dramatic arts.

Music

Music is organized sound. Music activities provide opportunities for children to learn how to control and respond to voices and instruments as they create rhythmic and melodic patterns through song and sound. Chapter 10 looks at ways to increase children's skill in listening to music, making music, and creating music.

Visual Arts

The **visual arts** draw on visual and tactile elements in order to communicate ideas and feelings. Children involved in visual arts activities use hand-eye coordination as they become skilled at manipulating materials and tools in symbolic ways. Two-dimensional and three-dimensional art activities for young children are provided in Chapter 9.

WHY SHOULD THE ARTS BE TAUGHT TO YOUNG CHILDREN?

We need to teach the arts to young children, first of all, because they are an integral part of our lives as human beings. Second, and just as important, the arts help children grow and develop into learners who are stronger—intellectually, linguistically, physically, emotionally, perceptually, socially, and creatively.

The Arts Stimulate Intellectual Growth

Because the arts are multisensory and interactive, they are an ideal way to help young children develop **cognitively.** Infants are born ready to make sense of the world. From birth, their brains absorb and process sensory and spatial information. Billions of neural connections grow rapidly as the child interacts with the environment. The arts can play an important role in enhancing this process.

The arts enrich learning. Eric Jensen (2005, 2008) suggests the following ways to strengthen learning based on recent brain research.

1. **Provide multisensory, interactive activities.** Because the brain is capable of simultaneously processing information from many senses, we learn best when sensory, visual, and spatial information are combined. Providing hands-on arts activities stimulates the senses and makes learning more memorable.
2. **Create an enriched environment.** Young children, and infants in particular, constantly seek stimulation and are attracted to novelty—loud noises, sudden movements, bright colors, and unique textures. Unusual events call forth excitement and curiosity. Enriched learning environments have been found to have a positive effect on brain development, physically changing the brain. Animals provided with many toys, for example, develop more brain connections than animals in bare environments (Carey, 2002, p. 11). Hanging intriguing artworks on the wall for children to look at, singing a wide variety of songs, offering intriguing props for dramatic play, and providing colorful, tactile art materials for them to explore are ways to enrich the learning environment and foster young children's brain development.
3. **Establish connections.** Searching for meaning is an innate process. The brain constantly examines incoming information, finding and creating patterns as it creates links to previous experiences. We help children learn when we draw on what they already know and present new information in integrated ways, such as when after a trip to the supermarket we set up a play store so children can learn more about money through their dramatic play.
4. **Build on individual interests.** Every child is unique. The child's memories are constantly changing as new connections are made between past experience and incoming information. Making and talking about their creative work is a positive way for children to share what they know and like. Based on what they tell us, we can create a more personalized curriculum.

The arts help children develop logical thinking. To grow intellectually means to become skilled at finding patterns, organizing them logically, and using reasoning to solve problems.

For example, arts activities invite counting, sorting, and classifying. Through questioning, children

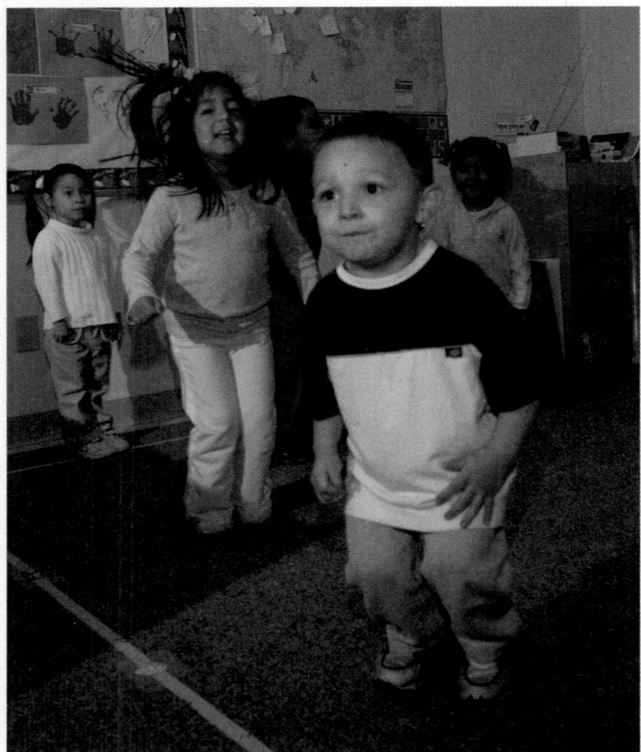

By participating in creative movement activities, these young children are not only increasing physical control over their bodies in space, but are also improving their health and well-being.

involved in arts activities can become aware of number concepts. They can count the number of flowers they have drawn. They can graph the shapes in their collages and sort the leftover paper scraps by color. They can represent the rhythm of a song with symbols, or map the pattern in the steps in a dance.

Well-designed arts activities require children to make their own decisions and to order their behavior to accomplish a goal. Children who are busy creating develop skill in planning and sequencing. They learn that they must put glue on the paper before attaching the piece of yarn. They must dip the brush in the water to clean the paint off of it. They must beat the drum in a regular pattern if they want to follow the rhythm of the song. They must move their arms in a special way to imitate flapping wings. When they are done, they must put their artistic tools in the proper place so they will be ready to use again.

Arts activities provide children with experiences in identifying how properties change and in discovering examples of cause and effect. Visual arts activities allow children to examine the properties of different substances—sticky glue, damp clay, shifting sand. Music activities let children play with changes in pitch, rhythm, and dynamics. Cause and effect are discovered when children explore how their fingers can change the shape of their play dough, or discover that spinning around makes them feel dizzy. Through discussion and questioning, we can help children formulate math and science concepts about these results.

The Arts Are a Child's First Language

Through the arts children's minds can demonstrate their concepts of the world long before they can put their ideas into spoken and written words. It is through the creative exploration of their bodies, the materials and tools of the art form, and the environment that child artists begin to develop visual, auditory, kinesthetic, and graphic symbols with which to represent their thoughts.

Children's language abilities are enhanced through the arts in many ways.

1. **Listening.** All of the arts require children to attend carefully to directions in order to be successful.
2. **Communicating.** Children share their art creations in a variety of ways—some nonverbally, some through sound effects or movements, and others with intricate oral explanations and stories. This is an important part of language development—the prewriting stage.
3. **Vocabulary.** Children learn new words and develop fluency when describing arts materials, processes, their own work, and the works of others.
4. **Symbolically.** Between the ages of two and eight, children acquire the ability to make symbols and learn that these symbols can communicate to others. Through the arts children develop writing skills by creating a graphic symbol system to record their inner and outer observations. When children are asked to respond creatively in response to an experience, they are being challenged to communicate their ideas and thoughts in a symbolic mode. Responsive activities, such as imitating the

The arts bring people together in ways that are enjoyable and fun. As these children learn to make music together, they are also learning how to listen to others and to work toward a common goal.

movement of animals after a visit to the zoo and then talking or writing about it or keeping an illustrated journal, help them use this developing symbol system and refine the nature of their communication.

The Arts Improve Physical Well-Being

Physical activity promotes fitness and health. This is particularly important at a time when our children are becoming increasingly sedentary. A 2006–2007 study found that 20 percent of two year olds watch two or more hours of television a day, which can lead to childhood obesity and slowed development (Kent, Murphy & Stanton, 2010, p. 837; Louv, 2008, p. 7).

The arts are a motivating way to get children moving. Arts activities help children improve their ability to control large and small muscles and refine hand-eye coordination. An infant shaking a bell, a preschooler jumping up and down to music, and a first grader acting out a nursery rhyme are all learning to manage the way their bodies move.

Soft, pliable play dough and clay improve finger strength. Using brushes at an easel develops control of the arm and wrist. Large and small muscles are exercised and challenged through the manipulation of materials and tools when children stack blocks or pick up tiny beads. Cutting a shape from paper or placing a leaf in a dab of glue requires the eye and hand to work together. Creative movement activities, such as imagining one's body as clay that can be made into different shapes, help the child relate physical movement and concepts.

The arts can also affect physical health in another way. Listening to different types of music has been shown to slow down or speed up a person's heart rate and lower blood pressure (Using music, 2009).

The Arts Foster Emotional Well-Being

The arts have always been valued for the self-expression they can provide. However, their importance in emotional health goes far beyond this. Purposeful and playful physical movement, such as is found in arts activities, improves emotional well-being by causing the brain to release mood-altering chemicals, such as endorphins, which can heighten attention and provide a sense of well-being.

This is supported by current research on the effect of creative arts expression on healing. Heather Stuckey and Jeremy Noble (2010), in a summary of research done between 1995 and 2007, found a strong connection between each of the art forms and emotional well-being.

- **Music**—Music, which is the most researched of the arts, can control pain and restore emotional balance.
- **Visual Arts**—The visual arts allow people to express feelings and thoughts that are difficult to put into words, such as grief, fear, and anxiety. Overall, creating visual art was found to be a positive activity that provided release from anxiety-producing situations, such as severe pain and health issues.
- **Creative Movement**—Creative movement not only improves physical condition but also improves self-awareness and body image.
- **Drama**—Theater training improves both long-term memory and feelings of self-confidence.

In all cases, participating in the arts reduced stress. Therefore, by providing a wide range of **open-ended,** developmentally appropriate arts activities, not only do we set the stage for young children to express their feelings, but we also gift them with a lifelong way to relieve stress and a source of self-healing that will improve the quality of their lives.

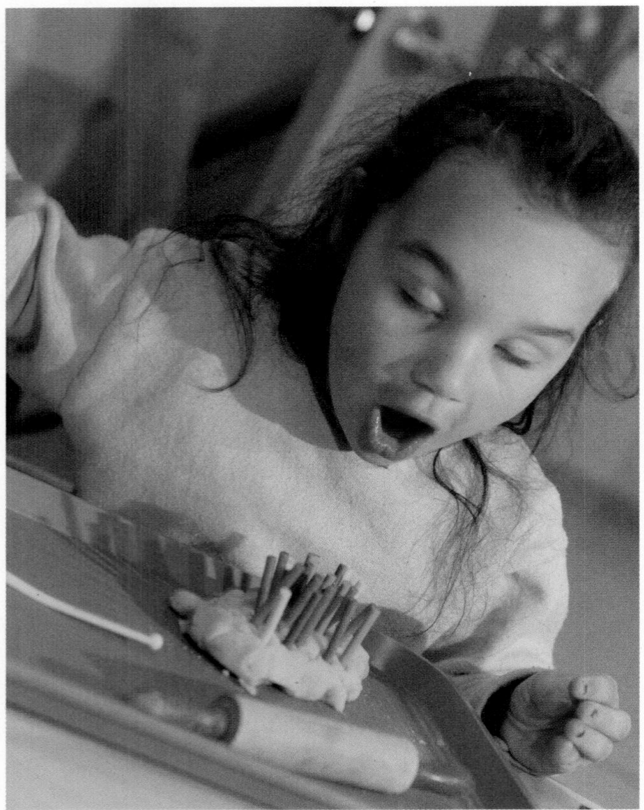

A little girl blows out the pretend candles on the play dough cake she has made. In this simple act we see the interrelationship among the arts. Playing with modeling materials and using her imagination helps this child grow intellectually, linguistically, socially, emotionally, perceptually, and creatively.

The Arts Build Sensory Perception

The arts help children develop perceptually. Children learn through their senses. They absorb information from the world through touching, seeing, hearing, tasting, and smelling. This is how they develop concepts about the nature of objects, actions, and events. Children learn better when teachers provide experiences that are sensually rich and varied, and that require children to use their perceptual abilities in many different ways. Children who have sung songs about, drawn pictures of, and acted out the metamorphosis of a butterfly will have a better understanding of the process than children who have only been told about the process.

The arts also enhance perceptive skills by teaching spatial concepts. Creative movement activities, for example, allow children to play with and use spatial concepts such as big/small, long/thin, and under/over as they reach high or crawl along the floor. Visual arts activities let children explore the visual and tactile constructs of color, shape, pattern, form, and placement in space as they draw, paint, and play with modeling clay. Singing and playing instruments provide opportunities for children to develop their listening abilities as they investigate pitch, rhythm, and melody.

Most importantly, the arts, especially when integrated with experiences with nature, allow children to use all their senses to develop a sense of wonder and appreciation for the aesthetic qualities of the objects in our world. Chapter 4 presents activities that awaken children to the sensory landscape around them.

The Arts Create Community

Arts activities can help children develop socially by teaching them to take turns, to share space and materials with others, and to make positive choices in personal behavior. Arts activities often require children to work with others to accomplish a project or to produce a single, unified piece of art or dramatic story.

Looking at artwork done by people different from oneself, taking a role in dramatic play, and experiencing unfamiliar styles of music are all ways to enhance children's understanding that each person has a different viewpoint and does not necessarily see things the same way they do. The arts provide the best entry point for developing media literacy (Nakamura et al, 2009). This is an essential skill in a society where visual images, music, acting, and dance are frequently used in commercials to entice us to buy something we do not need or propagandize one political point of view over another.

Sharing space and supplies, laughter and tears, and working on group projects with other young artists help children learn the power of cooperation and of empathy (Brouillette, 2010). Jessica Davis (2008) reminds us that the arts "excite and engage students, wakening attitudes to learning, including passion and joy, and the discovery 'I care'." Chapter 5 presents many ways to foster community through the arts.

Studying the arts of other times, people, and cultures is another way the arts can draw us together as we learn to appreciate and understand the fabulous diversity of creative ideas as represented by the unique art forms from around the world. In addition, sharing the arts from the cultures of students and their families is a respectful way to honor the diversity of our children. In Chapter 7 we will explore ways to present the art of others to young children.

Addressing bias and cultural differences. Our children come from different social and cultural backgrounds. Derman-Sparks and the A.B.C. Task Force (1989) encourage arts activities that help children accept racial and cultural differences and reject stereotypes. Selecting arts activities that show respect for their family backgrounds, home culture, and language can support children from diverse cultures. Activities should reflect appreciation for different cultural beliefs, holiday customs, and family traditions, and they should develop a sense of community. Visual art materials should reflect the many colors of humanity; drama, music, and dance activities should reflect the stories, sounds, and rhythms of the world, as well as the local community; and artworks that decorate the walls should represent people from diverse backgrounds. Through seeing, touching, and talking about a wide variety of art forms selected from both their own culture and different cultures, children learn that the arts reflect the ideas and feelings of other people. Field trips and guest artists can provide access to culturally diverse musical, dance, and dramatic performances.

Addressing english language learners (ELLs). Because the arts are a nonverbal way to communicate feelings and ideas, arts activities are an ideal way to integrate children who are non–English speaking or who are beginning to learn English into the community of the classroom. Directions to many arts activities can be given through modeling, physical clues, and hands-on demonstrations. Activities that are open-ended with no preconceived correct responses and that incorporate an element of play can allow ELLs to develop self-confidence and acknowledgment from peers. For example, because creative movement allows all children to express themselves nonverbally, it provides an ideal communication tool for children who are nonnative speakers or who have trouble expressing themselves orally (Koff, 2000).

The Arts Nurture Creativity

The arts are the realm of the imagination. The unstructured quality of well-designed arts activities allows children to experiment with their voices, bodies, and familiar materials in new ways. They can use their own ideas and power to initiate and cause change and to produce original actions and combinations. Paint that drips, block towers that fall down, whistles that are hard to blow, and all of the other small difficulties arts activities present challenge children to find their own solutions to emerging problems.

Torrance (1970) defined creativity as being able to see a problem, form ideas about it, and then communicate the results. When children are engaged in the arts, they are creating something new and unique; in doing so, they are being creative. As Chapter 2 will illustrate, creativity is not something that can be taught but, instead, is something that must be nurtured.

Book Box

The following children's books introduce children to the nature of the arts.

Catalonotte, P. (2006). *Emily's Art.* New York: Atheneum.
This beautifully illustrated book explores the idea that everyone has their own point of view when looking at art. Kindergarten and up.

Collins, P. L. (1992). *I am an artist.* Brookfield, CT: Millbrook Press.
In simple, poetic language, this book shows children that responding aesthetically to beautiful things is part of being an artist. A good read-aloud for a quiet time. Toddler and up.

Medeares, A. S. (1997). *Annie's Gifts.* East Orange, NJ: Just Us Books.
A young girl learns that there are many different ways people can express themselves through the arts. Four and up.

Raczka, B. (2003). Art is . . . . Minneapolis, MN: Millbrook.
Simple descriptions accompany a range of art work from African masks to cave paintings. Toddler and up.

Creativity is nourished when children are allowed the freedom to express their unique ideas in an accepting environment. Jason, age four, has painted his own idea of a cat.

WHAT IS THE RELATIONSHIP BETWEEN THE ARTS AND LEARNING?

Young children do not have a set goal in mind as they begin to create artistically, any more than they start the day with the goal of learning ten new words. They are caught up in the process of responding to and playing with the stimuli around them, such as the way paint drips, the way clay stretches and bends, and the way another child hums a tune.

As teachers we can see children growing and developing through the arts activities we design. We can watch the changes in behavior that come with increasing experience in the arts—from the first tentative brush strokes of the two-year-old to the tuneful singing of the mature eight-year-old. However, it is also necessary that children grow in ways that will make them more successful in their interactions with the world.

The nature of an early childhood arts curriculum is determined by our philosophy of how children learn. Visits to most preschools, child care centers, and primary school programs will find children drawing and painting, and singing and dancing. However, what the children are actually doing as they draw, paint, sing, and dance will vary widely depending on what the adults in charge believe young children are capable of doing, what they think is the correct way to teach them, and how they interpret the role of the arts in education.

To strengthen our philosophy and establish our goals, we need to examine learning theories, contemporary viewpoints, current research, and successful approaches to the arts in the education of children. These ideas will provide direction in the creation of a successful and meaningful arts program for children.

Piaget and Constructivism

In the early 1920s Jean Piaget, a Swiss biologist, began studying children's responses to problems he designed. Based on his now classic research, Piaget (1959) described how children develop their knowledge of the world. His findings have become the basis of the constructivist approach to early childhood education and include the following beliefs about how children learn:

- Children are active learners. They are curious and actively seek out information that helps them make sense of the world around them.
- Children construct knowledge based on their experiences. Because each child has different experiences, the understandings and misunderstandings acquired are unique to each child and are continually changing as the child has new experiences.
- Experience is essential for cognitive development. Children need to physically interact with the people and objects around them.

Thought becomes more complex as children have more experiences. Although Piaget proposed that cognitive development was age dependent, many researchers today have modified the rigid age categories and believe that complexity of thought follows gradual trends and may vary in different contexts and content areas (Ormrod, 2003).

Theory in practice. Constructivism views children as self-motivated learners who are responsible for their own learning. Open-ended arts activities that offer many creative possibilities are ideal for this purpose. Logical thought is developed by asking children to explain why they chose their particular creative solutions.

Vygotsky's Sociocultural Perspective and Social Cognitive Theory

Research on children's thinking in the 1920s and 1930s by Lev Vygotsky (1978) emphasized the importance of peers and adults in children's cognitive development. Vygotsky proposed that one way children construct their knowledge is based on past and present social interactions. His major points were the following:

- Complex thought begins through communication with adults and more knowledgeable peers. Watching and interacting with the people around them helps children internalize the thought processes, concepts, and beliefs common to their culture.
- Although children need to experience things personally and make discoveries on their own, they can also learn from the experiences of others.
- Children can perform at a higher cognitive level when guided by an adult or a more competent peer. Vygotsky defined the **actual developmental level** as what the child can do independently, and the **potential developmental level** as what the child can do with assistance.
- According to Vygotsky, most learning occurs when children are challenged to perform closer to their potential developmental level in what has come to be known as the **zone of proximal development.** It is when they are asked to perform tasks that require communication with more skilled individuals that children experience maximum cognitive growth.
- Vygotsky also thought that young children developed symbolic thought through play. Make-believe and dramatic play allow children to represent ideas using substitute objects (for example, pretending that a bowl placed upside down on their head is a hat) and so help children develop the ability to think abstractly.

Social cognitive theory emphasizes the role of modeling and imitation in children's learning. The well-known psychologist Albert Bandura (1973) found, for example, that children who watched a doll being treated aggressively repeated the behavior when alone with the doll.

However, for a child to learn from a role model, four factors need to occur.

1. **Attention:** The child needs to watch the role model perform the behavior.
2. **Motivation:** The child must want to imitate the role model. Bandura found children were more likely to imitate those they liked or respected, or who were considered attractive or powerful (Bandura, 1989).
3. **Remember:** The child needs to understand and recall what the role model did.
4. **Reproduce:** The child must repeat the behavior enough times to improve in skill.

Theory in practice. These theories help us see children as members of a social community in which adults as role models are an important source of information about the nature of the arts. As teachers we can model for children how artists think and behave. This is because the arts lend themselves to what is characterized as the "apprenticeship model" (Gardner, 1993). In an apprenticeship, the child learns not only how to do the task but also how experts think about the task. We can model artistic methods while thinking out loud about the process. We can make well-timed suggestions that guide the child to the next level of understanding, and we can ask children to explain what they are doing so that they make the learning their own. In addition, we can provide models of what the arts can be by introducing children to wonderful artists from all times and cultures. Doing these things will not only help children grow cognitively but will also nurture their ability to think and act as artists.

Multiple Intelligence Theory

Based on cognitive research, Howard Gardner (1983, 1991) has proposed that there are at least eight

Children learn by modeling their behavior on the peers and adults they know and by watching what goes on around them. From whom do you think this young boy learned about puppets and dinosaurs?

intellectual capabilities or **intelligences.** These intelligences represent biological and psychological potentials within each individual. Everyone has capabilities in each intelligence, with special strengths in one or more of them. Gardner has identified these intelligences as follows:

1. **Linguistic:** The ability to manipulate the oral and written symbols of language
2. **Logical-Mathematical:** The ability to manipulate numerical patterns and concepts in logical ways
3. **Spatial:** The ability to visualize the configuration of objects in both two- and three-dimensional space
4. **Musical:** The ability to manipulate rhythm and sound
5. **Bodily-Kinesthetic:** The ability to use the body to solve problems or to make things
6. **Interpersonal:** The ability to understand and work with others
7. **Intrapersonal:** The ability to understand oneself
8. **Naturalistic-Environmental:** The ability to sense and make use of the characteristics of the natural world

Traditional educational practice has focused mainly on strengths in the linguistic and logical-mathematical domains. Multiple intelligences (MI) theory provides a framework upon which teachers can build a more educationally balanced program—one that better meets the needs of children with talents in other areas. The arts as a learning and symbolic tool is particularly valuable not only because it embraces the talents often overlooked in education, but also because it crosses and links all of the intelligences.

It is important to note that Gardner (1993) does not believe that there is a separate artistic intelligence. Instead, each of the eight intelligences can be used for either artistic or nonartistic purposes. How an intelligence is expressed will depend on a variety of factors, including personal choice and cultural environment. Linguistic intelligence, for example, can be used to scribble an appointment on a calendar or to compose a short story. Spatial intelligence can be used to create a sculpture or to read a map. Conversely, to create a painting, a visual artist must draw not only on visual-spatial intelligence in order to visualize the artistic elements in the work, but also on bodily-kinesthetic intelligence in order to control the brush and logical-mathematical intelligence in order to plan the sequence in which the paint will be applied.

Theory in practice. **MI theory** broadens our view of children's abilities and potentials into a multidimensional view of intelligence. It means that we need to honor the special abilities of every child by creating an early childhood curriculum that includes many opportunities to use all of the intelligences in artistic ways.

Not every activity will engage all of the intelligences, but when activities are chosen that incorporate many of the intelligences, children can learn in whatever way best fits their intellectual strengths or learning style. In this book, Gardner's intelligences have been interrelated with the physical, linguistic, social, emotional, creative, and intellectual growth areas in order to create models of such balanced arts activities.

WHAT DOES A WELL-DESIGNED ARTS CURRICULUM LOOK LIKE?

The Task Force on Children's Learning and the Arts: Birth to Age 8 (1998) has laid out three curriculum strands for arts-based programs. These incorporate the need for artistic skills and judgments, while at the same time allowing for creative self-expression and cultural understanding. These strands are as follows:

- **Children must be active participants in the arts process**—They should create, participate, perform, and respond to carefully selected arts activities that reflect their culture and background experience.
- **Arts activities must be domain based, relevant, and integrated**—Arts activities should allow every child to be successful and reflect children's daily life experiences. The arts should be fully integrated into the rest of the curriculum and help children make connections with what they are learning. At the same time, these activities should build artistic skill and competence in the particular art form being used. Verbal and graphic expressive, reflective, and evaluative responses to arts activities can provide the opportunity to build literacy and intellectual skills.
- **The learning environment must nurture the arts**—Adequate quality materials, space, and time should be provided with the needs and abilities of the children foremost. Adult engagement should share in and support children in their artistic explorations and reflect input from current research in the field and artists, arts specialists, early childhood teachers, parents, caregivers, and other community resources.

The Reggio Emilia Approach to Arts Education

These principles are well illustrated by the preprimary program of the municipality of Reggio Emilia, Italy. In this program, the arts are highly valued. Each school has an *atelierista,* or art educator, who works directly with the teachers in designing the program. In addition, each school has a beautiful art room where supplies are arranged by color. This attention to aesthetic qualities carries over to the school itself, which is decorated with children's artwork that has been carefully mounted. Light, mirrors, and color produce wonderful spaces in which children can play and create. In the Reggio Emilia program, the arts are used as an important method of recording the observations, ideas, and memories of experiences in which the children have participated. The *atelierista* offers suggestions as the children work. The children also share their art with other children. Unlike in the United States, where arts experiences are often used as fillers and artwork is usually sent home at the end of each day, in Reggio Emilia, children are asked to return to their artistic works to reconsider, discuss and critique, and then to rework, or repeat their responsive arts activities.

The Reggio Emilia program is an example of **emergent curriculum.** Elizabeth Jones and John Nimmo (1994) describe this approach to teaching young children as one in which teachers are sensitive to the needs and interests of the children and then build on these through the provision of wonderful learning experiences. The teacher and children are coplayers sharing ideas and choices together in a curriculum that is open-ended and constantly adjusting

These preschoolers are pretending to be veterinarians. Here is a perfect moment on which to build an emergent curriculum. What activities in other areas of learning, such as mathematics and science, could expand on this interest?

to new ideas and needs. This does not mean that the teacher has no control over the curriculum. Rather the guiding adult is more like a stage director, the one who "sets the stage, times the acts, and keeps the basic drama together" (1994, p. 5). In such a curriculum, the arts can play a major role as is seen in the work done by children in the Reggio Emilia schools.

Another example of emergent curriculum in action is the Project Approach, as exemplified by the work of Lillian Katz and Sylvia Chard (2000). This approach will be examined more deeply in Chapter 8.

Goals for Learning

What do children need to learn about the arts? This is a key question in designing an effective arts curriculum for young children. According to Lillian Katz and Sylvia Chard (2000), there are four main categories of learning goals.

Knowledge. **Knowledge** includes the vocabulary and concepts we want our children to hear and use. In early childhood arts, this means that we must make sure that children will be learning to talk about and identify the elements of each art form, as well as the materials and methods belonging to each. We then want children to be able to apply what they have learned in their artistic performances and creations as well as in their responses to the artwork of others.

Young children construct this kind of knowledge from direct experiences and interactions with more expert peers and adults. It happens when we ask children to tell how they made a particular color in their paintings or when they learn a song from a friend. The knowledge to be imparted can be expressed in the vocabulary words selected, the concepts being applied, and the questions children will be asked as they are involved in arts activities. In the Exploring the Arts section of this book, examples of these are found under the "What to Say" heading.

Dispositions. **Dispositions** are the ways we behave as learners and performers. Examples of dispositions include being intellectually curious, using the creative process, thinking logically, and being generous and helpful. Another way to view dispositions is to think of them as preferred ways of thinking. We can think and make decisions, as would a creative musician, an inquiring artist, or an observant poet. Dispositions are nurtured instead of being taught directly. They develop best in carefully designed learning environments that allow creative exploration, provide safe risk taking, and foster creative problem solving.

Many different dispositions can be developed in the creation of art. First and foremost is the disposition to think and to act like a creative artist, musician, dancer, or actor. For example, a young child playing a drum may say, "Look, I am a drummer like in the band. You can march to the beat of my drum." This is nourished through open-ended arts activities using real art skills, materials, and tools presented by a teacher who is passionate about the arts and who verbally and visually models what these artists do. At the same time, thoughtful statements and questions can promote intellectual curiosity, and careful organization of the activity can promote cooperative behavior and nurture the growth of a caring and socially aware individual.

Feelings. Feelings describe how children receive, respond to, and value what they are learning and are reflected in the emotional state of the child. Positive feelings about the arts, or any other subject area, develop in an arts program that makes children feel safe; when activities are challenging but possible; when mistakes are seen as positive ways to grow; and where accomplishments are enthusiastically acknowledged.

Children come to value the arts when we prepare a curriculum that provides activities that share with them a sense of wonder and awaken them to the aesthetic qualities of the world in which they live, and encourages them to respond positively to the art of others. In such an arts program, teachers and peers respond to artistic endeavors with heartfelt, thoughtful comments, and provide open-ended arts activities that allow children to express their unique personal feelings and ideas. Most importantly, a well-planned arts program allows all children to feel successful as artists, thereby enabling them to see themselves as competent individuals.

Skills. Skills are the observable behaviors used in arts creation, such as cutting out shapes with a scissors or shaping clay into a ball. Although some skills are learned spontaneously, most develop through practice. If we want our children to be able to use paint skillfully, for example, then we need to give them lots of opportunities to explore paint. In addition, skills from the different growth areas can be practiced through the arts. For example, intentionally having two children use the same glue bottle provides them with an opportunity to practice sharing. Talking about how it feels to move like a drop of water allows children to develop their oral language skills. In fact, well-planned arts activities usually address skill development in all of the growth areas.

National Standards for Arts Education

Another way of looking at what children need to learn about the arts is to examine what children are expected to know and be able to do in the arts. The National Standards for Arts Education (MENC, 2007) address children from kindergarten to high school. Similar standards for the education of younger children have been developed by many states. Table 1-1 provides a sample set of standards for music from the state of Oregon. Links to other early childhood state standards can be found on the National Early Child Care and Technical Assistance Center (NCCIC) at http://nccic.acf.hhs.gov/pubs/goodstart/elgwebsites.html. All of them include the arts, some more and some to a lesser extent.

Based on the specific concepts and skills identified in the standards, we can make sure that young children are introduced to a breadth of rich arts experiences. In conjunction with forming teaching objectives, the content standards for visual arts, music, dance, and dramatics are listed in Chapters 9 through 12. The complete standards for kindergarten through fourth grade, as well as many resources for teaching the arts, can be found at http://artsedge.kennedy-center.org/.

Components of an Integrated Arts Curriculum

In an early childhood program that values the arts, music, dance, dramatics, and visual arts activities are inseparable from the total curriculum. It all seems so effortless. There is a rhythm and flow to a well-planned program that creates the sense that this is what will naturally happen if the children are just told

TABLE 1–1 Sample Early Childhood Arts Standards: Oregon

THE ARTS: Birth to Three

Early Childhood Foundation: Music
- Participating in numerous musical activities
- Playing with and making music with everyday items and musical instruments

Indicators: Observable Behaviors

The Child
Responds to sounds by change in expression or eyes widening.
Responds to music by cooing, becoming quiet or looking at sound source.
Bangs and shakes toys placed in hand.
Responding to and recognizing different types of sounds (loud/soft, fast/slow) by tapping feet, clapping hands, swaying with the body.
Uses everyday items to keep time to the rhythm of music (spoon, pan lid, toy).
Plays on rhythm instruments (tambourine or drum).
Hums or sings along to simple songs or rhymes.

The Adult
Provides opportunities to experience music throughout the day in the home or classroom.
Sings lullabies and simple songs.
Uses simple items in the environment to keep time with musical rhythm.
Uses musical instruments, where possible, to make music.

Supportive Learning Environments Include
Music on tapes or disks reflecting children's songs and rhyming music
Everyday items that can be used to make sounds in response

From Oregon Early Childhood Foundations: Birth to 3, available at http://www.ode.state.or.us/superintendent/priorities/ready4school/theartsbto3.pdf

Open-ended arts activities have no one right answer, but instead welcome the creative ideas of children. Nicole, age six, has imagined an animal with green horns and spots and then brought it to life using tempera paint.

to have fun with a lot of interesting materials. Nothing could be farther from the truth.

Behind that successful program is superb planning by a teacher who has knowledge about how children think, learn, and respond to stimuli in their environment. We can be that teacher. We can learn what to say about arts production and performance, how to say it, and when it is best left unsaid. We can know when to interact and when to wait and watch. We will seek to be judged not on the children's products but on their growth. We can continually learn and grow along with our young artists from the first contact to the last. We can constantly improve the program we offer, assessing each activity and noting how the children show growth in relation to the goals we have set for them. It is a program of our own creation, both meaningful and thoughtful.

WHAT IS THE TEACHER'S ROLE IN EARLY CHILDHOOD ARTS PROGRAMS?

Young artists need many things to be successful in the arts. They need safe, exciting art supplies; comfortable surroundings; ample space; and time to explore. They need activities that acknowledge their unique development, experiences, and skills. Most of all, they need a teacher who will enable them to be successful.

As teachers, we do not need to be professional musicians, dancers, artists, or actors to be effective teachers of the arts. Rather we need to design an art curriculum made up of activities that nurture young artists.

The teacher is the most important part of the arts curriculum. The teacher is like a gardener, providing the "fertile ground"—the enriched arts curriculum—that gives children a start in thinking and working as artists. As the children grow in skill and confidence, it is the planning, enthusiasm, and encouragement provided by the teacher that will allow the child's creativity to flower. It is the purpose of this text to help you become this teacher.

CONCLUSION: THE WELL-DESIGNED ARTS PROGRAM

> *A classroom for young children often looks for all the world like an artist's studio. The products that come out are children's products, but the process that goes on is the artist's process. The rich availability of easels, paints, brushes, paper, clay, and collage materials helps young children live like artists.*
>
> —*James L. Hymes (1989, p. 81)*

The stage has now been set for developing a rich and meaningful arts program for children. Children are natural artists, in the sense that they play creatively with the elements of the arts that they find in their surroundings. But those surroundings must be provided, determined by a philosophy of what child art is, and what it means. We need to consider why children should do certain arts activities, which ones should be selected, how they should be delivered, and what environment is most conducive to their performance.

This chapter has closely examined why the arts need to be taught. We have learned how the arts help children grow socially, emotionally, physically, intellectually, and linquistically. The following chapters will consider:

1. **How:** We will see how the delivery of arts activities affects what children learn, as well as how the way the child learns affects what activities will be successful.

2. **Where:** We will learn how to design the environment in which child artists will work.
3. **What:** We will investigate the appropriate selection and efficient delivery of arts concepts and skills.

It is the educator's role to nurture the artist within every young child. Although the focus will always be on guiding the artistic development of the child, in doing so the artist within the adult will also be rekindled. Adults and children must become part of the artistic continuum that stretches from our distant human past into the future. To guide young children as they grow through the arts is a deeply rewarding experience.

FURTHER READING

The books listed below illustrate the place of child art in human experience.

Eisner, E. W. (2002). *The arts and the creation of mind.* New Haven: Yale University.

Eminent art educator Elliot Eisner places the arts at the center of learning.

Gardner, H. (1993). *Multiple intelligences: The theory in practice.* New York: Basic Books.

This book presents Howard Gardner's theory of multiple intelligences and how it applies to educating children.

Davis, J. H. (2008). *Why our schools need the arts.* New York: Teachers College.

Davis explains why the arts belong in our children's lives and occupy a unique place in learning how to think, empathize, and imagine, and makes suggestions for ways to advocate for the arts.

Jensen, E. (2008). *Enriching the brain.* Hoboken, NJ: Jossey-Bass.

Eric Jensen presents current research on the relationship between the arts and the brain and offers reasons why the arts should be part of every child's education.

For additional information on the importance of the creative arts for young children, links to relevant websites and research, as well as arts standards and examples of children's arts visit the Growing Artists companion Web site at http://www.cengagebrain.com

TEACHING IN ACTION

An Integrated Arts Curriculum

The arts are integrated into the curriculum through emergent curriculum.

Children develop socially by working on a group project.

It is a warm spring day, and sunlight streams through the windows of the large bright room. Photographs of fish and sea creatures decorate one wall. Children's books about the sea are on display on the bookshelf. The teacher has already read several books about the sea to the children and talked to the children about experiences they have had during visits to the beach. Seashells, starfish, fishnets, floats, and other sea-related objects are placed around the room. It is easy to tell that the children have been learning about the ocean. In the center of the room an adult and several children, ages three and four, are hard at work painting a refrigerator box in which round windows and two doors have been cut. They are using yellow poster paint and large house paintbrushes. Newspapers cover the floor. One child is painting broad strokes of color across the box, while the other child presses the brush down again and again, making rectangular stamp marks in one small section. In the background, a recording of the Beatles' classic "Yellow Submarine" can be heard.

(continued)

TEACHING IN ACTION *(continued)*

The teacher enthusiastically responds to the artistic elements in the child's work with positive feedback.

While the painters work away on their submarine, other children are playing at the water table, experimenting with a variety of objects in different sizes, colors, and shapes that either sink or float. At an easel, a four-year-old has filled his paper with waving lines using mixtures of blue, green, and yellow paint. The teacher stops to help the painter at the easel remove his smock. "Look at all the blue-greens and turquoises you have made," she tells him, pointing to examples of those colors.

Arts activities are open-ended. Children choose to use the art supplies in their own creative way.

At a round table, three children have taken premade paper tubes from the supply shelf and are decorating them with paper, yarn, glue, and crayons. One child asks the teacher to attach a piece of blue cellophane to the end of his "scope." A second child puts her tube up to her nose. "I'm a swordfish. This is my sword. I have a beautiful sword," she tells another girl as she makes a roaring sound through the tube. A three-year-old is exploring what happens when he glues a piece of yarn on the tube and then pulls it off. In another corner, two boys are engaged in noisy, animated play with the trucks and blocks. At the computer, a four-year-old is making a multicolored line travel a wiggly path over the screen.

Visual images from diverse sources enrich the children's experience.

At the game table, two children are matching pictures. The cards have been made from prints of paintings, sculptures, and crafts from many cultures that illustrate subjects about the sea. These have been cut out of museum catalogs, glued to card stock, and laminated. On the wall behind them is a poster-size print of one of the artworks. One child finds a card that matches the poster and walks over and compares the two pictures. "They're the same, but this one is littler," he notes, holding the picture card up to the print.

Visitors provide common experiences that lead to integrated learning.

Suddenly everyone stops working. A special visitor has arrived! A father of one of the children brings in two plastic buckets, and all the children circle round. In the tubs are saltwater creatures borrowed from the pet store where he works. The children closely observe a sea urchin, an anemone, and a sea snake. One child looks at the sea urchin through his cellophane-covered tube. "It changes color," he states with wonder. He shares his tube with the others so they can see the change too.

Arts and language activities are unified.

When the visitor leaves, some children head off to a table where crayons, markers, and stapled paper booklets are set out. "I'm writing a story about a sea snake and an 'anoome,'" says one five-year-old girl. She draws a long wiggly line on one page. "Here he is very sad." Then she draws a purple circle. "This is his friend, the 'anoome.' Now he is happy!" When she finishes her book, she "reads" it to her teacher, inventing a long, detailed story to go with her pictures. "You made your anemone the same color as the one Sam's father brought to show us," the teacher says. The girl beams with pride and skips off to read her book to her friend.

Children explore sensory experiences.

A three-year-old has settled in with a lump of play dough. He rolls out a long "worm." "Look—I can make it wiggle like a sea snake," he says, as he twists and turns the play dough. Some children take cardboard tubes to decorate. They want to put cellophane on theirs so they can have their own "scopes." Several other children have taken colored paper, markers, and scissors. They talk quietly together as they invent new sea creatures.

"Mine has tentacles like the sea urchin."

"I'm going to give mine a big mouth and teeth," says another. They cut out their creatures and take them to the teacher.

TEACHING IN ACTION

Children initiate and choose what they want displayed.

"Let's put a string on them and hang them up so they can swim in our sea," says one. The teacher hangs their creatures inside a large glass aquarium that has been decorated with sand and shells on the bottom. They join other paper sea creatures, made by other children, which are already afloat on the air currents.

Meanwhile, several other children have moved into the submarine. They are busy arranging blankets and pillows.

"I think it is softer this way," says Peter. Sam lies down and tries it out. He curls up and sucks his thumb.

"I think we should have a yellow blanket in the yellow submarine," says Sue, bringing in a piece of yellow cloth from the dress-up box. Other children look in through the portholes and make faces at their friends.

Creative movement grows out of the children's dramatic play, and, combined with music, provides a smooth transition to story time.

"We will be the fish swimming around the submarine!" they tell them. The teacher observes the children's play and puts on Saint-Saens's *The Swan.* The music matches the children's actions as they move around the box inventing fish sounds and motions. The teacher joins the dancers and invites the children in the box to come out and swim in the sea with them. Sue swirls the yellow cloth behind her. "This is my tail," she sings.

Children have made plans and look forward to the next day.

"Story time!" says the teacher. "Let's swim to the rug." The dancing children and those working about the room move to the rug and settle around the teacher, who reads the story *The Rainbow Fish* by Marcus Pfister. The children gather round the aquarium and look at their floating sea creatures.

"We need a rainbow fish," says one boy.

"Let's make lots of rainbow fish tomorrow," joins in another.

"I will find some shiny rainbow paper for you," says the teacher. Full of excitement about the next day, the children help put away the materials they have used and then get ready to leave.

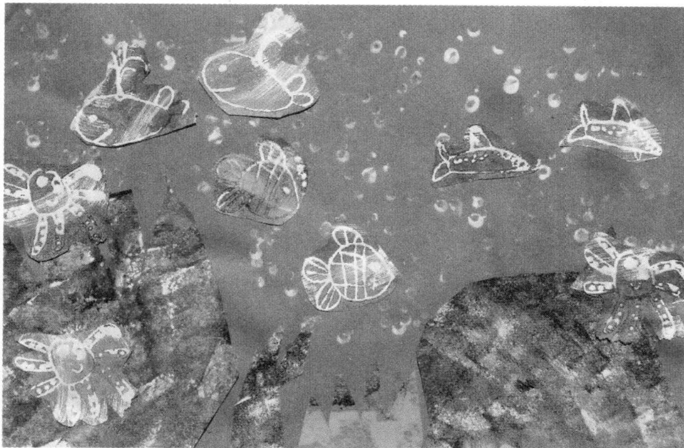

Inspired by the book *The Rainbow Fish,* primary students used carved Styrofoam and sponge printing to create an undersea mural. After studying live fish, Emma, Makenzie, Jason, and Jack worked collaboratively to place their fish prints into the seascape.

Studio Page

WHY THE ARTS?

All of the following have been suggested as important reasons children should be taught the arts. Think carefully about each item and then rank each by its importance. Write a number in front of each, with 1 being the highest rank and 9 being the lowest. Based on your ranking, write a statement that explains why you feel the arts are essential for young children.

_______ The arts are part of being human.

_______ The arts stimulate brain development.

_______ The arts promote early literacy.

_______ The arts improve physical health.

_______ The arts promote emotional well-being.

_______ The arts create community.

_______ The arts foster cognitive growth.

_______ The arts nurture creativity.

____

____

____

____

____

____

____

____

____

____

Studio Page

HOW TO HAVE A SUCCESSFUL OBSERVATION

Observing children involved in arts activities is an invaluable way to learn how children react to various kinds of arts experiences. As an observer, you are free of the pressure of performing and can devote your attention to the small details that busy, overworked caregivers often miss.

The following checklist will help you and the participants in the program you are visiting have a pleasant and rewarding experience.

Before the Visit

- Call for an appointment and get permission to visit.
- Write down the names of the people you speak to on the phone and those of the teachers whose children you will be observing.
- If you intend to use a camera or camcorder, make sure you have all the necessary permissions. In many programs, parents must be asked to sign a release form before you can photograph. Some schools may already have these on file.
- Prepare a form on which to record your observations.

On the Day of the Visit

- Arrive on time and introduce yourself to the teachers. If possible, have them introduce you to the children. If asked, give a simple explanation for your visit, such as, "My name is ____. I can't wait to see what you are doing today."
- Observe and record carefully. Do not bother the teachers. They are there to work with the children, not you.
- When it is time for you to leave, do not disturb the children or the teachers.

After the Observation

- As soon as possible, review your notes and add any special details you remember. Some people find it helpful to make an audiotape recording while the experience is still fresh in their minds.
- Write a note of thanks to everyone with whom you had contact. A special handmade card for the children is always welcome.

Studio Page

OBSERVATION: THE ARTS AND THE CHILD

The purpose of this observation is to observe young children in a typical learning situation. The observation will focus on the artistic behavior of the children in a group educational situation. This observation may be done in an organized school or a child care setting that services children between the ages of one and eight. The observation should last 40 minutes to 1 hour.

Date of observation: ______________________ **Length of observation:** ______________________

Ages of children: ______________________ **Group size:** ______________________

Observation

1. Which arts activities (creative dance, music, dramatic play, and visual arts) are the children involved in?

____

____

____

2. What are the adults doing?

____

____

____

3. How are arts activities made available to the children?

____

____

____

4. How did the children participate in these arts activities? (Examples: tried once then left; engaged in non-verbal or verbal interaction with children and/or adults; worked alone; length of time at activity)

____

____

____

Studio Page

ANALYSIS: THE ARTS AND THE CHILD

Based on your observation, write a response to these questions:

1. How do the arts activities of the children relate to the areas of artistic growth discussed in this chapter?

2. Which artistic goals for children were being met, and which ones were not? Why?

3. What do you think are the guiding principles of the arts curriculum in this program?

Chapter 2

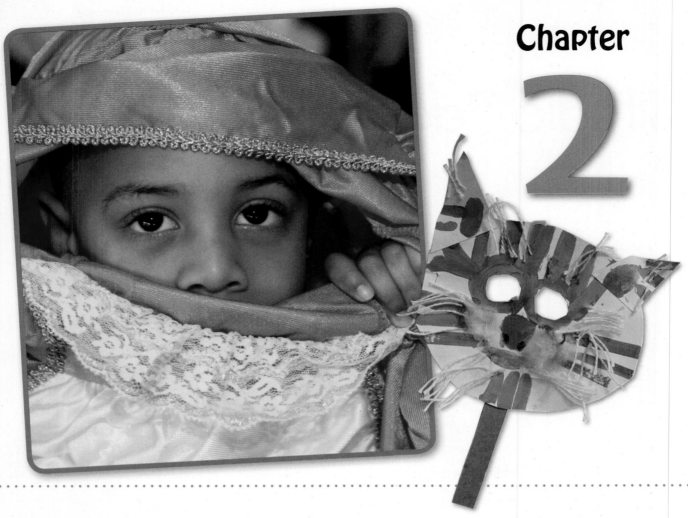

Nurturing Creativity

Questions Addressed in This Chapter:

- What is creativity?
- What does creativity look like?
- What is the creative process?
- How do teachers foster the creative process?

"Encouraging a person to discover their uniqueness and helping them develop its expression can be one of the greatest gifts we can ever give."

—*Fred Rogers (1982, p. 10)*

Young Artists at Work

Several four-year-olds are busy using paper and glue. The teacher has put out a tray of pre-cut yellow squares. Stephen spreads glue all over his paper and then slaps on several yellow squares haphazardly. He pokes at one square, sliding it around in the glue. Maryanne carefully makes small dots of glue. Then she selects a yellow square and places it over the glue dots. With a crayon, she draws eyes, a nose, and a mouth. Keith watches his friends at work, then picks up the glue bottle and makes a line of glue in the center of the paper. He chooses a square from the tray and sticks it in place. Then he adds more glue and another square. Soon his paper is covered with a line of gluey yellow squares.

WHAT IS CREATIVITY?

Genius often comes from finding a new perspective.

—Michael Michalko (2001, p. 19)

Even though children may be the same age and are working with the same materials, the artwork they produce is undeniably unique to each child. It is not enough to understand how a child grows developmentally. Adults who work with young children must also understand, and value, the nature of creativity and how it is expressed in the artistry of each child.

In this tempera painting, William, age five, shows creative thinking. To solve the problem of making a person, he has combined shapes in an original way and then elaborated on his idea by adding extra arms.

Defining Creativity

Creativity has been the subject of much research and analysis, yet there is no generally accepted definition. A creative act can be viewed in many ways. What is thought creative in one time and place may not be thought creative in another. Different researchers have pointed out important characteristics of creativity.

Uniqueness. Creativity is inventing something so unique that it is astonishing to the viewer or user and produces "effective surprise" (Bruner, 1979, p. 12). Thomas Edison's invention of the light bulb or Georges Seurat's use of tiny dots of color to create the style of pointillism are examples of unique products that are considered highly creative.

Rule breaking. Creativity is doing something that goes beyond the accepted rules but in a new way that is understandable and acceptable to a wider audience (Boden, 1990, p. 12). Jackson Pollock's drip paintings used familiar art materials in an unconventional way that grew out of the artistic trends of his time.

Problem solving. E. P. Torrance (1970) described creativity as the ability to see a problem, form an idea to solve it, and then share the results. The innovative American architect Frank Lloyd Wright thought houses should be inexpensive and fit their environment, so he developed slab construction and designed the "prairie home," which became the prototype for the contemporary ranch-style home.

Personal characteristics. Some researchers have concentrated on studying the lives and works of people who are considered highly creative and identifying those qualities that make them exceptional.

In their definitive research on creativity Theresa Amabile (1983) and Mihaly Csikszentmihalyi (1996) have identified the following basic characteristics of creative people:

- They are skilled in a particular area of learning, such as science, the arts, or writing.
- They have the ability to imagine a range of possibilities. They are playful, flexible thinkers who can generate many possible ways of doing something or of solving a problem.
- They are energetic and highly persistent and do not give up, even if they fail many times.
- They set high personal standards for themselves and push themselves to learn more and work harder.
- They are intrinsically motivated, willing to work hard and to struggle with frustration, and, yet, find great pleasure and satisfaction in the act of creation.

Divergent thinking. J. P. Guilford (1986) proposed a model of intelligence that included divergent thinking as one of the basic thought processes. Divergent thinking can be defined as the ability to generate many different solutions to a problem and is a key component of creative problem solving. It is characterized by

- **Fluency**—Being able to produce a multitude of diverse ideas or solutions. An example of fluency would be when a child thinks of many different ways to move like a bird.
- **Flexibility**—Being able to see things from alternative viewpoints. Flexibility is seen when a child plays several different roles, such as mother, child, and police officer, in pretend play.
- **Originality**—Being able to think of ideas or solutions that have never been thought of before. An example of this is when a child takes two magazine clippings of different objects, such as a clock and a bird, and glues them together to create a clock-headed bird.
- **Elaboration**—The ability to improve ideas by adding on or expanding them. Children building with blocks elaborate each other's ideas when they connect what they have made to someone else's creation, such as when one child makes the garage and the other makes the car to go in it.

An interactive process. Mihaly Csikszentmihalyi (1996, 1997) views creativity as a complex process that reflects an individual's motivation to solve a problem, not alone but in interaction with the requirements of a particular field of study and with other experts in that area of study as well as with the public. For example, a composer, in a desire to express a particular idea, might invent a new style of music. The resulting piece of music will reflect the composer's experiences and knowledge of music. This piece will then be judged and accepted or rejected by other composers, musicians, and the public.

Thinking process. In this view, creativity is an integral part of how all people think about and process information. Graham Wallas (1926), who created one of the first models of the creative process, identified four steps in creative thinking.

1. Preparation or the gathering of ideas
2. Incubation or subconscious pondering of the problem
3. Illumination or the "Aha!" moment when the solution is discovered
4. Verification when the solution is clear

Creativity, defined this way, can be seen as the human ability to see a problem or need, to use one's knowledge and skill to make plans, to try out ideas, and to come up with a solution. This creative process or set of behaviors can be seen operating whenever someone solves a problem or produces a unique product.

WHAT DOES CREATIVITY LOOK LIKE?

Most animals have inherited reflexes and responses that enable them to survive from birth. Human beings, on the other hand, must learn almost everything starting in infancy. Creativity is the mechanism by which people use past knowledge and learned skills to meet the needs of a new situation or to solve a problem. The result is a creative work.

Characteristics of Creative Works

How do we know when a performance or product is creative? Donald W. MacKinnon (1962) has proposed five characteristics that a creative solution to a problem or product should have.

- **It must be original**—This means it is something unusual or never before seen and experienced—a novelty.
- **It needs to be relevant**—The product must fulfill the need of the creator or solve the problem being addressed.
- **It defies tradition**—Nonstandard approaches, methods, or ideas are used to solve the problem or make the product.
- **It is elegant**—There has to be an aesthetic quality to the solution or product.
- **It must exist and be shared**—Recognition of creativity requires that the solution or product be evaluated and compared to others.

Creativity in Children

Because children are less familiar with the world, they are constantly dealing with fresh circumstances and problems and "creating" a unique response to the situation. The infant finds a dab of spilled milk and creates a design by swirling small fingers through it. The toddler rhythmically taps a spoon on a table. The preschooler finds a stone, adds some crayon marks, and imagines it is a "little creature."

The creative imagination is fueled by knowledge. What knowledge do these children need to have in order to pretend they are on a picnic?

The nature of the creative artistic responses children make will depend upon many factors. An infant does not yet have the ability to create a landscape painting. A toddler cannot produce a symphony. A preschooler cannot carve a marble monument. Nevertheless, even though the children are limited by their skill level and stage of physical growth, their artistic performances are still highly creative. At any moment, each child is at a precise point in development, has a unique set of experiences, and has a personal base of knowledge and skills. These combine to produce creative responses to each stimulus that the child confronts. We should not find it surprising that a one-of-a-kind child produces one-of-a-kind art, music, dance movements, and dramatic play!

At the same time, creativity in children looks different from that in adults. Adults bring to the creative process a reservoir of experience and skill. They have technical expertise in their subject matter and knowledge of other creative works. They also have years of living in a particular culture, which may set limits on what is deemed possible or acceptable. Children, on the other hand, are only beginning to obtain experience and expertise and are not yet bound by a rigid concept of what is possible. Therefore, their creative acts are characterized by spontaneity, imagination, and fantasy.

Spontaneity. Because children have less expertise than adults and have experienced less pressure to conform, they tend to be freer in their creative ideas and are more willing to share them. This leads to an open and bold approach to arts activities and an increased willingness to explore and take risks.

- **Imagination**—When we use our **imagination** or pretend, we are playing with mental images. These images are ideas of things that can be manipulated in the mind and can take visual, auditory, and sensory form. The ability to imagine is particularly strong in young children. Being able to pretend is a key feature of young children's play. A banana becomes a telephone; a bed becomes a boat. Indeed, Jane Piirto (2004) sees children's play as the "seed ground of adult imagination."

Young Artists at Work

"Look!" said the teacher after sharing the book *Planting a Rainbow* (Ehlert, 1988). "Here are some pictures of beautiful spring flowers for us to use in collages." He places a basket of magazine clippings showing flowers on one side in the art center. A group of children gather around and begin to cut and paste enthusiastically, while the teacher imagines a beautiful garden of finished collages to hang in the hall.

When the children are done, they hurry to share their creations with their teacher.

"Oh," said the teacher, seeing the finished collages. Where were the gardens? Instead of flowers, each child held a unique artwork. Some collages featured irregular shapes showing the backs of the clippings. Instead of flowers they were covered with print or a lopsided face encircled with pieces of an advertisement. Then the teacher looked again, and saw the children's creativity.

"Each one of you used the clippings in your own creative way," said the teacher enthusiastically. "That is what makes art so exciting. You never know what will happen."

- **Fantasy—Fantasy** is the creation of imaginary worlds. It is where the mental images of the imagination are brought to life through story. It is the realm of monsters, fairies, and flying elephants. For young children, the difference between reality and fantasy is not as strongly delineated as it is in adults. This allows children to be less stereotypical in their ideas than adults. This ability is often envied by adult artists. As Pablo Picasso said, "Every child is an artist. The problem is how to remain an artist once he grows up."

Nurturing Creativity

As the process of creativity is discussed in this section, it is important to remember that the creative behaviors being described come from within the child. These behaviors are not distinctly separate from each other, but are elements of the individual's whole approach to learning. Creativity is not a skill that can be taught directly but is nurtured by a teacher and an environment that is conducive to the creative process.

One of the more difficult things for adults to learn is when to set limits, when to offer direction, and when to stand back and let children do it by themselves. To nurture the creative process we must constantly set ourselves the task of providing safe stimuli and an enriched environment that allows young children to learn in creative ways.

In the following discussion of the creative process, we will see how our behaviors and attitudes, and the decisions we make, can create such a nurturing environment.

WHAT IS THE CREATIVE PROCESS?

The creative process can be viewed as being composed of a combination of mental processes that will lead to the final creative product or action. It consists of the following:

- **Knowledge—**What individuals already know about what they are exploring
- **Motivation—**The inner drive to accomplish something
- **Skill—**The development of expertise in using tools and materials or in carrying out an action
- **Immersion—**Being intensely focused on creating something unique with this knowledge and skill
- **Incubation—**A period of time in which individuals think and process what they know and what they wish to do
- **Production—**The tangible expression or product that is the end result of the creative process

Knowledge

Whenever people face a new stimulus or problem, the first thing that comes into play is what they already know. Young children have a much more limited knowledge base than adults, so their responses are often wildly different from those we might expect. The amount of knowledge children have about an arts technique or a concept will influence what their creative response will be. For example, given an assortment of rhythm instruments, a toddler might decide to bang the drum with a maraca.

Teachers help children gain knowledge about the arts in several ways.

Talking about the arts. Use a vocabulary rich in artistic language and point out how the children have used the different arts elements in their paintings, songs, dances, and make-believe play. For example, children who know what a line is and are aware that there are many different kinds of lines will be able to make a unique line. Activities to use in introducing the art elements are provided in Chapter 4.

Exploring the arts. To enhance fluency, provide a variety of arts experiences that allow children to explore new ways of using their bodies, their voices, and the materials and tools of the arts.

Experiencing the arts. Take children to music, drama, and dance performances and show them the works of visual artists. This encourages flexibility and elaboration as children can take what they experienced and build on it to create something new. For example, after seeing a children's theater production of *Little Red Riding Hood,* a group of children might decide to act out the story from the viewpoint of the wolf.

Accepting individual differences in knowledge. Each child brings different background knowledge to the arts experience. We must remember that a child's artistic responses may not be what we expect because their knowledge base is limited. Incorporating a used paper towel into a collage can be seen as a highly creative choice. It demonstrates an ability to categorize it as a piece of textured paper. This represents a highly creative action, equivalent to the famous Spanish painter Pablo Picasso using a piece of real newspaper to represent itself in his early Cubist painting—the result of which was equally unpleasant to art connoisseurs of the time.

Motivation

The inner drive that causes an individual to want to do something is called **motivation**. Young children are driven by intense curiosity about the world around them. Everything is new and exciting to them. They want to touch everything, see everything, and try everything. How wonderful for the teacher!

Often we have only to present the art materials or technique and give a few simple instructions, and the children's natural curiosity and desire to explore and play will do the rest. This is called **intrinsic motivation.** When intrinsic motivation is at work, smiling, laughing children gather excitedly around us. They ask curious questions and cannot wait to get started. They spend a great deal of time on their explorations, and want to do more and more.

Giving rewards and prizes is known as **extrinsic motivation.** Prizes or stars for "good" work or competition among students to win a ribbon replace intrinsic motivation with extrinsic motivation and do not belong in an arts program for young children. Such external rewards have been shown to have a limiting effect on creativity. Research by Therese Amabile (1983) found that children produced more artworks when engaged in an open-ended, free play environment than when offered rewards. Another study, in which children were asked to tell stories from a picture book, showed that the group that was rewarded produced stories judged less creative than those by children in the unrewarded group (Amabile Hennessey, and Grossman, 1986).

In order to create an intrinsically motivating environment, teachers need to be as creative as their students.

Provide choice. Intrinsically motivating activities are always **open-ended.** These are activities that have a multitude of possible results and ways of getting there. When children choose what material they will use or what idea they will express, they take interest in and feel ownership of their work, which will heighten their motivation.

Be sensitive. Unfortunately, intrinsic motivation is a delicate force. It may be easily lost through inappropriate organization or presentation of arts activities. Overly restrictive arts activities quickly dampen a child's natural curiosity. Self-motivation in children is

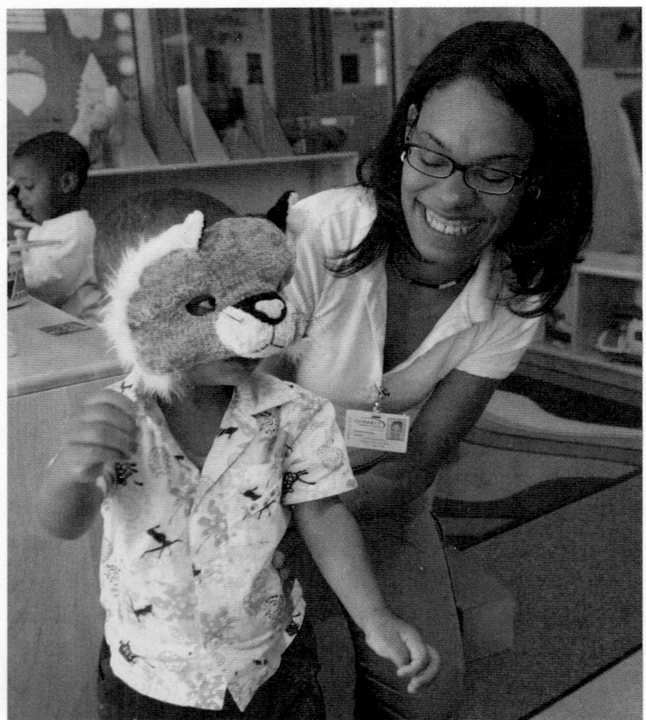

Motivation cannot be taught. It must be inspired. A child and a mask set the stage for a playful, imaginative interaction with a teacher who values creativity.

diminished by materials that can be used in only one way, projects that must match a teacher-made model, or actions that must conform to a fixed standard.

Be surprising. Intrinsic motivation occurs when the mind is active. Get children thinking and asking questions by making sure something new or surprising is always happening in the room. Display new artworks, introduce new materials, play unfamiliar music, wear unusual clothing, tell new stories, and constantly discuss new ideas and experiences.

Be flexible. Intrinsic motivation develops from within. Create child ownership of problems and ideas by being willing to change direction and follow up on their new interests. If a child arrives at school excited because he or she just saw the moon out during the day, take the whole group outside to see it and then make up stories, songs, and dances about the moon.

Be encouraging. Establish an environment in which mistakes are part of the learning process. Be willing to try a child's idea even if it seems it will not work. Teach children to respect the differing ideas and work of others in an atmosphere where insults and ridicule are discouraged. Anxiety about making a mistake can prevent children from fully exploring an arts activity.

Value difference. **Conformity** occurs when children feel they must be like everyone else. This can make children afraid to express themselves in a new way. For example, fear of getting dirty or ruining something can cause children to be unmotivated to try the messier art materials.

Show confidence. Teachers who nourish creativity demonstrate a high level of confidence in their students. Children do not worry about what the final products will look like or how other teachers and parents will judge them. They are more interested in the process the child goes through as they create than in the product that may or may not result.

Stand back. If children feel that they are constantly being watched and evaluated, they may be less willing to take risks and try new ideas. If they think we are going to interfere with their investigations, they will hesitate to pursue their own interests. If we solve the problem for them or do the work for them, they will expect that adults always will and will become complacent.

Act playful. Create opportunities for everyone to laugh, play, and have fun together. Intrinsic motivation happens when both teachers and children are relaxed and happy.

Be on the lookout for emergent problems. Problems that bring forth the most creativity are those that arise in the process of working. A problem that happens when trying to accomplish a task, such as mixing just the right color paint for a painting or attempting to play an original melody on the xylophone, is far more motivating to a child than solving a problem assigned by the teacher.

Show support for creativity. Cherish, honor, and display the creative ideas, actions, and works of the children. Instead of stereotypical commercial bulletin board patterns and ready-made pictures, make presentation panels that document in words and pictures the children's creative efforts, both failures and successes, and create visual displays that inform parents. Chapter 8 provides directions for making presentation panels.

Provide variety. Boredom arises when the child is constantly offered the same materials with little or no variation. For example, as wonderful as drawing with crayons can be, this cannot be a total visual arts program for young children. In the same way, a housekeeping corner is a great place for dramatic play but should not be the only play center offered all year. Ideas for dramatic play are provided in Chapter 12.

Teacher Tip

CHOOSING CREATIVE ACTIVITIES

When choosing motivating arts activities for young children, ask the following questions:

1. Can children explore on their own?
2. Can children go at their own pace?
3. Can children figure out their own ways to do things?
4. Are there many possible ways to do this activity?
5. Are the rules based on safety and management, not on the product desired?
6. Is it challenging?
7. Can children set their own goals?
8. Will it be fun—will they laugh, imagine, and play?

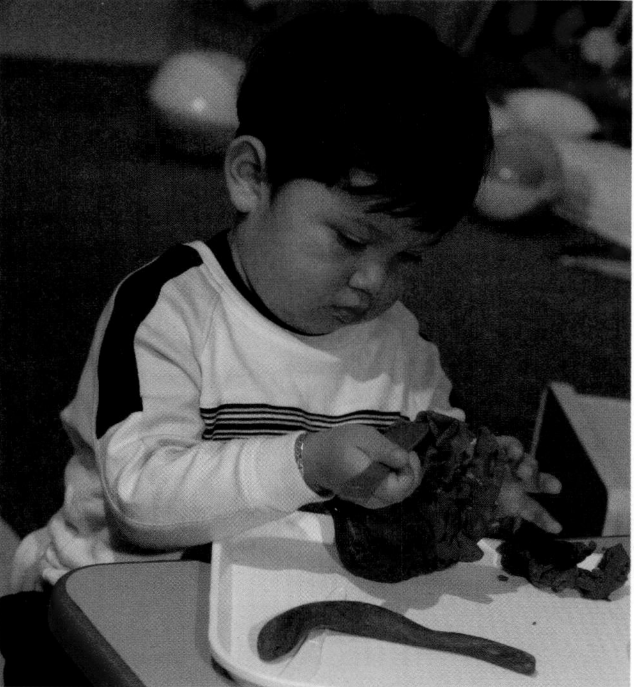

Exploration is the first step toward creation. This child discovers he can make holes in a piece of modeling clay using a tool.

Skill

The more skilled children are, the more they can concentrate on creatively using the artistic elements in their singing, dancing, drawing, painting, and more. We need to carefully organize activities so that the **skills** required to accomplish them are appropriate for ability of the young child. Activities requiring new skills must provide a significant level of challenge but be within the physical and mental capabilities of the child to learn. Materials should be aesthetically interesting and limited to those that can be easily handled by inexperienced children.

Children move through three levels of skill development as they investigate a new way of working or performing: **exploration, practice,** and **responsive.**

Exploration. The basis of all arts creation is the exploration of the medium. Exploration, therefore, must be the mainstay of early childhood arts programs. At this level the child is discovering what happens when they use the material or technique. The process of creating becomes secondary. Although this level is most common to infants and toddlers, it is found any time a child or adult tries something new. Even accomplished artists spend time exploring a new material or technique before using it in their work. Children need to know that it is okay to explore, and that these explorations will not be judged.

Selecting exploration activities. Exploration activities are open-ended and allow children enough time, space, and choice in which to develop comfort and control. For example, after a new puppet, art medium, musical instrument, or dance movement is introduced, provide an area or center where children can try out them out on their own.

Practice. Exploration must be followed by time to practice. At this level the child returns again and again to the same material or action, each time showing more organization and direction. For example, a child after several days or weeks of exploring the xylophone by randomly hitting notes may begin to tap two or three notes repeatedly in a rhythmic pattern.

Children need to be given many opportunities to use the same material over and over in order to develop control and skill. Putting out a new art material

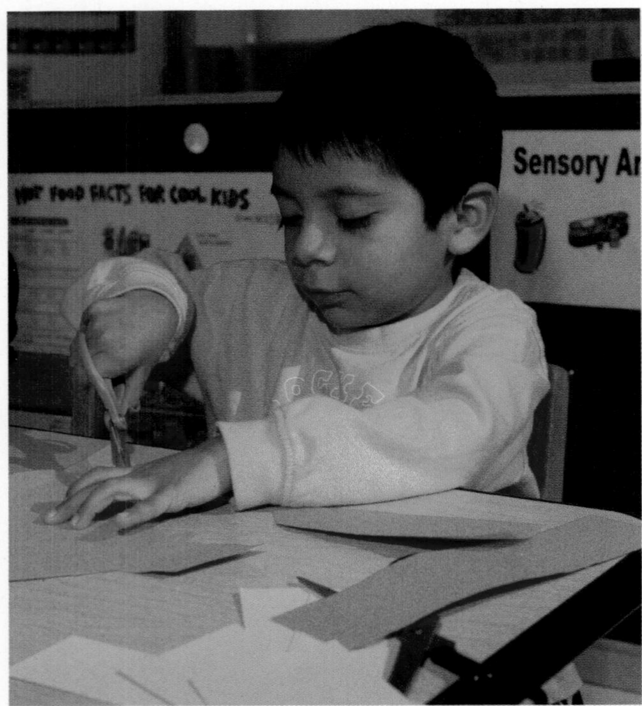

Children need many opportunities to practice new skills, such as cutting with scissors.

or musical instrument each day, for example, does not help children increase their skill using them to creatively express their thoughts and feelings.

Selecting practice activities. In selecting practice activities, make sure that they do, in fact, require the same skills that were introduced in the explorations, so that children develop confidence in their own abilities. Children who are able to attach paper to a collage may be able to glue down similar sizes and shapes of fabric as well, but they may find that the very different qualities of yarn make it more difficult to glue successfully.

Responsive. As children gain skill, their approach changes. They dive into the materials and techniques, no longer worried about how they will control them, but excited instead by the new way they can play and communicate their ideas. This is the responsive level where the artist is confidently in control and able to plan how to express ideas and feelings.

1. **Planning a responsive activity.** Responsive activities start with thought-provoking experiences, visual stimulation, and multisensory happenings, followed by opportunities to use the arts in all of their multimedia dimensions. For example, dramatizing how a letter travels from home to the post office and at last to the recipient stretches children's thought processes as they try to creatively represent what they know and feel about getting mail. Another name for responsive activities is **representation.**
2. **Selecting responsive activities.** Activities that require children to communicate ideas and feelings should use materials and techniques with which they are familiar. Making a mural or creating books about a trip to the zoo is not the time to introduce using chalk for the first time. Rather, select a drawing material the children have explored and practiced previously.
3. **Encouraging responsive activities.** Children are more likely to express an experience creatively when familiar visual arts, dramatic play, music, and dance activities are readily available following such events as visitors to the class, stories that are read or told, science experiments, exciting field trips, and all of the other daily experiences of a young child.
4. **Sharing responsive activities.** Encourage children to share their ideas by providing time to discuss the children's responsive arts creations and recording their oral commentary in class journals and as captions to their work.

Responsive activities ask children to recreate their experiences through the arts. Courtney, age five, uses chalk and tempera in her picture of an elephant she saw at the circus.

5. **Valuing children's own expressive forms.** Although children's responsive level to creative work may be starting to contain somewhat recognizable images, we must not demand that children produce a recognizable picture or imitate an event precisely. Activities that require children to produce or act like identifiable turkeys or rabbits or Christmas trees set both teachers and children up for failure. The fact that most young children cannot successfully produce such items on their own is what leads us to provide patterns, coloring-book pictures, or precut shapes to "help" the children. Such activities tell children that their creative ideas are unacceptable and not valued and should be avoided. To nurture the creative process, offer only those open-ended activities that develop skills without dictating the end result.

Immersion

Immersion is the state of being so completely focused on creating something that the passage of time is forgotten, as are personal needs and what is happening around us. In this state the artist feels relaxed and calm. Ideas seem to flow effortlessly from mind to hands. The artist is not concerned with the end product but only with the pleasure of the process itself. Creativity is at work! All of the knowledge, skill, and motivation of the individual have come together to make this moment possible. Mihaly Csikszentmihalyi (1997) calls this feeling of intense concentration and involvement the "flow."

Children need time to immerse themselves in creative activities. This child shows intense concentration as he moves the toy animals to match the story he is imagining.

It is much easier for children to enter this state of flow than adults. Adults rarely have uninterrupted, unlimited time in which to create. Some people, such as artists and writers, find that they have to go off by themselves to a "studio" or "garret" in order to work. Most people, however, spend their days surrounded by the pressure of social ties and job commitments and tending to basic human needs, with only rare moments to become immersed in the creative process.

Provide time to work. For creativity to happen, sufficient time must be planned to allow children to explore and experiment until satisfied. Young children cannot be rushed. Children who feel pressured to finish in a certain amount of time become frustrated, often to the point of crying. When offering an arts activity or center for the first few times, and it is unclear how much time the children will need, present it at the beginning of the session. If children want to start an activity when they will not have sufficient time, it is better to redirect them to something else.

Avoid interruptions. It is extremely frustrating for a child to be interrupted when immersed in the creative process. It will happen, despite the best planning, that children in the act of creating will need to be interrupted. If an individual child must be interrupted, do so gently. Try to make eye contact before giving a direction. Offer the assurance that the child can continue the activity at another time. It is essential to keep such interruptions to an absolute minimum. If this happens often enough, the child will eventually lose the motivation to create.

Incubation and Production

The creative process is like a stew in which knowledge and skill are the raw ingredients that are stirred together by motivation and immersion. **Incubation** is the slow simmering of this rich mix, which results in creative ideas and products. During the incubation

Young Artists at Work

A young child dabs some paste with her fingers and then begins to rub it across her paper in a swirling pattern. Although she is usually easily distracted, at this moment she pays no attention to the other children working beside her at the table. Instead of her perpetual chatter, she is silent. Her tongue projects slightly from her mouth as her eyes follow the movement of her hand. If we speak to her at this moment, she may not even hear us, and if she does, she may jump slightly or hesitate before responding to us. In the simple act of spreading the paste in a new way, this child has become immersed in the process of creation.

"Laurel, age five, inspired by a piece of embroidered cloth, has combined what she knows about cats and people to create something new: 'A Cat Lady.'"

stage, young artists are actively engaged in trying out ideas, asking themselves questions, and evaluating their actions. Outwardly, they may study the materials or handle them playfully. They may experiment with an idea or movement and try something new. They may test the limits of the material, the rules, or the teacher's patience. At other times, they may sit quietly and stare off into space or concentrate intently on what they are creating. Inside they may be thinking such thoughts as, "What will happen if I do this?" "How will these things go together?" "Wow, I didn't expect that to happen!" and "I never saw anything like this before."

All of this leads to **production,** when the ingredients in the stew blend together to form something new, a flavor that has never existed before. At this point, the children have become their creations because each child's knowledge, skills, and motivation are uniquely different from every other child who has ever existed. Children's creative production is an extension of all that they are at that moment. However, at all times we need to remember that it is the process the child went through to get to this moment that is key, not the final product.

HOW DO TEACHERS FOSTER THE CREATIVE PROCESS?

Adults will always be outside of the child's very personal creative process. However, the role we play is crucially important. Psychological studies carried out by Carl Rogers (1976) have shown that an atmosphere of psychological safety is necessary for creative processing to occur. Empathy and acceptance in a nonjudgmental setting lets creativity happen. It is the teacher's task to establish an environment and teaching approach in which these conditions can occur.

Becoming a Teacher of the Creative Arts

Helping children be creative in the arts does not require teachers to be highly skilled professional artists. What we do need to be is enthusiastic and passionate about the arts. For many people, feeling comfortable teaching the arts can be a challenge. How we see ourselves as artists, musicians, dancers, and actors depends on our past experiences in the different art forms and the judgments we or others have made about our artistic abilities. In some cases, we may feel more confident in one art form than another. This personal history sets the stage, but does not have to determine one's effectiveness as a teacher of the arts (Craft, 2002).

Acknowledge one's personal history. Becoming more comfortable with the arts begins first with understanding why we feel confident or hesitant about performing in the different art forms. Think back to your earliest experiences in the arts. Did you take dance lessons as a child? Were you told you had a beautiful singing voice? Did another child make fun of a picture you drew? Were you in a play and embarrassed when you forgot your lines? Understanding your own personal struggles and successes in the arts will help you be more aware of and sympathetic to the feelings the children you are working with may be experiencing.

Learn more about the arts. If there is an arts area with which you are unfamiliar or feel unsure about, try to learn more by attending a class or workshop, reading about it, and, most importantly, trying your hand at it. One of the best ways to learn something is to teach it to someone else. Select activities, such as those in this book, that expose children to the arts from a wide variety of times, cultures, and people, and develop an expanded view of the arts together with your students.

Create together. Children love when their teachers perform with them. They will not care how our voices sound, what we look like when we are dancing, how well we act out being the big bad wolf, or how well we draw a dog, because they will be busy singing, dancing, acting, and drawing, too.

Teacher Tip

A CREATIVITY-NURTURING TEACHER

Research in preschools by Angeloska-Galevska identifies the following characteristics of teachers who nurture creativity in their children (Craft, 2002).

- They value creativity.
- They have rapport with their students.
- They provide open-ended activities and materials that allow choice.

Model Being a Creative Artist

Children want to be like the adults they admire. They pretend they are grown-ups—a doctor making a sick doll better, a firefighter putting out a fire in a block building, a mom or a dad cooking dinner on the play stove. Most children are not often exposed to adults creating and talking about the arts. The arts for many

Teachers model creative behavior when they participate enthusiastically in arts activities.

young children is something children do at child care or school. Children, not adults, play with play dough; children, not adults, dress up and pretend. Because of this, many adults feel the arts are a childlike activity and have peripheral value to society. It is not enough for teachers to provide wonderful arts experiences for children—they must also model artistic behavior.

The teacher can model creative artistic behavior by exhibiting the following qualities.

Show self-confidence. No matter how you feel about your own arts skills, always model artistic self-confidence. Would a teacher say to a child, "I'm not a very good reader," or "I can't write the letter 'A' very well," and then expect the child to want to be a good reader or to make a well-formed "A"? However, many adults do not hesitate to tell children that they think themselves poor singers, or that they cannot draw. The child may well think that if this important adult who can read so well and knows so much cannot create in the arts, then it must be very hard to be good at any of the arts.

Be positive. Adults often say to children, "You're a much better artist or singer or dancer than I," even though they would never say to one child that her work or performance was better than her friend's. Putting themselves down in this way does not build up the confidence of children but instead introduces the element of comparative value. The child thinks, "How can I be better than the teacher? Can some art be better than others?" There should be no "better" or "best" in an early childhood setting, for either children or adults. Instead, differences in skill level should be explained as the result of experience and practice.

Exhibit enthusiasm. The children will mirror how we feel about the arts. If we are fearful and tentative about a project, then the children will react with hesitation. If we dislike the feel of a certain material, then the children will sense this and show discomfort. We should avoid using art media or offering activities that we personally dislike. It is important to be able to express enthusiasm. Words full of warmth and joy should be used, such as

"I can't wait to share this painting with you!"

"Look at how this hat makes you look just like a fireman!"

"Oooo, this play dough feels so smooth!"

"This music makes me feel joyous!"

Display the arts. Personal appearance is a way of showing how people value the arts and attracting attention to artistic elements and concepts. Dressing in shades of blue when studying the color blue or wearing a wool sweater when talking about fiber art can provide a catalyst for discussion. Appreciation of artwork from other cultures can be shown, for example, by displaying African prints, Guatemalan ikat weavings, Indian embroidery, and Native American jewelry and by playing music from around the world on a regular basis.

Participate fully. It is important for children to see that adults also enjoy the arts, and that they are not hesitant to join in with them. Nevertheless, teachers must be careful to model process and not product. There is a difference between showing children that adults enjoy the arts and providing them with a set model to copy.

Teacher Tip

MODELING PROCESS

- Sit with a group of children involved in an arts activity.
- Explore with the children.
- Watch the children's motions and use similar or slightly more advanced motions.
- Avoid doing something well beyond the children's skill level. For example, rolling balls of clay between the palms is beyond the capability of most two-year-olds and will frustrate them. Cutting out folded paper hearts is too difficult for most four-year-olds.

MODELING TECHNIQUE (DEMONSTRATION)

1. Ask if the child needs help.
2. Ask a leading question or suggest another approach.
3. Show only the part of the process that is needed.
4. Verbally explain as it is being done.

Communicating Empathy and Acceptance

We speak with more than words. Our whole body communicates our meaning. How close we stand, how we move our arms, and the expression on our faces tell children how we feel about them and their creative work. It is important for our nonverbal behavior to match what we are saying to children.

Faces are a mirror of our feelings. Smiling at a child tells that child that we are pleased with him or her and that we like what he or she is doing. Frowns and cold stares distance us from the child and show disapproval. We need to be aware of the messages we are sending. If a teacher says to a child, "You used the glue in an interesting way" but frowns at the same time because the glue is dripping on the floor, then the positive words do not foster creative development. It is better to react honestly. If the dripping glue is disturbing, deal with the problem first before commenting on the artwork. The teacher might say, "Let's put your collage over here and wipe up all the glue; then I can look at your collage."

How we move and gesture are also strong expressions of our feelings. It is important to remain at the children's level by sitting or stooping when interacting with them as they participate in the arts process. Using expansive arm motions can signal enthusiasm or inclusion. More subtly, hand signals and **American Sign Language** can be used to introduce the children to other ways of communicating while at the same time providing a quick and nonintrusive way to signal a child without disturbing the other children. For example, signing the word *thank you* can communicate to a child who is wiping up some paint drips that she is doing something that is appreciated.

Sharing Emotional Responses

No matter how hard we try to cover up our emotions, children seem to sense how we are feeling. It is often better to be open about how we feel. It is hard to shrug off the frustration of a car that would not start that morning or the anger left from sharp words with a friend. The arts can provide a way to express such feelings. Share with the children the source of the feeling and then say, for example, "That car is so frustrating, I'm going to act out a story about it to show how it is all broken," or "I am going to draw a whole bunch of angry lines on my paper and get rid of some of this angry feeling." Showing the children that adults use the arts as an emotional release lets children know that people of all ages use the arts to show their feelings.

Listening Actively

One of the most important ways a teacher or caregiver can respond to a child is through **active listening.**

Active listening is one of the most important ways to respond to young children.

This should be one of our first responses when children share information about their arts experiences. Especially with new children, it is extremely important to listen before responding verbally, in order to learn more about the artists' intent before deciding what to say to them. We also need to listen to the children we know well to show that we care about what they are saying. Active listening consists of the following components:

- **Waiting—**Do not always respond instantly and verbally to everything a child says. Establish eye contact, and wait for the child to speak. This will also provide time to formulate a thoughtful verbal response if the child does not offer a comment.
- **Looking—**Maintain eye contact with a child while she or he is talking. Remain at the child's eye level if possible.
- **Responding—**Respond with value-free head nods, appropriate facial expressions, and sounds as the child talks.

Responding Verbally

Words are powerful. They can transform a humdrum experience into an exhilarating one or destroy a special moment in a second. What we say to young artists can have a profound effect on how children view the arts for the rest of their lives. Many adults can trace the origin of their feeling of artistic incompetence to a thoughtless comment by a caring adult. We need to take care in offering comments to children, and not speak off the top of our heads or repeat the words spoken to us when we were children. What teachers say and how they respond to children is one of the most significant parts of the educational process, and it takes practice to choose words wisely and sparingly.

Importance of dialogue. Research indicates that the younger the child, the more important it is to communicate on a one-to-one basis rather than in a large group situation (Lay-Dopyera and Dopyera, 1992). Arts activities provide significant moments for personal dialogue between a child and a caring adult. This relationship is an important one. When there are many warm, positive interactions between adults and young children, there is a beneficial effect on social and emotional development.

In addition, by choosing words thoughtfully, we not only help children feel good about themselves but expand their thought processes and make the arts experience more meaningful to them.

Using Praise

Probably one of the most common responses to children's artwork is **unconditional praise,** in which a general phrase is said over and over regardless of what the child has done. "Good work!" "Great painting!" and "Nice singing!" are said quickly to the child as the teacher scoops up the drippy painting or hustles the child off to the next activity. The intent is to give encouragement and indicate to children that they have performed successfully.

However, studies indicate that consistent overuse of such praise actually diminishes the behavior being complimented (Kohn, 2006). Said over and over, the words become empty and meaningless. How can every picture be great or wonderful? The children come to believe that the teachers are not really looking at their work. In addition, unconditional praise does not help children think more deeply about their work or make the experience more educational for them.

Making Judgments

When teachers say, "I like it!" or "I like the way you— ," they are making judgments and expressing their personal values. Besides being overused, such terms open the door to more deleterious results. Many adults prefer realistic artwork that is neat and orderly, music that sounds familiar, and stories that follow familiar plots. They are more likely to respond positively to a painting of a house flanked by two trees and overlooked by a smiling sun than to a dripping paper covered in thick swirls of olive-green paint.

Expressing adult personal taste in young children's art can lead to some children believing that they are better artists and others feeling like failures. As many arts teachers who work with adults have noted (Cameron, 1992; Edwards, 1979), a large number of people have poor artistic self-images because as very young children a piece of their artwork or how they sang or danced was disliked or compared unfavorably to another's by a significant adult in their life.

In addition, Marshall (1995) and Kohn (2006) warn that by focusing the children's attention on whether or not their behavior is likable, they learn that they must perform to please the teacher rather than to successfully accomplish the learning task. The child's joy in self-expression through the arts is then replaced with the child's conscious effort to produce something likable.

Unfortunately, this sort of judgmental praise naturally flows from our lips. Arguments can be made that in some sense we do want children to behave in pleasing ways; telling them we like something may increase the likelihood that they will repeat the action. However, the creative arts are based on the expansion of new behaviors rather than the repetition of limited actions. Consider what meaningful information a child receives when a teacher says something such as, "I like the way you used green paint today." Does the teacher really want the child to repeat the same use of green paint in every painting, or is there some better way to respond to this child's work?

Using Positive Feedback

Positive feedback tells children precisely what they did well. Instead of saying "Great painting!" the thoughtful teacher says, "I noticed you wiped your brush on the edge of the paint container so the paint didn't drip." Positive feedback is best used to let children know when they have used a technique well or behaved in a way that will give them further success at the activity.

In order to respond specifically, teachers need to have a clear idea in their minds about what techniques and behaviors are appropriate and possible for the children, and then they must carefully observe the children at work. Positive feedback enhances children's feelings of self-confidence and creativity—it provides information on what they have done well, and communicates to them that adults are personally interested enough in their arts activities to observe specific things they have done.

Teacher Tip

Alfie Kohn (1993) suggests the following guidelines when praising children:

- Praise the behavior or product, not the child. Say, "That's a very unique brush stroke," not "You're a very original artist."
- Be specific. Say, "I hear you singing new words to the song," not "That's a nice song."
- Avoid phony praise. Use a natural, spontaneous voice.
- Avoid praise that creates competition. Praise the whole group, not one individual. Say "I see so many of you dancing to the music," not "Susie is being such a good dancer today."

Even though positive feedback seems more like a wordy description than praise, when it is delivered with the same facial expression and the same warm enthusiastic tone of voice that we would use for "Great job!" the child receives it as praise for being successful in a very specific way.

Positive feedback can take several forms, each appropriate in different situations. With practice, this kind of response can become a natural way of talking to children about their creative work in daily interactions.

Using descriptive statements. A **descriptive statement** can be used to make children aware of their behavior and of how they solved a problem creatively, or to increase their understanding of arts concepts. Such descriptive statements show children that teachers value their individuality, because careful observation is necessary to provide a meaningful description. Each child at the same activity can receive a different comment.

These kinds of statements refer to how the child is working either with others or with the materials. They are the easiest statements to formulate and can serve as a good entrance into a conversation with children about their work.

If children are working with a material, comment on how they manipulated it. For example,

> *"I noticed that you rolled the clay into a long snake."*
>
> *"You moved the (computer) mouse in a circular way to make those curved lines."*

When children work well with others, describe their behavior.

> *"I see that you are singing in tune with your partner."*

Statements can also refer to the amount of effort children have put into an activity.

> *"You spent a great deal of time working with Allan on your dinosaur project."*

Describing artistic decisions. Verbalizing the steps children have taken to solve a problem or summarizing their solutions are two important ways to make children aware of how they worked through a process.

If the child has struggled to find a solution to a problem, then describe the specific steps taken.

> *"I noticed that you tried several ways to attach the tubes together. First you tried gluing them, and then you tried bending them. Now you have pushed one inside the other, and they are holding together well."*

In responding to a finished piece of work, summarize what choices the child has made. Artistic decision statements often contain the following phrases: "you tried," "you found," "you discovered," "you chose." For example,

> *"You have chosen to use the drum to accompany your song."*
>
> *"I noticed you found a way to attach that unusually shaped button to your puppet for its nose."*

Describing arts concepts. Descriptive statements can increase children's vocabulary, further their understanding of the arts, and make them aware of the sensory qualities of their work. Everyone who works with children and the arts should be familiar with the artistic elements of each of the art forms. Chapter 4 provides a detailed description of these elements, and also of the sensory qualities that should form the basis of this kind of verbal description.

Using arts concepts as the basis of descriptions allows higher-level responses to toddlers' scribbles and arts explorations. For example,

> *"Look at all the swirling lines you have made!"*
> *"I hear you tapping the rhythm of the tune."*
> *"You are dancing with lots of energy!"*
> *"Look at the way the wet paint sparkles!"*

Paraphrasing and scaffolding. To **paraphrase,** teachers repeat what children have just said in their own words. This is an excellent way to show children that the teacher has been listening to them. For example,

> *Child: "I made lots of green lines."*
> *Teacher: "Yes, you made many green lines."*

To **scaffold,** the teacher adds to the child's thought. This helps increase the child's vocabulary and conceptual understanding. For example,

> *Child: "I made lots green lines."*
> *Teacher: "Yes, you painted many bright green lines with the wide brush."*

Talking to a child about their creative work is a wonderful way to communicate. What questions would you ask Elizabeth, age six, about her tempera painting?

Responding to meaning. When teachers respond to a child's artistic performance on a positive interpretive level, they model for the child the way the arts communicate to other people. We can refer to a personal sensation or a visual memory by saying, for example, "The story you told about your new puppy makes me remember my first puppy," or "The rectangles in your collage remind me of all the colorful windows in the apartment across the street."

Hall and Duffy (cited in Noyce and Christie, 1989, p. 46) found that when teachers initiated conversations with children by making a statement about their personal feelings or experiences, children gave less stilted, longer, and more spontaneous replies. Used appropriately, such responses can create a wonderful depth of communication between the child and adult.

Asking questions. Questioning or making a leading statement is one way to learn directly from the artists what their intent was. Questions can also be used to further children's understanding of the arts process, help them reflect on the consequences of their actions, and assess what they have learned from the arts activity. By encouraging children to verbalize about their artwork, we also help them develop language skills and clarify their thought processes. Questions must be phrased very carefully so that they are not intrusive, allow many possible responses from children, and make children feel comfortable talking about the arts.

Before we can expect a child to respond freely to our questions, we must create an atmosphere in which the child feels safe expressing his or her thoughts and feelings. There are four ways to do this.

1. **Provide plenty of opportunities for children to look at artworks, listen to music, and watch dramatic performances and dance.** This will make verbalizing about the arts a natural part of children's experience. If children are used to asking questions about someone else's art, then they will be more comfortable answering questions about their own work.

2. **Express comments about children's artwork in the form of positive feedback.** This

provides a model of how the children themselves can describe their own arts performances.

3. **Pay attention to the style of delivery in asking a question.** Questions need to be asked in a tone of voice that contains enthusiastic curiosity. Voices need to be soft, eyes need to make contact, and, once the child begins to respond, we need to practice active listening.

4. **Ask questions at the right moment.** Not every creative performance needs to be explained by a child. Choose carefully the moment to elicit a verbal response. If the child has just finished a painting and is eager to join some friends in the block area, it is not the time to engage the child in a deep conversation about the artwork. At this moment a simple descriptive form of positive feedback will suffice. On the other hand, if a child has been working a long time on a clay sculpture and has stopped for a moment to get another piece of clay, this may provide an opportunity for a discussion about the work.

Starting a conversation. It is important not to overwhelm children with a long string of questions. Use a question to begin a conversation. Continue the conversation only if the child is interested in doing so, and formulate responses based on the direction the child's answer takes. Learning how to phrase directed questions takes practice. Although when confronted with a dripping puddle of blue and purple paint, or noisy banging on a drum, our initial reaction may be "What is it?" or "What is that supposed to be?" such an intrusive, insulting question should be avoided. Not all child art is intended to be something. Much of a child's initial work with a medium will consist of exploration and experiments with the materials and tools and have no end result. This kind of question is limiting in that it puts all of the focus on the product and places children in the position of having to give an answer they think will please the questioner.

As an alternative to "What is it?" ask children to reflect on their creative performances in much deeper ways. Such questions can take several forms.

1. **Focusing on arts elements.** Questions can focus the children's attention on the arts elements in their work.

   "What kinds of lines did you make with the crayons?"

2. **Focusing on process.** The child can be asked to explain the process she or he used.

Teacher Tip

USING POSITIVE FEEDBACK

Typical examples of unconditional praise:	**Ways to use positive feedback instead:**
Good glue job!	I noticed you put the glue on the back of your shapes and then attached them to your paper!
Super playing!	I see you used the maracas to keep rhythm with the music!
Nice dancing!	In your dance you made a pattern with your feet.
Typical examples of judgmental statements:	**Ways to use positive feedback instead:**
You are a beautiful bird!	Your arms are moving like a soaring bird's wings.
Lovely work!	The lines in your picture swirl in and out like a maze.
Typical examples of imposing statements:	**Ways to use positive feedback instead:**
That's an angry picture!	I see you used lots of black and red and green to show your anger about the accident.
What a happy story!	Your story reminds me of a walk I took in my grandmother's garden.
It looks like your mother.	I see you used many interesting patterns and shapes in this picture. Is there a story to go with it?

"How did you make those sounds with the tubes?"

3. **Asking about decisions.** Artistic choices can be explained:

   "Where on your collage did you decide to put those interesting pebbles you found?"

Exploring relationships. Use questions to focus the children's attention on what they might do next and to see relationships between their behavior and the results. Kamii and DeVries (1993, p. 27) have postulated four types of questions that help children learn about how objects and events are related.

1. **Predicting:**

   "What do you think will happen when you press your fingers into the clay?"

   "What do you think might happen if you held hands and jumped together?"

2. **Creating an effect:**

   "Can you make different sounds with the bells?"

   "What do you think you could do if I gave you these pieces of yarn for your collage?"

3. **Connecting events:**

   "How did the character in the play turn into this puppet?"

4. **Finding the cause:**

   "Why don't the pebbles fall off your collage now?"

Book Box

CHILDREN'S BOOKS THAT CELEBRATE CREATIVITY

Pinkwater, D. M. (1993). *The big orange splot.* New York: Scholastic.
An exuberant story about a man who paints his house in his unique way, much to the initial distress of his neighbors. Children love the colorful language and exaggerated happenings in this book, which extols creativity. Follow up the story by encouraging children to paint a box or picture in their own way. Four and up.

Reynolds, P. H. (2003). *The dot.* Cambridge, MA: Candlewick.
In this award-winning book, a young girl who says she cannot draw is encouraged by what a teacher who says to just make a mark and find out where it takes her. Four and up.

Reynolds, P. H. (2004). *Ish.* Cambridge, MA: Candlewick.
A boy discovers that art does not have to always be realistic. Four and up.

Williams, K. L. (1991). *Galimoto.* New York: HarperCollins.
An African boy collects a variety of discarded materials to build a toy car. This is an excellent book to use with children to inspire them to be "creators." Four and up.

Young, N. (2010). *Zoomer*. New York: HarperCollins.
A clever dog surprises his family with the imaginative ways he avoids going to school. A great introduction to using the imagination. Four and up.

How Should Teachers Respond to Problems?

As children participate in arts activities, a variety of difficulties can arise that can limit children's creativity. Some of these are the result of the previous arts experiences children bring with them. If a program is designed around open-ended activities that draw on the children's interests, and if the teachers show children that they value their creative work through thoughtful conversation, then many of these problems will slowly disappear on their own.

Address fear. There will always be some children who hold back from participating in arts activities. They may be afraid to take risks because they have had a bad experience with that art form previously or are uncertain what to do. This fear must be respected. It is important to try to find out why they are afraid and then provide the needed assurance. Children may have been scolded for getting dirty or making too much noise, or they may have been made to copy art projects or perform arts skills too difficult for them.

Be patient. Never force children to participate in an arts activity. Allow them to watch others performing. If they seem interested, stay nearby and

To nurture creativity, teachers need to provide an accepting atmosphere where exploration and risk taking are seen as part of the learning process. Giving positive feedback is an essential part of this process.

invite them to investigate the activity. Be subtle and positive. Offer materials to use or actions to take, and then slowly withdraw. It is important to keep in mind that children do not develop skills when an adult does the work for them, nor do they develop self-confidence in their own abilities if their project is "improved" or "directed" by a teacher. Allow children to explore on their own terms. Remember that, like adults, each child will like some arts activities materials better than others.

Take care of personal needs. Sick, tired, or hungry children will not be able to concentrate and create. If children are worried or nervous, they will be unlikely to take the kinds of risks that creativity requires.

Provide comfort. Children cannot be creative artists if they are upset or worried. Teachers need to create a calm, accepting atmosphere that allows children to feel free to experiment and explore. This can be done by modeling an accepting attitude when interacting with children and their art. For example, if one child criticizes another's art performance by saying it is stupid or ugly, then respond immediately with a statement appropriate to the incident, such as in the following example:

- Start by making a positive statement about the artwork in question, such as, "Michelle has used many different textures in her collage." This provides assurance and comfort to the injured child.
- Make it clear that the comment made was hurtful and unacceptable, and that uniqueness is valued. For example: "It is hurtful to say that about how someone sings. Everybody sings in their own way."

Provide direction. If a child is misusing an art tool, musical instrument, or prop, or is struggling with a technique, intervene as subtly as possible. A quiet restatement of the directions, repetition of the safety rules, or quick demonstration is usually sufficient when given directly to the child. If it is not, redirect the child to another activity.

Build self-confidence. It is surprising that even very young children often exhibit a lack of confidence in being able to create in the arts. This is because it does not take much to make a child afraid to risk being unique. When a child participates in arts activities, often a product or performance of some kind results, and even if the child is just exploring, in some sense this is an extension of the child. An unkind word, an accident, a well-meaning attempt to make the product or performance fit a preconceived mold, or the attempt to imitate a model that is beyond the ability of the child to copy can all affect artistic confidence.

Offer open-ended activities. When children say, "Make it for me," there has been some interference in their natural desire to explore and play with art materials that has diminished their intrinsic motivation. These children need reassurance that their art is acceptable as they choose to make it. Make sure to provide many open-ended arts activities. It is also important to eliminate patterns to trace and models to copy and to maintain a "hands-off" policy. An adult should never work on or "fix" a child's art to make it better.

Ask questions. If children insist that they cannot create or perform in the arts, then affirm that difference is valued. For example: "Each artist creates in her own way. Look at all the different ways the other children have used the paint

TEACHER TO FAMILY

Sample Letter to Families: Responding to Their Child's Visual Art

Families also need to know how to respond to their child's artistic work, particularly in the visual arts. The following letter offers suggestions of ways parents can talk to their child about visual artwork.

Dear Family,

It is a special occasion when your child brings home a piece of art. Each child's artwork is unique, a special part of him or her. Please take a moment to share the art with your child.

Children have many purposes in creating art. Perhaps today was a chance to explore what happened when blue and yellow mixed together. On the other hand, maybe your child practiced using scissors and glue and discovered a new way to make shapes. To our adult eyes, we may see only some mixed-up colors or odd sticky shapes.

- Ask how it was done. You will help your child use words to describe what was learned.
- Ask if there is a story to go with the artwork. You will learn much more about the artist's imagination and assist in language development.
- Describe what you see in the artwork—the lines, colors, shapes, textures, and patterns—and ask your child to do the same. You will help your child build her or his vocabulary.
- Share a memory of a piece of art you created or have seen. You will be teaching your child that many people have created art.

After sharing a piece of art, hang it in a special place for the family to see, such as on a door or a refrigerator. When a new artwork comes home, remove the old one and store it away. Someday your child will enjoy looking at his or her art and remembering that special moment.

Your child's teacher,

(crayons, paper, boxes . . .)." Then ask an open-ended question:

"Can you invent a new way to . . . ?"

"What would happen if . . . ?"

"Have you tried . . . ?"

Offer timely help. When introducing new techniques, they should be within the skill range of the child, and the child must be really interested in learning them. It is helpful to ask, "Do you need help? You look frustrated. Would you like me to show you another way?" Children learn best when the technique that is being taught is delivered at just the right time—when they need it to solve a problem of their own creation.

Pair child with a partner. It takes a high degree of observational skill to be aware of the technical needs of a group of children all actively involved in arts processes. With experience it becomes easier to know which children are ready for a new technique and when they need it. In many cases, a simple pairing of two children of slightly different ages and/or skill levels may be the best way to increase the skill level of a child without direct adult interference.

CONCLUSION: CREATIVITY IN TEACHING

Creativity takes a long time and a certain amount of obsession.

—Jane Piirto (2004, p. 99)

Creativity is different from the other areas of growth that teachers try to develop in children. It is not something we can teach directly, but we must foster it through our attitude, behavior, and activity choices. Sometimes the children's creative solutions will challenge our tolerance for messiness and disorder. At other times, the inventiveness of a young child will fill us with awe. When selecting and designing arts activities for young children, remember that they will each respond creatively, based on their personally unique previous knowledge, not our preconceived idea of what they will do.

The entire learning environment must be designed around the elements that nurture creative processing. Teachers need to provide opportunities for children to gain knowledge and skill by exploring art media. Children need time to immerse themselves in arts creation, motivated by their boundless curiosity and the search for solutions.

Successful teachers of the arts value curiosity, exploration, and original behavior. They allow children to go at their own pace, figure things out for themselves, and encourage them to try new things. They refrain from making models; using children's materials in an expert, adult way; and requiring children to produce artwork that fits an adult idea of what it should look like. They listen to the children and pay attention to what they are thinking. They observe the process that children go through in dealing with problems, and pay less attention to the product of this process. Finally, an enthusiastic teacher of the arts provides the children with many opportunities in which they can safely explore and pursue creative activities without interruption.

The line between needed intervention and being directive is a fine one. Teachers do not want to miss the "teachable moment" nor interfere with the children's solving of their own problems. This is the art of creative teaching. Teachers must be in tune with children, understanding their past experiences, sensitivities, and desires. It is not easy. Children are always "dangerously on the brink between presence that they want and repression that they don't want" (Malaguzzi in Edwards, Gandini, & Forman, 1993, p. 58).

It takes a creative person to fashion such an environment. It takes knowledge, skill, and a great deal of motivation to fully bring out creative behavior in children. Like the child, the teacher will say:

> *"What will happen if I do this?"*
> *"How will these things go together?"*
> *"Wow, I didn't expect that to happen!"*
> *"I never saw anything like this before."*

No two individuals approach this task in the same way. This book and experience will provide the knowledge and the skills; teachers must provide their own motivation.

FURTHER READING

Bennett, C. (2010). *The confident creative. Drawing to free hand and mind.* Moray, UK: Findhorn.

Bennett's exercises combine drawing and yoga to develop artistic confidence.

Craft, A. (2010). *Creativity and futures.* London: Trentham.

Craft argues that creativity must be valued and nourished in today's schools in order to prepare our children for a rapidly changing future.

Michalko, M. (2006). *Tinker toys* (2nd ed.). Berkeley, CA: Ten Speed Press.

This book is full of exercises for developing creative thinking in adults.

For additional information on nurturing creativity in young children, visit our Web site at http://www.cengagebrain.com

TEACHING IN ACTION

Making a Shape Mural: An Interview

Q: *Have you ever done any printmaking with your child care children?*

A: Yes. One of the best experiences I ever had was one of those spur-of-the-moment things. There was only a half-day of school, and I ended up with eight children, ranging in age from one to eight. I didn't want them all just fooling around in front of the TV, so I looked around, and I happened to have some paper plates, some tempera paint, and a roll of brown kraft paper, so I decided to try a printed mural.

Q: *Do you always have art supplies like that?*

A: I have found that the arts are something that will get everyone involved. Even the littlest ones can have a part. I try

(continued)

TEACHING IN ACTION *(continued)*

to keep some paint in the cupboard along with other basic supplies.

***Q:** How did you get them started?*

A: It was a beautiful day, so I took everyone out to the yard, and I began by playing a game of shape tag. I called out a shape and they had to touch something with that shape.

***Q:** How did the toddlers participate?*

A: I had the older children hold hands with the one-year-old and the two-year-old and find a shape together.

***Q:** How did you transition into printmaking?*

A: I had brought out my box of printing objects. There were cardboard tubes and potato mashers and wooden blocks and sponges—big things even the little ones could handle. I dumped out the box and asked them to choose an object they thought would make an interesting shape. Then I put a small amount of paint on the paper plates and showed them how to dip an object into the paint and press it to make a shape. I used a piece of newspaper for my demonstration, and then I let them try their shapes on it. I asked the older children to work with the toddlers.

***Q:** How did you get the mural going?*

A: Well . . . while they were experimenting on the paper, I rolled out the mural paper on the picnic table and held it down with stones. Then I said, "Who is ready to make a shape trail with their printing tool?" Those who were ready—there were about four—came over, and I told them to start a trail on one edge and make it end on another edge. I challenged them to see how long they could make it. I told them they could cross each other's trails but not cover them up. When they finished, they rinsed their hands in a bucket of water and went to play on the swings and in the sandbox, while the rest came over and finished. The two little ones were in the second group, and I could give them the attention they needed.

***Q:** How did you end the activity?*

A: After everyone had made their shape trail, we went inside and washed up, and then I gave them some crackers for a snack. We talked about the shape of the crackers. It was neat. Some even made a shape trail with their crackers on their plate. Meanwhile, the mural was drying quickly in the sun. When snack was done, we went out and checked. It was dry, so we brought it inside, and the children had fun counting the shapes in their trails and seeing whose was the longest, whose had the most shapes, whose curved the most, and so on. Then three of the preschoolers played driving their cars along the shape trails. They had a lot of fun with it for many days afterward, and they learned more than if they had spent that time watching TV.

Because each child brings a unique set of skills, knowledge, and experiences to their creative efforts, the possibilities are infinite. Gadget print by Keith, age six.

Studio Page

EXPERIENCING THE CREATIVE PROCESS: WHAT IS IN A NAME?

In this box, write your name in as many different ways as possible. When the paper is full or you run out of ideas, make a list of all the ways they are different in terms of color, size, and thickness.

- How many different ways did you invent?

- How many look similar to your signature?

- How many look different?

- List the steps of the creative process you experienced.

Studio Page

SELF-EXPLORATION: MY FIRST ARTS EXPERIENCE

- What is the earliest arts experience you remember?

- What did you do?

- Where and when was it?

- What materials did you use?

- Who was there with you? What did they say?

- Did anyone comment on your work?

- What emotions did you feel?

Studio Page

SELF-EXPLORATION: MY PERSONAL ARTS TIME LINE

Fill in all of the arts experiences you remember, at about the age you experienced them. You can include such things as arts courses you have taken, museums and concerts you have been to, a specific artwork you made or performance you have given, a book about any of the art forms you have read, a movie related to the arts that you have seen, a comment made by a teacher or family member about your creative work, and so forth.

AGE	EXPERIENCE
Birth to age 5	
5 to 10 years	
10 to 15 years	
15 to 20 years	
20 to 30 years	
30 to 40 years	
40 to 50 years	
50+ years	

What Does My Timeline Tell Me?

Study your timeline and ask yourself the following questions:

1. Do you remember more experiences from your early childhood or more from your later years?

   ____

2. How many are happy memories?

   ____

3. Do any memories make you feel uncomfortable?

   ____

4. Do you remember any of the adults who participated in creating these memories?

   ____

5. How will these memories affect the way you will approach young children and their creative arts production?

   ____

Studio Page

SELF-EXPLORATION: DEFINING CREATIVE BEHAVIOR

> *Just how broadly creativity is defined is critical to any program planning, for far too often creative ideas are ignored, or worse yet, actively squelched when well-meaning educators are only watching for a creative product that matches their aesthetic standards.*
>
> —*Nancy Lee Cecil and Phyllis Lauritzen (1995, p. 28)*

Analyze each of the following behaviors in terms of whether or not you would consider it creative and what action you would take, if any, to change or control the behavior.

- A child eats a piece of play dough because "it looked like a banana."

  ____

  ____

- A child glues his paper to the table because he "didn't want it to slide off the table."

  ____

  ____

- A child runs around the room biting everyone with his imaginary "snake."

  ____

  ____

- A child drums on another child's head.

  ____

  ____

- A child uses a scissors to cut the hair of another child.

  ____

  ____

Chapter 3

Artistic Development

Questions Addressed in This Chapter:

- How do children develop in the arts?
- What factors affect development in the arts?
- What do developmental models tell educators?
- How do we assess children's growth in the arts?

"*The teacher who knows the difference between adult and child world views is likely to communicate and educate more successfully than one not so prepared.*"

—*David Elkind (1974, p. 134)*

Young Artists at Work

Andy picks up a crayon and grasps it tightly in his fist. He slowly approaches the large white paper before him. Arm held stiffly, he rubs the crayon on the paper. Lifting the crayon, he looks at the smudge he has left behind. With his other hand he touches it, rubs it, and looks at his fingers. The mark is still there. He bends over and sniffs it with his nose. Cautiously, Andy looks up. Is this all right? Can he do this? But no one is stopping him. He returns to the paper. With broad strokes, Andy makes his first true marks on the world. Broad sweeps of color up and down, back and forth. Again and again, on paper after paper, at the beginning of his second year of life, he draws . . .

HOW DO CHILDREN DEVELOP IN THE ARTS?

> *"Just as the first sounds that babies make are the same around the world, children's first scribbles are also the same."*
>
> *—Elaine Pear Cohen and Ruth Straus Gainer (1995, p. 28)*

It begins with the line—a line that reflects the child's physical control over the body. The one-year-old is at the beginning of a long and complex process, which in the eighth year of life will end with a mastery of line that is remarkably expressive and controlled. Toddlers do not know that this is where their explorations with line will lead; they only know the moment—this pleasurable and exciting moment in which they have used a tool and produced a result.

All of us were once infants, unable to move on our own. Step-by-step, we learned to crawl and then to walk. At first, we walked unsteadily, clasping a guiding hand. Soon we could take baby steps on our own, and in no time at all we could run and dance.

In the same way, each child grows artistically. Although no newborn is a musician or painter at birth, inside every infant is the potential to grow into one. When the time is right, the children start their artistic journey, tentatively making small marks upon the world. Their marks enlarge and change from wavy scribbles to enclosed shapes to symbols that encompass the child's experience. Their gurgling sounds coalesce, become organized, develop rhythm and pitch, and become song. Their random movements become coordinated, and patterned into a fluid dance. This pattern of increasing competence repeats itself in every young child, everywhere in the world mediated by the cultural background and personal experiences of each child.

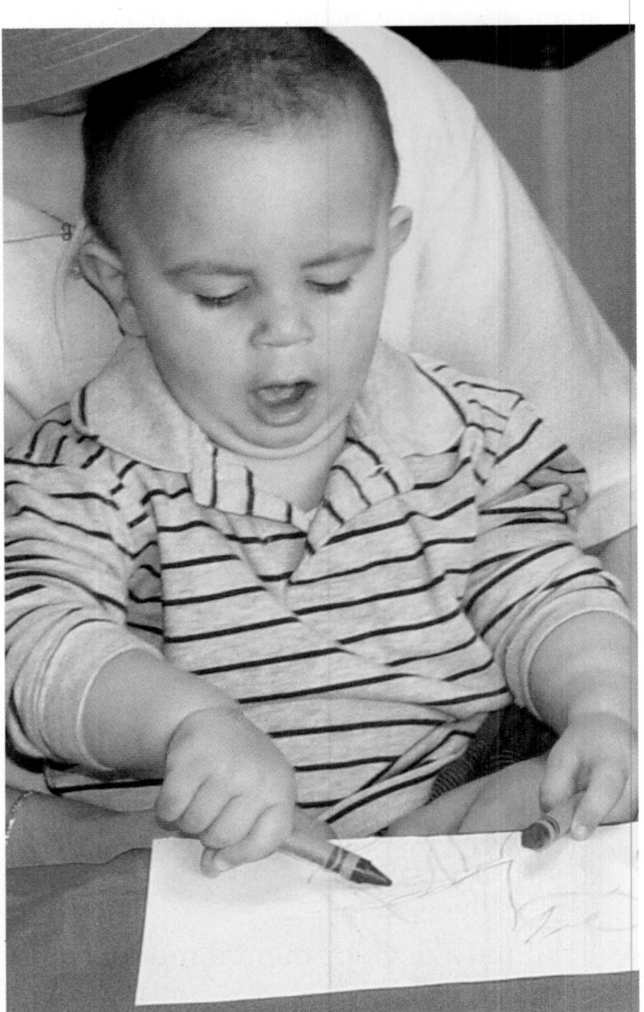

Young children's artistic work often reflects the physical development of the child. This infant grips the drawing tool in his fist and uses his whole arm to scribble.

Developmentally Appropriate Practice: DAP

> *"Developmentally appropriate practices result from the process of professionals making decisions about the well-being and education of children based on at least three important kinds of information or knowledge: . . . 1. What is known about child development and learning . . . 2. What is known about each child as an individual . . . 3. What is known about the social and cultural context in which children live."*
>
> —*Carol Copple and Sue Bredekamp (2009, pp. 9–10)*

Developmentally appropriate practice (DAP) is based on the idea that teachers need to know how young children typically develop, what variations may occur in this development, and how the learning and development of each individual child can best be facilitated. To determine the developmental level of a child, we need to ask two questions. The first directs us to look at the child's similarity to others the same age. The second asks us to look at those things that make the child uniquely different from others the same age.

How Is This Child Similar to Children of the Same Age?

According to the National Association for the Education of Young Children Position Statement on Developmentally Appropriate Practice the (Copple & Bredekamp, 2009, pp. 1–31), being knowledgeable about **normative development,** or what children are generally like at various ages, allows teachers to make decisions about which activities and experiences will be safe, but challenging, for young children.

The age divisions used in this text follow those of Copple and Bredekamp (2009). They are intended to provide general guidelines from which appropriate arts activities may be selected.

Infant. In this text, **infant** is used to refer to children from birth to 18 months. Infants have the following characteristics:

- Explore first with mouth and later with eyes and limbs
- Use movements, gestures, and vocalizations to communicate
- Have very limited self-regulatory skills and require constant supervision
- Show development of physical control from the head down and from the center of body out to the limbs
- Are strongly attached to caregivers and respond best in one-on-one settings
- Have short memories and attention spans
- Can learn to respond to simple commands

Toddler. Throughout this text, **toddler** is used to refer to children between the ages of 18 months and 3 years who may exhibit the following characteristics:

- Need to explore with all their senses and may still put objects in their mouth
- Have limited self-regulatory skills and require close supervision
- Engage in parallel play
- Show developing control over large muscles in the arm
- Have short attention spans, usually less than 10 minutes, and need simple materials to explore
- Need to repeat actions
- Say names of objects and understand more words than they can say
- Are developing a sense of self

Three- to five-year-olds or preschoolers. Most children of this age display the following characteristics:

- Show increasing self-control and can work side by side in small groups
- Usually will not put inappropriate items in mouth
- Show developing control over wrists, hands, and fingers
- Have an increasing attention span and can work independently for 10 minutes or more at a time

Five- to six-year-olds or kindergartners. Most children in this age range display the following behaviors:

- Show increasing control over wrists and hands and exhibit a more mature grip on drawing tools
- Can concentrate for a period of time, 30 minutes or more, on a self-selected arts activity
- Can work together in small groups of three to six on common projects and are able to share some supplies
- May dictate or be able to write stories with invented spelling
- Can follow a three-step direction
- Can classify objects and make predictions
- Can use words to describe the qualities of objects—color, size, and shape—and begin to sort them by those qualities

Six- to eight-year-olds or primary age. Most children in this age range show the following behaviors:

- Hold drawing tools with a mature grip
- Concentrate for an hour or more on a self-selected arts activity and return to an ongoing arts project over a period of several days
- Initiate, participate, and assume roles in cooperative group arts activities
- Begin to read and write stories with the majority using conventional spelling by the end of the eighth year
- Understand that objects can share one or more qualities and can use this knowledge to make predictions and comparisons and to draw conclusions

Children's Development in the Arts

Much of the artistic performance of young children is determined by their physical development. This is particularly true in the early years. However, as children get older, what they have learned influences their artistic performance as well. As children develop language skills and knowledge about the arts, their artistic performance and works become more complex.

Because each of the art forms requires different physical and language skills, we need to examine music, dramatics, creative movement, and visual arts development individually.

Musical Development

Musical development starts very early. Infants respond to music by turning their heads and making sounds and movements. Babies respond to music long before they can distinguish individual words. Even before birth, fetuses can differentiate between a familiar song and a novel one. At two months they turn to musically pleasant sounds and away from dissonant ones (Weinberger, 2004). Eight-month-olds can tell the difference between two complex musical works. In a study by Beatrix Ilari and Linda Polka (2006), the babies could distinguish between two orchestrated piano pieces by Ravel and recognize them again after a two-week hiatus.

Babies also notice changes in tempo and key changes in a melody. The rhythm and melodic quality of a mother's voice will keep a child's attention, the musicality of speech helping the child acquire language (Mithen, 2006). It is hypothesized that this is one reason adults in all cultures tend to talk to babies in singsong voices and to sing lullabies.

Young toddlers can repeat sounds, move to rhythms, and start to learn simple songs. By age three,

Development in the arts begins in infancy. This infant shows her responsiveness to music and rhythms.

children begin to make up their own songs, hold a beat, and match body movements to it.

At ages four and five, children can learn to match and classify sounds, can play singing and movement games, and can reproduce musical patterns. Five-year-olds are the perfect age to start a musical instrument, such as the piano or keyboard. Between ages six and eight, children improve in their ability to sing in tune and in large groups. They can learn to notate melodies and compose original musical pieces.

Musical development seems to reach a plateau by the age nine (Stellaccio & McCarthy, 1999). This means that the music activities we present to young children are vitally important. The early years are when children learn to sing accurately, acquire their vocal range, and learn basic concepts about melody (see Table 3-1).

By preschool age many children can create original dance movements based on the dances they have seen adults doing.

Creative Movement Development

Ability to control one's body in space is a key component of creative movement activities. In young children the development of physical control over the body is usually sequential and predictable. For example, children usually sit up before they walk. This sequence is illustrated in Table 3-2. However, physical development happens at varying rates in different children. There may be periods of fast growth followed by periods of slower growth.

TABLE 3–1 Musical Development in Young Children

Age	Rhythm	Listening	Instrument	Song
Before birth	Surrounded by rhythm of mother's body	Responds differently to familiar and novel music	Hears music	Hears mother's voice
Infants *Newborn to 6 months*	Respond differently to different types of music	Turn toward sounds Notice difference between melodies Respond to loud and soft Recognize and remember different complex musical pieces	Make sounds with objects such as rattles	Babble to musical stimulation Babble on own with pitch and rhythmic pattern Coo in open vowels
Infants *6 months to 1 year*	Rock and bounces to music	React to music with sound and motion	Show interest in instruments	Respond to singing by vocalizing
Toddlers *1 to 3 years*	Move feet with rhythm of music Cannot keep time Clap to music	Listen to music on radio and recordings Identifies types of sounds Show preferences for certain music Matches sounds and objects	Seek objects to make sounds	Real singing begins Tag on to the end of a song Make up songs and chants Sing on own with recurring pitch center and consistent tempo Have a five-note range Cannot match pitch

(continued)

TABLE 3–1 Musical Development in Young Children (*continued*)

Age	Rhythm	Listening	Instrument	Song
Preschoolers *3 to 4 years*	Begin to clap on beat Begin to echo clap	Can listen for longer periods while remaining quiet	Tap a beat on an instrument	May sing along with familiar songs with increasing accuracy
	Improvise complex rhythm Imitate simple rhythms	Can identify familiar songs Can talk about speed and volume of music Can identify musical phrases Can identify the source of a sound Can identify the sound of familiar instruments Can talk about what they hear using music vocabulary they have learned	Interest in real instruments increases Play simple instruments in small group Play short melodies on tonal instruments Can improvise melodies Can invent original symbols to represent sounds	Can sing in different keys Have a five- to eight-note range Begin to match pitch and echo words in rhythm Spontaneously invents new songs as they play Can sing along with a group
Kindergarteners *5 to 6 years*	Can march and clap at same time to music Keep time with music Improvise complex rhythm structure with a climax and conclusion	Identify change in music Recognize a familiar song played on an instrument without words Become active listener and can talk about music heard Can listen respectfully at concerts Can describe the elements and mood of musical pieces	Can tell sounds made by different instruments apart Play sequential and diatonic and chromatic tones on tonal instruments Can learn to read simple notation Focus on one instrument for extended time Can begin lessons on piano, violin, etc. Imitate a rhythm using a different instrument accurately	Make up own songs and write musical symbols Sing in clear tone taking breath at appropriate points Begin to know that a song's melody is fixed Sing in tune Whole steps easier to sing than half steps Descending patterns easier to sing than ascending ones Large intervals more difficult than close ones Most accurate in the A1D1 range (C1 is middle C) Add emotion through facial expression, pitch, dynamics, and tempo to voice
Primary ages *6 to 8 years*	Keep time accurately	Can hear harmony Recognize familiar songs played in different contexts Can differentiate between music reflecting different styles and moods	Can learn to read music Play parts on instrument	Can sing familiar songs accurately and has a repertoire of memorized songs Sing more accurately as individual than with group Can reach higher notes Can sing rounds and two-part songs Know that melodies are fixed

Note: As in all the arts, musical development is strongly influenced by experience. This chart is intended only as a general guideline to what skills might be mastered in terms of age. However, the basic sequence of skill acquisition will pertain to most children.

TABLE 3–2 Sequence of Physical Development in Young Children

Age	Arms	Head and Torso	Legs	Whole Body
At birth	Random movements	Need support	Random movements	
Infants *Newborn to 6 months*	Put hands in mouth Reach and grasp objects Bring object to mouth	Turn head Lift head Sit with support	Put feet in mouth Reach and kick objects with feet	Roll over
Infants *6 months to 1 year*	Pick up objects Drop objects Pass objects from hand to hand	Sit alone Roll	Can bear weight on legs Stand Walk holding on	Cross midline Crawl/creep Imitate actions Move whole body to music
Toddlers *1 to 2 years*	Throw objects Push and pull	Bend to pick up something	Walk "toddling" Kick object Run	Creep up stairs Climb up but may have trouble getting down Move mainly arms and legs to music
2 to 3 years	Catch large objects Throw underhand		Walk forward and backward Walk up steps Run with open stride Jump up and down Balance on one foot briefly	Climb up and down using alternating feet and hands
Preschoolers *3 to 4 years*	Throw overhand Bounces ball	Do somersault	Walk heel toe Balance on one foot Walk on a straight line Climb steps using alternative feet Jump over something Can do a standing broad jump Tip toe	Ride a tricycle Swing May have difficulty judging space and direction Switch quickly from one motion to another
Kindergarteners *5 to 6 years*	Hand dominance established		Hop on one foot Walk balance beam Skip a little Skate	Smooth muscle action Coordinate movements with others
Primary Ages *6 to 8 years*	Catch/throw small ball Know left from right Can dribble a ball		Skip on either foot Skip rope Walk forward/backward on balance beam	Remember dance steps Follow complex directions

Note: As in all the arts, physical development is strongly influenced by experience. This chart is intended only as a general guideline to what skills might be mastered in terms of age. However, the basic sequence of skill acquisition will pertain to most children.

In general, most children who do not have a physical or environmental disability develop bodily control from the head down and the center out. In the beginning, the newborn is all head, following objects with the eyes and turning the head toward sounds and objects with arms and legs moving randomly. For infants, initial movement activities focus on moving the head and then the whole body, followed by large arm and leg movements. We can build on this ability by moving together with the child, rocking the child, or moving arms and legs in rhythmic patterns or to music.

By six months the child has gained control over arms and hands, reaching for objects and grasping them. In the next six months the infant develops torso control, learning to sit, crawl, and stand. Older infants who are crawling, creeping, and pulling themselves upright are learning how to move their bodies in space. By holding them with feet barely on the floor and moving to music or hugging them to our bodies and swirling to a song, children can begin their first partner dancing. On their own, they may bounce to musical rhythms while sitting or hanging on the railing of crib or playpen.

Toddlers discover their legs, walking forward and backward with the characteristic toddling gait that gives this age group its common identifier. As they develop confidence they discover they can jump and climb, but they may still have trouble balancing and coming to a stop after running or jumping. With their increasing independence of movement, toddlers may invent motions to go with music. They are also primed to imitate dances and moves they see being done by others. Holding hands they can be led in simple group creative movements.

By preschool they are running around and going carefully up and down the stairs. With increasing control over their hands and feet and better balance, preschoolers can respond to suggestions that they move their arms, legs, or bodies in a particular way. They continue to imitate the creative movements of others, but can also initiate original moves in a process of discovery and by recombining movements already mastered. Simple, safe props, such as small scarves and short ribbons, can be held and used to enhance the child's natural movements. With the increasing ability to pretend, children can move as if they were somebody or something else.

Kindergartners and primary school students are beginning to have smooth control over their bodies. They can shift their weight from foot to foot, allowing them to skip and slide. The can coordinate their arms, legs, and sense of balance to move on a balance beam and climb effectively. They can follow directions to move in a series of patterns and can work together to learn repeated movements and simple folk dances. They can also use their new moves to invent dances of their own.

Dramatic Arts Development

Mirroring language development, dramatic skills develop rapidly in the early childhood years. Infants respond to facial expressions and gestures. Toddlers respond with words and actions to the behavior of others around them. They imitate things they see and combine these learned behaviors in creative ways, such as pushing a box while making car engine

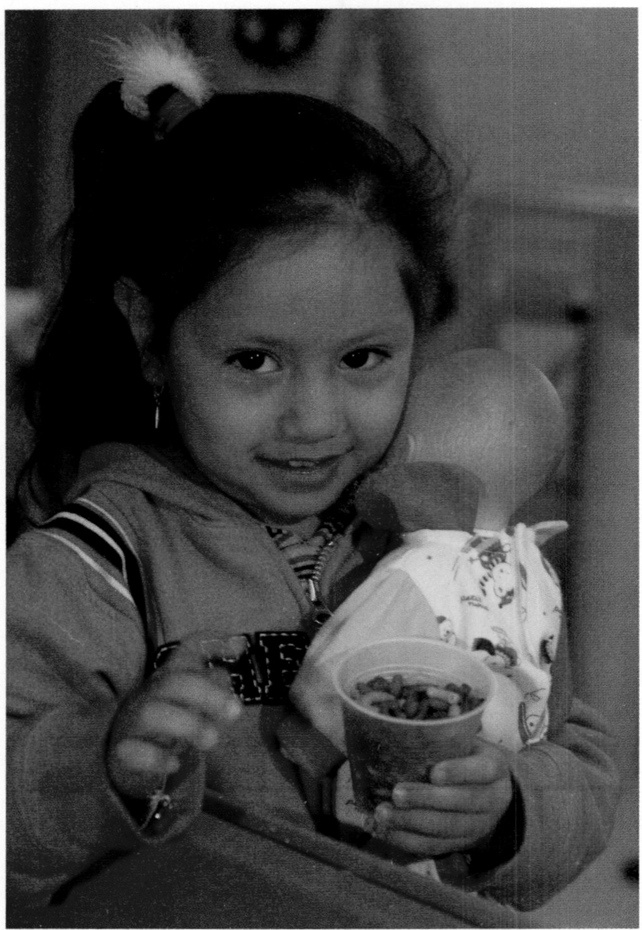

Through dramatic play, children use their developing imaginations to act out both familiar and imaginary roles. Here a kindergartner pretends that a cup of colored noodles is food for her "baby."

noises. Preschoolers enter the world of make-believe, creating dramatic play based on books, movies, and television shows they have seen. By the age of five most children are capable of creating and performing complex stories, often sustaining them over an extended time period. (See Table 3-3.)

The basis of current understanding about children's play and the development of young children is the work of Jean Piaget (1962) and Lev Vygotsky (1976).

Levels of play. Piaget identified three levels of play:

1. **Practice play,** in which infants and toddlers at the **sensorimotor level of development** explore and interact with objects and people using repeated actions, such as when an infant repeatedly knocks an object off the highchair tray.

TABLE 3–3 Sequence of Development in the Dramatic Arts

Age Group	Object	People	Language	Imagination	Narrative
Infants *newborn to 6 months*	Attracted to bright objects, mirrors, pictures, and rattles	Look at familiar faces	Babble Express feelings by crying, yelling, and cooing		
Infants *6 to 12 months*	Enjoy large toys that move	Play peek-a-boo Mirror facial expressions Solitary play predominates	Communicate with gestures, first words Imitates voices and sounds	Pretend familiar actions, such as sleeping, hiding, and talking on phone	Play is disconnected
Toddlers *1 to 3 years*	Like to play with real things, such as pots and pans	Rough and tumble play begins Solitary play leads into parallel play	Use words and simple sentences Name objects	Imitate familiar actions and events with realistic toys that resemble the real objects, such as sweeping with a broom Imitate familiar actions of people around them and seen on T V, movies Have make-believe conversations	Story play has no definite structure or end
Preschoolers *4 to 5 years*	Constructive play becomes most predominant, such as blocks and sand	Incorporate other children in play with increasing division of roles	Use voices to match character	Play becomes more fictional Can imagine one object is something else Imaginary playmates Role-play imaginary characters	Retell invent, and act out stories Stories have rudimentary plots Invented stories incorporate ideas from stories they have heard
Kindergarteners *5 to 6 years*	Object and constructive play becomes more orderly	Cooperative play in which there is a shared purpose	Talk about their play	Fantasy play is more complex and fluid	Use invented spelling and drawing to tell a story
Primary Ages *6 to 8 years*	Construction becomes more complex Create objects to go with story or play Like games with rules	Enact roles from life, fiction, and media Assign roles in logical, fair ways	Increased control over voice and matching it to role Evaluate dramatic performance	Can use very dissimilar objects to represent others Know difference between real and pretend Daydreaming replaces pretend play	Write invented stories from experience or picture Stories can have elaborate plots Create scripts for drama and puppet shows

Note: As in all the arts, dramatic arts development is strongly influenced by experience. This chart is intended only as a general guideline to what skills might be mastered in terms of age. However, the basic sequence of skill acquisition will pertain to most children.

2. **Symbolic play,** which happens when preschool-age children imitate things they have seen, heard in stories, or experienced. This can be observed when they enact make-believe scenarios such as playing house, taking care of their doll babies, and serving dinner, just like they see their families do.
3. **Game-based play,** which occurs during the **concrete operational** stage, when children's ability to think logically allows them to enjoy games with preset rules, such as board games and organized sports, and to re-enact the sequence of events in a story or movie they have seen.

Visual Arts Development

In the past 100 years, children's art has attracted the attention of many researchers. Some have collected samples of children's art and looked for patterns (Kellogg, 1969, 1979; Schaefer-Simmern, 1950, Sheridan, 2010). Others have tried to use it to measure intelligence (Cox, 1993; Goodenough, 1926; Harris & Goodenough, 1963). Many have used it to understand how children think (Gardner, 1991; Golomb, 1981; Winner, 1982; Hope, 2008). More recently, children's art has been used to assess emotional needs (Di Leo, 1970; Levick, 1986; Silver, 2002). Over the years, several models of artistic development have been created. These provide one perspective on the teaching of visual art to young children.

However, other research (Kindler, 1997; Wilson, Hurwitz, & Wilson, 1987) indicates that normative sequences do not always reflect the actual development of individual children, but rather development proceeds in stops and starts and is heavily influenced by a number of factors, including instruction.

Development in two-dimensional expression. From the 1950s to the 1970s, Rhoda Kellogg (1969, 1979) collected over 1 million drawings done by children from the United States and other countries. These drawings provided the basis for her in-depth analysis of the patterns and forms found in children's art and represent a commitment to the collection of child art unparalleled in early art education research. Kellogg was one of the first to recognize that the scribbles of young children were an important part of the child's development, and that the marks made by young children the world over were more the same than they were different.

1. **Basic Scribbles.** Kellogg isolated twenty kinds of markings (Basic Scribbles) made by children age two and under. The Basic Scribbles consisted of all of the lines the children make, with or without the use of their eyes, whether using a crayon on paper, fingerpaint, or scratching the lines in the dirt. She saw these strokes as representative of the neural and muscular system of the child and forerunners of all of the strokes needed to make art and language symbols. Her descriptions of these Basic Scribbles were offered as a way to describe the art of the very young child.
2. **Placement Patterns.** In addition, Kellogg looked at how children under age two placed these scribbles on their paper. She felt that the Placement Patterns were the earliest evidence that the child was guiding the initial formation of shapes. She hypothesized that children react to the scribbles they make by seeing shapes in the drawing itself rather than trying to represent the shapes seen in the world around them, and that visual and motor pleasure was a motivating factor in causing children to scribble.
3. **Diagrams and Combines.** Between ages two and three, Kellogg found that children began to draw shapes that they then combined into groups. She termed these groups Aggregates. At this stage, children move from unplanned scribbling to being able to remember and repeat shapes they have drawn previously. These shapes become the basis of all the symbols later found in children's drawings.
4. **Mandalas, Suns, and People.** Kellogg was most fascinated by the symbols that often emerged between ages three and four. She noted that the symbols seemed to follow a developmental sequence, and she felt that the mandalas and suns provided the stimuli for the child's first drawings of a person.

At the time Kellogg did her research, most adults considered child art a poor attempt to represent objects and persons in the child's environment and, therefore, worthless or in need of correction. Children

Mandalas, suns, and people. Marker–various children.

were discouraged or even forbidden from scribbling and were encouraged to copy adult models. Kellogg felt that drawing was an expression of the growth of the child's physical and mental processes; it was the process of drawing that was important. She argued that children need plenty of time for free drawing and scribbling in order to develop the symbols that will later become the basis of all drawing and writing.

More recently, Susan Sheridan (2010) has looked at the scribbles and drawings of very young children as brain-building behavior that she characterizes as "one of the predetermined ways a child's brain naturally builds itself" (p. 9). She proposes six stages of scribbling and drawing.

Matthew, age two, has used both broad strokes made with the whole arm, and smaller marks made with wrist movement in his marker drawing.

1. **Early Scribbling.** Up to the age of one year, children make only a few marks, usually lines and dots. They push and pull and stab at the paper without paying full attention to what they are doing.
2. **Middle Scribbling.** Between the ages of one and two, the child begins to make more and more complex loops and circles.
3. **Mature Scribbling.** The two- to three-year-old continues to develop more complex patterns using loops and circles and places them in a more controlled manner.
4. **Early Drawing.** Between the ages of three and four, the child starts naming the scribbles being made; this shows the beginning of representing the natural world and events.
5. **Middle Drawing.** Four- to five-year olds show a mix of scribbling and the beginning of recognizable shapes and images, which vary from child to child and drawing to drawing. The child's explanations of the work produced become more verbally complex.
6. **Mature Drawing.** Mastered shapes and movements are combined in new ways to create meaningful and imaginative images as children enter kindergarten and the primary years. They add marks that look like writing, which become words as they learn to write.

Development in three dimensions. As in their two-dimensional work, children go through modeling modes that mirror their physical and cognitive growth. The sorts of forms that children can produce are determined by the amount of control they have over their arms, wrists, hands, and fingers; by their mental ability to imagine a form and then produce it; and by their previous experiences with the material (see Table 3-4).

Initial exploration. When first confronted with a modeling material, children often approach it with a caution that quickly turns to abandon. They push their

TABLE 3–4 The Development of Modeled Form

Mode	Child's Behavior
1. Initial Exploration	Manipulates material using all of the senses; uses large motions of arm and hand
2. Controlled Exploration	Begins to make basic forms—pancake, worm, and ball; uses palms and fingers
3. Named Forms	Gives names and labels to modeled forms; begins to use them in symbolic play; uses fingers for shaping
4. Symbolic Forms	Plans the forms that will be used; can attach forms; can pull a form out of a larger piece of modeling material; can use fingers to create small details

fingers into it, pat it, pick it up and put it down, drop it, and squeeze it until it oozes out between their fingers. They may lick it and taste it, rub it on their faces, and stick it up to or into their noses for a good whiff. They will bang it with fists, peel it off their arms when it sticks, and throw it, if not stopped. There is no attempt to make the clay or dough into something but only a pure, multisensory exploration of this exciting material.

This purely exploratory behavior is seen in the youngest children, those between the ages of one and three, and it corresponds in some ways to scribbling in drawing. However, it is often seen in older children as well, especially as they first start to handle a new or an unfamiliar modeling material.

For toddlers, the behavior reflects their lack of small motor control, their reliance on large motor movements of the arm and hands, and their sensory approach to learning about their environment. For older children, this initial exploratory behavior reflects an attempt to understand the material's possibilities and limits. Even adult artists spend time working freely with a medium in order to assess its parameters before beginning to create a sculpture in earnest.

Controlled exploration. After the initial explorations of the modeling medium, children will begin to explore the clay or dough in a more systematic way. At this stage the children may flatten the clay into pancake-like forms using the palm of the hand. With their fingers, they may poke a series of indentations into the surface or pull off small pieces and flatten them. They may stick the pieces back together or create a stack of them. One of the first forms that they can make due to the increasing control over their hands is a long, thin cylinder created by rolling a piece of clay between the palms of their two hands.

One of the later forms that develops, sometimes in the fourth or fifth year, is the sphere or ball created by rolling the clay between the palms or between the table and one palm. This is a much more complex skill, as it requires the child to move the hand in a circular motion and is often preceded by much experimentation. Once the ball is perfected, it often becomes the object of manipulative play; it may be rolled across the table, or several may be lined up in a row.

For children who have had many opportunities to use clays, controlled exploration reflects their increasing control over hands and fingers. Older children and adults may also repeat these same manipulations as part of their preliminary explorations of modeling media.

Named forms. The difference between a named form and controlled exploration is not one of form or physical control. It relates instead to the cognitive development of the child. The long, thin cylinder becomes a "snake," the poked pancake becomes a "face," the clay balls become "snowballs." This naming of the modeled forms correlates to the naming of scribbled drawings and reflects the child's developing language skills and the growth of mental imagery.

Flattening and poking, as this boy does with his play dough, is an initial way young children explore modeling materials.

The manipulative nature of modeling materials allows children at this stage of development to pursue symbolic play in a way that they cannot with two-dimensional art media. Young children "cook" play-dough bits in the pots on a toy stove. They offer a "taco" to taste. They make mommy snakes and baby snakes that hiss and wiggle around the room and then turn into bracelets wrapped around active wrists. They "bowl" with their clay balls.

Although the child's creations may take on a life of their own, they still are, largely, the result of unplanned manipulation. Once made, they are then "seen" to resemble or represent something. As in drawing, children will repeat these behaviors as they perfect the skills needed to create the basic forms of sphere and cylinder at will.

Three-dimensional symbols. In the final mode of modeling development, children are able to plan the forms that they will need to create an object. Instead of using the clay solely as a vehicle for sensory sensation and the release of feelings, the modeling material now becomes a means of self-expression for internal images. These images can be formed in several ways. Some are created by bending, flattening, or distorting one of the basic forms; for example, making a "nest" by poking a hole in a clay ball. Others are produced by joining simple or distorted basic forms, as when a child creates a person from a clay ball and four flattened cylinders. As with the graphic symbols of drawing, the children are not trying to create actual representations of these objects but rather the idea of the object. Once created, they assume a major role in the symbolic play of the child. Airplanes fly and drop bombs; animals eat clay bits from the clay bowl; birds sit on eggs in the nest and then fly off to find clay worms.

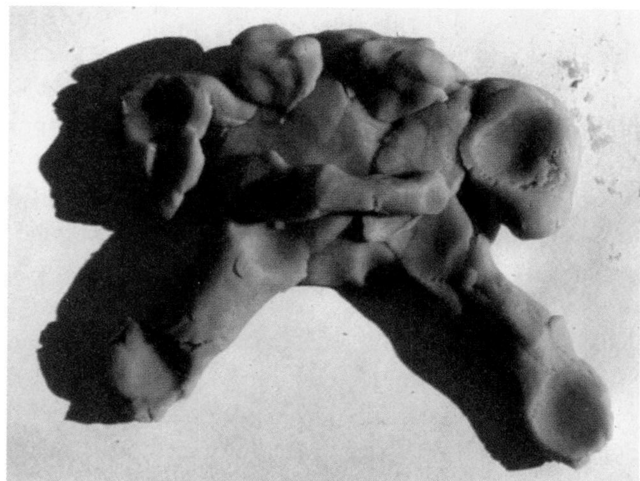

As children become more skilled with modeling materials, they begin to make recognizable forms. Tina, age three, creates a simple person shape from her play dough.

Elizabeth, age six, has used play dough to create a flower.

WHAT FACTORS AFFECT DEVELOPMENT IN THE ARTS?

As anyone who has ever worked with young children can verify, artistic development in individual children does not follow the nice neat patterns laid out in textbooks. Although developmental Tables 3-1 through 3-4 can provide useful guides in understanding what might be expected at various ages, they do not present the whole picture. Children are dynamic and ever changing. The second question we must ask as we design a developmentally appropriate arts curriculum is: What are the unique abilities of this individual child at this time and place.

DAP reminds us that children have unique strengths, needs, and interests. These may be due to maturational differences, developmental delays, physical challenges, or exceptional gifts. Development does not proceed in lockstep fashion, but rather in growth and spurts. Children also differ in the life experiences to which they have been exposed. Figure 3-1 illustrates the relationship among these uniquely personal factors.

Lillian Katz and Sylvia Chard (2000) call this the "dynamic dimension of development." Some children may have had negative early experiences that have a delayed impact on later functioning and personality development. Other children may come from rich arts backgrounds with parents who have given them many arts experiences from infancy. Some children may exhibit an extraordinary interest or skill in one particular arts area.

An examination of the social and cultural context in which young artists function reveals that there are many important ways in which variations in maturation, educational experiences, and other environmental factors influence young artists.

Physical Factors

Gross and fine motor development does not take place at a steady rate in most children. Instead, it proceeds in fits and starts. Sometimes a new ability will suddenly appear. At other times it will take the child months of trial and error before the behavior is exhibited. We see this in the variation that occurs in children learning to walk. Some stand up one day and take off at a run. Others take a step, fall down, crawl some more, and then try again over and over.

Growth patterns are strongly influenced by heredity, nutrition, and exercise. Poorly nourished children will exhibit delayed growth and physical coordination. For example, 40 percent of children in Head Start programs have been found to have delays in motor skill development (Woodward & Yun, 2001). Children who have the space, time, and encouragement to explore large areas physically, such as through creative movement activities, will be better coordinated and have stronger muscles.

Some children have physical challenges such as vision and hearing impairments or trouble controlling their bodies. These children need special consideration in planning arts activities so they can enjoy the arts and participate fully in them. In fact, for many children with special needs the arts can provide an alternate and meaningfully rich way to communicate with others.

Emotional Factors

How a child feels will greatly influence how the child performs in the arts.

Traumatic events. A child who has just experienced a disturbing event may use the arts as a way to express and release deep feelings. Tornados, earthquakes, accidents, and death often elicit scribbling,

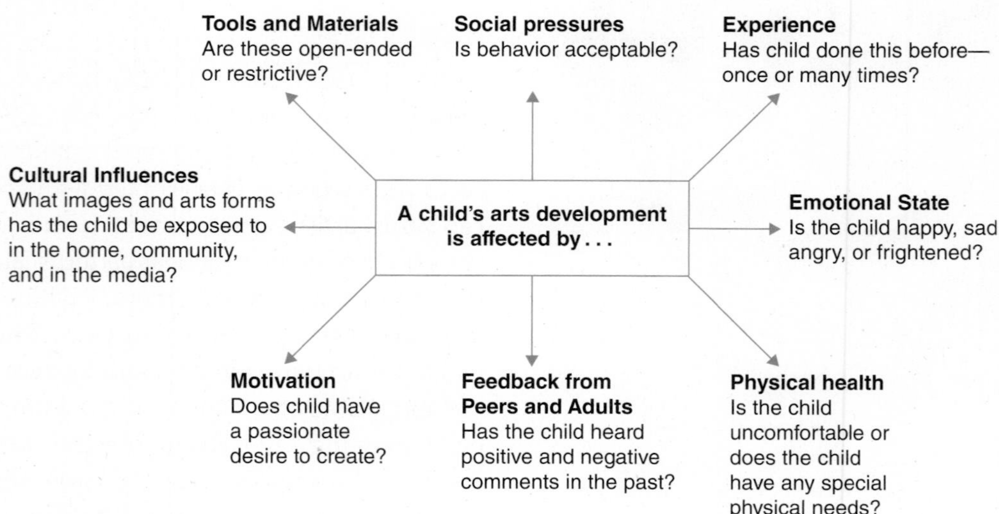

FIGURE 3–1 Factors affecting children's performance in the arts.

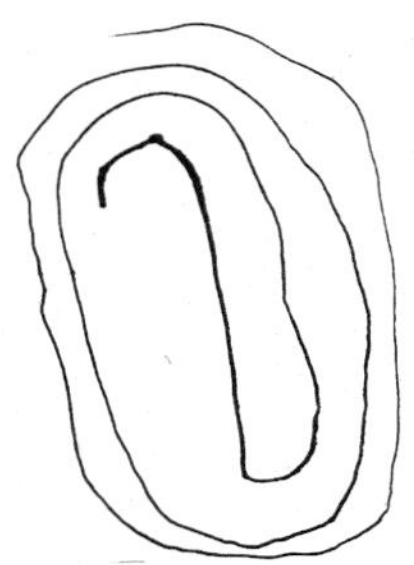

Within an age group, children will be found who are working in all of the modes. (1) Exploration. Marker—Andrew, age three; (2) Initial shapes. Crayon—Kelsey, age three; (3) Action symbol. Marker—Ross, age three; (4) Story symbols. Pencil—Michelle, age three.

stabbing at the paper, and splashing of paint from people of all ages. Because the arts can serve as an emotional release, we need to bring sensitivity to the artistic interaction. With understanding and encouragement, we can allow children to work through these deep feelings. Joe Frost (2005) has found that work, play, and the arts were significant ways to heal children who were affected by Hurricane Katrina. (See Chapter 5 for specific ways to address children's special needs through the arts.)

Social pressures. Teachers also need to understand how their own actions and those of a child's family can influence how a child feels about the arts. Children who are pressured to make their arts performance match an adult "ideal," or are frustrated by an arts material or skill that is beyond their physical ability to master, may develop feelings of failure. Such feelings may cause reluctance to participate in future arts activities.

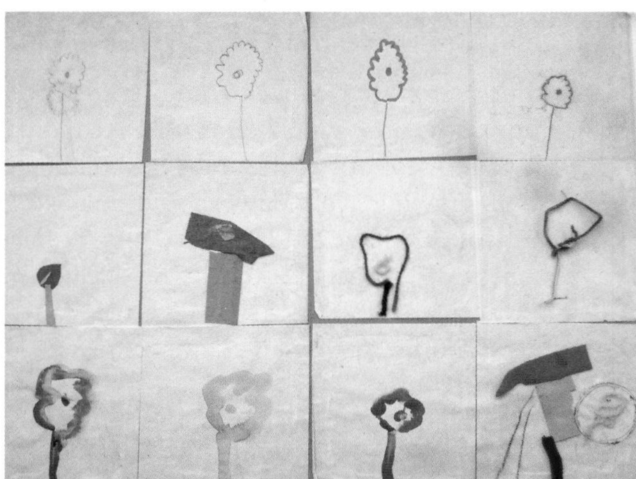

"A flower." These twelve pictures, done by the same five-year-old, show how skill and familiarity with media affect how the resulting artwork looks. The pencil and crayon drawings are far more controlled and flower-like than the cut paper, yarn, and collage pictures.

Rejection. Similarly, children who feel that their arts performance is rejected or unacceptable also retreat from arts activities. That is why it is equally important that teachers show their acceptance of the child's work and teach families how to encourage their young artists.

Environmental Factors

Young children may not see the world in the same way adults do, but they are influenced by the pictures they see, the kinds of objects that surround them, and the artistic reactions of their guiding adults to these things.

The role of culture. Children's development in the arts is strongly influenced by the culture in which they grow up. McFee and Degge (1981, p. 334) cite studies that indicate that children from cultures with particular stylistic ways of drawing will learn to draw in that style. Exposure to a wide variety of interesting musical styles challenges the child to invent new songs or refine existing ones.

Children who have seen examples of a variety of art forms and are taught to value them are more likely to incorporate elements from these examples into their own creative works. Dennis (1966) found that children raised in environments with plentiful visual imagery, surrounded by many drawings of people, had higher scores on the Goodenough-Harris Draw-A-Person Test (Harris & Goodenough, 1963).

The role of exposure. Adults determine which artistic behaviors and skills are acceptable for children to learn. They set the limits on what is a creative art performance and what is not. Smearing finger paint on paper is encouraged; smearing cereal on the wall is not. Are egg cartons an art material? Should we use food products in art? Is banging spoons on fine china making music? The adults' definition of what is and is not an arts activity will be transmitted to the child.

The Effect of Experience

Adults also determine how much experience children have with an art form. The more opportunities children have to use arts media, methods, and tools the more comfortable and skilled they will become in the creative arts. All individuals, regardless of their age, need to spend time exploring a medium before they can use it expressively.

Importance of practice. For example, if young children have many opportunities to draw, they will usually show their highest level of symbol development in their drawings. The same child may produce much less "competent" looking artwork if asked to use an unfamiliar material. Children will quickly revert to scribbles in their first finger painting or watercolor. Repetition and practice are the keys to improving skills at any level. Even adults with excellent fine motor control find themselves scribbling the first time they try to draw freehand with a mouse on a computer.

Importance of role models. Children are influenced by the people around them. They are more likely to be interested in creating art if other people around them are as well, and if arts are readily available and highly valued. Young children may make drawings in mud and hum made-up tunes on their own, but they are not going to choose formal drawing, singing, or dramatic activities unless parents and teachers have offered such opportunities to them.

Importance of real experiences. In the same way, the more opportunities a child has had to participate in real experiences, the richer and more meaningful their arts performance will become. A child who has seen a real chicken will more likely be able to imitate how it behaves in creative movement activities and draw it in more detail than a child who has not. Those who grow up in places where most houses have flat roofs draw house symbols that have flat roofs. Children who have seen that people come in many colors, whether in their community or in pictures, and are comfortable with that fact are more likely to include skin color in their artworks.

Giftedness

Young gifted children are those that exhibit an exceptional level of skill or the potential to learn rapidly in one area of the arts. Such high ability is often due to previous experiences and inner motivation.

Early exposure to the arts has been shown to accelerate artistic development. In homes where one or more of the arts are highly valued, children are introduced at earlier ages to more complex experiences and skills.

For example, all infants are born wired for music, but infants who are sung to and exposed to musical instruments at early ages begin musical expression earlier and are better able to match pitch than children raised in a nonmusical environment, whose only exposure to music was television and recorded music (Kelly & Smith, 1987). A 2003 research study found that three-year-old children who have more music in their homes had increased auditory sensitivity (Shahin, Roberts, & Trainor, 2003). An enriched music environment for toddlers produced increased voice production (Gruhn, 2002). A study by Christo Pantev found that the younger a child learned the piano, the larger the area of the brain that responded to music (1998).

Another factor that causes some children to excel in one of the arts is motivation. Some children develop a passion for one of the arts. One child may spend hours drawing every day. Another may sing and invent songs. Many children have rich fantasy lives and make up and act out stories. These children, on their own, put in many more hours practicing their chosen art than their peers and so have advanced artistic skills.

Gifted children may also exhibit earlier fine motor control. For example, one child might draw realistic-looking faces while most peers are still scribbling. Another child can finger a tune on a violin before others the same age can. Such exceptional abilities are quickly noticed and praised. However, it is important to remember that some children, particularly boys, cannot express their artistic gifts until later ages when physical development catches up with their creative potential.

Working with highly motivated and skilled children who learn rapidly can be challenging. They spend less time exploring and practicing with a material or technique and are ready to move on to responsive activities before their peers are. Open-ended arts activities that welcome many levels of responses are a good way to meet the needs of these gifted children.

Symbolic Communication Model

Incorporating these social and environmental factors, Kindler and Darras (1994; Kindler, 1997) have proposed a model of artistic development that presents artistic production as a two-fold process as depicted in Table 3-5. One part of the process is comprised of biologically propelled physical and cognitive growth. The other is the social and cultural learning, including formal teaching, to which the child is exposed. In this model, individuals do not lose their earlier approaches to arts production but incorporate them or return to them as needed throughout their lives.

As Table 3-5 indicates, there is a range of artistic behaviors that a child might exhibit. Rather than specific ages or levels, artistic production is organized by modes of behavior. During his or her lifetime, an individual may function in one or more of these modes in varying contexts. For example, upon meeting an unfamiliar medium, most children and adults will operate in the exploratory mode, making random movements as they try to assess the nature of the material. Once they have learned to control a material, they will attempt detailed, graphic, and symbolic expression.

The symbolic communication model shows how a child's arts performance can be viewed a multimedia blend of graphic, verbal, and kinesthetic communication that reveals the child's thought processes, rather than a lockstep process of growth.

TABLE 3–5 Multimedia Modes of Artistic Production, Based on Kindler and Darras (1994)

Child	Mode 1	Mode 2	Mode 3	Mode 4	Mode 5
Drama: Says. . .	Random sounds	Words	Matches sound and action	Naming	Story in cultural style
Visual art: Draws. . .	Random marks	Shapes	Action symbols	Object symbols	Pictures in cultural style (understandable without verbalization)
Creative dance: Moves. . .	Random movements	Conscious control	Self-imitation	Repetition	Imitation of cultural style of dance
Music: Makes. . .	Random sounds	Controlled sounds	Rhythmic sounds	Melody	Song in cultural style
ADULT	Media exploration	Simple doodles	Complex doodles	Shorthand symbols (e.g., stick figures)	Detailed, recognizable symbols in style of culture

WHAT DO DEVELOPMENTAL MODELS TELL EDUCATORS?

"One has to respect the time of maturation, of development, of the tools of doing and understanding, of the full, slow, extravagant, lucid and ever-changing emergence of children's capacities; it is a measure of cultural and biological wisdom."

—Loris Malaguzzi (in Edwards, Gandini, & Forman, 1993, p. 74)

All of these factors interact with each other in a multitude of ways, resulting in each child being a unique individual, as shown in Figure 3-1. We can never assume that if a child is a certain age, or is offered the same arts activities as another, we can predict exactly what that child will do with them. This is what makes teaching the arts to children so exciting. Every day is full of fresh, new creative arts performances for the teachers to enjoy.

The growth of young children, from exploring scribblers and babblers to symbol-creating artists, musicians, dancers, and actors, is an amazing journey. Understanding children's artistic development, and the factors that affect it, helps teachers better understand the artistic behavior of young children so that they can offer the most appropriate arts experiences.

Four Ground Rules

Based on what we know about how children develop in the arts, we must consider four things in selecting appropriate arts activities for our students.

1. **We must have realistic expectations.** Developmental stage models and an understanding of the factors affecting individual development enhance our understanding of why children's arts performance looks the way it does. Among young children, we should expect a range of behaviors, from simple exploration based on their level of physical control to complex expressions of their ideas. Within an age cohort, the creative arts produced by children will vary widely, depending on the children's cultural and social experiences and their familiarity with the art form. For example, it is not at all unusual in a group of four-year-olds to have some children scribbling, some using a limited number of symbolic forms, and some drawing complex graphic symbols. We must accept the scribbler's and babbler's artistic performances being just as valid and important as the more adult-pleasing recognizable pictures, songs, and stories, and select open-ended activities that allow all participants to be successful.
2. **We must value children's art production as a developmental process, not as a product.** It is essential to find ways of recording and presenting not just the final static product, but the whole process of creation. Anyone who has watched and participated in a child's arts activity knows that the final product may be a letdown. Young dancers may trip and hesitate as they attempt to glide around the room. Beginning singers may sound out-of-tune. Arts activities needs to be accompanied by a record of what the children said, the stages the works passed through, and how the children moved as they worked. This is a challenge for a busy, overworked teacher, but it is not impossible.
3. **We must understand better what the child is thinking.** Knowing the physical, social, cultural, and emotional factors affecting a child helps us better understand and accept the young artist's behavior and resulting creative work. For example, a child banging and stabbing the paper with a crayon is probably not being aggressive but more likely exploring the possibilities of the crayon.
4. **We must select activities that are suitable for particular children.** Because there will always be a range of abilities in any group, the arts activities that teachers select must be open-ended and allow every child to be successful. There must always be room for exploration as well as practice and responsive work.

HOW DO WE ASSESS CHILDREN'S GROWTH IN THE ARTS?

"Growth itself contains the germ of happiness."

—Pearl S. Buck (1967)

In assessing children's artistic growth, it is the process that is most important, not the end product. Therefore, we need to use methods that allow us to track children's behavior over a period of time. Two ways to do this are through careful observation and the collection of real records.

Assessing Artistic Growth through Observation

One of the best ways to assess children's behavior is to simply watch them. Watching children is an essential component of good teaching. Teachers can learn many things from how children behave and react artistically. To be useful, these observations need to be made regularly and carefully recorded. Two ways to do this are checklists and anecdotal notes.

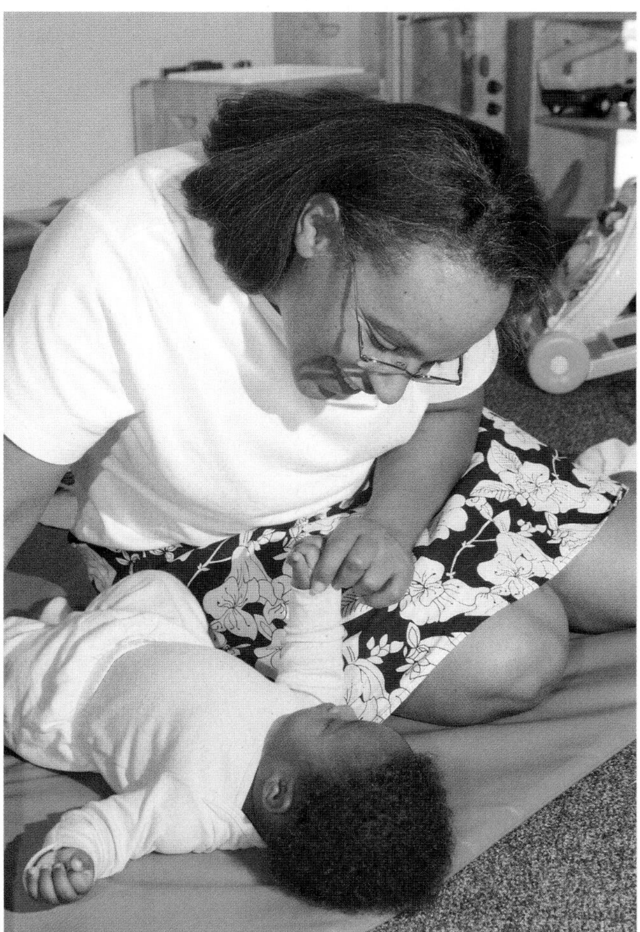

One of the best ways to observe children's growth and behavior is by carefully watching how they behave and react in different situations.

Observing the individual. Individual behavior patterns can give us information about the following growth areas:

1. **Physical:** The child's physical control of materials, methods, and skills
2. **Social:** The child's ability to work with others in arts activities
3. **Emotional:** The child's comfort level with arts materials and the art of others as expressed in arts activities
4. **Perceptual:** The child's visual and spatial perception skills
5. **Symbolic language:** The child's skill in understanding and creating ways to communicate through the arts
6. **Cognitive understanding:** The child's ability to express arts concepts graphically and through oral language

Observing group dynamics. No child functions alone. We must also place the child in the context of the group. Children learn as much from interacting with their peers as they do from adults. Every group has a unique dynamic, and no two groups react in the same way to the arts activities that teachers offer. Observations of the behavior of groups of children can help us see each child more broadly. Group behavior patterns can provide the following information:

- The suitability of the arts experience for the particular group
- The interests of the group
- The role of the child within the group

Assessing Artistic Growth through Children's Real Records

Children's creative behavior provides another way to observe their progress. These observations can include things such as the child's drawings, photographs of the child involved in arts activities, and recordings of the child singing or playing an instrument.

Using photographs. Anyone working with children should always have a camera close at hand.

Teacher Tip

SYSTEMS FOR RECORDING OBSERVATIONS

Checklists strategically placed around the children's environment can provide a convenient way to record behaviors. Make a list of the children's names and then hang it at the easels, by the blocks, near the listening center, and so on. Use Velcro to attach a pencil near each list. Develop a simple symbol for the behaviors being observed, such as the initial letters or a shape. Throughout the day, mark the lists with symbols to indicate that a child is in a particular area and what behavior is being observed. Done on a regular basis, these checklists provide a better picture of the child's daily behavior and skill development than memory alone (see Figures 3-2 and 3-3).

ANECDOTAL RECORDKEEPING

Anecdotal records provide an ongoing picture of the child's behavior at set times in specific settings. They can be made at the time of the observation or soon after the event. To be useful, the record should document the setting of the event (including the time), the children involved, and any other related information. Anecdotes should be objective, recording only observed behaviors and direct quotes of the children, not the teacher's opinion about the reason for that behavior. Figure 3-4 gives an example of a typical anecdotal note.

Index cards labeled with each child's name can be carried around in a pocket for a ready way to record quick observations. Having the names on them means no child is missed. Some teachers are more comfortable using clipboards or notebooks with one page divided into sections for each child. Another method is to write on large, self-stick labels, which can then be peeled off and attached to the child's folder.

Sample Checklist

Skills	Always	Sometimes	Not yet
Works independently			
Asks for help			
Cleans up after self			
Interacts positively with others			
Controls tools			
Cuts with scissors			
Stays on paper			
Verbalizes about work			
Observes cause and effect			

FIGURE 3–2 Sample behaviors and checklist system.

At the Easel Area

Child	Always	Sometimes	Not yet
Michelle	✓		
Nick	✓		
Stanley			✓
Berette		✓	

FIGURE 3–3 Sample checklist.

It does not have to be a fancy one, but it should be simple and foolproof to operate. Digital cameras are ideal for this purpose. Camera phones can be used as well. If the camera is convenient to use and nearby, then it is more likely to be picked up at opportune moments.

The uses of photos are multitudinous.

1. Photographs of block structures, sculptures, and other three-dimensional projects can be displayed long after the originals are gone.
2. Photo albums of children's artwork, field trips, and special events can be kept in the book area.
3. Photographs of children working can be saved in process folios and portfolios as a visual way to remember how something was done and as a way to emphasize process over product.
4. Photographs of class members, families, friends, and visitors, as well as the children's homes and family events, can be used in portrait lessons and family studies.
5. Photographs of familiar objects shown from unusual viewpoints can challenge children's visual perception.

Mario 2/4
At easel 10:04 to 10:10.
Started by making yellow line.
Then used blue. Touched where made green.
Put finger up to eye. Smiled.
Then took brush and smeared the colors together.
I asked, "What color is that?"
He said, "Green."

Susan 2/4
Drawing/cutting 10:50 to 11:05.
Took markers and went to block area.
Made a sign for building.
Said, "This is a supermarket."
Then drew rectangles and got scissors and cut them out.
Called them food.

FIGURE 3–4 Sample anecdotal records.

6. Photographs can be used to record arts activities, setups, and child interactions for teachers to use in later review of their teaching methods.
7. Digital photos can be saved to a flash drive, CD, or DVD for more compact storage.

For successful photographs, use the following guidelines:

- Try to get down to the children's level when taking photographs so the pictures do not all reflect an adult's perspective.
- If using flash, check the distance from the subject to avoid washed-out pictures.
- Do not shoot against a bright background, such as a window.

Videotaping. The availability of camcorders and the video function on digital cameras has made it possible to truly record the multimedia process of arts performances. If a camcorder is available on a regular basis, it can be used to create a time record of a child's artistic growth. At regular intervals, record the child dancing, singing, playing an instrument, and creating an artwork.

Photography is a great way to record the arts process. Allow children to get into the act by letting them film their own work and their peers using inexpensive cameras.

Videos can also be made to record group projects, as part of portfolios, and as a way to assess teaching style.

Obtaining releases. Before taking any photographs or making a video, it is essential to obtain a signed release from all families. Many institutions have parents fill out such forms upon enrollment. However, if special use is going to be made of the pictures, such as a public display in an exhibit or at a workshop presentation, then a more specific release should be obtained (see Figure 3-5). If a family refuses to sign a release, then that request must be respected. When shooting photographs and videos, be careful to avoid taking pictures of children without releases, except when shot from the back.

Portfolios

A **portfolio** is a collection of the child's work and related materials made over a period of time. Each child should have either a physical or digital arts folder in which a record of their arts process and development is stored either in the form of the actual artworks and photographs of performances, or, if the equipment is available, in a digitalized format.

Constructing a folder portfolio. A short-term portfolio can be made from a very large piece of paper folded in half, or from two sheets taped together. If it will be used for only a short time, then this will suffice. If the folder will be used over a long period, such as a year or two, then it can be made

Sample Model Release

The undersigned hereby grants ______________________ the right to make, publish, reproduce, use, and reuse photographs or likenesses of my child ______________________, in which my child appears, with or without his or her name, and to circulate and use the same for educational purposes. I further agree to hold ______________________ harmless from any claim action and damages based on a violation or alleged violation of these representations. All photographs, negatives, prints, transparencies, drawings, reproductions, and sketches made by ______________________ shall be the exclusive property of ______________________.

Parent's or legal guardian's signature ______________________

______________________ Witness

______________________ School official

______________________ Date

______________________ Title

FIGURE 3–5 Sample model release.

sturdier by using clear packing tape to protect the edges or it can be made from two corrugated cardboard pieces taped together along one side to form a hinge. The portfolio must be as large as the largest paper used by an individual child. For ease of use, color-code or mark the folders with special symbols as well as names so children and parents can quickly locate their own folders.

CDs, DVDs, and audiotapes that record music, dance, and dramatic activities can be stored separately in shallow gift boxes or trays labeled with the child's name. These boxes can be sent home for the family's enjoyment on a regular basis.

One of the reasons educators hesitate to initiate the portfolio is the problem of storing it while still retaining easy access. A pile of large floppy papers is unsightly and heavy. It becomes almost impossible to remove folders on the bottom without handling all of the folders above. One solution is the commercially made, vertical, divided storage boxes that are used to store art prints (see Appendix C).

Digital portfolios. Saving children's work in digital format solves many of the problems mentioned above. The arts, in particular, lend themselves to this method. Digital photos and video clips of an individual child and of whole group performances can be kept in a folder on the computer and, at the end of a set time period, saved to a flash drive, CD, or DVD to send home to the family.

However, digital portfolios do have some disadvantages.

1. Not all families have access to a computer. In this case a physical portfolio of actual artworks and photographs is a better choice.
2. Upkeep is more time consuming for the teacher, who must download and save the work to all the different children's folders.
3. It is the adult's task to manipulate the data on the computer, and the children become less involved in the care and organization of their work.
4. In terms of the visual art works, having the children look at a photo of their artwork on a computer screen is not the same as being able to touch the real work and experience its true texture, color, and size.

Combined digital and physical portfolios. To create the most effective and useful arts portfolio, digital recordings of music, dance, and dramatic activities recorded on a CD or DVD can be combined with a folder containing actual pieces of children's visual artworks.

Teacher Tip

MAKING A PORTFOLIO

Materials

1. Two pieces of corrugated cardboard, cut to the size of the finished portfolio (A), 24-by-36 inches, will hold all but the very largest pieces.
2. Two sheets of paper at least 2 inches larger in both directions than the cardboard (B) and two sheets the same size (C).
3. Two pieces of fabric, 4 inches wide and the length of the folding edge of the portfolio (D).
4. Six lengths of ribbon, about 12 inches each (E).
5. White glue.
6. Scissors.

WHAT TO DO

1. Before beginning, select matching paper, fabric, and ribbon colors.
2. Glue together the sheets of paper (B).
3. Place both sheets of cardboard (A) side by side on top of the paper. Leave an even amount of paper projecting on all sides. Leave a 2-inch space between the boards in the center.
4. Place a small line of glue on the outside edges of the boards. Flip and glue down.
5. Cut off the corners.
6. Fold over and glue down the flaps.
7. Attach ribbons, as shown.
8. Glue the sheets of same-size paper (C) over the glued-down flaps and ribbon ends.
9. Glue a strip of fabric (D) on the inside and outside of the folded edge. Make sure the glue is only on the edges of the fabric to maintain flexibility when folded.
10. Use your creativity to decorate the outside of the portfolio. Attach a pocket made from a large envelope to the inside to store a table of contents.

Selecting work for the portfolio. Having a portfolio does not mean that every piece of artwork, every song sung, every creative movement, and every story acted out needs to be recorded and saved. Once children have been introduced to the idea of making a portfolio, they should be asked on a regular basis if they wish to put their artwork or a recording of their performance into the portfolio. If artwork is three dimensional, ask if they would like a photograph taken for the portfolio. The teacher can also select pieces for the folder (see Figure 3-6). Children are more willing to part with their work if they know the reason why. For example, "This painting shows how you have learned to make orange and brown. Shall we put it in your portfolio? Would you like me to write anything about it to go with it?"

Preparing artwork for the portfolio. Artwork and photographs placed in a folder portfolio do not have to be mounted but should not be wrinkled. Each piece should be labeled with name, date, and any comments by the child. A simple preprinted form can be filled in and affixed to the back (see Figure 3-7). Camcorders and digital cameras can be set so the date is automatically included. Files are also dated when they are downloaded to a computer. When taking photographs and videos, be sure to include the child in order to make identification of the work or performance easier.

Timeline for collecting work. The portfolio should represent a natural timeline, such as one session, 3 months, or a half year. The time period should be long enough to show growth, but not so long that the collection becomes unwieldy. At the end of the time period, the work should be ordered by date to highlight the child's growth or changing interests. If the program is long term, extending over a year or more, then a few pieces from older portfolios can be selected to begin a new one.

Before sending the portfolio home, carry out a self-reflection interview as a culminating activity. Figures 3-8 and 3-9 suggest some possible questions to ask. This process helps children learn how to assess their own progress.

If using a physical portfolio, always send the entire folder home, and create a new one to use for the next time period. This provides families with a unified

Contents of an Arts Portfolio

Work samples
- ❍ Done in a wide range of media
- ❍ Done at different times

Photographs and videos of
- ❍ Creative dance activities
- ❍ Dramatic activities
- ❍ Three-dimensional projects

Audiotapes of
- ❍ Child telling stories
- ❍ Child singing
- ❍ Child talking about work

Anecdotal materials
- ❍ Child's comments
- ❍ Family's notes
- ❍ Teacher's notes

Checklist summaries
- ❍ Time spent at different activities
- ❍ Common choices of arts activities

Interviews with child and family
- ❍ Record answers to questions that inquire into what the child has learned about the arts
- ❍ Record biographical information about the child

Attitude lists
- ❍ Favorite arts activities
- ❍ Favorite works in the arts
- ❍ Favorite artists, musicians, dancers, actors
- ❍ Favorite books
- ❍ Home arts activities such as music lessons

Process folios
- ❍ Materials from special projects
- ❍ A series of works

FIGURE 3–6 What to include in an arts portfolio.

Portfolio Label

Name: ____________________

Date completed: ____________________

Title or comment by child: ____________________

FIGURE 3–7 Portfolio label.

presentation of the artwork rather than a hodgepodge of papers and keeps these simply constructed folders from becoming dog-eared. It is also beneficial for children to reestablish ownership of the portfolio concept through the creation and decoration of a new folder on a regular basis.

Using the portfolio. Whether in digital or folder format, the portfolio system allows arts experiences to be richer and deeper in many ways. Both formats allow the child, the teacher, and the family to look through the portfolio individually and/or together as a way to review past progress. There are also specific uses for each type.

The physical portfolio. Having the actual works of art available means that they can be manipulated in different ways.

- The child can decide to store a piece of artwork to be worked on another day.
- The teacher can suggest reworking a piece of artwork, such as using chalk over a painting or painting over a crayon drawing.

Attitude Toward the Arts

Conduct interviews at spaced intervals to assess changes in attitude toward the different arts forms. Some questions to ask include:

1. What is your favorite arts activity?
2. What do you like best about creating . . . (stories, paintings, dances, puppet shows, music, etc.)?
3. What is your favorite . . . (art print, dance, musical instrument, song, story, etc.)?
4. Who is your favorite . . . (singer, musician, dancer, composer, actor, storywriter, etc.)?
5. What is your favorite book about the arts?
6. Do you . . . (sing, dance, play an instrument, draw, use play dough, etc.) at home? Tell me about it.

FIGURE 3–8 Assessing attitude toward the arts.

Self-Reflection

Look through the portfolio with the child and ask questions that will help the child make sense of the collected work. Here are some possible questions to ask.

1. Which is your favorite work?
2. Which work shows something new you learned?
3. Which arts activity did you work on the longest?
4. Which arts activity did you do the most?
5. Is there any arts activity you would like to do again?
6. Do you want to add a story or comments to any of the works?

Is there anything you want to add to or remove from your portfolio? Why?

FIGURE 3–9 Self-reflection on portfolio contents.

- Work can be collected, categorized, and made into work logs, booklets, or series showing growth in skill or knowledge or variations on a theme.
- Work for display can be selected from a range of work rather than on the spur of the moment.

The digital portfolio. Once photographs and video clips are stored on the computer, they can be used in a variety of formats.

- Digitalized photos and video clips can be inserted into slide shows and PowerPoint-type presentations as well as newsletters and class Web pages.
- Digitalized photos, audio, and video clips can be saved on CDs, DVDs, and flash drives, and then viewed or listened to by the child as an activity choice.
- Digitalized photos and video clips can be inserted into dictated stories and autobiographies written on the computer.
- Digitalized photos can be printed out and used in a variety of creative ways such as in collages, class quilts, class books, cards, bookmarks, and identifying labels.

What Can Be Learned from a Child's Work?

Once we understand how children develop artistically, we can also look at the individual artistic performance as a means of assessing how a child is learning and thinking. Engel (1995) identifies two approaches to evaluating children's visual art, which can also be applied to work done in the other art forms as well. One way is to describe the individual work and what it says about how the child is communicating through that art form. The other is developmental—it looks at the work's similarities with the work of other children at the same level and uses this to place the child's work in perspective. These two descriptions can then be placed in context by referring to the process the child went through in creating the work as revealed in anecdotal notes, photographs, and digital media clips. A third approach looks at the process of creation. Using this evaluative approach, teachers can create a summary statement of a child's artistic growth.

The descriptive approach. Engel suggests that starting with a basic description of the work or performance forces teachers to look carefully before making interpretive statements. She offers a continuum of questions to ask about the work, from the most to least objective.

1. What is it made from? When and where was it or carried out? What did the child do? How did the child move or act or sing?

2. What are the basic arts elements used? What lines, shapes, colors, patterns, forms, textures, rhythms, and movements can be observed? What techniques did the child use (such as using the point or side of a crayon, or speaking in a voice to match the character being acted out)?

3. What, if anything, does the work or performance communicate? Is it something identifiable, or is it unidentifiable?

4. What is the organization of the work or performance? Where or how did the child use the elements? What is its purpose? Was the child experimenting? Does it tell a story?

5. Where did the idea come from? Is it a response to an experience? Does it reflect the child's interests? Has it been influenced by TV or other cultural factors?

The developmental approach. Although each creative work or performance is unique, it also reflects the developmental mode in which the child is operating. As we have seen, children's work can be viewed as a combination of normative and individual development. By looking at a selected work or performance and knowing something of the conditions under which it was created, teachers can compare it to the developmental models in order to place it in the general context of children's artistic development.

Developmental questions to ask about the work include the following:

1. Are the child's actions random or controlled?

2. Does the sample represent an action (such as driving a truck or going to grandma's)?

3. Does the sample show spatial understanding?

4. Does the sample show numerical concepts?

5. Is the meaning of the work or performance understandable to other observers from the same culture?

6. Does the sample use any of the conventions common to the arts of the child's culture?

7. Does the sample communicate the child's knowledge of the media or subject? Does it express how the child feels about the media or subject?

Assessing the process. A third approach is to examine a work or performance from the viewpoint of what the child's actions were during its creation.

1. What was the first thing the child did? The last?

2. How long did the child stay at this activity?

3. Did the child make any requests for assistance or other materials?

4. Was the child influenced by other children's actions?

5. Did the child change her or his actions during the activity?

6. Did the child express any feelings or ideas during the activity or in response to the work?

7. What was the child's body language and verbalizations while working?

Composing a summary statement. Using the responses to these questions, we can create a meaningful summary of the piece. Such a summary (see Figure 3-10) can be used as part of the portfolio presentation, as part of a display, in reports to families, and for our own records.

How Can Teachers Share the Arts with Families?

Families have a very different relationship with their children than do teachers and other caregivers. Children look to their families for exclusive attention and ultimate acceptance as capable people. When children share their creative work with a family member and say, "Look what I made!" they want more than a tepid "That's nice" or an ordinary "Good work." They definitely do not want criticism from this all-important person whom they wish to please. Children really want to know that their families have taken the time to acknowledge their efforts and joy.

Four-year-old Heather's painting of a cat is typical of her work over the last three months. It was done in tempera paint on smooth tag board. She used a stiff bristle brush and three colors of paint—red, yellow, and blue. Heather demonstrated that she has learned how to make green by putting yellow paint over the blue to make the green grass. She controlled the paint well, using the brush to keep the line size uniform throughout the picture.

She began by painting the sky and the grass. Then she made the cat's face. The shape of the head shows her spatial understanding that the ears are part of the cat. The cat is facing toward us, and the lack of a body may represent her inability to show it from the front, or her attempt to show that the body would be covered up by the head if viewed up close. Heather's number concept is strong. She shows three whiskers on each side, two ears and two eyes. The addition of the second sun represents a need to maintain the strong symmetry of the picture, rather than a lack of knowledge.

We can tell from the picture that Heather is familiar with and likes cats. Her cat and sun symbols are easily recognizable to the viewer. Heather's work is characteristic of early childhood art that uses simple, but recognizable, symbols to tell a story. As she learns to control the size of her painted line, we would expect that Heather will refine her symbol for a cat, using thinner lines for the whiskers and experimenting with views that would show more of the body. With time, she may also add more details to her painting to expand her visual stories.

FIGURE 3–10 Sample summary: Heather's cat.

Unfortunately, families are far less equipped to give the deep response that children are seeking than are teachers and other trained caregivers. Where the educator sees exploration and creative experimentation, the families may see only what they think is a visible (and perhaps an uncomplimentary) reflection on the quality of their children and their family.

It is the teacher's job to educate families about their children's artistic development. Remember, unless teachers make an effort to record children's creative arts process, family members will make judgments based only on children's products.

Ways to help families appreciate their children's arts process.

- Provide many opportunities for families to review portfolios.
- When talking to families about their children's arts activities, emphasize process and growth rather than the project, and then help family members see this in the artwork. Checklists and anecdotal records will prove invaluable in remembering the specific actions of the children. Instead of saying, "Mary made a painting today," say, "Mary used paint today and learned how to make pink. See the pink spots in her painting." Instead of saying, "Arturo sang a song," say, "Arturo explored the chimes in the music center and invented his own melody and words. He sang his song to the whole group at circle time."
- Schedule "Arts Happenings" throughout the year at which families are invited to create together. This is a good time for group projects, such as murals and rhythm bands, in which everyone can participate. Watching families interact also gives teachers a better idea of their attitude toward their children's artwork.

- Attach simple, prepared descriptions of arts processes to work being sent home.
- Send home letters or, better yet, institute a regular newsletter that describes the children's arts activities along with other class activities, in terms of process and growth.
- Prepare an attractive booklet, illustrated with children's drawings, that briefly explains the goals of the arts program, what children learn through the arts, and what kinds of arts experiences will be offered.
- Send home suggestions for setting up a simple visual art center in the home. It should not be project based but rather provide a few basic art supplies that are always available, such as crayons, markers, paper, glue, scissors, and a modeling material such as play dough that children can use in their own ways. Help families by suggesting ways that they can contain messes, such as by setting up a small area as an art studio, providing an "art table," or, if space is limited, designating a plastic tray as the art spot.
- Describe how to make simple homemade musical instruments, and send home copies of the songs the child has learned so the family can sing them together.
- Make up take-home bags containing a story and simple puppets so the child can dramatize the story for the family.
- Use a home arts survey to find out the artistic background and experience of individual children.

Ways to help families understand artistic development. Families often do not have other children's work with which to compare their children's, and so they cannot tell if what their children bring home is appropriate or not. Teachers need to help families understand the process of artistic development and have them come to understand that exploration in which no final product results is a natural part of every child's artistic performance. It is the teacher's job to assure families that their children are performing in ways that are to be expected. There are a variety of ways to do this.

- Display many examples of creative work of all kinds, by children of all ages, either in the public areas where parents congregate or through exhibits and open houses.
- Hold family workshops in which examples of child art and portfolios are shared and concerns about the arts are discussed.
- Send to families, on a regular basis, arts notes detailing what children have accomplished.
- Families gain a better appreciation for the creative process if they participate in workshops that allow them to draw, paint, sing, dance, play with puppets, and participate in arts activities similar to those of the children.

How Can Teachers Assess Themselves?

Probably the most important assessment we can do is of ourselves. Without self-assessment, teachers cannot grow and improve. Teaching is not a static profession with only one right way to get the job done. The most exciting educators are those who constantly tinker with their programs, try new methods, and are willing to take risks. Those educators must have methods of assessment to help them know what is working and what is not.

Because program self-assessment is done privately for ourselves, it is tempting for us to skip this crucial activity when we are exhausted from a busy day with energetic and challenging youngsters. Preplanned,

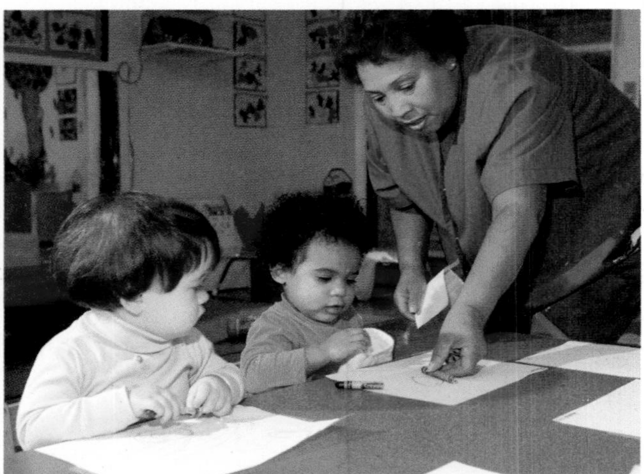

Assessing our successes and difficulties is vital for our growth as teachers of young artists.

easy-to-use assessment methods make it more likely that we will take the time to assess the programs we deliver. The following methods are suggested as ways to accomplish this task. Each provides a different viewpoint; when used in combination, they give an overall view of how teachers are doing.

Checklists. Checklists can be designed to quickly survey almost any area of the program. They provide objective information on the frequency of particular behaviors and areas that may require attention. Checklists do not work if they are buried on a desk or in folders. They need to be strategically placed where they can be seen daily and, once filled in, acted upon and then filed with program planning materials so that the information can be used in future planning. Checklists can be created for assessing activities and teaching methods (see Figures 3-11 and 3-12).

Feedback from the children. The checklists and anecdotal records that have been suggested for assessing the children can also be used for program assessment. These checklists reveal which activities attract interest and which are ignored. They document how many children choose to work in certain areas, how long they stay there, how much they interact, and what skills they are exhibiting. They also capture our interaction with the children and provide a picture of what we have said.

Personal arts notebook. Create a notebook in which to keep all of the materials generated in formulating the arts aspect of the total program. The notebook serves as a tangible memory of the form and nature of the program. Keep copies of plans, anecdotal records of how successful the activities were, and checklists and notes on actions taken to deal with difficult or unusual situations. Keep copies of all letters sent home to families. Looking back over this material will be invaluable in making better plans the next time.

Reflective teaching journal. A reflective journal provides a place for teachers to record their inner feelings about their work. Teachers need to set aside a time once a week, such as when the children are resting, to write a few reflective sentences on how they personally feel about what has been happening in this program of their creation. One way to approach this task is to respond to these sentence starters:

This week I felt competent when . . .

This week I felt frustrated when . . .

This week I felt exhilarated when . . .

"Terrific me" folder. Place a file folder labeled "TM" in a strategic place. Whenever complimentary notes from parents, children, or others are received, place them in this folder. Also include copies of materials from workshops attended or given, extra work done, notes about major accomplishments, and any other positive materials and activities. It is human nature to remember the negatives. Reviewing the materials in this folder every few months will provide not only an uplifting experience but also a more rounded view of one's accomplishments.

TEACHER TO FAMILY

Sample Arts Note (Attach To Paintings Going Home)

This painting was done at the easel using tempera paints and a variety of brushes. Painting helps children grow in many ways.

- They learn to use large and small muscles as they reach and stretch to make colorful strokes.
- Their hand-eye coordination improves as they move the brush from the paint container to the paper and back again.
- Their visual perception increases as they see how new colors are made as one color mixes with another.

Take time to enjoy this painting with your child. Some things to say include:

- You made many colorful lines.
- You made some interesting colors with the paint.
- Can you show me a yellow (or other color) line you made?
- Is there a story to go with your picture?

Through sharing this painting, you can discover what your child has learned and thought about today.

Your child's teacher,

Assessing an Art Activity

Arts experience: ____________________

Date(s): ____________________

Group composition: ____________________

ASSESSMENT AREA	CHECK IF PRESENT
Physical Growth	
• Required the use and control of large muscles	❍
• Required the use and control of small muscles of the hand	❍
• Required hand-eye coordination	❍
• Required the use of more than one sense	❍
Social Growth	
• Allowed children to work alongside others	❍
• Required sharing of supplies	❍
• Fostered positive peer interaction	❍
• Fostered positive child-adult interaction and dialogue	❍
Emotional Growth	
• Allowed children to work independently	❍
• Allowed children to express personal feelings	❍
• Provided time for introspection and concentration	❍
Cognitive Growth	
• Encouraged children to verbalize about their work	❍
• Fostered development of new way to show ideas	❍
• Provided opportunities to use the vocabulary of the art form	❍
• Enabled children to observe: Change	❍
Cause and effect	❍
Pattern	❍
• Enabled children to make comparisons	❍
• Provided experience with spatial concepts	❍
• Required children to make artistic decisions	❍
• Required children to order the sequence of their actions	❍
Creativity	
• Used and challenged existing skills and knowledge	❍
• Children were motivated to try activity	❍
• Provided sufficient time for immersion	❍
• Encouraged children to combine familiar elements in new ways	❍
• Required children to solve challenging problems	❍
Integration	
• Used knowledge from other curriculum areas	❍
• Enhanced knowledge of other curriculum areas	❍
• Enabled children to find connections among areas	❍
Arts of Others	
• Included opportunities to view arts of others	❍
• Included opportunities to discuss arts of others	❍
Reflection	
• Allowed children to talk about their own work	❍
• Allowed children to decide what to do with their work	❍
• Allowed children to participate in presenting the work	❍

Note: Few arts experiences include all of these areas. The more areas checked, however, the better designed and more worthwhile that arts experience is for children.

FIGURE 3–11 Arts activity assessment.

Assessing Your Own Teaching

Arts experience: ______________________________

Date(s): ______________________________

Group composition: ______________________________

ASSESSMENT AREA	CHECK IF PRESENT
Personal Behavior	
I showed confidence in my ability in the arts.	❍
I avoided terms of self-deprecation.	❍
I expressed enthusiasm for the activity.	❍
I wore clothing related to the activity.	❍
I participated in the activity by modeling process and/or technique.	❍
Nonverbal Responses	
My face mirrored my words.	❍
I lowered myself to the child's level.	❍
I shared my feelings.	❍
I allowed wait time.	❍
I made eye contact before speaking.	❍
Verbal Responses	
I used descriptive statements.	❍
I used paraphrasing.	❍
I made interpretive statements.	❍

ASSESSMENT AREA	CHECK IF PRESENT
I initiated artistic dialogue using questions based on:	
• arts elements	❍
• process	❍
• artistic decisions	❍
• predictions	❍
• cause and effect	❍
• connecting events	❍
• curriculum extension	❍
I elicited stories.	❍
I took dictation.	❍
Responses to Problems	
I gave encouragement when needed.	❍
I provided comfort when needed.	❍
I provided direction when needed.	❍
I fostered children's self-confidence by avoiding patterns and models.	❍

FIGURE 3–12 Teacher self-assessment.

CONCLUSION: THE CHILD ARTIST

"Once put down a line provokes thought."
—Sylvia Fein (1993, p. 16)

Artistic development models provide educators with a general overview of children and the arts. But we must remember that actual artistic development of each individual child is a combination of the biological maturation patterns of the body and brain, mediated by social and cultural factors and experiences.

Creative arts for the child is more than the simple manipulation of materials at an art table or putting on a funny hat in the dress-up corner. It is a developmental process. Children's artistic growth is not the step-by-step progress so carefully described by the early researchers. It is a multifaceted way for children to develop in the arts through new methods of expression and communication. This process can best be shared through the use of cameras, camcorders, and portfolios. It is our challenge to create the environment, to select the activities, and to devise a delivery system that nurtures this multimedia event.

FURTHER READING

These books will provide further insight into the artistic development of young children.

Lightfoot, C., Cole, M., & Cole, S. R. (2009). *The development of children.* New York: Worth.

This overview of development in children covers social, emotional, physical, and intellectual development.

Pica, R. (2009). *Experiences in movement: Birth to age eight.* Belmont, CA: Wadsworth.

Rae Pica provides a rich resource that relates physical development with development in the arts.

Sheridan, S. R. (2010). *Handmade marks.* West Conshocken, PA: Infinity.

Sheridan presents extensive research on the relationship among drawing, language, and other forms of communication. The book includes children's drawings from Rhoda Kellogg's collection, and a series of activities for teachers and parents to do with children starting at ten months that foster literacy.

For additional information on young children's development in the arts, visit our Web site at http://www.cengagebrain.com

TEACHING IN ACTION

Sample Newsletter

Dear Family,

This week we have been observing water—a perfect activity for such a wet, rainy week. We began by experiencing a variety of water activities. We put ice in the water on the water table, and the children had fun seeing how long it took for the ice to melt. We boiled water and observed the steam rising. Then we used the boiling water to make some delicious mint tea. At the easel, some children experimented with what happens when water is mixed with paint. Tuesday we went outside and splashed in the puddles on the playground. We observed the various ways water looked when it moved.

We talked about different ways to remember what we observed. Some children decided to make charts. Others made drawings of what they saw. Several decided to make books and used each page to draw pictures of different kinds of water. The children used creativity in inventing symbols to represent ice, steam, and water. They also had to decide which colors to use to represent water. We also imagined we were raindrops and moved creatively as we traveled from the ocean to the clouds and then down to the ground to water the flowers. We learned the song "Sun Soil Water and Air" by the Banana Slug Band and then invented our own movements to go with the song.

Please take time to talk to your child about what he or she learned about water as you enjoy the water projects that are coming home.

Your child's teacher,

These young children may all be the same age, however, each one learns and responds to arts activities in her or his own way.

Studio Page

LOOKING AT CHILDREN'S ARTISTIC DEVELOPMENT

Based on the models of artistic development described in this chapter, how would you characterize the artistic developmental level of the children described in the following examples?

- A child holds the paintbrush in his fist and moves it up and down, making large bold lines.

- A child taps a spoon on the table in time to a song on the radio.

- A child draws a detailed picture of her house that includes a ground line and skyline and writes a description below it.

- A child puts on a funny hat, makes a face, and says, "I'm a clown. I can make you laugh."

Studio Page

USING ANECDOTAL RECORDS

Based on the following anecdotes, describe the areas of artistic growth demonstrated by each child as you would explain them to the child's family.

Lien Age 2
Approached easel. Stirred paint in each container. Dipped brush into green and made a green line. Then dipped brush in red and smeared it over the green line. Exclaimed, "I made brown!"

____

____

Salvo Age 3 1/2
At collage center. Took tray and filled it with buttons. At table began to place buttons in rows. I suggested that he glue the row on a piece of paper. Shook head no. Five minutes later was still playing with the buttons. Cam approached and began to join in sorting. Together they made a row of buttons from one end of the table to the other. Very animated discussion about which button should come next in row. Cam invited me to see their "pattern."

____

____

Wendy Age 5 1/2
Wendy was wearing a lacy dress and a safari hat. When I asked her who she was, she replied, "I'm an explorer going to a party."

____

____

Loren Age 8
Loren sat under the table and worked on her story for all of the free time. Used crayon and marker. Worked very slowly and kept hesitating before selecting a color. Did not want to talk about it when I came by, so I left her alone. Later her two friends helped her dramatize the story for the class.

____

____

Studio Page

OBSERVATION: INFANTS, TODDLERS, AND THE ARTS

1. Plan an arts exploration or practice activity suitable for an infant or toddler.
2. Obtain permission to work with one infant or toddler, either at home or in a child care setting.
3. Set up your activity and observe the infant or toddler at work. Take anecdotal notes. If possible, take photos or videotape the activity (get permission first).

Age of child:
Setup of materials:
Length of time of observation:

---

1. What did the child do first?

---

2. What did the child say?

---

3. How did the child interact physically? (For example, describe position of arms and hands, grip, any other body parts involved.)

---

4. How long did the child work? (Measure periods of concentration. If child stopped, why? How did the child let you know he or she was finished?)

---

5. Describe the performance or work produced. (What did the child do first? How many drawings were made? What was repeated?)

---

6. Compare your observations to the mulitmediamodel of Kindler and Darras (1994). What behaviors did you see that support their ideas?

Studio Page

OBSERVATION: A CHILD AND THE ARTS

1. Plan an arts exploration or practice activity suitable for a child between the ages of four and eight.
2. Obtain permission to work with one child, either at home or in a school setting. If possible, take photos or videotape the activity (get permission first).

Age of child:
Setup of materials:
Length of time of observation:

---

1. What did the child do first?

---

2. What did the child say?

---

3. How did the child interact physically? (For example, describe position of arms and hands, grip, any other body parts involved.)

---

4. How long did the child work? (Measure periods of concentration. If child stopped, why? How did the child let you know he or she was finished?)

---

5. Describe the work produced. (What did the child do first? What was repeated?)

---

6. Compare the arts activity of this child to that of the toddler you observed. What similarities and differences did you notice?

---

7. How did this child's behavior fit the appropriate developmental stages?

Chapter

4

Awakening the Senses

Questions Addressed in This Chapter:

- What is beauty?
- How does an aesthetic sense develop?
- How is sensory perception developed in young children?
- What are the elements of the arts?

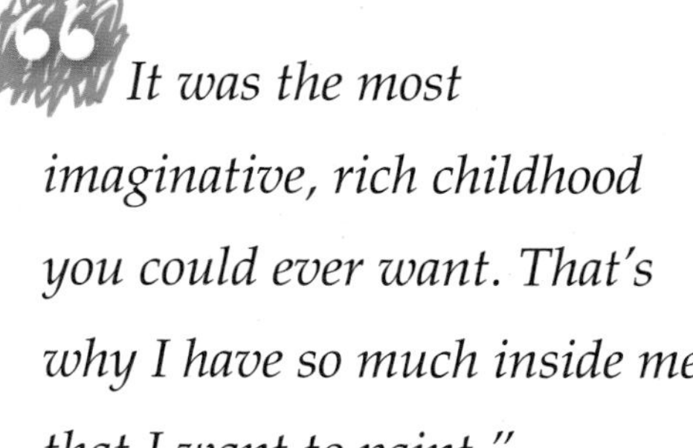

"It was the most imaginative, rich childhood you could ever want. That's why I have so much inside me that I want to paint."

—*Andrew Wyeth*
(Merryman, 1991, p. 21)

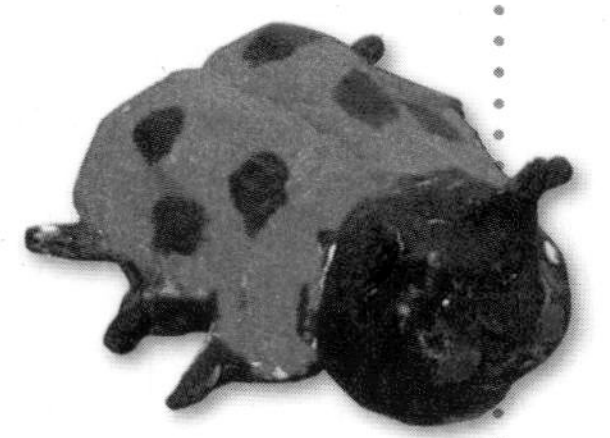

Young Artists at Work

"What a beautiful painting!" exclaims the preschool teacher, as she takes the dripping painting off the easel. Three-year-old Michelle smiles and runs off to the sand table, while the teacher carries Michelle's large sheet of newsprint covered with wiggly lines of lime green and black to the storage shelf. Soon Michelle's parents arrive to take her and her painting home. They too declare the painting beautiful and proudly hang it on the refrigerator door in the kitchen. When Michelle is eighteen and getting ready to study art in college, she finds her preschool painting. "Why did they save this old thing?" she chuckles.

WHAT IS BEAUTY?

Is this painting really beautiful? Why was it hung on the refrigerator instead of over the living room sofa? Why does grown-up Michelle no longer think it is beautiful?

When we judge something beautiful, we are describing its effect on our sense of sight, touch, smell, taste, and/or hearing—its aesthetic quality. But there are many other factors that determine what impact an artistic work or performance will have on our senses. No two people make identical judgments about the arts. People find beauty in different styles of painting, types of music, and ways of dancing because of their personal beliefs, knowledge, or experiences.

The preschool teacher thinks Michelle's painting is beautiful because she knows that it represents an initial experiment with crossing wet lines of paint. Michelle's parents think it is beautiful because it was their beloved child who created this new visual image. However, they will not hang it over the sofa, because the colors do not "go" with their beautiful living-room color scheme of rose and blue. Eighteen-year-old Michelle laughs, because she thinks her current art is so much more mature and, therefore, more beautiful than her childish beginnings.

HOW DOES AN AESTHETIC SENSE DEVELOP?

> *Aesthetics refers to a person's ability to sense and gain beauty and wonder from his environment. It can be done with any or all of a person's five senses as well as his imagination.*
>
> *—Mary Mayesky, Donald Neuman, and Ronald J. Wlodkowski (1990, p. 11)*

Children are not born knowing what is beautiful. If that were true, then every human being would have the same standards of beauty. However, children are born with a sense of wonder that makes them curious about their surroundings. As they explore with their senses, they learn to identify pleasing experiences with beauty. At first, children discover what the important people around them think is beautiful. Parents, siblings, grandparents, and peers express a personal view of beauty to the young child in statements such as: "Look at that beautiful sunset!," "Isn't that a gorgeous vase?," "There are wonderful designs on this sweater," and "Feel the beautiful quilt Grandma made you."

As children grow they are also influenced by the environment around them. The natural and human-made objects they encounter can provide pleasing or interesting sensory experiences that will shape their view of what is beautiful. Things that feel familiar, comforting, or exciting become incorporated into their own aesthetic belief about what is beautiful.

The Importance of Culture

Many ideas about beauty are held in common with other people with whom the child shares a similar heritage. When a group holds the same ideas about the beauty of some object or experience, this represents a **cultural aesthetic** or **style.** Ideas about style can be based on shared lifestyle, history, or experience. Styles can be handed down from one generation to another, as in the Amish tradition of making quilts from only solid-colored fabrics. Style can also denote works that are based upon a shared set of principles, such as jazz, an American musical style that features strong, flexible rhythms supporting solo and group improvisations.

Although childhood experiences and cultural styles form the core of an individual's aesthetic philosophy, each person's definition of beauty is always changing. Some cultural styles change over time. Eighteenth-century European men felt beautifully dressed when wearing long, curled, and powdered wigs. Sometimes one group of people or an individual will copy or adapt a style from another group, such as when non-Native Americans wear T-shirts decorated with traditional Native American symbols. Children are constantly bombarded with often conflicting ideas about beauty from books, television, and in movies and commercials. These, too, are added to their internal brew of aesthetic experiences and judgments. Taken together, all of these diverse influences form a personal aesthetic philosophy that determines what they think is beautiful and what they like.

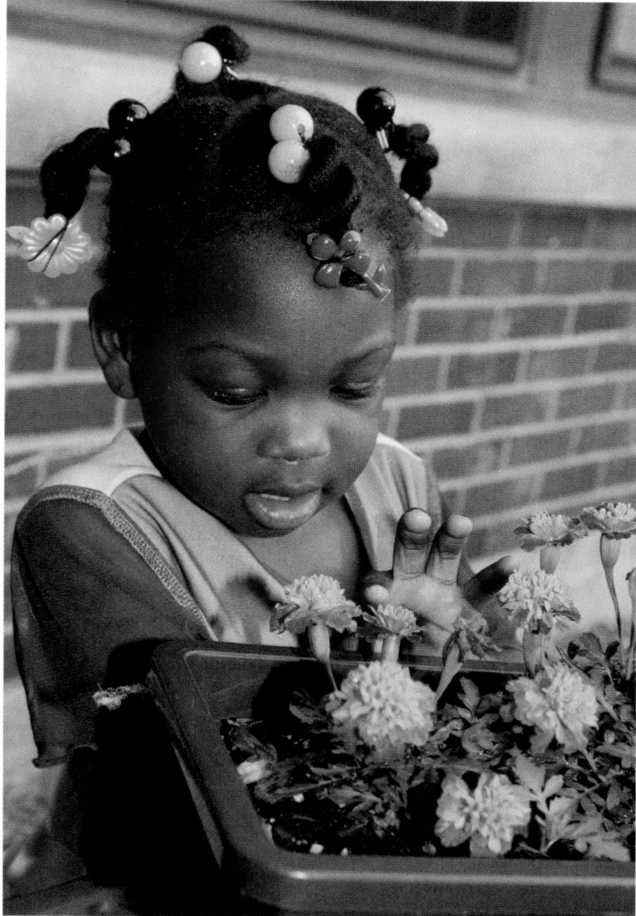

Children need many opportunities to discover the beauty in nature.

Art and Beauty

Liking a work of art, piece of music, style of dance, or story genre, however, is not the same as understanding and valuing it. The word *beautiful* is not a simple adjective but also a word of judgment. Not all creative works are intended to be beautiful. Some assail the senses with distorted or unpleasant images or strong emotional messages, which makes it difficult to separate how we personally feel about a work from its aesthetic value. Sometimes it is hard to separate our emotions about a piece or performance from its value as a creative statement by an artist. We may not like every creative performance done by the children with whom we work, but we can appreciate it, and we can help children appreciate the aesthetic elements in their creation by developing their sensitivity to the elements of the arts that are found in their environment.

The Role of the Teacher

We need to be aware of how we influence children's perception of beauty and the development of their aesthetic philosophy and judgment. This impact can be felt in two ways. One way we can affect young children's aesthetic perceptions is by creating a pleasing environment with carefully selected, beautiful objects. The other way is to expand children's definition of beauty by pointing out the aesthetic and sensory qualities in their creative works, performances, and in the environment, and by providing experiences that foster sensory awareness. The goal should be to help children grow into adults who love beautiful things, who value all kinds of art, and who can still find wonder in the beauty of the world.

HOW IS SENSORY PERCEPTION DEVELOPED IN YOUNG CHILDREN?

> *We know that children learn in active, not passive ways. The sense of belonging to the environment is part of each one. It is only later that children learn that it is often a do-not-touch, do-not-see, do-not-hear, do-not-taste world.*
>
> —*Larry Kantner (1989, p. 45)*

It is through the senses that we learn about the world. Born with the capacity to focus their attention and moderate their reactions to sensations, infants develop their ability to process sensory information through interactions with their caregivers and their environment (Cermak, 2009). When children are deprived of sensory information because of a physical issue such as blindness or from a lack of stimulating experiences, their understanding of the world is affected (Cermak, 2009). Children, therefore, need many sensory experiences in order to develop not only their aesthetic beliefs, but also a rich cognitive map of their environment.

For example, a child who has never seen, touched, smelled, heard about, or tasted ice cream will not have a concept of what ice cream is; will not be able to understand stories, poems, or songs about ice cream; and certainly will have no basis upon which to develop a symbol to represent ice cream in a creative work.

Sensory awareness is not something that can be put out on a table like crayons and paper. Our daily interactions with young children should be peppered with statements and questions that show the wonder and value of the sensory qualities of the environment. A sensory element exists in every activity in which children are involved. Instead of seeing blocks, see shapes and forms; instead of glue, notice stickiness. Listen and learn from children.

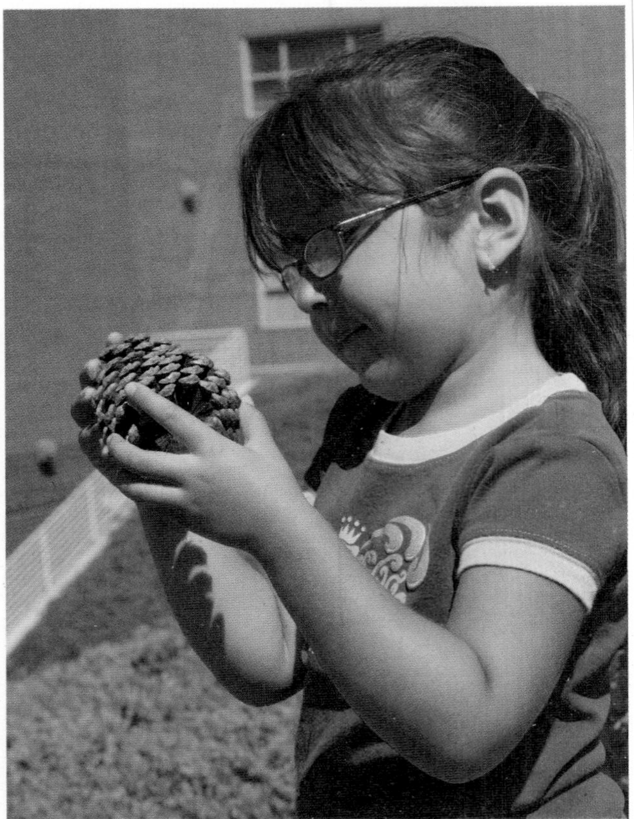

Sensory awareness cannot be put on the table. We need to provide intriguing objects and use rich language to describe how they look and feel.

Young children do not hesitate to invite us to "feel this" or "smell that," and we must do the same with them. Find a sensory element, and express it with rich language.

> *"Look at how the light is shining on your wet paint!"*
>
> *"Oh, the sand is so cool and damp today!"*
>
> *"These flowers smell like a summer day!"*

And, of course, lavish the young artists with comments about the sensory quality of their work.

> *"That red and green look beautiful together!"*
>
> *"Your clay ball feels so wonderfully round!"*

Developing Sensory Perception

In addition to finding and celebrating the sensory qualities of children's everyday experiences, we need to provide extraordinary and unexpected sensory experiences for them.

The experiences presented here are grouped by the **sensory mode** that is their main focus, although all are multisensory as it is almost impossible to eliminate the input from all senses but one, without placing great limits on the freedom of exploration of the child. In fact, many young children dislike being restricted from using their senses. They will peek over blindfolds and taste things before being told to do so. They should never be punished for such natural curiosity. Instead, take care in setting up these experiences, so that peeking and bold explorations are safely part of the fun.

Children may seem to spend only a short amount of time investigating these sensory activities before dashing off to something else. Remember that time for a young artist is not the same as time for an adult, and that the value of an experience cannot be measured by the clock. Even a minute or two of investigating an unusual sound or a visual texture is of utmost benefit to a child's cognitive growth. The child's new information about that exploration will enrich her or him in a way that constant exposure to familiar and everyday objects will not.

Therefore, we need to offer sensory activities regularly, change them often, and repeat them frequently. Young children grow quickly and will experience such activities differently at later stages of development. With careful planning and construction, many of the sensory activities suggested here can be reused many times over the years.

Special Needs

• SENSORY INTEGRATION •

Sensory integration refers to how we process information from our senses. All the sensations our body is feeling work together to help us understand and control our behavior and responses to stimuli. Children who have **sensory integration dysfunction (SID)** may be overly sensitive or under-reactive to touch, movement, sights, and sounds. Children exhibiting any of these characteristics may react strongly to arts activities by exhibiting fear, yelling, tantrums, or refusal to participate. These children need slow, careful exposure to many sensory activities with calm guidance from a facilitating adult. Many of the sensory and arts elements activities in this chapter provide gentle introductions to arts experiences.

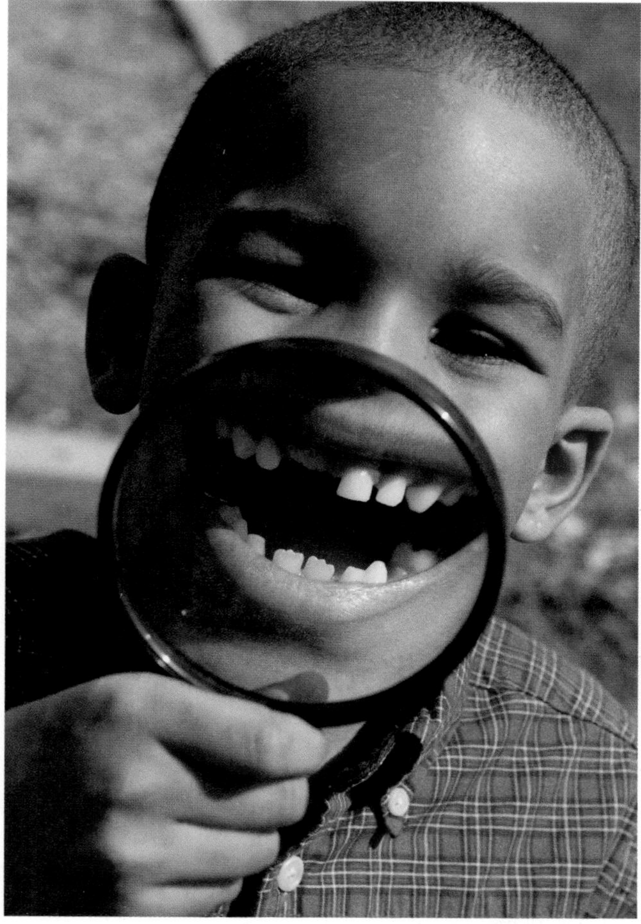

Invite children to look at familiar things in new ways.

Presenting Sensory Experiences

Sensory experiences can be offered in many ways so that they capture children's attention in the classroom.

Provide sensory bins. Place a sensory bin in a highly visible place where there is frequent traffic, perhaps near the door so it is one of the first things the children find when they arrive.

Set up an observation table. Place an unfamiliar object from nature on a small child-height table. Make a comment about it as the children arrive:

"Look, we have a beautiful conch shell from Florida! How do you think it feels?" "Can you guess what is in the sensory table today? What does it look like?"

Share something special. Present a unique item to touch, feel, and look at during circle time or to a small group. Then place it on the observation table, in the drawing center, or another selected location. For example, show a beautiful geode to the group, and have the children take turns describing what they see. Then show them where there are more in a basket for them to explore.

Visual Perception

Learning to discriminate between different colors and different shapes helps children see the world with more understanding. **Visual perception,** said the influential psychologist Rudolph Arnheim (1969), is really "visual thinking," a cognitive process that takes images perceived physically by our eyes and gives them meaning.

There are many ways to integrate visual perception activities into children's everyday experiences.

Book Box

Books that excite the senses.

Freeman, D. (1966). *A rainbow of my own.* New York: Puffin Books.
A little boy imagines that a rainbow is his friend in this time-tested book. Toddler and up.

Lionni, L. (1995). *On my beach there are many pebbles.* New York: HarperCollins.
Beautiful pencil drawings of pebbles, both real and amazing, show children how to look at simple things and see beauty. A quiet time read aloud to accompany sensory arts activities involving collecting, observing, and using pebbles and stones. Toddler and up.

Rotner, S. (2010). *Senses at the Seashore.* Minneapolis, MN: First Avenue.
Colorful photographs and simple text illustrate a day at the beach. Follow up by adding sea shells and water to the sand table. Infant and up.

Shaw, C. G. (1988). *It looked like spilt milk.* New York: HarperTrophy.
Free-form cloud shapes turn into ordinary objects. After reading the book, go outside and find pictures in the clouds. Also available as a big book from Scholastic. Infant and up.

Young, E. (1991). *Seven blind mice.* New York: Philomel.
Based on the classic tale of the blind men and the elephant, seven blind mice use their senses to investigate an elephant. Also available as a big book from Scholastic. Toddler and up.

Ziefert, H. (2006). *You can't taste a pickle with your ear.* Maplewood, NJ: Blue Apple.
A humorous introduction to the five senses. Preschool and up.

Describe what you see. Refer to visual elements when reacting to children's performances:

> *"The costume you are wearing has so many bright colors."*
>
> *"You made a pattern when you pressed the potato masher into the clay."*
>
> *"Look how our shadows change as we dance."*

Make "looking" tubes. Make plain tubes by rolling up a sheet of tag board into a cylinder and gluing or taping down the seam. Set out an attractive basket of long and short tubes, and encourage the children to look through them and describe what they see. Give them an attractive name such as "view scopes" or "looking tubes." For another experience, prepare some tubes ahead of time by taping colored cellophane to one end, or try taping black paper over an end, and poking several small holes in it. The children can use art materials to decorate their view scopes.

Create peep holes. Make openings to look through by cutting different shaped openings in stiff pieces of cardboard. The holes can be made small, for one-eye viewing, or large enough for the child to use both eyes. If possible, laminate these for durability, or cover them with clear package sealing tape or clear contact paper. Vary this activity by taping colored cellophane over the openings. Try overlapping several colors of cellophane in strips across the opening for another unusual effect.

Provide picture "frames." Prepare a set of construction paper or cardboard "frames" with varying sizes, shapes, and placement of holes cut out of them. These can also be laminated for durability.

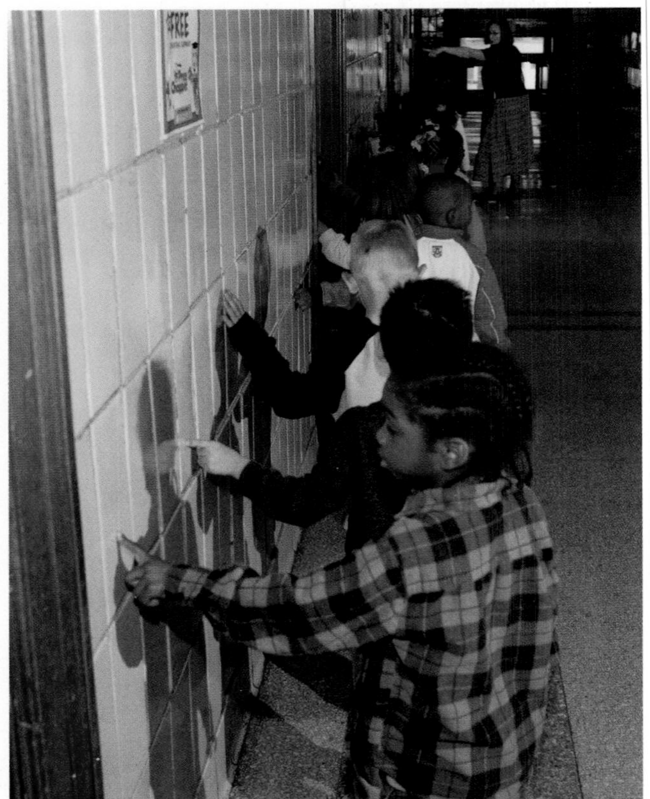

Having children trace their shadows on a wall helps them develop their visual perception and increases their understanding of light and shadow.

Children can use these to cover a piece of artwork, an illustration in a book, magazine pictures, or even games and puzzles for the thrill of seeing the detail of a small part. Young children love the peek-a-boo effect they can create. By turning the frame in different ways they can see how the effect changes. On occasion, add colored cellophane to these as well, or create frames with multiple openings for a different experience.

Make envelopes with holes. Cut out magazine pictures and mount them on heavy construction paper or poster board. Wildlife and nature magazines provide excellent sources of interesting scenes, animals, and people. The mounted pictures should be slightly smaller than an 8–1/2-by-11-inch brown mailing envelope. Study the picture and cut a hole in the envelope in a location where an interesting detail will show, such as an eye, a mouth, or a flower. Place the picture in the envelope. Children can study the detail and try to imagine the rest of the picture before pulling it out of the envelope and being surprised by the visual image they see.

Provide a book of holes. To make a visually enticing book, create "frames" by cutting holes in pieces of construction paper. Place two mounted magazine pictures back to back, add a frame, then two more back-to-back pictures, and another frame. Place the holes in creative and interesting ways, or try using more than one frame between pictures. Add a front and back cover, both with well-placed holes, and staple the book together.

Explore "shake" bottles. Fill plastic bottles with boiled water, food coloring, and small appealing objects that float and sink in the water in interesting ways. Try glitter, pompoms, beads, small plastic animals, marbles, and stones. Or try a mixture of oil and water for a different effect. Hot glue the lid securely on the bottle. Explore what happens as the bottle is turned and flipped. Safety note: Always supervise the child when using the bottles.

Provide a looking table. Set out, at the children's level, an object that encourages looking in new ways. Possible items include smooth and crinkled aluminum foil mounted on cardboard, crystals, **Fresnel lenses,** magnifiers, kaleidoscopes, fly's-eye viewers, liquid crystals, mirrors, optical lenses, colored Plexiglas, sunglasses, color paddles, holographic metallic papers, prisms, unbreakable mirrors, transparent colored or textured plastics, plastic water globes, or even a small fish bowl with fish.

Change the lighting. Set up a small table lamp in one corner of the room. Vary the color of the light bulb, and encourage the children to look at their familiar toys, book illustrations, and artwork in a "new" light. The book *Color! Color! Color!* by Ruth Heller (1995) uses color acetates between pages to create similar effects.

Change the room. For a special occasion, cover overhead lights or windows with loosely draped, colored tissue paper or cellophane. Encourage children to move creatively in the colored light and shadows.

Book Box

Books that develop visual perception.

Jenkins, S. (2003). *Looking down.* New York: Sandpiper.
Starting with a view of the earth, each collage illustration moves in closer and closer, ending with a close-up of a ladybug. Use this book to introduce the concept of enlargement. Follow up by displaying a poster-size print and a postcard-size reproduction of the same artwork. Four and up.

Jonas, A. (1987). *Reflections.* New York: Greenwillow Books.
This book features paintings that when turned upside down become different pictures. This book can inspire activities using mirrors and is a good companion to walks on which children study reflections in puddles and ponds. Six and up.

Tactile Perception

The entire surface of the human body is sensitive to pressure and temperature, as well as to the textural qualities of the matter that makes up the world. This is **tactile perception.** Young children rely heavily on tactile exploration to acquire knowledge about the characteristics of individual materials and objects and to develop an understanding of how things are spatially arranged. The environment and activities offered to young children should provide continuous opportunities to touch.

The following activities invite children to touch in safe, fun ways.

Use touch talk. Use textural words to describe the materials found in the classroom such as silky, soft, smooth, squishy, metallic, bumpy, and rough. Refer to the temperature of the materials: "Oh, this fingerpaint feels cold!" or "The play dough is warm from your hand." Make them aware of the pressure they are using: "You pressed hard with your feet on the floor when you marched," "You banged hard on the drum," or "Your puppet touched me very lightly."

Provide touch boxes. Touch boxes encourage children to concentrate on how an object feels without using the sense of sight. Cut a hole large enough for a child's hand to fit inside of a box (shoe boxes work well). Cover the hole by taping a piece of cloth over the top of the hole on the inside to form a flap. Glue an object with an interesting texture to the bottom of the box, put the top back on, and close with a rubber band. Encourage children to reach inside to feel the object first and then peek inside to see it.

Make a changeable touch box. Make your touch box more versatile by cutting pieces of cardboard the size of the box bottom and gluing a different object to each. Change the objects regularly by simply lifting out one cardboard piece and putting in another. Natural and man-made objects for touch boxes should be at least the size of the palm and durable enough to take a great deal of handling. Use both natural and human-made objects that have a variety of forms and textures. Check that objects do not have sharp or jagged edges. Some suggested objects include aluminium foil ball, block, bone, box, candle, coral, cotton, crumpled paper ball, fabric (especially velvet and corduroy), pinecone, plastic lid, plastic toy, polyester stuffing, netting, rubber ball, rug piece, screwdriver, shell, spoon, stone, twig, and wax (canning).

Try touch bags. Fill zip closure plastic bags with a small amount of hair gel colored with food coloring. Seal the opening with duct tape to prevent accidental opening. Although especially good for infants, children of all ages enjoy making marks and drawing letters and pictures by pressing the surface of the bag with their fingers.

Set up sensory bins. Partially fill a basket; dishpan; or large, clear plastic low-sided storage container with "stuff" through which the children can move their hands. A water table is ideal for wet items. Items for wet and dry sensory bins are listed in Table 4-1. Infants and toddlers will enjoy the physical sensation of moving their hands in the tactile materials. Hide interesting items in the bin, such as shells, plastic animals, or even their own photographs for children to search for and find. Add measuring cups and spoons to explore mathematical relationships.

A stuff bin filled with shaving foam provides a safe and exciting tactile experience.

Offer a please-touch table. Set up a small, low table on which to display one or a few items. Select these natural and human-made items with care. They should be individually beautiful items that are less familiar to the children and will attract their interest. To encourage a relaxed exploration, make sure the items are not very valuable and will stand the children's inexpert handling. Possible items might include a large conch shell, a piece of brain coral, a large rock with fossil impressions, a large gear from an old machine, the inside of a clock, a carved Peruvian gourd, a feathered mask, an African wood carving, or an intricately woven basket. Invite children and parents to contribute items to this table, too. Encourage children to make tactile observations of these items by asking questions such as the following:

> *"What part feels smooth?"*
> *"Is it cold to your touch?"*
> *"Are there places you can put your fingers?"*
> *"Does it feel differently on the bottom?"*

Go on a nature scavenger hunt. Take the children for a walk outside to find objects with interesting textures. Ask them to find objects with just

TABLE 4–1 Ideas for Sensory Bins

Dry Sensory Bins

cardboard squares	grass	oatmeal*	ribbons and bows
cornmeal*	gravel	pebbles	rice*
cotton balls	leaves (green or dry)	pennies	sawdust
craft sticks	lids (plastic, metal, juice)	plastic caps	short pieces of yarn or string
crumpled white tissue paper	macaroni*	plastic "Easter" grass	shredded paper
excelsior	marbles	polyester stuffing	Styrofoam packing material
fabric scraps	metal washers	popcorn*	tiles
flowers	nylon netting	raffia	wood shavings

Note: After being explored in the bin, these materials can be added to the collage choices. (Remember, if working with children under age three, use only items that pass the choke test. See Appendix A)

Wet Sensory Bins

bubble mixture (dish detergent and water)
cornstarch slurry* (heat while stirring: one part cornstarch to five parts water until creamy; let cool)
goop* (mix one part cornstarch to one part cold water)
shaving cream
unflavored gelatin mixture*
water (vary the temperature)
whipped soap (beat with hand mixer: two parts soap flakes to one part water)

Note: Food coloring may be used to color these materials to excite the visual sense. After initial explorations, cups, containers, and other tools for the children to use in manipulating the material may be added.

one texture, such as something smooth, shiny, or wet. Alternatively, say, "Find me all kinds of objects with different textures or that are interesting to touch." When they find items, describe the texture to them: "Oh, you found a very bumpy rock!" "What a shiny cap you found." Infants and toddlers can look for two contrasting textures such as something hard and something soft. Older children can find several objects and then sort and group them. Remind the children not to damage any living plants. Look over the area before taking the children out to make sure it is safe and to get an idea about what kinds of objects they might find. It may be necessary to limit the area of the search to just the grass or playground. Even in a small area, many interesting textures can be found, such as a rough piece of bark, a bottle cap with bumpy edges, or a smooth, shiny candy wrapper. Collect all of the objects the children find, and bring them inside to use in their collages.

Make texture cards. Glue pairs of sample textures to large cards made of heavy poster board or cardboard. If possible, try to use textured items that are similar in color. A variety of fabrics will work well. The children can try to match cards while closing their eyes and feeling the textures. You can also make oversize dominoes by gluing textures, instead of numbers, onto them.

Have a sand table. Few children can resist the tactile qualities of sand. Dry sand runs through the fingers; wet sand sticks. Sand is a material that young children feel that they can control. They can make their own textures in the sand by pushing and pulling and patting and pressing. They can pour it and mold it. A sand table or covered outdoor sandbox is an essential piece of aesthetic equipment for young children. To increase the children's tactile exploration of sand, vary the equipment and dampness of the sand. Remove the traditional sand toys occasionally and substitute more unusual items, such as natural objects (seashells, stones, twigs), large kitchen tools (slotted spoon, potato masher, spatula, turner), tools (screwdriver, mallet, wrenches, large bolts), cardboard (boxes of different sizes, strips, and squares of corrugated cardboard), and caps and lids of all kinds. To introduce sand play or to accompany it, read one of these delightful books about sand: *Sand* (Praeger, 2006) or *Ribbons of Sand* (Points and Jauk, 1997). If there is a beach nearby, take the children there to experience play in a giant sandbox. Encourage them to create bold sand drawings inspired by these experiences.

Olfactory Perception

Olfactory perception means using our sense of smell. Although the sense of smell is often less valued than the other senses, it is a very powerful one. A whiff of a familiar odor from the past can bring back a memory. The scent of school paste can make adults feel like they are in kindergarten again. Opening a box of new crayons can bring to mind a drawing made at age five.

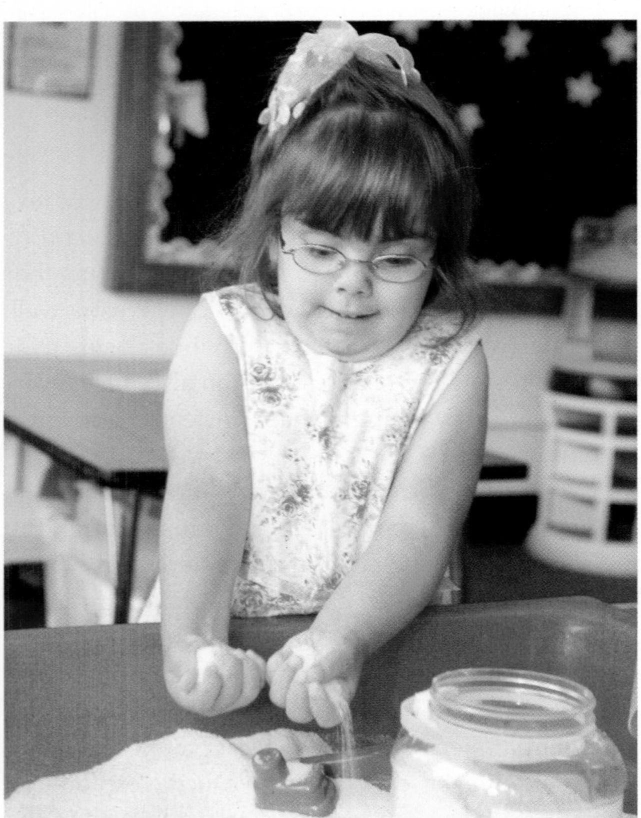

Tactile awareness is developed through sand play.

Special Needs

• SENSORY INTEGRATION •

Tactile defensiveness is when the child is overly sensitive to touch. Some activities that help children become more accustomed to touch sensations include:

- painting with shaving foam and pudding*
- playing in sand, finding hidden objects in rice* or beans*
- squeezing out white glue
- using play dough and clay
- drawing on touch bags

Book Box

Books to develop tactile percertion.

Adoff, A. (2000). *Touch the poem.* New York: Blue Sky Press.
Simple poems, illustrated with mixed media collages, celebrate all the senses, but particularly touch. Toddler and up.

Appel, J. (2006–2010). *Touch the art* series. New York: Sterling.
Famous artworks have an added tactile element in these board books for the very young. Titles include: *Feed Monet's Fish Pop Warhol's Top, Tickle Tut's Toes,* and others. Infants and up.

Cottin, M., & Faría, R. (2009). *The black book of colors.* Toronto, Canada: Groundwood.
Each page of this award-winning book is completely black with embossed pictures, Braille, and a simple text describing colors as a blind person might experience them.

Lee, H. V. (1998). *At the beach.* New York: Henry Holt.
In this story, children learn to write Chinese characters in the sand on the beach. The pictures are made of intricate cut-paper collages. Following a reading of this story, children may want to "write" in sand or sensory bins. Four and up.

Praeger, E. J. (2006). *Sand.* Washington, DC: National Geographic Children's Books.
Beautiful collages tell the story of how sand is formed and moved by natural forces. Four and up.

A research study by Schifferstein and Desmet (2007) found that when the olfactory sense was blocked, activities were less pleasant, less predictable, and less emotionally engaging. Experiences relating to smell may be more subtle, often in the background of other activities, but will make them more engaging.

Describe scents. As the children explore various common classroom materials, avoid references to foods that might cause the children to try to taste the material. Instead, make comments that compare the scents to nature, such as:

> *"The paste smells so fresh and clean!"*
>
> *"This play dough smells like pine needles."*
>
> *"The yellow paint smells like a field of flowers."*

Control the environment. The smells that surround the children as they listen to music and dance creatively will be also be associated with the arts for the rest of their lives. Make sure the classroom itself is always clean and fresh smelling. Check for allergies, and then select an air freshener, potpourri, or a disinfectant that leaves a pleasant odor. Open the windows in fair weather.

Add scents. Scents can be added to homemade materials or paints. Choose scents such as different shampoos, dish detergents, potpourri, and scented oils. Food-related spices can also be used—cinnamon, allspice, nutmeg, cumin, coriander, thyme, marjoram, cloves, savory, and the mints. These strong-smelling scents are not as likely to be tasted.

Use scented materials. Scented crayons and markers are available, but they should be used with great caution. The scents are too exciting for most children. They smell like candy, tempting young children to taste them, and they cause a problem when children stick them in their noses or someone else's for a better whiff. For children with limited vision, however, the scents help them identify the colors.

Make scent jars. Scent jars can be used as a focused exploration on the sense of smell. Prepare cotton balls by sprinkling each one with a liquid scent. Another method is to glue powdered spices to a piece of paper. Place the scents in plastic containers, such as yogurt cups or icing containers, which have tight-fitting lids. Cut a small hole in the lid, and tape the lid onto the container. The scents will remain strong for several days. Ask the children if the smells remind them of anything.

Pick favorite scents. As an extension for older children, mark each container with a different symbol. Make a chart with the children of the smells they liked the best. Use the most popular smells to scent paints or homemade recipes. Another variation on this activity is to make pairs of scents and have the children try to match the pairs.

Developing Taste Perception

Taste is not directly involved in most arts activities. Particularly in the visual arts, teachers must be concerned that children not ingest hazardous art materials. However, we can emphasize the aesthetic qualities of food as it is served and eaten at snack time and meals. Dramatic play provides another place where tastes can be imagined and acted out.

Use rich descriptions. Describe the visual and textural appearance of different foods, such as the rich pink and green of watermelon, the circle shape of a sliced orange, and the bumpy surface of a chocolate-chip cookie.

Concentrate on the act of eating and tasting. Think about the different ways we move our mouths when chewing different foods. Think of new ways to describe the tastes of familiar foods.

Book Box

Books about taste and smell.

Beaumount, S. (2005). *Baby senses taste* and *Baby senses smell*. New York: Make Believe Books.
The taste board book features eye-appealing photographs of foods. The smell book has scratch-and-sniff patches on large photographs of fruit. Infants and toddlers.

McMullan, K., & McMullan, J. (2002). *I stink!* New York: HarperCollins.
Take a ride on the garbage truck and discover all those incredible odors! Toddlers and up.

Wallace, N. E. (2005). *A taste of honey.* White Plains, NY: Marshall Cavendish.
A little bear learns where honey comes from. Toddlers and up.

Identify tastes. Put out three or four different familiar foods that children like. Have children cover their eyes and then give them one of the foods. See if they can identify it.

Compare tastes. Compare the taste of the same food in two or three different forms, such as an orange and orange juice.

Act out tasty pantomimes. Have children imagine they are eating a familiar or unusual food. Act out how it would look, sound, and feel.

Auditory Perception

Auditory perception is sensitivity to sounds and noises. It is a key skill in musical development. Some arts activities are very quiet; others are quite noisy. A young child painting at the easel is a model of quiet. That same child actively exploring a set of drums bangs and slaps with glee. The sounds that surround arts activities rise and fall as children enter the creative state of immersion or chatter happily with their friends.

Many activities encourage children to develop a closer awareness of sound.

Match sounds. Collect containers with tight-fitting lids. Let the children fill them with different small objects such as sand, rice,* beans,* or pebbles. Then put on the lids, shake them, and compare the sounds they make. Use tin cans and cardboard tubes for different sound effects. Cover the open ends with a piece of paper, and affix them with package-sealing tape. After they have explored the sounds made, hide one of the sound makers while shaking it and have children try to guess which one it is.

Respond to sounds. Set up a tape recorder or CD player while children are working in the easel area or at the drawing table. Play sound effects and have children draw a picture of what they think made that sound. Note: Royalty-free sound effects can also be downloaded from the Internet.

Recognize voices. Make a tape of each child and adult in the classroom talking or singing. Play the tape and have children try to identify whose voice it is.

Listen closely. Have children close their eyes and listen in silence for one minute. Then make a list of the sounds they heard. Repeat outside on the playground, under trees, near a street, and in any other place that will provide new sound sensations.

Provide a sound space. Create a semiprivate space by covering a table with a blanket that hangs down on three sides, leaving the front open as an entrance and for easy supervision. Place a soft rug on the floor underneath. On the rug set out a variety of gentle sound makers, such as dried gourds with the seeds inside, for the children to explore.

Book Box

Books for auditory perception.

Martin, B., & Archambault, J. (1988). *Listen to the rain*. New York: Henry Holt.
Poetical language describes all the sounds that rain can make. Four and up.

O'Neil, M. (2003). *The sounds of day. The sounds of night*. New York: Farrar, Straus, & Giroux.
Two poems evoke the sounds of daytime and nighttime. Have children close their eyes and visualize the scenes they hear described. Four and up.

Rylant, C. (1991). *A night in the country*. New York: Aladdin.
Spend a peaceful night in the country looking and listening to the sounds of the night. Four and up.

Showers, P. (1993). *The listening walk*. New York: HarperCollins.
This simple text describes a "listening" walk as a child walking outside hears different sounds in his environment. Use this book to accompany activities focusing on the sense of hearing. Also available in Spanish. Toddler and up.

Tresselt, A. (1990). *Rain drop splash*. New York: HarperTrophy.
Follow the sound of the raindrops as they pitter-patter and splash their way to the sea. Toddler and up.

WHAT ARE THE ELEMENTS OF THE ARTS?

When experiencing a beautiful artistic performance or a wonderful part of nature, we are overwhelmed by the total effect. But to re-create this experience for someone who has not seen it, we must describe it in terms of the artistic ingredients of which it is composed. These ingredients, or elements, are the building blocks of the artist, dancer, composer, and actor. When we react to something aesthetically, our senses are being affected by the way these elements have been brought together at that moment in time.

Creating with the arts is the process of playing with these elements and arranging them in an aesthetically meaningful way. This is what young children are doing when they explore different art forms. However, they also need to learn how to identify and describe these elements so that they can talk about, understand, and make aesthetic judgments about artistic works.

Although music, dance, drama, and visual art have elements that are unique to each, they also share many of the same ones. The following descriptions of these shared arts elements will increase your ability to describe children's creative work and to talk about natural forms. More detail about those elements that are specific to each of the arts is found in Chapters 9, 10, 11, and 12.

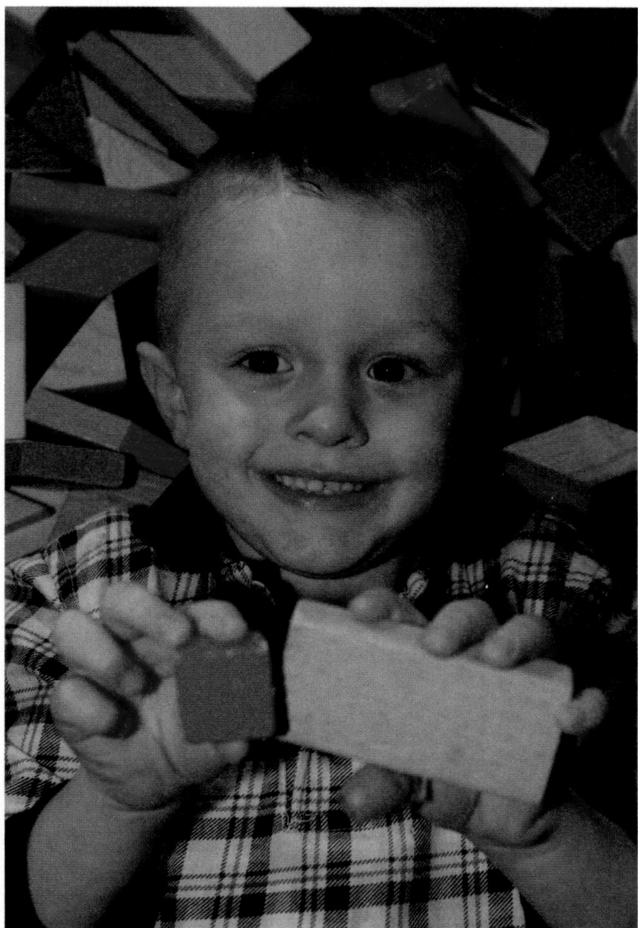

The arts elements are found in the clothes children wear and the toys they play with. We can find lines, shapes, colors, textures, forms, patterns, and spaces wherever we look.

Line

A **line** can be a mark made by a tool moving across a surface. It may be curved or straight or zigzag or wiggly. Lines can be thick or thin or long or short and are used by artists to make shapes and symbols and by writers to form letters, words, and numbers. Lines can show movement and direction—horizontal, vertical, or diagonal. Most importantly, lines are the mainstay of children's earliest drawings and will continue to remain an important element in all of their art.

Lines are present in visual artwork in all media, but we can also see lines in the positioning of the body in creative dance, in group movements, and in the order of notes in a melody. In nature lines are the edges and contours of objects and the paths and grooves in natural objects. The following line activities can be adapted for children of all ages.

Look for lines. Explore the environment, searching for different kinds of lines. Find straight lines between the tiles on the floor, curved lines hanging from the electric poles, and zigzag lines in the cracks of a frozen puddle.

Move in lines. Have the children line up one behind the other, and make a line that moves, wiggles, and sways as they walk in an open space or around furnishings.

Listen for lines. Play a simple melody and have children follow the melody by drawing a line in the air with their fingers, or give them paint and let them paint lines as they listen to music.

Draw with lines. Put out a variety of drawing materials, such as pencils, crayons, and markers, and compare the different lines they make. Tape two or more crayons or markers together and explore what happens.

Find lines in language activities. Read some of the many children's books that feature lines, and then put out blank booklets for the children to draw their own "line" stories. Study the different lines that make up the letters of the alphabet. Design new ways to write the letters using different kinds of lines.

Discover lines in math. Compare the length of different lines in the children's artwork or in line examples found in nature.

Use lines in science. Lay pieces of yarn along parts of the body, such as a leg, a finger, or around the head, and cut to length and then use them to make a graph, comparing whose are longer or shorter.

Explore lines in nature. Examine the veins of a leaf, the whorls on a shell. Classify objects by the types of lines you find.

Book Box

Books that celebrate lines.

Fox, M. (1997). *The straight line wonder.* New York: Mondo.

Tired of being straight, a line explores curves and points. Although his friend warns him against being different, his difference eventually makes him a success. Four and up.

Johnson, C. (1955). *Harold and the purple crayon.* New York: Harper & Row.

Using a purple crayon, Harold draws himself an adventure. This classic remains a child-pleaser. A good book to introduce the idea of drawing a story that continues from one page to the next when children begin "writing" their own books. Toddler and up.

Whitman, C. (2009). *Lines that wiggle.* Maplewood, NJ: Blue Apple.

A raised line runs across each page of this book of lively verse celebrating the many places lines can be found. Preschool and up.

Color

Teaching the colors has long been a basic of early childhood education. However, color perception is an extremely complex process about which we learn more and more each year.

Infants can see color at birth. In fact, they are born with a fascination for colors, particularly reds (Franklin, Bevis, & Ling, 2010). Infants physically process color with the right sides of their brains. As toddlers acquire language, color perception transfers to the left side (Franklin et al., 2008). In addition, people vary in how they see individual colors. A particular pink may look more orange to one viewer, more bluish to another.

Color perception is also influenced by the cultural and emotional context in which we learn those colors (Dedrick, 1996; Juricevic, 2010). This means that we need to be sensitive to young children's struggles to learn to identify their colors. The following activities provide ways to introduce and explore colors with children of all ages.

Look for color. Take time every day to notice the colors in the environment. For example, comment on the colors of the clothing children are wearing; the color of the grass, leaves, and sky when playing outside; and the colors of the fruits and vegetables in their snacks.

Describe colors. Use descriptive or comparative words to identify a color. For example, "Your sweater is as green as the leaves on our tree," and "Today the sky reminds me of the color of a robin's egg," and "The leaves on that tree are greener than on this one." Point out differences among **hues** in the same color family. Show how colors can vary in **intensity, tone,** and **value.**

Explore mixing colors. Finger painting with two or three colors is a very tactile way to combine colors, as is mixing several colors of play dough together. Colors also get mixed intentionally or unintentionally when painting and printing. Mixing new colors gives the child a sense of power. It is wonderful to be able to make such a noticeable change in the characteristics of an object in this simple way. Introduce the **primary colors** of red, yellow, and blue and let children discover how these three colors make the **secondary colors** of orange, purple, and green. Show how adding white makes a **tint**—a lighter version of the color and adding black makes a **shade,** a darker version of the color.

Dance in colored light. Project colored light on a wall during creative movement activities by placing colored cellophane or theater light gels in front of a bright light. Hang colored cellophane and prisms in the windows and let the sunlight create a light show. Dance in the light and study the colors of the ever-changing shadows.

Imagine color. Listen to musical pieces with your eyes closed and take turns describing the colors the music makes you visualize.

Book Box

Books about color.

Baker, A. (1999). *White rabbit's color book*. New York: Larouse Kingfisher.
Through simple text and charming illustrations, a white rabbit dips himself in different paint pots with predictable results. On his last dip into green and red, he turns into a brown rabbit. A good book for toddlers and preschoolers to lead into a discussion of browns. Toddler and up.

Carle, E. (1998). *Hello, red fox*. New York: Simon & Schuster.
A playful exploration of the effect of complementary colors on afterimages is beautifully integrated into a story of a frog inviting his friends to a party. It introduces the color wheel to young children. Four and up.

Heller, R. (1995). *Color! Color! Color!* New York: Grosset & Dunlap.
With rhythmic language, Ruth Heller presents a multitude of concepts about color. The book includes color acetates that overlap to show color mixing. A good book to share with one or two children so they can investigate the complex illustrations. Six and up.

Hoban, T. (1989). *Is it red? Is it yellow? Is it blue?* New York: Greenwillow.
Hoban's wordless books of magnificent photographs entice children's eyes to see the details of color, shape, form, and pattern in everyday objects. These are excellent books for toddlers and preschoolers to study on their own. They can also be used to introduce sensory activities involving the art elements. Infant and up.

Hoban, T. (1996). *Of colors and things*. New York: Greenwillow Books.

Walsh, E. S. (1989). *Mouse paint*. New York: Harcourt.
Three white mice discover the wonderful colors they can make. Toddler and up.

Dramatize and sing color. Make up dramatic skits in which children pretend to be different colors. Ask, "How would yellow sound? How would red move?" What would happen if green and blue touched? Make up songs about the different colors based on a familiar tune.

Address color blindness. Because everyone does not see colors in exactly the same way, color activities often need to be adjusted. Children who are **color blind** need to be identified so that they do not feel uncomfortable during color activities and games. Art materials can be scented to help children with visual difficulties. To help children understand that others may see color differently, tape red or yellow cellophane over a hole cut in an index card. Looking through this tinted window will make all of the colors look a little bit different.

Texture

Texture is the way something feels to the touch. Surfaces can be hard or soft, rough or smooth, or bumpy or jagged. Texture is found in all artwork and is an especially important element in collage and modeling activities. Texture plays a role in dramatic play as children dress up in costumes that can feel soft, rough, slippery, and so on against their skin. We can also see textures with our eyes.

Find textures. Invite the children to compare the textures of different items in the classroom or in the arts materials.

Use texture words. Ask, "Is it soft or rough?" and, "Which is stickier: the paste or the glue?" Use words that describe textures as the children play and eat their snacks.

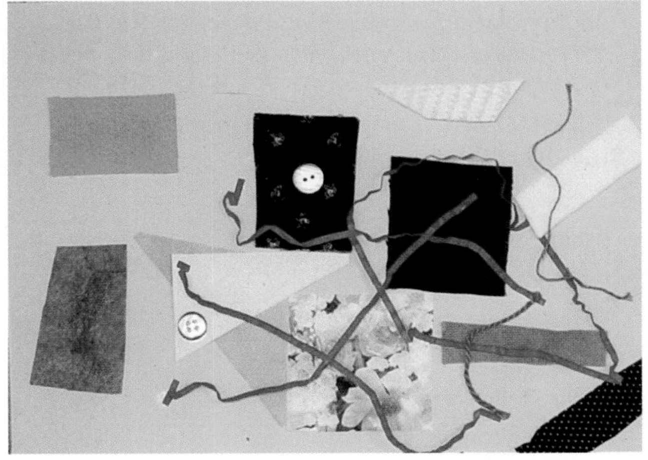

Making collages from a variety of materials is a great way to start a discussion about lines, colors, shapes, and textures. What questions could we ask Jori, age 4, about her collage?

Add more texture. Add different textured materials to the paints at the easel. Make sure collage boxes have a range of textured materials. Choose dress-up clothes that have a range of interesting textures.

Display texture. Make an aesthetic display of natural textured objects by placing rocks, feathers, bark, seeds, twigs, and so on in shallow open baskets.

Teacher Tip

GUIDE TO MIXING COLORS

Primary colors. The primary colors are red, yellow, and blue. Primary colors, when mixed, make the **secondary colors.**

- Red + Yellow = Orange
- Blue + Yellow = Green
- Red + Blue = Purple

Adding white. White plus any color makes a lighter or more pastel tint. Even a small amount of a color will change white. Add the color little by little until the tone is just right. More white will probably be used than any other color, so purchase double the amount of white.

- Red + White = Pink
- Orange + White = Peach
- Blue + White = Pastel Blue
- Purple + White = Lavender
- Green + White = Mint Green
- Brown + White = Tan

Adding black. Black plus any color makes it darker and duller. It takes only a small amount of black to change a color. Mix it in sparingly.

- Black + White = Gray
- Black + Yellow = Olive Green
- Black + Red = Brown

Other combinations.

- Orange + Yellow = Gold
- Red + Purple = Magenta
- Red + Green = Brown
- Blue + Purple = Deep Blue (Indigo)
- Blue + Green = Turquoise
- Yellow + Green = Chartreuse

Skin tones. Skin tones can be made by mixing different combinations of black, brown, yellow, red, and white. Always start with the lighter colors, and add the darker ones.

Making a Connection

EXPLORE COLOR IN MATH AND SCIENCE

- Provide premeasured amounts of different colors of paint, let children mix them, and then have children compare the results. For example, measure out a quarter cup of white to mix with a teaspoon of red, and vice versa. Make a labeled chart of the resulting colors, and then use them to paint with at the easel.
- Use prisms to see how white light contains a spectrum of colors.

Dramatize texture. Pretend to walk on different textured surfaces. Mime wearing clothing of different textures.

Read about texture. Toddlers will enjoy any of the books available that contain actual textures to touch. Older children can identify the different textures in the collages that illustrate many children's books. (See Book Box about textures.)

Group textures. Invite younger children to sort pieces of material with different textures. Glue them on a chart, or make them into a class book. Older children can find magazine pictures of things that have unusual textures, such as clippings of a dog (furry) or a pillow (soft), and can then make a similar chart or book.

Shape

Shape is a two-dimensional area or image that has defined edges or borders. Everything has a shape. A two-dimensional shape has height and width and may be geometric, organic, symbolic, or free form.

- Geometric shapes follow mathematical principles, such as polygons, squares, rectangles, circles, and triangles.
- Organic shapes come from nature, as in the shape of a leaf or butterfly.
- Symbolic shapes have a special meaning, such as that of letters or numbers.
- Free-form shapes are invented shapes that follow no rules.

Book Box

Books about texture.

Baker, J. (2002). *Window.* New York: Walker Books.
Three-dimensional collages of windows show an increasingly urban environment. Children enjoy identifying the different materials used in the pictures. Toddler and up.

Carle, E. (1996). *The grouchy ladybug.* New York: HarperCollins.
An aggressive ladybug challenges other creatures, regardless of their size. A clever book design shows the different sizes of the animals, which are illustrated with cut-paper collage. After reading this book, provide many different sizes and textures of paper in the collage area. Toddler and up.

Chase, E. N. (1992). *The new baby calf.* New York: Scholastic.
A simple story about a baby calf is special because of the textured illustrations made from modeling clay. This book will inspire young children to create picture stories from their modeling clay. Toddler and up.

Ehlert, L. (1991). *Red leaf yellow leaf.* New York: Harcourt Brace.
Richly textured collages of paper and objects illustrate autumn and the seasonal cycle of a tree. Toddler and up.

Fleming, D. (2007). *In the small, small pond.* New York: Henry Holt.
Bright handmade paper collages of nature and animals show a variety of textures. An excellent choice to accompany texture walks. Toddler and up.

Each of the four categories of shapes may contain some shapes that are **symmetrical.** If a straight line is drawn through the center of a shape, it will be exactly the same on both sides. Squares, butterflies, the letter "A", and hearts are all symmetrical shapes. All of these shapes will be found in children's artwork and in the classroom environment.

Playing with shapes. Play games with the children that involve finding shapes. Search the room and outside areas for types of shapes. Go on circle, rectangle, and triangle hunts. Hide shapes around the room for children to find.

Describe shapes. Talk about the qualities of these shapes. Are they big or small, short or tall, or colored or textured? Find shapes. Search the room and outside areas for types of shapes. Go on circle, rectangle, and triangle hunts. Hide shapes around the room for children to find.

Design with shapes. With infants and toddlers, use colorful wooden blocks to make shape designs. Older children can use pattern blocks and tangrams. Make mosaic-like designs by gluing precut shapes onto colorful backgrounds.

Hear shapes. Display pictures of different shapes and make up a different clap or vocal sound to go with each one. Point to the shapes in varying order, and have the children make that sound. Give children a chance to make up the sounds and point to the shapes.

Become shapes. Have children lie on the floor or stand against a wall and make their bodies into different shapes. With a partner, create symmetrical shapes. Project a light on the wall and make shadow shapes.

Special Needs

• COLOR BLINDNESS •

Approximately 6 percent of people have some form of color blindness. Color blindness is more common in boys than girls. Approximately 7 to 10 percent of men in the United States are color blind in the red-green area. Other color combinations, such as blue-yellow, are much more rare. Those color blind for red-green can often differentiate the colors when side by side, but not when the color is alone. Therefore, children who are color blind often have difficulty with color-related activities. These children quickly learn to try to hide their color discrimination difficulties, especially if they are laughed at by other children when using a color the wrong way, such as when drawing a purple tree. Often adults mistakenly think the child does not know the colors yet and will try to force the child to learn them. It is important to identify these children as early as possible. The Ishihara color test, which shows pictures made up of dots of different colors, is an example of a test for identifying color blindness that can be used.

Once identified, help these children by using scented crayons and markers and adding scents to paints. It also helps to always have the colors in the same order at the easel and to line up the markers and crayons in the same color order. When doing color games and activities, have these children work with the colors they can identify.

Hunt for shapes in books. Almost any children's book can be used for a shape hunt. Name a shape that is used in one of the illustrations, and then ask the children to look for it as they listen to the story.

Look at shapes mathematically. Geometric shapes are an important part of mathematical understanding. Identify the properties of different shapes. Let children sort shapes by size or the number of sides. Make charts or graphs based on the characteristics of shapes. Ask children to count the number of shapes they used in their artwork.

Book Box

Books featuring shapes.

Carle, E. (1972). *The secret birthday message*. New York: HarperTrophy.
A message, made from shapes, follows cut-out pages that repeat the shapes. An excellent book for older preschoolers who are beginning to use graphic symbols. Four and up.

Carle, E. (2005). *My very first book of shapes*. New York: Harper & Row.
The presentation of differently sized and shaped objects helps children become aware of the shapes found in the environment. Use this book to introduce the basic shapes to toddlers and younger preschoolers. Infants and up.

Carle, E. (1984). *The mixed-up chameleon*. New York: Crowell.
A chameleon wishes he could be another animal. Shapes are put together to make new creatures. Different shapes also form the borders of the pages. This book will inspire children to create their own creatures by combining cut-paper shapes. Toddler and up.

Hoban, T. (1996). *Shapes shapes shapes.* New York: Greenwillow.
Children are asked to find a variety of shapes in this beautifully photographed wordless book. Toddler and up.

Hoban, T. (1998). *So many squares. So many circles.* New York: Greenwillow Books.
Photographs of colorful familiar objects illustrate the different shapes in this wordless book. Infant/Toddler.

Seuss. (1997). *The shape of me and other stuff.* New York: Random House.
In his renowned rhyming style, Dr. Seuss introduces the shapes of all kinds of unexpected things. Infants and up.

Pattern and Rhythm

A **pattern** occurs when anything is repeated several times. In the visual arts a patterned design may be made from repeated shapes, lines, and colors. Musical patterns occur when the same note sequence or rhythm is repeated. **Rhythm** is a time-based pattern. Creative dance is built on the repetition of body movements that create patterns and rhythms. Patterns and rhythms occur naturally, as in the designs on a leopard's skin and the chirping of crickets, or can be invented by artists, dancers, and musicians. Patterns are important not only in the arts; being able to find and understand patterns is also the basis of mathematical understanding.

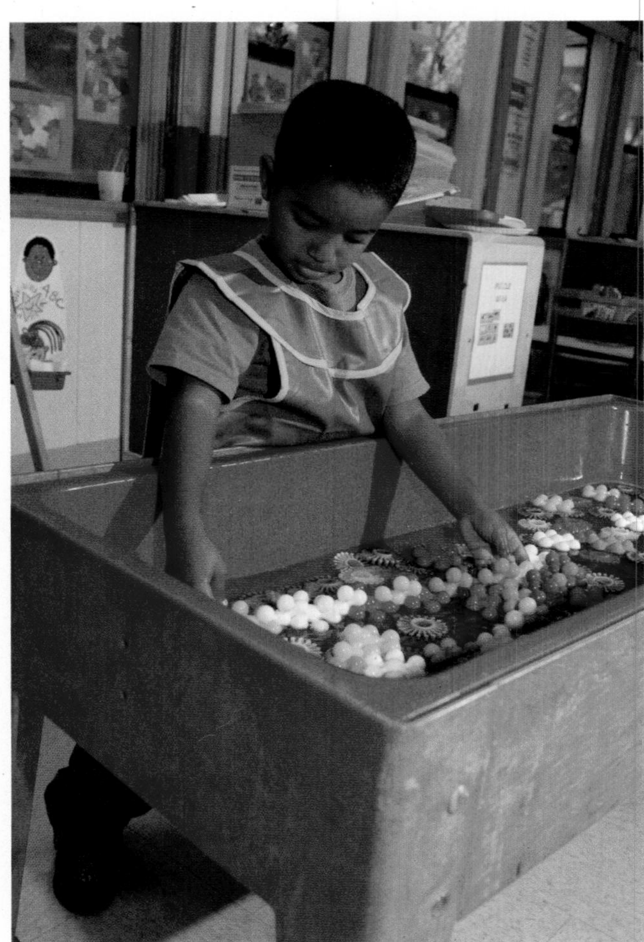

Pattern and rhythm can be found in the movement of familiar toys. A sensory bin filled with water and interlocking plastic loops entices children to make rhythmic waves and watch the resulting patterns.

Look for pattern and rhythm. Encourage children to find examples of pattern and rhythm in the environment. Find the shapes, lines, and colors in patterns on clothing, furnishings, and on nature objects.

Make patterns. Have children line up in ways that make patterns such as alternating tall and short or those wearing light colors and those wearing dark.

Talk about pattern. Comment on patterns found on the clothing they are wearing, the art they are creating, the music they listen to, and the objects in their environment. Help children see that a pattern is made up of smaller elements.

Listen for patterns and rhythms. Read a poem or dance rhythmically and follow the pattern by clapping or playing rhythm instruments. Listen for patterns in the words, melody, and rhythm of favorite songs. Clap and count the beats in a favorite song. Chart the patterns and rhythms using colors or shapes. For a responsive art activity, suggest that children record the song's pattern using art media.

Book Box

Books featuring patterns.

Crews, D. (1978). *Freight train*. New York: Greenwillow Books.

Crews, D. (1983). *Parade*. New York: William Morrow.

Crews, D. (1995). *Sail away*. New York: Greenwillow Books.
Crews' illustration style of airbrushed shapes provides a perfect way to introduce the concept of pattern as repeated shapes. All of these books feature repeated images of objects, creating visual patterns. Help children see the different repetitions in each book, and point out how the repetition makes the objects seem like they are moving. These books can also be used in related thematic units. Toddler and up.

Hoban, T. (1984). *Is it rough? Is it smooth? Is it shiny?* New York: Greenwillow Books.
Sharp, clear photographs present a wide variety of textured objects. After reading the book, go on a texture hunt. See how many different textures can be found. Toddler and up.

Polacco, P. (1996). *Rechenka's eggs*. New York: Putnam.
Patterns are everywhere in this engaging story of a magic goose and some beautifully decorated Pysanky eggs. An excellent book to encourage children to find patterns in illustrations. Four and up.

Find patterns in books. Share stories that are filled with pictures with patterns, such as the books of Patricia Polacco. Try to find all of the patterns in the illustrations.

Move in patterns. Make creative movement patterns by moving different body parts in repetitious ways, and, for primary children by moving in unison. Study the dance patterns found in traditional folk dances.

Form

Form is the three-dimensional quality of objects. Forms have height, width, and depth, such as found in spheres, pyramids, cubes, cylinders, and rectangular solids. Because most objects in our world are three-dimensional, children need lots of exposure to a wide variety of forms. Children's early physical handling and examination of many forms allow them as adults to recognize the nature of forms just by looking at them.

Talk about form. Forms are complex. They are not always the same in the back or on the bottom as they appear from the front. Point out examples of forms as part of other activities. Ask, "What form is your cup? What form is this block?" Use the correct geometrical term whenever possible.

Make forms. Block play and clay modeling activities are excellent ways for children to explore and to create their own original complex forms. Construction activities and papier-mâché also involve building in three dimensions.

Explore form with the body. Creative movement activities allow children to discover the flexible form of their bodies. Encourage them to stretch and bend, to curl up, and lay down to change the forms of their bodies. Older children can create more complex body forms by working together with a partner to make cubes, spheres, and rectangular solids.

Listen to forms. Look at the forms of different musical instruments. Compare how they look to how they sound. Challenge the children to think about why instruments such as a bass and violin sound different even though they have similar forms.

Explore forms mathematically. Fill hollow forms of different sizes and shapes, such as boxes, oatmeal containers, and bottles, with sand or

Styrofoam packing material. Have children predict which holds the most and which the least. Empty and measure to find out.

Study forms in nature. Help children see the beauty in shells, bones, rocks, and plants. Provide magnifying glasses and study the complex forms of insects and seeds. Make displays of natural objects that have complex forms such as wasp nests, bird nests, and pinecones.

Space

Artists do not just see shapes and forms; they also see the **space** that surrounds them. This may be the empty space of the paper, the open spaces in a sculpture, or the silent rests in a musical composition. Space is an absence of elements that provides a quiet focus in the midst of color, form, texture, line, and pattern. Young children discover space when they look through a tube and see the view contained in a circle, peer through a hole poked in play dough, or clap at the moment when everyone else has stopped.

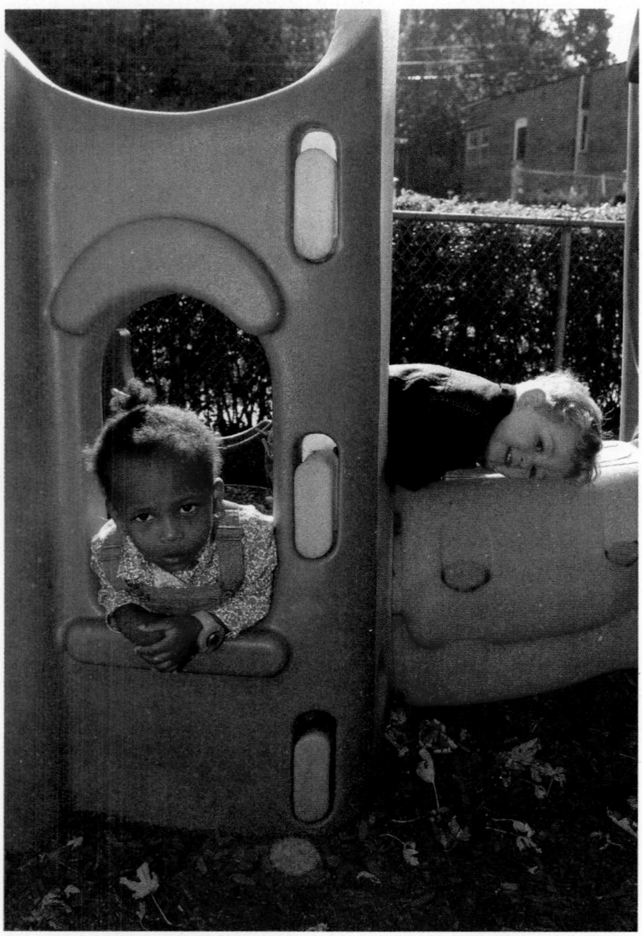

Actually getting inside three-dimensional forms and crawling through them on the playground is a wonderful opportunity to learn about form and space. Follow up by asking the children questions about the sensory qualities of the experience.

Because space is the absence of something, children need guidance in discovering the role of space in artistic creation.

Look for spaces. Cut differently shaped holes in pieces of poster board or cardboard covered with contact paper for durability. Encourage children to look through them at anything in the environment, including their artwork and block buildings.

Talk about space. Make comments such as, "You have left a rectangular space in the middle of your painting," "You have made round spaces in your play dough. Can you see through them?," "Listen for the silent part in this song," "Should you leave a big space between the blocks or a small one?"

Make spaces. Use arms and legs bent to touch the body to encircle different shaped spaces. Hold hands with a partner and make bigger spaces. Construct clay sculptures and block structures that are full of holes. Use different objects, such as sticks and geometric-shaped cookie cutters, to cut holes in the clay. Explore how many and how big holes can be before the structure collapses.

Move in space. Make tunnels from large boxes with the ends cut out or by draping cloth over tables and move in different ways through the spaces created. Have some of the children form pairs and clasp hands high while others move under the "bridge."

Listen for spaces. Using handmade or rhythm band instruments explore different rhythms. Point out that silent moments in a song (rests) are like holes or spaces. Listen for them in different pieces of music. Establish a stop signal, such as holding up a colored card with a rest drawn on it. Have children create and perform a rhythm. At set moments hold up the rest card and make a space in the music.

Book Box

Books about form and space.

Ehlert, L. (1989). *Color zoo*. New York: HarperCollins.
Layered openings in the classic book form abstract animals that change shape as the page is turned. The wordless book appeals to children of all ages and inspires them to create their own book of "holes." Infant and up.

Hutchins, P. (1989). *Changes changes*. New York: Aladdin.
A couple, made of blocks, build themselves a block house in this time-tested wordless book. A great book to use to name the different forms and to point out the spaces created when the blocks are stacked. Toddler and up.

Stevenson, R. L. (2005). *Block city*. New York: Simon & Schuster.
Robert Louis Stevenson's classic poem is illustrated with pictures of a little boy building a city with his blocks. Preschool and up.

Movement

Although **movement** is obvious in creative dance, all the arts are founded on movement. Visual art makes viewers move their eyes across the surface of the work. Dramatic works and stories move from introduction to climax. Music follows a similar sequence. Movement occupies space, takes time, and requires energy.

- **Space**—Movement can follow paths through space that are high, low, horizontal, vertical, and diagonal. They can consume the space or take very little.
- **Time**—Movement has speed and duration. It can range from slow to fast, brief to never ending. It can be rhythmic or arrhythmic.
- **Energy**—Movement can be fluid or sharp. It can flow gently like the melody of a lullaby or be as jerky as a puppet on a string. In the arts the energy most often comes from our bodies whether we are leaping across a stage, wiggling a puppet on our finger, acting out a story, or dragging a marker across a piece of paper.

Because movement is so much a part of all the arts, it will be found in every arts activity.

Describe movement. When talking about arts activities, try to describe the movement you are seeing. "You put a lot of energy into that high jump," "You are drawing a horizontal line across your page," "You are moving slowly just like the character in the story."

Ask questions about movement. Ask questions that help children discover the movements they are making. "Would a mouse make small movements or large ones?," "Is the music moving fast or slow?" "Are you putting a lot of energy into your brush strokes?"

Make movements. Describe a movement and have children respond through creative dance, dramatization, painting, clapping, or singing. For example, ask, "Can you make a jagged movement?," "Can you make a slow movement?," "Can you move diagonally?"

Add movement to language activities. Have the children suggest and carry out movements as a story is being read, such as shaking their heads every time the character makes a mistake.

Explore movement in math. Using age-appropriate manipulatives, such as pattern blocks or counters, have children explore moving them into groups in different ways, such as quickly making a group of ten or slowly making a horizontal line of eight.

Discover movement in science activities. Watch living creatures, such as snails, crickets, hamsters, fish, and snakes, and learn how they move. Imitate their movements, and then create a play pretending to be those animals. Roll and bounce different types of balls and compare how they move.

CONCLUSION: THE SENSITIVE TEACHER

Fifty percent of a child's learning capacity shuts off when made to sit still.

—Clyde Gillespie (Turner, 1990, p. 243)

All of us have treasured memories of something exceedingly beautiful. Perhaps it was a sunrise we saw driving to work or the image of our mother's face. Our children, too, deserve such memories. It is up to the adults who work with young children to help create these images. Some suggestions include:

- sharing beautiful objects from nature and artists' hands
- teaching children to see the elements of line, shape, color, form, space, texture, movement, pattern, and rhythm in the world around them
- providing activities that develop children's sensory perception skills
- creating opportunities for children to use their imaginations in new ways
- pointing out the sensory and aesthetic elements in the children's own work and in the artwork of others

The sensory activities presented in this chapter may seem different from more "traditional" arts activities for young children. Some of them may cross into other curriculum areas; others do not use the expected materials. Nevertheless, these explorations form the basis of what the arts will mean to young artists and upon which they will make aesthetic judgments about the world.

The guiding adults of early childhood are the most important ingredients in forming a child's initial opinion about art. It is only when children feel safe and confident that they are able to learn aesthetically. It is our job to create an environment that is open to exploration, full of wonderful experiences, allows children to gain pleasure as they use their senses, and that rewards children for using their natural learning style.

We must bring excitement and enthusiasm to the classroom daily. We must be open to the aesthetic wonders that surround us—the pattern of the raindrops on the windowpane, the rainbow in the spilled oil in a puddle, the warm fur of a kitten—and share these with children. Every experience can be an aesthetic one. Learn to see with the eyes of an artist and the heart of a poet. Anyone can walk on the ceiling, fly with a bird, or dance on the ocean floor through the power of imagination. If we visualize ourselves as enthusiastic nurturers of young artists' sensory and aesthetic development then the experiences and environment we provide will make every day special for a young child.

FURTHER READING

Jenkins, P. J. (1995). *Nurturing spirituality in children*. Hillsboro, OR: Beyond Words.

Contains many hands-on activities that develop sensory perception and self-awareness in young children.

Light, A., & Smith, J. M. (Eds.) (2005). *The aesthetics of everyday life*. New York: Columbia University Press.

Discusses the aesthetics of movies, food, walking in the woods, playing sports, and other everyday pursuits and helps clarify what is meant by beauty.

For additional information about sensory learning and the elements of the arts visit our Web site at http://www.cengagebrain.com

TEACHING IN ACTION

Sample Plans for a Celebratory Presentation

FESTIVAL OF LINES: A CELEBRATION FOR TODDLERS AND THEIR FAMILIES

AN INVTRODUCTION TO OUR STUDY OF LINES

Location: The playground

Time: 2:00 to 4:00 P.M.

Welcome Table: Program and map; painted or paper streamer lines for visitors to follow to the different activities.

Art Display: Children's drawings and paintings with associated dictation.

Photography Display: Photographs of children involved in the activities.

(continued)

TEACHING IN ACTION *(continued)*

Interactive Arts Display: Children's paintings with a set of brushes hung on string. Participants are invited to match the lines in the painting with the brush that created them.

Video: Creative movement and music activities are shown.

Participatory Arts Activity 1: Large sheet of mural paper, baskets of colorful markers, and an invitation to add some original lines.

Participatory Arts Activity 2: Partner loom is set up with a basket of colorful yarn and an invitation to weave a line.

Participatory Arts Activity 3: Children's paintings are interspersed with bold graphics showing different kinds of lines. Participants are asked to find the total number of each kind of line visible in the paintings. A box and coupons are provided for the guesses. At the end of the celebration, names will be drawn to receive door prizes.

Puppet Show: Put on by the children, the show features a simple tale about a magic string, based on the book *Billy and the Magic String* (Karnovsky, 1995).

Demonstration 1: High school student volunteers demonstrate and teach about string figures from around the world.

Demonstration 2: Professional spinner demonstrates how wool is turned into yarn. She gives pieces of yarn to participants to use on a partner loom.

Demonstration 3: Basket weaver creates willow baskets, surrounded by a display of photographs showing examples of lines in nature.

Demonstration 4: Washtub instrument. Participants can try making different tones by changing length of strings.

Measurement Table: Volunteers measure a length of string that is the height of each participant and tape it to a graph.

Musical Entertainment: Harp player and/or string players.

Dance: A parent volunteer teaches families line dancing.

Refreshments: Foods that resemble lines (pretzel sticks, liquorice sticks, breadsticks, carrot sticks and curls, spaghetti).

A huge sheet of paper, brilliantly colored tempera paints, and long-handled paintbrushes allow children a delightful exploration of line and color.

Studio Page

WHAT IS YOUR PERSONAL SENSE OF BEAUTY?

Make a list of things that you think are beautiful. Next to each item, record whether it is from nature or human-made. Also note how you decided it was beautiful and from whom you learned to appreciate its beauty.

Item of Beauty	Source	Why It Is Beautiful

Review your list. Can you find any relationships among these items? What senses do you use in experiencing these beautiful things? What has been the greatest influence on your personal sense of beauty?

Studio Page

REVIEWING THE ARTS ELEMENTS

Give an example of where you might find each of the following arts elements.

Line	Shape
Color	Texture
Pattern	Form
Space	Movement

Studio Page

DESIGNING A BIG BOOK ABOUT THE ARTS

A big book is the perfect size to read to a group of small children. The large pictures can be easily seen by everyone. However, you will not find big books on every topic you may need, nor will the books exactly fit your chosen activities. The ideal solution is to use your creativity and make your own!

Guidelines for Creating a Big Book on an Arts Topic

1. Select a topic based on one of the arts elements or the senses.
2. Limit the book to five or six one-sided pages.
3. Use just a few words.
4. Illustrations should be made from the same materials that the children will have to use.
5. Illustrations should be large, bold, and simple. Avoid cute, stereotypical, or cartoon-like drawings.
6. Plan the book so the children can interact with it. For example, include pockets that contain hidden shapes or holes to look through.
7. Make the pages from heavy oak tag, poster board, or corrugated cardboard. Join the pages with metal, loose-leaf rings.

Suggested Ideas for Your Big Book

Topic: Color. Feature a different color on each page. For each color, cut out a variety of shapes from different kinds of paper in that color. Write the color names in crayon and marker in that color. At the back of the book, attach an envelope containing shapes in each color. Have children find the correct page for the "lost" shapes.

Topic: Pattern. Use gadget or sponge prints to illustrate the following concepts:

- All patterns are made of repeated shapes.
- Some patterns are made from one repeated shape.
- Some patterns are made with two repeated shapes.
- Some patterns are made with three or more repeated shapes.
- Some patterns are made in only one color.
- Some patterns have lots of colors.
- Some patterns are made of different-sized shapes.

Use yarn to attach samples of the objects used to make the prints to the book. Invite children to match them to the patterns.

Topic: Line. Use marker, crayon, or paint to draw different kinds of lines on each page. Some lines to include are straight, curved, zigzag, jagged, thick, and thin. Try to have each line be a continuation of the one on the previous page. On the last page, put all of the different lines together in a wild line "party."

Studio Page

OBSERVATION: A SENSORY EXPERIENCE

Choose one of the senses, and design a sensory experience for children. Present the activity to two or three children, and record what the children do.

Date of observation:____________________ **Length of observation:** ____________________

Ages of children: ____________________ **Size of group:** ____________________

1. Describe the sensory experience.

2. What is the first thing the children do? How long do the children investigate the activity?

3. What do the children say?

4. Analysis: Using the information in this chapter and what you learned from the observation, defend the inclusion of sensory arts activities in an early childhood setting.

Section
2
Teaching the
ARTS

Chapter 5

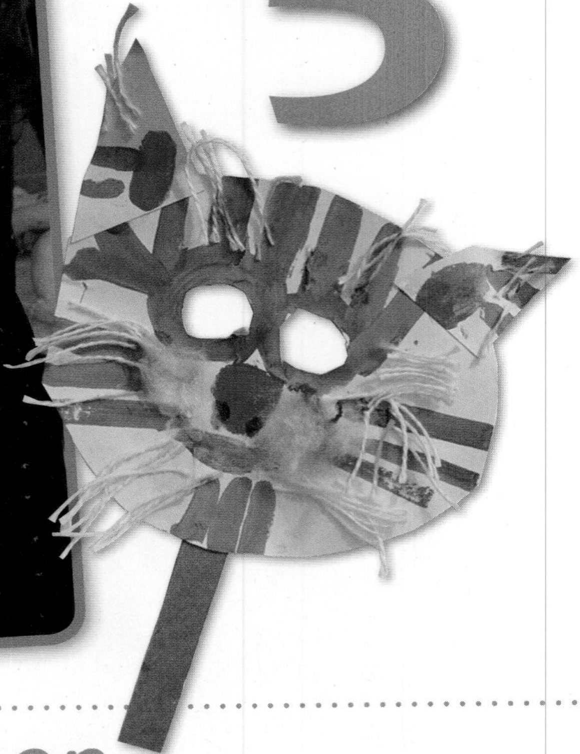

Coming Together Through the Arts

Questions Addressed in This Chapter:

- How can young artists work together?
- How are children with special needs included in the arts program?
- How can the arts be used in anti-bias activities?
- What is the role of holidays in arts activities?

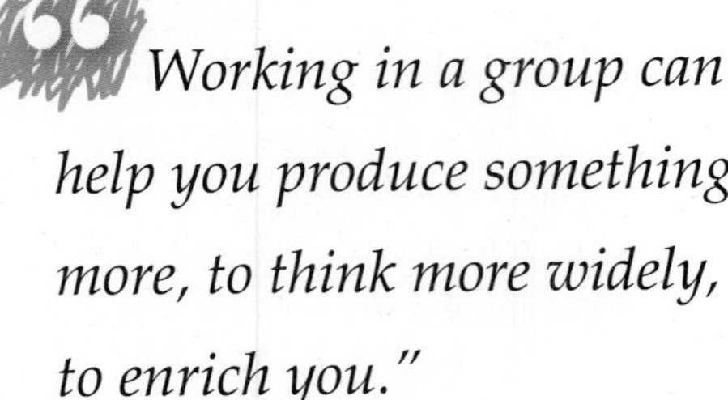

"*Working in a group can help you produce something more, to think more widely, to enrich you.*"

—*Tiziana Fillipina (Goleman, Kaufman, & Ray, 1992, p. 85)*

Young Artists at Work

"Your monkey has real long legs."

"So does yours."

"That's because he's trying to climb up this tree."

"My person is up in the air. He's jumping. You need long legs to do that."

"Yep. My monkey is going to jump when he gets to the top of the tree."

"Oops, the paint is dripping."

"Hurry. Catch it before it runs over Sari's picture."

"Sari will be mad if the paint drips on her dog."

"You are working hard on your paintings for our mural," says the teacher. "I see that you have used two different sizes of brushes."

"Yes, I used Mandie's little brush to paint the buttons, and she used my big brush to paint the long, long legs."

"See," says the teacher, "When we share things, we have more choices of things to use in our art."

HOW CAN YOUNG ARTISTS WORK TOGETHER?

Creative actions celebrate the individual, even when the actions are part of a group effort.

—Clare Cherry, Douglas Godwin, & Jesse Staples (1989, p. 133)

In our society, the arts are all too often seen as something a person does alone. Yet some of the most joyful arts experiences children can have are those in which they work in a group to create something greater than themselves—a mural, a box robot, a musical revue, or an original dance. Working together for a common purpose forges children into a group. It becomes "our mural," "our robot," "our songs," or "our dance." It is not surprising that so many of the "classbuilding activities" of cooperative learning programs are arts based. It is easy to incorporate the ideas and skill levels of each individual into an arts activity. Using themes and providing opportunities for arts projects are other ways to increase group bonding.

Although each child needs to explore the arts in a personally meaningful way, children also need to discover that the arts are not just for individual self-expression. This is best learned by participating in arts experiences as a member of a group. Well-designed arts activities allow children at different ages and skill levels to work together to create something uniquely different from what they would create on their own. When carefully planned, adults can even participate in many of these activities. Great satisfaction is felt when part of a successful group arts activity.

Group arts activities can help develop the social skills children need to become more understanding of others' special needs and more appreciative of the creative ideas of those whose background and cultural experiences differ from their own.

Accomplishing this requires the creation of an integrated cohesive unit in which both children and teacher smoothly work together. We need to take a group of unique, ever-changing individuals with different levels of social skills and turn them into a caring community.

Developing Social Skills

As children mature, their ability to interact effectively with others and work cooperatively increases.

Infants. Children begin life totally self-centered. For example, infants know when they are hungry and demand to be fed regardless of the time of day or night.

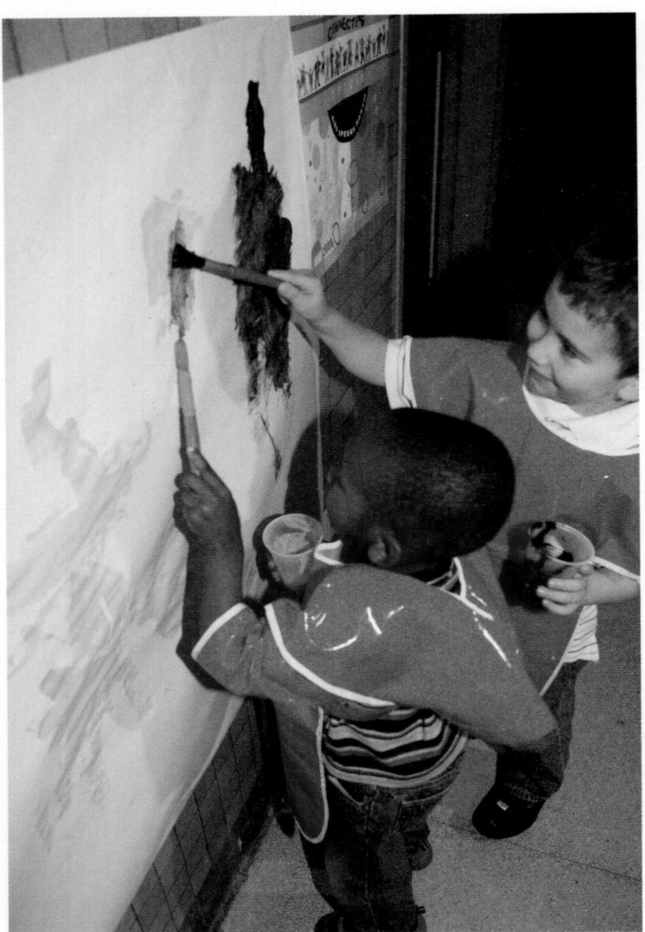

The arts provide time and space for children to learn from each other. These boys have just discovered they can make green by mixing blue and yellow together.

But as infants mature they slowly become aware that they are separate individuals and show increasing awareness of other people around them. Newborn infants, for example, have been shown to look longer at faces with eyes open than closed, as well as at those with a direct gaze as opposed to those looking toward the side (Bower, 2002). Starting at two to three weeks, infants imitate adult facial expressions and hand movements with increasing sophistication (Bower, 2003).

Erik Erikson (1963), in his classic analysis of children's social-emotional development, characterizes this period as one in which infants learn to trust other people. With attentive loving care from their caregivers, they will come to see other people as important companions and resources as they explore their world. It is not surprising, therefore, that the arts play a vital role in developing infants' social skills. Singing and moving together, looking at pictures in a book, and engaging in pretend play with a more knowledgeable peer or adult all help children learn how to explore and create joyfully together with one another in an atmosphere of trust.

Toddlers. Children from about eighteen months to three years are, according to Erikson, in the stage of autonomy versus shame and doubt. Toddlers want to be independent and in control, but cling to their caregiver when faced with new stimuli. They may see a toy they want and nothing short of physical restraint will prevent them from grabbing it from another child, or they may hide behind an adult when the booming drums pass by in a parade.

Toddlers work best in situations where they can pursue their arts explorations under the watchful eyes of caregivers. Adults can promote social growth by providing activities in which toddlers can work alongside others but have their own materials and space. Setting up activities in which two toddlers or a toddler and an older child are painting at adjoining easels or are smashing play dough together helps toddlers learn that they can do artwork in close proximity to other children.

Toddlers often engage in **parallel play** in which they imitate the actions of a child sitting near them (Einon, 1985). As toddlers work beside each other, they begin to become aware of each other's actions. One child will begin to pound the clay, and another child will imitate the same action. One child will see another using scissors and will demand a pair, too. Imitation is one of the ways that children learn skills and behaviors. Adults and other children can serve as artistic role models for the young child. Appropriate group arts activities for toddlers include singing with the teacher and another child, holding hands and dancing with the teacher, and building a block tower while sitting next to another child playing with the blocks.

Three- and four-year-olds. By the age of three children are beginning to play together. They will take on roles in pretend play and will work together to build a tower. By four many children can work together on all kinds of arts projects, from accompanying a song with handmade instruments to painting a mural. They become enraptured by the excitement of the collective moment and yet are interested in and "see" only the part they personally created. Cooperative activities for these children, therefore,

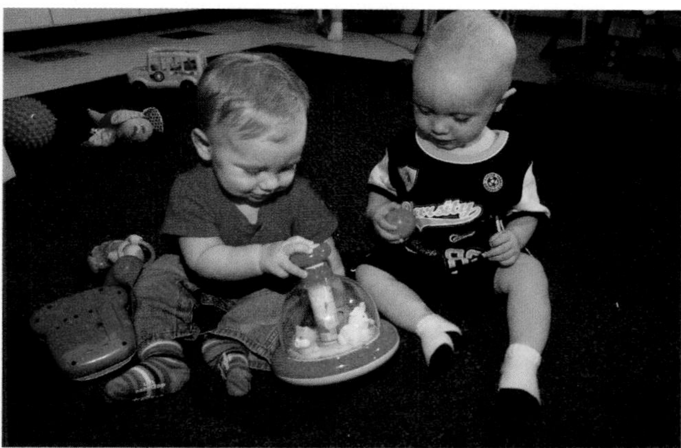

Playing side by side and watching each other is one way infants learn how to be social.

do not have the same meaning as those designed for older children and adults, in which ideas are arrived at jointly and the project is viewed as a whole. Young preschoolers work best on projects that do not have definite end goals but instead allow each child to play an individual part in the process. Appropriate group arts activities for young preschoolers include singing a song with others, moving in self-expressive ways to music as they circle around the room, taking a role and acting out a story, and cutting out a shape that will be added to a mural.

Five- and six-year-olds. When children gain the ability to value and differentiate their own products from those of others, they can start to see that each contribution is a part of something larger—a whole—that is different from each small part but is still partially theirs. Teachers can tell when children reach this stage, because they start to notice the artwork of the other children and will comment, "That is my friend's painting," or "That is Cheri's," when referring to a piece of art they see. They use the terms "we did" instead of "I did" when referring to group projects. They can identify who did the different parts of a project. When children reach this stage, they are ready for more cooperative group activities in which each child works on a designated part of the project sharing supplies or space. Appropriate group arts activities for these children include building a castle out of blocks, building a box robot together, painting a designated part of a mural, moving creatively with others as part of a dance, and painting and decorating a box to be a fire engine and then pretending to be firefighters.

Seven- and eight-year-olds. By this age children are capable of planning ahead of time what will be needed to accomplish their goal and which part of the project they will work on. However, they may still need adult guidance in learning how to incorporate the ideas of each member in a gracious way.

Primary students, who are busy learning about the broader world, enjoy working on long-term projects that involve a common idea, such as turning the classroom into a rainforest complete with a painted mural background, life-size painted animals and paper trees and bushes, accompanied by authentic Brazilian rhythms played on handmade instruments. They can perform parts in a play they have written, enjoy choral reading and group singing, learn folk dances together, and perform in small instrumental groups.

Teacher Tip

STAGES OF SOCIAL PLAY

Regardless of their age, children exhibit different levels of play depending not only on their social and cognitive development, but also on their previous experiences interacting with others. Observing how children play by themselves and with others can give us a better idea of their social skills.

Observing: The child watches others playing. This might be found in an infant who is not yet physically capable of joining in or in a child who is new to a group.

Solitary play: The child plays by him- or herself. The level of play can range from very simple, such as shaking a toy, to intense, focused imaginary play.

Parallel play: The child plays alongside another child, perhaps with very similar toys, but the children do not interact with each other. Parallel play usually begins around the ages of two to three years.

Cooperative play: Children play together first in pairs and then in larger groups. In cooperative play children develop language skills as they communicate ideas, needs, and desires. They develop social skills as they learn to share, come to agreement, and take group action. Cooperative play usually appears around the ages of three to four years.

Organized play: The ability to participate in games that have rules and winners, such as board games and sports, occurs slowly. It begins to develop around the ages of six to seven, but is most fully developed in eight- and nine-year-olds.

Creating a Positive Social Climate

As with creativity, social skills flourish in an environment where children feel self-confident, where they are relaxed, and where they feel secure.

A positive social climate develops when children feel that their ideas and feelings are accepted and valued. It is the teacher's task to model acceptance by giving appropriate time, attention, and assistance to every child. In carrying out arts activities, teachers have to consciously stay alert to their own biases. Research has shown, for example, that teachers often react differently to boys than they do to girls (Sadker & Sadker, 1995). Gender, race, and physical characteristics should not determine what roles children play in a story, or how they are expected to move in a dance. If children object to a child taking a certain role, share the book *Amazing Grace* (Hoffman, 1991) in which an African-American girl plays the role of Peter Pan in the school play. The open-ended nature of the creative arts allows children the freedom to challenge accepted ideas.

How Many Children Should Work Together?

Group size is a critical factor in determining if children will work together successfully. At the Reggio Emilia preprimary schools the teachers have found that different group sizes create different dynamics. For example, pairs of children engage in intense social and cognitive interactions. The addition of a third child can produce solidarity, but also conflict. Groups of four and five have other dynamics (Edwards, Gandini, & Forman, 1993). A general rule should be the younger the children the smaller the group.

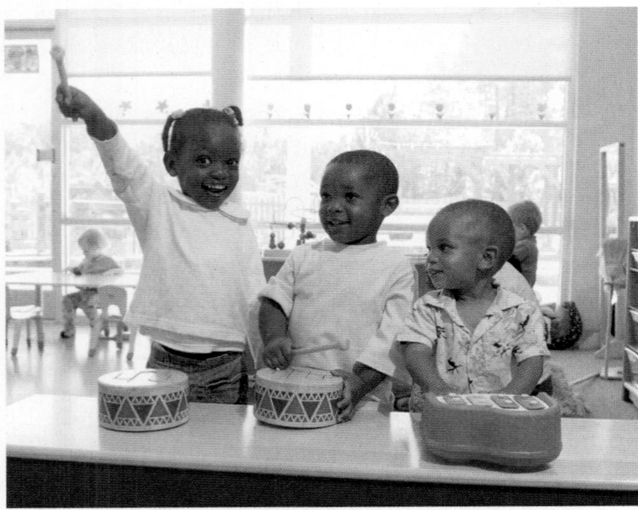

Arts activities provide a way for groups of children to interact creatively. These three children are discovering they can make music together.

Promoting Cooperative Behaviors

Learning how to work with others will make people more successful in life. Young children can gain skill in small behaviors that will help them grow to be more effective group members. Working on group arts projects will help children grow socially by gaining the following:

1. **Focus.** The ability to concentrate on a task in the presence of others.
2. **Patience.** The ability to wait for a turn.
3. **Cooperation.** The ability to share materials with others.
4. **Love of others.** The knowledge that working with others is a pleasant, joyful experience.

Teachers can encourage the growth of these preliminary cooperative skills in a number of ways.

Infants.

1. **Focus.** Use active arts activities such as singing or fingerplays that hold the child's attention.
2. **Patience.** Before handing the child an arts material, hold it for a moment and describe it in playful language and mime using it.
3. **Cooperation.** Hand the infant an arts material, such as a rattle, and then ask for it back. Give lots of positive feedback when the child responds appropriately.
4. **Joy of others.** Smile and laugh when singing, moving to music, and making sounds together.

Toddlers.

1. **Focus.** Provide arts activities that require toddlers to watch and pay attention such as listening to someone play an instrument or watching

an ethnic dancer. Start with short experiences of 5 minutes or less and slowly increase the length of time as they develop audience skills.

2. **Patience.** Remind children to wait until everyone in the group is ready to begin an arts activity. Encourage patience by giving positive feedback for success.
3. **Cooperation.** Provide opportunities for two or three toddlers to work at the same table. Place supplies in a common container from which children must select their pieces. Provide sufficient amounts of the supply so that children can have as much as they wish. Encourage children to take one item at a time. Have toddlers take turns working in pairs on a mural or a drawing or on painting a box. Make sure each child has plenty of space in which to work.
4. **Joy of others.** Introduce and carry out arts activities for two or three children with great enthusiasm and personal participation. March in noisy parades, use bold colors on a mural, and laugh together over silly songs. Use plenty of positive feedback.

Three- to five-year-olds.

1. **Focus.** Provide many occasions for children to hear and see performances by others. After the performance, ask questions that help them remember and understand what they experienced.
2. **Patience.** Offer supplies in common containers, and encourage children to develop the independent behavior of waiting a turn to use a tool or prop.
3. **Cooperation.** Have children work in groups of four to six at the same table or workspace. When a supply is limited, ask children to share fairly, such as having the children check that each has a red paper square or a similar supply of blocks.
4. **Joy of others.** Offer many activities in which children work together to accomplish something that is meaningful and valued, such as making a welcoming banner to the classroom for parents' night, or singing songs at a home for the elderly.

Six- to eight-year-olds.

1. **Focus.** Children should continue to attend arts performances of all kinds. Discuss and model what is expected of audiences. In addition, they can produce their own productions and take turns being the audience for each other.
2. **Patience.** Develop patience by having children plan and carry out a long-term arts project. Check off the days toward accomplishing their goal.
3. **Cooperation.** When working on group projects, always have the children meet and plan ahead of time what part each child will do. Teach children that in a team each member can contribute in different ways. Have children assume roles within their team. In a group of four, one child could be in charge of getting supplies, the second could be assigned to returning the supplies, the third could record the group's accomplishments—either by writing or making illustrative drawings—and the fourth could report orally to the class. A large body of literature is available on teaching cooperative group skills to children age five and up (Slavin, 1995). Children at these ages are also ready to participate in large-group cooperative behaviors. Have the whole class participate in deciding how the arts materials should be cared for and organized. Then have individuals or pairs of children assume responsibility for taking care of a specific supply.
4. **Joy of others.** Celebrate the completion of long-term projects with a party or exhibition.

Mixed-Age and Ability Groups

Groups that contain a range of ages actually offer one of the best settings in which to develop cooperative arts behaviors. The older children and adults can model respect for each other's work and at the same time supervise the more impulsive little ones.

Sharing space and materials helps children learn how to work together.

1. Select activities that each individual, no matter what his or her ability level, can participate in fairly equally.
2. Have members of the group take turns working in pairs or in groups of three. Pair a more expert peer with one who has less experience. The older members should help the younger ones find a place to work and supplies to use.
3. In the visual arts allow the youngest group members to go first, because older members will be able to work around one another, whereas the young children may not "see" the work already there and may work on top of it. In the performance arts, the older ones should go first to provide role models for the younger ones.

Ways to Promote Appropriate Behavior

Working together requires children to exert self-control. Groups of children involved in well-designed arts activities are usually so engrossed that behavioral issues do not play a large role. However, there will always be occasions when children overstep the boundaries of safety and propriety. Responding to inappropriate behavior during arts activities requires a gentle approach that addresses the behavior without restricting creativity. You can foster safe, creative behavior in three ways: **prevention, redirection,** and **removal.**

Teacher Tip

COMMUNITY BUILDING THROUGH THE ARTS

The following examples of drama and movement activities show how the arts can be used to help children get to know one another better.

Name Game. Sit in a circle and have the children call out their names. Repeat having the children call out their names in a new way each time—using a different "voice," adding a movement, showing an emotion, or making a funny face.

Greeting Each Other. Provide two greeting words, such as *hi* and *bye*. Have the children move around and greet each other. Repeat, adding a movement or singing the greeting.

What Happened? Have the children sit in a circle. Ask the first child, "What did you do when . . . ," adding an appropriate phrase, such as when you woke up, or when you met a new friend. That child then turns and asks the one sitting next to him or her the same question. Continue around the circle. When children are familiar with the game, try some fantasy phrases, such as what did you do when your house started dancing?

Watch Me. Stand so everyone can see everyone else. The leader mimes a brief action, such as meeting someone and shaking hands. The whole group copies the action. The leader then points to another child to be the leader who mimes a new action. Vary the activity by adding a sound to go with the action or mime the next logical step.

Guide Us. The leader thinks of a favorite place, such as a castle, park, or zoo, and then guides the group through it using words and movements for one minute. Then a new leader is selected and the group is guided to a new favorite place.

Is it Yours? Sit in a circle. Have everyone put a belonging, such as a shoe, piece of clothing, or jewelry into the center of the circle. One by one, have the children pick up an object and try to match it to its owner. Vary the activity by having the owner of the object tell a story about it and then see if someone can find the correct object.

I Know You. Have everyone sit in a circle with his or her eyes closed. Tap a child on the shoulder who should positively describe someone else in the group. When the other children think they know who it is, they should raise their hands. At an agreed-upon signal, all should open their eyes and the chosen child should share who was being described.

Prevention.

1. Offer only those activities, props, materials, and tools appropriate for the child's developmental level.

2. Keep materials and tools not on the child's developmental level out of reach and out of sight.

3. Provide each child with adequate space in which to work and move. Dangerous behavior often happens when children accidentally bump or push each other.

4. Provide sufficient supplies to prevent the children from grabbing for that one special item.

5. Closely supervise the children while they work, especially during initial explorations of new materials and tools.

6. Keep group sizes small until the children know how to work safely with a particular technique, material, or tool.

7. Keep arts supplies and tools orderly so children do not have to dig or grab for what they want.

8. Model safe movement and handling of tools and supplies at all times.

Redirection.

1. If a child begins to act or to use a tool or supply unsafely, gently restate the safe way to act or use it, and model the correct behavior, if necessary. For example, if the child puts play dough up to her mouth, say, "Play dough is not food, we use it to make art."

2. Older children can be asked to restate or read the rules or the directions given for the activity.

3. If two children want the same supply or tool, provide other similar ones or help them set up a fair way to share it.

Removal.

1. When a child's behavior is developmentally appropriate and not unsafe, but annoying to the other children, such as when a toddler draws on other children's papers, gently move the child to a place away from the others but too far away to reach someone else's workspace. Put the move in a positive light by saying, "You will have more space to draw over here."

2. If a child persists in unsafe behavior, redirect her or him to another activity that is more appropriate for that behavior. For example, if a child is snapping the scissors open and closed, explain that the scissors are too sharp to be used that way, but that she can open and close the toy pliers. Remove the scissors, and replace with the pliers.

3. When it is obvious that the activity, tools, or materials are inappropriate for the developmental level of the children, redirect them to another interesting activity, and then remove those supplies. Just because a particular activity may be recommended for children of a certain age or has been successful for others does not mean that it will be perfect for these particular children. It is better to say that this is not working and end it, than to set up a potentially dangerous situation or one that will cause children to misbehave.

Enjoying Working Together

On the other hand, many behavioral issues disappear when children are highly engaged in a well-designed open-ended arts activity. Well-designed

Large group activities, such as singing a song together, are an ideal way to learn how to work together to accomplish a goal.

activities are fun, flexible, relaxed, and based on a shared experience.

Make it fun. Always include an element of fun when working together. Songs, laughter, and excitement should all be part of the experience.

Be flexible and open to innovation. It is the group experience that is important, not the finished product. Avoid the trap of planning an end use for the cooperative project before it is started or having children practice lines of a play over and over for a formal performance.

Be a facilitator. The teacher's role is to be the guide, not the director. Provide the location, the materials, the excitement, and the beginning of an idea; then let the participants take over. Teachers can even participate themselves! The result will be a true expression of each individual's creative moment as a part of that group, at that time, and in that place.

Reduce stress. Well-designed group arts activities can provide an excellent way to introduce children to working in a group. However, it is important that children be familiar with the art form and materials to be used in the project and have had many practice experiences with it. A group activity is not the place to explore something for the first time, but instead provides an opportunity to take pride in using a skill and creating something that requires a level of comfort and control. It is also vital that these projects be designed as open-ended activities, so that every child can participate fully.

Provide a shared experience. A collective artwork needs to start out with everyone in the group sharing an experience. This common experience will combine the ideas and actions of each child into a unified whole. The experience should be one in which children participate directly, otherwise they will come to rely on stereotypes and teachers' examples rather than thinking on their own.

The shared experience forms the basis for planning and carrying out murals, creative dances, original songs and music, dramatic play centers, and group sculptures. For example, after a trip to the zoo, children share what they saw, and the teacher makes a class chart of their observations. That chart then becomes the source of ideas for what children will put in their re-creation of a zoo in their classroom.

The shared experience can be the following:

1. a field trip
2. an event that occurs, such as rain, snow, or a parade
3. observation of something real, such as nature objects, animals, machines, or a store
4. reading a story or poem together
5. a class project topic

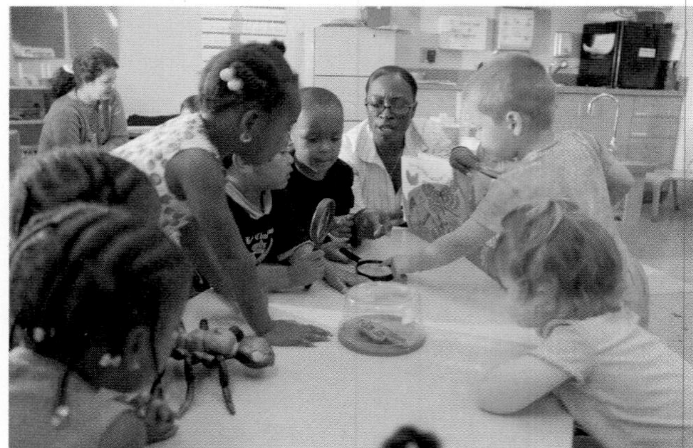

Shared experiences lay the groundwork for successful group activities. After observing insects, children contributed to a group display by making their own insects. These bugs were made from homemade play dough by Danita, Georgie, Jon, Noah, Mia, and Fajr, ages 3 to 5.

Encourage peer modeling. Imitation is one way that children learn new skills. Slightly more advanced peers provide better models for young children than adults, whose skills may be far greater than children need or are capable of imitating. Working together on a group arts project provides the perfect opportunity for children to learn from one another.

Group Arts Activities

Arts activities can offer many opportunities for groups of children to interact and develop cooperative skills.

Murals. The word **mural,** although technically defined as a "wall painting," in literature on children's art, usually refers to a very large, two-dimensional piece of artwork created by a group of children. That is the definition used here. Murals are ideal group projects for children and adults of all ages. They can either be created on the spot in response to an exciting experience, or carefully planned in response to a field trip, study topic, or piece of literature.

Any number of children can contribute to a collage mural as long as the background is big enough. Do not hesitate to add on to the background or to create several murals at the same time, if necessary. Murals enable children of different levels and abilities to work together successfully. One toddler can work with an older child or adult. Preschoolers can work in groups of three and four. Primary students can work in groups of four to six.

The group sculpture. When many hands contribute to an artwork, incredible energy results. Group sculptures make lively activities for mixed-age groups. Even the youngest child can be helped to place a part on a group sculpture. Group sculptures can be simple and immediate. For example, children on the playground can collect stones or sticks and arrange them into a design on the pavement. Wood scraps collected as part of a visit to a carpenter's shop or trip to a lumberyard can become an amazing structure.

Group sculptures can be built from any easily handled and joined three-dimensional material. Try boxes, paper bags stuffed with newspaper, chenille stems, straws, wooden blocks, corrugated cardboard, telephone wire, or Styrofoam packing material.

Just like murals, constructions need to grow out of a special experience. For example, visit a sculpture garden, and then come back and build a class sculpture out of corrugated cardboard. If children are using straws or toothpicks in a math counting activity, culminate with having the children glue them together into a linear sculpture using a piece of Styrofoam for a base. Walk through the neighborhood and identify different buildings. Then build a model of the community using boxes or pieces of wood.

As children work, encourage them to consider how their part will go with the rest. Describe the work as it changes with each addition: "Look, it's getting taller." Respond positively to each child's contribution: "Your piece helps make it stronger."

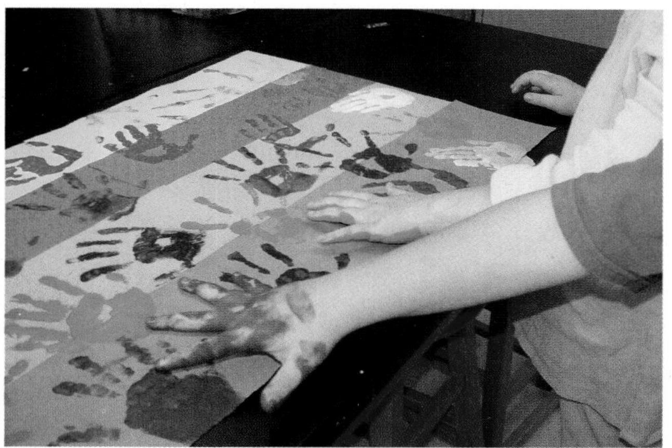

In mural making, children contribute in their own unique ways to create a marvelous whole. Handprint murals encourage children to consider the relationship of their print to those of others.

Making a Connection

IDEAS FOR MURALS BASED ON SHARED EXPERIENCES

Shared Experience	A Mural to Make
Rain: Rain is running down the windowpanes. It is a perfect day for drip painting!	Add water to tempera paint so that it drips slowly. (Try it out first.) Hang a long sheet of paper on a wall, and be sure to put newspaper on the floor. Show the children how the paint drips, and encourage them to make many raindrops on their own.
Clouds: Lie on the grass and watch clouds floating in a blue sky.	Give out white paint, and paint cloud shapes on a blue background paper.
Flowers: Walk in a garden, and talk about the colors and shapes of the flowers or study a bouquet.	Invite the children to paint flowers on a green background paper.
Bubbles: Blow bubbles with the children. Talk about their colors, sizes, and shapes. If possible, use a giant bubble wand.	Have the children think about ways bubbles could be shown in paint. Combine soap, water, and some tempera paint for color, and mix it to make it frothy. Then paint bubble shapes on the mural. (Remember, not all bubbles are round.)
Color: Hold featured color days. Ask everyone to wear something in a specific color. Fill the room with objects in that color.	Put out a collection of objects and art papers and materials in the featured color or, for a higher-level activity, have children find objects in that color. Use glue and scissors to create a collage mural.
Shape: Play a game about a shape. Offer precut paper in one basic shape (circle, square, etc.) in an assortment of sizes and colors, or let children cut their own shapes for the mural.	The children can glue the shapes directly onto the mural. More experienced children may create a piece of artwork on their shape before attaching it. They can draw, paint, or make collages or prints. If using printing, offer items that create prints in the featured shape.
Faces: Talk about facial features, and put out mirrors for the children to look in. Have a face hunt, and clip magazine pages that have faces on them.	Have the children tear or cut out the eyes, noses, and mouths to make their own faces on construction paper shapes. When done, have children sit in a circle and share their faces. Talk about places where crowds of people are seen, such as at a sporting event, at a show, or in a class. Then have each child in turn glue the face to the mural.
Mosaic: Take a walk and collect rounded or flat pebbles or stones. Toddlers should collect stones two to three inches in diameter; older children should find smaller pieces about one-half inch to one inch in diameter.	Have the students glue the stones on a heavy cardboard or wood base. (Variation: Have the children paint or color on them first, or use small blocks of wood, bottle caps, or seashells instead of stones.)
Snowflakes: Create this mural on a snowy day. Have the children play outside in the snow, and then come in and share how it felt.	Invite them to re-create the feeling of snow in a mural. Put out sponge balls or other objects to print with and white paint in trays to make snowflake prints. Have each child decide where to put his or her snowflake print in relation to the others.
Shoe prints: Collect some old shoes in different sizes, from baby shoes to high heels. On a day when a child arrives in brand-new sneakers and the conversation naturally turns to comparing shoes, make a shoe-print mural.	Bring out the paper and shoes, put colorful paint in several trays, and take the shoes for a walk across the paper.
Handprints: Use this activity to unite groups and become comfortable with their differences. Compare the size and color of everyone's hands.	Have each child mix up paint to match their skin tone. Then have the children paint their hands and make handprints across a long sheet of craft paper. Parents and visitors can be invited to add their handprints to the mural as well. If desired, label below the handprints with the child's name.
Wheels: Relate to children's interest in wheeled vehicles by closely examining a truck or visiting a tire store and then organizing a wheel mural.	Dip toy cars and trucks in shallow trays of paint and drive them around on a large sheet of paper. For variation, use small plastic animals and people instead of vehicles to make footprints, or draw roads first and then drive the cars on them.

Teachers Working Together

Educators also benefit from working alongside their peers. Teaching is often seen as an individual affair. We need to meet often with our peers to share ideas and frustrations. Projects are easier to plan when there are two or three minds brainstorming. We need to involve parents as partners in our programs. Foot painting, creative dancing, and nature collages are easier to manage when there are extra hands. Everyone needs to come together in order to grow together. The program will be richer, and the young artists will show more growth.

Teacher Tip

CAPTURE THE PROCESS

When engaged in group art projects, remember to record the process.

- Draw it: Encourage children to make drawings showing the sequence of steps they went through.
- Record it: Tape record children as they work. Display the children's own words next to the finished piece.
- Capture it: Take photographs and make video recordings.
- Write about it: Record the children's description of what they did on an **experience chart.**

HOW ARE CHILDREN WITH SPECIAL NEEDS INCLUDED IN THE ARTS PROGRAM?

Most important to remember is that they are children first, and they can learn.

—*Linda McCormick & Stephanie Feeney (1995, p. 16)*

Because of the open-ended nature of well-designed arts activities, children with special needs can participate fully in most arts programs and group arts activities, often without many modifications. If necessary, changes can be made in the tools and environment to allow active participation. The other children also need to be encouraged to accept and support those with special needs.

Defining Special Needs

Children with special needs are a tremendously diverse group. Some have obvious disabilities, and others have disabilities that cannot be seen by the casual observer. The **Individuals with Disabilities Act** (Public Law 105–17) has identified ten categories of children who can receive special education services. These include children with learning disabilities, speech and language disabilities, mental retardation, emotional disturbance, multiple disabilities, autism, hearing disabilities, visual disabilities, orthopedic disabilities, and other health disabilities.

Book Box

Books that celebrate working together.

Keats, E. J. (1987/2009). *Regards to the man in the moon*. New York: Viking.
Children paint a space mural, build spaceships out of junk, and then take an imaginary trip through space. Four and up.

Lionni, L. (1963). *Swimmy*. New York: Alfred A. Knopf.
A fish learns how to cooperate with others in this book illustrated with simple prints. Also available as a big book from Scholastic. Toddler and up.

Pfister, M. (1992). *The rainbow fish*. New York: North-South Books.
The most beautiful fish in the ocean discovers that by giving of himself he can find friendship and happiness. The scales on the rainbow fish that he shares with the other fish in the sea are made with real reflective foil. A powerful book to use to teach children the values of cooperation and sharing. Toddler and up.

Vazquez, S. (1998). *The school mural*. Milwaukee, WI: Raintree.
Colorful cut-paper illustrations show how a class plans and makes a mural to commemorate the school's 50th anniversary. Six and up.

In addition, the law mandates that children with disabilities be educated in the least restrictive environment. As a result of this law, many children with disabilities will be found in regular educational settings (Heward, 2000). This has led to many inclusion programs for young children where special provisions are made so that all children can achieve success.

Meeting Special Needs

Because children with special needs have unique developmental paths, inclusive early childhood programs need to focus on ways to help them become engaged in learning and in interacting socially with peers. Many of the techniques suggested for working with mixed ages and abilities will also help children with special needs be successful.

Select open-ended activities. Exploratory arts activities, which entice children with colors, textures, sounds, movements, and unexpected results, and which can be done alongside peers who are also exploring, can be vital to this process. Arts activities provide an opportunity for children to apply skills needed for further development. Grasping a marker or paintbrush prepares a child for holding a pencil for writing. Pushing and pulling play dough strengthens hand and arm muscles. Playing a xylophone improves hand-eye coordination.

Provide assistance. When a child needs additional help to be successful, try to provide it in a way that does not draw a lot of attention. Pairing a child with special needs with a knowledgeable child or adult, for example, who can either get the supplies or help the child move in a dance activity without constant teacher direction helps lessen the child being singled out.

Use role models. Because the child may need to approach the task differently from others, model the method or action in many different ways to the whole group.

Gentle assistance can help a child with special needs participate in arts activities. Here an adult helps a child clap along with a song.

Using the Arts to Facilitate Growth

Children with disabilities gain language and cognitive skills more readily when these behaviors are part of play (Davis, Kilgo, & Gamel-McCormick, 1998). Because the arts share so many qualities with children's natural play, they provide a wonderful way to help children with special needs improve in these needed skills.

This is important because children with developmental delays need more time and practice to accomplish educational goals. Therefore, every minute that the child is in an educational setting must focus on the basic skills and behaviors that the child needs to obtain. Teachers can facilitate needed development by joining the child in an arts activity and using the time to focus on general instructional goals. For example, if the goal for a particular child is to learn to ask for things rather than pointing, then as part of a collage activity, the teacher may sit beside the child and place some intriguing collage materials to the far side in order to elicit a request from the child.

Research also indicates that when a child talks more, language skills improve (Hart & Risley, 1995). For children with speech delays and disabilities, the teacher may encourage verbalization by asking targeted questions about their creative work and by responding to nonverbal child-initiated interactions by soliciting a verbal response. Talking about the child's creative process and work provides a nonthreatening environment in which to do this.

Special Needs

• BEING THE MOST SUCCESSFUL •

Linda Mitchell (2004) suggests using the MOST (**M**aterials + **O**bjectives + **S**pace + **T**ime) strategies in planning arts activities for all children, including those with special needs.

M Choose materials carefully so that all children will be successful using them. Make modifications as needed to meet individual requirements.

O Build into the activity objectives taken from individual children's **Individualized Education Plan (IEP).**

S Change the classroom setting to provide the best use of space for every child. This may require designating certain areas for specific activities.

T Children with special needs may require more time to engage in and complete an activity.

Adjusting the Activity

The teacher may also need to do a task analysis and break down arts activities into small steps so the child can achieve success. These steps can then be modeled and verbalized for the child, either one by one or in a series based on the child's needs. For example, an exploratory printmaking activity might be broken down into several parts:

1. The child selects a printmaking tool from a tray containing several.
2. The child dips it into the chosen paint color.
3. The child presses the tool onto paper that is taped to the table.
4. The child puts the tool back into the tray.

The steps are then repeated until the print is completed. At each of these steps, the guiding adult should give verbal and visual cues. With each succeeding repetition, the adult can withdraw some of the support until the child can carry out the tasks independently.

Book Box

Books that develop empathy.

Cottin, M. (2009). *The black book of colors*. Berkeley, CA: Groundwood.
Let children experience the world through all their senses, except sight, by sharing this book in which words describe colors in terms of touch, taste, and smell. Illustrated with embossed pictures on black pages that can be felt with the fingertips.

Moon, N. (1994). *Lucy's picture*. New York: Dial Books for Young Readers.
Lucy wants to make a gift for her grandfather, who is blind, but a painting is just not right. She decides to make a collage of things she collects inside and outside the schoolroom that her grandfather can feel. A perfect read-aloud for young children. It emphasizes that being aware of special needs is an important part of the arts process. Four and up.

Thomas, P. (2002). *Don't call me special.* Hauppauge, NY: Barons.
This book shows children with many different abilities learning and having fun together.

Getting Help

An important part of working with children with special needs is obtaining information and assistance from the child's family. Families play a major role in caring for the child, and they understand much about the child's needs and capabilities. They can share what interactions and modifications of the environment have been successful for them. In addition, an early intervention team or professionals with expertise in the child's area of need can also offer needed assistance.

The Role of Arts Therapy

All children find emotional release through the expressive nature of music, drama, dance, and arts activities, so it is not surprising that some children may use the arts to work through traumatic experiences. For example, a child who has experienced a natural disaster may draw pictures of houses and trees that are then scribbled over or "destroyed," as happened in the disaster. Gradually, such pictures decrease as the child comes to terms with the occurrence.

For some children, however, the release of otherwise unexpressed feelings and thoughts may require adult help. A child whose pet was killed in an accident may draw increasingly bloody pictures, indicating that the incident is still very disturbing and that there is a need to work through these deep feelings.

Gerald Oster and Parricia Crone (2004) identify several reasons why the arts are a useful way to engage children for therapeutic and psychological assessment purposes.

1. It is less threatening than verbally expressing deep emotions.
2. It provides a product that can be discussed in a variety of ways.
3. The act of creating allows the child to fantasize and try out solutions to problems.

However, it is dangerous for untrained observers to make judgments about a child's emotional state based on just one or a few pieces of artwork. The constant use of one color of paint may simply reflect what color was available or closest to the child. Research indicates that many young children often use paint colors in the order that they are arranged at the easel (Winner, 1982, p. 151). Pictures of family members may reflect attempts by children to control their world. The parents may be shown small and the child huge, a new baby may be left out, or divorce and remarriage may not be reflected at all in the child's "family" portrait. On the other hand, the arrangement of images may just indicate how well the child controls the art medium.

The teacher's role should be to allow children to use the arts as a personal way to express their thoughts and emotions—a safe place to show their feelings and, incidentally, give adults a peek inside of an often otherwise private world. However, in the case of serious traumatic experiences, arts therapy may be recommended. Arts therapy is a distinct field of study that requires expertise in both art and psychology. The **music, art,** or **drama therapist** functions as an educator who modifies arts activities to meet the emotional needs of troubled children. Qualified arts therapists work with a team of professionals to interpret the child's artwork, based on many samples. They then provide healing arts activities.

General Modifications for the Arts

All children with special needs are individually unique in terms of how they cope with arts materials and will require individualized adaptations. The following list provides some general ideas. Specific suggestions for each of the art forms will be found in the "Exploring the Arts" section of the book. See also Table 5-1.

Meeting needs for muscular control.

1. Put trays across wheelchairs.
2. Provide wheelchair-height tables.
3. Make sure there is sufficient space for wheelchairs to join in creative dance activities.
4. Use pillows to position the child to better manipulate materials and participate in singing and musical activities.
5. Art tools such as crayons, markers, pencils, brushes, and pens, and musical instruments, such as drumsticks, rattles, bells, maracas, and triangles, can be wrapped in foam hair curlers to improve grip. Velcro pieces can be attached to a cotton glove and the arts object.
6. Attach the drawing tool, paintbrush, or instrument to an arm, prosthesis, foot, or headgear. Some children without the use of their arms use their mouths. Drawing tools can be taped into cigarette holders, or a special holder can be made or purchased. Remember, children do not draw or make music with their hands, but with their minds.

TABLE 5–1 Examples of Ways to Adapt Arts Activities

Activity	Disability	Material Modification	IEP Objectives	Setting Modification	Time
Painting	Physical	Use thick-handled brush wrapped in foam	Child will strengthen right arm	Paper will be hung on easel at wheelchair height	Activity will be during open-ended center time
Singing a song	Hearing disability	Add signing to song	Child will use sign language to communicate	Child will sit near teacher in circle	Repeat song several times, adding the signs
Creative dance	Visual disability	Have children hold hands and move in a circle	Child will hold head erect when walking	Circle will be marked on floor in brightly colored tape	Children will practice walking around the circle
Acting out story	Autism	Use familiar objects the child is comfortable with as props	Child will look at others when speaking	Use tape to mark where actors will stand	Before activity have child visit area and see where to stand

Trays can help keep messy materials controlled.

7. To facilitate cutting, provide a rotary cutting wheel and a cutting mat instead of scissors.
8. Use no-spill paint containers and thickened paint. Choose brushes in a size that best matches the child's muscle control. Short, stubby brushes may work better than long-handled easel brushes. Foam brushes may make the paint easier to control.

Meeting visual needs.

1. Place a screen or textured surface under the paper to add texture to drawn lines.
2. Use a fabric tracing or marking wheel to create a raised line. Place pads of newspaper or rubber mats beneath lightweight paper.
3. Use scented crayons and markers; add scents to paint and glue.
4. Provide many tactile materials.
5. Place arts materials and props in the same locations every time, and attach tactile, identifying symbols on supply containers. For example, attach an actual piece of each collage material to collage storage bins. This will allow children to develop independence in obtaining their own supplies.
6. If the child has some vision, find out which colors are easiest to see, and provide many materials in those colors. For example, fluorescent colors and reflective safety tapes may appeal to some children. Mark bold lines on the floor to guide the child during movement and dramatic activities.

Behavioral and emotional needs.

1. Select activities that have few steps and instant results, such as modeling, painting, making sounds, and puppetry. Expect lots of exploration and physical expression of feelings.
2. For children who are easily distracted, provide work areas that allow plenty of space and that seem separate from the rest of the room.
3. Select and arrange arts supplies carefully to help limit distractions as well.

Teacher Tip

USING MODELING MATERIALS FOR EMOTIONAL RELEASE

The creation of modeled forms is often accompanied by children's enthusiastic destruction. Pliant modeling materials give children the power to control a small part of their environment. Clay and play doughs are regularly used by children to release strong feelings in an acceptable way. Clay, unlike other children, bossy adults, or precious belongings, can be hit and smashed, slapped, pinched and poked, and torn apart and put together again. Children who are having difficulty controlling their social behavior benefit from redirecting this behavior to the forgiving clay.

Other assistance.

1. Some children who have visual or motor difficulties may need hand-over-hand assistance. Place a hand over the student's to assist with such skills as dipping the paintbrush into the container and then onto the paper, or dipping a finger into paste and then applying it to the object to be glued.
2. Some children may need their base paper taped to the table to keep it from moving or wrinkling when they work.
3. Add picture clues and labels.
4. Use real objects to further understanding (i.e., a real apple as opposed to a picture of one).
5. Incorporate children's communication devices into the activity. For example, a child could play a sound on a communication board to accompany a song.

6. Use multiple delivery modes. Say the directions, show the directions in pictures and words, use sign language, and act out the directions.

Helping Other Children Accept Those with Special Needs

Although young children can be very accepting of individual differences, they may react in outspoken ways to things that are unfamiliar or strange. We need to be sensitive as we help children learn to live with all kinds of people.

1. Do not criticize children for expressing curiosity. When children notice and ask questions about disabilities and special equipment, answer matter-of-factly with a simple and accurate reply. It is important to be honest when answering. Use correct terminology whenever possible.

   Child: *"Why does Jared need a special holder for his crayons?"*

   Teacher: *"Jared uses a holder because he has trouble holding small objects tightly. Jared likes to draw like you do, but he has muscular dystrophy, so we figured out a way that he could do it."*

2. Do not deny differences, but help children see their shared similarities.

   Child: *"Maya just makes noises with the xylophone."*

   Teacher: *"Maya likes to make music, just like you do. She has learned how to do many things. Now she is learning how to play the xylophone. Would you like to play along on the drum with her?"*

3. Children need to become familiar with special equipment and devices but also need to learn to respect the equipment of a child with special needs. If possible, rent or borrow a variety of equipment for children to explore, but make it clear that they must respect the personal equipment of the child who must use it.

4. If children are comfortable doing so, have them explain how their special equipment helps them participate in the arts and why it is important to take care of it. If they cannot do this on their own, then have them demonstrate how the equipment is used while an adult explains.

5. Invite artists with disabilities to share their arts. Make sure they are prepared for the sometimes bold questions of children.

HOW CAN THE ARTS BE USED IN ANTI-BIAS ACTIVITIES?

It is not differences in themselves that cause the problems, but how people respond to differences.

—Louise Derman-Sparks & the A.B.C. Task Force (1989, p. 6)

Arts activities can be used to help children express their feelings about individual differences. They provide an opportunity for teachers to initiate a dialogue to correct mistaken beliefs and model respect for others.

In offering the arts to young children, teachers need to be sure that the choice of activities creates an environment in which children from all backgrounds feel comfortable and can be creative in their artwork. Children differ in their racial, religious, cultural, and ethnic backgrounds. Research shows that children begin to be aware of these individual differences by age two, and that between the ages of three and five they develop a sense of who they are and how they differ from others (Van Ausdale & Feagin, 2001). Before children can feel free to relax and express themselves in creative arts activities, they need to feel valued for who they are, not for how they look, talk, and behave. They need to be treated fairly and have their differences seen as strengths that enrich the learning of all of the children.

The visual, physical, and tactile nature of the arts allows children, regardless of their differences, to explore and learn together. Children who speak different languages can learn by observing each other as they create with the arts. Because the arts are common to all cultures, it can be a vehicle through which cultural differences can be explored.

Creating an Arts Environment that Celebrates Differences

Teachers must take action to encourage the development of an **anti-bias** atmosphere among children. They need to consider the materials they choose to supply and the pictures they display. Activities should be provided that foster discussion and the elimination of the misconceptions that are the basis of many prejudicial beliefs held by young children. The arts can be used in a variety of ways to support an anti-bias curriculum.

Selecting anti-bias visual images and supplies. Children need to see and become familiar with people who look different from them. They also need to develop an authentic self-concept based on liking themselves without feeling superior to others (Derman-Sparks & Ramsey, 2006). Taking the following steps will help children do this:

1. Provide arts materials that reflect the wide range of natural skin tones. Paints, papers, play doughs, and crayons in the entire range of skin colors need to be regularly available, along with the other colors.
2. Mirrors and photographs of themselves and their families should be available at all times for children to learn about themselves and each other.
3. Images of people who represent the racial and ethnic groups found in the community and in the larger society need to be displayed. There should be a balance in the images so that there is no token group. It is recommended that about half of the images should represent the background of the predominant group of children in the class. The remainder of the images should represent the rest of the diversity found in society (Derman-Sparks & the A.B.C. Task Force, 1989).
4. When selecting artworks, look for pieces that show a range of people of different ages, genders, sizes, colors, and abilities. Display photos of people who are involved in activities that depict current life. Many prints are available that reflect this diversity, including those depicting arts from Haitian, African, African-American, Native American, Mexican, and Asian sources. (See Chapter 7 for suggestions and Appendix B for sources.)
5. Artworks, music, stories, and dances should also represent artists of diverse backgrounds and time periods, including the present. This is particularly important for Native Americans.
6. Illustrations in the books read to the children and available for them to use should also reflect society's diversity.
7. Stereotypical and inaccurate images should be removed from display in the room and used only in discussions of unfair representations of groups of people. Avoid so-called "multicultural" materials such as bulletin-board kits and patterns that depict people from around the world wearing traditional clothing from the past. These materials leave children with the impression that, for example, all Native Americans wear leather and feathers, all Japanese wear kimonos, and all Africans wear dashikis.

Selecting anti-bias activities. Second, the arts activities can be chosen that help children acquire inner strength, empathy, a strong sense of justice, and the power to take action in the face of bias. Louise Derman-Sparks and Patricia Ramsey note that there are four basic goals of anti-bias education.

1. Help children develop self-confidence and a positive group identity with their home culture and with that of our society.
2. Develop empathy for, and a feeling of, commonality with those who are different.
3. Assist children in developing an understanding of fairness and the knowledge that discrimination and exclusion hurts.
4. Nurture children's ability to stand up for themselves and others in the face of unfairness and prejudice.

Anti-Bias Arts Activities

Arts activities, because of their open-ended nature and emphasis on working together to accomplish a creative goal are an ideal way to develop this inner strength. The following activities show how the arts can be used to address racial prejudice based on skin color.

Mixing my special color. Read a book about skin color, such as *All the Colors We Are* (Kissinger, 1994). Help children mix paint that matches the color of their skin. Place the paint in a container that closes tightly. Label the container with the child's name, and have the child give the color a beautiful name. Explain that whenever children want to paint a picture of themselves or their friends, they may use those special paint colors.

Valuing children's unique colors. Make sure skin-color paints are available at the easel. Then, when children use the paint color that is closest to their skin color, hair color, or eye color, make a comment about the beauty of that color and express its relationship to the children's coloring, such as: "You are painting with a beautiful almond brown (rich peach, soft beige, deep brown, etc.). It is the same color as your skin (hair, eyes)." Read the book *The Colors of Us* (Katz, 2002) in which different skin colors are given luscious names and then have children create their own names for their color skin.

Read a book that celebrates differences, such as *We Are All Alike . . . We Are All Different* (Cheltenham Elementary School Kindergarten, 1994). Collect a variety of paint-chip samples from a paint store. Have children sort them into groups. Then have them find the ones that match their hair, skin, and eye color. Make a graph or chart of the different range of colors in the group.

Washing up. This interaction can occur following any messy activity in which the children's hands get covered with an art material, such as finger painting, printing, clay work, or painting. When children are washing up at the sink, say, "What do you think might happen to the color of our skin when we wash the paint off? Look, it stays the same color. Our skin color doesn't come off, only the paint." Also, provide opportunities for children to wash dirt off dolls that have different skin colors.

Foster self-awareness. Read *Head to Toe* (Carle, 1999). Develop awareness of body parts and names by calling out a body part and a way to move it, such as, "Shake your arm up and down. Wiggle your toes. Put your hands on your head." Develop a rhythmic pattern, and repeat the actions several times. Another way to develop self-awareness is to encourage children to touch the different body parts on a life-size paper silhouette.

1. Invite a child to lie down on a sheet of kraft paper cut to her or his length, and trace around her or him. (Do not force a child to participate. This activity makes some children feel uncomfortable.)
2. Cut out the tracing for toddlers and preschoolers who have beginning cutting skills. More adept cutters can cut their own.
3. Help children select the color of paint or crayons that best matches their skin, hair, eyes, and clothing, so they may color in their "Me Persons."

"Me Persons" Children develop a better sense of their similarities and differences when they create art about themselves.

Color awareness collages. Children need to learn to cherish all the colors skin can be. Transition into a skin color awareness activity by reading a book that celebrates the colors brown and black, such as *Beautiful Blackbird* (Bryan, 2003). Have the children find or make a list of all of the beautiful black or brown things that they know. Take a neighborhood or nature walk and look for brown or black things. Look at the many different colors skin can be. Put out the collage items, exclaiming over the beautiful color of each material.

Talking to Children about Differences

When arts materials that reflect skin differences, images of a variety of people, and anti-bias arts activities are introduced to young children, occasions will arise in which biased or unkind remarks will be made, and a response will be required by the teacher. A child may not want to handle black play dough because it is "ugly," or another may say, "My skin color paint is prettier than yours." Whether it is during an arts activity, or at any other time of the day, children's discriminating behavior must be addressed. Such comments, even by very young children, must not be ignored or excused, nor is the teacher's personal discomfort in dealing with difficult subjects a reason not to act. Reacting strongly to biased statements shows children how to act when they see unfairness. The following suggestions may help:

1. Immediately address the child's negative response. A response to the aforementioned statements might be: "All colors are beautiful. Why do you say that?" If the comment is

directed to another child, say: "That is a hurtful thing to say. Why do you say that?"

2. Help children figure out why they are uncomfortable. Identify why it was unfair or based on stereotypes.
3. Explain why such remarks are hurtful, and give examples of things the child might say or do instead.

WHAT IS THE ROLE OF HOLIDAYS IN ARTS ACTIVITIES?

> *The overuse of holiday units interferes with a developmental approach to curriculum as too many "canned" activities take the place of activities tailored to the needs of specific groups of children.*
>
> —*Louise Derman-Sparks & the A.B.C. Task Force (1989, p. 86)*

In many early childhood programs, holidays have become a major focus for arts activities. Arts activity books abound that purport to deliver exciting new ways to create holiday art, and decorations, and perform festive songs and dances. Holidays are fun; they create rituals, which build a sense of solidarity; they are part of a society's cultural life, but there are dangers in relating arts creation so closely to holidays.

Fairness

First of all, how do teachers select which holidays to celebrate and which holiday arts activities the children will do? Not all holidays are celebrated in the same way by everyone. The holidays of all children in the group must be presented with equal emphasis. One holiday should not receive more time and attention than another.

Presenting Multicultural Arts beyond the Holiday

Presenting artwork and activities that relate to different cultures throughout the year rather than just in the context of a holiday helps prevent children from associating the arts of that culture with only the holiday. For example, Native American arts and culture should be displayed and discussed in many arts contexts—when making masks, working with beads, creating with clay, learning to spin and weave, and examining baskets—not just at Thanksgiving.

Avoiding Stereotypical Symbols

One of the hardest things to avoid when dealing with holiday-related arts activities is the stereotypical images related to holidays. These images limit children's creativity and visual imaginations, and they often undermine their artistic self-confidence as they quickly learn that they cannot replicate the commercial perfection of a holiday symbol.

The perfect Christmas-tree shape, for example, is impossible for young children to make successfully without resorting to patterns or step-by-step copying, and the image becomes so ingrained that many upper-level arts teachers find that they have to take their students on nature walks just to prove that all pine trees are not symmetrical, and that they can be represented in many other ways in their art. Hearts, egg shapes, bunnies, turkeys, and pumpkins all become bland, perfect symbols instead of reflecting the infinite variety of their actual forms.

It is hard to avoid these symbols because they permeate the markets and media of this society. However, we need to consider carefully which images we want to surround the children in our care. Teachers can take the following actions to expand children's artistic imaginations and fight the prevailing stereotypes.

1. In visual arts, activities provide geometric shapes that children can make into their own creative ideas instead of holiday-related shapes that limit what they can do. Let children draw their own versions of Christmas trees, turkeys, pumpkins, hearts, and other holiday shapes, instead of giving them holiday cutouts, coloring pages, or stickers.
2. At the play dough and clay center, instead of holiday-shaped cookie cutters, use simple geometric shapes from which children can build their own versions of these symbols if they wish.
3. Provide a range of color choices of materials, not just those of the prevailing holiday.
4. Instead of displaying stereotypical holiday images, provide aesthetic experiences with a collection of pumpkins, piles of pine boughs, a display of turkey feathers, a basket of eggs, or a cage of real rabbits, so the children can see and touch them and discover similarities and differences on their own.

Instead of using three perfect circles, snowmen can be made in many ways that allow children to express their own creativity as this snowman by Joseph, age 4, demonstrates.

Book Box

Books addressing physical and cultural differences.

Cheltenham Elementary School Kindergarten. (1994). *We are all alike . . . we are all different*. New York: Scholastic.
Children's drawings illustrate this book about how people are the same and different. Also available as a big book from Scholastic. Toddler and up.

Hoffman, M. (1991). *Amazing Grace*. New York: Dial.
A young girl with a flair for the dramatic wants to be Peter Pan in the school play, but is told she cannot because she is an African-American and a girl. With perseverance she stands up for herself and wins the role. Four and up.

Katz, K. (2002). *The colors of us*. New York: Henry Holtz.
A young girl discovers all the wonderful colors people in her neighborhood are. Three and up.

Kissinger, K. (1994). *All the colors we are*. St. Paul, MN: Redleaf Press.
Beautiful photographs illustrate this book that explains simply why people have different colored skin. Use this book to accompany mixing skin-toned paints. (Bilingual: Spanish) Four and up.

Lionni, L. (2006). *A color of his own*. New York: Alfred A. Knopf.
A lizard tries out many colors until he finds one just right for him. A favorite read-aloud. Also available as a big book from Scholastic. Four and up.

Nicola-Lisa, W. (1999). *Bein' with you this way*. Minneapolis, MN: Sagebrush.
A vibrant playground cumulative rap celebrates physical differences as children and adults dance through the park. An audio CD of the song is available. Toddler and up.

CONCLUSION: CARING FOR EACH OTHER

Art is an outlet that lets children convey what they might not be able to say in words.

—Diane Dodge & Laura Colker (1992, p. 161)

Group arts projects can take many forms. From painting a mural to acting out a story, working with others gives children a chance to interact with the arts in a way that is different from individual artistic pursuits. There must be a common vocabulary. "Should we put aqua paint on the fish?" There must be collaboration. "Should this character be a pigeon or an eagle?" And there must be cooperation. "I'll hold the paint for you, and then you can hold it for me."

The result is more than the sum of its parts. Group arts activities turn me into we and unite individuals.

Group arts activities can also be used to help children express thoughts and feelings that are hard to put into words. Teachers need to be sensitive to the personal needs and beliefs of their students. Children can and should talk about the differences among them, but actually painting with different skin tones, learning each other's personal likes and cultural backgrounds, and working on the same arts projects with those who are different helps children form tangible links. The arts activities that we choose can help children broaden their perspectives in ways that will make them more successful participants in the future.

This chapter has offered ideas that challenge the educator to address sometimes controversial issues. Overheard comments could be ignored. Black and brown play dough could be avoided, because it makes some children uncomfortable or makes them act silly. Teachers could focus on the more readily available "old masters" instead of looking for the harder-to-locate artwork of African-Americans, Latinos, and those of other cultures. Teachers could give in to the pressure to make commercialized holiday "art," or they can make the other choice, the one that takes a little more effort. They can make a commitment to do what is best for the children, knowing that change happens not all at once but a little bit every day.

FURTHER READING

For ways to help young children cooperate, read:

Kagan, S. (1994). *Cooperative learning.* San Juan Capistrano, CA: Resources for Teachers.

A systematic program for developing cooperative group behavior is presented in this comprehensive manual. Special suggestions are given for introducing cooperative skills to children age five and up.

Putnam, J. W. (1998). *Cooperative learning and strategies for inclusion. Celebrating diversity in the classroom.* Baltimore, MD: Brooks Publishing.

A research-based approach to addressing differences in the classroom.

The following references will help guide the development of an anti-bias program:

Bisson, J. (2002). *Celebrate: An anti-bias guide to enjoying holidays in early childhood programs.* St. Paul, MN: Redleaf.

This book looks at the meaning, purposes, and issues surrounding the celebration of holidays and provides ways teachers can incorporate them in a respectful way.

Derman-Sparks, L., & the A.B.C. Task Force. (1989). *Antibias curriculum: Tools for empowering young children.* Washington, DC: National Association for the Education of Young Children.

Using realistic examples, this book provides many positive ways that teachers can address bias in the classroom.

York, S. (2005). *Roots & wings: Affirming culture in early childhood programs.* NJ: Prentice Hall.

This book provides practical ways to address cultural differences and racial discrimination in the classroom.

For detailed information on modifying activities for children with special needs, see the following:

Rodriquez, S. (1997). *The special artist's handbook.* Palo Alto, CA: Dale Seymour.

This book is directed more toward children over age five, but it still has many usable ideas for the early childhood classroom.

Sobol, E. S. (2008). *An attitude and approach to teaching music to special learners.* Savage, MD: Rowman & Littlefield.

A carefully considered approach to teaching music to children with special needs.

To learn more about arts therapy, see the following:

Malchiodi, C. A. (2006). *Art therapy sourcebook.* New York: McGraw-Hill.

This book is an insightful introduction to what art therapy is and provides many self-awareness activities.

For additional information on teaching children to work cooperatively, visit our Web site at http://www.cengagebrain.com

TEACHING IN ACTION

Putting a Group Project Together: Our Neighborhood, Grade 1

This interview with a first-grade teacher shows how a cooperative arts project can incorporate learning in all the subject areas.

Q: How did you begin?

A: My first-grade class was very involved in learning about where we live. We began by learning about where each child lived. The children drew pictures of their houses and shared them with the group. We talked about who lived in the house and the things they did there. Some children brought in photographs of their homes, and we shared them. Then they wrote about their homes in their journals. Everyone had to learn to write their own address and phone number, and we displayed it with each child's house drawing. We emphasized differences a lot. I read the children the book *The Big Orange Splot* (Pinkwater, 1977), and we talked about the ways each of their houses is different. We put photographs of each of them with their families by their drawing and talked about how everyone's family was different, too.

Writing

Social Studies

(continued)

TEACHING IN ACTION *(continued)*

Mathematics
Visual Art
Creativity

We also went for a walk around the school and looked at the houses and stores. I told the children to look for different geometric shapes. Then when we got back we made a list of what they noticed and drew pictures. By now, houses were a popular subject at the easel and in the block corner. I was pleased to see that the children weren't just making the same old stereotypical house shape either, and they were combining the shapes in new ways and getting very colorful.

Q: How did you get them started on the mural?

Language

A: Well . . . I drew the streets we had taken on our walk on a large piece of cardboard. I traced our walk on the roads I had drawn and explained that it was like a map. Then I asked children to imagine our walk and to name the different streets, stores, and houses we had passed. I had them use their journals and our chart to help them remember. But it really was amazing how much of the walk they could describe. Next, the children each chose a building to make. They used small blocks of wood that a parent had donated. Doors and windows were drawn on with crayon and marker.

Q: Describe how you had the children put the model together.

Social Studies

A: We all sat around the cardboard base, with the children holding their buildings. I started at the beginning of our walk, and as I moved my finger along the road, I asked what buildings we would see along the way. The child with that particular building would then come up and place it along the road.

Dramatics

When we were done, we imagined we were walking around the neighborhood. One child would be the leader and guide up and down the streets describing things we might see.

Q: What do you think the children learned in making this model of their neighborhood?

A: They learned which houses and buildings are in the neighborhood of the school, and they were introduced to some beginning mapping. They learned that buildings can be made of many geographic shapes joined in different ways, and that this helped them make more accurate representations of houses and buildings. The children also learned how to work together in creating the model. I will build on this concept now by introducing how people need to work together to create a community in which all are safe and healthy, and where their rights are respected.

Working together, children can build marvelous group sculptures like this city built of wood scraps colored with crayon and marker.

Studio Page

SHARED EXPERIENCES

Think of one or more open-ended group arts activity that could be done in response to the following shared experiences.

Shared Experience	Activity Ideas
A sudden thunderstorm	
A trip to a shoe store	
Watching birds	
A zookeeper's visit	
Studying patterns	
Setting up a classroom fish tank	

Studio Page

OBSERVATION: CHILDREN WORKING TOGETHER

Observe two groups of two or three children playing together or working on a common arts project. Group A should be children under three years old. Group B should be children four years old and up.

Group A Composition:

Child A:	Age:	Sex:
Child B:	Age:	Sex:
Child C:	Age:	Sex:

Group A Observation:

1. In what activity were children involved?____________________
2. How long did children work together?____________________
3. What did children say to each other? (A tape recording can be used.)____________________
4. Which child/children imitated the actions of another?____________________
5. Which child/children initiated group actions?____________________
6. How often did an adult intervene, if at all?____________________

Group B Composition:

Child A:	Age:	Sex:
Child B:	Age:	Sex:
Child C:	Age:	Sex:

Group B Observation:

1. In what activity were children involved?____________________
2. How long did children work together?____________________
3. What did children say to each other? (A tape recording can be used.)____________________
4. Which child/children imitated the actions of another?____________________
5. Which child/children initiated group actions?____________________
6. How often did an adult intervene, if at all?____________________

ANALYSIS OF THE OBSERVATION

Based on your observations, defend or oppose the following statement:

> *When working in the same room or at the same table, each child speaks for himself, even though he thinks he is listening to and understands the others. This kind of "collective monologue" is really a mutual excitation to action rather than a real exchange of ideas.*
>
> —*Jean Piaget (1967, p. 29)*

Studio Page

DEALING WITH DIFFICULT SITUATIONS

Consider each of the following situations, and decide what you would say and do.

1. A parent picks up her son's painting and says, "Another painting all in black! Why don't you use some pretty colors when you paint?"

2. A little girl refuses to touch the brown play dough. "It's yucky!" she declares.

3. Michael, age five, draws only faces with blood coming out of their mouths.

4. An aide shows the children how to trace their hands to make turkeys.

5. A child with muscular dystrophy is having trouble holding her crayon.

space than older ones. Allow at least four square feet or more of table surface for each toddler, and at least three square feet for each older child.

Marlynn Clayton (2001) suggests that a large open space be used as the whole group meeting place. This should be the heart of the classroom. This multipurpose space allows everyone to sit in a circle, where every child can be seen and feel included. It also provides a special place for dance and dramatic activities. Clayton suggests the following guidelines in planning this meeting space:

- It should be inviting, with well-defined boundaries and clear of obstacles and distractions.
- There should be room for everyone in the class to sit in a circle without touching each other.
- Everyone should be able to see everyone else.
- It should have several entry and exit points that allow children to move in and out safely and quickly.
- It should be located near an easel or blackboard for displays and by a wall outlet so CD/tape players and other electrical equipment can be used.

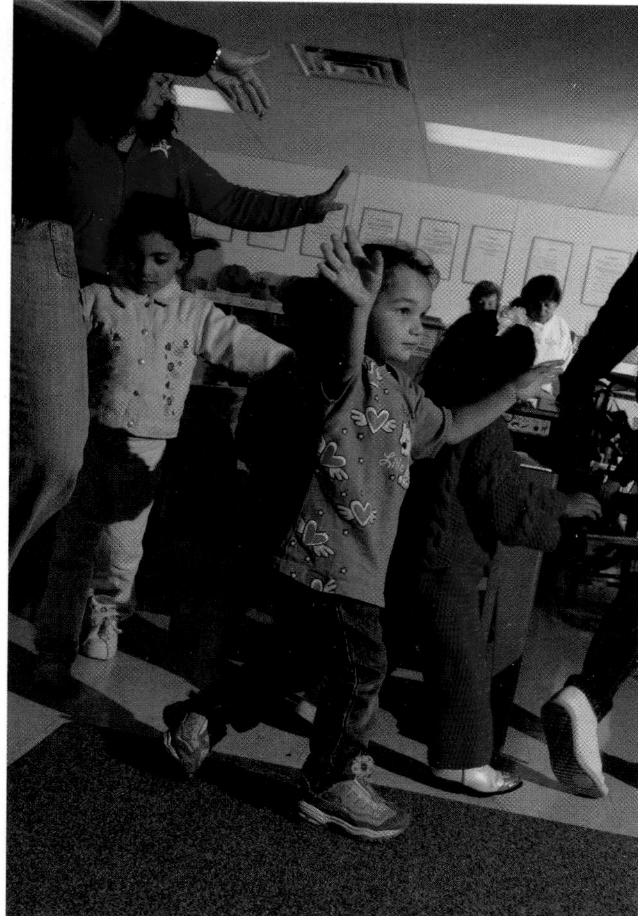

Creative dance and song games require enough space for children to hop, jump, leap, and fly.

Traffic Pattern

Consider how the children will move in the room. Will the activity areas attract them? Will there be sufficient room for children to gather around an interesting exploration? How many children can work in an area at a time? Ashley Cadwell (2005) suggests thinking of classroom spaces as streets and paths and organizing them as passages to the main "piazza, small meeting squares, and meeting spots."

The more flexible the room arrangement, the easier it will be if several children all want to work together. There should be ways to add more chairs, push two tables together, or even move all of the furniture out of the way to accommodate children who wish to explore an arts activity on the floor. Figure 6-1 analyzes the social arts environment.

Water Requirements

Those arts activities, such as paint and clay, which require water need to be located near a water source. The dirtier the children's hands get, the closer they need to be to a sink or washing area. Finger painting and printmaking in particular require an easy, clear passage to the sink. Dishpans and buckets of water can provide a preliminary rinse-off area when working outside or at a distance from a sink.

Separate Arts Activities from Food Areas

In all situations, arts activities, particularly gluing, painting, and clay, must be kept separate from cooking and eating activities. Children need to learn from the beginning that many art materials are never put in one's mouth nor eaten, and separating these two activities is one way to do this. In a home situation,

Category	Observation (check applicable description)
Space	__ Children have plenty of space for arts activities. __ Children interfere with each other during arts activities. __ Furniture constantly has to be moved to make room for arts activities.
Privacy	__ Many children utilize private arts spaces. __ Few children utilize private arts spaces.
Comfort	__ Children are quiet and calm in arts areas. __ Children are noisy and irritable in arts areas. __ Children avoid arts areas.
Social Interaction	__ Many positive interactions take place in arts areas.
Adult Usage	__ Many adult-child interactions take place in arts areas. __ Few adult-child interactions take place in arts areas.

FIGURE 6–1 Assessing the Social Arts Environment.

Teacher Tip

WAYS TO HELP CHILDREN DISTINGUISH FOOD FROM ART SUPPLIES

1. Avoid art materials that closely resemble foods or smell like foods.
2. Completely separate the areas that are used for food and art.
3. If the children will be making something from a food and eating it, it should be called "cooking" and done in the cooking area.
4. Never eat on tables that have been used for art projects. If tables must be used for both purposes, give the children trays on which to do their art, or cover the tables with plastic tablecloths when eating on them.
5. Enforce the rule that no art material is ever tasted, eaten, or drunk.
6. Supervise children, and do not let them put their fingers into their mouths when working with art materials, or before they have washed them.
7. Mix and store art materials in containers that are visually different from those used for food. If a food container is being reused, cover the outside with a label, or paint it.
8. Insist that children wash their hands after they finish using art materials and before they work with foods.

when the weather does not allow outside artwork, the kitchen may provide the only location for arts activities requiring water. One way to separate art from food activities is to have a special low table, tray, or mat that is used only for arts activities. If tables must be used for both food and art, then put down a special covering for one of the activities, such as a plastic tablecloth for eating or an old shower curtain for art.

HOW SHOULD ARTS SUPPLIES BE ORGANIZED?

How arts supplies are arranged in the environment is more than just a convenience. Carefully considered storage not only provides a more appealing appearance but also teaches. Materials and tools should be displayed and stored so that children learn how to get what they need and put an item back by themselves. Categorizing the materials by their unifying qualities teaches children visual perceptual skills as they learn to group similar items together. Toddlers do best

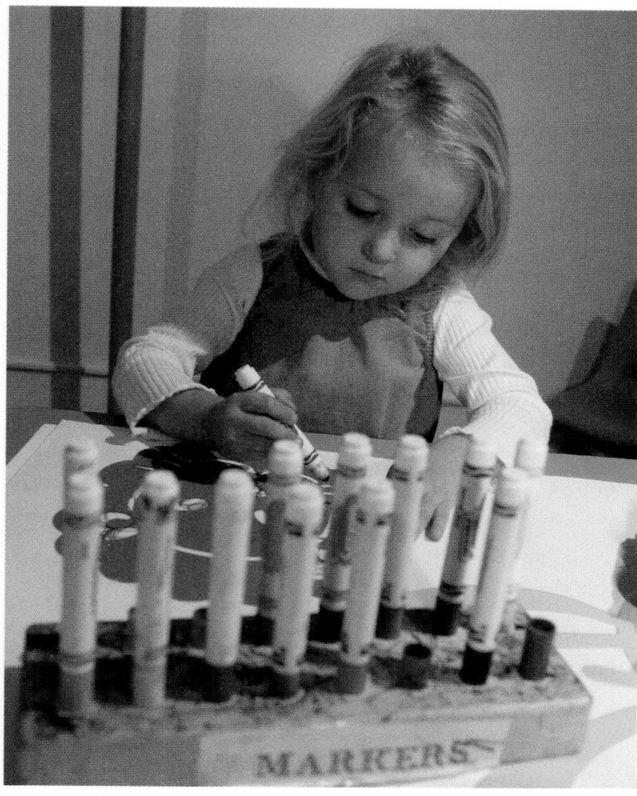

The orderly arrangement of supplies allows children to be more independent in their creative work. In addition, early literacy is enhanced by the use of a photograph and words on the label.

with broad categories of storage units with easily distinguished appearances, whereas older children can handle more complex storage systems. The order in which materials are arranged also teaches, as when materials used in a particular sequence are ordered from left to right.

Location

Not all work spaces for arts activities need to be at tables, nor do all arts activities need to be done in the same work space. Easels, for example, create a special place just for painting. Try to set them up in such a way that brushes and bottles of paint are beautifully displayed nearby.

Drawing has a far wider range of suitable places than some other, messier activities. Carpeted areas and durable pillows can entice children to sit and lie quietly while drawing. Places to crawl under and draw allow children private moments with their art. Encourage children to expand drawing activities by making small, portable containers of markers and crayons and by placing drawing materials in many areas of the room, such as by an aquarium or near a plant. Drawing should not be an occasional choice at the art table. Rather, it should be ever present throughout the room—available to record children's ideas and thoughts throughout the day.

Musical instruments should be stored on open shelves where they are easily seen and available for use as needed—to accompany an impromptu parade or to keep time with a counting activity.

Puppets and puppet-making supplies should be stored on racks near the puppet stage so they are

Teacher Tip

SHOULD FOOD BE USED IN VISUAL ARTS ACTIVITIES?
Teachers need to make their own decision about this tough subject. Here are some things to consider:

Pro: Why Food Can Be Used for Art

Many traditional adult art materials, such as egg tempera and casein paint, are made from food products.

Some modern art materials, such as play dough and white glues, are made from food products.

It is easier to determine the ingredients in food products than in real art supplies.

Food items are readily available at the supermarket. Sometimes it is hard to find safe art supplies.

You do not need to worry if children put their hands into their mouths after using food-based art materials.

Arts activities that use food products provide a multisensory experience in which children can use all of their senses in a safe way.

Children learn to appreciate the aesthetic qualities of the foods, such as the pattern inside of an apple.

Food used as art can be utilized to relate the activity to the theme of the class, such as making apple prints when reading about Johnny Appleseed.

Children are motivated by food and have a lot of fun doing these activities.

Con: Food Should Never Be Used in Arts Activities

Many children are severely allergic to some food items, such as milk, wheat, soy, eggs, and peanuts.

Most traditional art materials are not food based, such as crayons, chalk, and paper.

Food products used in commercial art supplies are usually inedible residues, such as sour milk or whey.

With a little research, the ingredients of all art supplies can be discovered.

Safe, commercial art supplies for children are widely marketed in department stores and drugstores, and through catalogs. Also, many free, "found" items can be used.

Children become confused when they are told that they can eat one art material but not another one that seems similar.

The aesthetic qualities of food should be investigated in cooking activities, not art.

Food is expensive and should not be wasted.

Many food/art projects involve sugary foods and reinforce poor eating habits.

People are hungry in our country and all over the world. Many children do not have enough to eat. It is cruel to have them make projects with food that could have fed them.

Some ethnic groups are offended if food that is valued by them is used for play and not shown respect.

near to hand for spur-of-the-moment improvised stories.

Costumes for dramatic play should hang on child-height hooks so each piece of clothing is visible for quick character changes. Store hats and shoes on nearby open shelves.

Supplies should be stored as close to the area of use as possible. Materials stored close to each other will tend to be used together. Paper, scissors, and drawing materials stored by the block area will increase the likelihood that children will make signs, maps, and other additions to their block creations. Locate puppets, costumes, and props near the class library or book corner to inspire re-enactments of favorite stories.

Ready for children, this well-organized and spacious dramatic play area includes colorful dishware, a mirror, and dress-up clothes on a rack, but is not so crowded as to overwhelm young children.

Displaying Materials

Supplies that are freely available to the children should be placed at child height and attractively displayed in sturdy containers, in baskets, or on open shelves. When supplies are carefully arranged, children are encouraged to treat them more respectfully. Children will, for example, carefully consider which piece to take when cut-paper shapes are ordered in containers by shape and color, but they will root and grab from a box of mixed-up scraps. Costumes thrown haphazardly into a cardboard box will receive less consideration than will those hung neatly from individual pegs.

Controlling amounts. Although supplies should be ample, avoid putting out huge amounts of any material. When children see large amounts of a material, whether paper or buttons, they are more likely to use the supply wastefully. It is better to display fewer supplies and refill the containers more often.

Using labels. Labels can be a way to introduce children to the printed word and should include both the word and a picture or sample of the object. Label storage containers, shelves, and hooks so children can match the item to its place.

Choosing containers. Even though labeled, containers should be low enough and wide enough so that children can easily see what is inside from their low vantage point. Clear plastic containers work well for many supplies, as do low baskets, cut-down cardboard boxes, and dishpans.

Storage

Whatever children see and ask for, they should be able to use, because this encourages creative growth. However, when there are insufficient supplies of a popular material, or when an item is not safe for children of that developmental level, then those materials should not be offered to that particular group of children. Such items should be stored completely out of sight in closets, cupboards, or boxes.

Storing Finished Work

Before selecting any visual art activity, consider carefully how the finished products will be handled. Nothing is more frustrating than trying to find space for items such as 25 dripping wet, papier-mâché covered boxes, or a 3-by-10-foot freshly painted mural.

Consider having multiple-use areas. Tables can be used for working on during the session and for storing projects at the end of the day. The area under tables or on top of shelves can also be used. It is often better to leave wet projects to dry where they are rather than risk damaging them. If projects must be moved, have the children work on trays or pieces of sturdy cardboard.

Cubbies or individual boxes for each child make a good place to store small projects, drawings, dry paintings, and collages. Placed close to the door, they help remind families to pick up their child's work. If cubbies cannot be used, a table by the door can hold work ready to go home.

HOW SHOULD CHILDREN'S WORK BE DISPLAYED?

> *It's important to keep in mind that how you handle children's art when it is finished says a lot about how much you value their efforts.*
>
> —*Diane T. Dodge & Joanna Phinney (1990, p. 175)*

No matter how much we recognize that process is more important than the finished product, at the end of each day we will be faced with many tangible arts products that will require attention. There will be paintings, child-made books, musical compositions, murals, videos of original playlets, and photographs of creative movements.

Visual Artworks

The visual arts, in particular, result in both two- and three-dimensional products. Infants and toddlers, who are immersed in explorations, may care little about what happens to their explorations of paint, marker, and play dough and may not even remember making them. Older children will have many different attitudes to their work, depending on their purposes. Some, like toddlers, may care little for exploratory

Teacher Tip

ORGANIZING ARTS SUPPLIES

Although each art medium has its own specific setup requirements, the following general guidelines apply to most arts activities.

- Allow plenty of space for each child to work. The younger the child, the more space is required.
- Protect any surface or clothing that might be damaged by the material in use. Make sure the protective covering is clearly different from any supplies being used. It is not necessary to cover surfaces that are easily washed.
- Provide a sufficient amount of supplies so that no more than two children have to share the same resource at a time. Certain supplies, such as scissors, should not be shared, because they can be dangerous when passed from child to child.
- Have plenty of cleanup supplies on hand for children and adults to use.
- Activities that make the hands messy should be set up very close to a water supply.
- Define areas in which certain materials must be kept. This can be done by such things as color coding the tables, hanging signs or symbols, placing tape on the floor, or teaching simple rules such as "clean hands only" on the rug, at the computer, or in the book corner.

pieces. Others may cherish every piece they have touched. Work that expresses a particular feeling or subject may be highly valued. Art that the child intends as a "gift" will be viewed differently than art that is done just because the materials are there and the mood struck. When children of all ages use the arts as an emotional release or to express feelings, the end result is viewed as an extension of themselves. Its treatment is taken personally.

Adults may have a difficult time ascertaining how a child feels about a particular piece of artwork. Often this is not verbalized by the child. It is always best if the adult treats all children's artwork with respect. This models for the children how deeply adults value them and the work they produce.

We need to keep track of our students' artwork and handle it with care.

Displays of children's work can have many purposes. Including an interactive component, such as the matching question on this printing display, invites the viewer to think about the work and will attract a closer look.

Put on names. Strive to put names on the back of all pieces of work. Attach pencils or markers to walls and easels with Velcro so that they are always handy. Develop a shorthand code, or use initials if pressed for time. If there are different sessions in the program, consider using a different-color marker for each session. For example, all of the green names might belong to the A.M. group, and all of the orange ones to the P.M. group. Label a shelf, cubby, or floor space with each child's name, and teach children to put their projects in their spots. Holding up children's artwork and saying "Whose is this?" tells the children that we did not care enough to notice what arts activities they were participating in that day.

Avoid folding artwork. If artwork is too large to fit in a space, then roll it up. Folded artwork can never be mounted properly. If stored for a period of time, it will tear at the folds. Arts portfolios need to be large enough to hold the largest-size paper that individual children use.

Discarding work. There will always be a few pieces of artwork that remain unidentified, no matter how hard we strive to label them all. If artwork must be discarded, do so discreetly. When children see artwork in the trash, they worry that the same thing may happen to theirs. Make sure parents are taught to do the same thing. Many children become disillusioned about creating visual art, because "it will just get thrown away at home."

Teacher Tip

MOUNTING TWO-DIMENSIONAL ARTWORK

Supplies Needed:
colored construction paper
scissors
stapler or white glue

METHOD 1: SINGLE MOUNT

1. Select a piece of construction paper slightly larger than the artwork. If the paper is the same size as the largest piece of construction paper, then overlap two sheets to make the mount larger. Artwork can be trimmed to make neater edges or so a smaller mount can be used. Trim up to one inch around the edges, as long as no part of the artwork is being cut off. Avoid cutting off any major part of the work, such as turning rectangular paintings into circles or bear shapes. Standard paper sizes can be mounted on the next size up (8-1/2 by 11 inches on 9 by 12 inches, 12 by 18 inches on 18 by 24 inches, and 18 by 24 inches on 24 by 36 inches).
2. Center the artwork. If desired, the bottom border can be slightly larger than the top.
3. Staple or glue the artwork to mount. If gluing, place a small line of white glue around the edge of the work. Never put glue in the center of the work, because it can cause wrinkles or discoloration.
4. Attach the child's name to the mount using a self-stick label or staple on a piece of paper.

METHOD 2: DOUBLE MOUNTS

1. Cut a piece of white or black paper so that it is one inch longer and wider than the artwork on all sides.
2. Center artwork and white/black mount on a larger piece of colored construction paper, and glue or staple.

OTHER METHODS

1. Commercial mats are available to fit standard sizes of paper. They give a finished look to the artwork and can be used and reused for exhibits or special displays (see Appendix C).
2. Small pieces by the same child or several children can be mounted on one large backing paper.
3. Glue a corrugated cardboard strip or dowel to the back upper edge of the artwork. Punch holes in each end of the cardboard, and attach a piece of yarn for hanging. This works well for projects done on cloth.
4. Purchase several glass or Plexiglas frames in a size that fits most artwork produced. Tape a selected piece into the frame. Change the framed artwork on a regular basis. This system works well for work displayed in offices and bathrooms.
5. Avoid using trash items, such as Styrofoam trays, that trivialize the artwork.

Prepare work attractively. Make sure that all artwork that goes home or is displayed is properly labeled and presented.

Keep hands off. Children's artwork is their own. Maintain a hands-off policy. Avoid drawing or working on a child's artwork to make it "better." This is insulting to the child artist and reflects a lack of self-confidence on the part of the educator.

Create a presentation center. An area may be set up where artwork is prepared to go home or to be put into the portfolio. This area can be a small table or shelf containing a stapler, colored paper in various sizes, markers, and preprinted labels.

When children finish a drawing or another dry project, or on the following day for projects that have been left overnight to dry (such as paintings, prints, and collages), the artwork is brought to the table. Ask the child to select a color for the background mount. Staple the artwork on the mount along with the label and any art notes for the family. The child then takes the work to a designated storage place or portfolio. If a child does produce a series of artworks on one day or over several days, they can be stapled together between two mounting sheets to form a book of art.

Photographs, musical compositions, and other arts creations can also be prepared at the presentation table.

Classroom Displays and Thematic Centers

In the classroom itself, we need to carefully consider our purpose in displaying the children's creative work. Some teachers do it as a form of self-flattery rather than as a way to educate the children. Hanging everyone's paintings or collages at the same time creates an overwhelming display—fine for a special occasion but hard to live with day after day. It does not take long for the art to be treated as just a colorful background.

Selecting work. Focus can be created by limiting classroom displays to a selection of works that illustrate the learning that is going on or that acknowledge the artistic accomplishment of one or a few children at a time. Remember that despite this seemingly limiting suggestion, each day the room will still be filled with art—art that is in the process of being made—paintings at the easel, sculptures of play dough on the table, and puppets on the stage.

Artist of the week. One way to create a purposeful display is to establish an artist of the week or month. Select one child to be "artist of the week," and put up a few pieces of child-selected artwork with accompanying photographs of the child involved in the process of creating it. It will make that one child's piece of work much more special and will eliminate the urge to compare the work of one child to another. Make sure the works are displayed at a child's height, and in a location where they will not be damaged by splashing water or wandering hands.

Accompany the piece with a photograph of the artist, a transcribed interview, and/or dictation about the piece. Take time to introduce the child and the artwork to the group. Discuss it with a group in the same way a print would be discussed. Chapter 7 provides lists of questions you can ask. Hang the artwork in a place of honor. Because the artist is present, in addition to descriptive questions and statements, questions about technique can be answered:

This same approach can also be used to present a group project.

Share the other art forms created by the artist of the week as well. Tape the child singing and playing musical instruments and set up a listening center with a CD or tape recorder and headphones. Display photographs showing the child dancing and participating in dramatic play activities.

Thematic Displays and Centers

Another method is to create a display of thematically related works that adds to or creates a unique environment and elicits the creation of more art. For example, for an underwater theme, turn one corner of the room into an undersea environment with child-created sea creatures displayed in a glass aquarium. Hang an undersea mural on the wall. Drape fishnets and shells on the shelving, and place sea-theme sculptures among them. Place the sand or water table in the center. Children's drawings of fish can be displayed by the aquarium, along with fish books and photographs of fish. Children should participate in creating these displays and deciding how they will look and where they will be placed.

Public Displays of Children's Work

The purpose of public exhibits of children's art is different from home and classroom displays. The public arena is used to present the program to people who have not participated directly in the children's arts process. Public exhibits can greatly benefit an arts program by showing parents and the community what the children have been learning.

The purpose of the display should not be for self-satisfaction or competition. When the sole purpose of presentations of child art is to boost the egos of the children or the educators, then they can create pressure situations that are detrimental to the arts

Thematic centers are an important part of the classroom and can be carefully planned or emerge from students' interests. Adding a class-made papier-mâché rocket ship to the creative environment inspires children's imaginations to soar.

process. Fearful of being judged by families or outsiders, educators exhort the children to do their best because their families are going to see it, or they select creativity limiting step-by-step projects for the children to do, which they hope will make a good impression. Teachers may display work that they think is most adult pleasing and reject work that looks out of control or unpleasant. Some teachers think, "I can't show this. Their families will be so disappointed in them. They'll think I'm not teaching anything."

Competitions and judged art shows also do not belong in early arts education programs. They emphasize adult-pleasing products and foster the attitude that certain types of art are better than others. Such events may have a positive effect on the winners but can cause the losers to give up on arts creation entirely.

Teacher Tip

MOUNTING THREE-DIMENSIONAL ARTWORK

WALL MOUNTS

For work that is relatively lightweight, such as papier-mâché or cardboard sculptures, bulky but lightweight collages, small modeled sculptures, and fiber projects:

1. Straight pins: Use to mount bulky or thick items in showcases or on bulletin boards outside of classroom areas where art is displayed to the public. If the pins are hammered into the cork, they will remain very secure and should pose no danger to young children.
2. Wire or chenille stems: Use to attach lightweight sculptures to a heavy paper or cardboard base, which can then be stapled to the wall.
3. String or yarn: Tie to sculptures, and then suspend from pins, nails, or thumbtacks.
4. Boxes: Staple small boxes to a wall, or join a group of boxes together with glue, wire, paper fasteners, or chenille stems. Paint the boxes a neutral color, such as white or gray. Place small sculptures in each box.

FLOOR MOUNTS

For heavy, large, and/or delicate sculptures:

1. Raise work to child's eye level by using cardboard boxes of various sizes, painted in neutral colors.
2. Place oversized work on a piece of large paper, a cloth, or a rug to set it off from the rest of the floor.

Positive Public Presentations

The public presentation of child creative work can serve several positive functions that enhance an arts program. All depend on having a portfolio folio system in place. Presentations with such carefully considered purposes will ultimately lead to more genuine ego building than those that have "ego boosting" as their main purpose.

Educational. Carefully designed exhibits can help families and friends learn more about how and why young children create art. They can also teach about arts concepts and techniques and other curriculum areas, and they can help introduce adults to the arts created by people from other places and cultures.

A multitude of ideas exists for educational displays.

Artistic growth. To show artistic growth, display a series of works done by one child over a period of time. Accompany the display with photographs of children's hands illustrating different grips on art tools or anecdotal descriptions of how the works were created.

Arts elements. To show the arts elements, display a series of works by different children illustrating the use of line, shape, color, texture, form, or pattern. Accompany the display with bold graphics representing the arts element and children's descriptions of the element in their artwork. Photographs of children exploring sensory experiences related to the particular element can be included, as can children's books about the element.

Artistic techniques. To demonstrate a particular technique, select artworks done using that technique, such as papier-mâché puppets, clay bowls, or dyed-wool collages. Accompany the artworks with step-by-step photographs of how the children made them and their dictated or written explanations.

Multidisciplinary. Learning from other curriculum areas can be displayed by hanging charts and graphs, sample experiments, child-created comments and stories (experience charts), and photographs accompanied by any illustrative artwork the children created.

Cultural experiences. Experiences with artwork from other cultures can be shown by displaying artifacts or prints of the featured pieces, accompanied by descriptions of the culture and how they were made, along with children's artwork and photographs that reflect a related concept. For example, combine printed cloth from India with children's prints and photographs of children playing bells and finger cymbals from India, or Mexican clay pottery with children's clay forms and photographs of children dancing a Mexican folkdance.

Promotional. A well-put-together public display can introduce a program's best aspects. It can be a multimedia glimpse into the children's daily pursuits. A promotional display should give a feeling for the experiences in which the children participate. Select one or more pieces of artwork showing a range of techniques and approaches. Accompany the works with photographs of children creating and children's comments or explanations. Label displays with bold signs that attract attention, such as "Our Artists at Work" or "The Wonderful World of Paint." Examples of the range of promotional presentations include brochures and calendars, showcases and bulletin boards, and badges and T-shirts, all featuring children's creative work.

Teacher Tip

GUIDELINES FOR CLASSROOM DISPLAYS

Avoid clutter.
Display only one or a few pieces of art at a time.
Change displayed artwork frequently.

Locating the display. Depending on their purpose, these kinds of public displays can be located in a variety of places.

Walls outside of the children's workspace are convenient for educational and promotional displays. Lobbies, hallways, stairwells, doors, offices, bathrooms, and any other space that is visited on a regular basis by the public can be used.

HOW IS AN AESTHETIC ENVIRONMENT CREATED?

A teacher as an artist thinks and designs the classroom differently from a teacher as a researcher or a teacher as an administrator.

—*Renate Nummela Caine & Geoffrey Caine (1974, p. 123)*

There is more to designing a space for living or working than arranging the furniture and displaying work in a functional way. This is particularly true of workspaces for children. In selecting the individual elements that make up the children's learning environment, we must consider the ways in which these elements will enrich the children's perceptions and thereby influence their aesthetic experience. Although people have different aesthetic senses, and room designs will reflect the uniqueness of personal experiences, the following guidelines, based on principles of color, design, and children's behavior, are intended as an initial direction from which we can create a beautiful workspace for children.

Guidelines for Establishing an Aesthetic Environment

Whether the workspace is a large, formal classroom or a corner of a family room or kitchen, the basic guidelines that follow can be used to provide an aesthetic place for children to create.

Floor and walls. The floor is an important working area of the room. Carpeted areas provide softness and absorb sound. They provide needed cushioning for energetic movement activities, and quiet musical activities. Tiles and linoleum areas are easy to clean up when wet or sandy and make a good surface for block building and painting. Area rugs provide the most flexibility and can be used to divide areas visually and texturally.

The walls are also a major teaching area. They provide a place for wall-mounted activities, such as easels and mirrors, as well as a display space for the children's work. But very often the walls are overused. When they are plastered with signs and artwork and garish commercial bulletin board displays, they overload the senses and make the room a tiring place.

Wall displays need to be carefully selected and hung at the child's eye level. It is an eye-opening experience to lower ourselves to the children's height occasionally and see the environment we have prepared from their vantage point.

Color and texture. View the walls and floor as background for the objects that will be displayed in the room. Bright or strongly colored walls or floors are limiting, especially if we consider that most children's toys and clothes are brightly colored. Bright intense colors can make a room seem smaller and are tiresome after a while. Light, neutral colors such as white, off-white, or soft gray can allow the color scheme of the room to be varied simply by changing the colors in the displays and will allow the colorful toys to stand out from the background. Brightly colored areas can be created by putting up a temporary covering of colored paper.

Consider the textures and patterns of the various materials on the floors and walls of rooms as well. It is good to have a variety, but, keeping the colors of these items closely related prevents the effect from being overwhelming. Here again, neutral earth colors, including beiges, grays, and browns, and pastels can provide an unobtrusive background for brightly colored toys and arts materials.

Work surfaces. Light, neutral-colored backgrounds not only increase the aesthetic quality of a room but can also make the space seem larger. They provide an unobtrusive foil to the children's own choice of colors in their artwork. Avoid the overuse of bright and saturated colors and patterns in areas where children are creating and performing. Although initially attractive, they may quickly tire the senses and make it hard for children to concentrate on their own color use in their creative work.

Storage. Storage containers should enrich the environment, not detract from it. Baskets are art forms that provide a beautiful way to store many items. If using cardboard boxes, take the time to paint or cover them. Choose a unifying color that goes with the colors of other items in the room. When using purchased plastic bins or containers, try to get them in similar colors, such as all blues or white. Clear containers are the most versatile and allow the children to quickly see the contents.

Materials. Arts supplies and props need to be presented in ways that catch the eyes and tickle the senses. Inspiration can be drawn from the Reggio Emilia program where small items in clear jars are arranged by color and carefully selected materials are arranged by shape and size. Lella Gandini calls this "a gesture of offering something precious" (Gandini et al., 2005, p. 123). Children are more likely to choose thoughtfully and treat materials carefully when they are beautifully arranged.

Details. As much attention should be paid to the small details as to the larger objects in the room. In the play corner, are the dress-up clothes and the dolls' clothes and bedding made from cloth that looks and feels beautiful? Are there a variety of textures? Do the dishes and tableware match? Are the blocks carefully arranged by size and shape? Are the puzzles, games, and toys displayed so that each one is separate and clearly visible instead of piled indiscriminately in a basket or box? It is better to put out a limited selection of toys and games at a time and rotate them when the children begin to lose interest. Remember to remove and replace worn and broken items frequently (see Figure 6-2).

Displaying Nature

Adding live plants, aquariums, terrariums, and other displays of natural objects can also enrich the aesthetics of the environment. Set up slowly changing displays of natural objects, such as shells, leaves, or rocks. Arrange the objects by size, texture, or color, and provide magnifying glasses so children can study them more closely. Quantities of small natural objects, such as acorns, seeds, and pebbles, can be displayed on a shelf or windowsill. Use clear plastic jars and containers that allow light to pass through and are safe for children to turn, shake, and study how the objects move and re-form.

Expressing Personal Taste

Our environments mirror what we are. The colors, shapes, and patterns that appeal to one person may differ from what appeals to another. What we consider the ideal environment for children may change as we learn new teaching approaches or visit other classrooms. In fashioning environments in which children will create, there are unlimited possibilities. All of the suggestions in this chapter are starting points, not unbreakable rules. No two early childhood environments need to be alike, nor should they remain static. The environment should change as the children's interests and activities change, or as we explore new ways to create the ideal environment for children. The key element is flexibility. When flexibility is built into the room, we can create the best environment for our children.

Adding plants, animals, and other natural objects enhances the aesthetic qualities of the classroom as well as encouraging children to help care for their environment.

Assessing the Physical Arts Environment

Area Observed	*Condition: Acceptable/Needs Attention**				
	Organization	**Safety**	**Upkeep**	**Cleanliness**	**Aesthetics**
Art Work Displays					
Blocks					
Book Displays					
Bookmaking					
Child Art Displays					
Collage					
Computer					
Dramatic Art					
Drawing Supplies					
Easel					
Movement Area					
Music Area					
Modeling					
Painting					
Printing					
Sand					
Sensory Items					
Sink					
Storage					

*If an area needs attention, take action as soon as possible:

- Organization: Areas that need major straightening up daily after the children leave require reorganization.
- Safety: Places where children were injured or nearly injured need to be checked for hazards.
- Upkeep: Items that look worn or broken should be removed or fixed.
- Cleanliness: Dirty areas need to be looked at for ways to make them easier to clean during use.
- Aesthetics: Cluttered areas may be distracting. Too many colors may assault the senses. Materials may need to be rearranged to improve appearances.

FIGURE 6–2 Teachers must create beautiful environments in which children are comfortable and ready to learn.

CONCLUSION: CREATING A SENSE OF PLACE

The space has to be a sort of aquarium that mirrors ideas, values, attitudes, and cultures of the people who live within.

—Loris Malaguzzi
(Edwards et al., 1993, p. 149)

For many years the emphasis on places for children has been on ease of cleaning and efficient functioning. This has been the model for most public schools in the United States. One large space is intended to serve all purposes. It is not surprising that in such an environment, visual arts activities are limited to a multi-purpose table that has to be cleared off at snack time, some boxes of junk, and perhaps a lonely easel.

Music and dance rarely occur, and dramatic play is found only in the dress-up corner. Cooking and art often go on at the same sink. In order to create an environment that is conducive to arts creation, some major changes must occur in how we build and equip the basic room.

The key to an enticing, functional place for children to create artistically is an environment where children can focus on the activities and supplies available, work independently, and clean up when done. Guiding adults want an environment that is safe and functional and in which children can learn. But most of all the space should show that adults value the role of the arts, not as a playtime activity, but as an important way that children show us what they are thinking.

Although every space is unique, with careful planning it can meet these requirements. It is well worth the effort.

- Children behave better in environments that consider their needs.
- Space that is arranged so that teachers can move about easily and find needed supplies quickly helps them become more relaxed and attentive to the children as they create art.
- Beautiful workspaces inspire both adults and children to create their best work.

On the whole, our society suffers from a lack of aesthetic vision. Many homes are decorated with an accumulation of well-liked things that do not relate to each other. Our educational settings mirror this. Adults often feel that children need all of these things to use. But do they?

Sandboxes are filled with so many shovels and containers that there is no room for a child to just play with the sand. Styrofoam trays, wrapping paper, strips of carpet remnants, and some old yarn bits are shoved in a cardboard box, and then children are expected to make something beautiful from them. Dress-up clothes are heaped together in a corner. Children are overwhelmed; they do not learn to focus in such an environment. Adults need to teach them that there is beauty in each part, and that each part relates to the others to make the whole.

FURTHER READING

Clayton, M. K., & Forton, M. B. (2001). *Classroom spaces that work*. Greenfield, MA: Northeast Foundation for Children.

This book addresses the different needs of children ages four to eleven and provides a wealth of ideas to make classrooms better places for learning.

Curtis, D., & Carter, M. (2003). *Designs for living and learning*. St. Paul, MN: Redleaf.

This book presents ideas for classroom design taken from exemplary early childhood approaches to classroom organization, such as Montessori, Reggio Emilia, and the Waldorf Schools.

Gandini, L., Hill, L., Cadwell, L., & Schwall, C. (2005). *In the spirit of the studio: Learning from the Atelier of Reggio Emilia*. New York: Teachers College Press.

This book tells the story of how a preschool in a church basement was transformed into a beautiful environment for learning by teachers inspired by the Reggio Emilia preprimary schools in Italy.

For additional information on creating beautiful environments for learning visit our Web site at http://www.cengagebrain.com

TEACHING IN ACTION

Spaceship Command Center: A Box Project

The following excerpts from a teacher's journal show how the project approach and a flexible approach to room planning was used in a prekindergarten class to correlate children's interests in space with the arts, science, and language studies.

Week 1

Day 1: The idea: Mike, Bobby, and Jeff arrived all excited. It seems there was a show about space on TV last night. At meeting, all they wanted to do was talk about the spaceship. At blocks, they built a launch pad and used cardboard tubes as rockets.

Day 2: Discovering the depth of interest: Today I decided to read Ezra Jack Keats's *Regards to the Man in the Moon* (1981). Then I asked: "What do you think we would need for a trip into space?" What ideas! I couldn't write them down fast enough on the chart. Toby said she has a cousin who went to NASA Space Camp. I wonder if she could come for a visit? I must get in touch. I noticed that many of the paintings and drawings were about space today.

Day 3: What do we already know? Today I asked: "What do we know about space?" I made a huge web of children's ideas. I can see they have heard about stars, planets, and the sun, but not much else. There was a discussion about aliens and Star Wars. I must find some factual books about space. Not surprisingly, everyone was building a launch pad today at blocks!

Day 4: Building on the interest: I found out about a space exhibit at the discovery center. I called and arranged for a visit the end of next week. That gives me time to plan the bussing and the parent volunteers. We will use this time to read more about space and make a list of questions. I put a sheet up labeled "Our questions about space" in the meeting area. I put up a big poster of the solar system. Then I pretended I was the sun and the children were the planets, and they had a grand time circling around me to the music of "The Planets" by Gustav Holst. I will try to read another two pages and do a movement activity each day at morning meeting.

Day 5: Small groups begin: At small group time, I started off by having my group of children look at a picture of the space shuttle and then figure out what the different parts were. I wasn't surprised when Mike, Bobby, and Jeff asked if they could build a spaceship. Everyone started to call out ideas. I said, "Why don't we draw some pictures of our ideas?" Boy, did they work on those pictures! So much detail!

Carol [the aide] had her group looking at photographs of each of the planets and talking about the sizes, colors, and names. Some children in her group wanted to make a mural about space.

Week 2

Day 6: Group work continues: We found a huge roll of black paper. I hung it on the wall, and the children sat in front of it, and we tried to imagine the blackness of space. I gave them each a tube to look through and turned off the light. It was very effective. At group time we continued to work on sketches for the spaceship. We put out gold and silver tempera paint at the easel, and the children had a grand time painting stars and comets of all kinds to paste on the mural. The spaceship group made tons more sketches. Carol's group made planets.

Day 7: Finding direction: I read Gail Gibbons's *Stargazers* (1992, New York: Holiday House). I simplified the text a bit. Then I passed around a telescope for children to look through. They cut out and pasted their stars on the mural. They even made a Milky Way! I can't believe they had such patience to cut out even their little tiny stars. We had so many we even hung some from the ceiling. Then we sat in front of the mural and sang "Twinkle, Twinkle Little Star" and made wishes. Suddenly someone said, I think it was Jeff, "Why don't we make our spaceship in front of the mural so we will be heading into space. . . like we could have a big window. The captain and his mates could sit here and look out."

Day 8: Building begins: Toby's cousin couldn't come, but she sent in a videotape of the training. We watched it twice. The second time we looked for ideas for our spaceship. We added seat cushions and seatbelts to the parent wish list by the door. We decided to move a table in front of the mural, and I cut open a large cardboard box. The children drew big windows, and I cut them out. Then they painted it. Now I have taped it to the table, and it looks great! They have already set up three chairs and sit there counting down.

Day 9: Our trip—What did we learn? It was wonderful! The children were so well behaved. I could see that all of our preparations made a big difference. They had a space shuttle model the children could go inside. When we got back, the first thing they wanted to do was make the control panel like the one at the museum. But I got everyone together first, and we wrote down the answers on our question chart.

(continued)

TEACHING IN ACTION *(continued)*

Then I got out some boxes, and everyone helped paint them. It was a good release after being so controlled all morning at the museum.

Day 10: The command center: It's done! I can't believe the children had such a great idea. We put some low boxes on the table and the bigger ones on the floor around it. Catie had the idea of using bottle lids for the dials. I attached them with chenille stems so they turn. Then the best idea of all was Louie's. He said, "Why don't we put the computer here?" At the museum, there was a computer in the spaceship. So we did! Some parents even brought in cushions and belts for the chairs. We all took a turn sitting in the command seats. Wow! Next week I will put out paper bags with pre-cut openings so they can make helmets if they wish. But the funny thing was when my colleague, Joanne, poked her head in and said, "What book gave you that neat idea for a computer center?" "It's not in a book," I said. "It grew in the children's imaginations."

Murals can be used as backdrops to creative play centers, such as "Wild Things" a marker and tempera mural created by children of mixed ages, 4 to 8.

Studio Page

BECOMING SENSITIVE TO OUR ENVIRONMENT

The following activities are designed to provoke thought about the environments in which we exist and the effect they have on our feelings and behavior.

1. Make a list of places where you feel most relaxed. Categorize them as soft or hard, open or closed, private or social.

    ____
    ____
    ____

2. Make a list of all of the different environments you spend time in each day, such as the bedroom, kitchen, classroom, bus, and so on. Describe your behavior in each environment in terms of how you move, talk, and dress, and whether you feel comfortable or not.

    ____
    ____
    ____

3. Based on what you wrote above, describe the perfect environment for you.

    ____
    ____
    ____
    ____
    ____
    ____
    ____
    ____
    ____
    ____
    ____

Studio Page

OBSERVATION: AESTHETICS OF AN ENVIRONMENT

Choose a room in a home or school where children do artwork. Examine this room's aesthetic effect. Use the information and Figure 6-2 in this chapter as a guide.

1. What are the background colors in this room?
   Walls: ______________________________
   Ceiling: ______________________________
   Floor: ______________________________
   Floor coverings: ______________________________
2. What is displayed on each wall? Be specific. Make a sketch if necessary.
   Wall 1: ______________________________
   Wall 2: ______________________________
   Wall 3: ______________________________
   Wall 4: ______________________________
3. Are there any sensory displays? If yes, describe them.
4. How are toys, games, and books displayed?
5. What is the total aesthetic effect of this room? Is there anything you would change to make it more aesthetically pleasing for children?
6. Do you think the room encourages or discourages children's artistic behavior? Is there anything you might change? Draw sketches of your ideas.

Studio Page

DESIGNING THE ENVIRONMENT

Keeping in mind what the children will be learning about the arts, design an ideal environment.

1. On this graph paper is outlined a room 14-by-20 feet. (Scale: one square equals one foot.)
2. Trace the scaled pattern pieces on Studio Page 24, or design your own.
3. Cut them out, and try several possible arrangements to create an environment that would be ideal for young artists.
4. Plan areas for activities that are wet and messy, quiet and comfortable, creative and dramatic, and involve kinesthetic movement.
5. Consider all of the different arts activities that could take place in each area, and then indicate where supplies would be located.

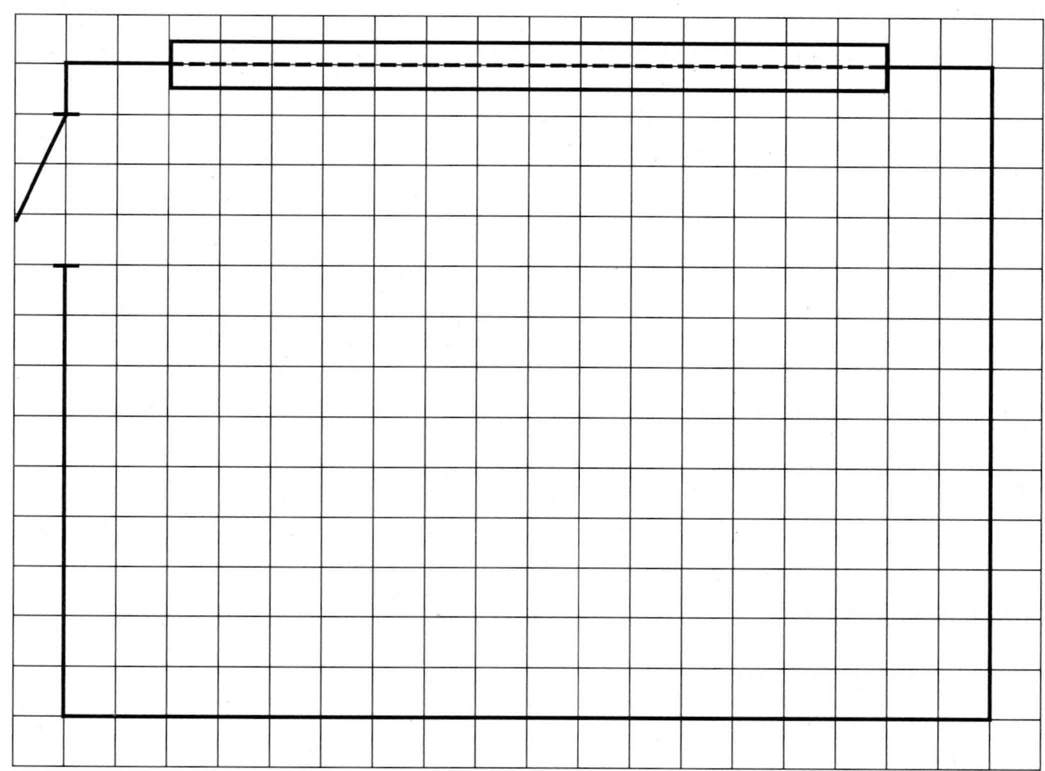

Studio Page

SCALED FURNITURE PIECES

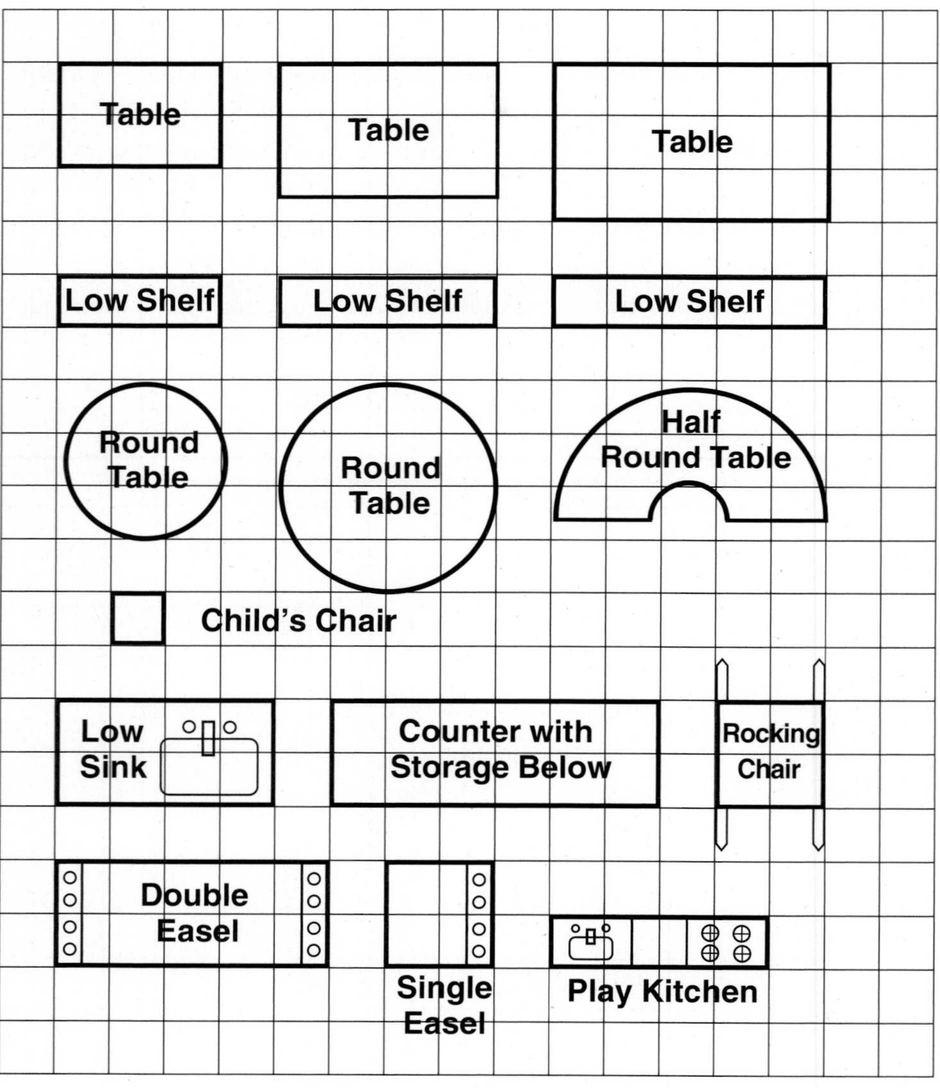

Chapter

7

Introducing the World's Arts

Questions Addressed in This Chapter:

- What do children learn from the arts of others?
- How should artworks be selected?
- Why include arts from other cultures?
- How can children's literature be used to teach about the arts?
- How are artworks, prints, and artifacts used with children?
- How can community resources be used?

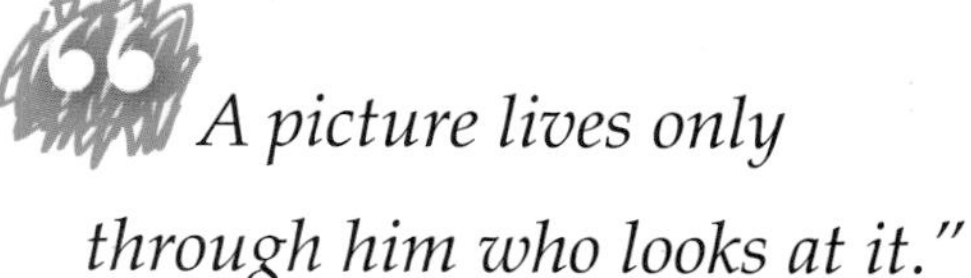

"A picture lives only through him who looks at it."

—Pablo Picasso (cited in Bruner, 1979, p. 22)

Young Artists at Work

"What are those things?" Brian whispers.

"I think they're spaceships," his friend Allen replies.

"No, silly, can't you see they're whirlies?" says Shannon.

"What's a whirly?"

"That's when you take a brush and whirl it all around."

"Oh," says Michael thoughtfully, "I do that when I paint, too."

"Well," says the teacher, coming up behind the children, "I see you have discovered our new print, Van Gogh's *Starry Night.* Come over to the rug, and I'll read you a story about the artist. It's called *Camille and the Sunflowers*" (Anholt, 1994).

WHAT DO CHILDREN LEARN FROM THE ARTS OF OTHERS?

> *Fine taste in the arts, or in any other aspect of life, cannot be specifically taught nor suddenly acquired. It develops slowly and subtly as a result of frequent exposure to examples which various cultures and generations have recognized as significant.*
>
> —*Aline D. Wolf (1984, p. 21)*

Children absorb many meanings from their environment. The songs teachers select to sing, the pictures they hang on the wall, and the knickknacks on the shelf all show what artistic styles and forms those teachers personally value. In selecting arts experiences, we must look not only to children's own creations but also to the music, dance, drama, and artwork that express their cultural and historical roots. The human-made creative works that surround children when they are young will impact how they will judge other artwork they encounter throughout life. People tend to like those things with which they feel comfortable and to reject the strange and unfamiliar. It is a basic principle of good advertising to bombard customers' senses until the product is so familiar that they choose it almost automatically. We must decide what we would like the objects and experiences in our children's environment to advertise.

After looking at Van Gogh's painting *Starry Night* this child painted her own version of a star-filled sky.

Expanding the Child's Definition of the Arts

Young children create their own drawings, paintings, songs, dances, and stories as part of their way of interacting with and learning about the world, but exposure to the arts of others helps them understand why artistic works are created, who is an artist, a musician, a composer, a dancer, a choreographer, a storyteller, or an actor, and how these art forms are a part of their everyday environment. By interacting with carefully selected creative works, children learn that the arts are more than just "messing around for fun." The children learn that the arts are not just what they do when they paint at the easel or beat on a drum. They learn that when they are exploring arts forms they are participating in a long chain of human creativity.

In addition, surrounding children with exciting artworks to explore with all of their senses provides them with the impetus to practice the cognitive skills of describing and responding to the arts. The ability to understand creative works extends far beyond experiencing them. Teaching children to notice the way different artists have created works of art, music, dance, and drama sets the stage for a more sophisticated understanding of the arts.

HOW SHOULD CREATIVE WORKS BE SELECTED?

If young children delight in looking at picture books of bunnies, babies, and bears, why not paintings such as Da Vinci's Mona Lisa, Van Gogh's Starry Night, Renoir's Girl with a Watering Can, or Chagall's Peasant Life?

—Joyce Mesrobian (1992, p. 19)

In order to select the best adult creative works to share with children, we must rely on more than our own personal values about what kind of art is pleasing to us. We must expand our own knowledge so children will be exposed not only to the styles of the arts with which their heritage and upbringing have made them comfortable, and the arts that reflect their background, but also those works that allow them to experience a wide range of artistic inventiveness across the spectrum of culture, age, gender, time, and technique.

Criteria for Selection

In selecting works to share our goal should be to help children value the very essence of artistic creation, regardless of the artist or the origin of the work. By exposing children to a wide range of art forms, we prepare them to be accepting of others' creativity wherever they encounter it, throughout their lives. As Gardner (1991, p. 101) states, "models initially encountered by children continue to affect their tastes and preferences indefinitely, and these preferences prove very difficult to change."

Begin by looking for works that reflect a range of styles. **Style** refers to the way something is done that is unique to the individual or culture that produced it.

Artworks from other countries and cultures can show children that artists use the same art elements they do. This Peruvian clay whistle shows color, form, pattern, and texture.

Tables 7-1, 7-2, and 7-3 list some of the many styles found in music, dance, and art.

As you select works to share with the children, strive for a balanced representation of different subject matters, media, styles, and places of origin. Make sure that each piece is engaging for young children. It does not matter if it is a great masterpiece, represents an important culture, or is a favorite song; it will not interest children if the subject matter or meaning is too complex for them to understand.

Selected works should illustrate the following concepts:

1. People of many different ages create works of art.
2. The arts have been made by people from many places and times.
3. The arts tell us about the lives of other people.
4. The arts are made using a wide variety of materials, tools, and instruments that reflect the environment and choice of the creator.
5. There are many ways or styles of art.
6. The arts are found in many places in our environment.

TABLE 7–1 Major Styles of Western Music

Caribbean:	Music from the Caribbean that incorporates elements from Native American, African, and European traditions. Percussion plays a major role as well as call and response vocals. Examples: salsa, reggae, Puerto Rican bomba, aguinaldo, jiharo, Cuban punto, mambo, rumba, and Jamaicas mentó.
Classical:	Music based on the Baroque style of the 1700s. Common forms include the concerto, piano sonata, string quartet, and symphony. Composers: Ludwig van Beethoven, Franz Hayden, and Wolfgang Amadeus Mozart.
Country:	Country music is a blend of musical forms found in the southern part of the United States. Its roots are from English and Celtic folksongs, blues, and gospel music.
Folk:	Music that is learned by ear rather than from printed music and is passed from generation to generation, undergoing changes in style and meaning over time. Folk music is usually performed by untrained singers and musicians and reflects the culture that created it.
Gospel:	Religious music based on African-American traditions, particularly spirituals sung by slaves and the tradition of sanctified churches in which members spoke and sung out spontaneously.
Jazz:	This style of music developed in New Orleans in the 1890s based on African-American rhythms. Musicians/Composers: Louis Armstrong, Bessie Smith, Theolonious Monk, and Charlie Parker.
Latin:	Music from Central and South America influenced by Spanish, African, and Native American cultures. Examples: bossa nova, Brazilian, calypso, flamenco, mariachi, merengue, and tango.
Marching:	Music composed with a strong regular beat, and almost always in a major key, to accompany marching. Composers: Kenneth Alford, Edoardo Boccalari, and John Phillip Sousa.
Modern Classical:	Music using classical forms but exploring unusual tonalities and combinations to achieve emotional self-expression. Composers: Benjamin Britten, Claude Debussy, Gustave Mahler, Joseph-Maurice Ravel, Arnold Schoenberg, and Igor Stravinsky.
Native American:	Choral vocals, rhythmic syllables, and antiphonal singing characterize traditional Native American music. Music is not always composed, but rather improvised to reflect spiritual and social needs. A wide range of drums, rattles, and flutes are commonly used instruments. Examples: Jay Begaye, Sissy Goodhouse, Six Nations Women Singers, and Judy Trejo.
Opera:	A type of theater in which almost the entire story is told through song and music. Composers: Georges Bizet, Wolfgang Amadeus Mozart, Giacomo Puccini, Richard Wagner, and Guiseppe Verdi.
R&B or Rhythm and Blues:	A musical form developed originally by urban African-American communities and found in rock, country, western, and gospel. It is characterized by a four-beat measure and a backbeat that is found in much popular music. Examples: blues, doo-wop, soul, Motown, funk, disco, and rap.
Rock & Roll:	Music growing out of African-American and country music influences in the 1950s. It features heavy percussion and electrified instruments such as guitars, keyboards, and synthesizers. Examples: Elvis Presley, the Beatles, and the Rolling Stones.
Romantic Classical:	1800s painted pictures. Composers: Georges Bizet, Frederick Chopin, Antonin Dvorak, and Edvard Grieg.
Show:	Music composed for musical plays in which the story is told through song and dance. Composers: Leonard Bernstein, Richard Rogers and Oscar Hammerstein, and Alan J. Lerner and Frederick Loewe.
Swing:	Dance music that grew out of the jazz tradition and performed by the big bands of the 1930s. Musicians/Composers: Glenn Miller and Benny Goodman.

Selecting Music

Many musical works pleasing to children have simple harmonies and patterns with a consistent beat. In general, it makes sense to introduce musical works played by a **solo** instrument or small group before listening to a **symphony.** However, this should not be the only music they hear. Children can also listen to and appreciate more complex styles, such as classical and jazz pieces. It is important to play many different styles of music as these early experiences help establish later musical preferences.

In particular, the baroque period of 1600 to 1750 produced music with rhythms that often match that of the heartbeat. This ties the music to the child's natural body

TABLE 7–2 Styles of dance

Style	Description
Ballet:	A formal form of dance based on precise movements.
Bolero:	A Spanish dance that has many sudden pauses.
Buck and wing:	An energetic tap dance style that involves leaps.
Cha-cha:	A fast dance in which you move backward and forward and side to side in a 1–2–123 pattern.
Conga:	An Afro-Congan dance performed by holding on to the person in front of you and moving side to side in rhythm to the music.
Hora or horo:	Circle dances traditionally performed in Israel, Greece, and the Balkans.
Hula:	A Hawaiian dance involving swaying of the body and graceful arm movements.
Limbo:	Dancers bend under a stick that is lowered each time while moving rhythmically to the music.
Macarena:	A Latin American–influenced line dance.
Minuet:	A very slow, stately Baroque dance in ¾ time in which couples move together in a line.
Polka:	A fast lively partner dance in ¾ time.
Salsa:	A fast jazz-influenced dance from Latin America.
Shuffle:	A dance in which the feet slide along the floor.
Square dance:	A dance in which two couples perform a series of formal moves announced by a caller.
Tap:	Fast complex footwork done wearing shoes with metal taps on the bottoms.
Twist:	A dance in which the torso is violently twisted.
Waltz:	A slow partner dance in ¾ time.

rhythms. The most famous composer of this period was Johann Sebastian Bach, and his work is considered the most musically complex. His original works, not those watered down for children, should be high on the list of what is played for infants and toddlers (Shore & Strasser, 2006). Chapter 10 provides more information on selecting musical works for young children.

Teacher Tip

SOME WORKS OF JOHANN SEBASTIAN BACH

- *Brandenburg Concertos Nos. 1–6*
- *Cantata: Sheep May Safely Graze*
- *Concerto for Two Violins in D Minor*
- *Keyboard Concerto #4*
- *Orchestral Suite No. 2 in B Minor*
- *Orchestral Suite No. 3 in D Major*
- *Violin Concerto No. 1 in D Minor*
- *Prelude in C Major*

Selecting Dance

Formal dancing instruction is not appropriate for young children. However, children can be introduced to styles of dance and then allowed to incorporate these styles as they move in their own ways to the music. Select dance forms that have a few repetitious movements that closely match the words or accompanying music, such as are found in folk dances. Choose works that allow individual creative movements, and do not require rigid conformity to prescribed dance steps or that are based on matching one's steps to that of another. For example, a Greek circle dance allows more freedom of movement than does a square dance.

Young children can also attend dance performances that feature ballet and cultural dance forms from around the world. Make sure such performances are geared for young children's short attention spans. Chapter 11 provides more information on selecting forms of dance for young children.

TABLE 7–3	Major Styles of Western Art
Abstract Expressionism:	Art having no recognizable subject, with a focus on color and media, often applied in a kinesthetic way. Artists: Willem De Kooning, Hans Hofmann, Jackson Pollock, and Wassily Kandinsky.
Abstraction:	Art that is based on real images but uses them as design elements. Artists: Constantin Brancusi, Lyonel Feininger, Paul Klee, Henry Matisse, Henry Moore, and Joan Miró.
Cubism:	Art that represents three-dimensional objects as if made of geometric shapes and forms. Artists: Paul Cézanne, Georges Braque, and Pablo Picasso.
Expressionism:	Art that focuses on showing emotions. Artists: Paul Gauguin, Edvard Munch, Vincent Van Gogh, and Georges Rouault.
Folk Art:	Art done by people who have not had formal training in art, or who use nontraditional art media. Artists: David Butler, the "Tin Man," Grandma Moses, and Henri Rousseau.
Impressionism:	Art that focuses on capturing the effect of light. Artists: Mary Cassatt, Edgar Degas, Claude Monet, and Pierre Auguste Renoir.
Kinetic Art:	Art that moves or has moving parts. Artist: Alexander Calder.
Nonobjective:	Art based on geometric and organic shapes and forms. Artists: Piet Mondrian, Hans Hofmann, and Franz Kline.
Op Art:	Art based on visual illusions and perceptions. Artists: Frank Stella and Victor Vasarely.
Pointillism:	Art that uses small dots of different colors that the eye blends together. Artists: Georges Seurat and Camille Pissarro.
Pop Art:	Art that is based on images from everyday life and popular culture, such as soup cans, clothespins, and cartoons. Artists: Jasper Johns, Roy Lichtenstein, Claus Oldenburg, and Andy Warhol.
Realism:	Art that focuses on showing reality. Sometimes it is also called representational. Artists: John Audubon, Leonardo DaVinci, Winslow Homer, Edward Hopper, Georgia O'Keeffe, Maxfield Parrish, Rembrandt Van Rijn, Grant Wood, and Andrew Wyeth.
Romanticism:	Art that attempts to make everything look more beautiful and wonderful than in reality. Artists: Albert Bierstadt, William Blake, John Constable, John Copley, Eugène Delacroix, Jacques David, and William Turner.
Surrealism:	Art that focuses on fantasies or dreams. Artists: Marc Chagall, Salvadore Dalí, and Frida Kahlo.

Selecting Dramatic Performances

Children's theater provides a wonderful introduction to the world of the stage. Short, interactive works performed by adults familiar with young children will provide role models for children's own dramatic play. Works that act out familiar stories and fairy tales are of particular interest, especially if we read the story to the children before they see it performed. Puppet shows, operas, and musicals are appropriate for young children. Although recorded productions can be shared, the experience lacks the reality of seeing a play performed on a stage, being little different from watching a television show. It is, therefore, worth the effort to take children to a performance or arrange for performers to visit your program. Investigate what is available locally by contacting local theater groups, high school and college drama classes, opera companies, and arts-in-education programs. Many non-profit traveling children's theater groups can be contacted as well.

Selecting Visual Artworks

No matter what style is used, children relate best to visual artworks that have subjects that they can identify with on a very basic level, such as faces, children, and people involved in activities, animals, nature scenes, and places. This does not mean that the pictures can only show familiar subjects, but they should have something on which children can base their understanding. Children who have never seen a red poppy can relate to the flower element of Georgia O'Keeffe's *Red Poppy*. They do not have to have lived in the sixteenth century to identify with the child in Rembrandt's *Girl with Broom*. They will also enjoy **abstract** and **nonobjective** works that resemble their own artwork, and works such as René Magritte's *Raining Cats and Dogs* that involve visual puns or tricks.

Sources of Information about Creative Works

We need to take the time to learn all that we can about the history and stories that relate to each creative we present to children. The more we know about a painting, **sonata,** or play, the more confidently we will be able to share it. Many wonderful children's books on artists, musicians, dancers, actors, and playwrights as well as about the many forms of art can be consulted. They can provide interesting facts to share about the selected pieces. Look in this chapter for specific books about artists and their art. These will help you become familiar with the major styles of **Western** and **non-Western art** and the different subject matter and media that artists have used.

Book Box

Books about artists.

Anholt, L. (1994). *Camille and the sunflowers*. Hauppauge, NY: Barron's Educational Series.

Anholt, L. (1996). *Degas and the little dancer*. Hauppauge, NY: Barrons.

Anholt, L. (1998). *Picasso and the girl with a ponytail*. Hauppauge, NY: Barrons.

Anholt, L. (2000). *Leonardo and the flying boy*. Hauppauge, NY: Barrons.

Anholt, L. (2003). *The magical garden of Claude Monet*. New York: Barrons.
This series of books by Anholt are fictionalized stories about famous artists, told through the experiences of a young child who befriends them. Four and up.

Collins, D. R. (1990). *Country artist: A story of Beatrix Potter.* New York: Carolrhoda Books.
A simple biography about Beatrix Potter and her wonderful stories for children. Four and up.

Hayward, J. (2005). *Come look with me: Discovering African American art.* Watertown, NY: Charlesbridge.
Thought-provoking questions accompany the work of African-American artists of the twentieth century. There are many other books in this series as well. Five and up.

Winter, J. (2003). *My name is Georgia*. New York: Harcourt Brace.
This book briefly tells about the life of Georgia O'Keefe. The illustrations are inspired by her paintings. Four and up.

Winter, J. (1991). *Diego*. New York: Random House.
This Spanish/English biography of Mexican muralist Diego Rivera focuses on his childhood and youth. Six and up.

Books about musicians

Ehrhardt, K. (2006). *This jazz man*. New York: Harcourt.
Using the children's song, "This Old Man," ten famous jazz musicians are introduced. A biography of each is found at the end of the book. Three and up.

Lach, W. (2006). *Can you hear it?* New York: Abrams.
Classical pieces of music are paired with well-known artworks in this book and a CD set that asks children to look and listen is included. Four and up.

Weatherford, C. B. (2008). *Before John was a jazz giant*. New York: Henry Holt.
In jazzy language John Coltrane is depicted as a young child surrounded by the sounds that later influenced his music. Four and up.

Books about dancers

Ancona, G. (2010). *Ole! Flamenco*. New York: Lee and Low.
Vivid photographs follow a young New Mexican dancer as she learns about the history and art of flamenco dancing. Four and up.

Reich, S. (2005). *Jose! Born to dance*. New York: Simon & Schuster.
The story of dancer and choreographer Jose Limon as he struggles to become a dancer. The sensory images of the brief text make this a good book for young children. Five and up.

Tallchief, M., & Wells, R. (1999). *Tallchief: America's premier ballerina*. New York: Viking.
Beautiful pastel drawings and a sensitive text describe Maria Tallchief's journey from the Osage Indian reservation to the New York stage. Five and up.

WHY INCLUDE ARTS FROM OTHER CULTURES?

How can we teach the essence of a people—Native American people, for instance? We can't, but we can do better than bows and arrows.

—*Patty Greenberg (1992, p. 30)*

It is important when selecting pieces to share to include examples of artwork from diverse cultures. The arts communicate more than stereotypes or bald facts. Children can learn about a culture and its people from looking at its arts and talking about how and why they are made. In the process they come to understand the use and importance of artwork in that culture.

When children see that the art of their culture and the art of other cultures contain many similarities, that culture becomes less strange and more appreciated. A simple woven basket from Botswana can link a small African village where baskets are used for carrying and storing grains, fruits, and peanuts to a preschool where similar baskets are used to hold some of the art supplies. African masks can be compared to those worn by people on Halloween, by characters on TV, and in plays and movies. All over the world artists have created art, music, dance, and drama for the same purposes—to beautify their homes, to make everyday things distinctive, to make a personal statement, to tell their stories or record their history, and to express their spiritual beliefs. The arts unite all of humankind.

When children see the arts of their heritage displayed and honored, they feel valued as people. When they see the arts of others treated with respect, they learn to value people who are different. Children model their behavior on adults' behavior. When we share the arts with children, we must consider the message our selection gives about which styles and cultures are important, and how the discussion of these works will affect the children. Before we can teach children to relate to the arts of the world, we ourselves must come to love and understand the arts of others. We will always have our personal favorites, just as the children will, but as we live and work with each piece, it will become an old friend from which we will not wish to part.

Look for interesting hand-crafted musical instruments from around the world to share with children. Here are an Indonesian frog rasp, a Peruvian shaker, a hand-carved Peruvian gourd, and a bell from India.

In selecting works of art, music, dance, and drama, make sure that they are representative of the culture, and that each piece is accorded respect and understanding.

1. Examples of **multicultural arts** should be displayed and performed in our rooms every day. Avoid trivializing the work of others by showing it only in the context of a particular holiday or art project.
2. Strive for balance. Collect examples from many racial and ethnic groups.
3. Respect the integrity of the works and the particular time, place, and person who created it. Avoid disconnecting the work from its creators by having the children copy the style, symbols, or the design of the work without exploring the original reasons the work was made. Making a paper copy of an African mask in a school setting is not the same as the ritualistic carving of a wooden mask by an African artist.
4. Avoid stereotypes. Collect works that show different racial and ethnic groups involved in all kinds of common activities. Make sure that the examples are not just from the past, but include creative works made by living artists, musicians, choreographers, and playwrights.

Book Box

Books about the world's arts.

Aliki. (2005). *Ah, music!* New York: HarperCollins.
Written in Aliki's signature style, this book introduces all aspects of world music in a child-friendly way. Six and up.

Levine, R. (2000). *Story of the orchestra.* New York: Blackdog & Leventhal.
Listen to the CD as you join Orchestra Bob in learning about instruments, classical music, and composers. Intended for older children, it is full of fun facts to share with younger children and is a great resource for teachers to learn more about classical music. Teacher resource.

Murphy, L. (2007). *A dictionary of dance.* San Francisco, CA: Blue Apple Books.
An alphabet of dance vocabulary is livened up with delightful illustrations. Four and up.

Sayre, H. S. (2004). *Cave paintings to Picasso: The inside scoop on 50 masterpieces.* San Francisco, CA: Chronicle Books.
Fifty artworks from many cultures around the world are explained alongside full-color illustrations of each one. An excellent timeline is illustrated with the works. This is an excellent book for teachers to use in learning about individual artworks. Seven and up.

Wolfe, G. (2001). *Oxford first book of art.* New York: Oxford University Press.
Artworks from around the world are grouped by themes, such as mother and child and patterns. Another excellent resource for teachers. Six and up.

HOW CAN CHILDREN'S LITERATURE BE USED TO TEACH ABOUT THE ARTS?

Even if we do not know any artists, musicians, dancers, actors, or if we live far from suitable museums and theaters, we can still introduce children to great art. Many books focus on the history of the arts or on individual artists and performers.

The picture books that teachers read to children are also pieces of art. For many children it is the picture that first entices them to the world of books, and books for the very youngest children are often wordless. In selecting books to share with young artists, always consider the importance of the pictures, not just as illustrations of the story but also as aesthetic statements.

Reading books about artists, musicians, dancers, and actors from many times and places is another way to bring the art of the world into the classroom.

Picture books should be chosen on the same basis as artworks. Make sure that a variety of artistic media, styles, and cultures are represented in the books that are offered. Specific descriptions of a multitude of children's books are found in the book boxes in each chapter. Make sure to have some examples from the following categories to introduce to the children.

- **Caldecott Winners**—The Caldecott award is given each year to an outstandingly illustrated children's book. Select those that are on the children's level.
- **Media**—Look for books that illustrate some of the less common art techniques, such as *Red Leaf Yellow Leaf* (Ehlert, 1991), which uses natural materials in collages to create three-dimensional images.
- **Multicultural**—Include books that feature art forms from other cultures, such as *Abuela's Weave* (Castaneda, 1993), which tells how weaving fits into the life of a girl and her grandmother in Guatemala.
- **Big Books**—For group sharing, have several big books in which the children can easily see the illustrations. More and more books are now available in this format.

Book Box

Recent Caldecott Award winners.

1990 Young, Ed. *Lon Po Po: A Red-Riding Hood story from China*. New York: Philomel.

1991 Macaulay, David. *Black and white*. Boston: Houghton.

1992 Wiesner, David. *Tuesday*. New York: Clarion.

1993 McCully, Emily Arnold. *Mirette on the high wire*. New York: Putnam.

1994 Say, Allen. *Grandfather's journey*. Boston: Houghton.

1995 Bunting, Eve. *Smoky night*. Illustrated by David Diaz. San Diego: Harcourt.

1996 Rathmann, Peggy. *Officer Buckle and Gloria*. New York: Putnam.

1997 Wisniewski, David. *Golem*. New York: Clarion.

1998 Zelinsky, Paul O. *Rapunzel*. New York: Dutton.

1999 Martin, Jaqueline Briggs. *Snowflake Bentley*. Illustrated by Mary Azarian. Boston: Houghton.

2000 Taback, Simms. *Joseph had a little overcoat*. New York: Viking.

2001 St. George, Judith. *So you want to be president*. Illustrated by David Small. New York: Philomel.

2002 Wiesner, David. *The three pigs*. Boston: Houghton Mifflin.

2003 Rohmann, Eric. *My friend rabbit*. New York: Roaring Book Press.

2004 Gerstein, Mordicai. *The man who walked between the towers.* New York: Roaring Brook Press.

2005 Henkes, Kevin. *Kitten's first full moon*. New York: Greenwillow Books/Harper Collins.

2006 Juster, Norton, and Michael di Capua *The hello, goodbye window*. Illustrated by Chris Raschka. New York: Hyperion.

2007 Wiesner, David. *Flotsam.* New York: Clarion.

2008 Sleznick, Brian. *The invention of Hugo Cabret*. New York: Scholastic.

2009 Swanson, Susan Marie. *The house in the night*. Boston: Houghton Mifflin.

Find more winners at www.ala.org.

Sharing Books with Children

It is not necessary to read every word or the whole book. Try some of these techniques to attract and keep their attention:

- If the children are wiggly, simplify the text or skip pages.
- Talk about the pictures. Point out the colors, the media used, and relate them to things the children know or have experienced. Use the illustrations to inspire storytelling and different uses for the book.
- Point to objects in the pictures, and say their names.
- If there are unfamiliar objects in the pictures, introduce them slowly—only a few at a time. Compare them to familiar things that the children know.
- Have one or more real objects that tie in with the story. For example, if the book features a trumpet, as in *Ben's Trumpet* (Isadora, 1991), then have a real trumpet to show the children.
- Invite participation by having children make appropriate sounds or motions as the text is read.
- Use an expressive voice. Change the tone for different characters.
- To develop literacy skills, ask children to predict what will happen next, before the page is turned.

Arts Books

Many children's books about the arts contain numerous illustrations of well-known works. When reading a book to a group of children, try to have a related large print or artifact to share with them as well as the illustrations. Children gain nothing from observing the small prints in a book when it is shared with a large group. Looking at a tiny picture of an African mask in the book will not convey the quality of the original work. For a child, the miniature picture in the book has no relationship to the powerful, life-size piece of art it represents.

Designing a Big Book about the Arts

If a children's book about a specific artist, musician, dancer, or actor or about a particular technique or instrument cannot be found, we can make our own big book for the children on the topic. Books can also be made to illustrate a song, to dramatize a story, or show a method or technique in the arts.

In designing such a book, try to find photographs in magazine articles or calendar illustrations, or draw simple pictures or make collages that illustrate the topic.

To construct the book, use half size sheets of poster board for the pages and bind them with loose leaf rings or yarn. Keep the book short—about eight pages work well, and the text simple—about one sentence to a page for toddlers and two for preschoolers and primary age. Consider adding interactive elements, such as a cut-out instrument which attaches to the musician's hands with hook-and-loop tape, or add flaps that lift up to reveal a surprise.

If the book is showing a method or technique, have each page illustrate one step. If possible, glue on real samples of the materials used, such as wool and yarn for a book about weaving, or palm leaves for a book about basket making. When presenting an artwork from another culture, research details such as children's names, customs, and daily life so that the story will be accurate. Use authentic materials, if possible. Many craft stores carry art materials from around the world.

Children like repetitive and cumulative text books. Here is a sample of a repetitive text suitable for a big book based on information about basket making in Botswana from *Native Artists of Africa* by Reavis Moore (1993):

Nangura of the Mbukushu goes to the river,

To get the palm leaves,

For a basket to store her grain in.

Nangura of the Mbukushu collects the bark

To dye the palm leaves,

For a basket to store her grain in.

A cumulative text is an excellent format for describing the creation of artwork that is done in a series of steps, and the repetition of each step helps children learn the sequence of how the article was made. Hand or body motions can be designed that mime the process to go along with the text. Using the same information as was used in the repetitive sample, here is a brief sample of a cumulative text.

Nangura of the Mbukushu goes to the river, [Mime walking.]

To collect the palm leaves, [Mime reaching up for leaves.]

For a basket to store her grain in. [Mime holding a basket.]

Nangura of the Mbukushu goes to the forest, [Mime walking.]

To collect the bark to dye the palm leaves, [Mime pulling bark.]

For a basket to store her grain in. [Mime holding basket.]

Nangura of the Mbukushu fills up the kettle, [Mime pouring water.]

To boil the dye, from the bark she collected, to dye the palm leaves, [Mime stirring a hot kettle.]

For a basket to store her grain in. [Mime holding basket.]

Nangura of the Mbukusku gathers up the dyed leaves [Mime gathering leaves.]

that were boiled in the dye, from the bark she collected, to dye the palm leaves, [Mime stirring the kettle.]

For a basket to store her grain in. [Mime holding basket.]

Making a Connection

THE ARTS AND BOOKS

Creative dance

Have children invent movements to go with the story.

Re-enact the story using no words, only movements of the hands.

Dramatics

Ask children to change who the characters are, such as turn a boy to a girl or a snake to a rabbit. Act out the new story that results.

Create a tableau. Have children take and hold the poses of the characters, as shown on one page in the story. Have other children try to guess which picture it is.

Music

Create an opera. Inspire children to turn the character's words into songs.

Listen to selections from *Peter and the Wolf* by Sergei Prokofiev and see how the composer used different instruments and melodies to represent the characters. Select an instrument and invent a rhythm or melody to represent the characters in another book you are reading them.

Visual Art

Draw a new ending for the story.

Make scenery and props and use them to retell the story.

Make a three-dimensional group sculpture.

HOW ARE ARTWORKS, PRINTS, AND ARTIFACTS USED WITH CHILDREN?

> *Children feel a certain magic about the real thing. You hear their breath draw in, see their eyes widen, hear their respect and wonder. . . . Nothing really substitutes for this experience.*
>
> *—Jo Miles Schuman (1981, p. 1)*

Children need to see and touch "real" pieces of art and actual musical instruments. They need to feel the texture of an oil painting, the flowing form of a stone carving, and the exhilaration of blowing on a mobile. They need to see real actors performing on the stage, and musicians playing in front of them. They will have many of these experiences in the context of creating their own art. They also need, however, to see that it is not just little children, in this room, at this time, who create artworks. In addition, there are many art media and forms that are not safe for or within the skill level of children but that they can experience on an aesthetic level, such as a welded metal sculpture or a symphony played by a full orchestra.

Original art forms can be obtained as follows.

Other children. Children's art can be permanently mounted, providing pieces for the current group of children to study. Permanently mounted in public spaces such as the hall and lobby, group-produced pieces such as clay tiles or sculptures provide a tie to the children who have come before. Audio and videos of past students singing, dancing, telling stories, and putting on puppet shows provide role models with whom the children can easily identify.

Artists in the community. Every community has wonderful artists, musicians, and dancers who work in all the art forms. Most of these people are willing to lend, donate a piece of art, or perform for the children.

Teachers' artwork. If teachers have studied music, dance, or drama or have created original art, music, dance, or dramatic performances of their own, they may have a piece or performance to share with the children. It could be a picture drawn as a young child, an original song written in honor of a special occasion, or a piece of pottery made in a workshop. Sharing a piece of our own creation is quite different from providing a model we have made and expect the children to copy. From your own work children will learn that people they know and care about create art.

Arts Words

ART SUBJECTS

Abstract: A picture emphasizing shapes, colors, lines, and texture over subject matter.

Cityscape: A representation of a city.

Interior: A picture showing the inside of a room.

Landscape: A representation of the outdoors.

Portrait: A picture of a person.

Seascape: A representation of the sea.

Still-Life: An arrangement of objects on a surface.

When sharing your artwork, model how artists share their creative efforts. Display or perform the work, and discuss it with the children explaining how you learned to do it. Share how it felt to create it, and tell why it is special to you. By being proud of our own work, we model artistic self-confidence. Use this experience to lead into a discussion about what the children might like to share about their own art.

Fine Art Posters

In recent years, inexpensive but high-quality prints of artworks from around the world have become widely available. Posters have the advantage of being large enough for a group of children to experience at one time and durable enough to take many years of handling. Fine quality prints can be purchased from most museum gifts shops. Sources for art prints are listed in Appendix C. Fine art prints can also sometimes be borrowed from libraries.

Medium-Size Prints

Smaller art prints can be obtained inexpensively by clipping pictures from some of the many beautiful calendars that feature artworks of all kinds, and from a variety of magazines and catalogs. These prints are too small for large group study or public display but are perfect for use with small groups of three or four children.

Mini Art Prints

Museum postcards and pictures clipped from catalogs and mounted on tag board can be used for a variety of activities by one or two children. These prints are just the right size for small hands, and the freedom they have to handle them makes them very popular with children.

Digital Images

The Internet is another source for pictures of artwork and instruments as well as videos of musicians and performers. Images can be viewed on the computer screen, projected, or printed out. DVDs are another possible source of images. However, digital media do not provide the same level of intimacy as does contact with a real work or performer, and, unlike a print, cannot stay on display for a lengthy period of time.

Artifacts

An **artifact** is a handmade, three-dimensional, cultural art form. Examples of artifacts include baskets, quilts, woodcarvings, musical instruments, and parts of dance costumes or dramatic performances, such as masks. They are often unsigned and made to be used. They may be considered a form of collective folk art. These are not usually museum-quality pieces but are representative of a class of articles from the everyday life of a people and represent the ethnic heritage of a group of people. They are often handed down from one generation to another and carry the family's story with them.

Look for unique works. Although they may not be considered fine arts because of the element of repetition of traditional forms and designs, high-quality handmade artifacts retain the creative touch of the artist. They are not made from precut or purchased patterns, but represent a creative variation on a piece that follows a cultural tradition.

When selecting artifacts, choose those that reflect the artist who created it. Each handmade and designed artifact will have a different color, form, and perhaps decorative element from the others. Artifacts are made from materials that are found in the locality in which they were made. A quilt might be made from a family's old clothing or a weaving from the neighbor's sheep wool. A whistle could be carved from a local wood or a mask decorated with native grasses.

If cultural artifacts are being sold, then the sale should benefit the family or community that made them. Beware of items made for the "souvenir" market. Especially on imported items, look for labels that indicate the country of origin. Avoid those that look like they were mass-produced. Before buying an artifact, research its culture to find out if the item is one that is used in the daily life of the people.

Sources of art artifacts. The best examples of cultural artifacts are items intended for home, community, or ritual use, not for public display outside of the culture. Teachers may have some artifacts that belonged to their own families, or that they have made themselves and can share with the children. If teachers are willing to share personally valued artifacts, such as grandmother's patchwork quilt, then others are more likely to do so. The families of the children may wish to bring in a special artifact to show the group. If friends have traveled widely or are collectors of a specific type of artifact, then they may be willing to let the children see one or two pieces or might invite the children to visit the collection. (See the following section on using community resources for specific guidelines.) Sharing cultural artifacts is an excellent way for people of different heritages to bond.

On occasion, a particular artifact may be purchased that will either expand the cultural experience of the children or relate to an activity. For example, share an Indonesian shadow puppet before making shadow puppets with the children.

Artifacts of all kinds are available from many sources, such as department stores, importers, charitable organizations, and craft fairs. Charitable organizations are a good source, because they usually provide information about who made the item and how the money will be used to help the artisans. Craft fairs provide the opportunity to buy directly from the creator and collect the story that goes with the piece.

Using artifacts. Many artifacts are relatively low cost and durably made. After all, they are intended to survive the wear and tear of a normal household. Children will especially benefit from being able to touch and perhaps even to use the artifact, such as using an African basket to serve crackers for snack, eating soup from a hand-thrown tureen, wearing a hat from Peru in pretend play, or sitting under a handmade quilt made by a grandparent for story time. Table 7-4 suggests some of the types of artifacts that teachers might seek. Appendix C provides a list of artifacts and their sources.

TABLE 7–4 Multicultural Artifacts

Aprons	Lacquerware
Banners	Kimono
Baskets	Knitted items of original design
Beads	Masks
Beadwork	Mats, woven fiber
Calligraphy	Mosaics
Crocheted items	Musical instruments
Cloth, hand-painted, hand-dyed, handwoven, or hand-printed	Papier-mâché
Cornhusk items	Pottery, hand- or wheel-built, not slip cast
Dance shoes	Puppets
Decorated eggs	Quilts
Dolls, handmade	Rattles
Drums	Rugs
Embroidery	Sand painting
Ethnic clothing	Saris
Figurines, modeled clay, stone, wood	Scarves
Flutes	Scrimshaw
Furniture, handmade	Straw designs
Games, hand-carved or modeled	Tapestries
Glassware, hand-blown	Tin ware
Gourds, carved	Tutus
Handmade papers, also cast paper	Weavings
Hats and head coverings	Whistles
Inlays, wood or stone	Wrought iron
Jewelry, handmade	Yarn paintings

Teaching Appreciation with Artworks, Prints, and Artifacts

How a work of art is presented is as important as the selection process that went into obtaining it. Hanging a Van Gogh print on the wall, playing a Beethoven symphony, or displaying a piece of Burmese lacquerware is just a start. If teachers do not focus the children's attention on the work and relate it to their lives and artistic heritage, then it will have no more meaning than the cartoon characters that decorate so many classrooms. Teachers must engage children in the process of looking, questioning, and thinking about each piece. The following activities will provide ideas that can be expanded to accompany any artwork, print, or artifact.

Setting Up a Masterpiece Corner

Select a prominent place in the room in which to display a featured piece of artwork, artifact, or to play a musical work on a regular basis. The area should be free of distractions such as toys, competing signs, and other wall decorations and should be in a "clean-hands" area. Store related fine-art manipulatives, related books, and prints on nearby shelves. There should be room for several children to gather. Like the sensory table, a good location is near the entrance to the room where it will attract the children's attention as they enter with fresh eyes and ears each day.

It is important to place the work or artifact at the children's eye level. Leave it on exhibit for a length of time. If the subject corresponds to a topic being studied, leave it up during that unit. After several days of display, or if several children become very interested in the piece, involve the children in one of the following suggested arts appreciation activities.

Using a Puppet or Stuffed Animal

The key to engaging the children's interest in a work or artifact is in the way we express our personal enthusiasm and interest in the work. Our voices need to be full of energy and excitement as we discuss the artwork with the children. Some people find it helpful to use a puppet or stuffed animal. Just like children, adults often feel less inhibited when having "Rembrandt Bear" or "Musical Mozart" talk to the children.

Convert a simple stuffed animal or purchased puppet into an "arts expert" by adding a few small details such as a beret and a smock (with paint splotches, of course) for the "visual arts" or a tux and baton for music. An original puppet can be created using a sock, papier-mâché, or cloth. It helps if the "arms" can be moved so more expression can be added to the presentation. The "arts expert" should be constructed durably, as it will prove a popular friend to the children, who will often model the teacher's art discussions in their play. Make sure to give it a personal history that tells how it came to be so expert in the arts.

Questions to Ask

Although the specific questions will depend upon the particular piece of music, visual art, dance, or drama that has been selected, the following will offer some ideas to get started.

What does it tell you about? These questions focus on the subject matter or the story of the artwork.

- What is the season? Weather? Time of day?
- What kind of place is this?
- What is happening in this work?
- Who is this person? Who are these people? What are they doing?
- What is this animal? Tree? Plant? Building?
- What objects in the work do you know? Use? Are there any you do not know? Use?

How was it made? These questions help children learn about the different arts techniques.

- How do you think this was created? How can you tell?
- Does this look like it was made with any arts materials that we use?
- What tools do you think the artist used?
- What instruments do you think the musician used?
- How did the artist make this texture? Color? Line? Shape? Pattern? Sound? Movement? Rhythm?

Can you find? These questions give the children practice in using arts vocabulary.

- Can you find a line? Shape? Color? Texture? Pattern? Rhythm? Pitch? (Be specific, for example, red rectangle, rough texture, accented beat.)
- Can you trace with your finger a line? Shape? Melody?
- Can you touch or point to a line? Shape? Color? Texture? Pattern?
- Did you hear a high pitch? A low one?
- How is the dancer moving? High? Low? Energetically? Slowly?

How does it make you feel . . . ? Young children are not always able to express their feelings verbally. Be accepting of any responses that the children make to these questions. Trying to imagine how the people in the artworks, particularly portraits, and how the artists feel helps children become more sensitive to the feelings of others.

- If you were in this place, how would you feel?
- How does the person in this play feel?

- How was the artist feeling when she created this?
- How do you feel when you look at this? Hear this?
- Do you ever feel that way when you paint? Draw? Model? Dance? Sing? Act?

What comes next . . . ? These questions challenge children to make predictions based on the visual clues they see and allow them to practice creative visualization. In designing these questions, make sure there are enough clues to give direction to the child, but that there is no one right answer. Be accepting of all responses.

- What do you think will happen next? Happened before?
- What do you think this person (animal) will do next? Did before?
- What notes will you hear next?
- How will the dancer move now?

How many . . . ? Questions can also relate to other curriculum areas, such as math, language arts, social studies, and science.

- How many red circles (blue squares, etc.) can you find? (math)
- Tell me a story about this artwork. (language arts)
- Why are these houses made from reeds? (social studies)
- Do these clouds look like rain clouds? (science)

Can you do . . . ? Asking children to respond through creative movement to artworks helps them develop their mental imaging skills and allows them to become more involved in the artwork. There are no right answers to these questions; accept all of the children's responses.

- Can you make your face look like this one?
- Can you stand (sit) in the same position as this person? How would this person walk?
- Can you imagine you are doing what this character is doing? (Mime the character's actions.)
- Can you imagine opening and closing this door? Looking in this window? (Mime.)
- Can you imagine you are touching this animal? (Mime.)

What is the same or different . . . ? These questions encourage the children to develop skill in visual comparison. For very young children, keep the comparisons general and obvious. Older children will enjoy trying to solve trickier ones.

In a single work:

- In this picture, which person (house, animal) is bigger? Older? Younger? Smaller?
- Can you find the biggest (smallest) square (triangle)?
- Can you find the longest (shortest, thickest, thinnest) line?
- Can you find the brightest (dullest, lightest, darkest) color?
- Can you find the pattern in the song?

Comparing two artworks:

- In which story is there a person? A house? An animal?
- Which picture looks more real?
- Which artwork is round (three-dimensional)? Which is flat?
- Which artwork makes you feel happy? or sad?
- Which artwork have we seen before?

Personal taste. These questions allow children to express their personal reaction to an artwork based on their aesthetic response of the moment. Asking children to pick their favorite is a good way to spark interest in an artwork. It is a useful assessment technique to ask children for their personal opinions when first displaying an artwork, and then again after it has been on display awhile and discussed. Notice if negative initial reactions have changed or become tempered as children become more familiar with the piece. Be accepting of all responses.

Do not tell children that they must like something, but do make them justify their response by asking

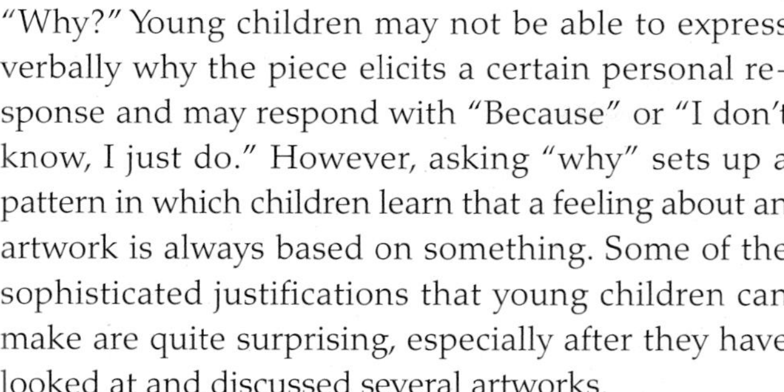

"Why?" Young children may not be able to express verbally why the piece elicits a certain personal response and may respond with "Because" or "I don't know, I just do." However, asking "why" sets up a pattern in which children learn that a feeling about an artwork is always based on something. Some of the sophisticated justifications that young children can make are quite surprising, especially after they have looked at and discussed several artworks.

- Do you like this? Why?
- Which of these is your favorite? Why?
- Would you like this artwork to hang in your home? Bedroom? Why?
- Would you like to meet this artist, musician, dancer, or actor? Why?
- Would you like to make an artwork like this? Why?

Presenting Artwork and Artifacts from Another Culture

When presenting an artwork and artifacts from another culture, have the children focus on its universal artistic qualities first so that it is clearly identified as a piece of art. Ask a selection of questions from any of the arts categories before asking about the cultural element. Questions should focus on finding similarities with familiar art forms and investigating possible uses.

- How is this artwork similar to the one we use? Make? Perform?
- How do you think it is used?

Remember that young children under age eight have a minimal knowledge of the world. They do not know specific geographical information. They respond best when descriptions of how something is made and used in another place are embedded in a story. Children can identify with common human themes such as family, food, and homes; and they love stories that contain animals.

Engaging Children with Art Prints

The following activities are designed to help a small group of toddlers or a larger group of older children become engaged with an art print.

Book Box

ARTS OF THE AMERICAS

Castaneda, O. S. (1993). *Abuela's weave.* New York: Lee & Low.
A young Guatemalan girl and her grandmother grow closer as they weave beautiful cloth to sell at the market. This book helps children understand why some artists sell their work. Six and up.

Garza, C. L. (2005). *Family pictures/Cuadros de familia.* Chicago: Children's Book Press.
Paintings by Mexican-American artists tell the story of a child growing up in a Hispanic community in Texas. Four and up.

Kleven, E. (1996). *Hooray! A piñata!* New York: Dutton.
A little girl wants a piñata for her birthday party. Colorfully illustrated with painted collages. A note at the end explains the Mexican custom of the piñata. Four and up.

Lessac, F. (1987). *My little island.* New York: HarperTrophy.
Brilliantly colored folk art paintings illustrate the life and culture on a Caribbean Island. Four and up.

ARTS OF ASIA

Hoskins, W. (2005). *Asian kites.* Boston, MA: Tuttle. Ages seven and up.
Plans for fifteen kites from China, Japan, and Korea are accompanied by detailed descriptions of how they are used in each culture.

La Fosse, M. G. (2003). *Origami activities.* Boston: Tuttle.
An introduction to the art of origami. Simple folding projects are explained. Five and up.

Merill, Y. Y. (1999). *Hands on Asia: Art activities for children of all ages.* New York: Kitts.
This excellent resource for teachers provides detailed information on the cultural setting and techniques used to create the folk art of Eastern Asia. Teacher resource.

Using a peek-a-boo window. This activity can be done with a large print (12-by-18 inches or larger) that has been on display or one that the children have never seen. From a sheet of paper the same size as the print, cut out a "window" in any shape that corresponds to a particularly interesting part of the picture. For example, in a painting such as Matisse's *Goldfish,* highlight one of the fish. In a portrait or mask, accent an eye, a mouth, or a decorative element. In

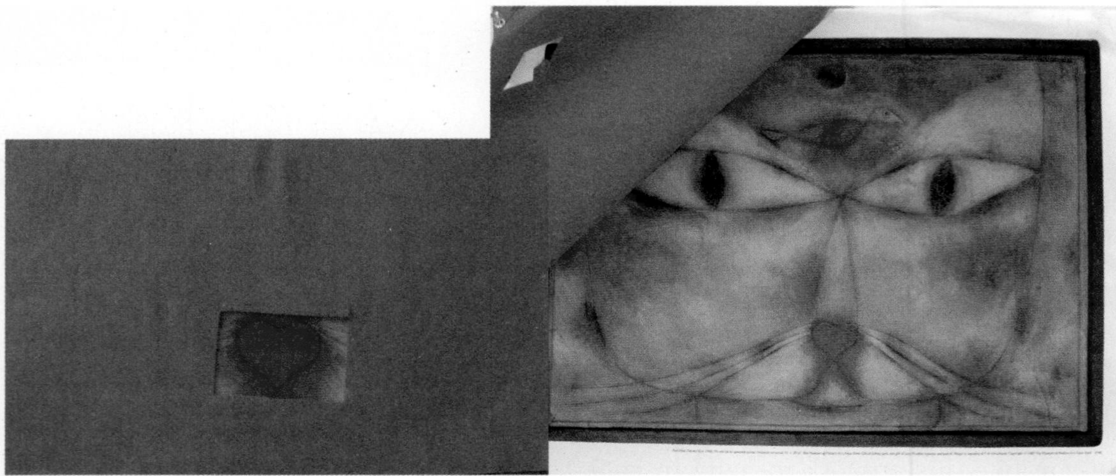

There are many ways to share fine art with young children. Showing just a tantalizing part of an artwork adds an element of surprise. A peek-a-boo window shows a tiny red heart. Lift it up and surprise—it's a cat's nose in this painting by Paul Klee.

a nonobjective artwork, choose a shape or a color. Place the window paper over the print, and fasten it securely at the top so it lifts easily. Then ask a series of thought-provoking questions about that part and what might be in the rest of the picture.

If they have seen the print before, ask children questions that challenge their memories.

- Do you remember what this ____________ was a part of?
- What other ____________ are in this artwork? (colors, shapes, lines, details, textures, animals, people, plants, or any other visual element that relates to the artwork)
- What is special about this one part of the artwork?

If it is new to them, ask children questions that entice them to predict.

- What do you imagine this ____________ is part of?
- What else do you think might be in the artwork?

It is not necessary to ask many questions. If the children are very excited about seeing the rest of the artwork after only one or two questions, then end the questioning by saying: "Let's look at the artwork and see what the artist chose to do." The children will respond by comparing what they see or hear to what they thought. This is an excellent way to develop mental imagery skills. Often children like to raise and lower the window several times. They also like to be able to touch the artwork. Leave the print covered for a while after the session so children can explore the window effect on their own.

Envelope (or book) of holes. Medium-size prints (about 8-by-10 inches) can be used in a cutout envelope or window book, as described in Chapter 4. Medium-size prints are easy to find. Many calendars contain reproductions of art, and people are happy to donate them when the year runs out. Magazine pages are just the right size, and a wide range of art is found in magazines such as *The Smithsonian* and *Natural History*. The National Gallery also sells inexpensive prints in this size.

Art to hang. Mount four or five medium-size prints on cardboard and laminate or cover with clear contact paper. Punch two holes in the top of each print, and attach a string or piece of yarn. Hang a child-height hook in the home life area or play corner, and let the children select and change the displayed art at will. If possible, try to get copies of the larger prints that have been discussed with the group, making sure the assortment represents a variety of art forms. Store the prints in an attractive basket or a box decorated with a collage of mini art prints. On occasion, substitute or add a new print.

A blank wall or divider in one area of the room can be turned into a "museum" by providing a group of varied medium-size prints and a row of child-height hooks. Large blocks can be used as bases for any three-dimensional artworks that are durable enough for the children to handle, such as baskets, weaving, and tin ware.

Two books to share with the children as they explore the museum area are *Matthew's Dream* (Lionni, 1991), in which a young mouse decides to become an artist after visiting a museum, and *Visiting the Art Museum* (Brown and Brown, 1986).

This area can also become a gallery or crafts fair. Children can "buy" new art to hang in the home life area, or they can select favorite pieces to take home to share and enjoy for several days. The yarn hanger makes it easy for parents to display the print on a doorknob or other convenient hanging place. Attach a brief history of the artwork, the artist's name, and any special facts about it to the back of any artwork that is sent home.

Art bags. Sew simple cloth bags with a handle, or decorate sturdy paper bags with mini-print collages. In each bag, place a medium-size print; an audio or video recording of music, drama, or dance; or a durable, inexpensive artifact along with a book that relates to the work and a toy, game, clothing, or food item that relates to the theme (see Table 7-5). It is important to select works from a variety of heritages, so parents as well as children become familiar with the world of the arts.

Children can take a bag home for a special treat such as a birthday or holiday. Set up a sign-out system. Make sure that the artwork is labeled, and provide a notebook in which parents can write their comments before they return the bags.

Living portraits. After sharing several prints of portraits, place an empty, unbreakable picture frame in the area where the dress-up clothes are kept. Children can take turns "posing" behind the frame. Keep a camera handy so as not to miss some of these creative portraits.

I see a. . . Play a game modeled on "I see a color. . . ," in which one child names a detail in the artwork, and others have three guesses to find it. The one who finds it goes next. If it is not found, the same child goes again. Encourage the children to select arts elements such as "I see a red square," or "I hear a. . . ." An exciting variation is to give each child a cardboard "looking" tube to use while playing this game.

Puzzles. Glue an inexpensive, medium-size print to a piece of corrugated cardboard. Laminate or cover with clear contact paper. Cut it into a few simple shapes that follow the shapes in the picture. Make a frame for the pieces with two sheets of cardboard slightly larger than the print. In one piece, cut a window the size of the print. Glue the window frame to the base, and fit puzzle pieces inside (see Figure 7-1).

Using Postcard-size Prints

Postcard-size prints can be purchased or made. To make your own, glue small copies of prints from art magazines, calendars, museum catalogs, or from the Internet to postcard-size tag board. Look for musical instruments, scenes from plays, and **ethnic folk art,**

TABLE 7–5 Suggestions for Arts Bags

Artwork or Artifact	Book	Real Object
Still-Life with Apples on a Pink Tablecloth by Henri Matisse	*What am I? Looking through Shapes at Apples and Grapes* by Leo Dillon and Diane Dillon (1994)	Apple wrapped in a pink piece of cloth
Girl with a Watering Can by Auguste Renoir	*Planting a Rainbow* by Lois Ehlert (1988)	Packet of flower or vegetable seeds and small plastic watering can
Diamond Painting in Red, Yellow, and Blue by Piet Mondrian	*Color Zoo* by Lois Ehlert (1989)	Set of colorful blocks
Wood carving of an elephant from Kenya	*I Am Eyes * Ni Macho* by Leila Ward (1978)	Small African drum or kalimba
Native American pot	*When Clay Sings* by Byrd Baylor (1987)	A piece of modeling clay or bag of play dough
Peaceable Kingdom by Edward Hicks	*Chester Raccoon and the Big Bad Bully* by Audrey Penn (2008)	Animal finger puppets

Note: All prints mentioned are available in 11-by-14-inch sizes from the National Gallery of Art.

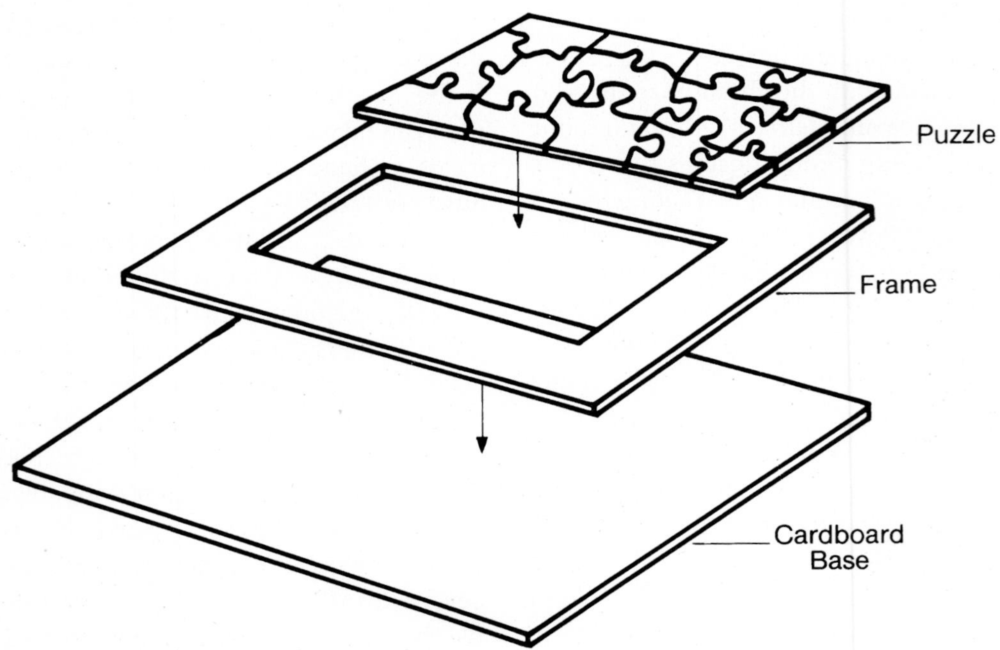

FIGURE 7–1 Puzzle Construction.

as well as works by famous artists. If possible, have the cards laminated for durability. Aline Wolf, in her book *Mommy, It's a Renoir!* (1984), explains how to prepare special folders to store sets of mini-art prints, and how to create sorting activities for children that increase in difficulty as the children become more familiar with the artworks. Sorting sets can consist of two to four pairs of mini-prints in a variety of groupings.

For example:

- pairs of duplicate pictures
- pairs that are predominately the same color, such as two mostly blue artworks and two mostly yellow
- pair a print that features mostly one color with a card bearing a shape in that color
- pair a print of an artwork that has a basic shape—round, square, and so on—with a matching shape card
- pairs of different subjects, such as two portraits, two still-lifes, and two landscapes
- pairs that show different art forms, such as two African masks, two Navajo weavings, and two Kuna Indian **molas**
- pairs that show the same art form created by different cultures, such as two baskets from Kenya, two Micmac baskets, and two American willow baskets
- pairs that show the same subject, such as a sun or face, done in different media, styles, or cultures

Sorting sets are most appropriate for children, ages three and up. Three-year-olds will probably enjoy just looking at the mini-prints and doing the simplest matching activities. Older children will enjoy working alone or in pairs trying to match the more challenging sets. Place the sets in attractive folders, clear plastic page protectors, small baskets, or decorated card boxes, and keep them in the "clean-hands" area. To make the sorting activity self-checking, place matching symbols on the back of each pair of prints. When children think they have a match, they can peek on the back to check themselves.

Sorting game board. A variation on this sorting activity is to create a game board by gluing six mini-prints on a piece of cardboard and laminating it or covering it with clear contact paper. The board can be decorated to resemble a museum with different wings, such as painting, sculpture, antique musical instruments, Asian art, and so on. For an easy level, provide duplicate mini-prints for the children to match with the ones on the board. For a more advanced level, provide mini-prints that are similar to the ones on the board. Glue a sturdy envelope on the back of the board to store the cards.

Hot and cold. Postcard-size prints can be used to play the traditional game of "Hot and Cold." Instead of using a piece of colored paper, a child places a mini-print in plain view somewhere in the room, while one or more children leave the room or cover their eyes. Then they try to find the print, while the other children tell them if they are getting warmer (closer to the print) or colder (farther from the print).

Print match. If several mini-prints that match large or medium prints are available, then play this matching game. Hang the large or medium prints on the wall, and have the children sit in a circle in front of them. In the center of the circle, place the mini-prints face down in a basket. Place all of the children's names in a basket, or use choosing sticks. (Choosing sticks are craft sticks with the child's name written at one end. Place the sticks name-end down into a small container. Pull a stick to choose a child.) The chosen child picks a mini-print and tries to match it to the larger print.

This game provides an excellent opportunity to explain to the children that prints are photographs of real artworks that are in museums. Demonstrate this by showing a real basket and a print of a basket or some similar artwork, or if there are prints that match some of the artifacts, play the Match Game and have children match the print to the real object. To demonstrate enlargement, show a snapshot-size photograph of something familiar to the children (such as themselves) and an 8-by-10-inch photograph of the same subject. Matching commercial big books with the regular versions is another way to reinforce the concept of enlargement. Give the children plenty of time to explore these examples. These are new and difficult concepts for many young children, especially if they have not had much experience with photography.

Mini-print gifts. Another way to bring the art of the world into the children's lives is to give them gifts that feature great art. Birthday cards and bookmarks can be made by gluing reproductions of prints clipped from magazines and catalogs onto various sizes and types of paper. Very small prints can be glued to heavy tag board and made into magnets by sticking magnetic tape on the back. If there is access to a badge maker, make art pins for gifts as well. Whenever giving a print as a gift, be sure to label it with the artist or culture that made it.

HOW CAN COMMUNITY RESOURCES BE USED?

> *Trips . . . give children an opportunity to see for themselves something they will learn more about later in pictures or in books or through conversation.*
>
> —*Rhonda Redleaf (1983, p. 3)*

One way for children to learn about other art forms and the role of art in adult life is for them to meet working artists and to see the arts in the community. Because most young children have short attention spans, these kinds of activities need to be carefully planned. Although a bad experience can do more harm than no experience, it is not difficult to organize a successful artist visit, an arts-related field trip, or a museum experience. The key is to design the experience so it meets the attention level of the particular children.

Guest Artists and Performers

The guest artist or performer can be a friend, a colleague, a family or a community member who creates original art that is relatively portable and not injurious to the children's health. It would not be a good idea to have someone oil paint or solder stained glass in a room used by children. The person should genuinely like young children and their infinite curiosity.

When inviting artists and performers to visit, make sure to prepare them for the particular group of children, and explain clearly what they should share and say. Have an information sheet prepared ahead of time to give to families and artists who will visit the class. The information sheet should list the times of the various daily activities, the number of children, their ages, and any particular information about items, such as special needs. There should also be a brief outline on how to design a program for children this age.

Presenting to Toddlers

Toddlers respond best to visual artists who create fairly large pieces that change appearance quickly. Basket making, painting, drawing, pottery, weaving, and sewing quilt squares together are examples of this kind of art activity. Musicians, dancers, and actors should choose short pieces that children can participate in through movement or singing.

Setup. Squirmy toddlers respond better if the teacher announces the visitor's arrival and directs the artist to a quiet corner, rather than having the visitor offer a group program. The artist then sets up and gives a short performance or begins to work on a sample piece of art. This kind of presentation mirrors Gardner's "skilled master" model (1991, p. 204).

Teacher Tip

It is well worth the effort to create an information sheet to send to guests before they visit. A sample follows:

GUIDELINES FOR GUEST ARTISTS

1. Visual artists: Bring an unfinished piece to work on and samples of your artwork at various stages. Musicians: Bring an instrument that children can touch and explore. Actors and dancers: Bring costumes or props that children can try on and use.
2. Avoid dangerous items if possible. If you must bring anything sharp or hot, make sure you have a childproof container for it.
3. Children are more sensitive to toxic materials than adults. Do not bring any solvents, permanent markers, solvent-based glues, oil paints, varnishes, sprays, or dusty materials.
4. Bring only one or two finished pieces that you feel will appeal to young children. Consider how you will display them safely.
5. Bring objects or samples that the children can touch.
6. If possible, bring a "souvenir" of the process or performance that the children can take home.
7. Keep your presentation simple. Prepare questions about your art that you could ask young children. Because children have short attention spans, plan for no longer than 15 minutes.
8. You may also wish to write a letter telling families about your demonstration for the children to take home.

What the guest should say. Toddlers can gather around to watch and ask questions. The visitor should be prepared to answer the children's questions in a simple, understandable way without talking down to them.

Samples. The visitor should bring sample materials and child-safe tools that can be touched by the toddlers. Any dangerous tools should be put away out of sight after each use or, if possible, not used during the demonstration. For example, a quilter could substitute small, blunt scissors for sharp shears when cutting threads.

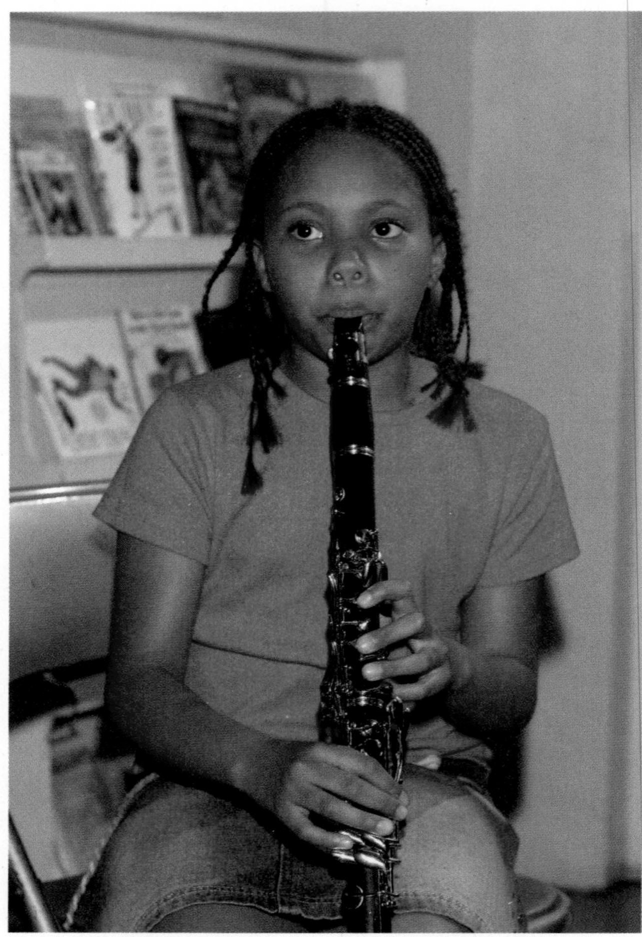

Visits from guest artists teach children that many different people create art. Ask families if there are any members who play an instrument, sing, paint, work in clay, dance, or act. An older sister, who plays the clarinet, makes an ideal role artistic model for young children.

Presenting to Three-Year-Olds and Up

Children, ages three and up, can benefit from a slightly longer and more complex visit. Before the guest arrives, tell the children about the visit, and ask questions to find out what they already know about this art form. Relate the visit to any explorations or arts activities that the children have done by asking intriguing questions such as, "Mrs. Kahn will be showing us how she paints landscapes today. I wonder if she will use an easel like you do when you paint?" or "Mr. Chang will be showing us Chinese calligraphy today. Calligraphy means beautiful writing. Do you think he uses a paintbrush or a pencil?" or "Ms. Ganesh will be showing us a dance they do in India. What do you think she will be wearing?"

Setup. When visitors arrive and have set up their work, gather the children around and introduce them. Let the guests explain what they do, and give a brief demonstration if the art form is suitable for a large group to see clearly, such as working on a large painting or making a good-size basket. The toddler format described earlier can be used for demonstrations that are best viewed by small groups of children at a time. In the case of visual art, if the process is very long, the guest might bring several samples in various stages of completion and then work on one that is just about complete.

What the guest should say. Rather than a lecture, the guest should be prepared with interesting questions to ask the children. For example, a quilt maker might ask, "How many pieces do you think are in one square?" or "How big do you think this quilt will be when I have sewn these six squares together?" A calligrapher might ask, "Do I hold the brush the same way you do?" An instrument maker might say, "What do you use drums for?" Teachers may want to offer possible questions to the guest ahead of time.

The guest or teacher may want to read a children's book that relates to the visit, or visitors may have interesting stories to share about when they were young, or how they became artists.

Samples. Just like toddlers, older children need to be able to use their sense of touch as much as possible. Invite the guest artist to bring a sample of materials that the children can touch. For example, a calligrapher could let the children touch the brush and the ink stone instead of the finished calligraphy.

If possible, see if they can give the children a small sample that they can take home with them. A quilter could offer a scrap of cloth that matches the quilt, a basket maker a piece of reed, and a weaver some yarn. Painters can apply paint that matches the painting to a piece of paper; when dry, they can cut it into simple shapes and sign them for the children.

Concluding the Visit

Prepare a brief letter to send home to families about the child's experience. This helps families understand the child's new knowledge. The child's "souvenir" can be attached to the letter as well so that it will have a context of meaning once it is home.

After the guest has left, have children participate in making a thank-you card. A nice thank-you is a photograph of the visit. Also take photographs to keep in a scrapbook so children can "read" and remember the experience.

Visiting an Artist's Studio

Taking a group of young children to an artist's studio can be a major undertaking and is most suitable for older children or a small, mixed-age group with ample supervision. The advantages of such a visit are that artists are often more comfortable working in their own surroundings with all of their supplies on hand. The children also get to see the working environment that the artist has created.

The disadvantages are numerous. The workspace may not be large enough or safe enough for young children, and there may be many items that they cannot touch. In cases where visual artists use materials that are hazardous for young children, a visit to the studio is not advised unless those materials can be cleaned up and put away. The workplace of a painter, an **illustrator,** a **calligrapher,** a **weaver,** a **spinner,** a basket maker, a **quilter,** a woodcarver, and a stone sculptor should be relatively safe, with minor adjustments. A printing studio, stained glass studio, pottery studio, or metal workshop may need to be carefully cleaned up, certain processes not demonstrated, and the children closely supervised.

In considering such a field trip, always visit the artist's workspace ahead of time. Check for the following features:

- **Space—**Is there a space large enough for all of the children to gather and observe the artist, or must they take turns? What can the children who are waiting their turn look at or do?
- **Safety—**Are there any dangers that cannot be removed? What areas does the artist need to clean up? What parts of the process are dangerous for the children?
- **Preparation—**What do we need to tell the families and children so they will be prepared? Do they need special clothing? What should they look for and point out to the children?

Field trips provide children with rich, sensory experiences that add meaning to their artistic work. A visit to a local high school band room can introduce young children to a variety of band instruments such as these kettle drums.

Make sure there is ample supervision for children. Families and other supporting adults should be invited to come and oversee one or two children each. Use the guidelines for guest artists to plan the actual presentation.

Visiting Museums

Most museums are not set up to deal with groups of young children. The "look-but-don't-touch" nature of the displays usually means that the children cannot use their natural learning impulses and thus spend the visit constrained and unhappy, leaving them with a dislike for museum going that may last all of their lives. The exception is the children's museum or children's wing, of which numerous versions have sprung up around the country. These are set up to engage children of all ages in activities that involve the arts and sciences. If such a museum is in the vicinity, do take advantage of the wonderful features it offers. Again, make sure to visit the site ahead of time, and arrange for adequate supervision.

Attending Performances

Preparation is key in taking young children to musical, dance, and theatrical performances. Select programs that are especially designed for children and which relate to themes and projects that are ongoing in the classroom. Beforehand, read books about the art form and the artists. See if you can schedule time to meet with the performers after the show or invite them to visit the classroom. After the performance spend time talking about it with the children and then set up a center at which there are props that children can use so they can re-enact what they experienced.

Other Places to Visit

Many other places allow children to experience the arts. Explore the neighborhood and community for possible experiences for children. Here are some possible ideas:

- **Art store—**Children will enjoy seeing the many different kinds of paints, brushes, papers, and pencils available for visual artists.
- **Music store—**Here is an opportunity to examine instruments up close. If the store gives permission, have children take paper and pencils and draw pictures of what they see.
- **Public sculpture—**Young children may also enjoy a visit to a piece of public sculpture if there is an example within walking distance. Public sculptures are often found in parks or near government and university buildings. Outdoor sculpture gardens attached to museums may also make a good experience. When visiting these locations, go prepared with a list of questions to focus the children on the visual elements of the pieces, and find out something about the artist who made it. Because these sculptural forms are separated from the artist and very different from their own art, children often have difficulty recognizing them as art and treat them more like unusual playground equipment. Expect such visits to be brief, and perhaps tie them in with a trip to another location.
- **Historic sites—**Reconstructions of older historical homes or farm sites may demonstrate traditional handicrafts from earlier times, such as wool spinning or candle making. These places are usually set up to handle groups, and they may shorten and customize their presentation for young visitors. There is often a real story to make the place come alive for children.

CONCLUSION: BECOMING A LOVER OF THE ARTS

> *When children are surrounded by artworks, photographs, collections of beautiful things—and all their own attempts are encouraged—they will begin to value art.*
>
> —*Gaelene Rowe (1987, p. 5)*

The arts are much more than the personal act of creating something. Art is also looking at, talking about, and appreciating the art of others. If we are dedicated to educating the whole child, we must provide children with opportunities not only to explore the process of the arts but also to experience a broad range of artworks and performances. In doing so, we will introduce children to the artistic heritage of humankind and the long continuum of creativity that it represents.

It will take effort on our part to do this. Letting children beat on a drum in the classroom is easier than taking a group of wiggly toddlers to experience a drum circle performance in the park. Putting markers out on a table is simpler and more immediate than learning about a piece of artwork and the culture that created it, and then designing a way to explain it to young children. But adults who work with children must never stop making the effort. We must dedicate ourselves to becoming as knowledgeable about art as we can be. Our lives will be richer, as will the lives of the children we touch. Together we will approach the crayons on the table, the play dough on the tray, and the dress-up clothes in the housekeeping corner with a new respect and sense of purpose.

FURTHER READING

Barbe-Gall, F. (2002). *How to talk to children about art.* Chicago, IL: Chicago Review Press.

Barbe-Gall begins with an overview of how children at different ages respond to artworks. He then uses a question-and-answer format to address the why, how, and what of understanding Western art. The book ends with color reproductions of masterpieces of European and American art, each with typical questions or comments that might be asked about it.

Robinson, D. (1996). *World cultures through art activities.* Portsmouth, NH: Teacher Ideas Press.

Use this book to gain a deeper knowledge of a wide variety of cultures. Suggested activities include ideas for crafts and puppets that bring the culture to life. But be sure to supplement these with real examples of art and artifacts from the culture.

Saccardi, M. (1997). *The art in story.* North Haven, CT: Shoestring Press.

This book is an invaluable teaching resource containing original stories to tell children about the art of the world. It covers both ancient and modern art, including Egypt, Greece, Asia, Africa, the Middle Ages, the Renaissance, Impressionism, and computer art. In addition, it provides ideas for related activities and a comprehensive bibliography of both children's and adult books.

Schuman, J. M. (2003). *Art from many hands.* Worcester, MA: Davis.

Provides a basic overview of artifacts from different parts of the world and then presents activities related to them.

For online resources for teaching about the world's arts to young children visit our Web site at http://www.cengagebrain.com

A visiting artist, such as this guitar player, needs to customize his or her performance to fit the attention span of the children.

TEACHING IN ACTION

INCORPORATING THE WORLD OF ART

Why Do We Wear the Clothes We Do? An Integrated Unit of Study for Preschool and Up

INTRODUCTION TO STUDY

The type and kind of clothing worn daily is an important facet of a young child's life. Getting into and out of complicated clothing, bundling up in cold weather or dressing lightly in the heat, and feeling comfortable or irritated by the fit or texture of a garment all directly influence how a child feels. Begin the study by building on this interest. We can do this in many ways. One way is to wear an unusual handmade garment, or comment on a new outfit that a child is wearing, and then follow up with any or all of the following:

- Compare this piece of clothing with that worn by other children. Notice the colors and textures in the different garments.
- Make charts and pictographs of the clothing children are wearing.
- Make a web of all of the different items of clothing children can name.
- Ask children how they think clothing is made and how it is colored, and record their ideas on a KWL (what we Know; what we Wonder about; what we want to Learn) chart to return to later in the unit.
- Have children draw pictures of themselves wearing different types of clothing in different settings, such as in school, at night, on a cold day, or at the swimming pool or beach.

INITIAL EVENT

Follow up the introductory activities with a visit by a fiber artist, such as a weaver, a knitter, an embroiderer, a quilter, or a dressmaker. Try to have this visitor come over a period of several days, and make a complete garment from beginning to end, so children can see the entire process. A small piece of clothing for one of the children's dolls or stuffed animals would be particularly motivating for children. Document the visit by taking photographs or making a videotape of the visitor at work, and have the children record what they see by drawing in theme journals.

UNIT ACTIVITIES

- Visit a children's clothing store. Have children make drawings of the clothing displays. Older children can put together an outfit and calculate the cost.
- Put out long pieces of wildly printed and richly textured fabric, such as velour and taffetas, and encourage children to make up new outfits for the dramatic play area.
- Investigate special clothing worn for different occupations. Have a fire-fighter, football player, ballet dancer, or construction worker come and explain why he or she dresses the way he or she does.
- Invite children to wear certain colors or types of clothing on special days, such as sweat suit day or beach day. Plan special activities to go with the clothing. Sweat suit day, for example, could focus on exercising activities.
- Cut out simple vest shapes from brown paper grocery bags, and have children decorate them with printed designs or drawn symbols representing possible future careers.
- Make an attractive display of cloth scraps, laces, ribbons, yarns, and trims, arranged by color and texture, for the collage area.
- Display paintings showing people from different times and places wearing a variety of clothing styles. For example, introduce some of the following (all from the National Gallery): *The Hobby Horse* (Anonymous), *Anne with a Green Parasol* (Bellows), *Little Girl in Lavender* (Bradley), *White Cloud* (Catlin), *Italian Girl* (Corot), and *Marchesa Brigida* (Rubens).
- Explore different ways clothing is fastened—zippers, buttons, laces, and hook-and-loop tape. Add buttons to the collage offerings.
- Extend the study to include footwear, jewelry, hairstyles, and masks.
- Sing the song "Go In and Out the Windows" with children, standing in a circle with their arms raised. Choose one child in turn to weave in and out the "windows" going under the arms of each pair. Compare this play dance to weaving cloth.

Studio Page

ARTWORK STUDY

Select an original piece of art, a print, or an artifact that interests you. Record the following information:

Title ______________________________

Artist/Culture ______________________________

Media ______________________________

Description/Story ______________________________

____

Based on this artwork, write an example of each type of question you could ask children.

1. What does it tell you about?

   ____

2. How was it made?

   ____

3. Can you find? (arts elements)

   ____

4. How does it make you feel?

   ____

5. What comes next?

   ____

6. How many? (related curriculum question)

   ____

7. Can you? (kinesthetic response question)

   ____

Studio Page

COMPARING CREATIVE WORKS

Select two pieces of work representing any of the arts that have some similarity, such as subject, media, colors, artist, material, use, or culture. Describe each piece.

Art Work 1: Title ______________________
Artist/Culture ______________________
Media ______________________
Description/Story ______________________

Art Work 2: Title ______________________
Artist/Culture ______________________
Media ______________________
Description/Story ______________________

Write three questions that would help children focus on the similarities in the artwork.

1. ______________________
2. ______________________
3. ______________________

Write three questions that would help children focus on the differences in the artwork.

1. ______________________
2. ______________________
3. ______________________

Studio Page

SELF-EXPLORATION: MY ARTISTIC HERITAGE

What is your cultural background?

What arts did you have in your home when you were growing up?

As a child, did you know anyone who was an artist, musician, actor, or dancer?

As a child, did you visit museums or attend performances?

As a child, did you have any favorite piece or type of art, music, dance, or drama?

As a child, was there any artwork you hated?

In your home now, do you have pieces of artwork, or musical instruments?

Do these pieces reflect your artistic heritage, another family member's, and/or choices made based on what you have learned about the arts as an adult?

Studio Page

SELF-EXPLORATION: MY VIEW OF THE ARTS NOW

I think it is important to learn about the arts created by others because:

I would like to learn more about the art, music, dance, or drama of:

If I could own any piece of artwork ever created, I would choose:

Chapter 8

Integrating the Arts into the Curriculum

Questions Addressed in This Chapter:

- Where do the arts belong?
- What is emergent curriculum?
- What is the project approach?
- What is an integrated learning unit?
- How can we share learning through the arts?

"*Through the multiple threads of many activities, learning can be woven into a whole cloth.*"

—*Pearl Greenberg (1972, p. 85)*

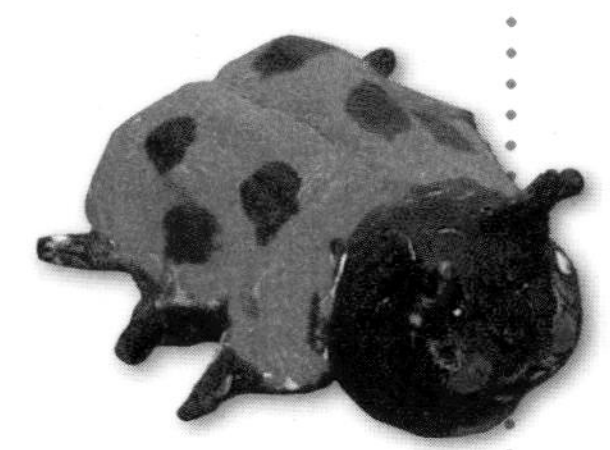

Young Artists at Work

Dennis has found a dead butterfly in the grass by the swing. He bends over and picks it up gently. "Look!" he says, "I've found a butterfly." Several other children gather around.

"I've seen one like that."

"My sister caught a butterfly."

"Can I have it?"

The teacher notices the group of children and approaches. "Look at my butterfly," Dennis says proudly.

"It has so many colors!" responds the teacher. "I see gold and blue. What do you see?"

"Here's some red and yellow," answers Dennis.

"It has lots of feet," Tomas adds.

"Wow, there is so much to see! Why don't we take it inside and look at it with the magnifying glass?" suggests the teacher.

Inside, Dennis places the butterfly on a soft cushion of paper towels, and the children take turns looking at it through the magnifying glass. Some children begin to pretend they are butterflies fluttering around the room. The teacher says invitingly, "Would you like to paint with butterfly colors?"

"Yes," say the children.

Gold, blue, red, yellow, and black paints are put out at a table. A group of children begins to paint enthusiastically. One paints a huge head and body with many legs and swirls of color around it. Another dabs his brush up and down lightly across his paper. "My brush is a butterfly flying from flower to flower," he says.

Another girl studies the butterfly, then runs over to the table. She makes a tiny dab of paint on her paper. Then she goes back and observes again. Back and forth she goes, choosing each color and stroke with deliberation. "My butterfly is the same size," she states with assurance.

Dennis is painting too. His paper is covered with bold strokes of lines and colors. "This is a butterfly day," he declares.

WHERE DO THE ARTS BELONG?

The arts are a powerful learning tool. They develop physical, emotional, language, social, and intellectual skills. They activate the spatial domain and stimulate the senses. They are a creative playground for the growing mind. Young children need to use the power of the arts to express their ideas and knowledge and to respond to their experiences. An integrated arts program provides children with the opportunity not only to explore the different art forms in open-ended ways, but also to express what they are learning through the arts. In such a program, arts activities radiate into all areas of learning.

Steps toward Integration

Many educators would agree that learning is best accomplished when children are surrounded by activities, objects, and active experiences that relate to each other in a meaningful way. Caine, Caine, McClintic, and McKlimek (2004) find that when an integrated learning approach is used, conditions are created that match optimum requirements for "brain-based" learning. As integrated curricula designs have become widely accepted in early childhood education, teachers have found that unifying the activities presented to young children is both challenging and very rewarding. Integrated activities stimulate both children and teachers to look at the environment around them in new ways.

Integrating the arts into the curriculum requires the teacher to approach the arts in different ways for distinctive purposes. Lessons can be intertwined, so that children acquire arts concepts and skills, while using the arts to connect and increase learning across the disciplines.

Step 1: Teaching about the arts. The arts disciplines are discrete subject areas. Dance, drama, music, and visual arts each have unique concepts and skills. A lesson in which the teacher presents a new song and then asks children to invent a way to notate it, or one that has children look at a sculpture and then asks them to imagine how the artist made it, is a lesson that addresses the concepts, skills, tools, and work of artists.

Children who have disciplined, specific artistic skills and knowledge can use the arts more effectively and creatively to communicate their ideas. To nourish creative artists, musicians, dancers, and actors teachers must plan thoughtful, well-organized arts lessons with clearly stated objectives that focus directly on the arts and artists and that provide many opportunities for arts exploration and practice. The "Exploring the Arts" section of this book suggests ways to meet these objectives. Appendix B explains how to write an activity plan like the ones featured in the Making Plans boxes.

Step 2: Connecting the arts. Next, the arts can connect with learning in other subject areas. When children sketch the parts of a flower or sing a song about the seasons they are using the arts to enhance learning in another subject area. These kinds of connected lessons allow children to use skills and techniques of the different art forms to practice and communicate concepts and ideas learned in other subject areas.

Connecting the arts in this way enriches the child's learning experience by providing multiple pathways for children to make what they are learning about more meaningful. The arts can be connected in this way to math, science, social studies, literature, and to each other. The Making Connections boxes found throughout this book provide many examples of ways to connect the arts with other subjects.

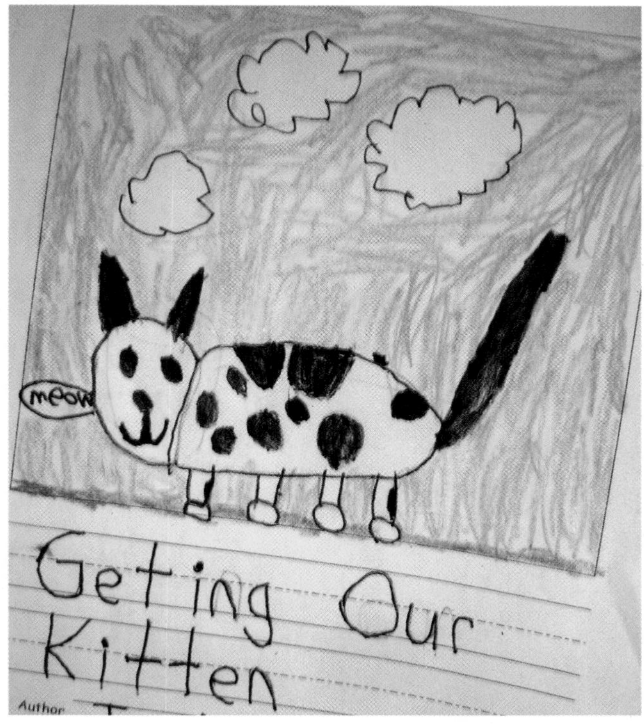

Art can be used to expand and enrich the words of beginning writers. "Getting Our Kitten" Marker—Elizabeth, age 6.

Connected arts lessons can develop in several ways. They may be carefully planned as part of the curriculum. Children studying trees might be asked to imagine they are trees in a creative movement activity. On the other hand, sometimes a wondering question may set the stage for an activity. For example, children measuring water at the water table might wonder aloud what happens when different amounts of water are added to paint. The alert teacher quickly sets up a paint and water mixing activity and invites the young scientists to come explore. Arts activities can also lead to lessons in other curriculum areas. The butterfly painting activity described at the beginning of the chapter could be connected to reading books about butterflies, dramatizing their life cycle, hatching a cocoon, or creating a graph of the different butterflies observed by the children on the playground.

Step 3: Learning through the arts. In a fully integrated arts program, the arts are found everywhere in the classroom. Arts pursuits flow into and out of the daily classroom activities as children need them. For example, instead of children passing through a visual art center, each taking a turn at the art medium being offered that day, they are offered a well-stocked art supply center from which they can select familiar tools and media that best meet their expressive needs at that moment.

1.

2.

The children in this kindergarten class made a special visit to their playground. Together, with their teacher, they looked carefully at the different shapes and forms and noticed the spaces as well. Then they came back to the classroom and drew pictures. They used art to communicate their ideas.
1. "My friends and I like to ride the swings." Marker—Brittany, age 5
2. "I like to run and jump all over the playground." Marker—Joe, age 5

In such a classroom children's projects incorporate the arts. Children studying about homes, for example, may make crayon sketches of the houses near the school. In the same class another group might choose to put on a puppet show about building a house. Individual arts pursuits are also facilitated. One child may spend several days building a complex house of Styrofoam pieces, whereas another paints houses at the easel one day and creates a house from collage materials the next.

In order for this level of integration to occur, children must have ideas and experiences to express. The curriculum can be organized in several ways to provide unifying experiences that inspire children to communicate their learning artistically. In this chapter two of these ways will be examined in detail—**emergent curriculum** as represented by the **project approach,** and the **integrated learning unit.**

WHAT IS EMERGENT CURRICULUM?

Emergent curriculum is created by teachers and children working together to explore ideas that interest them. Topics for study develop from events in the children's lives, daily happenings, and concerns that develop as children work and play.

An emergent unit might begin with listening closely to what children are talking about and observing what they are doing. For example, Dennis's discovery of the butterfly and the children's interest in it could be the start of learning more about insects. The teacher increases the children's interest by modeling enthusiasm and wonder. Tantalizing questions can make children look more closely or think more deeply. Instead of dismissing Dennis's discovery of the butterfly with a "That's nice," the teacher draws the children in by pointing out the colors and asking questions about what they see.

If the children continue to show interest in butterflies, the teacher might then start to gather resources and think of experiences and activities that relate to this interest. A web about butterflies could be created to help

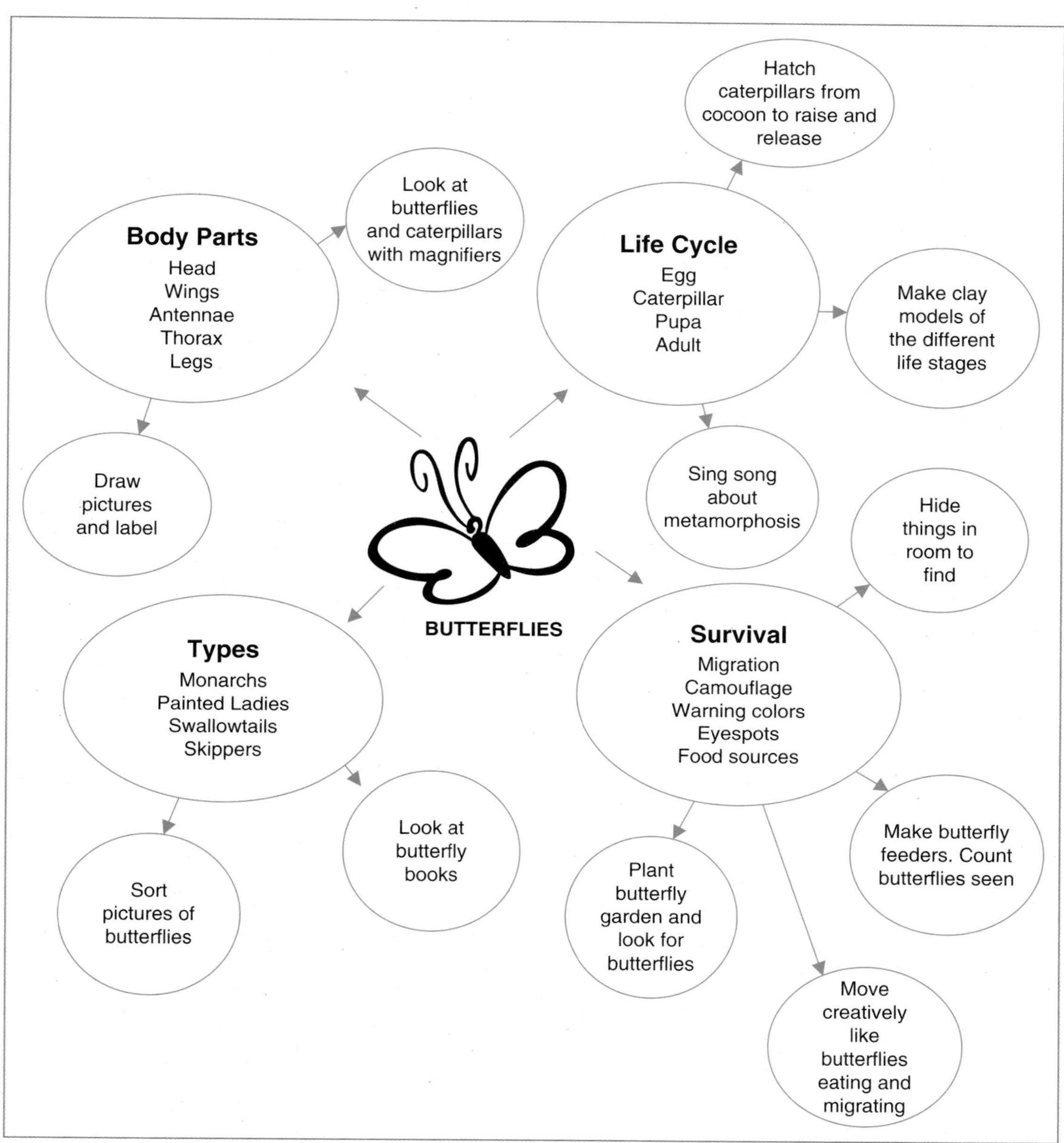

FIGURE 8–1 Butterfly brainstorm web.

discover ideas to pursue further with the children (see Figure 8-1). Experiences chosen must be rich in sensory and visual stimuli. They should be memorable—full of opportunities for asking questions and making observations. Most important, the experiences should flow directly from the children's questions and interests.

Throughout an emergent unit the teacher needs to be on the lookout for things that spark children's interest. It is handy to have a reservoir of ideas, books, songs, and arts materials on hand that can be drawn upon at a moment's notice.

WHAT IS THE PROJECT APPROACH?

The project approach is an example of one way to organize and carry out an emergent curriculum. Katz and Chard (2000, p. 2) define a project as "an in-depth study of a particular topic that one or more children undertake." Howard Gardner applauds the project approach, as demonstrated at Reggio Emilia, for the way it guides children in using all of their "intellectual, emotional, social, and moral potentials" (Edwards, Gandini, & Forman, 1993, p. xii).

The project approach starts with a topic of interest to the children and then fosters the children's exploration of that topic as they apply already acquired knowledge and skills in making sense of new material. It is particularly designed to meet the needs of children in prekindergarten, kindergarten, and the primary grades, and it can be very effective in multiage classes, because it draws on the differing skills and knowledge of each child.

In the project approach children work in small groups of two to five on a project that reflects their personal interests, some of which may be far removed from their everyday experience, and from what the teacher might select. These groups establish a relationship with the teacher in which the teacher not only facilitates but also collaborates in the process directly by supplying the needed skills and direction.

The Value of the Project Approach

The project approach engages children's intellects by widening their knowledge and skills at their individual levels of understanding. The traditional format of learning through play, although beneficial, lacks intellectual challenge and underestimates children's ability to acquire wider meaning from their experiences. An academic approach, on the other hand, forces children to proceed in a lockstep sequence of learning skills and concepts, whether or not these skills are relevant or appropriate for the individual child.

Katz and Chard (2000) believe the following benefits are best achieved through the project approach:

1. Project work helps children learn in an integrated manner and breaks down the divisions between subjects or play areas.
2. The use of projects challenges teachers to be creative and to devise constructive solutions to educational problems.
3. Project work relies on the children's intrinsic motivation because it allows for a much wider range of choices and independent efforts on a topic of their choice.
4. Children can select work that matches or challenges their skill level.
5. Children can become expert in their own learning. They are in charge of finding information and using it in new ways.
6. When children reflect on and evaluate their contribution to a project, they become accountable for their own learning.

Project Approach in Action

In the project approach topics rather than themes form the framework. Topics, unlike themes, can be very specific and are chosen because they relate closely to the children's interests.

Teacher Tip

DRAWING AND THE PROJECT APPROACH

Sylvia Chard recommends that drawing to record information plays an important role in project work. Drawing can be incorporated in the following ways:

1. The first stage in a project is to draw upon the children's existing knowledge and experience. To begin a project, tell a story that relates to the topic to be studied, and then ask children to share their own stories. For example, if the topic is shoes, tell the children about a special pair of shoes and how you felt when you wore them. Follow storytelling by having the children draw memory pictures about their shoes.
2. In the second stage, children do fieldwork to learn more about the topic. In this stage, they can make drawings from direct observation, such as taking off their shoe and drawing it. They can make sketches on field trips, such as at the shoe store, by attaching a few sheets of paper to a clipboard or to a piece of cardboard with a pencil attached.

Choosing the topic. One way to find a topic is to listen to what interests or concerns the children. Did someone just get a letter from a relative who lives far away? That could start a project on the post office. Is a child going to the hospital for surgery? That could begin a project on hospitals. Teachers can also initiate a project by selecting a topic about which everyone has a story or experience to share. For example, the teacher might begin by telling a story about a time

What we Know K	What we Wonder about W	What we have Learned L
Snakes are long and skinny	What do snakes eat?	Snakes are reptiles
Snakes live in the grass	How are baby snakes born?	Snakes shed their skin when they grow
Snakes can bite	How can you tell if a snake is dangerous?	Snakes eat mice
Some snakes are dangerous	Why are some people afraid of snakes?	
Some of us are scared of snakes		

FIGURE 8–2 Sample KWL chart: snakes.

she lost her shoe. Then the children talk about and draw pictures of their experiences with shoes.

Facilitating learning. Based on what the children say and draw, learning activities are planned that relate to each individual child's ideas and questions. These activities should allow open-ended exploration of topic-related ideas, encouraging the child to observe, sense, explore, and experiment, both individually and with others. For example, after several children participating in a project on plants comment that all leaves are green, a variety of plants with different color leaves can be put on display alongside containers of different green materials for collages. These activities are then available as a choice for any child to investigate.

Organizing activities. Although flexibility is a principle feature of the project approach, projects usually follow a set course. The first phase is devoted to memory work. Children are invited to tell personal stories, to make drawings, and bring in things from home that relate to the topic. The children's knowledge and questions can be made into a KWL chart (see Figure 8-2).

The second phase is devoted to gathering data from observation and experience. During this week children go on field trips, make drawings from real things, and talk to experts. Children record what they learn with drawings, creative movement, music, dramatic play, and constructions.

The third phase is concluding the project. At this time the teacher helps children select from the work they have done, what they want to share with other classes, and their families. Time is also taken to record conclusions and evaluate what was learned. Figure 8-3 gives an overview of what happens in the different phases.

Through drawing children can record what they have learned. Elizabeth, age 6, made this crayon drawing to show what she observed about vegetables after a trip to the farm.

Small group work. One of the key features of the project approach is the importance of working with children in small groups. Teachers meet on a regular basis with groups of children. Together they discuss the initial experiences and pursue questions and ideas that lead into a variety of independent investigations or projects. Small group projects can range from writing a book to making puppets and putting on a puppet show. Children are limited only by their imaginations.

As they work on their projects, the teacher offers guidance, provides requested materials, directs the children to sources of information, and teaches specific skills as needed.

Discussion/representation. Time is set aside to talk about and share the children's ideas

Phase 1 Beginning	Phase 2 Data Collecting	Phase 3 Conclusion
Topic ideas are investigated	Resources are collected	Plan culminating event
Topic selected	Fieldtrips taken	Complete activities
Topic web created by teacher	Guest experts visit	Set up event displays
A common experience is shared with the group	Books are read	Discuss and evaluate
Stories are shared	Examine artifacts	Create presentation panels
Ideas about topic are shared through the arts	Learning is represented through writing and the arts	Invite parents
KWL chart created	Revisit KWL chart	Celebrate learning

FIGURE 8–3 Life cycle of a project.

daily. These can be recorded by the teacher in various ways—in charts, graphs, dictation, and through audio taping. The children's changing ideas can also be documented through their drawings and constructions and through photographs and videotapes made of their activities. This is a very important part of the process; it is the way the different groups' learning is made visible to all of the children.

Culminating Projects

Completed projects need to be recognized in a special way. One of the main dangers with the project approach is the temptation to focus on the finished products and to ignore the thought and process that went into it. Plan ways to share the children's work through displays of not only the project, but also all of the documentation of the process that went into it. This will be further explained later in this chapter.

A project on how animals survive in the wild emerges when a teacher finds abandoned baby rabbits and brings them to school.

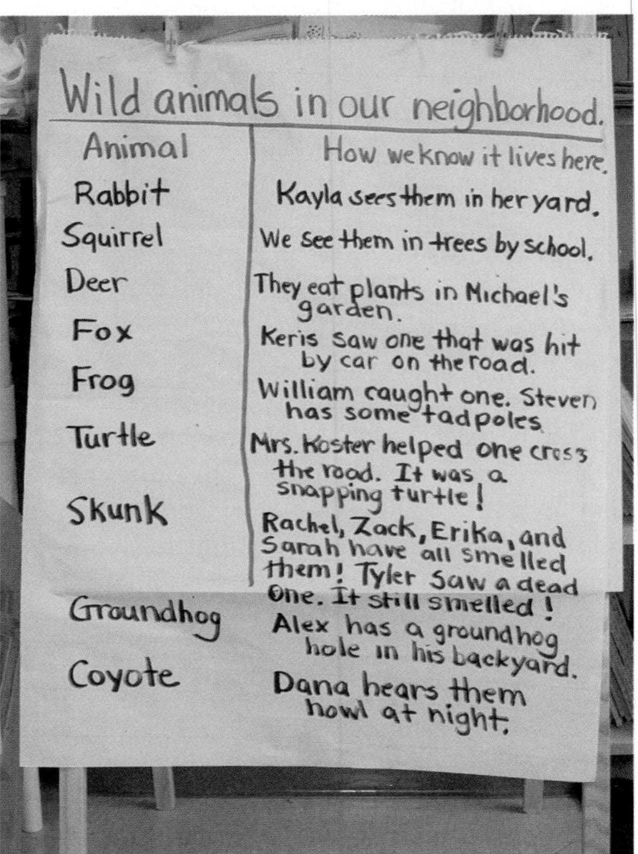

Memory work, the first part of a project, acknowledges what children already know and sets the stage for further research.

A mural is a great way to culminate a unit of study. "Wild animals in our neighborhood" Tempera—Kerris, William, Zack, Carolyn, Sabrina, Tyler, Alex, Mackenzie, Jenna, Taylor, Erika, and Dana, ages 6 to 8.

WHAT IS AN INTEGRATED LEARNING UNIT?

> *Life should be a single whole, especially in the earliest years, when the child is forming himself in accordance with the laws of his growth.*
>
> —*Maria Montessori (1967, p. 164)*

An integrated unit is one in which many different subject areas are tied together by relating them to a carefully selected, broad-based concept or theme. This is expressed in the form of an overarching question or a metaphor that ties together the learning areas. For example, if the chosen question is "What is water?" then books about water will be read. Children will experiment with water. They will paint with water, wash the dolls and toys in the play area, and splash in water at the water table. They may take a field trip to a stream or lake and talk about the animals that live in the water.

Selecting a Unifying Question

Visualizing the possible ways that all the subjects can be integrated around a common question enables teachers to see beyond the isolated arts activity of the day and allows arts concepts and techniques to be introduced, explored, practiced, and mastered in concert with all the other subject areas. The following guidelines will aid in the selection of appropriate questions for integration.

Is the question broad-based? Decide if the question is one that is rich in possibilities for expansion to the different subjects or growth areas and any standards that must be addressed. A concept web, such as illustrated in Figure 8-4, can be used to explore the depth of the unit. Once the concepts to

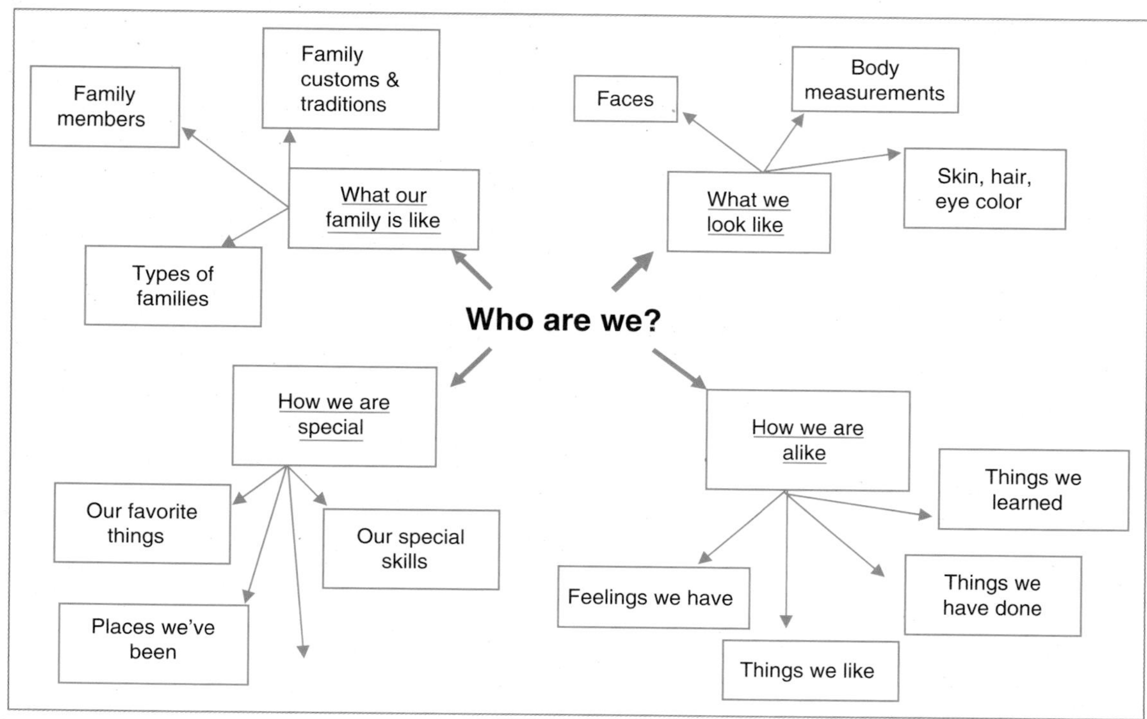

FIGURE 8–4 Sample concept web.

be learned are laid out on the web, try to brainstorm the activities you might use to teach them. Are there wonderful books to read? Are there related songs and poems? Will there be things to explore through science, visual art, drama, and play? Will children be able to use skills from all of the multiple intelligences to explore this question? Some questions for integrated units have more potential than others (see Figure 8-5).

What resources are available? Are needed supplies available for certain activities? Are there places to visit or people who could talk to the children about this? Where can books be found that address this question?

How much time is there? The question should be open ended enough so if the children's interest wanes it will be easy to move on to something else. There should be sufficient time, however, so if the children become highly interested they do not have to be cut off to "move on." It is not the specific content that teaches. The goal in early childhood education is not to make children experts. Rather the question should be a vehicle that will allow children to explore and learn about their environment within a meaningful context.

The Arts in Integrated Units

Integrated teaching provides an excellent way to unify the child's arts experiences with the rest of the curriculum. However, it is very important to make sure that the arts activities are open ended. It is a real temptation for the teacher, for example, to want to give the children unit-related pictures to color and patterns to follow, but it must be remembered that such directive activities do not foster artistic growth, no matter how attractive the results may be.

Do not expect or demand that every child make the same arts projects to take home. The arts allow each child to express a unique view of the unit concepts. Open-ended arts activities can be integrated into integrated units in many ways (see Figure 8-6).

Through everyday creative arts activities. Make sure basic, familiar arts supplies and props are always available. During the unit, children should be free to choose to draw, paint, make a collage, move creatively to music, or create a puppet, whether as a personal exploration or as a reaction to a unit-related experience.

Through special materials. Unit-related materials can be offered as a choice. For example, for the unit "What is a tree?" pressed leaves can be added to the collage area, twigs for painting can be placed alongside brushes at the easel, and drums made from hollow tree trunks added to the sound center.

Through responsive activities. Encourage children to use the arts as a way to record and respond to special events and experiences by providing a special time during which the children "write" and share their ideas. For example:

1. Make individual journals by stapling together several sheets of blank or partially lined paper. Then set aside a daily five minutes for children to record in pictures and words their ideas about what they are learning. Have children share their journals with a partner or a small group.

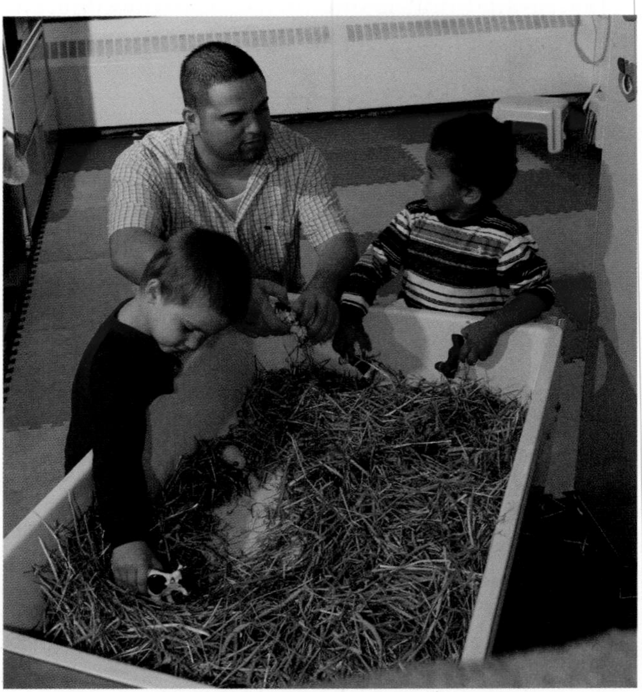

Integrated arts activities will be found in all areas of learning. Here children play with plastic farm animals in a sensory bin full of hay as part of an integrated unit on farming.

Questions for Integrated Units	Possible Topics	Related Arts Activities (Note: See Exploring the Arts sections for more ideas)
How do animals live?	Habitat, shelter, food, food chains, behaviors	**Dance:** Move like prey and predators; pretend to find food and shelter. **Drama:** Act out stories of animals' lives. **Music:** Sing animal songs, such as *Animal Fair** and make up new words. **Visual art:** Sketch live animals, make clay animal models, paint animals. **Group:** Create an animal habitat mural. **Art to view:** Edward Hick's *Peaceable Kingdom* and the art of Henri Rousseau.
How do our bodies work?	Body parts, exercise, jobs	**Dance:** Invent new ways to move different body parts. Attend a ballet. **Drama:** Pantomime doing different jobs using simple props. **Music:** Sing *Dry Bones* and *Head, Shoulders, Knees* and *Toes* adding more body parts. **Visual art:** Draw people, draw playgrounds, build models of imaginary playgrounds, cut out people pictures from magazines and make collages. **Group:** Make a mural of people doing things. **Art to view:** Paintings of people doing things, such as those by William Johnson, Jean Millet, and Edgar Degas.
How do we get there?	Transportation: boats, cars, trucks, maps, bridges, stairs, ramps	**Dance:** Move as if driving different types of vehicles. **Drama:** Act out a trip. Add suitcases and tickets to play corner. Use chairs to make a train or make trucks and cars from large boxes. **Music:** Sing *The Wheels on the Bus, The Walking Song,* and *Going on a Bear Hunt*. Add more ways to travel to the songs. Use instruments to create vehicle sounds. **Visual art:** Draw vehicles and maps. Print using toy car wheels, and build vehicles from blocks and boxes. **Group:** Build model of local roads and places. **Art to view:** *California Crosswalk*, by Outerbridge (MAPS).
How did these buildings get here?	Architecture, construction equipment, building materials, carpentry, mapping	**Dance:** Imagine building a house—carrying, lifting, hammering, and more. **Drama:** Act out *The Three Little Pigs*, inventing new houses for them. **Music:** Use safe tools to make sounds and rhythms. **Visual art:** Blocks, papier-mâché buildings, wood sculptures, sketching houses. **Group:** Build a city or town model. **Art to view:** cityscapes by Romare Bearden, Childe Hassam, and Edward Hopper.

FIGURE 8–5 Sample questions and activity ideas.

Questions for Integrated Units	Possible Topics	Related Arts Activities (Note: See Exploring the Arts sections for more ideas)
What can we see?	Eyes, colors, shapes	**Dance:** Move in different colored lights, with eyes closed, or in darkened room. Explore shadows. **Drama:** Act out a story of someone who is blind. **Music:** Sing *Color Doesn't Really Matter* (Wood, 2001) and *Pretty Colors*. Explore how the shape of instruments affect how they sound. **Visual arts:** Paint with different colors, shape/color collages, gadget prints, paint on wet paper, color mixing experiments, sensory experiences, peek boxes. **Group:** Make a shape or color mural/quilt. **Art to view:** works by Stuart Davis, Paul Klee, Hans Hofmann, and Piet Mondrian, Amish quilts
What is a family?	Family members, foods, customs	**Dance:** Learn simple dances from family cultures. Attend folk dance performances. **Drama:** Add props to play corner representing cultures of families. Tell stories. **Music:** Learn family favorite songs. Listen to music from families' cultures. **Visual arts:** Draw family portraits, make collages using food clippings, or family photos. **Group:** Make a quilt, mini-box, or plastic bag mural. **Art to view:** family portraits by Mary Cassatt and John Singer Sargent, folk art from many places.
What is water?	Water sources, uses	**Dance:** Move like water; swim like fish Put glass pan of water on overhead and move creatively in the projected ripples. **Drama:** Set up a small rowboat or life raft and add life preservers and fishing poles with magnets to catch fish. **Music:** Sing *Row Your Boat* and make up new words. **Visual art:** Use watercolors. Sketch at a pond/puddle/creek. Make water creature mobiles, nature collages, boats, and pipe maps. **Group:** Make a refrigerator box submarine or boat. **Art to view:** Works by Winslow Homer, Claude Monet's *Water lily series.*
Where do we live?	Community, mapping, homes	**Dance:** Pretend to dance through the neighborhood. **Drama:** Set up play stores and add shopping props. **Music:** Change *Round the Mulberry Bush* to Round the Neighborhood. Visit music stores and performances in neighborhood. **Visual art:** Sketch stores/houses (inside and outside), draw signs and maps, build box buildings and houses. **Group:** Make a model neighborhood, box house, or store. **Art to view:** Interiors by Albrecht Dürer, Vincent Van Gogh, and Henri Matisse. Study homes in other cultures.

*Note: Unless otherwise indicated, lyrics and tunes for songs mentioned above can be found at http://www. theteachersguide.com/ChildrensSongs.htm

Question	Subject	Activities
What do we look like?	Dance	Set up floor mirrors; dance in front of them using different body parts; pair children and have them mirror each other's actions.
	Drama	Put mirror in play area. Make funny faces in mirror.
	Language Arts	Tell stories about selves.
		Read books such as *We Are All Alike. We Are All Different* (Cheltenham Kindergarten, 1994)
	Math	Measure body parts and graph.
		Count numbers of hands, feet, arms, fingers, etc. in class.
	Music	Sing *If You're Happy* and add different facial and body expressions.
	Science	Study how the different body parts work and help us survive.
	Social Studies	Display photographs of class members. Have them learn to identify each other. Hang up photographs of all kinds of people from all over the world.
	Visual Arts	Make self-portraits.
		Make tracings of bodies and add personalizing details.
		Look at portraits by Rembrandt Van Ryn, Amedeo Modigliani, and Pierre Renoir

FIGURE 8–6 Sample arts activity brainstorm chart.

2. Set up a storytelling center, such as described by Vivian Paley (1992). This is a center where children can dictate their unit-related stories to the teacher. Later the class can help act out these stories for everyone to enjoy.

Through group activities. Plan one or more group activities that relate to the unit concepts. Quilts, murals, and box sculptures can be designed to relate to many theme concepts. Whole group singing and creative movement activities can help make concepts come alive.

Organizing Integrated Unit Activities

The unit activities selected should span the range of developmental growth areas and tap into all of the domains of the multiple intelligences. Consider questions to be addressed, explorations and experiments to be done, vocabulary to use, and assessments to be made. One way to organize this material is to use a planning web or grid (see Figure 8-7).

1. **Put activities in developmental order.** Activities should be planned to logically build on each other. Skills acquired in one activity should recur again at slightly more challenging levels in the next activity. One way to do this is to use index cards or sticky notes on which are written the different activities being considered for the unit. Categorize each activity as introductory, exploratory, practice, and responsive, and then lay out the activity cards in sequence from least to most complex on a calendar or grid. As the unit progresses, move the cards to extend or repeat activities as needed. At intervals, take time to revisit the plans and notice what is going well. Do not be afraid to discard some activities or add others to better match the learning needs of the children. The goal is to produce an integrated unit that flows across the disciplines in concert with the children's developing skills and interest.
2. **Check for comprehensiveness.** The developmental growth areas, in concert with Gardner's Multiple Intelligences (MI), can be used as an organizing framework to make sure that no area of learning is more heavily emphasized than another. Figure 8-8 provides an example of an MI planning web.
3. **Determine the amount of time needed.** It is important to plan how the activities will unfold over time. Figure 8-9 shows how the arts could be integrated into one week of a unit focusing on the question, "How do our bodies work?"

Language Objectives	Cognitive Objectives	Emotional Objectives	Social Objectives
These are behaviors and skills that help children receive and communicate ideas through listening, speaking, reading, and writing.	These are behaviors and skills that help children develop the ability to reason, to think logically, to organize information, to understand mathematical relationships, and to solve problems.	These are behaviors and skills that help children develop independence, understanding, and confidence in their own feelings, preferences, decisions, and abilities.	These are behaviors and skills that help children get along better with others by showing appropriate reactions to others, such as kindness, acceptance, respect, and affection.
Linguistic Activities Naming, telling, discussing, describing, defining, retelling, answering, matching lettters to sounds and words, using handwriting, using correct language forms, writing stories, poems, and reports, using the writing process—drafting, editing, and revising own writing and that of others	**Logical-Mathematical Activities** Identifying properties of objects, predicting, researching, using and manipulating number concepts, measuring, ordering, comparing, contrasting, finding patterns, using graphic organizers, making graphs, planning and carrying out tests	**Intrapersonal Activities** Identifying and expressing personal feelings and preferences, controlling one's feelings and behavior, setting a goal or making a plan and then working to accomplish it, assessing or judging one's own work or efforts	**Interpersonal Activities** Sharing, helping, taking turns, performing a role in a cooperative activity, using manners, making moral decisions, settling conflicts, making rules, playing games, and learning about other people and cultures
Integrative Question: A broad, overarching question that addresses an important idea **Concepts:** The specific ideas and information children learn through this thematic unit			
Musical/Rhythmic Activities Identifying and using rhythmic and musical elements, critically listening to music, solving aural problems, singing, playing, and composing music, participating in musical performances	**Visual/Spatial Activities** Identifying and using the art elements, looking closely at and evaluating artworks, creating original drawings, paintings, sculptures, and so on, reading and making maps, solving spatial problems and representing ideas using graphic images	**Naturalistic Activities** Observation, classification and grouping, expressing feelings about nature based on sensory perceptions and outdoor experiences, taking action to protect and care for living things, natural resources, and the environment	**Bodily/Kinesthetic Activities** Sensory activities, exercising, doing physical work, using tools, dancing, moving creatively, dramatizing, cutting, pasting, painting, playing an instrument, doing puzzles, block building and other constructions, driving, and playing sports
Musical Skill Objectives These are behaviors and skills that help children express their ideas through rhythm and music.	**Art Skill Objectives** These are behaviors and skills that help children express their ideas through visual imagery, two-dimensional graphic images, and three-dimensional forms.	**Environmental Skill Objectives** These are behaviors and skills that help children understand, appreciate, and care for the natural world.	**Physical Objectives** These are behaviors and skills that help children develop their coordination, physical strength, balance, and use of the sense organs for taste, smell, touch, sight, and sound.

FIGURE 8–7 Sample MI planning web.

Language Objectives	Cognitive Objectives	Emotional Objectives	Social Objectives
Children will • Increase their vocabulary • Improve their writing skills • Improve their listening skills • Improve oral language skills	*Children will* • Learn to measure using body parts • Practice counting • Practice telling time • Compare and contrast sensations • Learn to classify	*Children will* • Become more confident in their movements • Feel more relaxed moving • Be more self-aware	*Children will* • Improve ability to wait turns • Improve ability to share space and materials • Know safe ways to move around others
Verbal/Linguistic Activities • Name parts of body and describe use • Listen to stories about the body • Dramatize their own body stories • Write a class Big Book	**Mathematical/Logical Activities** • Measure tracings of their bodies • Count and graph different body motions • Time races • Explore textures, different temperature liquids, and so on at sensory center • Classify bones using bone puzzle	**Intrapersonal Activities** • Practice movements until they can perform them expertly • Do many movement activities and talk about how they make us feel • Draw pictures of the insides of our bodies and minds	**Interpersonal Activities** • Play group games • Take turns telling body stories, adding to class book, making measure-ments, and so on • Work together on hand-footprint mural • Act out safe ways to behave on field trip so no one is hurt

Integrative Question: How Do Our Bodies Work?

Theme-related concepts and facts: Our bodies can move in different ways. Our bodies bend at the joints. Inside our body is a skeleton made of bones. Muscles help our body move. Skin protects our bodies. Our bodies can sense temperature, hunger, thirst, tiredness, texture, and so on. Body parts have special names. We can do work with our bodies. Exercise makes our bodies strong.

Musical/Rhythmic Activities	Visual/Spatial Activities	Naturalistic Activities	Bodily-Kinesthetic Activities
• Sing body-related songs • Add own words • Move to music in different ways • Paint to music	• Draw people moving • Make paper fastener "joint" art • Trace body and paint • Make hand-footprint mural • Make stick puppets • Look at X-rays • Look at full-length portraits • Look at Mexican Day of the Dead sculptures	• Take a "Watch Your Step" walk in the woods • Observe animals' movements, bones, and body structures	• Sensory table experiences • Move to music • Daily exercising • Relay races • Acting out stories with movements • Watch gymnastic demonstration • Trip to museum—Inside the Body exhibit
Musical Skill Objectives *Children will* • Improve ability to identify sound patterns • Improve ability to match rhythms	**Art Skill Objectives** *Children will* • Visualize the shape and form of the body • Use the creative process to solve open-ended problems • Practice mixing paint colors • Appreciate how other people represent the body	**Environmental Skill Objectives** *Children will* • Learn how to control body so as not to disturb natural environment • Appreciate similarities in human and animal bodies/movements	**Physical Objectives** • Use senses to gather information • Perform coordinated body movements • Strengthen muscles • Develop safe control over body in space and around others

FIGURE 8–8 Sample integrated unit MI planning web.

MONDAY	TUESDAY	WEDNESDAY	THURSDAY	FRIDAY
Introductory experience Demonstration by gymnast. **Language** Discuss how he moved. Imitate motions. Ask: How do our bodies move? Chart their ideas. **Journal time** Record what they saw. **Read-aloud** *Head to Toe* (Carle, 1997, Scholastic) Do motions. **Art center** Put out bendable materials such as chenille stems, yarn, and cardboard strips. Encourage children to compare the different ways these bend. Ask: How can you make art that moves? (Exploration) **Music** Teach the "Hokey Pokey." Do motions. **Math center** Put out light and heavy things to explore and move. **Science center** Put out bendable model skeleton, X-rays, and drawing materials. **Blocks** Put out bendable plastic action figures.	**Introductory experience** Display photos of gymnastic demonstration. **Language** Talk about photos. Name body parts, and tell how they move. Review visit. Write thank-you note together. **Journal time** Draw thank-you pictures. **Read-aloud** *Me and My Body* (Evan & Williams, 1992, Dorling Kingsley) **Art center** Put out materials for making stick puppets. Set up puppet theater. (Exploration) **Music** Review "Hokey Pokey." Do motions. **Math center** Add scale to center. Sort items by weight (*small group*). **Science center** Have children match skeleton's bones to their own bodies (*small group*). **Blocks** Ask children to describe motions of figures.	**Introductory experience** Display paintings showing people in action, such as Homer's *Crack the Whip* or a Degas ballet scene. **Language** Look at paintings. Ask: What are the ways we can move? Add ideas to word chart. **Journal time** Show yourself moving in a special way. **Read aloud** *The Skeleton inside You* (Balestrino, 1990, Scholastic) **Art center** Introduce paper fasteners. Show how to use to make a bendable "joint." Encourage them to make moving parts on their puppets. (Practice) **Music** Add children's own words and motions to song. **Math center** Have children select object, weigh it, and record it on chart (*small group*). **Science center** Have children find their joints and bend them. Draw pictures of the skeletons inside them. (*small group*). **Blocks** Watch how children move and talk about figures.	**Introductory experience** Have children show actions using their puppets. **Language** Describe ways the puppets moved. Find the ways on the word chart. Look for word patterns such as*ing*. **Journal time** Show how the puppets moved. **Read aloud** *All about My Skeleton* (Black & Ong, 1995, Scholastic) **Art center** Encourage puppet making to continue. (Practice) Add other materials for puppets such as yarn, foils, sports insignia clipped from magazines. Invite interested children to create a play using their puppets. (Responsive) **Music** Use word patterns from word chart to make up a chant. *Example: Running, jumping, hopping, skipping, bending, stopping.* Clap the rhythm, and add body movements. **Math center** Have children select objects of different weights from chart, push them on flat surface, and describe how it feels and the motion they see. Add information to chart (*small group*). **Science center** Add boiled chicken bones. Provide mat for sorting bones by size and shape. Ask them to guess what part of a chicken they come from. **Blocks** Encourage children to draw pictures of their figures and their block structures.	**Sharing** Have children put on playlets using their puppets. Videotape them. **Language** Show tape and have children identify movements. **Journal time** Show your favorite part of the show. **Read-aloud** *I Can Be the Alphabet* (Bonini, 1986, Viking) Do motions. **Art center** Put out paint and play music. Encourage children to move their brushes in different ways as the music changes in pitch, speed, and rhythm. (Exploration) **Music** Recite chant from yesterday. Have children substitute other words and movements. Sing "Hokey Pokey." **Math center** Offer a new set of objects. Have children sort them by what they predict they weigh, then weigh them. **Science center** Put out drawing of chicken skeleton. Invite children to place matching bones on drawing. **Blocks** Challenge children to think of other ways to move the figures.

FIGURE 8–9 Sample week of an integrated unit plan for kindergarten or grade 1.

The Integrated Unit in Action

Integrated units consist of the following components:

Setting the stage. Before beginning the unit, allow the children to become familiar with how the workspace or room is organized, what behaviors are expected of them, and how the time is divided during the day. Once the unit begins, the children will already know where the basic supplies are and which areas are used for certain activities. Taking time to allow for basic exploration of the environment and getting to know each other beforehand will make it easier for everyone to concentrate more on the theme.

The initial event. Once a question is selected, plan an initial event that will be stimulating and provocative, and will get the children excited about the theme. It should focus everyone's attention on the theme and be full of images, ideas, and feelings. The event may be one that takes the children beyond the walls of the room, such as a walk or field trip, or it may involve bringing something special to the children, such as a visitor, an animal, or an object. Rearrange the room, and put out new materials and play items that relate to the unifying theme of the unit. The idea is to raise the interest of as many children as possible.

Activity integration. In a play-based program unit activities should be integrated into each of the learning centers offered but should not replace them. Children need the continuity of knowing that sand, blocks, home-life/dramatic play, and easel painting will be waiting for them every day. Integrate the unit activities into these areas in small ways such as changing the paint color or texture or the paint tools offered at the easel; providing different containers or toys in the sand; putting out topic-related toys; or providing different dress-up clothes, art to hang, or play food. Although it may not be possible to integrate unit

Making Plans

UNIT QUESTION: WHAT DO WE SEE?

WHO? **Group composition age(s):** Toddlers and preschoolers

WHEN? **Time frame:** Each week materials in a featured color will be displayed and discussed.

WHY? **Objective:** Children will learn to identify different colors.

WHERE? **Setup:** Learning centers

WHAT? **Materials:**

Sand Play: Put out containers and shovels, and/or hide blocks or plastic objects of the featured color in the sand.

Block Play: Put out pieces of cardboard that have been covered on both sides with paper or contact paper, and/or add plastic toys of the featured color to the block area.

Dramatic Play: Offer dress-up clothes in the featured color. Put out play food, dishes, or art prints in the featured color.

Easel: Put out the featured color paint, plus white and black.

Music: Put out chimes or a xylophone with different color keys.

HOW? **Procedure:** To begin -As children explore the centers first point out the featured color objects, and say the color name (s).

ASSESSMENT OF LEARNING 1. Can the child find and name the color(s)?

Making Plans

UNIT QUESTION: WHO ARE WE?

WHO?	**Group composition age(s):** Older infants, toddlers, preschoolers
WHEN?	**Time frame:** Daily
WHY?	**Objective:** Children will learn to recognize each other and to accept individual differences.
WHERE?	**Setup:** Play areas
WHAT?	**Materials:** Photocopies or digital prints or photos of the children's faces
	Sand Play: Mount the photos on cardboard, and hide them in the sand for the children to find and play with.
	Block Play: Glue photos to well-sanded blocks of wood and add to regular blocks.
	Dramatic Play: Put out masks and mirrors. Frame and hang photos on the wall.
	Art: Provide small digital prints for children to glue onto their collages.
	Music: Put out chimes or a xylophone with different color keys.
HOW?	**Procedeure:** Show children the photos. Play a matching game where the children pick out their photo from the others. At the play areas ask them to find their own face and that of any other children. Encourage them to say each others' names.
ASSESSMENT OF LEARNING	1. Can the child find his or her own face among the others? 2. Can the child name any of the other children?

concepts into every area every time, try to find creative ways to touch as many areas as possible.

In the primary grades integrated activities can be used to unify the different subject areas. For example, if the question is "How do living things survive?" then a science lesson in which children plant seeds and water some of them will tie in math as they measure the growth of the new plants, writing as they keep a journal, and visual art as they draw pictures of the different stages of growth.

Ending the unit. After all the time and effort spent on an integrated unit, it should not be allowed to fizzle away at the end.

- **Share—**Provide time for the children to share what they have learned with each other. Children can show artwork or projects they have done and tell how they made them. Consider trying a variety of formats. Although having the child stand up in front of the group is a common method, other possibilities include audio taping or video recording the child's presentation for sharing with the others. These tapes can then be shared with parents as well.

- **Display—**The children can also make displays that show what they have learned, and the children can circulate among them asking questions and making comments. To keep the group focused on the presentations, provide a simple checklist to mark or coupons to collect to show which displays they visited.

- **Evaluate—**The end of an integrated unit is a time for evaluating what has happened. What were the children's favorite activities? What do they remember best? What new things did they learn? What do they want to tell others about their experiences? What have the children learned and accomplished?

Integrated Units and Projects in Combination

Although the project approach and integrated learning unit have been discussed separately, they are not mutually exclusive. Within the presentation of an integrated unit, topics of interest to one or more children may emerge. For example, during a unit focused on the question "What is water?" three children might become interested in bubbles and want to learn more about them. If the teacher is flexible, these interests can become independent projects.

Whether used separately or in combination, both of these approaches integrate the arts into the total learning of the child. The arts provide the symbolic medium through which children can express what they have observed and thought about. In a dinosaur project drawings might record how a dinosaur model was built. An original song and creative movement might re-create what was learned about how dinosaurs moved. A puppet show might act out how paleontologists dig up fossils. Nevertheless, these artworks do not stand alone. They are richer and more intense because they are part of a total experience.

A unit on life in the oceans becomes more meaningful when children are given the opportunity to move creatively. Here children imagine they are fish wiggling through the water without help from arms or legs.

HOW CAN WE SHARE LEARNING THROUGH THE ARTS?

There are many ways to share what children have learned.

Documenting Learning

Documentation of what has been learned is an essential part of both integrated and project approaches to curriculum design as well as for individual arts activities. When done well, such documentation provides a rich, thought-provoking, and memorable record of the learning process the children went through.

Julianne Wurm (2005) describes how the documentation kept by teachers in the Reggio Emilia program is used to create documentation or **presentation panels** that contain photographs, children's artwork, and written descriptions of what the children said and did. Hung in the classroom, these panels show the children that the process they went through in an arts activity, an integrated unit, or a project is important and provide opportunities for them to revisit their work. Displayed in public spaces for parents and community, the panels show what children can accomplish as they learn.

Project documentation. In order to create these kinds of presentation panels, materials that record how the learning was accomplished must be collected throughout the unit, project, or activity. These records can be anecdotal notes, tape recordings, photographs, and samples of children's work. Materials should be collected at all the stages of the unit or project. Figure 8-10 provides examples of what might be collected.

Recording group work. Group work can be recorded on a specially designed sheet that allows input from the children. A large sheet of paper is divided into days. Each day the group dictates its accomplishments. Children can also be encouraged to record on the sheet in their own way. Alternatively, each day's work can be recorded on separate sheets that are later bound to create a book about the project.

Creating a panel. A meaningful presentation panel should include most or all of the following documents:

1. **A large, easy-to-read title.** A good title draws the viewer to the presentation and places the work in context.

DINOSAUR PROJECT RECORDS
Calendar showing days and time project was worked on
Child-dictated anecdotal records (see Figure 8-11)
Teacher's anecdotal records
Photos of dinosaur being built
Photos of finished dinosaur and everyone who worked on it
Class graph comparing heights of dinosaur and children in class
Michelle's drawings of finished dinosaur
Frank's story about the dinosaur (dictated and illustrated)
Margo and Toma's story about the dinosaur (recorded on audiotape)
Sheet of comments about the dinosaur written by families and visitors to program

FIGURE 8–10 Project Documentation: The dinosaur project.

Our Dinosaur Project	
Day 1:	We have decided to build a dinosaur. Michelle is making a head out of a box. Frank is making a big tail.
Day 2:	Michelle's mom gave us a big box for the body.
Day 3:	We decided to paint our dinosaur purple. We painted the head today.
Day 4:	Toma and Mark helped us paint the body and tail. Michelle made neat teeth out of a Styrofoam tray.
Day 5:	We tried to put our dinosaur together today. First we tried glue, but it fell off. Then Michelle thought we should use tape. So we taped it, but when Mrs. Denali moved it so we could have reading time, the head fell off. Everyone laughed. Frank was upset. He went and played with the blocks.
Day 6:	Mrs. Denali showed us how to use wire to attach the parts of our dinosaur. She made the holes, and we pushed the wire through. Now our dinosaur is really strong. His head even moves because of the wire.
Day 7:	We named our dinosaur "Purple." Margo wrote the name for us, and we hung it on a string around his neck. We measured him, and he is four feet high. He is taller than we are. We pretended he was wild, and Kate, Toma, and Frank built a pen for him out of the big blocks. We knocked it down and let him out. He is really friendly and guards our room when we aren't here.

FIGURE 8–11 Sample project group work anecdotal note.

2. **Parent information.** There should be brief descriptions of what the children did and learned that make clear the value of doing the project. Unit goals and objectives can be restated in clear, direct language.
3. **Visuals.** The panel should catch the eye. Children's artwork and photographs of the children involved in the processes of learning are an ideal way to do this. Photographs of science experiments, creative movement activities, and other hands-on activities bring what happens in an active classroom to life. The visuals should be carefully mounted on color-coordinated backgrounds.
4. **Captions.** The photographs and children's work should be boldly labeled with quotes made by the children. These can be obtained from anecdotal notes, tape recordings, or by having children offer their own comments (see Figure 8-11).
5. **Artifacts.** Actual samples of tools and materials used, artifacts related to the theme, and three-dimensional constructions can be attached to the panel or displayed on a table nearby. For example, for a project on the ocean, shells can be glued to the panel.
6. **An interactive.** The best way to involve those looking at the panel is to make sure they are intellectually involved. Ask them to look for particular things or to answer a question, or think about another way to do the same work. For example, for a documentation panel about farming, samples of farm products, such as wool, corn, and hay, can be attached with the question "Can you identify all these farm products?"

Celebratory Events

Another way to share the learning of integrated units and projects is to stage a celebration. It takes extra effort, but a celebration of learning or a culminating activity helps solidify all the learning that has taken place. The event may consist of special activities that relate to the topic of study, and/or it may include displays of work and photographs that reflect the activities that have taken place. The entire environment of the room may be changed for the day, and visitors may be invited. It should be a party that celebrates the joy of learning.

Celebrations provide opportunities for parents and children to interact in ways not afforded in the classroom. Celebrations provide a way to display more than presentation panels. For example, large play spaces and constructions, such as a store or a hospital, are often created during project work and integrated units, which must be removed to make way for the next learning experience. These can be shared with families during a celebration. A celebration also allows children to share what they have learned directly as they explain the work they have on display or put on performances. Families can also take an active role. Invite parents to help prepare and present the different activities.

Staging a celebration. A celebration can have all or most of the following:

- artwork—with descriptions (by children or adults)
- banners and signs
- demonstrations—of technique and/or of art forms
- presentation panels
- guest performers—artists, musicians, dancers (children or adults)
- interactive exhibits (viewers are asked to respond to a question or survey, or to decide which tool or method was used to make an artwork)
- invitations
- musical and dramatic performances (children, adults, mixed groups, professional)
- participatory activities (such as a mural to which every guest contributes something)
- photographs
- posters
- video of children at work being shown

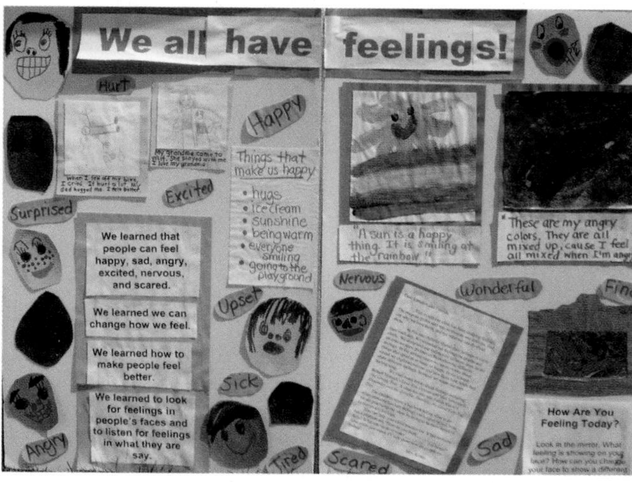

Every study unit should culminate with a presentation panel that visually summarizes what the children have learned. In this panel self-portraits, paintings, and drawings by first graders are displayed along with what they said and learned about their feelings.

CONCLUSION: MAKING THE CONNECTION

> *Let the main ideas which are introduced into a child's education be few and important, and let them be thrown into every combination possible.*
>
> —*Alfred North Whitehead (1929, p. 2)*

The arts, as a way of learning and communicating about the world, can enrich every aspect of an early childhood program. Presented with activities that are unified by a deep-seated question, children learn to see and react to the world as an interconnected place. When children's interests provide the starting point for designing arts activities in emergent curriculum, the children see them as meaningful. Self-initiated projects help children develop independent thinking and working skills.

Setting up these kinds of opportunities takes a great deal of work, effort, and creativity on our part. No published unit or project list will work with every group of children every time. Each class is unique in its interests and skills, and the integrated units teachers create must be customized accordingly. It is well worth the effort. When children's interests are aroused, when they are full of enthusiasm, and when they know they have a choice, they respond by thinking more deeply. They care more about what they are doing, and they understand the world better. Integrating the arts into the curriculum also means that all learning becomes more meaningful.

FURTHER READING

Chard, S. (1998). *The project approach: Making the curriculum come alive.* New York: Scholastic.

This book details ways to initiate projects in the classroom. Sylvia Chard also has a wonderful Web site (http://www.projectapproach.org/) that presents many examples of actual projects.

Helms, J. H., & Beneke, S. (Eds.). (2003). *The power of projects.* New York: Teachers College Press.

This book provides many examples of actual projects carried out by teachers of young children.

Stacey, S. (2008). *Emergent curriculum in early childhood settings.* St. Paul, MN: Redleaf.

Wein, C. G. (2008). *Emergent curriculum in the primary classroom: Interpreting the Reggio Emilia approach in schools.* New York: Teachers College Press.

These two books show how to design and carry out an emergent curriculum.

Wurm, J. P. (2005). *Working in the Reggio way.* St. Paul, MN: Redleaf.

This is an intensive analysis of how integrated curriculum is designed at the Reggio preschools in Reggio Emilia, Italy.

For additional information on integrating the arts into the curriculum visit our Web site at http://www.cengagebrain.com

TEACHING IN ACTION

A Preschool Teacher's Project Log
The Store Project: The First Two Weeks

Monday 10/7. We took a walk to the store on the corner to buy the ingredients for our fruit salad snack. When we got back, I noticed that the children in the dramatic play area were pretending to go to the store.

Tuesday 10/8. I brought in some shopping bags and empty cereal boxes to add to the dramatic play area. Some of the children asked me to help them make a store. We sat in a small group and talked about what we might need in a store. I listed their ideas. They had a pretty good idea about the need for shelves and a cash register. When I asked what we should sell in the store, they had a lot of disagreements.

Later I thought about this and decided we needed to take another trip to the store.

Wednesday 10/9. I called the market and made sure we could visit. Then I asked some parents if they could come on Friday for our trip to the market. I announced our trip at the meeting and explained that some children wanted to make a store in our classroom. I read them the book *On Market Street* (Arnold Lobel, 1989, New York: Mulberry).

Thursday 10/10. At the meeting we talked briefly about our trip and what we might see. Later, I met with small groups and made lists of what they thought they would see. I gave them stapled "journals" to record what they did see, and they wrote their names and decorated the covers with their ideas about the store. Today we read *Tommy at the Grocery Store* (Bill Grossman, 1991, New York: HarperCollins). They loved the rhymes in this book.

Friday 10/11. We visited the market early in the morning when there was hardly anyone else there. The children loved talking to the produce manager, cashiers, and the butcher and drawing in their journals. The store gave us paper bags and hats. When we got back, we shared about the trip. We listed all of the products we saw being sold. Many children drew more pictures in their journals. Now everyone wants to help make our own supermarket.

Monday 10/13. Wow, such enthusiasm. I shared the photos from our trip, and the children helped me write labels for them. We hung them on the bulletin board. I read the book *Something Good* (Robert Munsch, 1990, Toronto: Annick).

TEACHING IN ACTION *(continued)*

We talked about where our store should be and what kind of furniture we needed. Later, some children helped me clear out the area. Now lots of shoppers are in the dramatic play area.

Tuesday 10/14. Today I read the book *Not So Fast Songololo* (Niki Daly, 1989, New York: Aladdin), and we talked a little about how people shop in different places. We made a list of different types of stores. We talked about what we wanted our store to look like. Tom, Inga, and Monica drew the front of the store on a large paper. Then several other students helped them paint it. Other students made a big sign. Henry and Aaron cut out "cookies" from paper. I sent home a note asking for empty food boxes for the foods on our list.

Wednesday 10/15. Anna's mom came in and helped four children make fruit by covering balls of newspaper with papier-mâché. A parent also donated a printing calculator to use as the cash register. I put it out for the children to explore.

Thursday 10/16. It is starting to look like a store. Several children arranged the boxes on the bookshelf. The papier-mâché fruit was finally dry, and the group painted their fruit very brilliant colors and patterns. Children are very busy making play dough cakes, pies, hot dogs, and tacos to sell. The best thing was when Susi announced that she was making books to sell in the store. Two other girls and she started a book factory. They spent over an hour folding paper into booklets and drawing pictures inside. I recorded them talking about what to draw in the books so that they would sell—such entrepreneurs!

At the class meeting we talked about how people buy things at the store. The topic of money came up. The children shared about their allowances and times when they lost money. I quickly decided to read the book *Bunny Money* (Rosemary Wells, 1997, New York: Dial).

Friday 10/17. I put out a bin of plastic coins for the children to explore and sort at the math center. I hung up some oversized coins nearby. The coins quickly ended up at the store. Some children spent a lot of time cutting out paper dollar bills and drawing "presidents" on them. Then they had a great time counting them. We put them in a box by the cash register.

I had brought in a price stamper and some labels. Several children were fascinated with these and made labels for the boxes in the store. I spent some time with them and asked them how they knew the price. They had some interesting ideas about what made something more valuable. Gina thought that the lasagna should cost more than the spaghetti because the noodles were bigger. Michael thought the papier-mâché fruit should be very expensive ($1,000,000) because it was hard to make. Luis said we had the best store because we just could make the money when we wanted to buy something. Michael thought about that and noted that it would take a long time to make a million dollars to buy his fruit. Many children spent time buying things at the store.

Next week I can see we will spend quite a bit of time on money. This will be great for practicing counting skills.

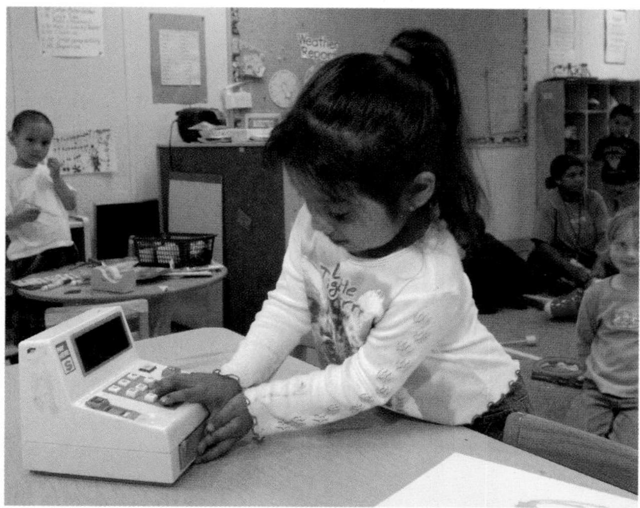

Integrating the arts is a wonderful way to make learning meaningful and memorable.

Studio Page

MY INTEGRATED UNIT FRAMEWORK

Select a project topic or integrated unit question of your choice and complete the framework below:

Language Objectives *Students will*	**Cognitive Objectives** *Students will*	**Emotional Objectives** *Students will*	**Social Objectives** *Students will*
Verbal/Linguistic Activities	**Mathematical/ Logical Activities**	**Intrapersonal Activities**	**Interpersonal Activities**
Question: **Concepts:**			
Musical/Rhythmic Activities	**Visual/Spatial Activities**	**Naturalistic Activities**	**Bodily/Kinesthetic Activities**
Music Skill Objectives *Students will*	**Art Skill Objectives** *Students will*	**Environmental Skill Objectives** *Students will*	**Physical Objectives** *Students will*

Studio Page

ARTS ACTIVITY PLAN

Plan an arts activity for the integrated unit you planned. (See Appendix B for specific guidelines.)

Activity title

Who? Group composition age(s):
Group size:
When? Time frame:
Why? Objectives: In this activity the child will develop . . .

- Socially . . .
- Emotionally . . .
- Physically . . .
- Cognitively . . .
- Linguistically . . .
- Perceptively . . .

Arts skills and knowledge . . .

Where? Setup:
With what? Materials:
How? Procedure:

- Warm-up:
- What to do:
- What to say:
- Transition out:

Assessment of learning

Studio Page

PREPARING A PRESENTATION PANEL

Select a topic and plan the layout and contents of a sample presentation panel. Include the following:

A large, easy-to-read title

Parent information

Visuals (artwork, photographs)

Captions

Artifacts

An interactive activity

Studio Page

PLANNING A CELEBRATION OF THE ARTS

Select a topic or integrated unit question, and plan a celebratory presentation.
Title:

Welcome:

Educational Arts Displays:

Dramatic Performances:

Musical Performances:

Interactive Exhibits:

Participatory Displays:

Demonstrations:

Graphic Elements (invitations, brochures, posters, signs, banners):

Section 3

Exploring the ARTS

Chapter

9

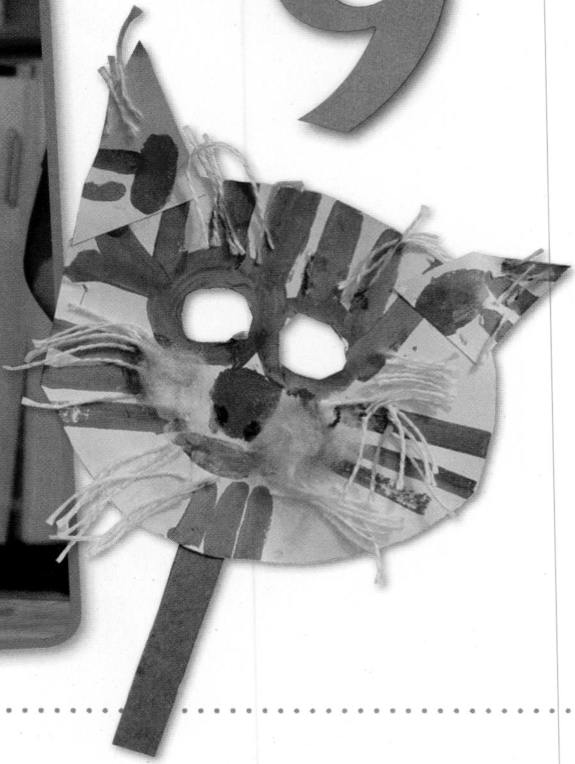

Creating Visual Art

Questions Addressed in This Chapter:

- What are the visual arts?
- How do the visual arts help children grow?
- How are two-dimensional arts activities designed?
- How are three-dimensional arts activities designed?

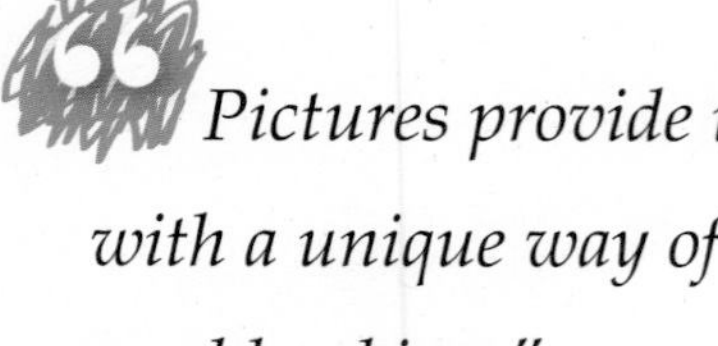

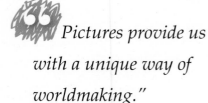

"Pictures provide us with a unique way of worldmaking."

—Bent Wilson, Al Hurwitz, & Marjorie Wilson (1987, p. 14)

WHAT ARE THE VISUAL ARTS?

The *visual arts* involve the creation of two- and three-dimensional images that communicate ideas and emotions. The traditional media for doing this includes drawing, painting, collage, printmaking, and sculpture, but in fact, visual art can be made from almost any material imaginable, ranging from natural fibers to industrial waste. The key ingredient is the manipulation of the visual and tactile elements of line, shape, color, form, texture, pattern, and space. These elements are arranged by the artist into a composition, which combines the selected materials into a unified whole.

HOW DO THE VISUAL ARTS HELP CHILDREN GROW?

Through the visual arts children will develop

- **Physically—**By using the large and small muscles of the arm and hand and eye-hand coordination to handle the different art media. (Bodily-Kinesthetic)
- **Socially—**By working alongside other children and sharing arts materials. (Interpersonal)
- **Emotionally—**By learning to enjoy the act of creating visual art and by developing self-confidence in their ability to control a part of their environment as they handle challenging tools and materials safely. (Intrapersonal)
- **Visual perception skills—**By exploring new ways to make graphic symbols in two- and three-dimensional space, and by responding to the visual effects they have created. (Spatial)
- **Language skills—**By learning a vocabulary of visual art words, and by learning how to communicate about their artwork and the work of others, orally, with graphic symbols, and, at the primary level, through writing. (Linguistic)
- **Cognitively—**By seeing that their creative actions and decisions can cause the effect of producing a visual image, and by developing the ability to compare and evaluate their own work and the work of others. (Logical-Mathematical)
- **Visual art concepts and skills—**By meeting the National Standards for Visual Art (Ponick 2007, pp. 33–35). By the end of the primary years children should meet the following content standards:

Content Standard 1: be skillful with different art media and tools.

Content Standard 2: understand the basic elements, concepts, and structures of art.

Content Standard 3: be able to identify, describe, and analyze the use of symbols, subjects, and ideas in artworks.

Content Standard 4: be knowledgeable about artists from many times and places.

Content Standard 5: be aware of historical, cultural, and social factors that have influenced artists.

Content Standard 6: understand the relationships among the arts, and with disciplines outside the arts.

The visual arts provide another way for children to express their thoughts and feelings. Ryan, age 5, has used marker to create a picture of his mother and himself in their kitchen.

HOW ARE TWO-DIMENSIONAL ACTIVITIES DESIGNED?

Drawing, painting, collage, and the other art media can be used by children of all ages, but children vary greatly in maturity level and ability to concentrate on a visual arts activity. The choice of an activity should be based, first of all, on each child's day-to-day behavior rather than on chronological age. In the following activity plans, ages are given only as a guideline.

The presentation of the activity should also be adjusted to the developmental level of the children.

One-on-One

For infants and young toddlers, who still put things in their mouths, the best way to introduce arts materials and tools is to work with just one child at a time. This allows the child to work under close supervision with a caring adult who can provide immediate positive feedback and share in the child's joyful creation.

Exploration Centers

Older toddlers and preschoolers will need to spend time discovering how the different art media work. This is the exploration stage. At this level visual art is best presented through art centers where arts materials are arranged in attractive and organized ways. Children should be able to freely choose from a variety of materials and explore on their own in a playful atmosphere.

Practice Activities

Once they are familiar with a material, they will need plenty of opportunity to practice learning how to hand the different materials. This is the practice stage. Art centers, stocked with familiar materials and which allow choice and continued exploration, should continue to form the backbone of the visual art program from preschool to the primary grades. Centers allow children to return again and again to familiar materials and tools. In addition, children can select materials from centers for use in small group or class projects.

Responsive Activities

Once they have gained skill, children will be able to focus the ideas and feelings they are trying to communicate in their compositions. This is the responsive stage. Responsive activities are often based on common experiences shared by the whole class. In these cases, opportunities for the whole class to make paintings or work with clay at the same time make sense. Working together in this way allows children to see how each of them responds in different ways to the same stimuli. Preschoolers, kindergarteners, and primary age children can participate in large group discussions about art. First and second graders can write about their own artwork and the work of others. Nevertheless, art centers should still be available to provide tools and media for individual projects, continued exploration and practice, and as a resource to draw upon as needed.

THE DRAWING EXPERIENCE

Drawing is the most basic of all the visual arts. It is usually the first art experience young children have and is the first step toward literacy.

Selecting Drawing Materials

Because many ways of drawing are simple and safe, drawing can be offered to even the youngest of children.

Drawing is one of the first visual arts experiences young children have.

Crayons. Crayons have been the mainstay of early childhood drawing for many years. Their durability, relative safety, and ease of use will continue to keep them popular. The thick kindergarten size will prove most sturdy for grasping fists. However, other shapes and sizes can be slowly introduced over time. Breakage is to be expected, and removing the paper wrappers expands their creative possibilities. As the children gain better finger control, provide regular-sized crayons as well. Children can also be offered a much wider variety of colors. Fluorescent crayons, metallic crayons, and multicolored crayons will provide great enjoyment for children at this level. Two or three notches can be cut in the side of a large unwrapped crayon. Rubbed sideways on the paper, it will produce an interesting effect.

Markers. Unscented, water-based markers should be the backbone of the drawing program. The smooth, fluid nature of markers allows a level of detail not possible with other drawing materials. Markers are much loved by toddlers. Choose water-based, broad-tipped markers. They create broad sweeps of vibrant color with little pressure. Taking off and putting on the caps provide small muscle practice, although some youngsters may need help doing this for a while.

Pencils. Look for pencils with very soft leads. Using pencils makes young children feel grown up and lets them draw finer lines than they can with the other materials.

Chalk. Chalk is not suitable for infants. If toddlers are able to keep their hands out of their mouths while working, thick sidewalk chalk used outside on the pavement will provide an interesting color and texture change from using crayons and markers. Avoid the use of chalk on paper or any other surface when working with toddlers. The dust created is hazardous to their health (see Appendix A).

For preschoolers, kindergarteners, and primary age children, regular white and colored blackboard chalk can be offered, but only if the children draw outside or on paper that has been moistened with liquid starch, milk*, water, or thinned white glue. Alternatively, the chalk can be dipped into the liquid and then used for drawing. To prevent inhalation of dust do not use dry chalk or artists' pastels.

Selecting Drawing Surfaces

Changing the drawing surface changes the way drawing materials work.

Paper. There are many ways to vary the paper offered to children. The size and shape of the paper will affect how the child uses it. Generally, the younger the child, the bigger the paper should be, because smaller paper requires more muscle control to stay within its borders. Newsprint and 50-lb. manila and 50-lb. white drawing paper should be provided for basic drawing activities. Paper can be cut into squares, rectangles, triangles, and circles. Use paper of different colors and textures as well.

Mural paper. Long, rolled paper can be hung on a wall, inside or outside, to create a "graffiti" mural. A large sheet can also be laid on the floor, and several children can draw together.

Other surfaces. For infants zip closure plastic bags can be filled with hair gel colored with food coloring and taped closed. Infants can use their fingers to make marks. Older children will enjoy drawing on rocks, on the sides of cardboard boxes, and in sand and rice. With increasing fine motor skills, they can also work on materials with more confining shapes and sizes, such as strips of adding machine tape and sandpaper. Scrap pieces of wood that have been sanded on the edges make an interesting drawing surface. Small, decorated pieces may then be used in wood sculpture constructions.

Drawing Activities for Infants

Provide one-on-one drawing explorations daily or as often as possible. As infants mature and gain experience, offer more choices of drawing materials and times and places to work.

All one color. Offer a combination of markers, crayons, and pencils in the same color range, such as all reds or all blues. Then talk about dark and light, and dull and bright.

Contrasting colors. Use dark-colored paper with light-colored or metallic crayons.

Drawing Activities for Toddlers

Set up a drawing area supplied with large paper and sturdy crayons and pencils so toddlers can draw when they choose. Continue to supervise them as they work

Making Plans

ONE-ON-ONE ACTIVITY PLAN: First Drawings

WHO? **Group composition age(s):** Older infants and toddlers

Group size: One-on-one

WHEN? **Time frame:** 10 minutes

WHY? **Objectives:** Children will develop

- physically, by using the large and small muscles of the arm and hand to draw. (Bodily-Kinesthetic)
- socially, by interacting with adult. (Interpersonal)
- emotionally, by learning to enjoy the act of drawing and the ability to control a part of their environment. (Intrapersonal)
- visual perception skills, by exploring new ways to make visual marks and responding to the visual effects they have created. (Spatial)
- language skills, by learning a drawing vocabulary and using sound and language in combination with graphic production. (Linguistic)
- cognitively, by seeing that their motions can cause the effect of making visual lines. (Logical-Mathematical)
- art awareness, by becoming familiar crayons and the types of lines they make. (Content Standard 1)

WHERE? **Setup:** For infants—at a highchair or seated in adult's lap. For toddlers—at a child-size table.

WHAT? **Materials:** Several thick crayons and large sheets of paper 12 by 15 inches or larger.

HOW? **Procedure:**

Warm-Up: Show child a crayon and make some lines. Place crayon in child's hand and ask, "Can you make lines, too?"

What to Do: Sit with the child(ren) while they are working; smile and point to the lines and marks they have created.

What to Say: It is not necessary to talk constantly while the child(ren) are working, but occasional statements or questions can increase the toddler's enjoyment and learning.

1. When speaking, be enthusiastic and descriptive: "Look at that red line!" "What a long line!" "What kind of line will you draw next?" "That's an up and down line!"
2. Use drawing as an opportunity to develop the child's vocabulary. Words to use include: *draw, drawing, write, writing, line, lines, long, short, thick, thin, dark, light, colorful, the color names, crayons, dots, marks, paper*.
3. Toddlers love songs and rhymes. Make up little poems, using the descriptive words, to go along with their art explorations, and sing them to traditional tunes.
4. To build vocabulary, look for examples of lines in the environment, such as cracks in the pavement or veins on a leaf. Use the same terms to describe their drawings.

Transition Out: At this young age the child(ren) will spend only a relatively short time, by adult standards, drawing. When the child loses interest, let him or her wander off to the next activity. If the drawing activity must end, do so by providing an attractive alternative, such as "Let's read a story now."

ASSESSMENT OF LEARNING

1. Does child show some control over crayon?
2. Does child say and use some of the drawing vocabulary words?

TEACHING IN ACTION

Drawing with Preschoolers, Kindergarteners, and Primary Age Children: From Exploration to Responsive Drawing Activities in Five Weeks.

WEEK 1: On the first day of class, sit on the rug and open a brand-new box of crayons. Have children name their favorite color. Ask: "How do we use crayons?" Talk about how, when, and where they can be used. Show children where crayons are kept. Have children model getting crayons from the supply area and going to a worktable, and then putting them away. Keep this brief—no more than five minutes. For the rest of the week, have white paper and crayons on the storage shelf. Encourage children to get them and draw. Monitor proper use. Save their drawings for the next lesson.

WEEK 2: Start the week by reviewing what the children did with the crayons. Sitting together on the rug, make up a song or movement about lines. Say, "Last week you learned how to get and use the crayons. Here are some drawings you made. What do you see? Do you see lines? What colors do you see?" Let children respond.

"I will be putting different kinds of papers on the shelf this week. Do you think the crayons will work the same way on them?" Each day put out a different color or texture of paper. Encourage children to compare these to drawings on white paper. Save their drawings.

WEEK 3: Work with a different small group each day. Begin by looking at their drawings. Ask, "What was your favorite paper?" Then say, "Now you know how to get crayons and choose paper. Today I will show you our drawing boards. You can use the drawing board to draw anywhere in the room. You could draw a picture of your block tower. You could draw the fish. You could find a quiet place to draw an imaginary picture. This is how you get a board (demonstrate). Take a crayon container and find your very own drawing place. Draw a picture, and then put away the board and crayons. Gina, can you show us how to put the board and crayons away? Now let's have everyone try it. Find your special place to draw." During the week, encourage children to use the drawing boards.

WEEK 4: Start the week by introducing drawing outside. Say, "Today when we go outside, I will take the drawing boards and crayons. Maybe you will find a special place to draw outside." Continue to encourage children to draw inside and outside. By the end of the week, children should be able to get their own drawing supplies and find a place to draw. Now they will be able to do responsive drawings or keep journals as part of thematic units or during projects.

so they do not put things in their mouths or draw on walls and other surfaces.

Shaped paper. For toddlers paper can be cut into a variety of geometric shapes, but keep these large and simple. Squares; long, thin rectangles; and large triangles are easy to prepare. A paper cutter is invaluable when working with a large number of children.

Share drawings by well-known artists. Select art prints that have subjects of interest such as the cave art of the Paleolithic or Picasso's drawings, to share with your group of young children. Encourage them to trace the drawn lines with their fingers.

Drawing Activities for Preschoolers

By preschool children are usually familiar with drawing tools. The following activity ideas provide ways to keep them excitedly drawing.

Drawing everywhere. Put paper and crayons or markers in various places around the classroom, such as at the science center and block center. Encourage children to record what they see and do.

Bookmaking. Booklets can be made either from 9-by-12-inch paper or in big book size from 12-by-18-inch sheets. Staple the paper together on either the long or the short side. Start with two pages; as the children develop their story-making skill, increase the number of pages. Tell the children that pages can be added if they need more to complete their story. Show the children how to fold back the pages so the booklet lies flat while they are drawing.

Drawing Activities for Kindergarten and Primary Age

Increased fine motor control allows older children to explore more responsive activities.

Portraits. Set up mirrors and invite children to draw self-portraits.

Pictographs. Have children draw self-portraits or other personal pictures on small squares of paper. Laminate them, and use them to create pictographs reflecting the children's interests.

Draw what you see. Set up a still-life arrangement of fruits or flowers or display a live animal. Put drawing materials nearby and invite children to sketch what they see.

Drawing boards. Provide large clipboards with an attached pencil so children can sketch anywhere. Take these on field trips to record what they observe.

Featured artists. Introduce art prints that illustrate more complex drawing techniques, such as the work of Albert Durer and M. C. Escher. Challenge children to figure out what drawing material the artists used and provide similar materials for them to use.

Book Box

Books celebrating drawing.

De Rolf, S. (1997). *The crayon box that talked*. New York: Random House.
Sing along with the book as the crayon colors learn to get along with each other. Two and up.

Druscher, H. (2006). *Simon's book*. San Francisco, CA: MacAdam/Cage.
A boy starts a drawing of a monster and then goes to bed. During the night, the pen, the ink, and the monster come alive and finish the drawing, with surprising results. The simple, animated text enchants children of all ages. This book can be used to lead into a discussion of how a book is made. Four and up.

Gilliland, J. H. (2002). *Not in the house, Newton!* New York: Clarion.
Using a magical red crayon, Newton fills his house with drawings turned real. Use this book when focusing on the color red. Four and up.

Snyder, I. (2003). *Wax to crayons*. New York: Scholastic.
Colorful, sharp photographs show the complete process of making crayons. Children love learning how those mysterious and ever-present crayons are really made and may be inspired to reinvestigate their artistic possibilities. Four and up.

THE PAINTING EXPERIENCE

There is nothing else quite like it. Long tapered brushes dip into liquid color that flows and falls with abandon across a white rectangle of paper. For a moment, the young artist is alone, focused on the interplay of mind and muscle, action and reaction. Painting provides the sensory link between the childish finger that plays in the spilled milk and the masterly hand that painted the Mona Lisa.

Before beginning a painting exploration with children, take a moment to make a tempera painting. Swirl and spread the paint, and concentrate on the way the brush responds to muscular commands and the visual result that is created. Feel the way the brush glides over the surface, and watch how the wet paint catches the light and glistens. Creating a painting is the perfect way to appreciate the importance of process over product to the young child, for whom painting is first and foremost a sensory experience.

Selecting Paint

A variety of paints are available that are safe to use with young children.

In addition to liquid tempera, other types of paint can be offered. Most of these will work better if used on a table rather than at the easel.

Painting at the easel develops physical control over the arm, the hand, and the unpredictable paint. "My rainbow." Tempera painting by Katie, age 3.

Fingerpaint. Commercial **fingerpaint** provides vibrant color in a smooth, easy-to-clean formula and should be the main fingerpaint used. For other fingerpaint explorations, try shaving cream, whipped soap flakes, or liquid starch colored with a small amount of food coloring or tempera paint.

Tempera blocks. This paint comes in dry cakes that fit in special trays. The children must wet the brush to dampen the cube for use. Choose the larger sizes in basic colors and fluorescents (see Appendix C for sources). Some adults like the fact that these do not spill. However, the colors and texture of the block paints are not as exciting as liquid tempera paints, so these should never be the only type of paint the children use but, rather, an interesting addition to the program.

Paint "markers." These small plastic containers have felt tips. Fill the container with tempera paint, and use like a marker. The stubby shape of the bottles fits well in little hands, and the paint flows out easily. Keep them tightly capped in a resealable plastic bag when not in use (see Appendix C for paint marker sources).

Watercolors. The small size of the individual watercolors in a set, even in the larger half-pan size, makes them suitable only for preschool and primary age children with well-developed fine-motor control. Watercolors are also more likely to stain clothing than tempera paint. Before giving watercolors to the children to use, wet the color pans and let them sit a short time to soften the paints. Watercolors produce interesting effects when used on wet paper or on top of crayon drawings. Paper can be dampened with a sponge or paintbrush before painting.

Artist's Tool Box

SELECTING BRUSHES

A multitude of commercial paintbrushes are available on the market. Always buy the best quality you can afford. A good brush that is regularly washed out will hold its point and last many years. Poor quality brushes lose their hair rapidly and do not come to a point. Brushes usually come numbered. The higher the number the larger the brush. Offer children an assortment of brushes to choose from when painting.

SHAPES AND SIZES OF BRUSHES

Flats. These brushes are rectangular shaped and have a straight edge, instead of a point. They are good for painting in broad areas of color, edges, and for making thick even lines.

Rounds. These rounded brushes come to a point. These are good for detail work and painting thin lines and dots.

Easel brushes. These brushes have a long handle. They are best used when painting at the easel.

TYPES OF HAIR

Bristle brush. A stiff brush made from hog hair.

Fine hairbrush. A brush made from ox hair or in the more expensive ones, from sable.

Polyester or nylon. A brush made from synthetic material. These are usually very durable.

Stencil brush. This is a stubby round brush with very stiff hair. It is a good brush for infants and toddlers who can stamp it up and down to make dots.

Sumi. A soft-haired brush with a bamboo handle, traditionally used in Japanese painting. It works best in watercolor.

Selecting Surfaces for Painting

Although plain white paper provides an adequate surface for most types of paint, create exciting sensory experiences by providing a variety of surfaces for children to paint on.

Brown paper. Brown kraft paper (or a cut, flattened paper bag) provides an absorbent surface with a color that contrasts well with the lighter colors that are often lost on white paper. Try it with pink, yellow, and white paint. Try wrinkling the paper and then smoothing it again to create a bumpy texture that is fun to paint on, too.

Colored paper. Colored construction paper in dark colors also offers a good contrast for light-colored paints.

Commercial fingerpaint paper. This is heavy, with a smooth, shiny surface. Although relatively expensive, children should occasionally have the opportunity to fingerpaint on this paper. Freezer paper, shiny shelf paper, and other sturdy papers can also be used. Paper may be dampened with a wet sponge to make the paint spread more easily.

Fabric. Burlap or fabric glued to a cardboard base serves as a challenging texture for painting. This would be a good choice when exploring texture.

Teacher Tip

PAINTING SMOCKS

A good smock that will cover most of the child can be made from a large adult's shirt that buttons up the front.

1. Cut the sleeves very short.
2. Put it on the child backwards, and fasten it together in the back with a spring clothespin.
3. Make sure the child's sleeves are pushed up above the elbows.

Special Needs

• DRAWING AND PAINTING MODIFICATIONS •

Visual: Children with limited vision should work on a tilted surface or easel so they may have their eyes closer to the work surface. Choose the colors of crayons, markers, and paint that they can see best, and add sawdust or sand to the paint so they can feel their finished painting. Different scents can be added to the paint to help in color identification.

Physical: Some children with orthopedic handicaps work best if they can lie on the floor when painting. Tape paper to the floor or other work surface so that it does not move while they are working. Wrap foam around the handles of the brushes or drawing tools to make them easier to grip. Use wide, low-sided containers for the paint, such as cut-down margarine or frosting containers. If necessary, use tape to hold paint containers in place.

Accommodate children in wheelchairs by hanging the paper on the wall at a height that allows them to work comfortably. Provide plenty of room for them to extend their arms out full range. If necessary, attach a brush or marker to a dowel to extend the child's reach. Keep the paint thick, and make sure all children have ample working space, so if there are involuntary movements or lack of control, paint does not splatter on the paper or clothing of other children. (See Chapter 5 for more ways to meet special needs.)

Paper products. Paper placemats, coffee filters, shelf paper, and thick paper toweling offer different textures for painting.

Wood and stone. The varying texture and absorbency of wood scraps and stones provide an interesting contrast to flat paper.

Other papers. Some papers are more difficult to paint on for young children. Tissue paper dissolves when it gets wet. Metallic papers and aluminum foil do not take water-base paint well and when dry the paint flakes off.

Setting Up a Painting Center

A painting center for preschool and primary classrooms should have both a table and easel. Provide a ratio of one easel for every five children (i.e., if there are 20 children, have four easels set up), or a table on which four children can paint at one time. Side-by-side easels provide the most opportunity for the children to interact. Cover the table and easel surface with newspaper, and put a piece of heavy plastic under the easels. Use spring-type clothespins to clip the paper to the easel. Provide a place for children to put wet work to dry. To attract children to the center, display bottles of paint on open shelves and hang children's paintings and works by famous artists as well.

Painting Activities for Infants

Painting activities for infants need to be safe and carefully supervised but allow plenty of free exploration.

Paint bags. Add 1 tablespoon of cornstarch to 1 cup of water and heat until thick. Cool. Fill a zipper plastic bag with a small amount of the liquid and add some drops of different color nontoxic food coloring or tempera paint. Zip closed and seal with tape. Infants can use fingers to mix colors.

Finger water paint. Put a small amount of water on a white plastic dish or tray and add a few drops of nontoxic food coloring. Encourage children to mix colors with fingers.

Painting Activities for Toddlers

Toddlers need many explorations of painting.

Water painting. Give toddlers large brushes and buckets of water. Go outside and paint walls and pavement.

Foam painting. Spray a small amount of shaving cream on a colored tray or tabletop and let toddlers fingerpaint.

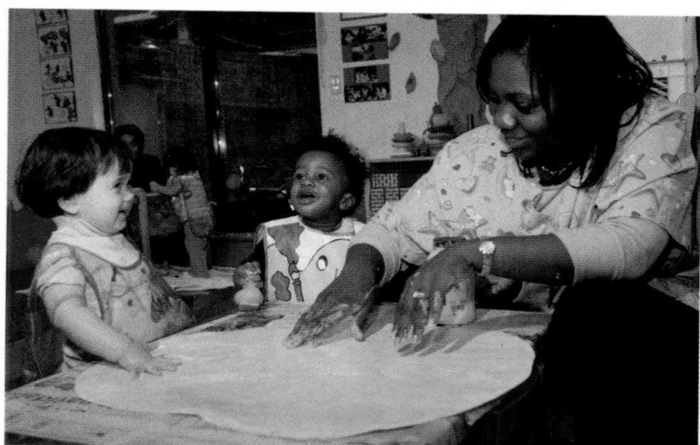
Fingerpaint provides a wonderful sensory experience for young children.

Table painting. Put fingerpaint on a smooth, washable table top and let children explore. To save artwork, place a piece of paper on top and press to capture the child's work.

Lots of colors. Once the child understands painting procedures, offer new colors. There is no rigid formula for selecting the colors. The primary colors of red, yellow, and blue are good choices to start with, because these three colors provide exciting color mixes. As the children gain experience, increase the number of colors offered to include four or five colors, such as brown, green, purple, orange, black, or white.

Brush exploration. Try unusual brushes, such as new toothbrushes, bottle brushes, toilet brushes, and vegetable brushes.

Famous painters. Introduce toddlers to colorful works with bold shapes such as the work of Wassily Kandinsky, Joan Miró, Georgia O'Keefe, and Vincent Van Gogh.

Painting Activities for Preschool

By preschool, painting should be a regular activity. Set up easels and make sure everyone gets a chance to paint often.

Paint patterns. Make paint design scrapers. Cut notches in the edge of a sanitized Styrofoam tray, and pull it through wet paint. Try foam rollers and daubers, pattern painters, and fingertip design makers. (See Appendix C for sources.)

Drop painting. Use eyedroppers and small basters to drop paint on paper.

Book Box

Books that celebrate painting.

Demi. (1980). *Liang and the magic paintbrush*. New York: Henry Holt. (Media: painting; Multicultural: China)
A Chinese boy is given a magic paintbrush that can make his pictures come alive. Six and up.

de Paola, T. (1988). *The legend of the Indian paintbrush*. New York: G. P. Putnam's Sons.
This retelling of a Plains Indian tale of the origin of the flower "Indian paintbrush" explains the role of painting in the life of the Plains tribes. This book relates well to painting activities involving different types of paintbrushes or using natural materials such as twigs and grasses to apply paint. Also available as a big book from Scholastic. Four and up.

Gibbons, G. (1998). *The art box*. New York: Holiday House.
Collage and drawn illustrations show the tools and materials used by artists for drawing and painting. Six and up.

Moss, S. (1995). *Peter's painting*. Greenvale, NY: MONDO.
Colorful and eye-catching, Peter's paintings look like splashes and dots, but in his mind they show incredible things. Each painting he makes appears on the walls of his room on the next spread. Toddlers and up.

Celebrate a color. Offer the featured color and related **tints** and **tones** at the paint setup. On purple day, for example, put out purple, lavender, and white paint.

Add textures to the paint. A variety of materials can be mixed into the liquid paint to give it a different feel.

Watching a young child paint is the perfect way to learn to appreciate process over product.

Making Plans

ONE-ON-ONE ACTIVITY PLAN: First Painting Experience

WHO? **Group composition age(s):** Infant old enough to sit up and hold brush or young toddler

Group size: One child

WHEN? **Time frame:** 5 to 15 minutes depending on child's interest

WHY? **Objectives:** Children will develop

- physically, by using the large and small muscles of the arm and hand to draw. (Bodily-Kinesthetic)
- socially, by interacting with adult. (Interpersonal)
- emotionally, by learning to enjoy the act of drawing and the ability to control a part of their environment. (Intrapersonal)
- visual perception skills, by exploring new ways to make marks and responding to the visual effects they have created. (Spatial)
- language skills, by learning a drawing vocabulary and using sound and language in combination with graphic production. (Linguistic)
- cognitively, by seeing that their motions can cause the effect of making visual lines. (Logical-Mathematical)
- art awareness, by becoming familiar with crayons and the types of lines they make. (Content Standard 1)

WHERE? **Setup:** A high chair, a child-size table, or seated in an adult's lap. Put a smock on child. In addition, have wet paper towels ready to wipe hands.

WHAT? **Materials:** One thick-handled paintbrush, a stable cup of paint in one color, large sheet of newsprint.

HOW? **Procedure:**

Warm-Up: Show the child the brush and say, "Let's paint!"

What to Do: Dip the brush in paint and model how to make a mark on the paper. Hand the brush to the child and let the child try.

What to Say: Emphasize the sensory experience by excitedly describing the texture, color, and movement of the paint. "Ooo, look the paint is shiny." "Wow, see how the brush makes a thick line." Use words like *long, short, round, curved, spot, high,* and *low* to describe the marks the child makes.

Transition Out: Children are usually delighted with the effect they can create using colorful paints. Let them paint until they feel they are finished, then guide them to the place to wash their hands. Put the painting out of the way to dry. It is best if it can dry flat, to minimize drips.

ASSESSMENT OF LEARNING

1. When paintings are compared to ones done previously and stored in portfolios, do child(ren) demonstrate increasing control over the brush and paint?
2. Do children use descriptive language, as modeled by the teacher, to describe the painting experience?

1. The simple addition of a little more water makes a thinner paint and changes the sensory response of the brush as it moves across the paper.
2. Detergent, liquid starch, and corn syrup* added to the paint will make it spread differently.
3. To make the paint thicker and textured, add sand, sawdust, cornmeal,* flour,* oatmeal,* dry cereal,* or soap flakes.
4. Salt* added to the paint will produce a bubbly effect.
5. Salt* and Epsom salts sprinkled on the paint produce a glittery effect.

Famous paintings. Use art prints and art cards to introduce different styles of painting. Select works that are noticeably different in style, such as a painting by Vermeer and one by Monet.

Varied papers. In addition to the large newsprint, vary the painting surface by providing colored paper, cardboard, and smooth shelf paper. Cut the paper into a variety of large rectangles and squares, or occasionally into a triangle or circle.

Make magic pictures. Draw a picture using white candle stubs. Then paint over the picture with a very watered down tempera paint.

Painting Activities for Kindergarten and Primary Age

Painting activities for this age group should still be open-ended, but increasing hand-eye coordination enables older children to work smaller and in more detail. Paintings can be done to illustrate stories and record experiences.

Making Plans

CENTER ACTIVITY PLAN: Fingerpaint Color Mixing

WHO? **Group composition age(s):** Preschool

WHEN? **Time frame:** 15 to 20 minutes

WHY? **Objectives:** Children will develop

- physically, by controlling and strengthening their fingers. (Bodily-Kinesthetic)
- socially, by working side by side with other painters and sharing materials and space. (Interpersonal)
- emotionally, by feeling trusted to paint with their hands. (Intrapersonal)
- visual perception skills, by observing the different colors they can make. (Spatial)
- language skills, by using descriptive words to describe the experience. (Linguistic)
- cognitively, by learning how to make different colors. (Logical-Mathematical)
- art awareness, by identifying colors, textures, and patterns in their work and that of others. (Content Standard 2)

WHERE? **Setup:** Start on the rug with the whole group. Later, students will work at low newspaper-covered tables in the painting center. Students will wear their smocks with sleeves pushed up high.

WHAT? **Materials:** Fingerpaint paper or other smooth paper as large as possible, preferably 9-by-12-inches. Fingerpaint in the three primary colors. When the child is ready to paint put a tablespoon of each color on the newspaper above their paper.

HOW? **Procedure:**

Warm-Up: Have children on the rug facing the chart. Hold up cards or pieces of paper—one orange, one green, and one violet. Ask, "Do you know how to make these colors?"

Place color sample at top of column on chart paper and record their ideas. Explain that at the painting center they will be able to try to make these colors using fingerpaint. Say "Let's get ready to fingerpaint!" Have them hold up their hands and wiggle them. Ask them to imagine they are painting in the air.

What to Do: When children come to paint at center time, put the three colors of paint on their paper.

What to Say: At the center as children dip their fingers in the paint and mix the colors on their paper, ask them to describe the colors they are using and what happens when they mix them together. Ask them to find patterns and textures, too.

Transition Out: Have children put paintings to dry. When work is dry, have children sit in a circle with their fingerpainting on the floor in front of them. Discuss the differences and similarities in the colors. Ask, "What colors made orange (green, violet)?" "Is everyone's green (orange, violet) the same?" "Why might the colors be different?" "What other colors did you make?" "Did you see any textures or patterns in others' work?"

ASSESSMENT OF LEARNING

1. Children can explain how they made their colors, textures, and patterns.
2. Children work safely and thoughtfully with each other.

Making Plans

RESPONSIVE ACTIVITY PLAN: Making a Paintbrush

WHO? **Group composition age(s):** Primary class

WHEN? **Time frame:** 45 minutes to an hour

WHY? **Objectives:** Children will develop

- physically, by using fine motor skills to direct self-made brush. (Bodily-Kinesthetic)
- socially, by working side by side with other painters and sharing materials and space. (Interpersonal)
- emotionally, by practicing evaluation of their own work. (Intrapersonal)
- visual perception skills, by comparing the visual images created using different tools. (Spatial)
- language skills, by answering questions about their work. (Linguistic)
- cognitively, by observing cause and effect when using different brushes. (Logical-Mathematical)
- art awareness, by exploring how the tool affects the way the painting looks. (Content Standards 1, 2, and 4)

WHERE? **Setup:** Students will work at their own newspaper-covered desks. Students will wear their smocks.

WHAT? **Materials:** Students will be given craft sticks, scissors, a piece of masking tape, and an assortment of materials (cloth, Styrofoam, sponge, yarn, etc.) cut into small rectangles. Six colors of paint will be available in sanitized Styrofoam egg cartons that have been cut in half (see Appendix C). Sheets of 9-by-12-inch paper should be used.

HOW? **Procedure:**

Warm-Up: Show a paintbrush. Ask, "How do you think this brush is made?"

What to Do: Write children's ideas on chart paper. Next, show children a painting with lots of texture, such as Van Gogh's *Starry Night*. Ask, "What kind of paintbrush did this artist use?" Explain that they will be inventing their own paintbrushes today. Demonstrate how to wrap the materials around the end of the craft stick and attach using the tape.

What to Say: As children make brushes ask them, "How do you think your brush will work? Will it make thick lines or thin ones?" As they start to try to paint with their brushes ask, "Is it working the way you thought? How can you change it to make it work better?"

Transition Out: Have children put paintings and brushes to dry on a sheet of newspaper or in a drying box. When work is dry, have children sit in a circle and show their brushes and the resultant painting. Discuss the difference and similarities in the brush strokes. Ask, "Did your brush work as you expected?" "Why do you think commercial brushes are made from hair?" "Based on your exploration of brush design, what can you say about the brushes used by Van Gogh and other artists?" "Can you tell from the finished painting what kind of brush was used?"

ASSESSMENT OF LEARNING

1. Do children make usable brushes?
2. Can children name two or more similarities or differences about the brushes?
3. Do children make reasonable predictions about the possible painting tools used by other artists?

Different sizes of paper. Older children can begin to use smaller sizes of paper, but continue to offer large sheets as well. They need to use their whole arm as part of the painting process, just as adult artists do. Many of the paintings adults are familiar with from small reproductions are in reality quite large. Monet's *Water Lilies,* for example, are over five feet long.

Make your own textured surface. Children can make their own textured painting surface by gluing textured materials such as sand, fabric, and ribbon pieces to a sheet of construction

TEACHER TO FAMILY

Sample Letter to Families about Painting

Dear Family,

Painting is an important part of our art program, and the children will be painting almost every day. In order for your child to have a wonderful time painting, please dress him or her in clothing that is easy to wash. It is important that sleeves can be pushed up above the elbows to prevent them from dragging in the paint.

Children will be wearing smocks when painting. However, accidents do happen. The water-based tempera paint we use will come out of most fabrics if it is washed in the following way:

Apply detergent to the spot and rub.

Wash normally.

If the spot still shows, repeat rubbing and washing.

Line dry. Do not put in the dryer until the spot is gone, as the heat will set the color.

It may take several washings to remove the stain completely.

Painting activities help your child grow in many ways, as he or she learns to control the paintbrushes and other painting tools. Please help your son or daughter enjoy painting without the worry of getting paint on clothing.

Your child's teacher,

paper on one day and then painting over it the next.

Explore style and technique. Compare art prints, art cards, or digital images of artworks done in different styles or techniques, such as a portrait by Rembrandt and one by Amedeo Modigliani. Then challenge children to make two paintings of the same subject using two different styles or techniques.

Put chalk over paint. Encourage children to use chalk to add more details to their dry paintings.

Explore other ways to apply paint. Paint can be applied with all of the following items: branches, pieces of cardboard, twigs, feathers, feather dusters, squeeze bottles (such as empty mustard or shampoo containers), and more. Encourage children to be inventive in figuring out new ways to apply paint.

Straw blowing. Use an eyedropper to make a spot of thin watercolor paint on the paper. Use a straw to blow the paint in different directions. Note: Make sure children do not blow too hard or too long as they may feel dizzy from hyperventilation.

Crayon resist. Draw a picture in crayon, pressing hard. Then paint over the picture with watercolor or a very watered down tempera paint.

Make colorful fingerpaint paper. Cover regular paper with colorful crayon shapes. Try to fill in the whole paper. Then fingerpaint on top of the crayoned colors.

THE COLLAGE EXPERIENCE

Every art program for young children includes the art activity called "collage." Children are offered various papers, magazine pictures, and small objects to glue onto their pictures. Collage has become one of the most popular art forms for young children. It is also one of the most creative. Young children can arrange their bits and pieces of collage materials in a multitude of ways. Adults do not expect children to produce "realistic-looking" collages and do not evaluate them in the same way as drawings. Teachers and parents are often more accepting of the exploration process and the resulting products in collage than they are in drawing or painting. Children are extraordinarily free of restraints as they become immersed in the creative process of making a collage.

Every collage experience can be new and different. It is easy to vary the materials that are offered so the children's motivation to explore and practice will remain high. Children will steadily develop more control over the paste and glue if they are given many opportunities to make collages. The challenge of applying paste to objects of different textures and forms will help develop their hand-eye coordination.

Artist's Tool Box

SOURCES OF COLLAGE MATERIALS

From Nature

acorns, feathers, flowers, leaves, pebbles, sand (under special conditions), seashells, seeds, stones, twigs, walnut shells

From Home

aluminium foil, bottle caps, cardboard, carpet pieces, cork pieces, cotton, cotton balls, dried beans*, jar lids, macaroni, nails and screws, tubes from paper toweling (cut into short, 1½ to 1-inch slices), rice*, string, Styrofoam packing beads

From Crafts

beads, buttons, cotton and polyester batting, craft sticks, fabric, foam pieces, fun fur, gift wrap bows, jewelry pieces, leather scraps, paper confetti, pompons, ribbon, rickrack, sponge pieces, spools, stuffing (polyester), tiles, wood scraps, wood shavings, wooden ice cream spoons (also called craft spoons), wool fleece, yarn

Selecting Pastes and Glues

Glue Sticks

- **Advantages—**Large glue sticks are easy for young toddlers to use. Children can grasp them in one or two hands and easily rub the glue on the backing paper. Disappearing-color glue sticks help the child see where the glue has been put. Glue sticks work best for most paper and fabric.
- **Disadvantages—**One major difficulty is that caps are difficult for young children to remove and put back on. Often the stick of glue is damaged in the process. This is a skill that needs to be taught and practiced. In addition, children often push up the stick more than needed and over apply the glue. Glue sticks do not work well for three-dimensional objects, so they are limited to only certain types of collage. Compared to bottled glue, they are also expensive.

Paste

- **Advantages—**White paste or school paste has many advantages. It is easy to use because it is thick and does not run. Paste holds a variety of materials well. It can be placed on a piece of paper or in a plastic lid and applied with the fingers

Artist's Tool Box

SUGGESTED COLLAGE PAPERS

Advertising brochures	Art boards	Marble paper	Mat board
Binders' board	Blotter paper	Metallic paper	Napkins
Candy wrappers	Cardstock	Newspaper	Newsprint
Cereal-box cardboard	Charcoal paper	Oak tag	Paper placemats
Chipboard	Coffee filters	Paper plates	Paper towels
Computer paper	Construction paper	Photographs	Poster board
Corrugated cardboard	Corrugated paper	Rainbow	Rice paper
Doilies	Drawing paper	Construction paper	Shelf paper
Fluorescent paper	Foil paper	Sandpaper	Tracing paper
Fadeless construction paper	Gift wrap	Tag board	Velour paper
Holographic foils	Graph paper	Typing paper	Watercolor paper
Magazine pages	Kraft pages	Wallpaper	White tissue paper
	Manila	Waxed paper	

or a craft stick. It provides a wonderful tactile experience for young children.

- **Disadvantages**—It has a tendency to crack and flake off when dry if applied too thickly.

White Glue (also called School Glue)

- **Advantages**—This is a strong, durable adhesive that can be used to glue all kinds of objects. Choose only the type that indicates it washes out of clothing. White glue can be thinned with water and spread on a base to provide a pre-glued surface for collage. It will stay wet for 5 to 10 minutes. It easily cleans up with water, and is available in a wide variety of sizes and bottle designs. It dries clear.

- **Disadvantages**—The runny consistency makes this glue more difficult for young children to control. When applied heavily, it wrinkles the paper. Its major disadvantage is that it dries very slowly. Projects must be dried flat for at least 30 minutes before they can be handled. (Tacky or craft versions of this glue can be used in specific situations when instant adhesion is required, but it does not wash out of clothing.)

Gel Glue

- **Advantages**—This glue is transparent and may be lightly colored. It dries clear, leaving a shiny mark on the paper. It is strong enough to hold a variety of lightweight- and medium-weight objects. It cleans up with water and does not stain clothing. It is available in bottles similar to that of the white glue, as well as in roller and tube forms.

- **Disadvantages**—This glue is runnier than white glue and is hard for children to control. When gluing fabric, for example, the glue quickly comes right through and wets the fingers. It dries slowly and wrinkles the paper.

Other adhesives. Many other pastes and glues are available on the market. Some of them are not safe for young children (see Appendix A). Others are difficult for the children to handle, such as the mucilage, cellulose, and wheat pastes, which are very sticky or runny. Glue pens and rollers are much more expensive (often three times the cost of white glue!) and work best with children who are skilled in handling drawing tools. See Appendix D for recipes for homemade pastes.

Tape. Avoid masking tape and transparent tape. Even though tape is easy to use, it is neither a permanent nor an artistic way to hold arts materials together. Many times, once children become accustomed to using tape, they do not want to use the messier and more challenging paste and glue.

Selecting Collage Materials

Fascinating materials for collages can be found in nature, from around the house, and from craft activities. See the Artist's Tool Box for ideas. Look for interesting papers as well. Send a letter home to parents asking them to contribute found items to the collage center.

Selecting Cutting Tools

Select scissors that are lightweight and move easily at the pivot. They should be sharp enough to cut paper with very light pressure. They should have a blunt tip. Scissors are traditionally designed for use in the left or right hand, but many children's scissors are now on the market that can be used with either hand. Select ones that work with both left- and right-handed children, if possible. If separate left- and right-handed scissors are used, then color code them so children know which they should select.

All-plastic, blunt-tipped scissors are a good choice for toddlers and younger preschoolers. These scissors will not cut hair, skin, or fabric. Older children can use pairs with lightweight stainless steel blades and plastic handles. They can also use the new children's scissors that make decorative cuts. Other cutting tools include the following:

Training scissors. For toddlers or children with impaired finger dexterity, select training scissors that have blunt tips and spring-apart, plastic-coated handles.

Double-ring training scissors. These scissors have a pair of outer rings so that as the child holds the scissors, you can guide the actual cutting. They are most useful for children who have dexterity and strength but do not turn the wrist enough to hold the scissors vertically to the paper. This problem is usually manifested when the child tries to cut, but instead the paper folds. Usually the child needs to use them only once or twice. If there continues to be a problem, have the child try the training scissors.

Rotary hand cutter. This cutting tool, similar to ones used by quilters, is very sharp and must be used with close supervision. However, this may be the only way some children with special needs can cut. Look for ones designed for use by children that have a protective cover over the blade. Make sure the blade is covered and the handle is easy to grasp. It should have an automatically closing cover. It must be used with a cutting mat underneath at all times. This setup will allow a child who can grip only with a fist to become quite proficient at cutting.

Teacher's scissors. Adults are always cutting many unusual items for collages. Invest in the best quality, all-purpose snips to be found. These usually have stainless steel blades, spring-apart blades, and a lock mechanism, which makes them safer to have around young children. They should be able to cut through heavy cardboard, all fabrics, carpet, leather, branches, pipe cleaners, wire, and more.

Dealing with Cutting Problems

Children face a variety of challenges when learning to use scissors.

- **Hesitancy—**If children have been forbidden to use scissors in the home, they may be hesitant to begin at first. Give them gentle encouragement to try the scissors.

- **Difficulty holding scissors—**Watch for children who are having difficulty holding the scissors vertically to the paper. Check that they are using the thumb on top and opposing fingers on bottom to hold the scissors. If they are, gently guide their scissors into the correct position. It may help to hold the paper for them to practice the first few snips. The training scissors can be used to give them a start.

- **Difficulty controlling scissors—**Sometimes the scissors are too heavy or large for the child's hand. In this case, the scissors will tip or wobble unsteadily, and the child will not be able to cut paper. Light plastic, appropriate-sized scissors should be made available to these children.

- **Hand position—**Some children may need help positioning the hand that is holding the paper. Make sure that they learn to keep their fingers out of the path of the scissors.

- **Paper bends—**One of the most frustrating things for a young child is when the paper bends instead of being cut. This often indicates that they are not exerting enough pressure as they close the scissors. If they keep trying to cut in the same spot, they will never succeed. Suggest that they try cutting in another place or using a different piece. Check that the child is holding the scissors in the correct position, as poor hand position often causes the paper to bend.

- **Wrong paper—**Paper that is either too thin or too thick is difficult for beginner cutters to use. Avoid tissue paper, thin gift wrap, and cardboard when children are still learning. White drawing paper and construction paper have the right amount of stiffness for first-time scissors users.

- **Weak grip—**Children who have difficulty using their fingers, hands, or wrists will find cutting with traditional scissors difficult. Scissors that are squeezed together between the thumb and all of the opposing fingers, and that open automatically with a spring, work well for some children. These are often called "snips." Try to select the lightest-weight pair with the bluntest point. Another option is the use of a rotary cutter.

Setting Up the Collage Center

Provide a low table where the children can comfortably stand or sit. The tabletop should be bare and easy to wash. If the table must be covered, use an old shower curtain or a plastic tablecloth rather than newspaper, which can stick to the projects. A laminated sheet of construction paper also works well.

Because pasting and gluing with young children is a "messy" activity, and one that can be confused with food, it is important to set up a place where collages can be done away from food areas. This can be a special table that is near a water source. If working in a kitchen area, a large plastic tray or plastic tablecloth can be designated for collage activities, and pasting and gluing can be done only when that surface is set up.

As children gain skill, set up a permanent collage center with attractively displayed paper and objects grouped by texture and color, and set out on low shelving in shallow trays or clear plastic jars and bins.

Collage Activities for Infants

Although infants are not ready for glue and scissors, they can participate in simple collage activities.

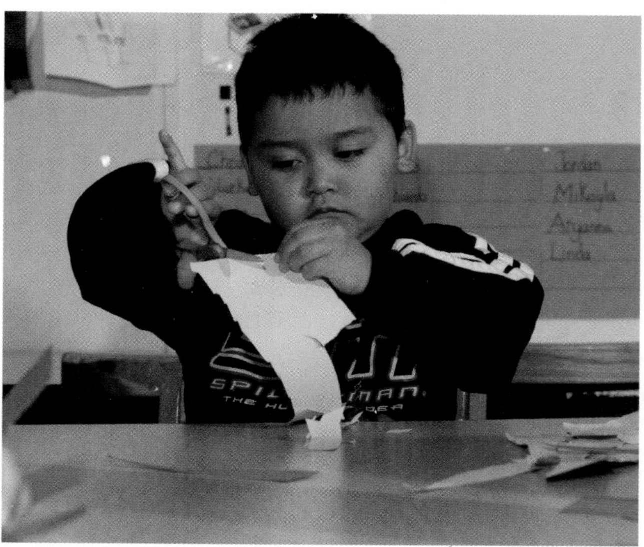

Making a collage is the perfect way to practice using scissors.

Paper shape play. Prepare children for future collage activities by cutting out a variety of colorful shapes from heavyweight tag board. If possible, laminate them or use foam. Together, play with the shapes on the high chair tray or table. Describe the shapes and arrange them in different ways. Let the child decide where to put them.

Tearing. As a precutting activity, give an older infant strips of easy-to-tear paper and let the child tear them into small pieces.

Paper balls. Show infants how to squeeze small pieces of light-weight paper into balls. Drop balls onto contact paper or preglued paper.

Collage Activities for Toddlers

Toddlers can begin to explore collage using white paste to glue down simple shapes.

Counting collage. Have children select paper shapes from the collage box and paste to paper. Together, count the shapes used.

Photo collage. Print out digital photographs of family and familiar objects. Let children paste pictures onto a stiff paper or tag board background.

Picture collages. Preselect pages from magazines and cut them into simple shapes. Initial selections should focus on color, texture, or pattern rather than on objects. Be prepared for the children to paste them down with either side facing up.

Collage Activities for Preschool and Kindergarten

In the beginning, offer only limited types of materials at a time. Slowly, as the children grow in skill, introduce materials that are more difficult to paste or glue.

Glue experiments. Offer glues and paste with different consistencies and textures. Investigate which ones work the best.

Topic collages. Offer preselected pages from magazines and invite children to look for pictures that go together to make a collage. For example, they could look for faces, animals, colors, or shapes.

Cloth and yarns. Textiles make interesting additions to collages. Most young children cannot cut such materials, so precut them into simple shapes. In addition to fabric, offer ribbon pieces, rickrack, lace, thick yarns, and strings. Cut all of these linear items into short lengths, no longer than 6 inches, to make them easier for young children to handle.

Include assorted objects. Many three-dimensional items, such as buttons and pompoms, can be added to collages once white glue has been introduced and handled successfully.

Try homemade pastes. Mix up some paste using the recipes found in Appendix D.

Making Plans

ONE-ON-ONE ACTIVITY PLAN: First Collages

WHO? **Group composition age(s):** One older infant or toddler

WHEN? **Time frame:** 5 to 15 minutes

WHY? **Objectives:** Children will develop

- physically, by developing their hand-eye coordination. (Bodily-Kinesthetic)
- socially, by sharing the experience with a caring adult. (Interpersonal)
- emotionally, by practicing self-control. (Intrapersonal)
- visual perception skills, by observing the different colors, textures, and shapes in their own art. (Spatial)
- language skills, by learning new descriptive words. (Linguistic)
- cognitively, by learning to differentiate different colors and shapes. (Logical-Mathematical)
- art awareness, by learning how a collage is made. (Content Standard 1)

WHERE? **Setup:** Infant—in high chair or adult's lap. Toddler—at child-size table.

WHAT? **Materials:** Sheet of contact paper with the backing peeled off. Tape paper to table, sticky side up. A paper plate with precut geometric paper shapes in different colors, patterns, and textures.

HOW? **Procedeure:**

Warm-Up: Hold up one of the paper shapes. Say, "Look at this square. Do you know what color it is? Where will you put it on your collage?"

What to Do: Hand the child the shape to place on the sticky surface. If the child is not sure what to do, help guide him or her. Repeat with some other shapes. Then let child make some choices independently.

What to Say: After the child puts the shape down, describe where it was placed. "You put it near the top or next to the blue triangle." Repeat with the other shapes. Encourage the child to help self from the plate. Describe the colors, textures, patterns, and shapes.

Transition Out: When the child tires of the activity or all shapes and space are used, hold up the collage and say, "Look at the collage you made. Can you find the square (circle, etc.)?" Hang the collage up and return to it often. Continue to help the artist find the different shapes in the picture using descriptive terms.

ASSESSMENT OF LEARNING

1. Can the child place shapes on paper without help?
2. Can the child identify the named color or shape?

Offer other papers. Once the children have become competent using scissors to cut construction paper, offer different weights and textures of paper for them to try.

More practice. In addition to cutting shapes for collages, children can practice cutting in other arts activities, such as puppet making, mask making, and constructed sculptures.

Classroom Museum

When doing collage share the work of Picasso's Cubist period, in which he used collage, such as *Three Musicians*. Children like to hunt for the different materials, such as pieces of newspapers, that he used in his work.

Making Plans

PRACTICE ACTIVITY PLAN: Leaf Collages

WHO? **Group composition age(s):** Toddler group 1-1/2–2 years (Can also be adapted for preschool and kindergarten)

WHEN? **Time frame:** 45 to 60 minutes on a fall day

WHY? **Objectives:** Children will develop

- physically, children will develop small motor skills by handling and gluing down leaves. (Bodily-Kinesthetic)
- socially, children will develop social skills by participating in a group experience. (Interpersonal)
- emotionally, children will develop self-confidence by successfully making a collage. (Intrapersonal)
- visual perception skills, children will develop skill at identifying leaf shapes. (Spatial)
- language, children will develop vocabulary by describing leaves. (Linguistic)
- cognitively, children will develop patterning, sequencing, and computation skills when they compare, order, and count leaves. (Logical-Mathematical)
- art awareness, children will practice controlling the amount of glue they apply. (Content Standard 1)

WHERE? **Setting:** With assistants holding their hands, toddlers will go outside under the big maple tree in the yard. Then they will return and use the leaves at the collage center.

WHAT? **Materials:** Need a basket, leaves, paper, and glue (or contact paper with the backing peeled off).

HOW? **Procedeure:**

Warm-Up: Take toddlers outside on a fall day. Try to have one adult or older child paired with one or two children. Together, collect leaves.

What to Do: As children find leaves, help them name the colors and describe how beautiful they are. Put the leaves in an attractive basket. Inside, put the basket of leaves on a table. Have the children come to the table one at a time. Model how to spread glue on a piece of paper. Have children select several leaves and place them on the paper.

What to Say: Talk about the colors and shapes. Count them. Help children remember how it felt to collect them. Ask them why they chose the leaves they did. Describe the colors in exciting language, such as golden reds and brilliant yellows.

Transition Out: When all children have made a collage, read *Red Leaf Yellow Leaf* (Ehlert, 1991) or *Leaf Man* (Ehlert, 2005). Have children point out the leaves in the collage illustrations and see if they match any they found.

ASSESSMENT OF LEARNING

1. Can the children use descriptive terms for color, texture, and shape of leaves?
2. Can the children explain why they chose the leaves they used?
3. Can the children successfully glue the leaves to paper?

Making Plans

RESPONSIVE ACTIVITY PLAN: Creating Painted Paper for Collages

WHO? Group composition age(s): Primary

WHEN? Time frame: 45 to 60 minutes

WHY? Objectives: Children will develop

- physically, by developing their hand-eye coordination and fine motor control. (Bodily-Kinesthetic)
- socially, by sharing ideas and materials with others. (Interpersonal)
- emotionally, by evaluating their own work. (Intrapersonal)
- visual perception skills, by observing the relationship among the different colors, textures, and shapes in their compositions and in those of artist Eric Carle. (Spatial)
- language skills, by answering questions about their work. (Linguistic)
- cognitively, by testing out different ideas. (Logical-Mathematical)
- art awareness, by developing an understanding of value and color in their own work and that of other artists. (Content Standards 2 and 4)

WHERE? Setup: Children will start on the rug for the whole group experience, then work at the tables, then return to the rug for sharing.

WHAT? Materials: White and colored paper, paint, brushes, scissors, and glue (Optional: printmaking objects)

HOW? Procedeure:

Warm-Up: Hold up a sheet of white paper. Ask, "How can we change the color of this paper?"

What to Do: Record their ideas on chart paper. Then read a book illustrated with collages by Eric Carle, such as *The Tiny Seed* (1987) or *The Grouchy Ladybug* (1977). Study his illustrations and see how he made his collages. Return to the tables and paint on the white and colored paper to make interesting paper for collages. Let them dry. Then have each child cut the papers into four parts and put them in color-sorted bins. Have children illustrate a story they have written with a collage made from their hand-colored papers.

What to Say: Ask children to describe the colors and patterns they paint. When they work on their collages, ask them to think about the importance of value. "Do those two colors go together? Is there a lot of contrast in value between them? Can you see the one shape when it is on top of another?"

Transition Out: Have children share their collages. If desired, make a class big book of their collages and stories.

ASSESSMENT OF LEARNING

1. Are children able to compare the values of different colors?
2. Do children work cooperatively with others?
3. Can children successfully use collage to illustrate a story?

Teacher Tip

CHOOSING SAFE MATERIALS FOR COLLAGES

Make sure objects offered for collage are safe for children under age three. Use the choke test to be sure (see Appendix A). Glitter and metallic confetti are not recommended for young children. These items stick to children's hands and can be rubbed into the eyes. Lick-and-stick papers are not recommended. They give the children the impression that it is all right to put arts materials into their mouths.

Collage Experiences for Primary Students

Primary students can use collage in more sophisticated ways.

Nature scenes. Use natural materials to create landscapes and pictures of animals.

Homes. Use collage materials to make furnishings inside a low-sided box.

Maps. Use collage materials to create maps of real and imaginary places.

Mosaics. A **mosaic** is a picture made from small objects. Make mosaics from paper cut in 1-inch squares, or any small items, such as seeds, small pebbles, buttons, or tiles.

Invent paste. Set up a center with flour*, cornstarch*, sugar*, water, and milk* and small cups for mixing. Provide measuring spoons and explore making a new recipe for paste.

Book Box

Books illustrated with collages.

Bunting, E. (1994). *Smoky night*. New York: Harcourt Brace. A fire in the night drives a young African-American boy from his apartment during the 1992 Los Angeles riots. He overcomes cultural differences to help his Asian neighbors. It is illustrated with paintings framed with textured collages that give a feeling for the chaos and scariness of the riot. This Caldecott-winning book will give children ideas for ways they can "frame" their artwork. Six and up.

Snyder, I. (2003). *From tree to paper*. New York: Scholastic. Photographs show the process by which a tree becomes a sheet of paper. Use this book when introducing different kinds of paper for collages. Four and up.

Ehlert, L. (1998). *Mole's hill*. New York: Harcourt Brace. Based on a Native American folktale, this story is illustrated with paper collages inspired by Woodland tribe beadwork and ribbon appliqué. Toddler and up.

Keats, E. J. (1962). *The snowy day*. New York: Viking Press. In this Caldecott winner, painted cut paper collages detail the experiences of an African-American boy as he explores the snow. Also available as a big book from Scholastic. Toddler and up.

Keats, E. J. (2003). *Jennie's hat*. New York: Puffin. Jennie does not like her new hat. Delightful collages show her "improving" the hat. Toddler and up.

Laden, N. (2000). *Roberto, the insect architect*. San Francisco: Chronicle. A termite who loves to play with his food becomes a philanthropic architect. The book is illustrated with fantastic collages made from unusual materials. Four and up.

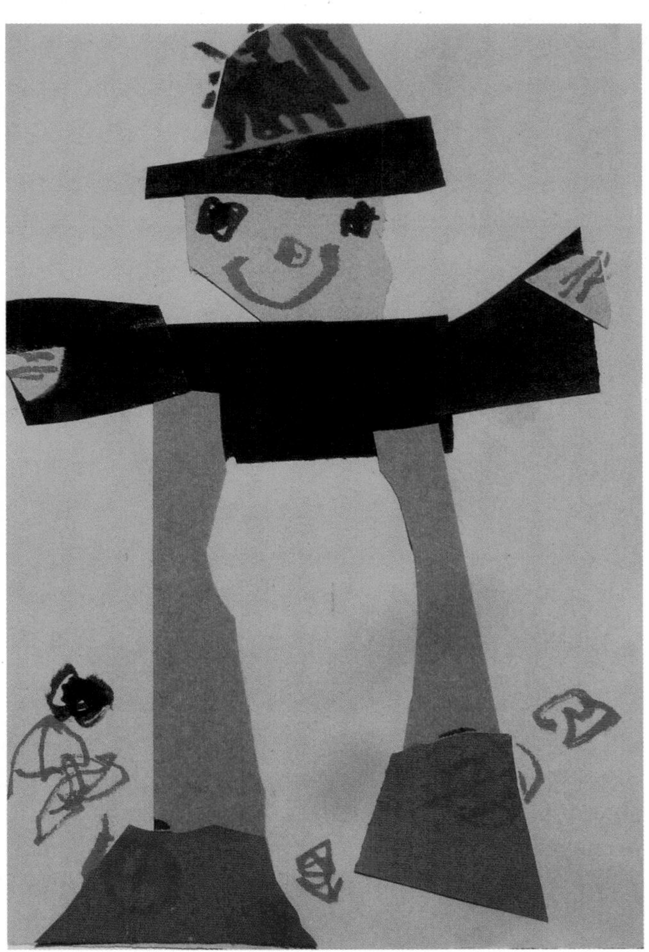

Because there are no preconceived ideas about what a collage should look like, creating a collage is a very open-ended activity that allows unlimited choices. Colin, age 4½, has glued down precut paper in his own unique way to make a "Dancing Man."

THE PRINTMAKING EXPERIENCE

Printmaking is any art form that involves making a copy of something. Some printing techniques can produce multiple prints, others only one copy (**monoprint**). Printmaking can provide another way for young children to explore the sensory characteristics of objects. The children use their sense of touch as they handle the object and apply pressure to make the print. They can compare the stiffness of the object with the slippery wetness of the paint. The print provides a visual image of the texture, pattern, and shape of the object, and the stamping process often creates a rhythmic sound. Printmaking is also a very active art form that requires the children to move their arms with vigor and apply pressure sensitively.

Teacher Tip

AVOIDING FOOD ITEMS FOR PRINTMAKING

Many books recommend using fruits and vegetables for printmaking. Consider carefully the message children receive when told to put food in paint and then see the food thrown away. (See Chapter 6 for further discussion on this topic.) The Artist's Tools: Printmaking Objects offers plenty of ideas for printing objects that do not use foods.

Selecting Printmaking Materials

Printmaking requires three basic materials—paint, paper, and something with which to make a print.

Paint. Choose several colors of very thick tempera paint or fingerpaint. Make sure that the paint colors will not stain hands. White is always a safe choice, as are pastels that are mixed using white and a few drops of a color. If the paint is thin, thicken it with flour. Place a small amount of paint in each tray.

Trays. Put the paint in low-sided trays. Use Styrofoam or plastic food trays that have been sanitized (see Appendix A). Ensure that the sides are no higher than half an inch, or try paper plates.

Printing tools. For the first explorations, provide the children with large, easily grasped objects that they can dip in the paint, such as a variety of potato mashers or long, cardboard tubes. Place one tool in each tray. As children grow in skill, smaller objects can be added (see Artist's Tools Printmaking objects).

Paper. Use paper in the 9-by-12-inch size range. Larger paper makes it difficult for the children to reach the trays and objects without leaning into their prints. Have plenty of extra paper so that children can make more than one print if they wish.

Drying rack. A cardboard box drying rack (see Figure 9-1) or other wet project storage unit placed near the printmakers will provide a quick place for the prints to dry while still supervising the children. With experience, the children can put their own prints away.

Printmaking allows children to explore how shapes can be put together in new ways.

Setting Up a Printing Center

For initial printmaking explorations, provide a low table that the children can work at while standing. Children usually spend only a few minutes making prints and can do so standing up. This also enables them to reach the trays of paint and objects more easily. Cover the table with newspaper. Have all materials set out before inviting children to begin. Place the trays between the papers or down the middle of the table, depending on the size and shape of the table. Have smocks ready for the children to wear.

Limit the group to one or two toddlers or four older children. Once the children are familiar with the technique and can work more independently, the group size can be increased for the practice activities.

Once children are skilled at printing, consider merging the printmaking center with the painting

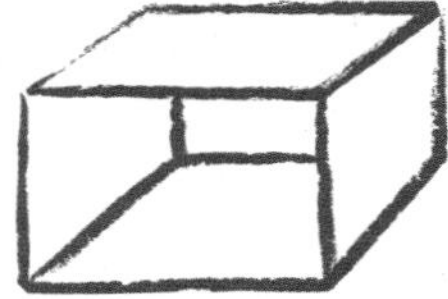

1. Select a box that is slightly larger than the paper children usually use.

2. Draw lines two or three inches apart on opposite sides of the box.

3. Cut halfway in on each line.

4. Cut " shelves" (from cardboard) that are four inches longer than the box. Measure in two inches from the edges and draw lines.

5. Cut halfway in on each line on the shelves.

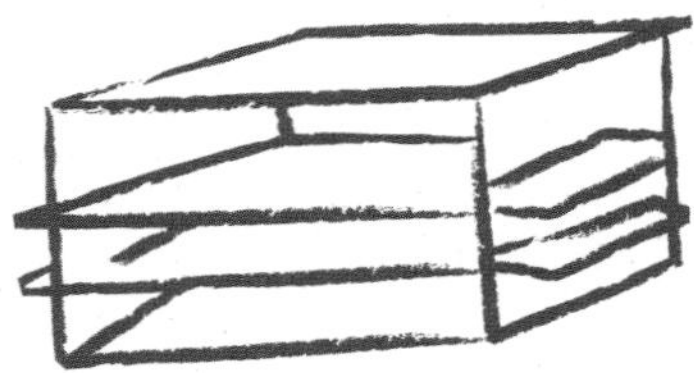

6. Slide each shelf into the corresponding slots.

Figure 9–1 Making a paint-drying box.

center by putting the printmaking tools and plates with small amounts of paint near the easels and painting table. This will encourage more innovative work because children can add printed shapes to their paintings.

Artist's Tool Box

PRINTMAKING OBJECTS

- Berry baskets
- Blocks (building or interlocking)
- Bristle blocks
- Cans (with smooth edges)
- Corks
- Corrugated cardboard (cut into rectangular pieces)
- Erasers
- Feet
- Film cans
- Forks
- Garlic press
- Hands
- Juice cans
- Lids and tops
- Ornamental corn
- Pinecones
- Plastic cups and containers
- Potato masher
- Rocks
- Shells
- Shoes
- Sponge ball
- Sponges (in simple geometric shapes, not pictorial)
- Spools
- Toy trucks
- Tubes
- Wooden blocks

Printmaking Activities for Infants

Handprints and footprints make a good introduction to printmaking.

Water printing. Provide a tray of water and let the child make hand or foot prints outside on the pavement.

Sand prints. Press a hand or foot into the damp sand. Note: The print can be preserved by pouring plaster over it.

Printmaking Activities for Toddlers

Toddlers can begin to explore different ways to print.

Gadget prints. Provide large items that the child can easily grasp such as small plastic water bottles, spice jars, and potato mashers and use flat trays or paper plates of tempera paint. Vary the printing tools, combining new ones with familiar ones.

Making Plans

ONE-ON-ONE ACTIVITY PLAN: Handprints

WHO? **Group composition age(s):** One infant or toddler (Note: This can be done as a mural activity with each child being given a turn to participate)

WHEN? **Time frame:** 5 to 10 minutes

WHY? **Objectives:** Children will develop

- physically, by using the large and small muscles of the arm to place a hand in the paint. (Bodily-Kinesthetic)
- socially, by interacting with a caring adult. (Interpersonal)
- emotionally, by growing in self-confidence by being trusted to use the paint. (Intrapersonal) visual perception skills, by matching a hand to its matching print. (Spatial)
- language, by hearing and repeating sensory descriptive words. (Linguistic)
- cognitively, by seeing cause and effect as the hand makes a print. (Logical-Mathematical)
- art awareness, by learning how to make a print. (Content Standard 1)

WHERE? **Setup:** Have the child sit in a high chair or on an adult's lap. For a mural the child can be carried or stand.

WHAT? **Materials:** Paper plate with small amount of tempera or fingerpaint. Sheet of paper or mural paper. Wet paper towels for clean up.

HOW? **Procedure:**

Warm-Up: Show the child the plate with paint. Ask, "How do you think the paint feels?"

What to Do: Gently place the child's hand palm down onto the paint. Then place the hand on the paper to make a handprint. Encourage the child to repeat independently.

What to Say: Ask the child to describe the sensory experience. Use words like *wet* and *sticky*. Point out the visual effect, "Look your hand is all _____(chosen color)!" "Look at your handprint. See all your fingers." Note the process, "You put your hand in the paint and then touched the paper. See what happened?"

Transition Out: When child is done, wipe the hand with wet towels. Say, "Look at the print(s) you made!" When the paint is dry, have the child match his or her hand to the prints.

ASSESSMENT OF LEARNING
1. Can the child make a handprint on his or her own?
2. Can the child match his or her hand to the print?

Sponge prints. Sponges make great printing tools. Cut the sponge into simple geometric shapes. Attach a clothespin to the top of the sponge shape, or, using craft glue, attach a spool"handle"to the sponge.

Tire tracks. Dip the wheels of toy cars and trucks in tempera paint and drive around a piece of paper.

Printmaking Activities for Preschoolers

After exploratory activities, offer printmaking on a regular basis.

Monoprints. Make a painting on paper or on a smooth washable table top. While still wet, place a piece of paper on top. Lift to see its print.

"Rubber" stamps. Commercial rubber stamps are too small for little hands to grasp, but larger ones are easy to make. Cut out simple geometric shapes—square, circle, triangle, rectangle, oval, and so on—from sticky-backed foam. Peel off the backing and affix these shapes to sanded wooden blocks.

Splatter prints. Make a screen box by cutting an opening in a cardboard box and fastening a piece of screening over it. Tape edges well so there are no rough places. Remove the bottom of the box. Place paper and washable or disposable objects, such as shells, plant stems, lacy dollies, and plastic spoons, under the screen box. Dip a toothbrush in tempera paint and rub across the screen. Remove objects carefully.

String monoprint prints. Dip a piece of yarn or string in tempera paint. Drop the string onto a sheet of paper. Place another piece of paper on top and press. Remove to see the print.

Marble print. Place a piece of paper, a marble, and a squirt of paint in a box with low sides. Encourage the child to roll the marble around the box to capture its movement. Add other colors or more marbles to extend the experience.

Making Plans

CENTER ACTIVITY PLAN: Gadget Prints

WHO? **Group composition age(s):** 2–3 preschoolers or 4–6 kindergarteners

WHEN? **Time frame:** 30 to 40 minutes

WHY? **Objectives:** Children will develop

- physically, by using the large and small muscles of the arm to press the object in the paint and on the paper. (Bodily-Kinesthetic)
- socially, by sharing the printing tools and paint trays. (Interpersonal)
- emotionally, by learning to enjoy making prints and by seeing themselves as trusted with "messy" paint. (Intrapersonal)
- visual perception skills, by matching an object to its print. (Spatial)
- language, by learning a vocabulary of printing words and by describing their prints. (Linguistic)
- cognitively, by learning that different objects and materials make print marks. (Logical-Mathematical)
- art awareness, by learning ways to make prints and by becoming familiar with prints used in book illustrations and other artwork. (Content Standards 1 and 4)

WHERE? **Setup:** Start the whole group on the rug, then move them to the printmaking center.

Optional: A large piece of paper for a group print can be hung on the wall or laid on the floor nearby.

WHAT? **Materials:** On a newspaper-covered table set trays with small amounts of tempera or fingerpaint in three to six different colors, paper, objects for making prints, wet paper towels and sponges for clean up.

HOW? **Procedure:**

Warm-Up: On the rug, use guided discovery to unveil the different printmaking gadgets.

What to Do: Ask them to predict what marks they will make. Model how to make a print. With the class, develop guidelines for working at the center. Have some children act out using the center. At the center: Children will explore the different prints the objects make. They can then select the object they like best to make some prints on the class mural.

What to Say: Use a vocabulary that describes the marks made by the objects and the actions the child has used. Words to use include *shape* (and all of the shape names), *pattern, texture, repeated, lift, press, stamp, hold, move,* and *place*. Comment on the shapes they have made: "Look, you made circles," or, on the way they moved the tool: "You moved the tube up and down."

Transition Out: As the children finish, help them put their prints in a place to dry. After the printmaking experience, set up a matching activity in which the child matches a print with the object that made it. Hang up the mural or make a presentation panel along with photographs of the children printing and examples of the gadgets they used for the prints. Look at the printed illustrations in the children's books of Bernard Waber and Ezra Jack Keats and try to guess what they used to make their prints.

ASSESSMENT OF LEARNING

1. Can children match an object to its print?
2. Do children use printmaking terms?

Rubbings. Place flat textured objects, such as pieces cut from plastic berry baskets, under a piece of paper and rub with the side of a peeled crayon to capture the texture. Commercial textured rubbing plates are also available (see Appendix C).

Classroom Museum

Look for silk-screen prints by Native American artists of the Northwest coast, such as Tim Paul, Bill Reid, Tony Hunt, and others. Also, seek hand-printed fabric from India and Africa. Indian wood blocks, used for printing the cloth, can be found in import stores.

Printmaking for Kindergarten and Primary Age

With improved fine motor control, older children can handle smaller objects. They can also coordinate multistep process printing.

Roller prints. Dip string, yarn, or rickrack in white glue and then wrap around cardboard tubes or juice cans. When dry, roll the decorated cylinder in paint, and then roll it on the paper. This is a very messy but exciting exploration.

Big books. Make a big book about patterns, using prints made from the same objects the children have used, and share it with them.

Printing plates. Cut flat, highly textured objects, such as corrugated cardboard, yarn, and burlap, into interesting shapes, and glue on a cardboard base. When the glue is dry, paint over the entire cardboard surface using a brush. Press a piece of paper over it and rub with hands to make a print.

Styrofoam prints. Cut out flat pieces from the bottoms of sanitized food trays (see Appendix A). Use a pencil to draw on the tray. Roll tempera paint with a little detergent added over the drawing, and place a piece of paper on top. Rub well with flat of hand to produce a print.

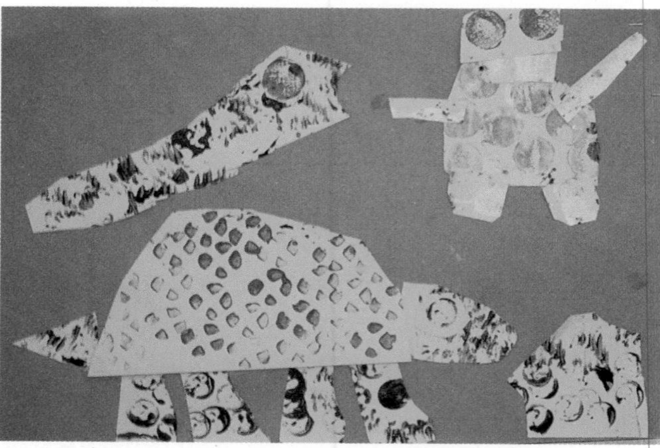

The repetitive quality of printmaking provides the perfect opportunity for children to work together. Inspired by the printed collage illustrations of Leo Lionni, Emily, age 5, used her carved clay and gadget printed papers to make a collage of animals.

More to do with rubbings. Go on searches around the room and outside for textured objects. Place paper on top and rub with crayon to make a texture collection. Rubbings can be enjoyed because they are or can be cut into shapes and used to create a collage.

THE FIBER ART EXPERIENCE

Fiber art refers to any art form that involves the use of yarn, cloth, or the raw materials that are used to make them. Because fabric plays such an important role in everyday life in terms of clothing and furnishings, it is often seen as a functional object rather than an art form. Yet, even the simplest piece of clothing bears the mark of unnamed artists who determined the shape of its pieces, the drape of the fabric, and its texture and pattern.

Introducing fiber art to children helps them appreciate this often "hidden" and ancient art, which has found unique expression and form throughout time and across cultures. It is an excellent example of an art medium that can serve as a unifying theme for young children. Fiber activities can be used as part of the study of texture, line, and pattern.

Making Plans

RESPONSIVE ACTIVITY PLAN: Printed Undersea Mural

WHO? **Group composition age(s):** Primary students

WHEN? **Time frame:** Three 45-minute blocks of time and a ½-day field trip

WHY? **Objectives:** Children will develop

- physically, by using hand-eye coordination and fine motor control to make prints. (Bodily-Kinesthetic)
- socially, by sharing mural space, the printing tools, and trays. (Interpersonal)
- emotionally, by feeling pride in accomplishing a task as part of a group. (Intrapersonal)
- visual perception skills, by observing the relationship between the object and its print. (Spatial)
- language, by orally explaining their decisions and by writing labels and captions for their mural. (Linguistic)
- cognitively, by comparing and contrasting different compositions. (Logical-Mathematical)
- art awareness, by learning how to organize visual images into a composition and by becoming familiar with prints used by book illustrators. (Content Standards 2 and 4).

WHERE? **Setup:** Gather the whole group on the rug to hear a story. Then take a trip to the aquarium. Next, wear smocks and work in small groups at desks covered with newspaper. Then go back on the rug to put the mural together.

WHAT? **Materials:** Trays with a wide range of tempera paint colors. Objects for making prints and small sponges for the background. Wet paper towels and sponges for clean up.

HOW? **Procedure:**

Warm-Up: *Day One:* On the rug, share several items from the sea, like a seashell, a crab shell, some seaweed, etc. Then read the stories *I Was All Thumbs* by Bernard Waber (1975) and *Swimmy* by Leo Lionni (1963). Discuss the sea life in the stories and prepare students for a fieldtrip to the aquarium by making a KWL chart (see Chapter 8).

What to Do: *Day Two:* Trip to the aquarium. Have students make pencil sketches of sea life they see.

What to Do: *Day Three:* On the rug, students will reflect on their trip and share their sketches. On chart paper list things to include in their mural. At desks or art center explore making sea life prints.

What to Do: *Day Four:* Students cut out the dry sea life prints and bring them to the rug. On the rug is a large sheet of blue paper for the mural backing. Students take turns putting their prints on the paper and trying different arrangements. When happy with the composition, several students can glue the prints in place. Another group can sponge paint the water around the prints. Other students can write labels and captions.

What to Say: Give students lots of positive feedback. On day 4 help students create their composition by asking questions such as: "Does putting the octopus there help tell the story better?" Use placement words: *top, bottom, near, far, overlapping, behind,* and *in front*.

Transition Out: Complete the KWL chart. Hang up the mural, along with photographs of the children on the field trip.

ASSESSMENT OF LEARNING

1. Does the artwork reflect careful observation of sea life?
2. Do children share ideas and work cooperatively?

Book Box

Books about the fiber arts.

de Paola, T. (1999). *Charlie needs a cloak*. Minneapolis, MN: Sagebrush.

Charlie is a shepherd who needs a new cape to wear in the winter. In simple language, the story describes the basic processes of turning wool into a finished garment. At each step, the sheep "help" Charlie. This book is an excellent introduction to fiber processing for all children, who particularly love the antics of the delightfully illustrated sheep. Toddler and up.

Johnston, T., & de Paola, T. (1985). *The quilt story*. New York: G. P. Putnam's Sons.

A treasured quilt provides comfort to two little girls from different times. Also available as a big book from Scholastic. Four and up.

Jonas, A. (1994). *The quilt*. New York: Puffin.

An African-American girl sleeps beneath a quilt made by her mother and father and has fantastical dreams. Toddler and up.

Kurtz, S. (2001). *The boy and the quilt*. Intercourse, PA: Good Books.

A little boy collects fabric squares of many colors and sews his own crazy quilt. It shows, step-by-step, how the quilt is made and combats the stereotype that only girls make quilts. Four and up.

Selecting Materials

Yarn and cloth form the basis of most fiber activities and are readily available. People who knit and sew will often donate leftover yarn and cloth to schools.

Yarn. Provide children with a wide range of yarns in different colors and textures. Look for one- and two-ply yarns made from cotton, acrylic, and wool. For very young children use the thicker yarns.

Cloth. Burlap is a sturdy, textured cloth that can be used as a base in **stitchery** and **appliqué** activities. Unbleached muslin is an inexpensive cotton cloth that can be used to draw on and as a background. Felt is easy to cut and handle. More elaborate cloth, such as satins and brocades, provides sensory stimulation. It can often be obtained in discarded sample books from upholstery and carpet stores.

Needles. Choose long 2- to 3-inch plastic needles with large holes for most stitchery activities that use burlap as a base.

Fiber Activities

Fiber activities share many commonalities with collage. Once stitchery and appliqué have been introduced as an activity, yarn and cloth can easily be added to the collage center and cloth cut in the size for backgrounds can be offered alongside paper.

Most fiber arts activities require specific fine motor and visual perception skills. In order to be successful at most of these activities, the children need to have certain abilities. They should be able to:

1. pick up or grasp small objects with thumb and index fingers.
2. push and pull small objects with thumb and index fingers.
3. identify top and bottom, front and back, and inside and outside.
4. repeat a patterned motion.

Fiber arts activities are particularly successful with mixed-age groups. Some of the activities here may be too complicated for toddlers or younger preschoolers to do on their own, but they may be able to do a part of the activity when paired with older children or adults.

Look at clothing. Talk about the different articles of clothing that can be woven or knitted from

Weaving on a simple frame loom allows children to explore pattern and texture as they move rhythmically.

yarn, such as sweaters, socks, and hats. Bring in examples from different places in the world, and look for similarities and differences.

Move creatively. Have children hold hands in a line. The first child is the needle and threads through the line, ducking under the uplifted arms. Still clasping hands, the others follow.

Make a wall hanging. Join the children's cloth stitchery or appliqué to create a large group piece, or have children take turns working on a large piece of burlap.

Making Plans

CENTER ACTIVITY PLAN: First Stitchery

WHO? **Group composition age(s):** Preschool or primary age 4 to 6 at center

WHEN? **Time frame:** 10 to 20 minutes

WHY? **Objectives:** Children will develop

- physically, by using fine motor control and hand-eye coordination to place yarn in glue. (Bodily-Kinesthetic)
- socially, by helping each other glue the yarn. (Interpersonal)
- emotionally, by feeling successful when getting the yarn to stick. (Intrapersonal)
- visual perception skills, by observing how lines become shapes. (Spatial)
- language, by describing lines. (Linguistic)
- cognitively, by measuring the yarn. (Logical-Mathematical)
- art awareness, by learning how to handle yarn and looking at stitchery by other artists. (Content Standards 2, 3, and 5)

WHERE? **Setup:** Children at the stuff bin and later moving around the room. Then working at the center, and then back at the rug for sharing.

WHAT? **Materials:** Thread a large number of 3-inch plastic needles with different colors of yarn, in 12- to 16-inch lengths. Double the yarn, and make a large knot at the end. These can be stored ready for use by pushing the needles into a thick piece of Styrofoam. Sanitized Styrofoam trays for each child.

HOW? **Procedure:**

Warm-Up: Children do not often notice how clothing is put together. Have an embroiderer, a seamstress, or a tailor visit and demonstrate sewing work, or wear an embroidered garment or point out one a child is wearing. Take an old garment apart at the seams to see how it is put together. Have children find seams and stitches on their own clothing.

What to Do: On the rug, show examples of stitchery and the threaded needles and explain they will be added to the collage center. Model how to push the needle through the tray and then back to make a "stitch."
At the center, help children select threaded needles and emphasize going from front to back and back to front by making up a chant or song together to sing as they work. Invite children to select a threaded needle, and push it in and out of the tray. Do not expect children to make neat stitches. For most, this will be an exploration. It will take many stitching explorations before a child understands how to go from front to back in a patterned way. If children are to acquire this skill, they need many opportunities to practice it. When the yarn is used up, cut off the needle and tape the end to the back of the tray.

What to Say: Ask, "How many stitches have you made?" and "Look how the yarn makes lines." Words to use include *in, out, front, back, needle, stitch,* and *yarn.*

Transition Out: When done, gather on the rug and have the children describe one of the lines in their stitchery. Join the trays together with stitches into a wall hanging.

ASSESSMENT OF LEARNING

1. Can children successfully measure, cut, and stitch the yarn?
2. Can children describe the lines and shapes they have made?

Making Plans

RESPONSIVE ACTIVITY PLAN: Weaving

WHO? Group composition age(s): Primary

WHEN? Time frame: 45 to 60 minute blocks of time for 2 to 4 days

WHY? Objectives: Children will develop

- physically, by using fine motor control and hand-eye coordination to weave yarn. (Bodily-Kinesthetic)
- socially, by cooperating with a partner to reach a goal. (Interpersonal)
- emotionally, by feeling pride in accomplishing a challenging task. (Intrapersonal)
- visual perception skills, by observing how the weaving process itself creates texture and pattern. (Spatial)
- language, by communicating directions to each other. (Linguistic)
- cognitively, by working in sequence to create a pattern. (Logical-Mathematical)
- art awareness, by learning the weaving process and studying woven cloth made by other artists. (Content Standards 1, 4, and 5)

WHERE? Setup: Children will move creatively about the room and then sit on the rug for introduction. The weaving will be done in pairs on a loom set up in the corner of the room.

WHAT? Materials: Chicken wire, rough edges covered with masking tape, stretched on either a large wooden frame and mounted vertically or a partner or frame loom. Yarn, ribbon, shoelaces, or string.

HOW? Procedure:

Warm-Up: Have children imagine that they are pieces of yarn that are stretched, bent, folded, twisted, and woven. Have them join hands to form longer pieces of yarn, and then weave around the furniture in the room or trees and playground equipment.

What to Do: On the rug, pull apart a piece of cloth (burlap works well) to see the yarn from which it is made. Show the loom and demonstrate how to push the yarn in and out to create patterns. Explain that the children will weave in pairs.

At the center, have two children face each other with the loom between them. One child pushes a piece of yarn or other material through the holes in the chicken wire or between the stretched yarns. Then the other child takes the end and pushes it back through to the partner. If necessary, wrap tape around the ends of the yarn. Use the song "Go in and out the Windows" to reinforce the pattern. Children may weave in any direction.

What to Say: Ask "What is the texture of the weaving?" "How do the different yarns change how it feels and looks?" "What patterns do you see?" Words to use include *over, under, back, front, yarn,* and *weave*.

Transition Out: When all children have had a turn, gather on the rug, and study the weaving looking for patterns. Introduce small handlooms made from cardboard with notches cut in each end and yarn wrapped around on which children can do their own individual weavings.

ASSESSMENT OF LEARNING

1. Do children work successfully with their partners?
2. Can children follow the over/under weaving sequence, and vary the colors to create patterns?
3. Can children identify similar weaving patterns in the artwork of others?

Making Plans

RESPONSIVE ACTIVITY PLAN: Class Quilt

WHO? **Group composition age(s):** All. This activity works particularly well in mixed age groups.

WHEN? **Time frame:** 40 minutes

WHY? **Objectives:** Children will develop

- physically, by using hand-eye coordination to place the quilt squares. (Bodily-Kinesthetic)
- socially, by coming to consensus on the quilt design. (Interpersonal)
- emotionally, by feeling pride in accomplishing a large cooperative task. (Intrapersonal)
- visual perception skills, by observing how parts make up a whole. (Spatial)
- language, by telling a story about their square. (Linguistic)
- cognitively, by comparing colors and designs and creating a pattern. (Logical-Mathematical)
- art awareness, by learning how to make a quilt square and studying quilts made by other people. (Content Standards 1, 2, and 4)

WHERE? **Setup:** Children on the rug in a circle, then at tables. Then back at the rug.

WHAT? **Materials:** Squares of muslin cut into 9-by-9-inch squares, crayons.

HOW? **Procedure:**

Warm-Up: Show children a handmade quilt. Have them point out any patterns they see.

What to Do: Give each child a cloth square and use crayons to make a design or picture. (If desired, the quilt can have a theme related to something being studied, such as flowers, animals, or stories read.) When done, have children return to the rug and sit in a circle. Take turns telling about one's square and then putting squares side by side in rows to create the quilt top. Have children stand in a circle with their quilt squares. Invite them to take turns placing their square on the floor so that it touches the other ones. Challenge the children to place their squares so that a rectangle is formed. Have children retrieve their squares, and then create a new arrangement. This can be repeated several times in a row, or on different days. Use this opportunity to develop two concepts: (1) a whole is created from its parts, and (2) a pattern is created from the repetition of an element. After several rearrangements, ask the children to make a final arrangement for the finished quilt. If the quilt will be glued together, put out a large sheet of paper. As children place their squares, apply glue to the paper in those spots. Emphasize that each piece must touch another. If the quilt will be sewn, arrange the pieces on the floor, and then gather them up by rows. Have a parent or volunteer sew the pieces together during class time, so the children can participate in the excitement of seeing the quilt grow together.

What to Say: Ask, "Can you count the squares?" "How many are in a row?" "What patterns do you see?" "Does this square look better here or over here?" Words to use include *quilt, pieces, pattern, row, repeated, stitch,* and *bind.*

Transition Out: Display the quilt in the room. The quilt top can be left as it is and used for dramatic play, or it can be stuffed and finished, destined to become a favorite spot to cuddle. Alternatively, give it as a gift to a nursing home or other group with whom the children have a relationship.

ASSESSMENT OF LEARNING

1. Do children work together cooperatively and come to a consensus with no disagreement?
2. Do children see larger patterns created by the placement of the pieces?
3. Do children use the quilting terms introduced?

Classroom Museum

Story Cloths: Display and discuss Huichol yarn paintings (see Appendix C for sources). Hmong embroidered and appliquéd **story cloths** can be displayed and discussed. Embroidery is also used in the traditional dress of many cultures such as Ukrainian, Greek, Chinese, and Indian. Find lines, shapes, symmetry, and patterns in these works.

Tie-dye. Give children muslin rectangles to tie in knots and wrap tightly with rubber bands. Dip in strong tea. Untie and unwrap, then iron dry.

Design patterns. Offer pattern blocks and color tiles with which to make sample quilt patterns.

Weave. Plastic berry baskets can be used for weaving by individual children. Poke thick yarn, ribbon, or cloth strips in and out of the openings. A commercial freestanding weaving frame loom is also available that works well with young children.

Sing and move. Play "In and out the Window." Have all the children but one stand in a circle holding hands. Children lift their arms as the child weaves in and out between them as the song is sung. Continue until all children have had a turn to be the "weaver."

Arts Words

FIBER ART

Appliqué: A design made by attaching pieces of cloth to a fabric background.

Basket: A container woven from twigs, reeds, or other sturdy fiber.

Carding: Brushing wool fibers to straighten them.

Dye: Any substance that changes the color of a material.

Embroidery: A design made with thread on cloth.

Fiber: A fine, threadlike material.

Fiber art: Art forms that use fibers or materials created from fiber such as weaving, appliqué, and embroidery.

Handwoven: Cloth that has been created on a loom.

Hand spun: Yarn that has been made by hand.

Loom: A frame or machine on which yarn is stretched for weaving cloth. Also called a *handloom*.

Natural dye: A dye obtained from plant materials, such as flowers, leaves, or bark.

Quilt: A fabric design created by piecing together smaller bits of fabric.

Spindle: A stick used to twist and hold yarn as it is spun.

Spinning: The process of turning fiber into yarn.

Stitchery: A design made with yarn or cloth.

Story cloth: Appliquéd and embroidered textiles, made by the Hmong people of Southeast Asia, which record traditional folktales and personal life stories.

Table loom: A loom small enough to be used on a table.

Textile: A woven fabric.

Tie-dye: A design made by tying parts of a cloth together and then dying it.

Vertical loom: A loom on which the yarns for weaving (warp) are held vertically to the ground.

Weaving: The process of creating fabric by interlocking threads and yarns.

Whorl: A weight on the end of a hand spindle.

THE COMPUTER ART EXPERIENCE

Very sophisticated conversations about art happen not only at the art table but also between children working at the classroom computer. Computers have found their way into the hands of the very young, and they are providing an interactive medium unlike any other art form. Like collage, computer graphics provide an avenue of art exploration that challenges both child and teacher to accept new ways of thinking and working with the elements of art. This section will look at how the use of computers can enhance the art program offered to children.

The Computer as Art Medium

When the computer is viewed as an art medium rather than as a teaching tool, the logic of its inclusion in any art program involving children becomes apparent. A computer loaded with a simple graphic "paint" program is just another way to create lines and shapes. The monitor screen is the "paper," and the mouse is the tool for applying the lines and shapes and colors. The child manipulates colored light rather than pieces of paper, paintbrushes, or glue, but the artistic decisions are the same.

The computer provides the perfect place for an art conversation. An older computer loaded with an open-ended drawing program and with the keyboard placed on top is ideal for young artists.

In this technologically sophisticated society, even very young children are often familiar with computers. Being able to create their own "television" picture makes children feel independent and powerful. Properly selected and set up, computer art software provides a wonderful way to introduce children to the computer, beginning a pattern of comfort and success with this technology that will play such a large role in children's futures.

The computer can be viewed as another component of the arts program, just like easels and collage centers. It is neither more nor less important than any of the other arts activities offered to children. Like the other arts activities, the computer allows children to play with the art elements in a creative way. Opportunities to work at the computer can be offered as one of the children's daily play choices.

Selecting Art Software

The computer **software** discussed in this section is of one type only. These are often called "paint," "**graphic**," or "drawing" programs and may come as part of the initial software on the computer; may be the graphic part of "works" programs that combine word processing, spreadsheets, and data processing; or may be purchased in special versions designed just for children. Because the specific software programs available change rapidly, use the following general guidelines for making sure the one selected will work well for young artists.

1. There should be a large workspace of white or black on which to draw.
2. The **cursor** should be large and easy to see.
3. The **menu** of color, shape, and line choices should be visible at all times, either at the side or top of the screen.
4. Menu choice boxes should be large, with logical symbols for line types, shapes, and fill options.
5. The program should have a limited number of menu options. Children do not need such things as multiple pages, graduated colors, and inversions.
6. Programs that load quickly are most convenient. If the only one available requires a complicated loading procedure, be sure to load the program before the children arrive. Turn the monitor off until it is time for the children to work.
7. The ability to save and print the children's pictures allows the children to review what they have done or to put on a computer art show. Some programs save groups of pictures with a "slide show" feature.
8. Most importantly, the program should be open-ended. It should not have pre-drawn coloring-book-style pictures to color, nor should it involve the manipulation of shapes or pictures on an already drawn background. Just because the words *draw, paint, picture,* or *art* are in the title of a program does not mean it is a true art program. Always preview a program before offering it to children.

Locating the Computer

The computer should be located away from heavy traffic and in a "clean-hands" location. There must be an electrical outlet capable of handling the necessary power, preferably with a surge protector. Make sure the computer area will be visible from all parts

Deanna, age 8, has made many pictures using the computer. Her picture "Houses and Sun" was made using Microsoft Paint a basic program found in Accessories on many computers.

of the room so that assistance can be offered when needed.

Choosing Equipment

Consider the following equipment when setting up a computer art program.

Computers. Any computer that runs the appropriate software can be used. Many child-appropriate art programs can be put on older, lower-powered machines. If the right combination of a program and an older machine can be found, then that may allow one computer to be dedicated to art exploration alone.

Printers. A printer is a nice addition, as it provides a way to capture the children's work, but it is not essential. For young computer artists, just as in all of the other art forms, process is more important than product, and the printed versions of children's art are often pale imitations of the glowing images on the screen anyway. For many children, part of the fun seems to be making their pictures disappear when they are done.

Input devices. A **mouse** is the best way for young children to draw on the computer. Joysticks can also be used. A cordless mouse provides more freedom of movement. Try to put the keyboard out of the way so that the child can focus on the mouse and the screen. On some computers, the **keyboard** can be placed on top of the monitor, or it can be removed and the mouse plugged in directly. If the keyboard is not removable, then it is essential to cover the keys with a protective skin. This will keep sand and other deleterious items out of the keyboard. The keyboard can also be covered with a cardboard box when children are using the mouse to draw.

HOW ARE THREE-DIMENSIONAL ACTIVITIES DESIGNED?

It is important for all children to have many opportunities to work in three dimensions. Infants can explore form by building with blocks and boxes, and through closely supervised one-on-one activities with play dough. By giving children the opportunity to explore a material that has many sides, that can be turned over and around and looked at from different points of view, teachers strengthen children's understanding of the spatial realm in which they exist. Three-dimensional art forms call upon different perceptual modes and different areas of skill development than do drawing, painting, and other two-dimensional activities.

THE MODELING EXPERIENCE

Modeling, or working with three-dimensional pliable materials, is one of the great joys of early childhood. Soft, smooth clays and play dough are just waiting to be squeezed and poked, to the great delight of the young artist.

When children draw or paint, there is a strong visual response to the marks they make on the paper. In working with modeling materials, although the visual element is still there, the children respond first to the tactile qualities of the forms as they create them. Young children working with play dough or clay will often manipulate the material vigorously while focusing their eyes on something else or staring off into space.

A great deal of talking and noisemaking goes on as children explore clay. Children working on drawings or paintings will perhaps make a comment or two while they work or add a special sound effect, but many at the clay table will pound, slap, and talk

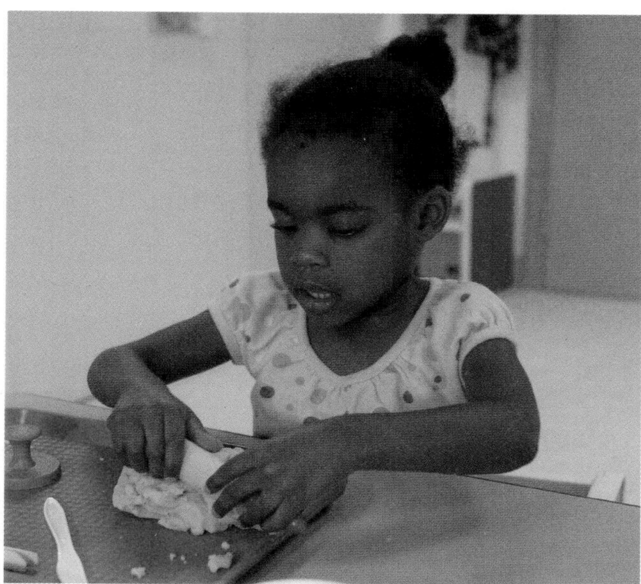

Pat it. Poke it. Squash it. Modeling provides a rich tactile experience.

incessantly. Modeling materials will provide an opportunity for children to practice their social skills as they respond to each other's actions and exchange pieces of clay or tools.

Modeling Center Design

Like paste and glue, modeling materials are quite often tasted or eaten. Provide constant close supervision until children have learned not to eat the material. A low, smooth-topped table that is easily washed makes the best working surface. There should be plenty of space for each child. If the tabletop is not appropriate for modeling, or when working at home in a kitchen area, provide each child with a large tray to be used whenever he or she models or does other artwork. Pottery clay requires a different setup because of the need to keep dust to a minimum (see Appendix A).

Selecting Modeling Materials

A range of pliable materials is available.

Play dough. The safest, most pliable modeling material for young children, especially infants and toddlers, is play dough. Use a commercial brand, or produce a homemade version. Many recipes are available in books on art for children, or consult Appendix D: Recipes.

For the child's initial exploration, the dough should be a nonfood color and have a nonfood scent. A homemade dough has the advantage of being able to be made without scent for the first few explorations. Use only one color of dough for the first experience so the child can concentrate on the tactile qualities of the materials. Provide each child with a baseball-size piece of the modeling dough. If the dough will be reused, offer separate, tightly lidded containers or resealable plastic bags, clearly labeled with each child's name. Preschoolers and primary-age children can be given several colors of play dough at a time, which they will mix with great enthusiasm. Try to pick colors that when combined form attractive new ones, such as red and yellow to make orange, or blue and yellow to make green.

Salt-flour dough. Children can also mix their own play dough. A salt-flour* dough is the easiest for children to use independently. Note: Salt may cause a burning sensation or irritate any small cuts or scrapes that children have on their hands. Check the children's hands first. If children complain about burning, let them wash their hands right away.

1. Work with a small group of three or four children that can be closely supervised.
2. Give each child a bowl, and help each child measure and pour one cup of flour and one-quarter cup of salt. Add one-quarter cup of warm water, and let them knead it together.
3. If the dough is too dry, add some drops of water. If it is too wet, add more flour.
4. Children can add liquid tempera, food coloring, or unsweetened powdered drink mix to the dough to color it.

Non-hardening clay. This is an oil-based modeling material, also called *modeling clay*, that does not dry out when exposed to the air. It is more rigid than play dough and suitable for older children who have more developed finger strength. Non-hardening clay, like play dough, is suitable for individual or large group work. Modeling clay should not be ingested. It is not appropriate for children who still try to taste or eat modeling materials. It works best on a smooth, washable surface such as a plastic laminate tabletop, a plastic placemat or tray, or even a laminated piece of construction paper. Do not use it on newspaper, as it picks up the ink.

Pottery clay. This is the real clay that comes from the earth and from which pottery is made. It has been used for thousands of years by people around the world. The china dishes we use every day are made from it. Purchase only talc-free, moist clay (see Appendix C for sources). Avoid all powdered or dry clay mixes. Figure one pound of moist clay per child. Store unused clay in double plastic bags that are tightly closed and placed inside a covered plastic can. When used clay is returned to the bag, add a half-cup of water per piece to replace evaporated moisture. Clay will keep a very long time this way.

Special Needs

Children who have limited vision love the tactile nature of modeling materials. Provide a large tray with slightly raised sides for the child to work on—it will make it easier to find small pieces of the modeling material.

Modeling Activities for Infants

Because infants readily put things in their mouth, most modeling activities are not suitable for them. Begin with brief one-on-one experiences with unscented homemade play dough.

Modeling Activities for Toddlers

Once children are familiar with safe ways to use play dough, the activity can be varied in many ways.

Add scent. Once children have learned not to taste the dough, add nonfood scents. (See Chapter 5 for a list of possible scents.)

Add textures. Find a recipe for homemade play dough that has a different texture, or add a material to commercial play dough to provide a different tactile experience. Try adding coffee grounds or sand.

Provide tools. The majority of a child's modeling experiences should be done with the fingers only. Manipulating the play dough directly is the best way to develop hand and finger strength. On occasion, provide some very simple tools. Little children love to cut up play dough. A plastic knife provides a safe way for the child to feel grown up and trusted. A small wooden or plastic rolling pin is another tool that children enjoy, and one that helps them develop hand-eye coordination.

Teacher Tip

COOKIE CUTTERS

Hold back on giving the children cookie cutters. Although these are commonly used in early childhood programs, in many ways they are similar to giving the children precut paper patterns on which to draw. They tell the children that adults do not think the forms they create on their own are as good as the commercial cookie-cutter designs. Cookie cutters also reduce the wonderful three-dimensionality of the play dough to two dimensions and so do not help develop the child's spatial abilities.

Modeling Activities for Preschoolers

Preschoolers love using play dough. Although just having colorful lumps of dough available is sufficient to motivate most children, try some of these activities too.

Play with color. Let the children color their own dough by squeezing a drop or two of food coloring or liquid tempera paint onto uncolored, homemade dough and then mixing the color with their hands. (Homemade play dough recipes are in Appendix C: Recipes.)

Try impressions. Give the children objects with interesting textures to press into the dough and clay. Try berry baskets, plastic food trays, plastic forks, lids, bottle tops, potato mashers, keys, coins, and any other washable items. Compare the impressions with prints made from the same items.

Making Plans

ONE-ON-ONE ACTIVITY PLAN: Introducing Play Dough

WHO? **Group composition age(s):** Older infant or toddler

WHEN? **Time frame:** 5 to 15 minutes

WHY? **Objectives:** Children will develop

- physically, by using the large muscles of the arm and the small muscles of the hand to manipulate the modeling material. (Bodily-Kinesthetic)
- socially, by interacting with a caring adult. (Interpersonal)
- emotionally, by developing self-confidence from being allowed to handle the dough. (Intrapersonal)
- visual perception skills, by exploring three-dimensional forms from differing viewpoints and learning that pliant forms change shape. (Spatial)
- language skills, by verbalizing how the dough feels and learning words for size and shape. (Linguistic)
- cognitively, by observing cause and effect as their manipulation changes the nature of the form. (Logical-Mathematical)
- art awareness, by learning how to work in three dimensions Content Standard 1 & 2.

WHERE? **Setup:** Child in a high chair or on an adult's lap at the table. Low-sided tray, such as a cookie sheet for the dough.

WHAT? **Materials:** Soft homemade, unscented play dough.

HOW? **Procedure:**

Warm-Up: Place a lump of dough in front of child. Model how to poke it and pat it. Explain that it is not food but something with which to play. Let the child see it, smell it, and touch it.

What to Do: Children will react differently to the stimulus of the play dough. Some will dive right in; others will approach cautiously. Some will pat and poke gently; some will squeeze it tightly in their hands. Often the first response is to try to taste or smell it. Only interfere with children's exploration for safety reasons. Be ready to stop them from putting the dough into their mouths. Remember that it is important from the start to emphasize that arts materials are never put into the mouth.

What to Say: Use this activity to talk about the tactile qualities of the play dough. In an excited voice, use words such as *soft, squishy, pat, poke, push, pull, sticky, press, squash,* and *flatten*. Modeling is a wonderful time to chant or sing with toddlers. Make up some modeling chants to accompany this wonderful activity.

Transition Out: Let the child spend as much time as he or she wishes exploring the nature of the dough. When done, store the dough in a plastic bag to use again.

ASSESSMENT OF LEARNING

1. Does child respond positively to the play dough?
2. Does child have sufficient hand strength to change the shape of the play dough?
3. Does child repeat and use the descriptive terms modeled by the adult?

Making Plans

CENTER ACTIVITY PLAN: Using Non-Hardening Modeling Clay

WHO? **Group composition age(s):** Preschool, kindergarten, or primary age children in a group of 4 to 6 at the center

WHEN? **Time frame:** 15-minute introduction, then 10 to 20 minutes at the center

WHY? **Objectives:** Children will develop

- physically, by using the large muscles of the arm and the small muscles of the hand to manipulate the modeling material. (Bodily-Kinesthetic)
- socially, by sharing workspace and materials. (Interpersonal)
- emotionally, by using self-control while working independently at the center. (Intrapersonal)
- visual perception skills, by exploring three-dimensional forms from differing viewpoints and learning that pliant forms change shape. (Spatial)
- language skills, by explaining the changes in the forms and by answering questions about their actions and choices. (Linguistic)
- cognitively, by comparing changes in the tactile quality and form of the clay. (Logical-Mathematical)
- art awareness, by learning ways to work with clay and by comparing their clay work to that of others. (Content Standards 1, 2, and 3)

WHERE? **Setup:** Low, smooth-surfaced table near the sink.

WHAT? **Materials:** Individual pieces of modeling clay in a basic color such as beige, gray, or brown. A low-sided cardboard box divided into sections, one for each child. Plastic zipper bags for each child's clay.

HOW? **Procedure:**

Warm-Up: Use guided discovery to introduce the clay. Wrap a piece of modeling clay in fancy paper with a bow. Pass it around and let children guess what it might be. Slowly open it until they guess what it is. Pass it around and let children touch it and make suggestions for how to use it. Write guidelines for its use on chart paper.

What to Do: Explain how to store their individual piece of clay in a bag placed in the box. Have children model how to get clay, use it, and put it back. Children can then work at the center in small groups at center time.

What to Say: Encourage children to describe what they are making, and engage in pretend play with them. Use words that describe the forms they are making, such as cone, cylinder, and sphere. Introduce the word *coil* to describe the long snakes children love to roll out. Ask them to tell you how they made certain forms and how they were able to attach them. If a child loses self-control with the clay, point out the class's guidelines for working.

Transition Out: Invite children to put finished sculptures on display in an area set aside for this purpose. Then take photographs of the works so children can reuse the clay.

ASSESSMENT OF LEARNING

1. Can children describe their actions and what happened?
2. Do children use modeling vocabulary to describe their work?
3. Do children exhibit self-control and follow modeling guidelines?

Modeling Activities for Kindergarten and Primary Age

Play dough is always popular with older children, but their stronger hands and better fine motor control means they will also enjoy using all types of modeling materials.

"Stick" sculptures. Use a lump of air-drying dough (see Appendix D) as a base in which to insert materials such as sticks, toothpicks, pipe cleaners, cardboard strips, craft sticks, beads, buttons, drinking straws, and nature materials, such as pinecones, acorns, shells, dried grasses, and twigs. When the dough has dried, the objects will be securely fastened to the base.

Geometric forms. Older children can use non-hardening modeling clay to make forms such as cubes (made by tapping a sphere on the table to create the sides) and slabs (flat, rectangular "pancakes"), which can be used in building structures.

Classroom Museum

Share the sculptures of Henry Moore. His gently rounded human forms are appealing to young children. Compare them to work by other sculptors. If possible, visit a sculpture in the neighborhood, and study and sketch it from different sides.

Pottery Clay for Primary Age Children

Working with real clay from the earth is an exciting, yet very technical procedure. Present the pottery clay to the children as an exploration to start without expectations of making finished works. Encourage them to try different ways of using it, and let them explore on their own. Show the children how to return the clay to its storage container when they are done.

Guidelines for Working with Pottery Clay

1. **Joining.** Two pieces of clay will not join and stay together when dry without special preparation: To join: apply **slip**—a watery clay mixture—to each piece. Press together. Smooth joint so it cannot be seen.
2. **Dampening.** The more the clay is handled, the more it dries out. Overly dry clay cracks and will not stay together. Small amounts of water should be added as needed. It takes a lot of experience to know just how much water to add. Children will quickly learn that too much water reduces the clay to a mud pile. Use this experience to help children see cause and effect. Help them learn to add just a little at a time.
3. **Location.** Avoid using pottery clay in any multipurpose room or where food is eaten. If possible, use pottery clay outdoors. Indoors, because the fine dust spreads easily, cleanup is very important. The clay-covered newspaper will need to be folded up slowly to not spread the dust. Inside there will be less mess if they work standing at a table covered with several layers of newspaper.
4. **Clean up.** Wash all tools and wipe down all surfaces. Use buckets for the initial hand and tool rinsing so the clay-filled water can be dumped outside on the ground where it will not clog the sink drain.

Pottery Clay Activities

Bring in experts. Visit a pottery studio, invite a guest potter, or share a special ceramic bowl or dish.

Observe changes. Discuss how pottery clay changes when it is baked at a hot temperature, and show examples of **unglazed,** baked clay and **glazed,** fired clay. Compare how the firing clay differs from the other modeling materials the children have used.

Make clay tiles. Most creations by young children are too fragile to survive firing in the **kiln.** Again, they are best saved through photography. If, however, a kiln is available, a wonderful, cooperative culminating activity for the pottery clay exploration is to make clay tiles.

1. Make one or several large flat squares of clay, about 1½ inch thick, and 4- to 6-inches per

side. Children can help roll out the clay using rolling pins.

2. Have the children take turns drawing an original design or picture on the tiles using pencils or craft sticks. Caution the children not to press too hard.
3. Alternatively, wet the clay surface and have the children attach small pieces of clay, such as flattened balls and skinny snakes, combined to make a picture. Keep the height under 1 inch.
4. Poke holes in the top of the tiles so they can be hung up after firing.
5. Air-dry completely—at least one week.
6. Low-fire the tiles in the kiln (1100°–1500°F).
7. After firing, the tiles can be painted with watercolors or tempera paint or left natural.

Make wind chimes. Clay slabs can also be made into wind chimes. Have children make flat pancakes with the clay, and then cut them into three or four different shapes. Impress designs in the clay, or draw in the clay with a pencil. Poke a hole in the top of each piece. After firing suspend with yarn or leather thongs from a tree branch or dowel. A group wind chime can be made by having each child contribute one shape.

Make coil pots. Show children how to roll out ropes of clay using the palms of their hands. Make a base by cutting a circular shape from a slab of clay. Attach a thick coil to the outside edge of the base using slip. Smooth the inside so that no joints show.

Make animals. Children love making animals from clay but often have difficulty making the legs and necks strong enough to support the body and head. Talk about how large animals need strong legs. Offer the idea of attaching the animal to a slab base or making it sitting or lying down. Emphasize the importance of using slip to attach limbs and details, and make sure the child smoothes the joints. If clay animals will be fired in a kiln, make sure to hollow out any thick bodies so that they will dry better and be less likely to crack during firing.

Making clay tiles and firing them in a kiln is an excellent introduction to the wonders of pottery clay. These were made by Laurel, age 6.

Classroom Museum

Display brightly colored Mexican figurines of roosters and other common animals. Talk about why artists might use color on some sculptures and not on others. Also, share handmade pottery pieces. Have a potter visit and demonstrate making a pot, or visit a potter's studio. Use handmade pottery to serve snacks.

Making Plans

CENTER ACTIVITY PLAN: Pottery Clay

WHO? Group composition age(s): Preschool, kindergarten, or primary age children in groups of 2 to 4

WHEN? Time frame: 15-minute introduction, then 10 to 20 minutes working with clay

WHY? Objectives: Children will develop

- physically, by using fine motor control to shape the clay. (Bodily-Kinesthetic)
- socially, by sharing the materials and their experiences with the clay. (Interpersonal)
- emotionally, by showing pride in their work. (Intrapersonal)
- visual perception skills, by learning to look at all sides of a form. (Spatial)
- language skills, by describing the clay experience. (Linguistic)
- cognitively, by comparing and contrasting the clay as it dries. (Logical-Mathematical)
- art awareness, by developing skill in handling the clay and in studying the purposes of pottery made by people in other times and places. (Content Standards 1, 2, 4, & 5)

WHERE? Setup: Newspaper-covered table set up outside on a warm, sunny day.

WHAT? Materials: Individual pieces of talc-free pottery clay. Clay tools. Cups of water. Bucket of water and paper towels for cleanup.

HOW? Procedure:

Warm-Up: At snack time use a handmade pottery bowl. Ask children if they know from what it is made. Explain that they will have a chance to use pottery clay when they go outside. Read the book *The Pot That Juan Built* (Goebel, 2002).

What to Do: Outside show them the clay table. Choose several children. Hand each one a piece of clay and have them describe how it feels. Model how to use water to soften the clay and to make slip to attach two pieces together. Then let the children explore using the clay. When done return the clay to the storage bin, and introduce the next group to the process.

What to Say: Emphasize keeping hands away from nose and mouth. Ask children to describe the forms they make and what happens when they add water to the clay. Use clay words such as *pinch, coil, slip,* and *slab*.

Transition Out: Leave some pieces of clay out to dry and to be discussed the next day when children share their clay experiences. Set up a pottery clay area whenever there is good weather. As children gain in skill, model how to make animals, and pinch coil pots.

ASSESSMENT OF LEARNING

1. Do children observe safety rules?
2. Do children have hand strength and fine motor control to shape the clay?
3. Do children repeat and use clay terms?

Firing Pottery Clay

The following guidelines will help make the firing experience more successful:

1. Work to be fired should be fairly uniform in thickness so that it dries evenly.
2. Place clay pieces to be dried in a location where they cannot be handled by the children. Greenware is very brittle.
3. Clay should dry slowly. The location needs to be away from the sun and any heaters.
4. Check pieces daily, and gently turn them, if necessary, to allow drying on all sides.
5. Work can be fired only when it is completely dry. Damp spots will cause the piece to crack during firing. Damp clay feels cold to the touch. Dry clay feels room temperature and has a chalky texture.

Arts Words

TALKING ABOUT POTTERY CLAY

Bisque: Unglazed clay that has been fired in a kiln. It is hard and porous.

Coil: A long rope of clay made by rolling it on a flat surface with the palms moving outward.

Firing: Slowly heating clay in an insulated oven called a *kiln.*

Firing clay: Modeling compound formed from earth that dries out in the air and becomes hard when fired in a kiln. Also called *pottery clay.*

Glaze: A finely ground mixture of minerals that, when fired to a high temperature, forms a glassy coating on clay.

Greenware: Clay that has air-dried. It is very brittle and easily broken.

Hand wedging: Kneading clay to bend it and remove pockets of air.

Kiln: An oven made from firebrick in which clay can be fired to temperatures over 1000°F.

Leather hard: Clay that is still damp but no longer flexible. It can be cut and carved.

Scraffito: Using a stick or pointed tool to scratch designs into the surface of the clay.

Slab: A flat piece of clay made either by pressing with the palms or by using a rolling pin.

Slip: Liquid clay made by combining clay with water to form a thick, custard-like substance. It is used to join clay pieces.

Wedging: Kneading and pressing clay to remove air pockets and to create an even texture.

Teacher Tip

USING CLAY SAFELY

Have children wear smocks to prevent dust from collecting on clothing. Wash smocks after use.

Remind children to keep their hands away from their faces and to dampen them when they are dusty and dry. Children must never put their hands into their mouths or touch their faces when using the clay. They must clean under their fingernails as well as clean their hands when they are done. Do not allow children to clap their hands together, raising dust.

Kilns must be located in areas far away from where children are working. They must be fully ventilated to the outside. Never use a kiln that does not meet these requirements.

6. Allow plenty of time. It usually takes one week for clay work to dry completely, but this depends on the weather. It is better to wait longer before firing to be sure, rather than to rush the process and risk a ruined project and a disappointed child. Stack unglazed pieces in the kiln with the heavier ones on the bottom.

Book Box

Books about clay.

Baylor, B. (1972). *When clay sings.* New York: Aladdin.
A classic about the pottery of the early inhabitants of the American Southwest told poetically.

Hill, L. C. (2010). *Dave, the potter.* New York: Little, Brown.
Simple, poetic language tells the story of Dave, a gifted potter, who was a slave 200 years ago in North Carolina. Kindergarten and up.

Carolina, Goebel, N. (2002). *The pot that Juan built.* New York: Lee & Low.
On one side of the page is a cumulative story about a clay pot being made by a Mexican potter. On the opposing side is a detailed text, which explains the process. Three and up.

Hughes, L. (1997). *The sweet and sour animal book.* New York: Oxford University Press.
Lively two- and three-dimensional artwork by children illustrates Langston Hughes's alphabet book of poetry. Very suitable to share with children of all ages. Four and up.

THE CONSTRUCTED SCULPTURE EXPERIENCE

> *The smooth shape of the blocks gave me a sense that never left me—of form becoming feeling.*
>
> —*Frank Lloyd Wright (Willard, 1972, p. 7)*

Children, too, are builders. They create environments. They are the architects of the spaces they inhabit, often creating complex arrangements of toys and

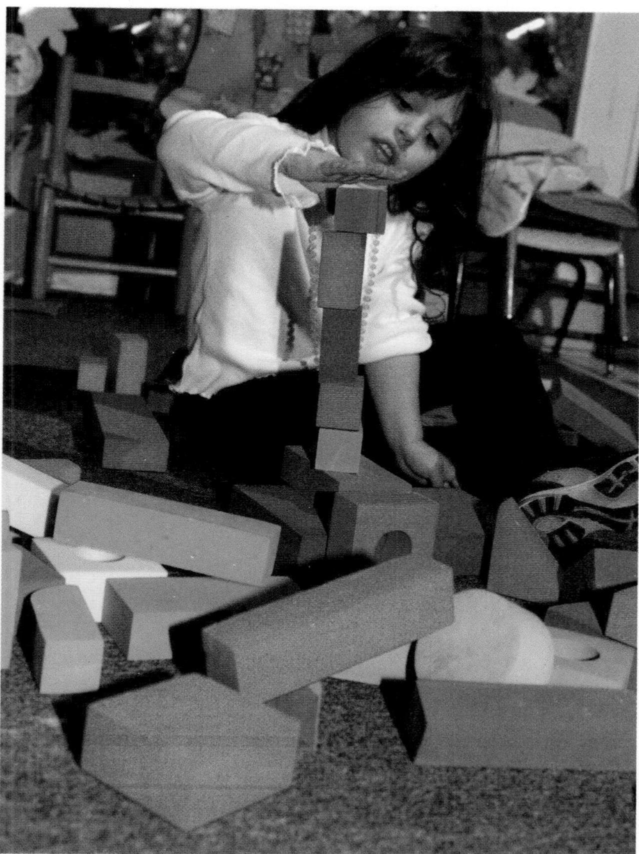
Blocks allow children to creatively investigate form and structure.

furnishings indoors and shelters of sticks and grass outdoors. Frank Lloyd Wright (Willard, 1972, p. 7) attributed his interest in architecture to the gift of a box of Froebel blocks from his mother. Much has been written on the importance of block play for young children (Chalufour and Worth, 2004; Church and Miller, 1990; Gelfer, 1990). In this section, the focus will be on the artistic and creative learning that is developed in building structures with blocks and other materials.

Selecting Construction Materials

The first construction materials usually offered are blocks. Many different kinds are available from which to choose. Other construction materials can later be added to the block center or used on their own.

Large blocks. Made of plastic, wood, cardboard, or foam, large blocks allow children to build structures they can sit on or go inside. They are excellent for dramatic play and for balancing towers. They provide a fun way to discover spatial relationships by building walls to peek over, through, and around.

Boxes. Empty cardboard boxes provide both units to stack and spaces inside which to build. Jewelry or pudding mix boxes can be used to make miniature houses to be arranged in a model of the neighborhood or town. They can also be made into homes for tiny toys or special treasures, or glued together into unique, three-dimensional structures. Small boxes can become homes for beloved stuffed toys. Shoe boxes and cereal, pasta, and oatmeal containers can also be made into houses, homes for treasures, and creatures of all kinds. Giant boxes are instantly appealing to young children, providing an immediate sense of privacy and drawing forth imaginative play. Painting larger boxes provides large motor movement for young children. Appliance boxes can be turned into spaceships or submarines.

Pattern blocks. These small, flat, colored blocks of wood or plastic demonstrate many mathematical relationships. They are excellent for developing ideas of symmetry and pattern, as well as for inventing creative designs and patterns.

Unit blocks. These blocks are usually wooden and come in a variety of geometric and architectural forms. They represent mathematical concepts, such as two right triangles aligning to form a rectangle the same size as the rectangular unit block. This offers the children an excellent opportunity to investigate symmetry and geometric relationships.

Large cardboard. Pieces of cardboard cut from boxes can be used to create walls, roofs, and ramps. They can also be fastened together using paper fasteners or chenille stems to make structures that are more elaborate.

Wood scraps. Collect small leftover pieces of wood from carpenters or lumberyards for children to glue or nail together.

Classroom Museum

Architecture. Display a print of one of Frank Lloyd Wright's buildings. Tell the children about how he loved to build with blocks.

Constructions. Share the box assemblages of Duchamp and Nevelson, such as Nevelson's *Case with Five Balusters* (Take 5: Collage and Assemblage).

Papier-mâché. Share prints or actual papier-mâché artifacts, such as masks from Mexico. (See Appendix C for sources.)

Making Plans

CENTER ACTIVITY PLAN: Building Blocks

WHO? **Group composition age(s):** Preschoolers, kindergartners, or primary age—small groups of two to six depending on the amount of space and number of blocks available

WHEN? **Time frame:** 10 to 30 minutes

WHY? **Objectives:** Children will develop

- physically, by using large muscles in moving blocks and boxes, by using the small muscles of the hand and arm in controlling the placement of smaller three-dimensional objects, and by using eye-hand coordination to effect careful placements. (Bodily-Kinesthetic)
- socially, by sharing space and materials with others and by working cooperatively on large constructions. (Interpersonal)
- emotionally, by gaining confidence through building substantial structures. (Intrapersonal)
- visual perception skills, by learning to see three-dimensional structures from a variety of viewpoints. (Spatial)
- language, by learning a vocabulary for concepts of size, form, shape, location, and relationship. (Linguistic)
- cognitively, by sorting objects by categories, by organizing them into patterns, by counting them, and by observing cause and effect as they try different solutions to problems. (Logical-Mathematical)
- art awareness, by learning about architecture and three-dimensional design principles. (Content Standards 2, 3, and 5)

WHERE? **Setup:** A large area visually separated from other centers by a low-pile rug.

WHAT? **Materials:** Shelves hold sorted wooden blocks in many sizes and shapes. Plastic bins have small animals and vehicles. Blue paper and white pencils sit nearby.

HOW? **Procedure:**

Warm-Up: Have children sit in a circle with blocks in the middle. Place a block in the middle and have the children add a block to build a structure. Then model how to put the blocks away.

What to Do: In the beginning allow children plenty of time to explore. As children start to build structures, enter into children's play by modeling ways of building and asking questions to help them solve problems.

What to Say: Use a vocabulary of spatial terms, such as form, space, shadow, balance, symmetry, top view, and side view. Offer description. Say: "You are making your tower symmetrical. See, you have the same blocks on each side." Provide direction. Ask: "What size block will you use next?" "How can you make the base stronger?" "Give encouragement. Suggest to children that they include art in their building projects. Ask: "From which view will you draw a picture?" "Can you make a roof with this cardboard?" "Do you want to make some signs for your road?" Ask them how they solved particular problems. "What did you do to keep that from falling down?" "How did you decide to make the tower base so wide?"

Transition Out: Take photographs of the structures. Encourage older children to draw blueprints of their buildings. Create a presentation panel showing photographs of the children's constructions together with their drawings.

ASSESSMENT OF LEARNING

1. Do children build structures that are creative and sturdy?
2. Can children identify and name three-dimensional forms?
3. Can children describe decisions they made, and problems they solved?

Setting Up a Construction Center Featuring Blocks

The number of children who can be in a block area will be determined by their ages and the size of the area. Infants work best one-on-one with a caring adult. Two toddlers can work side by side if there are enough blocks and space. If there are only a few blocks in a small, enclosed area, then bumping and grabbing may result. Preschoolers and primary children, who may become involved in cooperative building projects, often can work in larger groups, but attention must always be paid to each child having enough room to move around and get more blocks without knocking over someone else's structure. Use masking tape to mark off a distance from the shelves in which building is not allowed, so that children can get blocks off the shelves without knocking someone's structure down.

Other factors that affect the group size are the size of the blocks and the floor surface. A flat, low-pile carpet makes a good surface because it muffles the blocks when they fall. It is also more comfortable for the children to sit on while working. A smooth wood or tile floor, however, provides a slightly more stable base on which to work and allows smooth motion for wheeled vehicles. A well-designed block area should include both types of surfaces.

Teacher Tip

BLOCK SAFETY

Like other supplies, blocks need to be arranged aesthetically and safely. Low shelves are essential. Blocks stored higher than the child's waist can fall and cause injuries. On the shelves, the blocks should not be stacked more than several high, and each type of block should have its own location. Create a label for each location by tracing the shape of the block on paper and then attaching it to the correct shelf. Put the heaviest blocks on the bottom. Use the top of the shelves for accessories stored in clear plastic bins.

Construction Activities for Infants and Toddlers

Safety is the first concern when building with infants. Provide soft blocks with no hard edges or use boxes. Boxes are also perfect for toddlers. Small ones can be stacked. Large ones can be used to build mazes and tunnels. A refrigerator-size box makes a cozy house.

Make it move. Attaching a string turns a box into a vehicle in which stuffed toys can ride.

Decorate it. Art can be created inside of the box as well as outside. Color boxes with crayons and markers. Let children glue colored papers to the sides or paint the box using large paintbrushes.

Arts Words

ARCHITECTURAL STRUCTURES

Arch: A curved structure supporting the weight of part of a building.

Beam: A long, straight piece of solid material, such as wood or metal, that supports the weight of some of the building.

Column: An upright support.

Post and lintel: Two upright supports (posts) that hold up a horizontal piece of solid material (lintel), such as wood, stone, or metal, to create an opening such as a door or window.

Teacher Tip

ADDING ART TO THE BLOCK CENTER

Art materials can be added to the block area to increase the dramatic and architectural possibilities.

1. Paper, markers, and crayons for making maps, and drawing pictures of the buildings.
2. Blue paper and white pencils or crayons to make "blueprints."
3. Cardboard pieces, tubes, and scissors for the construction of roofs, signs, ramps, and more.
4. Fabric pieces to use for rugs and furnishings in houses.
5. Non-hardening clay to make people and animals.
6. Bottle caps and thread spools to add decorative patterns.
7. Aluminum foil to cover blocks for a sparkling effect.

Note: These materials should be slowly added to the block area, so that children have time to investigate the possibilities of each before being overwhelmed by too many choices.

Construction Activities for Preschoolers and Kindergarteners

Blocks and boxes introduce children to the world of architecture. It is natural for young children to build structures that mirror the buildings they inhabit and see around them. Encourage this connection by pointing out the relationships between the basic forms and their architectural counterparts (see Figure 9-1).

Take a walk. Explore the neighborhood, and find cylindrical columns, triangular roofs, rectangular

Making Plans

RESPONSIVE ACTIVITY PLAN: papier-Mâché

WHO? Group composition age(s): Primary age small group of four to six at a time

WHEN? Time frame: 6 days of 45 to 60 minutes each

WHY? Objectives: Children will develop

- physically, by using hand-eye coordination to place the paper strips. (Bodily-Kinesthetic)
- socially, by sharing space and materials with others and by working cooperatively on a large group project. (Interpersonal)
- emotionally, by feeling pride in accomplishing a large cooperative task. (Intrapersonal)
- visual perception skills, by observing how parts make up a whole. (Spatial)
- language, by describing the process they went through to create their dinosaur. (Linguistic)
- cognitively, by sorting objects by categories, by organizing them into patterns, by counting them, and by observing cause and effect. (Logical-Mathematical)
- art awareness, by comparing their sculpture to that of other artists. (Content Standards 3, 4, and 5)

WHERE? Setup: A large area covered with newspaper.

WHAT? Materials: large boxes, newspaper, art paste (see Appendix C), individual containers with tight lids for the paste, large brushes, and tempera paint.

HOW? Procedure:

Warm-Up:

- *Day 1*—A letter arrives from the class next door. They have found a dinosaur skeleton. They have sent a description and measurements and challenge them to build a model of it. The children try to image which type of dinosaur it is.

What to Do:

- *Day 2*—The children use dinosaur books to do research and make drawings of what it should look like.
- *Day 3*—The children sit in a horseshoe shape and take turns trying out different ways to use the boxes to build a model of the dinosaur. When satisfied, they then tape the boxes together.
- *Day 4*—The teacher models how to wrap the boxes with glued newspaper strips. Then children, working in small groups, take turns applying the strips. It then is allowed to dry for several days.
- *Day 5*—Class decides what color and pattern the dinosaur should have, and taking turns, small groups begin to paint it.
- *Day 6*—Children write letters inviting the class next door to come and measure their model and see if they followed the directions. Take photographs and video of the project.

What to Say: Give lots of positive feedback and encourage children to work together. Ask questions that help them solve problems as a group. "How can we stabilize that leg?" "What could we use to support the neck?"

Transition Out: Have children create a display about how they built the dinosaur. These could be drawings, books, stories, and PowerPoint presentations.

ASSESSMENT OF LEARNING

1. Do children work well together to solve the problem?
2. Does the finished dinosaur reflect the information the children were given?

bricks, arches, and more. Note how doorways are created by placing a crosspiece over two vertical supports (post and lintel), and point out similar constructions in children's block buildings.

Find boxes. Take a field trip to the local grocery store, and have each child select a carton to bring back. Find out what the store does with the empty cartons.

Ask an expert. Invite an architect or architecture student to come and share his or her sketches, plans, and models of buildings. Such a visit will inspire the children to draw "blueprints" of their own.

Design a personal space. Plan a day for older children to each be given a small section of the room in which to build her or his own private place using blocks, moveable furnishings, and other delineating materials to form the walls. Share the story *Roxaboxen* (McLerran, 1991) as the perfect complement to this activity.

Plastic blocks. Preschool-size interlocking blocks of different designs, such as Duplo® or bristle blocks, allow children to investigate other ways to support what they build.

Construction Activities for Primary Age

By the ages of six to eight, children are developing more fine motor control and can handle construction materials that are much smaller.

Architectural blocks. Wooden blocks in the style of Egyptian, Greek, Roman, and Middle Eastern styles allow children to explore columns, lintels, and domes.

Interlocking blocks. Plastic and wood blocks, such as LEGO® and Lincoln Logs®, allow children to build on a smaller scale. When offering these, try putting them out without directions and let children create their own designs.

Add on. Provide precut pieces of flat cardboard that can be glued onto the boxes in various ways.

Draw it. Encourage children to make drawings showing the sequence of steps in building their sculpture(s). Display these near the piece.

Talk about it. Tape-record children as they work. Replay the tape, and have children try to identify the speaker. Display selected quotes next to the finished piece. Record the children's description of what they did on an experience chart.

Working with Papier-Mâché

Papier-mâché is a wonderfully sticky material that dries hard and paintable. It is a good way to convert flimsy cereal boxes into sturdy constructions. Papier-mâché should be seen as a medium to be used when children have a specific problem or project in mind. For example, if children are frustrated because paint will not stick to the box they are painting, suggest papier-mâché. If some children want to build a box robot and the boxes will not stick together, suggest papier-mâché.

For the paste use thinned white glue, plain flour, or one of the special art pastes available (see Appendix C for suppliers). Do not use wall paper paste as it contains toxins. If using flour, be on the alert for gluten-sensitive children who may have severe allergic reactions.

Book Box

Books about building.

Barton, B. (1990). *Building a house.* New York: Mulberry.
Clear colorful pictures show the steps taken in building a house. Infant/Toddler and up.

Crosbie, M. J., & Rosenthal, S. (1993). *Architecture COLORS.* Washington, DC: Preservation Press.
This board book illustrates each color with a photograph of an architectural feature on a home or building opposite the word for the color and the feature. This is a good read-aloud for toddlers and a read-it-myself book for preschoolers. Follow up reading this book with a walk through the neighborhood, looking for the colors and architectural features mentioned in the book. One of a series published by the National Trust for Historic Preservation that also includes Architecture SHAPES, Architecture COUNTS, and Architecture ANIMALS. Infant/Toddler and up.

Komatzu, E. (2004) *Wonderful houses around the world.* Bolinas, CA: Shelter Publications.
Photographs show families outside their home and then cutaways show what is inside. Discusses how environment affects home design. Six and up.

Maddox, D. (1986). *Architects make zig zags: Looking at architecture from A to Z.* New York: John Wiley.
Detailed drawings introduce different architectural features. Five and up.

McLerran, A. (1991). *Roxaboxen.* New York: Lothrop, Lee, & Shepard.
On the edge of the desert, a group of neighborhood children builds "houses" out of stones, sticks, old pottery, and crates. Using their imaginations, a town is created. Four and up.

Morris, A. (1992). *Houses and homes.* New York: Mulberry Books. (Art Awareness: architecture; Media: construction)
Photographs show homes from many different places in the world. Toddler and up.

Using papier-mâché requires children to follow a set of orderly steps:

1. Demonstrate how to dip a strip of paper into the paste, and then place it on the box or tray.
2. Children should keep their hands over their paste buckets, which should be set directly in front of them in order to catch drips.
3. Encourage the children to cover the box or tray completely, so that nothing shows. One layer is usually sufficient for the first papier-mâché experience. In future experiences, children can be encouraged to put on more layers to make the base sturdier.
4. Place finished projects on a sheet of plastic to dry. They will stick to newspaper. Place them in a safe, dry place near a heater or in the sun to speed drying time.

When the papier-mâché is dry, the form can be painted and/or collaged.

Two girls get ready for takeoff in their class built a papier-mâché rocket ship.

Papier-Mâché Activities for Primary Age Children

The easiest activity for the first time using papier-mâché is to have children cover a box.

Make buildings. A walk on the street could lead to a project for some children who want to make houses and buildings. To make a building base, cover a box with two layers of pasted paper strips. When dry, paint and then paste on door and window shapes.

Create puppets. Use glue-soaked strips to cover a cereal or spaghetti box, left open at one end so that it will turn into a puppet form that fits over the child's hand. Paint on a face and add yarn hair.

Make a mask. A tray can be used to make a mask-like shape. Cover the tray with two to three layers of strips. Let dry several days. When dry, the tray will fall away. Trim edge into shape for mask and cut out eyeholes. Finish by painting and adding yarn hair.

CONCLUSION: THE POWER OF THE VISUAL ARTS

Visual artists have been creating with paper, paint, clay, fiber, and more for thousands of years. Much of what is known about civilizations of the past has been bequeathed to us through the culture's visual artworks. Providing young children the opportunity to work with a wide variety of visual arts media in open-ended ways facilitates the growth of both the mind and hand; it is also a link to our past and our future. As teachers, we need to be sure that all children have the opportunity to explore new media, create graphic symbols, and develop technical skill.

FURTHER READING

To learn more about teaching drawing, read:

Smith, N. (Ed.) (1998). *Observation drawing with children.* New York: Teachers College.

This book gives an overview of drawing development and an analysis of the role of drawing that will be of interest to all teachers working with children. It suggests many activities based on studying real objects.

To learn more about teaching painting, read:

Topal, C. W. (1992). *Children and painting.* Worcester, MA: Davis.

This book lays out how to have successful painting experiences with children. Although it has an elementary focus, it will provide many ideas for working with all children.

To learn more about teaching clay, read:

Topal, C. W. (1998). *Children, clay, and sculpture.* Worcester, MA: Davis.

A detailed guide to working with potters clay and children, this book shows how to use all the basic techniques to be successful and to have fun using clay.

Kolh, M. F. (1994). *Mudworks: Creative clay, dough and modeling experiences.* Bellingham, WA: Bright Ring Publishing.

A multitude of play dough recipes and open-ended modeling experiences make this book a rich resource for teachers of young children.

For additional information on teaching the visual arts to young children visit our Web site at http://www.cengagebrain.com

TEACHING IN ACTION

A Day with Clay: A Teacher's Notebook Entry

My friend Julian, who is an art student at the local college, came today and showed the children how he makes a clay pot. We set up a table out on the grass by the playground fence. We all gathered around and watched. Outside was perfect. It was very informal and open. The children would watch awhile, go play, and then wander back.

All the while Julian worked he kept describing how it felt. He said things such as, "This is bumpy; I must make it smoother." He also described what he was doing, as in, "I am pushing the clay with my fingers." He was so patient and answered all of the children's questions. He let them touch the clay and the pot he was making, too.

When Julian was done, he invited the children who were standing around him to make pots also. He gave them each a piece of clay and guided them in making it rounded and pushing a hole in the middle with their thumbs. When they were finished, a few others came over and made some pots. Several just wanted to pound the clay flat. Julian showed them how to press sticks and stones into the clay to make impressions. Some children decided to do that to their clay pots. He carved the child's name on each one and took all of the projects to fire in his kiln. He said he thought they would turn out fine. I had a bucket of water for the children to rinse their hands in, and then they went inside to wash up at the sink.

I took lots of photographs. I can't wait to get them back. Then we can make a class book about our Clay Day!

The flexible nature of clay lets imaginations soar. These firing clay pieces have been fired in a kiln and then painted with tempera paint.

Studio Page

THE ELEMENTS OF ART

In Chapter 4 we learned about the elements of art. For each of the elements listed below give an example of a related visual art activity you could do with children in the age groups indicated.

Element	Toddler	Preschool	Primary
Color			
Shape			
Texture			
Form			
Line			
Pattern			

Studio Page

PLANNING AN ART CENTER

Select an age group and art media. Explain how you will set up the center and introduce the children to it.

Age Group: ____________________ **Media:** ____________________

Where will the center be located?

____

____

What materials will be there?

____

____

How will these be aesthetically arranged?

____

____

How will you introduce the children to the new center?

____

____

Studio Page

OBSERVATION: CHILDREN DRAWING

1. Plan a drawing exploration or practice activity suitable for an infant or child up to the age of eight.
2. Obtain permission to work with the child or children, either at home, at school, or in a childcare setting.
3. Set up your activity and observe the child or children at work. If possible, take photos or videotape the activity (get permission first). With the child's permission, save one or more of the drawings for your own collection.

Age of child(ren):
Setup of materials:
Length of time of observation:

---

1. What did the child(ren) do first?

___

2. What did the child(ren) say?

___

3. How did the child(ren) manipulate the drawing tool(s)? (For example, describe the position of the arm and hands, grip, and any other body parts involved.)

___

___

4. How long did the child(ren) work? (Measure periods of concentration. If the child stopped, why? How did the child(ren) let you know the drawing was finished?)

___

___

5. Describe the art produced. (What did the child(ren) draw first? How many drawings were made? What was repeated?)

___

___

___

___

Studio Page

OBSERVATION: CHILDREN AND CLAY

1. Plan a drawing exploration or practice activity suitable for a child between the ages of three and eight.
2. Obtain permission to work with one child, either at home or in a school setting. If possible, take photos or videotape the activity (get permission first). With the child's permission, save one or more of the drawings for your own collection.

____

____

Age of child(ren):
Setup of materials:
Length of time of observation:

____

1. What did the child do first?

____

2. What did the child say?

____

3. How did the child manipulate the drawing tool(s)? (For example, describe the position of the arm and hands, grip, and any other body parts involved.)

____

4. How long did the child work? (Measure periods of concentration. If the child stopped, why? How did the child let you know he or she was finished?)

____

5. Describe the art produced. (What did the child draw first? How many drawings were made? What was repeated?)

____

6. Compare the art activity of this child to that of the toddler you observed. What similarities and differences did you notice?

____

____

Chapter

10

Making Music

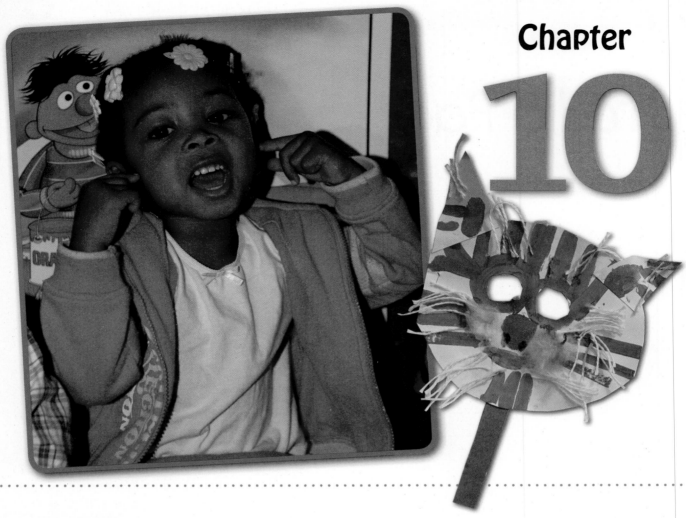

Questions Addressed in This Chapter:

- What is music?
- How does music help children grow?
- How are music activities designed?

"*Children need music every day and every year of their learning lives, and the more complex the better!*"

—Rebecca Shore & Janie Strasser (2006)

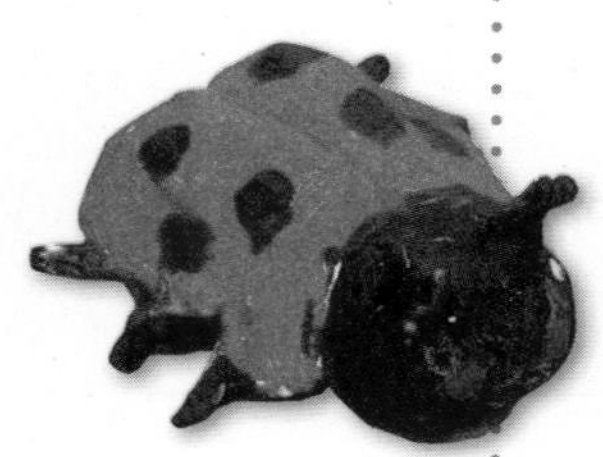

WHAT IS MUSIC?

Music is organized sound. One of the tasks of teaching music is to introduce children to the different ways in which music plays with and orders sound. Listening, rhythmic activities, singing, and playing instruments form the basis of creative music experiences, through which the elements of music—rhythm, timbre, dynamics, form, melody, and harmony—are organized into compositions that speak to our mind and body.

Music has been part of human society since the dawn of culture over 30,000 years ago. It has the power to make us cry and to make us feel joy. A 2002 study by Carol L. Krumhansl found that different types of music actually produced physiological changes in the listener (Weinberger, 2004).

HOW DOES MUSIC HELP CHILDREN GROW?

Music can positively affect health and brain development and can enhance growth in the physical, social, cognitive, and language areas.

Music and the Brain

Music has the power to change the brain. Musicians who began their training before age six have hyper-development in some parts of their brains (Rauscher & Hinton, 2003). Babies who were exposed to a complex work by Ravel paid more attention to this longer, more difficult piece of music than they did to unfamiliar ones indicating growth in neural networks (Ilari, Polka, & Costa-Giomi, 2002).

Music has also been shown to enhance long-term memory. Long-term memory is always forming and reforming interconnections with the information being absorbed (Caine & Caine, 2004). Adding music to learning activities helps establish memories more quickly and firmly (Stuckey & Nobel, 2010).

Music and Well-Being

Listening to music has been shown to lower levels of stress, affect the heart rate, and aid healing (Harvard Health Letter, 2009; Nakahara et al., 2009). Research has shown that when premature babies were exposed to music daily, they grew faster and went home earlier than those who were not (Sousa, 2001, p. 223).

Music and Developmental Growth

Music affects a child's total development. Through music activities children develop:

- **Physically**—By using the body to participate in and create music. Physical development occurs when children listen, sing, and move to music. Music stimulates and develops a child's auditory perception. Making music with hands and instruments foster the control and coordination of large and small body movements. Research has shown that musicians who play instruments have more ability to use both hands (Weinberger, 2004).
- **Socially**—By learning music skills with and from others. For thousands of years music has drawn groups together in song and performance. Young children learn about their culture as they sing traditional songs, and they develop cooperative skills as they work together to create a musical moment. At the same time, music ties together all humanity. All societies have tonal music and sing lullabies to their children (Wade, 2003).
- **Cognitively**—By developing the **auditory discrimination** and spatial relationship abilities of the brain. Music allows children to investigate sequencing, and cause and effect. Jensen (1998) notes that playing an instrument helps children discover patterns and develop organizational skills. Although simply listening to music seems to "prime" children's spatial thinking abilities, numerous studies have found a stronger correlation between spatial reasoning and early instruction in music, particularly as related to learning the piano or keyboard (Costa-Giomi, 1999; Graziano, Peterson, & Shaw, 1999; Hetland, 2000; Rauscher et al., 1997).

- **Language skills—**By talking about and listening to music. Oral language is developed as children compose their own rhythms and songs to express their ideas. Listening skills increase as children pay attention to the music they hear and play. Research has shown that music can help make information more memorable (Wolfe & Horn, 1998). Many adults, for example, rely on the ABC song, learned during childhood, to assist in alphabetizing. Causal relationships have been found between music instruction and reading skill (Butzlaff, 2000). The fact that music perception skills have been found to predict reading success indicates that similar auditory processing is needed for both (Anvari et al., 2001). Music has also been found to help English language learners. Songs can help children gain skill in pronunciation, grammar, vocabulary, phrasing, and speed of delivery (Scripps, 2002).
- **Emotionally—**By using music to express and respond to feelings. Music provides another way for children to express their feelings. Listening to music can also soothe and help children focus better on other tasks (Hetland, 2000). A case study of students who were emotionally disturbed found that they wrote better and had an improved attitude when listening to music (Kariuki & Honeycut, 1998).
- **Music concepts and skills—**By meeting the National Standards for Music (Ponick, 2007, pp. 26–29).

By the end of the primary years children should be able to do the following:

Content Standard 1: Sing, by oneself and with others, a wide range of music.

Content Standard 2: Play a variety of music on instruments by oneself and with others.

Content Standard 3: Improvise and create variations on rhythms and melodies.

Content Standard 4: Compose and arrange music to accompany stories, events, or in specific styles.

Content Standard 5: Read and notate music.

Content Standard 6: Listen to, identify, analyze, respond to, and describe music.

Content Standard 7: Explain preferences and evaluate music and music performances.

Content Standard 8: Understand the relationships among the arts and with disciplines outside the arts.

Content Standard 9: Be aware of the relationship between music and historical and cultural influences.

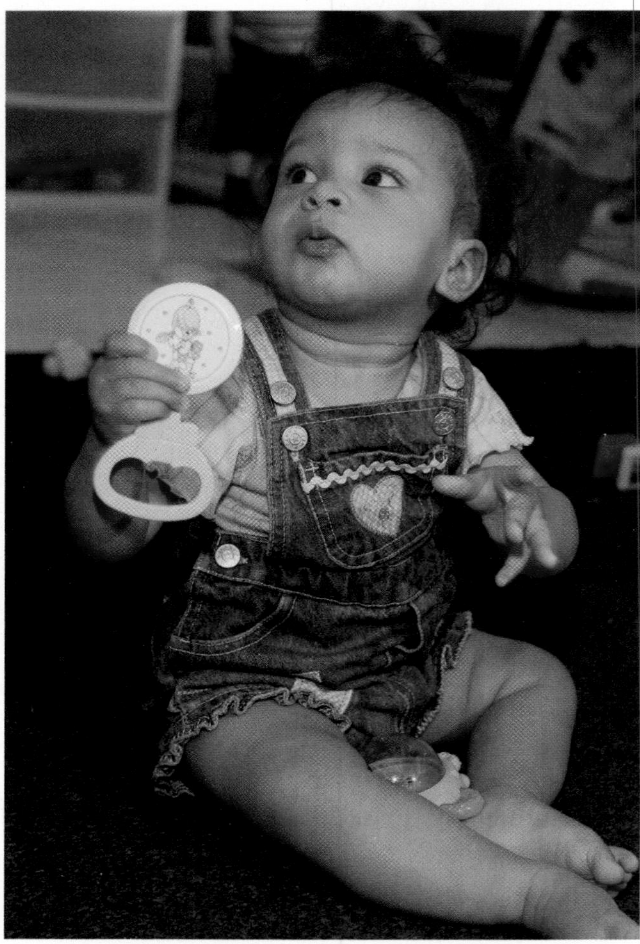

Infants are naturally musical, moving with delight to simple songs and rhythms.

Arts Words

TALKING ABOUT MUSIC

Accent. The beat that gets the strongest emphasis in music as in *one* two, *three* four, or *one* two three, *one* two three.

Beat. The regular rhythmic pattern of the music. There are strong beats (down-beat) and weak beats (up-beat).

Compose. Create an original piece of music or adapt a familiar piece.

Dynamics. Changes in volume from loud to soft and the accenting of certain tones.

Form. The structure that organizes the elements of music.

Genre. A type of music (e.g., gospel, jazz, lullaby, opera, rock and roll, sonata).

Harmony. A sequence of tones that enriches a melody and makes the sounds blend. Harmony is often created by using chords—several notes played together at the same time.

Key. The tone or chord that is the focal point or center of a musical piece. It is often the notes on which the piece ends.

Melody. A sequence of tones that changes or repeats.

Meter. The organization of rhythmic beats in a musical piece. It is shown by a fraction. The denominator is the unit of measurement and the numerator is the number of beats in a measure.

Mood. The way a particular combination of music elements affects the listener.

Notation. Writing down music using some kind of a symbol system. Staff notation in which notes are indicated on a five-line staff is the most common system used today.

Note. A single sound or tone.

Pitch. How high or low a sound is.

Rhythm. Time-based patterns that order sounds.

Scale. An ordered set of notes.

Staff. The five parallel lines on which music notes are written. Plural of staff is staves.

Style. The special way a musical piece is created. Style may be influenced by culture or period in which the musician works, or it may be unique to a particular musician.

Syncopation. A rhythm that puts the beat in a place it is not usually found. Syncopation makes music with a steady beat more interesting.

Tempo. The speed at which a musical piece is played. This is usually indicated by a term written at the beginning of the piece. Largo, for example means slow. Allegro means lively and fast. Presto means very fast.

Timbre. The unique quality of a sound.

Tonality. A system of writing music around a center key, such as middle C.

Note: An excellent glossary of musical terms can be found at http://www.naxos.com. Under Education click on Glossary.

HOW ARE MUSIC ACTIVITIES DESIGNED?

Musical activities can be organized in three ways: as individualized instruction, as open-ended, independent exploration, and in organized groups. An effective music program needs to incorporate all these approaches into the curriculum in order for children to develop fully as confident musical creators.

One-on-One Interactions

For infants and toddlers, in particular, but for all children as well, interacting one-on-one with an adult has been shown to be vitally important in acquiring musical competence. Children, for example, sing more accurately when singing individually than with a group (Goetz & Horii, 1989). Learning to play an instrument proceeds faster when the child receives intensive one-on-one lessons.

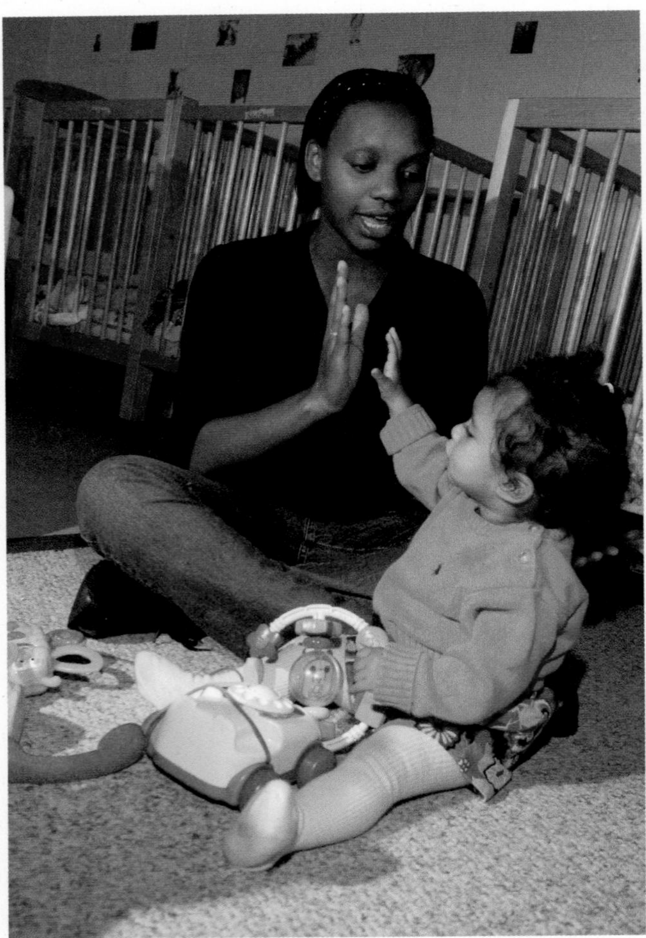

Interacting one-on-one with an adult is essential to music skill development.

One-on-one interactions can occur throughout the education of young children. Singing to an infant or toddler while going about daily activities, such as dressing, diaper changing, putting on outerwear, eating lunch, walking places, and so on fit naturally into adult-child interactions. In preschool, kindergarten, and primary classrooms one-on-one echo singing and instrumental solos can be purposely planned into group activities.

Exploration Centers

Music centers allow children to explore sound, rhythm, and music in playful, creative, and open-ended ways. A center for exploring sound can be problematic in a busy, noisy preschool and primary classroom. However, it is possible. To muffle the sound, include soft items such as a pile rug, pillows, and draped fabric. A sturdy table covered on three sides with heavy cloth and open in front makes a cozy "music house" in which to listen to music and explore making sounds, but still allows teacher supervision. Several types of music centers address different components of music education.

Listening center. Stock the center with a child-friendly CD/music player, or tape recorder, and earphones.

Conducting center. To the listening center add flashlights covered with different-colored cellophane that children can move in concert with the music. Provide a metal tray and magnet-backed notes, or paper with staves for older children so they can try their hand at composing.

Sound discovery center. Set out different plastic containers with easy-to-close lids and a variety of small objects, such as pebbles, jingle bells, and buttons that fit inside. Children can use these to make their own shakers to keep time to the recorded music or their own singing.

Instruments. Provide handmade and commercial instruments to accompany the recorded music or to use in making up original songs. Make sure there is an assortment of percussive, drums, shakers, and so on, and melodic instruments, such as a xylophone or handbells.

Responsive Group Activities

Music is mainly a social activity. Although individuals may play or sing for their own personal enjoyment, music is usually experienced as part of a group. However, the size and purpose of musical groups can vary.

Small group. Small groups of children can participate in listening, singing, and composing activities as part of projects and at centers. For example, primary students might compose a song to accompany a skit, or a group of preschoolers may sing a lullaby to the dolls in the housekeeping center.

Whole group. Many music activities lend themselves to whole group presentations. Children can listen to music during a nap or snack. They can sing favorite songs together as part of group meetings as a way to build community. New songs can be taught to large groups. A rhythm band in which everyone participates can show children what can be accomplished when every member works together.

Transitions. Music as a form of communication can be used to signal changes in activities, mood, and behavior. Playing calm music while children work and play can create a peaceful, relaxing environment.

THE LISTENING EXPERIENCE

According to Shore and Strasser (2006), an effective music curriculum starts with a developmental series of listening activities. It should include a wide range of music, including complex music. This is based on the research that shows that early listening to complex music by infants leads to richer cognitive and language development. Music activities should also include music from other times and cultures, as well as listening to natural sounds.

Arts Words

SOME MUSICAL FORMS

Aria. A song for a solo voice, usually found in an opera.
Cannon. A musical form in which a tune is repeated at regular intervals, like a round.
Cantata. A vocal work that can be religious or secular.
Choral. A hymn.
Concerto. A musical piece written for one instrument, accompanied by an orchestra.
Duet. A piece of music written for two instruments or singers.
Fugue. Similar to a cannon, but it has intervals of repeated passages and then free-form passages.
Gregorian chant. Voices in unison with no regular beat.
Improvisation. Music created spontaneously as it is played.
Jam session. When two musicians improvise together.
March. Music with a strong beat designed for marching.
Mazurka. A Polish dance in triple time.
Medley. A group of tunes played together.
Opera. A play in which the actors sing, accompanied by an orchestra.
Orchestra. A large group of musicians, grouped by instrument, and playing parts together.
Quartet. A musical work designed to be played by four instruments.
Quintet. A musical work designed to be played by five instruments.
Raga. A musical form based on the classical melodies of India.
Recital. A performance by one musician, who may or may not be accompanied.
Rhapsody. A free-form musical work that feels like it is spontaneous in design.
Riff. A repeating melody or refrain in jazz and contemporary pop music.
Score. The complete work of music in written form.
Solo. A performance by one singer or instrument.
Sonata. A musical form composed for two instruments and having three or four movements played at different tempos.
Suite. A musical work consisting of several shorter pieces.
Symphony. A musical piece written for an orchestra. It usually has four parts, with the first part being a sonata.

Selecting pieces for listening. Music intended solely for children is commonly part of most preschool and primary music programs. However, regardless of the children's ages musical selections should never be limited to only simplified pieces, because all children are capable of more sophisticated listening. Without exposure to complex music, not only in the Western classical tradition, but also that of other cultures, they will not develop the aesthetic awareness and close listening skills needed to truly appreciate and love music. Table 10-1 presents a sampling of music from many cultural traditions that will both appeal to young children while challenging their listening skills.

TABLE 10–1 Music for Listening and Study

Artist	Title
Africa Fete 99	*Selections*
Benedictine Monks of Santo	*Chants*
Frederick Chopin	*Sonata No. 3 Op. 58*
Hamza El Din	*The Water Wheel*
Edward Grieg	*Peer Gynt*
Gustav Holst	*The Planets*
Tokeya Inajin	*Dream Catcher*
Inti-Illumani	*Imagination*
Thelonious Monk	*My Funny Valentine*
Wolfgang Amadeus Mozart	*Symphony No. 39 in E Flat*
Modest Petrovich Mussorgsky	*Pictures at an Exhibition*
Michael Oldfield	*Tubular Bells 1 and 2*
Nikolai Andreyevich Rimsky-Korsakov	*Scheherazade*
Wayna Picchu	*Folk Music from Peru*
Igor Stravinsky	*Petrushka*
Vangelis	*Antarctica*

Note: These are just a few of a multitude of musical selections that can inspire young children.

Listening Activities for Infants

Sensitivity to sound is one of the most highly developed senses in infants. Listening activities help them learn to focus attention and make sense of the many sounds in their environment.

Lullabies. Lullabies are a very special category of song. To soothe infants, play lullabies and rock them gently. Brahms, Handel, and Mozart all wrote wonderful lullabies. Traditional lullabies are available from all cultures. Alice Honig (2005) points out that it does not matter to infants in what language the lullaby is. Nevertheless, families will appreciate a caregiver's initiative in learning lullabies from the child's culture. Try to memorize several to sing often to the infant. Vary saying the words and humming the melody.

Attention getters. Sing, hum, or play a lively song to get the baby's attention.

Clock. Place a loudly ticking clock near the infant.

Mobiles. Hang a mobile that makes soft sounds or plays a lullaby.

Shakers. Shake a rattle, set of keys, or bells to attract attention. Move the shaker around so the baby follows it with eyes and head. With an older infant, play peek-a-boo with the noisemaker.

Listening Activities for Toddlers

Toddlers are becoming more aware of the sounds around them and can begin to identify the sources of many of them. They are also starting to develop preferences for certain music.

Sound walk. Take a walk outside in the neighborhood or in a park and notice the different sounds heard. Look for other places to visit that have interesting sounds, such as a kitchen, a factory, a pool, or beach.

High low. Choose a fun word or the child's name and repeat it over and over. Start low and get higher and higher in pitch. As you get higher, raise arms over head. As the sound gets lower, lower arms to side.

Identify sounds. Make a sound using an object, then hide it, and have the children try to guess what it is. When they are familiar with several, see if they can pick out one from the others only by listening.

Loud and soft. Explore ways to make sounds louder or softer. Cover and uncover ears. Whisper and yell. Turn the volume up and down on the player.

Listen to music. Play and sing many different kinds of musical pieces from all over the world. Continue to soothe the child with lullabies and gentle classical music.

Listening Activities for Preschoolers and Up

With their longer attention spans, preschool children can participate in individual and group activities that ask them to compare and contrast sounds and music. They can also describe what they hear and share their ideas with others.

Body sounds. Explore all the different sounds you can make with your body—rubbing hands; slapping chest, thighs, or floor; snapping fingers; clapping hands; tapping fingers; stamping feet; clicking teeth; popping cheeks; and so on.

Collect sounds. As new sounds are discovered, record them on a class chart.

Find the sound. Have the children close their eyes while one child makes a sound somewhere in the classroom. See if they can identify from where the sound came. Try this game outside as well.

Listen to relax. Provide quiet times when music is listened to solely for enjoyment and relaxation. For preschoolers this can be at naptime.

Make it memorable. Tell a story about the music that makes it come alive and be memorable. For young children this could be a simple made-up story, such as "Can you hear the birds flying to their nests?" For older children tell stories about the composer, how and why he or she wrote it, and the instruments used to play it.

Sound scavenger hunt. Go on a scavenger hunt outdoors. Collect nature objects that can be used to make interesting sounds.

Tapping walk. Give each child a rhythm stick, sanded dowel, or wooden spoon. Go outside and tap gently on different objects, such as walls, fences, and garbage cans, to hear the sounds made. Discuss how the sounds are the same or different. Which are high pitched? Which are pleasant or unpleasant? Which last for a long time?

Introduce new tunes. Slowly introduce new music styles so children have time to become accustomed to them, but keep coming back to tunes they already know to maintain recognition.

Special Needs

• PROVIDING ASSISTANCE TO CHILDREN WITH AUDITORY PROCESSING NEEDS •

- If the child has partial hearing, the use of earphones and preferential seating near the player may help. The child may also respond to low-pitched drums.
- Children with cochlear implants have poor pitch resolution, which limits recognition of melodies played on a piano or single instrument, although they have normal responses to rhythm. More complex musical pieces that contain multiple clues, such as voice and definitive patterns, are easier for them to recognize and enjoy (Vongpaisal, Trehub, Schellenberg, & Papsin, 2004).
- Children with no hearing respond best to rhythmic pieces, which they can feel through vibrations. If possible, let them touch the speaker as the music plays. Providing a visual element may also help. Media players on the computer often have wave visuals that can accompany the music. The 1995 movie *Mr. Holland's Opus* provides insight into how musical performances can be presented visually to the deaf using lights and visuals.

Listening Activities for Kindergarten and Up

Kindergarteners are much more sophisticated listeners. They can recognize the **timbre** of different instruments and identify instrumental versions of familiar songs.

Create sound signals. Use certain sounds to indicate a change of activity or to get the children's attention.

Making Plans

ONE-ON-ONE ACTIVITY PLAN: Listening Together

WHO? **Group composition age(s):** Infants and young toddlers

Group size: One adult and one child

WHEN? **Time frame:** 5 to 10 minutes

WHY? **Objectives:** Children will develop

- physically, by using gross motor movements to turn toward or move to music. (Bodily-Kinesthetic)
- socially, by responding to prompts from a caring adult. (Interpersonal)
- emotionally, by learning to relax while listening to music. (Intrapersonal)
- auditory perception skills, by improving auditory discrimination skills. (Musical)
- language skills, by orally communicating responses to the music. (Linguistic)
- cognitively, by hearing repeated patterns and responding to them. (Logical-Mathematical)
- music skill and knowledge, by listening to music. (Content Standard 1)

WHERE? **Setup:** Soft, cozy area near an electrical outlet furnished with pillows and with room for both child and adult to sit or lie down. It could be under a table or canopy to provide a feeling of safety, quiet, and closeness. A rocking chair could also be used.

WHAT? **Materials:** Music player and a work by Bach

HOW? **Procedure:**

Warm-Up: Play the carefully selected musical work with the volume set to low. Bring the child to the area and sit or lie down with him or her.

What to Do: As music plays massage the child's arms and legs or hold the child in your lap and rock in time to the music. Talk softly in a soothing voice. Allow moments of quiet.

What to Say: Describe the music. "Can you hear the high notes?" "Can you feel the rhythm?" "Is the music moving fast or slow?" Talk about how it makes you feel.

Transition Out: If the child becomes restless or the music ends, assure the child that there will be time to listen again and then move together to the next activity. Return to this center often and play the same music or other pieces.

ASSESSMENT OF LEARNING

1. Was the child relaxed?
2. Did the child move in time to the music or repeat patterns heard in any way?
3. Did the child's attention span show interest and appreciation of the music?

Making Plans

CENTER ACTIVITY PLAN: Sound Makers

WHO? **Group composition age(s):** Preschool, kindergarten, or primary

Group size: Whole group on rug. Later at sound-making center—four at a time.

WHEN? **Time frame:** 15 to 20 minutes at center

WHY? **Objectives:** Children will develop

- physically, by using fine motor control in making sound makers. (Bodily-Kinesthetic)
- socially, by sharing space and materials and by listening to each other's sound makers. (Interpersonal)
- emotionally, by feeling trusted to work independently. (Intrapersonal)
- auditory perception skills, by distinguishing different pitches, tempos, and dynamics. (Musical)
- language skills, by describing the sound made by their sound makers. (Linguistic)
- cognitively, by matching the materials to the sound they make. (Logical-Mathematical)
- music skill and knowledge, by learning and using the terms pitch, dynamics, and tempo. (Content Standard 6)

WHERE? **Setup:** A table on which to make the sound makers. Two chairs or pillows with a cloth or cardboard screen set between them.

WHAT? **Materials:** Plastic eggs that can be opened, preferably in the largest size, and/or margarine-type containers with tight lids. Trays with a variety of materials to put inside the containers, such as small pebbles, larger stones, rice*, sand, wood beads, marbles, toothpicks, macaroni*, washers, and buttons.

HOW? **Procedure:**

Warm-Up: On the rug, play the game "Mysterious Sounds." Collect a group of objects to make sounds with, such as a pie tin and a wooden spoon, rocks in a glass jar, or bubble wrap to pop. Place the objects behind the screen that will be used at the center and make a sound. Have children make guesses as to what it might be. After several guesses show the object, and then do the next. Describe the sounds using the terms *pitch,* and *dynamics*. Have these words written on a chart and point to them as you use them. "It has a high pitch sound." "What is the dynamic of this sound. Is it soft or loud?" Explain that they will make their own mystery sound makers at the sound center.

What to Do: At the center help the children select materials and fill their containers. Tape the containers closed and label with the child's name. Then encourage the children to sit behind the screen and guess what is in each other's containers.

What to Say: To develop vocabulary, continue to use the terms *pitch,* and *dynamics*. To develop cognitive reasoning, ask "Does the type of container you use make a difference in the sound?"

Transition Out: At the next whole group time have the children share their sound makers. Together, decide which ones have the same pitch, dynamics, or tempo. Encourage children to add their sound makers to the "music house" or music center. The sound-making center should be available daily for a lengthy period of time to allow ample exploration. Vary the containers and materials offered. If space is an issue, combine it with the collage center because many materials can be used for both activities.

ASSESSMENT OF LEARNING

1. Do the children become better at comparing the sounds?
2. Do the children use the terms correctly in their descriptions?
3. Are the children motivated to make more sound makers and compare the sounds?

Making Plans

GROUP ACTIVITY PLAN: Name It

WHO? **Group composition age(s):** Kindergarten and primary

Group size: Whole group on rug

WHEN? **Time frame:** 10 to 20 minutes

WHY? **Objectives:** Children will develop

- physically, by using their bodies to help identify the musical works. (Bodily-Kinesthetic)
- socially, by listening to each other's ideas about the music. (Interpersonal)
- emotionally, by using self-control as they wait their turn to share ideas. (Intrapersonal)
- auditory perception skills, by distinguishing different pitches, tempos, melodies, and dynamics. (Musical)
- language skills, by describing music using descriptive language and music terms. (Linguistic)
- cognitively, by comparing and contrasting different musical works. (Logical-Mathematical)
- music skill and knowledge, by classifying musical works by shared elements. (Content Standard 6)

WHERE? **Setup:** Students seated on rug.

WHAT? **Materials:** CD player and a selection of unfamiliar pieces with different structures, kinds of instruments, and from different cultures (see Table 10-2).

HOW? **Procedure:**

Warm-Up: Hum or play a musical piece that is very familiar to the students and you are sure they can identify. After they identify it, ask them to tell you how they knew it was that piece.

What to Do: Write the title of the piece on chart paper and note their description after it. If they do not use the musical terms—*pitch, tempo,* and *dynamics*—add them to the chart and review their meaning. Have children clap and move to the music to help identify rhythms and patterns. Next, play two new pieces that are very different in sound. Have students describe each one and add to the chart. Now, using the three pieces, play "Name That Tune." Play pieces at random and have the children try to identify them.

What to Say: Use the terms on the class chart. Encourage students to use comparative words like *faster* and *slower*.

Transition Out: Play the pieces often and tell the children to be listening for these new pieces when they are at the music center or when played as background music. If desired, have them raise their hands or make a special signal when they hear it. Research shows it takes years of exposure to develop melody recognition and that culturally standard tunes are easier than atypical ones (Schellenberg & Trehub, 1999). As children learn to recognize the new pieces, slowly add new ones.

ASSESSMENT OF LEARNING

1. Do the children become better at identifying the pieces?
2. Do the children use the elements of pitch, rhythm, and tempo to help identify the pieces?
3. Do the children notice similarities as well as differences?
4. Create a class chart of the musical pieces the class can recognize.

Listen for the line. Give children paper and a marker. As a musical piece is played, have the children draw to the music, making a continuous line without taking the marker off the paper. Discuss why they choose to make the lines they did.

Ordered sound. Fill small metal cans or film containers with different materials so there is a range from soft to loud. Seal containers shut so the children cannot open them. Let the children explore them at the sound center and think of different ways to group them. Encourage them to put them in order from softest to loudest. Make another set that has matched pairs and see if the children can match them up.

Listen closely. Play a piece of music while the children close their eyes. Have them raise their hands when they hear a preselected part, melody, or pattern, or when they hear a change in pitch, tempo, or dynamics. At first play a sample of what to listen for before beginning. Later as the children get more accurate, try it without a sample.

Attend concerts. Take the children to a wide range of musical performances so they can hear a variety of instruments and types of music.

Classroom Museum

Display beautiful objects that make interesting sounds such as a conch shell to hold up to the ear, glass bottles to blow across the tops, and beach pebbles to roll against each other.

Listening Activities for Primary Age

In addition to discussing music, primary students can begin to write about their listening experiences. This, plus increasing knowledge in the different subject areas, allows activities to become more integrated into other areas of learning.

Let children choose. On a daily or weekly basis, select a child to be the music master or disc jockey whose task it is to select and play the background music for daily activities.

Favorites. Have the children tell and/or write about their favorite musical piece, style, or composer and then make a class graph showing their preferences.

Write a sound story. Talk about different sounds and the words that describe them, such as *honk* for a car horn and *toot* for a whistle. If there is no word, invent words for them. Then have the children write stories that include as many sound words as they can.

Classify sounds. Collect items and/or instruments that make interesting sounds. Group them by loudness, length of sound, timbre, and pitch.

Invent sound machines. Using boxes, paper, sandpaper, tin foil, Styrofoam, cardboard, straws, and other similar materials build machines that make an interesting sound.

THE RHYTHMIC EXPERIENCE

Rhythm is fundamental to life. Each of us carries our own natural rhythm in our heartbeat. Develop children's sense of rhythm, and introduce them to ways to create sound patterns by providing safe, simple objects for them to shake and tap, such as spoons, margarine containers, and wooden dowels. Set up a sound center where

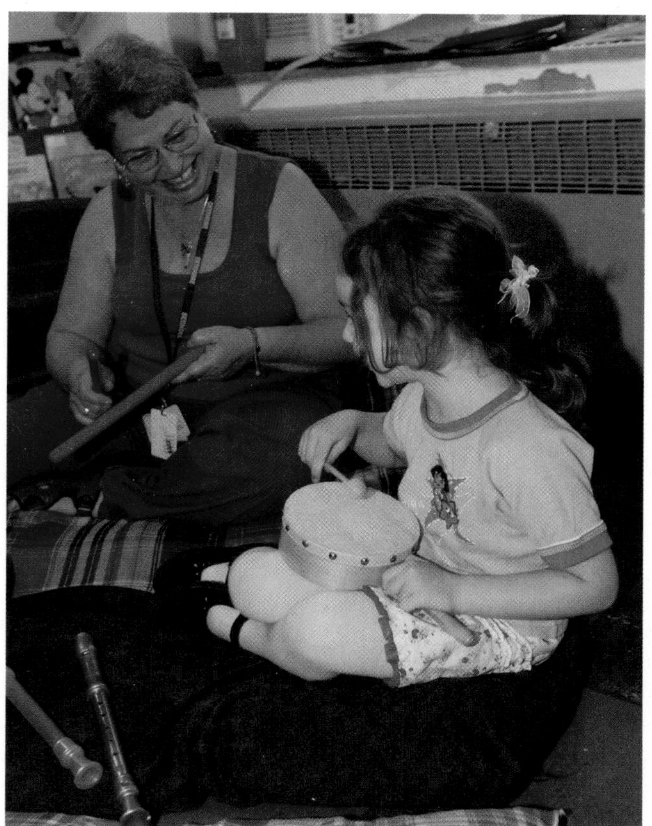

Try to match children's rhythms with your own.

children can explore the sound and rhythms they can make. Provide older children with a tape recorder so they can play back their rhythms. Carry around a small drum or tambourine to catch and mirror the rhythms of the children. For example, as children paint at the easel, tap out a rhythm that matches the movement of their arms.

Selecting Rhythm Instruments

Rhythm instruments for young children are usually **percussion** type instruments, although any instrument can be used to create a rhythm or steady beat. Percussion instruments create sound by being struck or shaken. Although many items found around the house can be used to provide rhythm experiences, a wide range of traditional and nontraditional rhythm instruments can be purchased reasonably. Others are easily made. However, do not rely solely on ones you can make; children need to experience real instruments as well as homemade ones.

Bells. All varieties of bells can be used, such as sleigh bells, cowbells, brass bells from India, and gongs. Jingle bells can be attached to elastic wristbands for children who have not yet developed fine motor control or attached to arms or legs to allow infants and toddlers to move their bodies in rhythm.

Claves. Made from thick polished sticks, one is held in the palm and the other used to tap it. Explore the sounds made by tapping different sizes and shapes of wood.

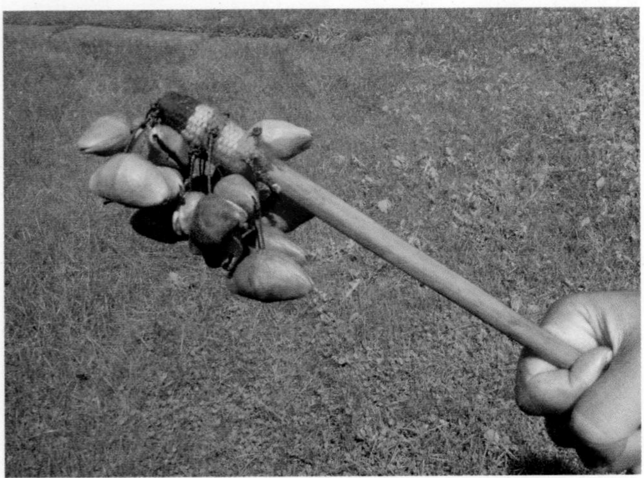

Look for instruments for other cultures to share with children. This is a cacho shaker from Peru.

Cymbals. Children love the large sound they can make with cymbals. Child-size cymbals usually have handles and are designed to fit little hands. Louder cymbals can be made from old pan lids. Finger cymbals come from Asia and because of their small size and high pitch, are ideal for young children.

Drums. Drums come in all sizes and shapes ranging from the bass drum to the hand drum. Drums for children should be stable and make a good sound without too much effort. Bongos, tom toms, and the different African drums, such as a *doumbek* or *djembe,* add variety to drumming activities. Drums can also be made from margarine and larger plastic containers with lids, plastic and metal pails, steel pie plates and pots, and five-gallon clean plastic buckets, such as used for pool chemicals and paint. A quiet drum can be made by stretching a balloon over the top of a coffee can using lacing, elastic bands, or heavy tape to hold it in place. A community drum can be made by using rubber roofing scrap and attaching grommets. Stretch the rubber over a large 3-gallon water tub. Heavy-duty plastic water tubs, intended for farm animals, come in very large sizes and make pleasant-sounding drums when turned upside down.

Maracas. Originally made from a dried gourd with the seeds still inside, today they are often plastic. Similar shakers can be made from soda and water bottles filled with different materials, with the lids hot glued on. Preschoolers can fill plastic eggs, and margarine-type containers with lids. Put out a selection of items from which to choose, such as sand, gravel, and marbles that make interesting sounds. Paper plates, filled with rice or beans, can be stapled together to make easy-to-use shakers.

Rainstick. Purchase a traditional one from the rainforest or make your own. Insert nails at regular intervals in a cardboard tube, fill with rice, and seal both ends well. Wrap the entire tube in sturdy tape so nails cannot be removed.

Rhythm sticks. These are ubiquitous in children's rhythm bands because they are inexpensive and easy to use. They can be made from well-sanded wooden dowels or wooden spoons. Sometimes they are grooved and a different sound results when the sticks are rubbed up and down against each other.

Sand blocks. Two wooden blocks can be wrapped in sandpaper and rubbed together to create a soft scratching sound.

Strikers. Depending on the instrument, most percussion requires something with which to tap or hit. Drumsticks are usually too large and loud for children. Hard rubber mallets can be purchased for a softer tone. Soft sounding mallets can also be made by attaching a tennis ball or rubber ball to the end of a heavy wooden dowel. Cut a hole in the ball, insert the handle, glue, and then wrap in duct tape or cloth so it is firmly attached.

Tambourines. A tambourine is a hoop with jingles set into the frame. Some tambourines have a skinhead; others are open. It is an easy instrument for young children to play because it can be either shaken, tapped, or both. Its very pleasant sound makes it ideal for creating rhythms to accompany children's activities or for rhythmic transitions.

Tappers. A number of instruments make tapping sounds. Castanets are clamshell-shaped wood; although for children, they usually are made of plastic. They are held in the palm and clicked by opening and closing the hand. Spoons made of wood, plastic, and metal also make good tappers. The spoons, an American folk tradition, are played by holding two metal spoons back to back with one between the thumb and the index finger and the other between the index finger and the middle finger. Hold the palm of the other hand above the spoons and hit the spoons against the knee and the palm to create a clicking rhythm.

Triangles. A favorite of young children because of its pleasant high pitch, the triangle is made of a bent piece of metal hung from a string and tapped with a metal stick. Explore the sound made by other metal objects, such as pie tins and old spoons. Suspend pie tin from a string so it can vibrate so they can vibrate.

Wood blocks. These are hollowed pieces of wood that create a pleasant sound when tapped. The pitched tongue drum is made from hollowed wood and is of Aztec origin. It has wood "keys" that make different pitches when tapped.

Teacher Tip

CHILD SAFE INSTRUMENTS

Select safe materials for sound makers and homemade instruments.

When working with infants and toddlers choose objects that meet the choke and poke test. They should be longer than 2 inches in length and 1 inch in diameter.

- Sticks and handles should have smooth, rounded ends and be at least 1 inch in diameter.
- Wrap handles in foam for added protection and ease of handling.

Rhythm Activities for Infants

By the age of six months, many infants already respond to rhythms by rocking and bouncing. Rhythm activities for this age focus on helping the child discover the rhythm and respond to it.

Foot dance. Attach rattles or bells to an infant's ankles and encourage the child to kick.

Exercising. Play a lively tune with a distinct beat. Move an infant's arms and legs in time to music. If the child is able to move on his or her own, model moving to the rhythm.

Keeping time. As the child plays, watch for natural rhythms, such as when walking, and clap or tap them out as the child moves.

Rocking. Hold the child and rock back and forth in time to music or singing.

Rhythm instruments are ideal for young children.

Special Needs

• ADAPTING RHYTHM INSTRUMENTS •

Limited hearing. Percussion instruments are ideal for children with limited hearing. A visual effect of tapping and shaking accompanies the vibrations produced. Sprinkling small pebbles or rice on the top of a drum is a fun way to see the beat.

Physical disabilities. For children with limited motor control select rhythm instruments that require little energy to produce a large effect. Bells and shakers can be attached to arms, legs, or head. Triangles can be suspended from a stand or chair back. An open tambourine is easy to grasp and shake.

Rhythm Activities for Toddlers

Toddlers are beginning to develop a sense of rhythm. In the beginning, they will rock and move their feet to music, but not be able to keep the beat. Activities should focus on making rhythms more noticeable and helping the child find the beat.

Name rhythm. Clap out the syllables of the child's name.

Nursery rhyme rhythms. Select a familiar nursery rhyme or poem and follow the rhythm clapping or using rhythm instruments. Listen for the accented beats.

Word play. Add fun to daily activities by repeating a pair of words or a phrase in rhythmic ways, such as "line up, line up, line up," "let's eat, let's eat, let's eat." Have children join in or suggest some words to try. Vary the rhythm by changing the speed, accented word, loudness, and softness.

Making Plans

ONE-ON-ONE ACTIVITY PLAN: Move to the Beat

WHO? Group composition age(s): Infant or toddler
Group size: One adult and one child

WHEN? Time frame: 5 to 10 minutes

WHY? Objectives: Children will develop

- physically, by using gross motor movements to move to the beat. (Bodily-Kinesthetic)
- socially, by matching the motions of a caring adult. (Interpersonal)
- emotionally, by gaining in self-confidence by controlling the body. (Intrapersonal)
- auditory perception skills, by matching movement to the rhythm. (Musical)
- language skills, by responding to an adult's prompts. (Linguistic)
- cognitively, by hearing repeated patterns and responding to them. (Logical-Mathematical)
- music skill and knowledge, by performing on instruments alone and with others. (Content Standard 2)

WHERE? Setup: Infant: Soft, cozy chair near an electrical outlet furnished with pillows with room for both child and adult to sit. Toddler: Large, open area that allows movement.

WHAT? Materials: Music player and musical pieces with a strong beat, such as marches and dances. A variety of rhythm instruments for child and adult to use. For an infant, attach bells to arms and legs or use a rattle. A toddler can use any tapping or shaking instrument.

HOW? Procedure:

Warm-Up: Put on music. Bring the child to area. If it is an infant, hold child in your lap. Start moving the infant's arms and feet so the bells sound to the beat of the music. For a toddler, model tapping or shaking the instrument to the beat, then let the toddler try. When child knows what to do, take an instrument of your own and play along together. You can also sing and play the rhythm at the same time.

What to Do: Continue keeping time to the beat. Count the beats. Explore other rhythm instruments. Stop when the music stops.

What to Say: Describe the sound of the instruments. "The bells make a high sound." "The drum is very loud." To challenge the child cognitively, ask, "Which instrument is louder?" "Can you move your feet to the beat, too?"

Transition Out: If the child is not tired when piece ends, try another. If moving to another activity, try to march there using the same beat. Return to this center often and play the same music or other pieces.

ASSESSMENT OF LEARNING

1. Did the child try to move to the beat?
2. Did the child repeat rhythmic patterns in any way?
3. Did the child gain in confidence through practice?

Making Plans

CENTER ACTIVITY PLAN: Rhythm Makers

WHO? **Group composition age(s):** Preschool, kindergarten, or primary

Group size: Music center—four at a time

WHEN? **Time frame:** 10 to 15 minutes at center

WHY? **Objectives:** Children will develop

- physically, by using gross and fine motor control to control percussion instruments. (Bodily-Kinesthetic)
- socially, by working together to make a new rhythm. (Interpersonal)
- emotionally, by expressing their feelings and preferences. (Intrapersonal)
- auditory perception skills, by matching rhythms. (Musical)
- language skills, by describing their rhythms. (Linguistic)
- cognitively, by inventing a pattern. (Logical-Mathematical)
- music skill and knowledge, by performing and improvising on instruments. (Content Standard 2)

WHERE? **Setup:** The music center.

WHAT? **Materials:** Music player and a recording of rhythmic music such as *Planet Drum* by Mickey Hart. Rhythm instruments, including ones the children made, carefully arranged. They can be displayed on low open shelves or placed in a large pocket chart hung on the wall.

HOW? **Procedure:**

Warm-Up: Play the recording to attract the children to the center.

What to Do: At the center let the children explore the instruments and try different rhythms.

What to Say: To develop vocabulary use the words *tempo, beat, rhythm, keep time,* and *accent.* Encourage the children to describe and compare their rhythms. "Is that a fast beat or a slow one?" "Can you match your beat to your friend's?" "How does it sound if you play together?" "Can you hear the accented beat?"

Transition Out: Invite the children to play their rhythms for the whole group at circle time. Chart their rhythms using a simple notation system—making vertical lines to show the beats and a U shape to show the rests.

ASSESSMENT OF LEARNING

1. Do the children invent their own rhythms or are they influenced by the music?
2. Can they identify an accented beat?
3. Can the children use the notation to play a rhythm?
4. Are the children willing to share what they did with the others?
5. Record and photograph the children playing their rhythms for their portfolios.

Making Plans

GROUP ACTIVITY PLAN: Body Percussion

WHO? **Group composition age(s):** Kindergarten and primary

Group size: Whole group on rug

WHEN? **Time frame:** 5 to 15 minutes

WHY? **Objectives:** Children will develop

- physically, by using their fine and gross motor control to play the instrument. (Bodily-Kinesthetic)
- socially, by listening to each other and sharing their ideas. (Interpersonal)
- emotionally, by using self-control as they wait their turn. (Intrapersonal)
- auditory perception skills, by distinguishing different rhythms. (Musical)
- language skills, by reading the words and describing the rhythm orally. (Linguistic)
- cognitively, by comparing and contrasting different rhythms. (Logical-Mathematical)
- music skill and knowledge, by improvising new rhythms. (Content Standard 3)

WHERE? **Setup:** Students seated on the rug in a circle.

WHAT? **Materials:** A pocket chart, Velcro chart, flannel board, or magnetic board. Cards with the words and/or pictures depending on the reading level of the group labeled—legs, cross, head, shoulders, nose, and hands. Have some blank cards as well for unexpected ideas. Have several cards for each word. Note: The cards can be reused many times so make them sturdy.

HOW? **Procedure:**

Warm-Up: Say, "Today we will play our bodies like a drum. Sit with your legs crossed like mine." Then say and slap out a rhythmic pattern, such as: Say "leg" and slap each thigh with the corresponding hand. Then say, "cross," and cross arms and slap the opposite leg. Invite children to imitate the pattern. On the chart put two each of the word-pictures for leg and cross and have children do the leg slap and cross slap twice.

What to Do: When children can do the pattern confidently, ask them to select another body part and make a new pattern, replacing the word *leg* with the new body part. Repeat until the children are confident with all the body parts. Then encourage them to invent more complex patterns, such as leg cross, cross cross, head cross, and so on. When a child suggests a pattern, allow the child to demonstrate it for everyone.

What to Say: Say the words aloud as you slap the rhythm. Give lots of positive feedback. "I see everyone keeping the beat going." Explore different tempos and change the dynamics. "Can we do this faster?" "How does it sound if we do it slower?" "Let's start soft and then get louder and louder." Ask open-ended questions that allow choice. "What body part should we do next?" "How can we change this rhythm?"

Transition Out: Signal the end of the session by having everyone drum with both hands on the floor in front of them. Repeat the activity often using the cards.

ASSESSMENT OF LEARNING

1. Can the children maintain the rhythm after some practice?
2. Do the children vary the tempo and dynamics?
3. Can the children describe the differences in the patterns?
4. Can the children follow the rhythm using the cards alone?

Classroom Museum

Display rhythm instruments from other cultures, such as Tibetan singing bowls; carved frog and cricket wood rasps from Indonesia; rain sticks and goat hoof chachas rattles from Bolivia; the telavi from Ghana; and woven shakers from Africa, Brazil, and India.

Rhythm Activities for Preschoolers

By preschool, children have a much better ability to respond on the beat. They can mirror back a rhythm and invent rhythms of their own.

Body talk. Select a word of two or more syllables. Say the word and match its syllables by clapping or moving a body part, such as nodding the head, stamping the feet, waving the arms, clapping the thigh, and so forth. Try it using two or more words.

Name rhythms. Have the children clap out the syllables of their names. See whether children can identify a name just from hearing it clapped. Look for names with the same or similar rhythms.

Nursery Rhymes. These old favorites are ideal for introducing rhythm and pattern. Have younger children clap or keep the beat using rhythm instruments. Teach older children to write new versions of the rhymes and then add their own rhythmic accompaniment.

Clocks. Find a clock with a loud tick. Have the children say "tick tock" and keep time with claps or rhythm instruments. Follow up by introducing a **metronome,** a device that produces a regular beat that can be changed. Show how the beat can be sped up and slowed down.

Heartbeat. Have the children sit very still and silent, put their hands on their hearts, and feel their heartbeats. Have them tap the floor or their thigh, and shake an instrument with the other hand to match the rhythm. Investigate: Is the rhythm the same for everyone? Does the speed change if you jump up and down?

Rhythmic transitions. Play a rhythm on a small drum or tambourine to signal transition to a new activity.

Stop and go. Together with the children, invent stop and go hand signals. Have the children play a rhythm, using the signals to tell them to stop and play. Let the children take turns signaling the group.

Rhythm Activities for Kindergarten and Up

By kindergarten, children are often able to perform complex rhythms. They can start to compare and contrast rhythms and combine rhythms in new ways.

Accompany music. Play music from different times and places and keep time using an assortment of rhythm instruments.

Bubbles. Blow bubbles. Ask each child to select one bubble to watch. When that bubble pops, they are to say "pop." Repeat, having them make different sounds when the bubble pops. Ask them to listen for any rhythms or patterns that they hear. Do the "pops" come faster as all the bubbles disappear? Follow up by creating a bubble song.

Echo clapping. Echo clapping is when the teacher or child leader claps a rhythm, and everyone else claps the same rhythm back. This is an excellent way to get the attention of a group even when they are deeply involved in another activity because they must focus.

Identify rhythms. Introduce the terms **tempo** and **dynamics.** Play two different rhythms and have the children describe differences in them using these words.

Improvise rhythms. Read rhyming books and invent rhythms to go with the words.

Explore rhythm instruments. Provide plenty of time for the children to explore rhythm instruments on their own before starting any group activities. Introduce new instruments one at a time to the sound center. Provide instruction as needed.

Pass patterns. With the children in a circle have one child start clapping or tapping a rhythmic pattern of beats. Pass the pattern around the circle. Then have another child start a new pattern.

Rhythm Activities for Primary Age

By this age children usually can keep time fairly accurately, especially if they have had many rhythmic experiences earlier. They can now play complex rhythms in group activities.

Rhythm band. Have children sit in a circle and hand out the instruments. Play or sing a familiar song and keep time. At intervals have the children pass their instruments to the person sitting next to them so everyone gets a chance to play every instrument.

Drum circle. Provide each child with a commercial or homemade drum. Ideally, there should be drums in an assortment of sizes, and hands should be used instead of drumsticks. Sit in a circle and have one child start a rhythm, which is picked up by everyone else. In turn, signal a different child to change the rhythm.

Rhythm stories. Have the children write stories on a specified topic such as animals or cars, or choose a story from a book. With a partner, add rhythms to parts of the story that reflect what is happening. For example, if a character is walking, then play a slow, even beat. If the character is running away from a predator, play a quick, heavy rhythm.

Write the rhythm. Have children create rhythms and invite them to invent a way to write it down using symbols so their friends can play it.

Compare rhythms. Play two different musical works and listen to the rhythm. Make a chart listing how the rhythms sound.

THE MUSICAL INSTRUMENT EXPERIENCE

Rhythmic activities naturally grow into explorations of musical instruments. First experiences with musical instruments should allow children to explore the different sounds they can make. Expand the sound center into a music center, and provide simple, durable instruments, both homemade and purchased.

Help children learn to identify the instruments by name. Ask them to describe the shape and sound of each. Make a recording of each instrument's sound, and place it in the music center so the children can explore timbre, the quality of the sound, by matching the mystery sound to its instrument.

As children gain skill and confidence, stage impromptu parades and concerts. Add child-created sounds to a favorite story or poem. Always remember to keep these activities open-ended and flexible. Performances that require hours of rehearsal and create stress are inappropriate for young children and steal away the child's natural affinity for making music.

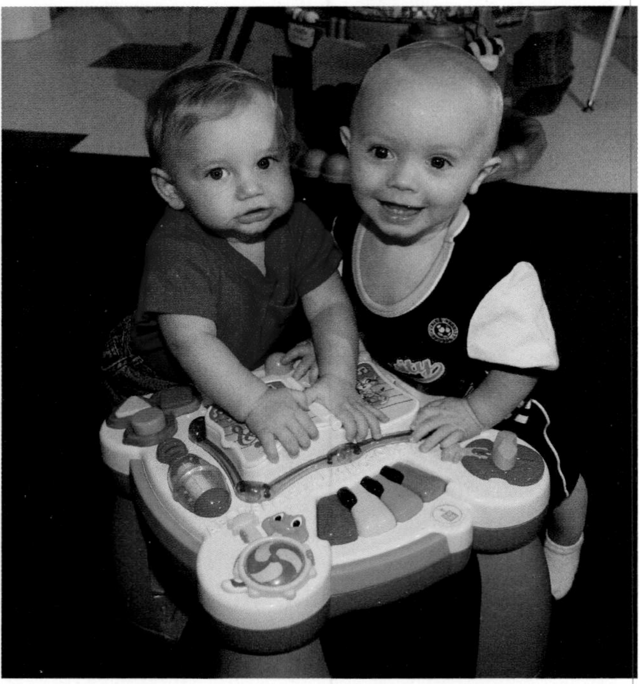

Tonal instruments allow children to explore melody.

Teacher Tip

CHOOSING AN INSTRUMENT

When selecting musical instruments for children to explore on their own, consider the child's experience and motivation. Instruments for young children must meet the following guidelines:

1. They should be sturdy and durable.
2. They should be fairly easy to learn to play.
3. They should be safe with no sharp edges.
4. They should be inexpensive.

Some appropriate tonal instruments include

Infants: Chimes and xylophone

Toddlers: Add the electronic keyboard and piano

Preschool: Add the autoharp, thumb piano, simple ukulele, and handbells

Kindergarten and Primary Age: Add the penny whistle and recorder

Selecting Musical Instruments

Although rhythm instruments are the most convenient and usually least expensive instruments for children, young children also need opportunities to explore tonality. Providing tonal instruments allows children to discover melody.

Bells. Pitched bells can be a wonderful instrument for young children because they are similar to rhythm instruments and yet they can be used to play a melody. Handbells are widely available and can be used with all ages. A double set of Montessori bells can also provide excellent training in learning to identify the different pitches.

Keyboard. These instruments usually have black and white keys. The white keys are in C major scale and the black keys are sharps and flats. The piano and electronic keyboard can be used even with very young children for a variety of music activities. They have the advantage of making it easy to name the notes and play harmony. Other keyboard instruments include the accordion, harpsichord, clavichord, and organ.

Pitched percussion. The xylophone and chimes are pitched instruments struck with mallets. Rubber and plastic mallets can be used to soften the sound. Simple eight- and twelve-note xylophones allow children to compose and adapt simple melodies as well as explore rhythms. Other pitched percussion instruments include the bell lyre, and vibraphone. These are usually found in full orchestras. The thumb piano or kalimba is an African instrument that is easy for children to play. A simple chime can be made by laying nails in a range of sizes from 10 to 60 penny on a piece of foam and tapping with a pencil.

Strings. String instruments feature vibrating strings. Guitars and autoharps can be used to accompany children singing and to introduce playing simple melodies. Violin, viola, cello, bass, and harp are usually found in orchestras. Folk string instruments include the ukulele, dulcimers, banjo, and mandolin.

Wind instruments. These instruments are played by blowing air across or into the instrument. The pitch changes either by varying the amount and direction of the breath or by pressing down keys which change the length of air in the instrument. Woodwinds have keys, which release the air at different lengths down the tube of the instruments. Many woodwinds also have a reed, which vibrates when blown. In order of descending pitch, there is the fife, piccolo, flute, oboe, clarinet, saxophone, and bassoon. There are also many folk wind instruments, such as the bagpipes, harmonicas, penny whistles, and recorders. Brass instruments are played by putting lips into a metal mouthpiece, such as the trumpet, trombone, French horn, and tuba. The sound is created by the vibration of the lips.

For health reasons, children need personal wind instruments. Because of this, wind instruments are rare in most preschools and general classrooms. Inexpensive penny whistles and plastic recorders are sometimes used in the primary grades.

Combining tonal handbells with rhythm instruments allows children to explore playing parts and harmonies.

Teacher Tip

THE SUZUKI METHOD

Dr. Shin'ichi Suzuki believed that any preschool child could learn to play a musical instrument, usually the violin, but others as well, if the right environment was created. This environment consists of the following:

1. Beginning formal lessons between the age of three and five.
2. Teachers who are well trained in the method.
3. Learning by ear before learning to read music and all pieces memorized and reviewed regularly.
4. Playing the same piece together in a group.
5. Frequent public performance so children become accustomed to it.
6. The expectation that parents will attend lessons and supervise daily practice.

The Suzuki method has had much success in getting young children started on instruments, but it has also been criticized for requiring too much formal practice for such young children (Bradley, 2005).

Instrumental Activities for Infants

Infants up to the age of one explore the world with all their senses. Instruments are particularly fascinating to them because the child's actions create marvelous sounds. Safety, of course, is the number-one issue and instruments offered to this age group should be sturdy with no sharp edges. Close supervision is vital and the best experience is one-on-one with the infant in the adult's lap.

Chime blocks. Commercial pitched chime blocks make a wonderful introduction to melodic instruments for the infant. If these cannot be found, similar blocks can be made by putting pitched bells inside small sturdy boxes, which are securely taped closed.

These should be used only with adult supervision. Make sure the bells being used pass the choke test.

Keyboard play. Play a melody on any keyboard instrument while holding the baby on your lap. Let the child "play" along, but never allow the child to bang on the keys.

Stringing along. Let the child pluck the strings of any stringed instrument. Be sure the instrument is secure—often you can wedge it between pillows and the hold the child on your lap. As the child plucks a string, finger some notes so different pitches result.

Chimes. Simple chimes set in foam rubber are available for older infants. These should still be used with close supervision.

Instrumental Activities for Toddlers

Toddlers are curious about everything, and instruments are no exception. They are still at the exploratory stage and are more likely to just want to make noise than to create actual melodies. Opportunities to play with sturdy instruments are very important. However, one-on-one activities are a very effective way to guide the child into discovering the melodic possibilities of the instrument.

Exploring instruments. Create a music play area and provide sturdy toy instruments, such as chimes, xylophone, plastic guitar, handbells, and a child-size piano or keyboard instrument as well as the more common rhythm instruments. Tape the child making music often.

Teacher Tip

READING MUSIC

Introduce older preschoolers, kindergarteners, and primary students to the staff and the names of the notes. The spaces are FACE, easily remembered as face. The lines are EGBDF, for which there are several different phrases of which "Every Good Boy Deserves Fudge" is an example. Once these are known, the whole keyboard makes sense because the white keys go from A to G and then repeat in the same pattern.

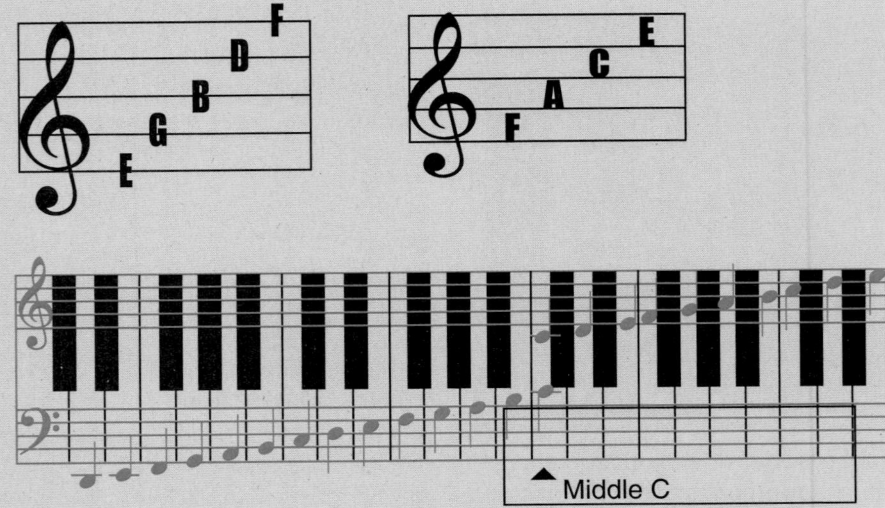

Making Plans

CENTER ACTIVITY: Composing A Melody

WHO? **Group composition age(s):** Preschool, kindergarten, or primary

Group size: Four at the center

WHEN? **Time frame:** 10 to 20 minutes

WHY? **Objectives:** Children will develop

- physically, by using their fine and gross motor control to play the instrument. (Bodily-Kinesthetic)
- socially, by sharing ideas with others. (Interpersonal)
- emotionally, by developing confidence in their ability to make music. (Intrapersonal)
- auditory perception skills, by listening for repeated melodic patterns. (Musical)
- language skills, by putting words to their melodies. (Linguistic)
- cognitively, by comparing different melodies and making decisions about their own melody. (Logical-Mathematical)
- music skill and knowledge, by improvising and performing an original melody. (Content Standards 2 and 3)

WHERE? **Setup:** At the music center. This area is in a corner of the room. It is carpeted and has instruments displayed on low shelves. On the walls are posters of musical instruments. Children should be familiar with the rhythm instruments at this center.

WHAT? **Materials:** Child-size xylophone with colored keys labeled with their note names and soft rubber mallets on a low table. A child-friendly music recorder is nearby. Crayons and paper.

HOW? **Procedure:**

Warm-Up: Share the xylophone when the children are gathered on the rug. Tap out a short simple melody line of a familiar song like *Row, Row, Row the Boat.*

What to Do: Let the children explore the xylophone when they visit the music center. Visit the center regularly and demonstrate how to tap out a melody line while pointing out the key colors and names. Encourage the children to use crayons to write their melodies on paper in colored lines or dots and the note names.

What to Say: Help the children listen closer. "Does your melody go up or down?" "How many notes do you hear in your friend's melody?" "Are those notes close or far apart? How do they sound different?" Encourage them to write down their melodies. "What color is the first note? What is its letter name?"

Transition Out: Collect the melodies the children write and staple them into a class music book. Keep the book in the center for all to use. Play some of the melodies at group time and have the children add words to them. Try joining some of the melodies together into a song.

ASSESSMENT OF LEARNING

1. Do the children create original melodies?
2. Can the children record the melody using symbols?
3. Can the children read their symbols and play their melodies?

Making Plans

RESPONSIVE ACTIVITY PLAN: Watch the Conductor

WHO? **Group composition age(s):** Kindergarten and primary

Group size: Whole group on the rug

WHEN? **Time frame:** 10 to 20 minutes

WHY? **Objectives:** Children will develop

- physically, by using their fine and gross motor control to play the instrument. (Bodily-Kinesthetic)
- socially, by working together to create a group musical project. (Interpersonal)
- emotionally, by developing pride in accomplishing a cooperative task. (Intrapersonal)
- auditory perception skills, by listening closely to stay in time. (Musical)
- language skills, by describing the sound of the music. (Linguistic)
- cognitively, by creating and copying patterns. (Logical-Mathematical)
- music skill and knowledge, by performing on instruments with others. (Content Standards 2 and 5)

WHERE? **Setup:** Students seated on the rug in a circle

WHAT? **Materials:** A conductor's baton—this can be made from a dowel painted black. An eye-catching object, such as a shiny star or colorful ribbons can be attached to the top. Assortment of instruments. There should be at least three to four of each kind. Chart paper.

HOW? **Procedure:**

Warm-Up: Attend a concert where the children can watch a conductor. If that is impossible, watch a short video of someone conducting.

What to Do: Ask the children to describe what the conductor does. Write their ideas on chart paper. Ask the children to select an instrument. Then invite the children to sit together with the other children who have the same instruments and make up their own rhythmic pattern and melody. With the children in instrumental groups go around the circle and have each group share their pattern. After a pattern is shared, have the whole group practice it. When every group is comfortable playing, introduce hand signals for starting and stopping. Practice these several times. Next, introduce signals for loud and soft, fast and slow. When everyone understands what to do, model conducting a short piece using one of the groups' rhythms. Give a signal to start. Use hand signals to tell some groups to play and others to rest. Explore playing loud, soft, fast, and slow. Now let children have turns being a conductor.

What to Say: Ask the children to listen to the performance. "How does it sound when one group plays at a time?" "What happens when several groups play?" Evaluate the conducting and give positive feedback. "Can you see the baton move?" "Could you tell when to start playing?" "How could we make it easier to see the conductor?" "When we were all playing our parts, the pattern was easy to hear."

Transition Out: Record the children playing. Then play the tape and ask them to identify patterns, rhythms, and changes in dynamics and tempo. Repeat this activity often, until children are confident in their conducting.

ASSESSMENT OF LEARNING:

1. Do the groups work cooperatively in creating their unique rhythm?
2. Do the children use music terms to describe the music they make?
3. Do the children follow the conductor?
4. Does the conductor give clear, easy-to-follow signals?

Making Plans

RESPONSIVE ACTIVITY PLAN: Music Makes Me Feel

WHO? **Group composition age(s):** Kindergarten or primary

Group size: Whole group on the rug. Then at tables working.

WHEN? **Time frame:** Two to three 40-minute blocks of time

WHY? **Objectives:** Children will develop

- physically, by using cutting and pasting skills. (Bodily-Kinesthetic)
- socially, by working together to create a cooperative group project. (Interpersonal)
- emotionally, by learning to express how music makes them feel. (Intrapersonal)
- auditory perception skills, by learning to recognize particular works. (Musical)
- language skills, by describing how music makes them feel. (Linguistic)
- cognitively, by making choices as to what pictures match which music. (Logical-Mathematical)
- music skill and knowledge, by identifying music by style. (Content Standard 6)

WHERE? **Setup:** At start, students seated on the rug. Later at desks.

WHAT? **Materials:** Tape or CD player. Carefully chosen music that shows different moods. *Pictures at an Exhibition* by Modest Mussorgsky is a good choice. Preselected photographs from magazines or old calendars. Large sheets of paper, scissors, and glue. Chart paper and markers.

HOW? **Procedure:**

Warm-Up: Have the children close their eyes. Play a short selection from the recording.

What to Do: *Day 1*—Ask the children to share how the music makes them feel. Accept all responses. Write down their ideas on the chart paper. Repeat with several other selections. Discuss similarities and differences in their responses to the same and different pieces.

What to Do: *Day 2*—Group the children into cooperative teams of three or four. Place the magazine and calendar pictures on the children's desks along with scissors, glue, and one large sheet of colored paper. Assign each group one of the musical works. Have everyone close their eyes and listen to all the pieces again. Then, using the pictures, they should work together to create a collage that shows the way the music makes them feel.

What to Say: Encourage the children to use descriptive words to describe their feelings. If they say sad, ask how sad? Introduce the term *mood*.

Transition Out: *Day 3*—Have the children share their posters and explain why they chose the pictures they did. Label each poster with the name of the musical selection and the mood. Join them together to make a mural.

ASSESSMENT OF LEARNING

1. Do the children use rich descriptive language?
2. Do the children work cooperatively in their groups?
3. Do the finished collages match the mood the children chose?

Music mats. Large piano-like mats that children can walk on to make notes let toddlers explore melody bodily.

Making music together. Continue the one-on-one activities listed above for infants, but as the child explores say the name of the note being played. Together with the child, make up a song using that note.

Matching game. Have the child close her or his eyes or turn the head while you play one of two different, but familiar, instruments. Challenge the child to guess which one made the sound. Then let the child challenge you in turn.

Name the instrument. Make large cards with photographs of familiar instruments. Start by showing the card and the actual instrument together. Say the instrument's name. Then put out the cards and see how many the child can remember. Make a game of it and repeat often.

Instrumental Activities for Preschoolers

By preschool children are able to handle instruments more carefully. They still like to explore and need plenty of sturdy instruments, such as listed above for infants and toddlers, but they can also be trusted to handle a guitar or piano with supervision. Preschoolers will freely compose original melodies and songs if given the opportunity to use melodic instruments. A music center for preschoolers should include, if possible, a piano or electric keyboard.

First concerts. Begin exposing preschoolers to short performances where they can see the different instruments being played. Sometimes high school students are willing to come perform on their instruments for a preschool. Contact the local high school band and orchestra teachers and arrange regular visits. Remind performers to play a very short piece and to share how the instrument is played with the children. If possible, see whether the children can touch the instrument or try it out under supervision. Do not allow the children to blow into a wind instrument, however, for sanitary reasons.

How does it sound? Play an instrument and have the children describe how it sounds using descriptive words. Make up sound words if necessary, such as the violin sounds like "eeeeee." Paste a picture of the instrument on a poster and write the children's descriptions around it.

Instrument timbre match. Perform a melody on a familiar hidden instrument and let them try to guess which instrument it is. Once they can do this regularly, try identifying the same instruments being played on recordings of music by famous composers or from other cultures.

Match the note. Place two xylophones or chimes on opposite sides of a screen. Have one child play a note and see whether another child can play the same note back. As children grow in skill, challenge them to match two or more notes up to an entire line of a familiar melody.

Name the note. This is the age when it is important for children to hear the names of the notes. Provide many opportunities for children to say the note names. Label the notes on keyboard instruments too.

Instrumental Activities for Kindergarten

By kindergarten, children have the hand-eye coordination to handle more complex instruments, and can identify many instruments by sound. They can add harmonies to songs they improvised and, if given the opportunity, can start to read music.

Guess the instrument. Share a variety of instruments and hang up posters or photos of them. Play notes on the instruments so the children learn how each one sounds. When the children are familiar with them, hide the instrument and play it or play a recording and see whether children can identify it.

Name that tune. Make a list of songs children know. Play one of these familiar melodies on a keyboard, piano, xylophone, or guitar. See whether the children can select the song from the list. Vary the game by playing the tune on less familiar instruments, such as a thumb piano.

Notate a melody. Give the children paper and crayons and then play a short simple melody. Challenge them to write the melody. When they are done, compare the different symbols they invented. Tell them that all of these are great ideas. Then show them sheet music and explain that most composers use the same symbols so that other people can read and play the music. After this experience, be sure to put paper and drawing materials in the music center so the children can notate their original melodies.

Playing with notes. Make large different-colored notes and a large staff labeled with the letter names of the notes. Put Velcro on the back of the notes and laminate the staff. Hang it in the music center so the children can explore composing a melody and then playing it on a xylophone labeled with the note names. If the xylophone has color keys and note labels, make sure the notes you make match in color as well.

Teacher Tip

ABSOLUTE PITCH

Absolute or perfect pitch is the ability to identify or sing a named note without reference to other notes. Those with this ability may be able to name all the notes in a chord and even identify the pitch of everyday sounds, such as a car horn. It is a cognitive process of memory that is much like identifying a color. It is believed that there is also a genetic component because children with autism, Well's syndrome, and savants have a much higher incidence of perfect pitch than people in general.

Some research has shown that absolute pitch is a combination of inborn ability and very early exposure to music during a critical period of development in which children between two and four are taught the names of musical tones (Chin, 2003). However, absolute pitch is not required to be a musician or composer. Although Mozart, Beethoven, and Listz all had perfect pitch, Hayden, Ravel, and Wagner, for example, did not. Most trained musicians have relative pitch in which they can identify notes in comparison to others.

IMPLICATIONS FOR TEACHERS

Early childhood programs put great emphasis on teaching color names, but almost none on learning the names of the notes. Between the ages of two and four, try to expose children not only to the sound of notes, but also their names. This is done most easily with a piano or keyboard, but any tonal instrument can be used. If you do not know the names of the notes, refer to the piano illustration in this chapter, or use a child's xylophone that has the notes labeled. Sit the child on one's lap, play a note, and sing its name. Also, play each note in a selected chord, such as C E G, as you sing the letter names. Encourage the child to sing the names, too. Such early exposure may not necessarily result in perfect pitch, but will certainly help in developing relative pitch.

Instrumental Activities for Primary Age

Primary age students can identify instruments by timbre. They can start to understand how instruments work. With instruction they are capable of reading music, and playing the piano and violin on their own and in organized groups. Handbells and recorders can also provide opportunity for group musical experiences. Although usually formal instruction on the larger string instruments, viola, cello, and bass, and the wind instruments does not begin until the end of the primary years, younger children will benefit from many opportunities to explore the basic instruments.

Make string instruments. Create a finger harp by wrapping rubber bands around a very sturdy piece of cardboard or wood. Make a guitar by cutting a hole in the top of a sturdy box and wrapping rubber bands around. Explore how the sound box changes the dynamics of the rubber bands. Explore what happens with different thicknesses and sizes of rubber bands.

Make wind instruments. Make flutes from marker tops. Blow across the top to create a sound. Select several different types and tape them together in a row from shortest to longest to make panpipes. Plastic water and soda bottles of different sizes can also be used to create different tones.

Water bottle tunes. Fill five or more identical glass bottles with narrow necks (beer bottles work well) with different levels of water. Change the levels until you have them close to a musical scale. Tap the bottles with xylophone mallets or a metal spoon to play notes and melodies. Explore what happens when you add or take away water in the bottles. Try blowing across the top. How does the sound change? Try other shaped glass jars and glasses.

Recorder lessons. Although some children have families who can afford private lessons on piano or violin, many children do not have this opportunity and yet, this is the age when children should begin to learn an instrument. Inexpensive plastic recorders are available along with excellent teaching materials (see Appendix C). Starting a class recorder band is an excellent way to introduce children to playing an instrument in a group.

Finding the meter. Use nursery rhymes to help children learn about meter. Start by saying the rhyme together. Say it again accenting the main beat. This is the start of the measure. Next, tap the beat using rhythm instruments. Finally, decide whether the rhythm moves in 2's (strong| weak strong| weak) or 3's (strong weak weak |strongweak| weak). Some nursery rhymes with a strong meter are *Humpty Dumpty*, *Jack and Jill*, and *Jack Be Nimble*.

Book Box

Books about famous musicians and composers.

Orgill, R. (1997). *If I only had a horn: Young Armstrong.* New York: Houghton-Mifflin.

Pinkney, A. D., & Pinkney, B. (2007). *Duke Ellington: The piano prince.* New York: Jump at the Sun.

Raschka, C. (1992). *Charlie Parker played be bop.* New York: Scholastic.

Venzezia, M. (1995). *Wolfgang Amadeus Mozart.* Chicago, IL: Children's Press.
This is one of a series that includes stories about Aaron Copeland (1995), George Gershwin (1995), Peter Tchaikovsky (1995), Duke Ellington (1996), Ludwig von Beethoven (1996), Johann Sebastian Bach (1998), and John Phillip Sousa (1999).

Keyboard fun. The pentatonic scale only has five notes. On a piano the black keys form a pentatonic scale. On a xylophone it is the first, second, third, fifth, and sixth notes. This set of notes always sounds harmonious together and is the basis of many traditional songs, such as *Mary Had a Little Lamb.* Have the children compose melodies using only these notes.

Music note blocks. Make a set of music note blocks. You will need eight wooden blocks of the same size. On paper that fits one side of the block draw a staff with a note and its letter name. Glue the paper to the block and cover with clear sealing tape. Or draw directly on the block with indelible pen. Have the children rearrange the blocks in different ways and then play the tune they created on the xylophone or a keyboard.

THE SINGING EXPERIENCE

Children sing spontaneously from as early as age two. They often make up little tunes based on simple, repetitive words while playing. However, it may take longer for them to become comfortable singing with others. Singing daily helps develop self-confidence, expands vocal range, and helps draw a group of children together into a cohesive group.

Many adults, however, may feel uneasy singing aloud. Nevertheless, all teachers can teach children to enjoy singing. Although we may not like how our voices sound, that does not mean we cannot sing with children. As is true in all arts activities, our level of enthusiasm is far more important than having a trained voice. Children will be more involved in their own participation and learning a new song than in criticizing their teacher's voice.

To develop confidence, always practice a song first. If possible, learn the song from a fellow teacher or friend. If that is not possible, sing along with a recording. Many children's songs are now available on the Web. The National Institute of Health Sciences has an extensive collection of children's songs, lyrics, and MIDI files. Most of the songs suggested in this chapter can be found on their Web site at http://www.niehs.nih.gov/kids/home.htm.

Book Box

Books about musical instruments.

Kroll, V. (1995). *Wood-Hoopoe Willie.* Watertown, MA: Charlesbridge.
A young African-American boy saves a Kwanza celebration by playing the drums when the adult drummer is incapacitated in a car accident. The book describes and illustrates many African instruments. Richly patterned African cloth is featured throughout the book. Four and up.

Krull, K. (2003). *M is for music.* New York: Harcourt.
A brightly illustrated alphabet of musical terms. Infant and up.

Le Frank, K. (2006) *Jake, the philharmonic dog.* New York: Walker.
A dog enjoys listing and woofing along with an orchestra when each of the instrument groups practice. Then he comes to the rescue when the conductor's baton goes missing. Four and up.

Moss, L. (1995). *Zin! Zin! Zin! A violin.* New York: Scholastic.
The sounds of the orchestra fill this book. Two and up.

Peles, L. C. (1996). *Long live music.* New York: Harcourt Brace.
A colorfully illustrated history of music and an introduction to the different classes of instruments. Five and up.

Williams, V. (1988). *Music, music for everyone.* New York: Greenwillow.
Rosa's grandmother is ill so she organizes a group of her friends to play their instruments for her in this classic follow-up to a *Chair for My Mother.* Four and up.

Selecting songs

Choose songs that are short, easy to sing, have a steady beat, and lots of repetition. Children (and adults) usually learn the chorus of a song long before they know all the verses. For example, many people know the chorus to *Jingle Bells*, but how many know more than one verse? Use the following guidelines when choosing a song to sing:

- **Infants**—Songs for infants are often very short with lots of repetition. Lullabies are soothing melodies with a slow beat. Teasing songs, such as *This Little Piggy Went to Market*, allow adults to interact with the child physically through tickling, finger actions, and sound effects.
- **Toddlers**—Songs for toddlers should have a limited range. The majority of children will sing most comfortably from middle C to G. Middle C is the 24th white key from the left-hand side of the piano (see Teacher Tip: Reading Music). Nursery rhymes and folk songs are often in this range. To appeal to active toddlers, select songs that have interactive elements and movements that draw the child into the song and make it more memorable. Toddlers also love nonsense songs and songs that involve moving their bodies.
- **Preschool and kindergarten**—For preschoolers, look for songs that tell a story or have words strongly tied to the beat and melody. Many of these are traditional folk songs that have been passed down for generations. Preschoolers particularly like songs that are personal and relate to their everyday lives. Make up songs that feature their names, feelings, body parts, daily activities, and special occasions such as birthdays: Songs can also help them learn to count, spell, and learn other rote material (Wolfe & Hom, 1993; Wolfe & Stambaugh, 1993). Interactive elements and movement are still an important element in songs for this age and help children remember the words better. Song games encourage children to practice singing and moving to the music.
- **Primary age**—As children get older their vocal range extends to as much as an **octave** above and below middle C. Songs for primary children should use this range because children will lose the high and low notes if they do not use them regularly. As children learn more about the world, they enjoy learning the story behind the song. Songs in foreign languages fascinate them. They also enjoy songs from their favorite movies and from radio (see Table 10-2).

Children sing better when you sing with them than when singing along with a recording.

Teacher Tip

SINGING WITH CHILDREN

Jan Wolf (1994) makes the following suggestions for singing successfully with children:

- Show expression on your face.
- Maintain eye contact with the children.
- Be enthusiastic.
- Signal when to begin, such as with a "Ready, go!"
- Really know the song. Practice it many times beforehand.
- Pictures and props will help the children (and you) remember the song better.
- Choose simple, repetitive songs that are easy to remember.

Chanting. *Chanting* is half speaking and half singing in a rhythmic way. Sometimes a chant is performed on just one note and sometimes on two or more notes. Nursery rhymes, such as *Jack and Jill*, and traditional fingerplays and jump rope rhymes such as *Pat-a-Cake*, are good examples. Chants are poems spoken in rhythm with no or limited change in pitch. Many traditional chants were jump-rope rhymes. Some familiar ones are

Miss Mary Mack; My Name is Alice; Lady, Lady; and *Touch the Ground*. See the Arts Tools Box for ideas. In addition, numerous books and web sites list jump-rope rhymes.

Chants provide a bridge between early language development and singing and, as such, are very appropriate for infants and toddlers. Because of their simplicity, these are often the first "songs" children sing. Young children will also make up their own chants as they play. Chants are easy to invent on the spot. To help develop a child's singing voice an adult can chant a request to a child and the child can chant it back.

Invented songs. Music naturally engages children in learning. In particular, there is a strong link between literacy development and singing. Shelly Ringgenberg (2003) found that children learn vocabulary words better through a song than through conventional storytelling. She suggests that teachers take the melody and rhythm from familiar songs, such as *Mary Had a Little Lamb* or *Twinkle Twinkle Little Star,* and add new words based either on a story in a book or that use the concepts or vocabulary being taught.

Arts Tool Box

SOME TRADITIONAL HAND PLAYS

This little piggy went to market.
This little piggy stayed home.
This little piggy has roast meat
This little piggy had none.
And this little piggy cried Wee Wee Wee,
All the way home.

One potato two potato three potato four.
Five potato six potato seven potato more.

Rain, rain go away
Come again some other day.
Little Johnny wants to play.
So rain, rain go away.

I have hands that clap clap clap
I have feet that tap tap tap
I have eyes that see you too
__________ (child's name) I see you!

More chants can be found at http://www.songsforteaching.com/chantsraps.htm.

SOME TRADITIONAL JUMP-ROPE RHYMES

Jelly in the dish,
Jelly in the dish,
Wiggle-wiggle
Wiggle-wiggle
Jelly in the dish.

Ladybug, Ladybug, turn around,
Ladybug, Ladybug touch the ground.
Ladybug, Ladybug shine your shoes,
Ladybug, Ladybug read the news.
Ladybug, ladybug, how old are you?
One, two, three, four . . . . .

Sixteen black birds sitting on a fence.
Flapped their wings and started to dance.
Upward, downward,
All along the line,
Brightly feathered and looking fine!
Count 1, 2, 3 . . . . .

Teddy bear, teddy bear,
Turn around.
Teddy bear, teddy bear,
Touch the ground.
Teddy bear, teddy bear,
Show your shoe.
Teddy bear, teddy bear,
That will do.
Teddy bear, teddy bear,
Go upstairs.
Teddy bear, teddy bear,
Say your prayers.
Teddy bear, teddy bear,
Turn out the light.
Teddy bear, teddy bear,
Say good night.

More traditional jump-rope rhymes and clapping games can be found at www.gameskidsplay.net.

TABLE 10–2 Some Songs for Children

Age group	Song Examples*
Infant	**Lullabies** *All the Pretty Horses, Brahms' Lullaby, Irish Lullaby, Michael Row the Boat Ashore, Rock-a-Bye Baby, Hush Little Baby Don't You Cry* **Playful Songs** *Hickory Dickory Dock*—Walk fingers up the child's body and then quickly down *Pat-a-Cake*—Hold the child's hands and clap them together, then act out patting the cake and putting it in the oven *Pop Goes the Weasel*—Make a circle on the child's tummy; on word *pop* clap *Pony Boy*—Bounce the child on your knee
Toddler	**Five-note songs** *Alouette, Baa Baa Black Sheep, Farmer in the Dell, Five Little Ducks, London Bridge, Row, Row, Row the Boat, Sing a Song of Six Pence* **Action Songs** *Animal Fair*—Act out the different animals *Ants Go Marching*—A song for marching *Coconut*—Put the lime (thumb) in the coconut (semi-closed hand); then rub belly *Down by the Station*—Add hand actions to go with the lyrics Act out the lyrics of the following songs: *Do Your Ears Hang Low? Happy and You Know It, If You're Wearing Red, I'm a Little Teapot, It's Raining Its Pouring, Itsy Bitsy Spider, Let's All Sing Like the Birdies Sing, Loop de Loop, Ring Around the Rosies*
Age group	**Song Examples***
Preschool and Kindergarten	**Traditional songs** *Camptown Races, Clementine, Frere Jacques* (Are You Sleeping), *Oh Suzanna, Oh Where Oh Where Has My Little Dog Gone? Polly Put the Kettle On, Sailing Sailing,* and *See Saw Margery Daw* **Learning Songs** *Alice the Camel; Alphabet Song; Do Re Me; Head, Shoulders, Knees and Toes; B-I-N-G-O; Hot Time in the Old Town; Oompa Loompa Song; The Rainbow Song; Six Little Ducks; Ten Little Monkeys; Vowel Song; What's the Weather?* **Cumulative Songs** *Little Cabin in the Woods* *Little White Duck* *Old Woman Who Swallowed a Fly* **Work Songs** *Heigh Ho; I've Been Working on the Railroad; Sing, Sing Your Way Home;* *Whistle While You Work* **Special Occasion Songs** *A Very Merry Unbirthday, Happy Birthday to You, You Say It's Your Birthday* (Beatles song), *For He's a Jolly Good Fellow, More We Get Together* **Game Songs** *A Tisket a Tasket, Bunny Hop, Farmer in the Dell, Here We Go Round the Mulberry Bush, Hockey Pokey, Jack and Jill, John Jacob Jingleheimer Schmidt, Michael Finnegan, Miss Molly, Old MacDonald Had a Farm, Paw Paw Patch, She'll Be Coming Round the Mountain, Skip to My Lou, Wheels on the Bus*

(continued)

TABLE 10–2 Some Songs for Children *(continued)*

Primary Age	**Learning Songs**
	Social Studies
	America the Beautiful
	Columbia Gem of the Ocean
	Erie Canal
	Science
	Come Little Leaves, Dry Bones, Little April Shower, Over in the Meadow
	Songs in Parts
	The Bear in Tennis Shoes
	Rounds
	Frere Jacques
	Hey Ho Nobody Home
	Kookaburra
	Row, Row, Row the Boat
	Twinkle Twinkle Little Star

**Words and music for these songs and many more can be found at http://www.niehs.nih.gov/kids/home.htm and at http://www.theteachersguide.com/ChildrensSongs.htm.*

This type of song is also known as a "story song," "zipper song," or "piggyback song," and many examples can be found in books and on the Web. However, it is just as easy to invent your own to fit the needs of your own children. In addition, allowing children to participate in making up songs based on old favorites is a powerful way to begin a creative music community. Children, if allowed to contribute to the writing of the song will take ownership and pride in the song (Hildebrandt, 1998). Shelly Ringgenberg (2003) points out some other advantages as well:

- The melody will be familiar, making it quicker and easier to learn the song.
- Because you choose the content, speed, and length, the song can be tailored to fit the needs of the moment.
- It saves time that would be spent searching for an existing song that might fit.
- No materials are needed except voices and creativity.

Teaching a New Song

The best way to introduce a new song is spontaneously when it fits what is happening in the children's lives. Singing *Rain Rain Go Away,* for example, will be far more memorable when first heard on a day when rain has spoiled an outdoor playtime or event. Teach a lullaby when children are resting quietly. Introduce a silly song when they need cheering up. Tie songs into integrated units and projects. Sing songs to help chores get done faster.

Children learn a song first by hearing it, then by tagging on to an accented word or phrase, then by joining in on a repeated or patterned part like the chorus, and finally, they can sing it on their own (Wolf, 1994). There are many approaches to introducing a song. Using a combination of them is most effective, but remember, singing with children should always be fun and spontaneous. Do not expect young children to learn all the words of a song. It is fine if they chime in on the chorus or on silly words or sounds, and let the teacher sing the verses. Do not expect or demand perfection. If the same song is practiced over and over, it will become boring or a chore to sing. If children become resistant to singing, or lack enthusiasm for a song, it is time to teach a new song.

Songs can be taught to one child, a small group, or a whole class depending on the age of the children and the situation. Children learn songs best from another person's singing rather than from a recording. This is because they are best at matching pitches in their own vocal range and you are free to match their pitch, whereas a recording is preset. Men may find that singing in falsetto may help children sing in better tune. Nevertheless, most young children only begin to sing in tune in the primary grades.

Here are some ways to introduce new songs:

Teacher Tip

INVENTING A STORY SONG

Shelly Ringgenberg (2003) makes the following suggestions for creating an effective story song:

1. Make sure it is developmentally appropriate.
2. Use short, familiar melodies.
3. Choose a key that is comfortable for the children and you. If you are not sure, listen to the children sing and join in with them.
4. Keep it short and rhythmic to hold the children's attention and make it easier to learn.

Sample story song. To the tune of *Mary Had a Little Lamb*

This is how we make an A,

Make an A; make an A.

This is how we make an A,

Up Down Across.

(Note: On the last three words, act out making an A: Move fingers up and down to make the point of A. Then draw a finger across it.) Continue the song using other letters of the alphabet.

Whole song method. Sing the song two or three times. Then sing it again and leave out a key word for the children to fill in or have the children join in the chorus or last line.

Call and response. Sing one line of the song and have the children sing it back to you.

Say it first. Sometimes it helps to say the words before or after singing the song to help the child understand them better. We are all familiar with the child who thinks that "Oh say can you see" in the *Star Spangled Banner* is "Jose can you see?"

Write it out. For older children, write the words on large chart paper. For beginning readers use a combination of pictures and words. Point to the words as you sing the song.

Clap the rhythm. Particularly in songs with a strong beat, clapping or tapping the rhythm helps children feel where the words fit best.

Act it out. Many songs lend themselves to movement and dramatic performance. Adding movement helps children remember the words better, as do open-ended songs to which children can add their

Teacher Tip

THE KODÁLY METHOD

Zoltan Kodály (1882–1967) was a Hungarian composer and educator. Kodály believed that every person was a musical being and that singing was the foundation of music education because the voice is the one instrument everyone has. His approach to teaching music has been widely adopted, particularly in public schools. The Kodály approach is founded on the following:

- Music instruction for children should focus first on the folksongs of the child's culture, followed by the works of great composers.
- Music training should be active, using folk dances, singing games, and moving to music.
- The goal of music education is music literacy—the ability to look at written music and hear it in one's head.
- Pitch, intervals, and harmony are taught using hand signals based on the sofège syllables (*do re me fa so la ti do*) that visually show the relationship of the notes. Using hand signals helps make learning to sing a more concrete experience.
- Instruction starts with *sol* and then adds *me* and *la*.
- Visit the Organization of American Kodály Educators Web site for more information: http://www.oake.org/.

Making Plans

EXPLORATION CENTER ACTIVITY PLAN: Mini-Theater

WHO? **Group composition age(s):** Preschool and kindergarten

Group size: Four at a time at the center

WHEN? **Time frame:** 15 to 20 minutes

WHY? **Objectives:** Children will develop

- physically, by moving and acting out their songs. (Bodily-Kinesthetic)
- socially, by sharing their songs with each other. (Interpersonal)
- emotionally, by developing self-confidence as performers. (Intrapersonal)
- auditory perception skills, by listening to each other's songs. (Spatial)
- language skills, by describing their performances. (Linguistic)
- cognitively, by choosing and learning a selected song. (Logical-Mathematical)
- music skill and knowledge, by singing expressively and from memory. (Content Standard 1)

WHERE? **Setup:** The mini-theater center features lightweight draperies hung from rods suspended from the ceiling about 4 feet away from the wall. Large curtain rings at the top of the draperies will make them easier for children to open and close. A low platform serves as a stage. If a platform is not available, a rug can be used to delineate the performing area. The audience can sit on the floor in front of the curtains. (Note: This center can also be used for dramatic play performances; see Chapter 12.)

WHAT? **Materials:** Provide props that would be used by singers—a toy microphone, a toy piano, chairs. Children can also select their own props and use dress-up clothes to enhance their performance. For example, they may want to be a rock band with toy guitars and drums.

HOW? **Procedure:**

Warm-Up: Model how the center can be used by performing a song for the whole group.

What to Do: Remind children, who seem unsure, of songs they already know. Support children who want to make up their own songs. Encourage children to sing together. Videotape the performances.

What to Say: Give positive feedback to the singers, such as "You sang very clearly. I could hear all the words." "You remembered the entire chorus." "You acted out the words of the song in a new way."

Transition Out: Record the performers and the songs they sang in a class music log. Provide time later in the day for children to watch themselves on videotape.

ASSESSMENT OF LEARNING

1. Do the children remember the songs learned in the whole group setting and sing them confidently?
2. Do the children create their own versions of familiar songs?
3. Are the children a good audience for each other?

own words. For example, *Pop Goes the Weasel* is easily acted out.

Substitute meaningful words. Making the song personal also makes it more memorable. The words can be varied by substituting a child's name, a familiar place, or a daily event. For example, instead of singing "Mary had a little lamb" sing "______(child's name) has a little ____ (substitute child's pet)."

Tell the story. Explain the song as a story, or for primary students, talk about the history of the song. For example, explain that the song *Yankee Doodle* was composed by British soldiers to make fun of the poorly dressed, uneducated Americans, who then adopted the song as their own.

Make it familiar. When introducing a new song, play it in the background for a while then sing it in its entirety. However, children will not learn a song heard only in the background. There has to be active listening by the child. After all, no one can learn a language just by hearing it in the background while concentrating on something else. To learn a song, active involvement in the singing is needed.

Add signs. Sing the song accompanied by American Sign Language (ALS). The hand movements make the song easier to remember as well as introduce children to a way they can communicate with those who are deaf. Videos are available for learning how to sign familiar songs (see Appendix C).

Singing Activities for Infants

Singing activities for infants should build on their developing verbalization skills.

Sing along. Accompany the child's movements and activities by humming and singing familiar songs.

Match it. Sing along with infant vocalizations. If the child says, "Ba ba" sing "ba ba" back.

Singing Activities for Toddlers

Toddlers are just beginning to sing. Activities for this age group should help them become familiar with the words and melodies of songs.

Add movements. Help active toddlers learn new songs by adding motions to accompany the song.

Teacher Tip

Take children to performances by local singing groups or have groups visit the program. Children may be familiar with popular singers and groups featured on television and radio. Introduce them to different types of performing groups, such as choirs, barbershop quartets, and a cappella groups.

Sing it. Instead of talking, sing to the child while involved in daily activities.

Singing Activities for Preschoolers

Preschoolers are ready to learn to sing songs on their own and in groups. Design activities that help them remember the words and melodies and that encourage them to create their own songs.

Picture it. Use props or a flannel board to dramatize a song. Make a simple flannel board by gluing felt to a thick piece of cardboard. Make your own figures or let the children draw their own ideas on tag board and attach felt to the back.

Use puppets. A puppet makes an ideal companion with whom to sing. Use the call-and-response method, with the puppet echoing the song line along with the children. Encourage the children to sing to puppet friends by keeping the puppets at the music center.

Hands free. Tape yourself singing a song you want the children to learn as you accompany yourself on an instrument. Play the tape as you teach the song. This will leave you free to add gestures and movements.

Arts Words

PARTS OF A SONG

Break. A section in which only instruments play.

Bridge. An optional part of a song that harmonically joins two different sections. A song only has one bridge, and it often comes between the last verse and the final chorus and may be instrumental or sung.

Chord. Three of more notes played together at the same time.

Chorus. A melody line or group of lines that repeats at the end of every verse, emphasizing the theme of the song. It is sometimes called the **refrain,** although a refrain, being two lines, is usually shorter than a chorus.

Lyrics. The words of the song.

Verse. Groups of two or more lines that have the same melody, but different words.

Singing Activities for Kindergarteners

Singing to learn. Make letter, word, and number cards to accompany songs. Hold up the card at the appropriate time. Once the children are sure of the song let them hold up the cards.

Singing games. Play traditional and original singing games with the children. For kindergarten, keep the game simple, active, and noncompetitive. A good example is *Farmer in the Dell*. To play the game, sit or stand in a large circle. The child chosen to be the farmer walks around the circle and chooses the wife. The wife then chooses the animal named next and so on. The game ends when all children have been chosen. It is easy to change the subject of simple songs such as this and keep the game the same. Instead of a farmer, try a zookeeper, or a school bus driver. For example,

The keeper of the zoo
The keeper of the zoo
Heigh ho the derry oh
The keeper of the zoo.
Along comes a camel
Along comes a camel
Heigh ho the derry oh
Along comes a camel.

More singing games are found in Chapter 11.

Singing Activities for Primary Age

Primary age children can sing much more accurately in a group setting. Singing activities for this age group can begin to introduce part singing as a way of developing the ability to create harmonies.

Use cue cards. Chart the song using words and pictures, such as a rebus as a guide for more accurate group singing and to develop literacy. If singing a song in parts, have separate cards for each part.

Taking a part. Introduce part singing by having some of the children chant a simple phrase while the others sing the melody. For example, for the song *Hickory Dickory Dock* have half the children sing the song and the others chant "tick tock." It helps if the two groups sit together with space separating them.

Rounds. Start with very simple rounds based on the most familiar songs. *Row, Row, Row Your Boat* and *Frere Jacques* are commonly two of the first rounds children learn. Start with two groups and as children gain experience divide them into three and four groups.

Book Box

Books based on popular songs.

Collins, J. (2010). *Over the rainbow.* Watertown, MA: Charlesbridge.

Denver, J. (2003). *Sunshine on my shoulder.* Nevada, CA: Dawn.

Guthrie, W. (2008). *This land is your land.* New York: Little, Brown.

Taback, S. (2007). *There was an old lady who swallowed a fly.* New York: Viking.

Hoberman, M. A. (2002). *Eensy-Weensy spider.* New York: Little, Brown.

Peek, M. (1988). *Mary wore her red dress.* New York: Clarion.

Raffi. (1990). *Wheels on the bus.* New York: Crown.

Rogers, R. (2001). *My favorite things.* New York: Harper Collins.

Songs, S. (2009). *Knick knack paddy whack.* Cambridge, MA: Barefoot Books.

Warhola, J. (2007). *If you're happy and you know it.* New York: Orchard.

Books about singers and singing.

Izen, M., & West, J. (2004). *The dog that sang at the opera.* New York: Harry Abrams.

Ryan, P. M. (2002). *When Marion sang.* New York: Scholastic.

Weaver, T. (2002). *Opera cat.* New York: Clarion.

Yarrow, P. (2010). *Songs for little folks.* New York: Sterling.

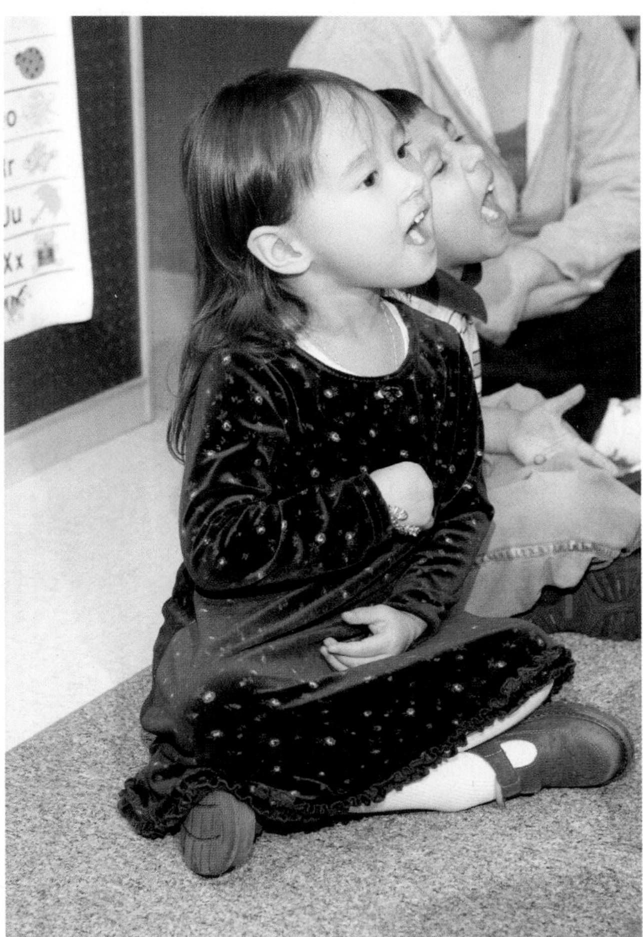

Adding movement to songs helps children learn the song faster.

CONCLUSION: BECOMING MUSICAL

> *Remember the music; remember the bond singing and shared experience create. Choose songs you love the most. Joy will follow.*
>
> *—Jan Wolf (2000, p. 30)*

The goal of music experiences for young children is to develop each child into a musical person. A musical person is not a just a consumer of music, nor a professional musician. A musical person is someone who is tuneful, beatful, and artful. A tuneful person carries the melodies of wonderful songs in their head. A beatful person feels the beat of music of all kinds and the natural rhythms of the world around them. An artful person responds to the expressiveness of all music with all their body and soul.

We owe it to the children we teach to give them the gift of music. Music education must start before the child is born and be intensive through the early years. To do this we need to become comfortable ourselves in the world of music. We do not need to be virtuosos. However, we do need to become enthusiastic and confident. Teachers must also be learners. It is never too late to learn to play an instrument or take voice lessons.

FURTHER READING

Fox, D. (2003). *Treasury of children's songs.* New York: Henry Holt.

This book contains 40 of the most well-known traditional children's songs and nursery rhymes.

Jensen, E. P. (2000). *Music with the brain in mind.* Thousand Oaks, CA: Corwin.

Eric Jensen shows how music helps children learn and provides useful tips for classroom teachers.

Levitin, M. (2006). *This is your brain on music: The science of a human obsession.* New York: Dutton.

Professional musician, music producer, and scientific researcher Michael Levitin reviews current research and presents his own music experiments, explaining how music affects our brains.

Mither, S. (2006). *The singing Neanderthal: The origin of music, language, mind, and body.* Cambridge, MA: Harvard.

Archeologist Steven Mither combines prehistory and current neurological research to explain why we make music.

Newcome, Z. (2002). *Head, shoulder, knees, and toes and other action rhymes.* Cambridge, MA: Candlewick.

This is a collection of songs and rhymes that involve rhythm and movement suitable for infants and up.

Perret, P., & Fox, J. (2006). *The well-tempered mind: Using music to help children listen and learn.* Washington, DC: Dana.

This book reports on the results of the Bolton project in which 30 minutes of music education three times a week improved academic learning for "at-risk" children. It explains the philosophy behind this program.

Seskin, S. (2008). *Sing my song: A kid's guide to songwriting.* Berkley, CA: Tricycle Press.

Steve Suskin shares how to write original songs with children. The book includes the lyrics and a CD with many of the songs he has written about acceptance, respect, and hope being sung by schoolchildren.

For additional information on teaching music to young children visit our Web site at http://www.cengagebrain.com

TEACHING IN ACTION

A Literacy-Based Integrated Music Activity

"What do you think is in this box?" I ask my class of prekindergarteners.

"A dog!" Billy yells out, forgetting to raise his hand.

"No way. It's too small." Amy says, her large eyes fixed on the box.

"Can I shake it?" Hughie, my little scientist, asks.

I hand him the box.

"Hmmm. Sounds like there's lots of small things inside."

The box passes around the circle of children. Each holds it to his or her ear and gives it a shake.

"They don't bang like metal."

"It's a soft sound."

"I think it's not so many—maybe three or four things."

"I'll give you a hint," I say, after everyone has a chance to listen. "Today we are going to read the story *My Crayons Talk* by Patricia Hubbard."

"It's a box of crayons," everyone says at once. "Open it, Miss Giradi. Open it, please!"

With great majesty I unwrap the box, and show them the nine crayons inside. I hold each one up and the children call out the colors: red, blue, green, yellow, brown, orange, black, pink, and purple.

I read the book to the children, holding up the appropriate crayon when its color is named.

"Now we will read it again in a different way." I open up the plastic container that holds our rhythm instruments. Chloe claps her hands. "Oh, we're going to make music."

"That's right. We're going to make the colors talk. Let's decide which instrument reminds us of each color."

"Yellow goes with the bell, because it's yellow too." Latasha says.

I hand the bell to Latasha.

"I think the drum goes with black, because they are both loud," Billy says.

As each child makes a suggestion, I hand the instrument to them.

"We are going to need some yackity clackers too," I say. I hand out the claves and castenets to the rest of the children.

Now we are going to read the book again. This time when we say a color, if you have the instrument we chose, make a loud sound. When we get to the yackity clakity parts, everyone will play together."

Highly motivated and intently focused each child listens for her or his cue to play as we bring the words in the book to life through the rhythms of the children.

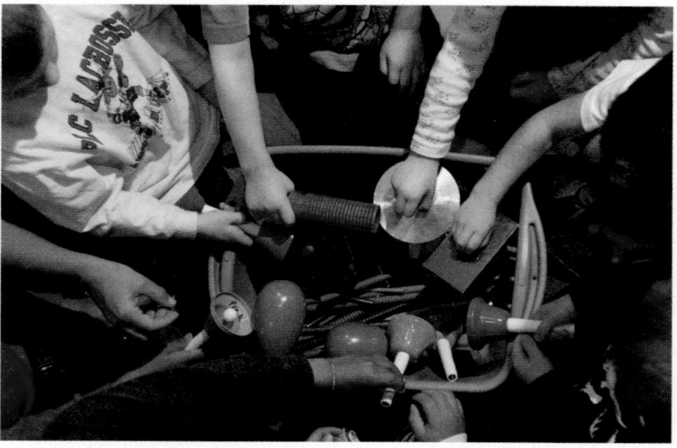

When instruments are handy, music happens naturally.

Studio Page

DISCOVERING ONE'S MUSICAL HERITAGE

What factors have influenced how you feel about music?

1. What are some family songs you learned as a child? Do they reflect any special ethnic or cultural influences?

2. Were any members of your family involved in music? What did they do?

3. Have you ever studied any instrument or had voice training?

4. What are some of your favorite pieces of music? How often do you listen to them?

5. What area of music would you like to learn more about?

Studio Page

SELECTING APPROPRIATE MUSIC ACTIVITIES

Based on the information in this chapter, decide what would be the most appropriate age group (s) for each suggested music activity below and list the Music Content Standard the activity addresses.

1. Clap a rhythm and have the children echo it back to you.

   Age group: ______________________ Content Standard ______________________

2. Move a maraca around a child's head while shaking it.

   Age group: ______________________ Content Standard ______________________

3. Hide a familiar instrument behind a box. Challenge a child to guess which instrument it is.

   Age group: ______________________ Content Standard ______________________

4. Have the children write stories and then add rhythms and songs.

   Age group: ______________________ Content Standard ______________________

5. Have the children make up new words for a familiar song.

   Age group: ______________________ Content Standard ______________________

6. Play a musical work by Sebastian Bach while the child is relaxing.

   Age group: ______________________ Content Standard ______________________

7. Have the children invent their own way to write the melody of a song.

   Age group: ______________________ Content Standard ______________________

8. Sing songs in a limited range, such as nursery rhymes.

   Age group: ______________________ Content Standard ______________________

Studio Page

MEETING SPECIAL NEEDS

How would you adjust these activities to meet the special needs of each child?

Child	Activity	Adjustments that might be made
A child with a cochlear implant	Listening to music	
A child with some hearing loss	Playing rhythm instruments	
A child with total hearing loss	Having a musician visit the class	
A child with poor coordination	Playing a tonal instrument, such as the xylophone	
A child in a wheelchair	Playing rhythm instruments while marching around the room	

Studio Page

SUPPORTING MUSIC EDUCATION FOR YOUNG CHILDREN

Why is it important to teach musical skills and concepts in early childhood? Write a letter to the families of an early childhood program, explaining why music activities are part of the curriculum. Justify your reasons using research cited in this chapter.

Chapter 11

Moving Creatively

Questions Addressed in This Chapter:

- What is creative movement and dance?
- How does creative movement help children grow?
- How are creative movement activities designed?

"Dance is the most immediate and accessible of the arts because it involves your own body. When you learn to move your body on a note of music, it's exciting. You have taken control of your body and, by learning to do that, you discover that you can take control of your life."

—Jacques d'Amboise (2006)

WHAT IS CREATIVE MOVEMENT AND DANCE?

The ability to move is a function of three interacting bodily systems. First, our muscular and skeletal system provides support and a framework for action. This framework is guided by kinesthetic awareness, the system of sensors found in our muscles, joints, and tendons, which provides information on posture, equilibrium, and the effort required for a motion to occur. Both these systems are kept balanced by the vestibular sense located in the inner ear, which keeps track of the motion and position of the head relative to the rest of the body. All these parts work together to create the simple and complex actions that we perform unthinkingly each day of our lives.

Our capacity to move allows us to interact with the world and people around us. However, when these movements are organized into a work of bodily art we come to understand how marvelous our bodies are. Through carefully chosen creative movements, we can communicate feelings, tell stories, and become part of the music. We dance.

Creative movement and dance are inherently human and incredibly ancient. Paintings on pottery indicate that dance was as much a part of life in Neolithic times as it is today. Then as it is now, the creative movement of the body was tied to social and spiritual rituals. In the past these rituals were often related to everyday life and needs. The first dances probably imitated the movements of activities such as hunting, harvesting, and planting. Today we dance to feel part of a group, to make friends, and to release bodily tensions.

Is It Creative Movement or Dance?

The art form based on moving our bodies has been called both *creative movement* and *dance*. Usually in early childhood education, the term *creative movement* is used to emphasize the open-ended nature of movement activities that are developmentally appropriate for young children. Dance, on the other hand, more often refers to formalized styles of movement in which children are taught specific ways to move and particular dance positions and steps, such as ballet or the polka. In truth, both aspects of movement are essential in the education of young children.

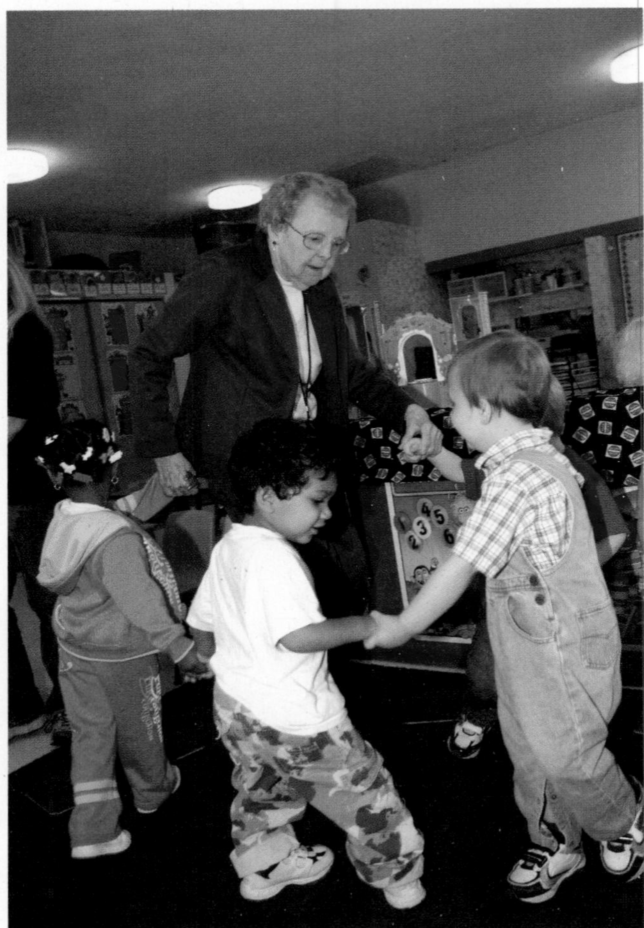

Creative movement activities draw children together and create relationships.

All children need the opportunity to use the creative process in discovering their own original ways to move and in using their bodies to communicate their emotions and ideas. However, as they grow they also need to learn how to control their bodies and match their movements to rhythms, music, and the movements of others by participating in simple dances from our own and other cultures. For this reason the term **creative dance** can be used to encompass both these aspects of the movement arts.

The Elements of Dance

The elements of dance are body, movement, time, space, and energy. See Table 11-1.

- **Body—**The body is the tool we use to create dances. It is our muscles, bones, tendons, reflexes, and breath. It is the medium through which our ideas and feelings are expressed. This makes dance "the most personal of all the arts" (Walter, 1942).

- **Movement**—We use our bodies as an art medium when must move them. Creative dance is made up of these movements, which consists of streams and pauses in sequence. Locomotion means the movement moves from one place to another as when we leap, hop, and run. Nonlocomotion refers to those moves we can do standing in one place such as bending, twisting, and swings. Movements can go in any direction, any distance, and be balanced or unbalanced, large or small.
- **Time**—We can move our bodies slowly or quickly using varying speeds and duration.
- **Space**—Space refers to how we position our bodies in the space that surrounds us. Our bodies can occupy different levels and be open or closed.
- **Force**—This is the effort we use as we move our bodies through distances in that space. Our body can move in a relaxed way or under tension. We can attack and release.

TABLE 11–1 Describing Movement

Space	Effort	Connection
Place Size Distance	**Time** Speed Duration	**To body** Balanced Unbalanced Stretched Compressed
Direction Forward/back Left/right Up/down Clockwise/counter clockwise	**Force** Attack Tension Release Relax	**To objects** Close/far On top/underneath Side-by-side Inside/outside In front/behind Around Through
Level High Middle Low	**Flow** Open Closed Rhythmic Accented	**To people** Partnered Leading Following Solo
Path Straight Bent Curved	**Distance** Near/far Short/long Wide/Narrow	

HOW DOES CREATIVE MOVEMENT AND DANCE HELP CHILDREN GROW?

Movement is basic to life. From birth children spend their waking moments in constant motion. The newborn waves arms and legs, the infant crawls, the toddler toddles, and the preschooler jumps, runs, and climbs. Even in the womb, the fetus swims and kicks.

Movement and the Brain

Being able to move is essential for normal brain development. Research shows that young children use motion cues in developing concepts about objects (Mak & Vera, 1999; Newell, Wallraven, & Huber, 2004). We also know that children with physical disabilities must compensate for their limited motor abilities in order to develop normally (Bebko, Burke, Craven & Sarlo, 1992).

In addition, physical movement increases oxygen to the brain, which produces enhanced cognitive functioning (Sousa, 2001, p. 230). According to Jensen (2001, p. 94), academic achievement is better in schools that offer frequent breaks for physical movement.

Movement and Developmental Growth

Movement affects a child's total development. Through creative movement activities children develop

- **Physically**—By using the body to move with control in the performance of creative movement. Creative movement is a powerful form of exercise in which the body is strengthened and made fit. Introducing young children to creative dance teaches them a pleasurable way to stay fit and healthy. This is especially important because so many of us are prone to be inactive most of the time. A 2004 government survey found that 30 percent of Americans participated in no leisure-time activities and another 30 percent participated only minimally (National Center for Health Statistics, 2006). Moving through dance helps regulate weight, maintain glucose metabolism, and fosters heart health as well. Endorphins are released, which create a state of well-being. Dancing improves posture, balance, physical endurance, and flexibility.

- **Socially**—By learning how to move in concert with others. Creative movement creates social unity. Moving with others is an opportunity for children to experience the role of both leader and follower. Children learn how to communicate their ideas to others using only their bodies. Group dances instill collective discipline on the children and make cooperation physically visible as they focus on each other's roles in the performance and note each other's relative position in space to their own. Creative dance also provides the opportunity to learn about and experience culturally different ways of moving as children move creatively to music from other places, and perform folk dances from other parts of the world.
- **Cognitively**—By developing thinking and problem-solving skills. Sensorimotor learning has long been recognized as central to early cognitive development in young children (Piaget, 1959). More recently, the powerful relationship between movement and thinking has been supported by the evidence presented by Howard Gardner (1993) for a separate bodily-kinesthetic intelligence. Jay Seitz (2000) outlines two components of bodily thinking that support the deep connection between mind and body. First is the ability of the brain to order movement through motor logic. Kinesthetic thinking integrates cognitive, sensory, and emotional experiences, and then responds with the best physical action. Second is kinesthetic memory, which allows us to remember how to move in specific ways, such as dancing a waltz, by reconstructing the effort, position, and action needed to be successful, even if one has not waltzed in years. In addition, the close relationship between mind and body is shown in the ability to mentally rehearse a physical action through mental imagery so that without actual practice one can improve that physical skill.

Open-ended creative dance exercises also provide the opportunity for children to use problem-solving skills as they match the movement of their body to the physical challenges being asked of them. For example, if children are asked to move as if they were a cloud, they must first think what a cloud is and how it moves and then decide how they might make their body imitate that movement. Next, they must actually perform that movement, and follow up immediately with self-assessment to see if they have accomplished their initial goal and then make any needed correction. Because dance extends over time, this self-correcting feedback between mind and body can continue throughout a dance sequence in a way not always possible in music or fine art.

Spatial and mathematical concepts require children to be aware of their orientation to the environment and how objects behave in space. They need to have a physical understanding of distance, force, and time in order to figure out how objects

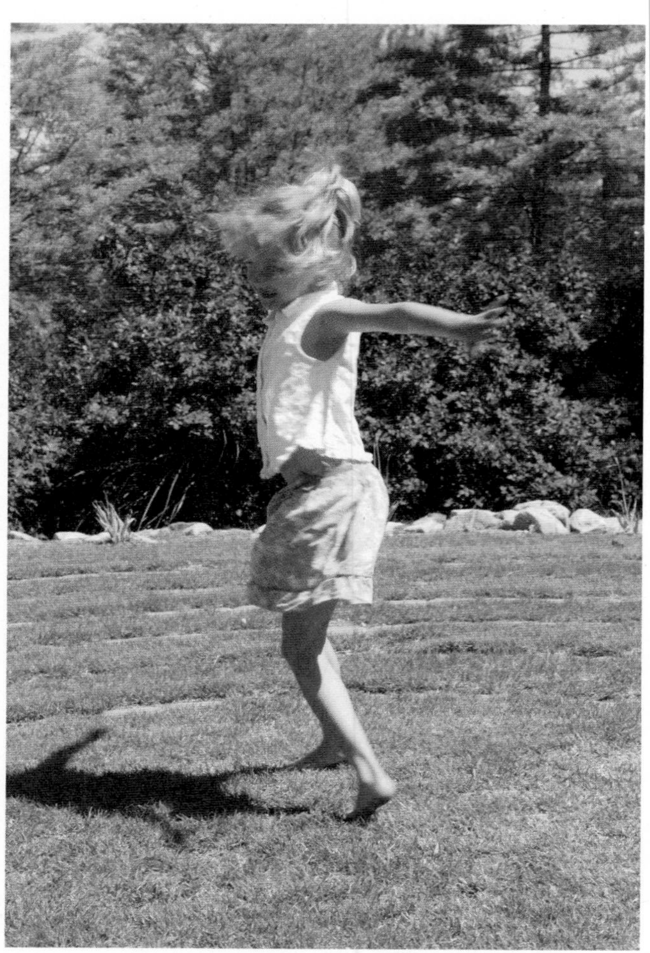

Creative movement and dance is a powerful form of exercise.

around them move. This knowledge is obtained by physical investigation and body memory. Dance provides many opportunities for children to move in, around, under, and above the things in their environment cementing these important words in place.

- **Language skills**—By using their bodies to communicate ideas and by a developing vocabulary related to mathematical and spatial concepts. Movement is an essential part of language and communication. Studies show that hand control and speech develop from the same neural systems as evidenced by the fact that gesture precedes speech in infants, and even toddlers will ignore a vocal command if it conflicts with a physical gesture (Seitz, 1989, p. 31). Gesture remains an important form of communication even in adults. Creative movement activities provide an opportunity for children to explore gesture and body position as a way to express feelings and ideas.
- **Emotionally**—By improving self-confidence and allowing self-expression. Being in control of one's body and feeling fit are essential components of positive mental health. In adults physical fitness has been strongly linked with lower incidences of depression and reduced stress (Fox, 1999). Children who are overweight, clumsy, or uncoordinated are at a disadvantage in most sports activities. Creative dance, which welcomes all bodily responses, provides a safe, pleasurable way for all children, regardless of ability, to release inner emotions and feel successful.
- **Dance concepts and skills**—By meeting the National Standards for Dance (Ponick, 2007, pp. 23–25).

By the end of the primary years children should

Content Standard 1: Understand and use the elements of movement and the techniques and skills of dance.

Content Standard 2: Create original dance sequences and improvisations alone and with others.

Content Standard 3: Know that creative movement and dance are ways to create meaning and communicate ideas.

Content Standard 4: Compare and evaluate creative movement and dance with reference to the elements of dance.

Content Standard 5: Understand and perform dances from many times, cultures, and places.

Content Standard 6: Know the connection between good health and dance.

Content Standard 7: Connect creative movement and dance with the arts and other subjects.

Teacher Tip

ASSESSING PROFICIENCY

Creative dance activities should closely match children's physical development. Careful observation of a child's movements can provide important clues to the child's level of physical skill. Graham, Holt-Hale, and Parker (2001) have identified the following four levels:

Precontrol: The same movement cannot be repeated in succession.

Control: The same movement can be repeated somewhat consistently but cannot be combined with another movement or object.

Utilization: The same movement can be repeated consistently and used in new situations and combinations.

Proficiency: The movement is automatic and effortless and can be performed at the same time as other actions as well as modified to fit planned and unplanned situations.

HOW ARE CREATIVE MOVEMENT ACTIVITIES DESIGNED?

Creative dance is concerned with the role of movement in artistic creation. Activities that support this differ from physical exercises and sports, which are also concerned with physical development. In creative movement activities children are asked to imitate and expand on everyday behaviors and actions using their bodies, sometimes with music and props, to create what Jay Seitz (1989) calls a "metaphorical twist" in which the body part is no longer itself but rather a representation of something else. For example, waves can be represented by gently undulating one's arms. Even formal dance has this aesthetic element to it. As the dancers move in choreographed motion, geometric and symbolic patterns are created.

Creative movement activities are best organized by the skill, attention, and experience level of the children.

One-on-One Activities

Creative movement is by its very nature a social activity and most movement activities for young children are usually done in a group setting. Infants and children with limitations on their motor control are often best taught first in one-on-one and then pair situations where they can practice and develop the skills needed for successful participation in a larger group. For example, an infant's arms might be gently moved to a lullaby while being held in one's lap. An older child might play a game of hand mirrors with an adult where they sit or stand opposite each other and place hands palm to palm, while they take turns being the leader and moving the hands in different ways.

Exploration Exercises

Explorations are activities that allow children to explore the possibilities of how they can move their bodies. These can be done one-on-one or with small or large groups of children. In the beginning, these may form the entire movement experience. Later on, they can be used as warm-up exercises for more complex movement experiences.

Group Movement Sequences

The richest creative movement experiences are those in which a whole group participates. Depending on the age of the children, these can range from having the whole group responding to the same open-ended prompts to elaborate story dances in which individuals and small groups play different roles. Movement sequences can be based on or include traditional and formal dance forms familiar to the group as well and are best improvised or choreographed by the children themselves.

Large group creative dance activities require an open space that allows children to move freely and safely.

Creating a Space for Creative Movement

Movement activities require a carefully prepared environment in which children have plenty of space to move boldly and freely. This requires careful structuring of the environment and the creation of safety guidelines.

Floor. For very young children who are not yet walking steadily, a carpeted area provides the best surface for movement activities. Once children can walk steadily, a bare floor, preferably wood, provides more stability. However, if the surface or underlayment is cement, some kind of cushioned surface or carpet is essential. Movement activities can also be performed outside on the grass in good weather.

Children's shoes should match the surface on which they are dancing. Bare or stocking feet might work on a carpet or carefully prepared grass areas, but be sure nonslip soles are worn on smooth surfaced floors.

Space requirements. Depending on the ages and sizes of the children more or less space will be needed. A general rule is that the children should be able to spread out their arms in any direction and still be an arm's-length away from anyone else, a wall, or object.

Safety requirements. Furniture and objects along the edges of the movement area should be closely checked for sharp edges. For example, metal shelving can cut a child who slides into it. The corner of a bookcase can injure a child's eye. It may be helpful to outline the edge of the area with tape or paint so children know where to stop or the edge of the carpet can be the stopping point.

Creating signals. As anyone who has worked with young children knows, having a whole group of them in motion at one time can be harrying. Before starting any creative movement activities, it is necessary to have in place easily recognized signals or rituals for starting, stopping, listening, and resting. These signals should be ones you can do easily while dancing yourself, such as a voice command, clapping, or a particular tap on a small drum or tambourine.

No matter which signaling method is chosen, use it consistently and take sufficient time to practice it separately and then together. One of the goals of first movement explorations should be to have the children internalize the signals. Ruth Charney (1992) suggests the following steps in teaching children to respond quickly and efficiently to signals:

1. First, explain why a signal is needed. "Sometimes we will need to stop dancing and listen so I can give you new directions."
2. Sound the signal and then model the expected behavior as you explain it.
3. Sound the signal and have individual children model the behavior for the group.
4. Now have several children model the behavior for the group.
5. Last, have the whole group respond to the signal.
6. Repeat as many times as necessary until the whole group performs the task in the expected way.
7. At the start of future activities always review the signals and have the children practice them.
8. If at any time the children do not respond to the signal as expected, then take time to practice the behavior again.

Moving in Concert

Creative movement activities require both sharing space and moving in conjunction with others. Before beginning, set up simple, positively worded behavior rules that foster cooperative behavior and have children role-play what to do in situations such as bumping into another child. Keep the rules simple. It is generally recommended not to have more rules than the age of the child. A good rule for one-year-olds might be "Be safe." Then as children get older add, "Be a friend." "Be a listener." "Be a thinker."

A sheet of bubble wrap adds sound effects to a child's movement while at the same time providing a designated spot in which to move.

THE CREATIVE MOVEMENT EXPERIENCE

Creative movement may be done with or without music. It is an open-ended approach to moving the body that asks children to solve a problem while making independent choices. It differs from formal dance because it allows many possible responses. At its simplest it asks children to explore the elements of dance or parts of their body as they develop physical and mental control. Complex creative movement activities let children create a sequence of movements with a beginning, middle, and end that express an idea or feeling.

Teacher Tip

LEARNING TO RELAX

To move creatively with young children the teacher needs to feel relaxed and calm. Try these relaxation exercises to get ready to move:

1. Wear loose clothing and sit in a comfortable chair.
2. Inhale through your nose and exhale through your mouth.
3. Inhale slowly, counting to four. Imagine the air flowing to all parts of your body.
4. Exhale, imagining the tension flowing out.
5. Next, as you breathe in, tense one muscle group. As you breathe out, relax.
6. Repeat often.

Selecting Music for Creative Movement Activities

Movement activities are often accompanied by music. In selecting music, look first of all for pieces that make you feel like moving in different ways. The music should be mostly instrumental because lyrics can be distracting unless they relate directly to the movements being done. Symphonies can also be overpowering in their complexity. Short, carefully selected selections are often more effective. Solos and ensemble performances, for example, have a clear sound quality that makes moving to them easier. In addition, be sure to expose children to a range of musical styles and instruments because each evokes different emotions and ideas (see Table 11-2).

Using Silence and Body Percussion

Movement activities do not need to be accompanied only by music. Sometimes it is best to begin with silence so children can focus on the signals, your guiding questions, and their own movements. Next, try adding body percussion—clapping and tapping various body parts—or vocalizations—catchy sound effects such as pop, bing, and swoosh. Rhythmic poetry can also be used.

Adding Props

Props are anything held by the children while moving. Props take the focus off the child's own movements and allow the children to move more freely and with more force. For this reason, they are particularly useful when working with children who are shy, self-conscious, or who have a physical disability. Props enlarge the child's movements and add fluidity. For example, although children can certainly imagine they are moving as if they were planting flowers, holding and manipulating long-stemmed artificial or real flowers will help the child better visualize the needed movements (see Table 11-3).

Props can also be used to literally tie a group together. Have young children hold on to a jump rope or scarf as they move to keep everyone together. Hula hoops, boxes, carpet squares, and even bubble wrap can be placed on the floor to provide a spot for each child to move within. If using bubble wrap or carpet squares on a slippery floor, be sure to use double-sided tape to hold them in place.

Planning Creative Movement Activities

Creative movement activities work best when presented in a flexible format that allows the activity to

TABLE 11–2 Some Music for Moving

Artist/Composer	Album	Musical Work	Movements to Explore
Beethoven	*Sonatas for Piano & Violin*	No. 5 "Spring" Allegro	Flowing, high and low, tension and release, bent, straight, curved, mirroring
		No. 9 "Kreutzer" Presto	High and low, quick and short motions, skipping, galloping, leaping
John Coltrane	*My Favorite Things*	My Favorite Things	Tiptoeing, hopping, bouncing, short and quick motions, high and low
Enya	*Shepherd Moons*	Shepherd Moons	Slow, graceful, rocking, high and low, open and closed
		Book of Days	Contrasting motions—large and small, high and low, fast and slow, short and long, open-closed, accented, rhythmic
Gustave Hoist	*The Planets*	Mars	Large, smooth, forceful motions, marching, twirling
Maria Kliegel	*Le Grand Tango Dances*	Gavotte Tarantella	Tiptoeing, floating, high and low
Carlos Nakai	*The Best of Carlos Nakai*	Shaman's Call	Long extended motions, gliding, bending, relaxing, curving
Pachelbel	*Pachelbel's Greatest Hits*	Canon in D	Gliding, bending, stretching, shrinking, floating, waving
Bill Whelan	*Riverdance*	The Countess Cathleen (2nd half)	Stamping, waving, shaking
		Marta's Dance	Hopping, jumping, bouncing, fast stepping
Various	*Dances of Spain and Latin America*	Cubana Tutu	Slow and rhythmic
		Mirimba	Walking, hopping

adjust and change in response to the movements of the children. There should also be plenty of opportunity for children to provide input and be leaders as well.

TABLE 11–3 Props for Creative Movement Activities

Adding machine paper	Jump ropes
Artificial flowers	Paper shapes
Balls, all sizes	Plastic tablecloths cut in strips
Bells	Puppets
Boxes, all sizes	Stuffed animals
Carpet squares	Thin scarves
Cloth squares in unique colors and fabrics	Toile streamers
Chair	Tubes
Hats	Yarn
Hula hoops	

1. Start with a guided exploration: How would it feel to be an animal? What animal would you be? How would it walk if it were tired? Hungry? Happy? Allow children to make their own decisions about how the movement should be expressed. Do not say, "Move like an elephant" which makes it sound like there is only one way elephants move. Instead, say, "How do you think an elephant would move?" (See Table 11-4.)

2. Then provide plenty of free practice time during which children work individually creating their movement. Take time to allow the children to share their movements with each other by having them pair up and perform them for each other. This is quicker and less frightening than having each child perform before the whole group.

TABLE 11–4 Some Guided Explorations

Element of Dance	Category	Movement Quality	Guided Explorations to Try
Space	Place	Size Distance	• What are biggest/smallest steps, hops, leaps, bends, etc. you can make? • What are most/fewest steps, hops, leaps, etc. you can make?
	Direction	Forward/backward Left/right Up/down	• Start on line and ask them to move forward/backward, left/right, up/down by walking, hopping, etc.
		Clockwise/counter clockwise	• In circle, move clockwise to music. At signal change to counterclockwise. Imagine you are hands on a clock, water going down the drain, planets circling the sun.
	Level	High Middle Low	• Stand in place and move up and down to music.
	Path	Straight Bent Curved	• Line children up one behind the other and walk, skip, hop, crawl around the room in straight/curved/bent line. End where you started. What shapes do the paths make?
Effort	Time	Speed	• Move at different speeds to the accompaniment of a drum or music. Imagine you are an ice-cream cone melting, a rocket blasting off, an animal running.
		Duration	• Have children strike a pose. Time how long they can hold it. Repeat each day to see if they can hold it longer as they gain control and strength.
	Force	Attack Tension Release Relax	• Stand in place and make a sharp movement with their arm, hold it and feel the tension, release it and let it relax. Repeat with other body parts. This can be a good relaxation exercise or done to music.
	Flow	Open/Closed	• Wrap limbs close to body and then open them out in different ways—slow, fast, high, and low. Imagine you are a sleeping creature waking up, butterfly emerging, or a Jack-in-the-box. Repeat to music.
		Rhythmic Accented	• Move to the tap of a drum or a poem being read making bigger movements on the accented beat. • Imagine you are popcorn popping.
	Distance	Near/far Short/long Wide /narrow	• Move creatively back and forth from near objects to far ones. • Take short steps and long steps. • Push tables together to create narrow and wide passageways. Move creatively through the spaces.
Connection	To body	Balanced/unbalanced Stretched/compressed	• Figure out how many different ways you can balance yourself on one foot. • Imagine you are a rubber band, a slingshot, dirt under a shoe, and a paper at the bottom of the stack.
	To objects	Close/far On top/underneath Side-by-side Inside/outside In front/behind Around Through	• Call out a location as children use a prop, such as a scarf or chair, and place their bodies in relation to it as directed. Move to a rhythm at the same time. • Crawl or wiggle around the room going around and through things.
	To people	Partnered Leading Following Solo	• Hold hands with a partner while doing any of the ideas above. • Give each child a turn to lead the group in the movement using the agreed signals. • Provide opportunities for individual children to show their invented movements.

3. If it seems appropriate, consider adding a rhythmic accompaniment such as beating a drum or shaking a tambourine or related prop.
4. Finally, if the children seem to be deeply involved add some music that matches the movement.
5. Repeat this or similar movement explorations on a regular basis.

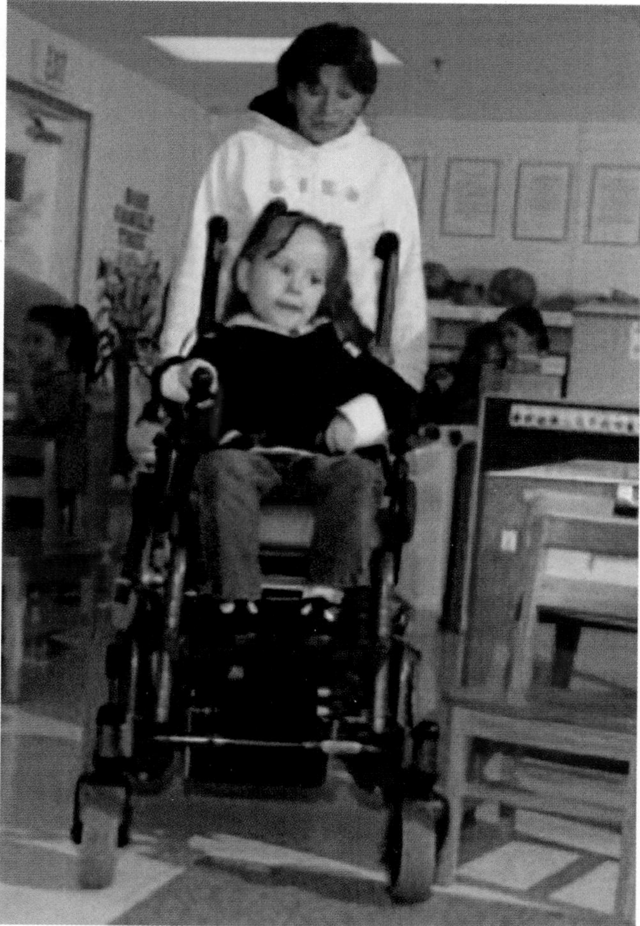

Make sure there is room for children in wheelchairs and with walkers to dance with the group.

Adapting to Special Needs

Creative movement activities are easily adaptable to meet special needs. Susan Koff (2000) points out that the power of creative movement is that it allows all children a way to express themselves nonverbally.

Physical limitations. For children with limited physical control or strength alter the environment.

Eliminate hazards, such as low objects that could trip children. Make sure there is room for wheelchairs and walkers to move in the same way as the rest of the children.

Keep the environment consistent so children come to know where furniture and objects are located.

Reduce distances and heights that might be expected in the activity.

Put low-pile or indoor/outdoor-type carpeting on the floor to cushion falls and prevent slippage.

Use helpers, either peers or adults, to provide gentle support by holding a hand or shoulder or to push a child in a wheelchair.

Spatial awareness. For children having trouble maintaining their position in an open space, try moving in circles or along the edge of an area rug. Make lines and shapes using tape or paint on the floor for children to follow.

Visual disabilities. Have children hold on to a rope, ribbons, or scarves. If children have difficulty balancing their bodies, provide a bar or study table they can hold onto as they move or alternatively, pair children up so everyone, including the child with limited vision, has a buddy.

Deafness. Children who are deaf can participate fully in creative movement activities with minimal changes. Naomi Benari (1995) notes that having in place large clear visual signals for starting and stopping are essential. She suggests a raised arm or drumstick. Take extra time to be sure children who are deaf understand what each sign means. Play games such as "Follow the Leader" or "Eyes on Me" which require the children to keep their eyes on the teacher as they move. Benari advises using music with a low, loud beat such as Caribbean and African music. Children can also hold on to a piano or kettledrum while moving.

Making Plans

ONE-ON-ONE ACTIVITY PLAN: Body Part Match Up

WHO? Group composition age(s): Infant 6 months to 12 months
Group size: One infant one adult

WHEN? Time frame: 5 minutes

WHY? Objectives: Children will develop

- physically, by learning how to move different parts of the body. (Bodily-Kinesthetic)
- socially, by responding to the motions of others. (Interpersonal)
- emotionally, by developing confidence in their ability to control movements. (Intrapersonal)
- spatial awareness skills, by locating the position of body parts. (Spatial)
- auditory awareness skills, by moving to music. (Musical)
- language skills, by learning the names of body parts. (Linguistic)
- cognitively, by answering a question using movement. (Logical-Mathematical)
- dance skills and knowledge, by learning how to control arm movement. (Content Standard 1)

WHERE? Setup: Sitting opposite each other on a mat, blanket, or rug

WHAT? Materials: None

HOW? Procedure:

Warm-Up: Adult touches nose and says "Nose." Ask, "Can you touch your nose?"

What to Do: Touch another body part such as the ear. If the child can imitate two motions, add a third, such as head. Now repeat, saying each body part as you touch it. Slowly create a rhythmic pattern that the child can follow, such as nose, ear, head, head, ear, nose, and so on. To add to the activity play a rhythmic piece of music to accompany the game. If the child cannot touch his or her own body part, then the adult can guide the child's hand. Encourage the child to initiate touching another body part and add it into the movement pattern.

What to Say: Give lots of positive feedback. "Yes, that's your nose. You found it!" Ask, "What other body parts can you touch?"

Transition Out: End the movement activity by saying, "Now we know more about our body. Next time what body part should we touch?" Repeat this activity often until the child reaches a level of proficiency.

ASSESSMENT OF LEARNING

1. Does the child touch the body part that is named?
2. Can the child repeatedly touch the body parts in order?
3. Does the child initiate touching other body parts?

Creative Movement Activities for Infants

Creative movement is a natural way to interact with infants and young toddlers who are still mainly sensorimotor learners.

Monkey see. Make a movement and encourage the child to imitate you. If the child does not respond, imitate the motions the child is making. This can be done with or without music in the background.

Rock together. Hold the child's hands and move together to music of different kinds. The child can be lying on a blanket, sitting, or standing for this activity.

A rope or tape on the floor helps children control their movements and guides those with special needs.

Making Plans

GROUP MOVEMENT SEQUENCE: *Space Ball*

WHO?	**Group composition age(s):** Preschool **Group size:** 7 to 10
WHEN?	**Time frame:** 15 minutes
WHY?	**Objectives:** Children will develop • physically, by learning to control the position of their body in space. (Bodily-Kinesthetic) • socially, by sharing their creative ideas with others. (Interpersonal) • emotionally, by developing confidence in their ability to control their movements. (Intrapersonal) • spatial awareness skills, by learning how their body occupies space. (Spatial) • auditory awareness skills, by matching movements to a rhythm. (Musical) • language skills, by learning the words for above, below, in front, and behind. (Linguistic) • cognitively, by planning a sequence of movements. (Logical-Mathematical) • dance skills and knowledge, by learning about the element of space. (Content Standard 1)
WHERE?	**Setup:** A large, open carpeted area
WHAT?	**Materials:** A hula hoop for each child
HOW?	**Procedure:** **Warm-Up:** Hold up a large ball and ask, "How is our body like a ball?" Today we are going to imagine we are Space Balls. **What to Do:** Place the hula hoops on the floor and have a child stand inside each hoop. Check to see that everyone is an arm's-length away from each other. Explain that the hoop is their planet and they cannot leave it. Have them explore the ball of space that surrounds them by reaching out in all directions to touch the inside of the ball. Remind them to reach above, below, and behind themselves. **What to Say:** "What are some ways you can move inside the ball?" "How fast can you move?" "How small can you make your ball?" Give plenty of positive feedback as well, such as "You are really stretching high." "I see everybody inside their hoops." **Transition Out:** Give the stop signal followed by the listen signal. Give the whole group positive feedback on responding to the signal and then describe what you saw happening. Ask children what else the hoop could be and choose an idea to try the next time they are Space Balls.
ASSESSMENT OF LEARNING	1. Do the children stay inside of the hoops? 2. Do the children move smoothly from one level to another while stretching? 3. Take a video of each child for their portfolio to be compared to their performance after five or more body-in space-exploration experiences.

First counting. Ask the child to move a certain number of body parts in a specified way, such as "Wave one hand" or "Shake two feet." With young infants gently help them respond.

Creative Movement Activities for Toddlers

Energetic toddlers are always moving. Tap into that energy with movement activities that let them jump and wiggle.

Play pretend. Together, pretend to be some familiar thing that moves in interesting ways and invent movements to express it (see Table 11-5).

Beginning balance. Develop balancing skills by placing a rope on the floor and have the children imagine it is a "tightrope" to walk.

Beanbags. Try moving in different ways with a soft beanbag on the head, arm, shoulder, foot, and so on. Stay relaxed; part of the fun is having it fall off again and again.

Making Plans

RESPONSIVE GROUP ACTIVITY PLAN: Under the Sea

WHO? **Group composition age(s):** Primary age—1st or 2nd grade

Group size: Whole class 20 to 25

WHEN? **Time frame:** Three days, about an hour a day

WHY? **Objectives:** Children will develop

- physically, by moving their bodies with varying force in rhythmic ways. (Bodily-Kinesthetic)
- socially, by combining their ideas to create a unified presentation. (Interpersonal)
- emotionally, by developing self-confidence in their ability to communicate through movement. (Intrapersonal)
- spatial awareness skills, by learning how to locate their bodies in relation to one another. (Spatial)
- auditory awareness skills, by listening and moving in concert with the music. (Musical)
- language skills, by describing their ideas and how they used the element of force. (Linguistic)
- cognitively, by designing a sequence of movements to express an idea. (Logical-Mathematical)
- movement skills and knowledge, by creating an original creative dance sequence using the element of force, which communicates an idea. (Content Standards 1, 2, and 3)

WHERE? **Setup:** Large, open space in the classroom, outside, or in a gym

WHAT? **Materials:** A small glass fishbowl with a goldfish, an overhead projector, a clear glass pan, chart paper, and markers

HOW? **Procedure:**

Warm-Up: Set up a small fishbowl with a goldfish in it. Place it on the overhead projector. Have students observe the fish and describe how it moves. On chart paper write down their descriptions.

What to Do: *Day 1*—Following the fish observation, lead an open-ended guided movement activity: If you were a fish, how would you move? Before starting, review the start/stop/listen/rest signals. Have students stand in a large circle and remain in the circle as they move. After guiding them, play the musical selection *The Swan* from the *Carnival of Animals* by Camille Saint-Saens as they swim around the room. After a few minutes, have the children sit on the rug and share how it felt to be a fish.

What to Say: Guiding questions: "How would you swim?" "How would you turn?" "How would you move if you were resting?" "How would you move if you were being chased by a predator?" "How would you eat your food?"

What to Do: *Day 2*—On chart paper write the heading Effort and the words *attack, tension, release,* and *relax* below it. Have different students act out these different words with their bodies. Put students in groups of three or four and pass out books about sea life. Have students choose a fish or sea creature from the book and then as a group work out how that creature might move. Challenge them to include all four of the effort words in their movement. Allow about 10 minutes for them to explore different ways to move. Then have the group come together on the rug and have each group share the movement they created. Look for examples of effort.

What to Say: "When would a fish be relaxed?" "How does your body feel when you attack or when it is under tension?" "Does it feel similar or different?" "Does it feel good to release the tension from your body?"

What to Do: *Day 3*—Set up the overhead projector and place the glass dish on top with a small amount of water in it. Project it on a screen or bare wall. If possible, darken the room. Stir the water to create ripples on the wall. Have the groups from the day before get together and perform their movement in the ripples. Signal listen and have the students decide how they could all move together in a beautiful, safe way to create a sea scene. Play *The Swan* again as they dance in and out of the ripples. Videotape the performance.

What to Say: Point out examples of the different forces. Give lots of positive feedback.

Transition Out: Give the stop and listen signal and have the students gather together to watch the video of themselves.

ASSESSMENT OF LEARNING

1. Can the students incorporate the different forces into their movements?
2. Do they include everybody's ideas in their movements?
3. Do they move in rhythm to the music?

Teacher Tip

IS IT CREATIVE MOVEMENT?

Creative movement activities allow children to be creative and make kinesthetic decisions. In selecting activities, ask the following questions:

1. Are the children free to move all parts of their bodies within safe limits?
2. Can the children make their own decisions about how to move?
3. Can the children express their own ideas?
4. Can they do it without tedious practice?
5. Are there a multitude of acceptable movements and few or no incorrect ones?

TABLE 11–5 Creative Movement Starters

Here are some ideas to get the children moving. Ask them how would it feel to be a __________? How would it move?

Cloud blowing	Parachute collapsing
Balloon escaping	Plane flying
Bird peeking	Popcorn popping
Cat washing itself	Puppet collapsing
Butterfly fluttering	Snake wriggling
Detective sneaking	Snowflake floating
Egg hatching	Spider creeping
Gelatin wiggling	Turtle lumbering
Helicopter hovering	Water dripping
Ice cube melting	Wind-up toy running down
Leaf falling	Worms burrowing

Partner up. Hold the child's hands and have child put their feet on top of yours. Then move together in different ways. Try sliding, hopping, and wiggling.

Creative Movement Activities for Preschool and Kindergarten

For older children it is an excellent way to use kinesthetic memory in learning facts and concepts in all subject areas.

Body shapes. Have the children try to make their bodies into different shapes, such as a ball, a square, and a triangle.

I can be the alphabet. Have the children lay flat on the floor. Call out a letter of the alphabet and have them try to make their bodies into it. For some letters, such as M and W, have them work in pairs.

Balancing challenge. Lay out a rope or piece of tape on the floor. Challenge the children to try to move in different ways while keeping one or both feet on the line, such as hopping, walking backwards, walking with eyes shut, and so on.

Worms. After looking at worms, snakes, snails, or other wiggly creatures, have the children hold hands at their sides and wiggle around on the floor. Explore the forces of tension and release. Have the children think of other wiggly things they could be. Add rhythmic music as they explore this way of moving.

Growing. Have some children imagine they are seeds or baby animals and have the rest walk around pretending to water them or feed them. Each time they get nourished they should grow a little bit. Slowly tap a drum as they grow.

Floating. Have each child stand in a hula hoop or designated spot and imagine how a feather, balloon, winged seed, leaf, or other floating, falling object would move. Focus on moving from level to level smoothly with control. After they have explored their ideas, add clapping, drum beats, music, or props for practicing.

Tip tap. After the children have had time to explore the different levels with their bodies, have them practice moving from level to level by tapping a drum and calling out up, middle, or down. Vary the speed of the taps, getting faster as they gain more control. Use the same method to practice other contrasting movements, such as turning left and right, forward and back, attacking and releasing, and so on.

Left-right. Put a sticker on every child's right hand. Have the children stand in a circle. Ring a bell or make some other kind of a signal to indicate when to move. Call out "right leg" as you signal and everyone should put in their right leg. After a few times have the children be the leaders. As they gain control add more movements, such as "right leg then left leg." Older children can work in pairs to invent their own right-left movement pattern to try with the group.

Teacher Tip

PLANNING CREATIVE MOVEMENT ACTIVITIES

Component	Question to ask yourself
Exploration	How will you introduce the movements?
Free practice	What will the children do to practice?
Rhythmic accompaniment	What instruments, music, or body sounds will you add?
Movement control	What signals for start, stop, listen, and rest will you give?
Props	What can children use to emphasize or enrich the movement?
Extensions	What other themes or topics using these movements can you do?

Shadow wall play. Shine a bright light on a plain colored wall or sheet. Have the children move with their backs to the light watching the shadows they create.

Weather walk. Have the children move as if they were walking through heavy rain, strong wind, snow, or hot sun.

High-Low. Make a syllable sound, such as "aaa" or "eee," sliding your voice up and down. Vary the speed and intensity. Encourage the children to move up and down with the sound. Let them try making their own sliding sound to accompany their movements. When they have good control, try moving to simple music pieces that go up and down in pitch (see Table 11-2).

Statues. Have the children move in place or about the room as music plays. When it stops, they must freeze. Give the relax signal, and then start again. Focus on the feeling of tension and release.

Wave it. Wave a scarf, flag, or long piece of paper and have the children imagine they are that object and express the movement they see through their bodies.

River crossing. Put two pieces of tape on the floor about 3 feet apart to be the banks of a "river." Walk around the room in a line and when the children come to the river invent new ways to get across, such as crawling, swimming, or using pretend "stepping stones."

Creative Movement Activities for Primary Age

All the activities for preschool and kindergarten can also be used with older children. Because creative movement is often neglected in the elementary school, children may need to start with simpler activities before trying the more complex ones suggested here. Remember to establish signals and behavioral guidelines at the start. Once in place, using movement to enhance learning is very effective.

Guess the leader. Sit in a circle. Have one child leave the room. While the child is out, select a leader who begins a dance movement. The leader changes movement at random. When the child returns, he or she watches to see whether or not the leader can be identified. When pointed out, that leader then goes out of the room, a new one is chosen, and the game continues.

Cycles. After studying one of the natural cycles, such as the water cycle, the rock cycle, the movement of the sun and moon, or the life cycle, have students work in teams to create a sequence of movements that illustrate it. Children can add props and music to

Creative movement activities bring learning alive and reinforce what children have been taught. As they move their bodies we can assess this knowledge. Here two preschoolers demonstrate that they know how frogs leap.

enhance their performance. Remember to point out how they use the different dance elements in their creative movements.

Systems. Have individual or groups of students read and learn about one part of a system being studied, such as the solar system, a bee hive, a transportation system, a machine, the rainforest, and so on. After learning about the specified part, the students should create a creative movement sequence to represent that part. When everyone is ready, call each part in a logical order. Have each add their unique movements until the whole system is up and running.

Making a Connection

TRANSITIONS

Use movement to transition from one activity to another.

Rest time. Move slower and slower until you come to a complete stop at the resting place.

Quiet moves. Tiptoe from place to place or imagine being a quiet animal like a bunny or mouse.

Lining up. Form a train with the teacher or child leader as the engine.

Gathering on the rug. Move in slow motion or, in contrast, imagine being rockets blasting off and landing on the rug.

Leaving the rug. Take tiny steps or giant steps to the next activity.

THE CREATIVE DANCE EXPERIENCE

Dancing is moving to music in a repeated pattern or using formal positions. Knowing the steps to a dance allows us to easily move in concert with other people. However, for young children, learning to dance should not be for the purpose of public performance or learning perfect steps, but rather to learn how to better control their bodies, and thereby find joy in moving to the music with others.

Selecting Developmentally Appropriate Dances

Young children learn to dance much as they learn to sing a song. They begin by tagging on, repeating one or two of the main movements of the dance over and over. A child attempting to waltz may sway back and forth. Over time and with practice they will slowly add more parts to the dance until they have mastered the entire piece. Dances for the very young should consist of one to three basic movements that match the beat of the music and be open-ended enough that children can invent other ways for doing the dance for themselves. This turns what could be a lockstep performance into a creative arts activity. A danceable song for young

Book Box

Books to inspire creative movement.

Aardema, V. (1992). *Who's in rabbit's house?* New York: Puffin.

The characters in this tale from the Masai of Africa are shown as people wearing masks. Four and up.

Brown, M. (1982). *Shadow.* New York: Macmillan.

A mystical view of shadows, set in Africa and featuring African dance and masks. A perfect book to accompany children's mask-making activities. When their masks are done, turn off the overhead lights, set up a spotlight, and let the children create their own shadow dance. Four and up.

Jonas, A. (1989). *Color dance.* New York: Greenwillow Books.

Three children dance with transparent cloth that overlaps to create new colors. Follow up by giving children transparent or translucent materials, such as cellophane, sheer cloth, or tissue in a variety of colors to explore in movement activities. Toddler and up.

Shaham, S. (2004). *Spicy hot colors: Colores picantes.* Little Rock, AR: August House.

This bilingual book has a jazzy rhythmic beat that interweaves nine colors and four dance steps. Illustrated with cut paper computer-enhanced collages. Toddler and up.

Taylor, A. (1998). *Baby dance.* New York: Harper.

This book is a great example of ways to dance with infants. A father moves his baby as he recites a rollicking poem. Toddler and up.

children has a strong beat with lots of repetition. Some children's songs provide directions for how to move. An example of this type of song is All Around the Kitchen by Pete Seeger in which the lyrics provide directions for the movements. There are many wonderful children's albums that feature danceable songs from around the world (see Table 11-6).

However, do not be afraid to invent ways of moving to any favorite song or piece of music. Many songs have obvious places to insert a repeated motion. For example, Woody Guthrie's *Car Song* lends itself to driving motions. There should also be plenty of opportunity for children to make up their own dance moves to teach to others.

TABLE 11–6 Music For Dancing

Artist	Album	Description
Kimbo and others	*Folk Dance Fun*	Very simple dances with directions.
Pete Seeger	*American Folk, Game, and Activity Songs for Children*	These are all the traditional dance songs of early childhood.
Raffi	*Raffi's Box of Sunshine*	A collection of all of Raffi's most well-known songs. Many are suitable for inventing simple dance steps.
Various	*Putumayo World Playground* *Putumayo Caribbean Playground*	These two albums will introduce children to the sounds of dance music from other parts of the world. Many are very danceable.
Various	*Smithsonian Folkways Children's Collection*	This contains classic children's songs sung by famous folk artists such as Woody Guthrie, Leadbelly, and others. Many are suitable for simple dances.
Dan Zanes	*Family Dance Rocket Ship Beach*	Original songs very suitable for making up your own dances. Some have motions as part of the lyrics.

Book Box

Books that celebrate dancing.

Acherman, K. (2003). *Song and dance man.* New York: Knopf.
Grandpa is a former vaudeville performer who loves to dance for his grandchildren. Four and up.

Andreae, G. (1999). *Giraffes can't dance.* New York: Orchard.
A clumsy giraffe takes dance lessons from a cricket and becomes a confident dancer. Four and up.

Boyton, S. (1993). *Barnyard dance.* New York: Workman.
Slip, slide, and jump with the farm animals in this simple board book. Infants and toddlers.

Compestine, Y. C. (2006). *D is for dragon dance.* New York: Holiday House.
A simple text and vibrant pictures tell the traditions surrounding the Chinese New Year dragon dance in this ABC book. Four and up.

Cooper, E. (2001). *Dance!* New York: Greenwillow.
A choreographer plans a dance, helps dancers practice it until perfect, and then proudly puts on the final performance. Five and up.

Gollub, M. (2000). *The jazz fly.* Santa Rosa, CA: Tortuga Press.
Animal sounds and rhymes create jazzy text as a drummer fly starts his own jazz band. A danceable CD accompanies the book. Four and up.

Isadora, R. (1993). *Lili at the ballet.* New York: Putnam.
A young aspiring ballerina shares her determination to be a dancer as she goes to practices, has a role in the school play, and goes to ballet performances. Five and up.

Reich, S. (2005). *Jose! Born to dance.* New York: Simon & Schuster.
A biography of José Limón, a Mexican-American dancer, shows how the sounds of his childhood became part of the movements in his dances. Five and up.

Making Plans

ONE-ON-ONE ACTIVITY PLAN: *Wiggle Jiggle*

WHO? **Group composition age(s):** Infant and toddler

Group size: One child and one adult

WHEN? **Time frame:** 5 to 10 minutes

WHY? **Objectives:** Children will develop

- physically, by moving their body to the music. (Bodily-Kinesthetic)
- socially, by moving together with someone else. (Interpersonal)
- emotionally, by gaining self-confidence to move independently. (Intrapersonal)
- spatial awareness skills, by experiencing different ways to move in space. (Spatial)
- auditory awareness skills, by matching movement to the music. (Musical)
- language skills, by tagging in on the song lyrics. (Linguistic)
- cognitively, by deciding how to move to the music. (Logical-Mathematical)
- movement skill and knowledge, by using the techniques and skills of dance while improvising creative movements. (Content Standards 1 and 2)

WHERE? **Setup:** Child can be on a blanket or rug. There should be space to move.

WHAT? **Materials:** A danceable song on tape, MP3 player, or CD—*Clap Your Hands* by Pete Seeger would work well for a starter.

HOW? **Procedure:**

Warm-Up: Sing the song with one simple motion such as clapping or waving or wiggling a foot.

What to Do: Sing the song again, but this time encourage the child to join in on the motion. If the child is very young, you can gently help the child move. For an older infant or toddler cue them with a sign or brief reminder: "Let's wiggle and jiggle! Move with me now!"

What to Say: "Can you hear when to move?" "Can you think of another way to move?" "Do you want to dance some more?" Be enthusiastic and encouraging with playful comments, such as "Clap those wiggles out!" "Wave those jiggles all about."

Transition Out: Stop when the child loses interest or seems tired. Repeat this activity often, introducing new songs and movements when the child is comfortable with those already learned.

ASSESSMENT OF LEARNING

1. Does the child respond with motion at the appropriate time?
2. Can the child improvise a motion?
3. Videotape the child performing for the portfolio and compare to other dance activities to assess growth in motor control.

Creative Dance Experiences for Infants

Dance experiences for infants should focus on the joy of moving together with a caring adult.

Hug me. Name a body part and hug it in a repeated pattern. Say: "I hug my leg, leg, leg. I hug my head, head, head" and so on. For very young infants, hug their body part for them. Older infants can hug themselves or their caregiver. Make up a song to sing during this dance.

Classroom Museum

Display reproductions of paintings of dancers by Edgar Degas as well as posters of famous dancers, such as Alvin Alley, Fred Astaire, George Balanchine, Milkhail Baryshnikov, Isadora Duncan, Martha Graham, Rudolph Nureyev, Anna Pavlova, Bill Robinson (Bojangles), and Maria Tallchief.

Making Plans

CENTER ACTIVITY PLAN: Dance Band

WHO? **Group composition age(s):** Preschool
Group size: Four to five

WHEN? **Time frame:** 20 minutes

WHY? **Objectives:** Children will develop
- physically, by moving their bodies in new ways. (Bodily-Kinesthetic)
- socially, by dancing together. (Interpersonal)
- emotionally, by developing self-confidence as performers. (Intrapersonal)
- spatial awareness skills, by moving within the confines of the center. (Spatial)
- auditory awareness skills, by matching movements to the music. (Musical)
- language skills, by using comparative words to describe their dances. (Linguistic)
- cognitively, by planning a sequence of movements. (Logical-Mathematical)
- movement skill and knowledge, by using the elements of dance to improvise dance sequences based on dances from other places in the world. (Content Standards 1, 2, 3, and 5)

WHERE? **Setup:** The dance center will be in a corner of the room. There is a rug on the floor and a low shelf on one side and a sturdy divider on the other.

WHAT? **Materials:** On the shelf is a simple tape or CD player featuring several Latin American dances the children have learned in a large group. There are also maracas, small drums with quiet mallets, and tambourines. Books about Mexico are displayed as well. Hanging from the divider are colorful ponchos, shawls, and Mexican-style hats. There is a child-safe mirror on the wall and posters of Mexico.

HOW? **Procedure:**

Warm-Up: Using guided discovery, introduce the center after the whole group has done one of the dances. Explain that they will be able to dance to the same music at the center.

What to Do: Children will choose this center at free choice time. They can dance and play along to the music.

What to Say: "Do you remember the steps we learned?" "Can you invent or add new steps for this dance?" "Can you teach the steps to your friend?" "Is this a fast dance or a slow dance?"

Transition Out: At the end of the day at class meeting ask the children who were at the center if they want to share any new dance steps they created. Over time add other tapes with dances from other places for children to explore. Include relevant props.

ASSESSMENT OF LEARNING
1. Can the children repeat the steps learned in a large group with a high level of control?
2. Do the children readily improvise? Do the new dances match the music?
3. Do the children have the confidence to perform their dances for the whole group?

Bouncing. Place the infant on one's lap. Put on a catchy tune and bounce the infant gently up and down to the music, providing any needed head and back support. An older child can sit face-to-face holding your hands. Bounce up and down to the music. Say "up" and "down" as you move together. Then explore other ways to move together to the tune.

Dancing feet. Play a danceable song and hold the infant upright so that the child can wiggle and kick its feet to the music.

Dance Experiences for Toddlers

Toddlers with their newfound independence need open-ended dance experiences that let them join in as they wish.

Making Plans

GROUP ACTIVITY PLAN: Learning a Dance

WHO? **Group composition age(s):** Primary
Group size: 20 to 25

WHEN? **Time frame:** 40 minutes

WHY? **Objectives:** Children will develop

- physically, by controlling the motions of their bodies. (Bodily-Kinesthetic)
- socially, by working together with others to create a unified movement. (Interpersonal)
- emotionally, by developing confidence in their ability to dance with others. (Intrapersonal)
- spatial awareness skills, by keeping their movements within a defined space. (Spatial)
- auditory awareness skills, by matching the size and speed of their movements to the music. (Musical)
- language skills, by explaining their dance step ideas. (Linguistic)
- cognitively, by repeating a pattern of movement. (Logical-Mathematical)
- movement skill and knowledge, by comparing their dances to others and making connections with other art forms. (Content Standards 4 and 7)

WHERE? **Setup:** Large, open area big enough for all children to stand in a circle at arm's-length apart.

WHAT? **Materials:** A three-foot ribbon for every child. Tape of *Jim Along Josie* by Pete Seeger or any other simple dance song.

HOW? **Procedure:**

Warm-Up: Play a brief game of "Simple Simon." Ask: "How do we all know how to do the same thing?" Talk about the role of communication in maintaining the pattern in dance activities.

What to Do: Have children sit on a rug and listen to the tape of *Jim Along Josie*. Identify the different movements of the dance—jump, tiptoe, crawl, etc. Have some children demonstrate what these might look like. Now have everyone stand up in a circle and take hold of the end of a ribbon so that all the children are joined one to another by their ribbons. Remind the children of the signals and behavior guidelines. First, play or sing the first verse of the song, practicing how to jump into the circle while still holding the ribbons. Stop and have the children evaluate their motions. If the ribbon pulled out of someone's hand, determine why. Next, practice the other motions in the same way. Finally, play the whole dance through several times until everyone is confident and having fun. If there is time, have the children suggest other verses and moves for the dance.

What to Say: "Does everyone move together?" "How far can we move and still hold on to the ribbon?" "How do we know when to jump, tiptoe, etc.?" "What other ways can we move to this song?"

Transition Out: Give the stop and listen signal. When ready, ask them to describe how it felt to all move together at the same time. Write the pattern of movement in this dance on chart paper. Ask them to find other examples of patterns in music and artwork they know.

ASSESSMENT OF LEARNING

1. Do the children adjust their movements so they all move together to the music?
2. Can most children perform their movement at the utilization level? How many are at the proficiency level?
3. Can the children find examples of patterns in the other art forms?

Buddy dance. Have the toddler put his or her feet on your shoes as you move gently to a dance tune. Then let the toddler dance on his or her own.

Shake a leg. Put on a peppy instrumental piece of music and do a leg and arm shaking dance. Toddlers may have trouble moving each limb separately and keeping their balance. Make sure the floor is cushioned and all forms of movement are accepted.

March. Put on a John Phillip Sousa march and parade around the room. Add props and rhythm instruments.

Creative Dance Experiences for Preschoolers and Kindergarteners

With their better physical control and more fluid movements, three- to five-year-olds are ready to learn simple repetitive dances that they can use as springboards to inventing their own dances.

Slow motion. To increase body control, take any dance the children are familiar with, such as *Head, Shoulders, Knees, and Toes,* and do it in slow motion. Then do it as fast as you can.

Chain dance. Have the children join hands. Put on a tune with a regular beat. The leader starts the chain off by moving the free arm in an interesting way as he or she leads the group around the room. The rest of the children then copy that movement. Have different children take turns being the leader, each of whom improvises a new dance movement.

Creative Dance Experiences for Primary Age

Children who can perform a sequence of movements are ready to learn and remember more formal

Putting a CD player in the dress-up center encourages children to create their own dance moves.

dances. Even so, start with dance games and open-ended dances before trying fancy footwork. Use creative movement activities as warm-ups. Remember that the goal is feeling part of a group, not public performance.

Open-ended line dancing. Have the children line up one behind the other. Then have the leader improvise a pattern of changing movements. Play a drum or put on a piece of music and have everybody follow his or her lead. Give everybody a turn at being a leader. Next, try an improvised dance in which everyone holds hands and moves around in a circle.

Free waltzing. Play a waltz and have the students invent a dance step that matches the one two three beat. Try other types of dances.

Obstacle course dance. Create an obstacle course in a large space such as a gym. Include cloth tubes to crawl through, small trampolines, balance beam, ramp, and so on. Put mats down anywhere children are likely to tumble. Have the children improvise a dance step to a selected piece of music. When they have practiced enough, challenge them to do the obstacle course while dancing to the music. When done, discuss how they had to change the movement to get through the course.

Foot mat choreography. After the children have invented a dance step, give them a large sheet of paper and, working with a partner, have them trace their feet in the various positions, and then number the steps taken in order. Give the mat to another student to try. Does the mat dance match the original dance step?

Folk Dancing for Children

Folk dance refers to dances that are at least one hundred years old and are not copyrighted. They are usually danced at informal gatherings and have as many versions as the people who dance them. In a folk dance the dancers can stand in many different ways: in a circle, a square, a spiral, a line, or two facing lines. Sometimes there may be a caller or leader, and selected participants may dance in small groups of four, as partners, or as solo dancers.

Folk dancing teaches children how to move in a pattern while maintaining a constant rhythm.

The predictability and rhythm of the movement and the accompanying song or music helps children learn the sequence of steps and practice counting.

The best way to introduce young children to this kind of dancing is to start with simple singing games in which the song cues the children how to move. Examples of these kinds of games include the well-known *Ring-Around-the-Rosie* and *London Bridge is Falling Down* See Table 11-7 for other examples.

Follow this by introducing the concept of line dancing by having the students march to different dance tunes. When they seem comfortable with the rhythm of a tune, have them form two lines and face each other when dancing. This naturally leads into circle dances. Finally, introduce four- and two-partner dances.

The Dance Steps

When selecting folk dances, look for ones that use basic movements. If you wish to try a dance and the moves are too complicated, don't be afraid to simplify them or even invent your own steps to a song or type of music. Here are some basic steps found in many folk dances:

- **Slide**—In this move one foot moves away from the other and then the other foot moves over to join it. You can slide in any direction and for any number of steps. This is best taught by standing with your back to the children.

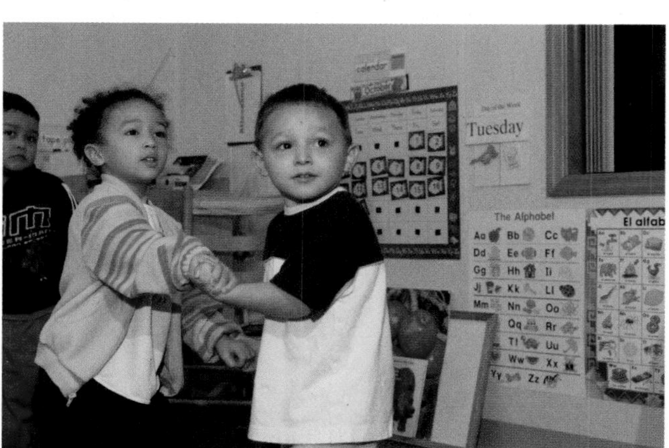

Working with a partner, such as in simple singing games and folk dances, allows children to match their movements with one another.

- **Skip**—This move is very hard to describe in words. Basically, you take a step, hop with a rocking motion on the back foot, then bring that foot forward so you can hop on the other. The hop is shorter than the move and uneven in feel. Skipping is one of the last large motor skills children develop, so be accepting of all children's attempts. Holding a child's hand and slowly skipping with him or her as the motion is rhythmically described is one way to help children improve their skipping.
- **Step-Hop**—Although like a skip, the step-hop is evenly balanced. The step and hop are equal in timing. Once children can skip, play an even 1-2 beat on a drum or clap until they can match the beats.
- **Cross-Kick**—The foot is kicked out and across the body with the toe pointing outward at a slight angle to the body. Other kicks include back and front. This step requires children to be able to balance on one foot. It helps to have children hold hands or lock elbows in the beginning.
- **Jumps**—Some dances involve jumping in place or forward or back on both feet. The Bunny Hop is an example of a dance built on jumps.
- **Taps**—The dancer taps toe or heel on floor to make a tapping sound. This is the basis of tap dancing in which shoes have metal plates to emphasize the sound.

Dealing with Gender

Many traditional dances specify different roles and positions based on gender. However, there is no reason to follow these dictates. Instead of separating them into boys and girls, have children line up randomly or have them count off by twos.

Process Not Performance

For children, moving creatively through dance is the process of learning how to control their bodies in space as well as a delightful way of expressing themselves. As they whirl about the room with their peers,

TABLE 11–7 Dances for Young Children

Singing dance games	*Looby Lou* *London Bridge is Falling Down* *Muffin Man* *Pop Goes the Weasel* *Pussy Cat, Pussy Cat* *Ring Around the Rosie* *Round and Round the Village* *Skip to My Lou* *The Snail* *Thread Follows Needle* *Farmer in the Dell* *Head, Shoulders, Knees, and Toes* *Hokey Pokey*
Line dances	*Grand March* *I See You* *Virginia Reel* *Noble Duke of York*
Ethnic Folk dances	*Ach' Ja!* (German) *Carnavalito* (Bolivia) *Chiapanecas* (Mexico) *Chimes of Dunkirk* (Belgium-French) *Danish Dance of Greeting* (Denmark) *Hora* (Israeli) *Swedish Clap Dance* (Sweden)

Dance steps and recommended music for these dances and many others can be found at http://lloydshaw.org/Catalogue/Alpha_Index.htm.

they do not need to worry about how they appear to others. However, expecting them to perform these same movements in front of an audience instantly changes the focus from process to product.

Anyone who has ever attended a dance recital for young children knows that children and teachers become nervous and stressed in such situations. As an alternative to staged performance, consider having parents partner with their children, and together perform creative movement activities or learn simple dances.

CONCLUSION: LET'S DANCE!

> *We do not simply inhabit our bodies; we literally use them to think with.*
>
> —*Jay A. Seitz (2000, p. 23)*

The power of creative movement and dance is immense in terms of developing children's ability to think spatially. Yet, it is often the one art form that is missing from young children's educational experience. If children do movement activities, it is usually in the form of simple dance games with little input from the children themselves. Although *Head, Shoulders, Knees, and Toes* and *Ring Around the Rosie* are perfectly fine simple movement activities for young children, they are not all that creative movement education can be. Creative movement and dance must allow children to think with their bodies. The teacher of creative dance must be willing to improvise along with the children. The best dance activities happen when the teacher watches what the children are doing and builds on their ideas, adding props, music, and enthusiasm as needed.

Remember too that dance happens in a fleeting moment. Unless it is caught on video, there is no record of it happening. There is no artwork to hang on the wall or tune to hum. Today with digital photography, there is more opportunity than ever to capture the imagination of children as they discover the potential of their bodies to communicate ideas and express feelings.

FURTHER READING

Brehm, M. A., & McNett, L. (2007). *Creative dance for learning*. New York: McGraw-Hill.

This comprehensive book on dance covers all the theory and techniques as well as explains how to use creative movement to enhance learning and foster group cooperation.

Fraser, D. L. (2000). *Danceplay: Creative movement for very young children*. Lincoln, NE: Author's Choice Press.

This book provides simple ways of moving creatively with infants and young toddlers.

Goldman, E. (2004). *How others see us: Body movement and the art of communication.* London: Routledge.

Take an interpersonal journey of discovery as you explore how you communicate through your body. Goldman explains the complexity of gesture and how to blend the movement of our bodies into a unified whole.

Kaufman, K. A. (2006). *Inclusive creative movement and dance*. Champaign, IL: Human Kinetics.

Karen Kaufman gives a detailed overview of creative movement for children and adults and then explains how to adapt movement activities for those with physical disabilities.

Sanders, S. W. (2002). *Active for life: Developmentally appropriate movement programs for young children.* Washington, DC: National Association for the Education of Young Children.

Although focused on physical development rather than artistic expression, this book provides useful information on selecting, organizing, and assessing movement activities for young children.

For additional information on teaching creative dance to young children visit our Web site at http://www.cengagebrain.com

TEACHING IN ACTION

Open-Ended Creative Movement in Action

The Bridge: After visiting a bridge or learning about bridges, have children stand in two lines about 3 feet apart. Play a slow, gentle piece of music and ask children to slowly reach across to the child opposite and join hands to make a bridge. They can make their bridge at any height. As the music plays they should sway with their bodies. Now, have the children go under the bridges one at a time to get to the other end where they form a new bridge with a partner.

The Machine or Robot: Have each child think of a machine-like movement and a sound to go with it. Establish a start and stop signal and then have them practice their movement. Now ask everyone to touch someone else to become part of a giant machine or robot.

Dancing Dolls: Put out a variety of materials, such as paper, wood, metal, cloth, stuffing. Have children feel these and study how they move. Ask: "Which are rigid?" "Which are flexible?" Have children choose one of the materials and imagine how they would sound and move if their bodies were made out of it. Have them explore their creative moves and then share with others. To extend the activity, have two different materials join together and move in a new way reflecting that combination.

Dance Cards: On large paper or poster board, draw different kinds of lines, swirls, spirals, dashes, and dots in different sizes, weights, and directions, as in these examples.

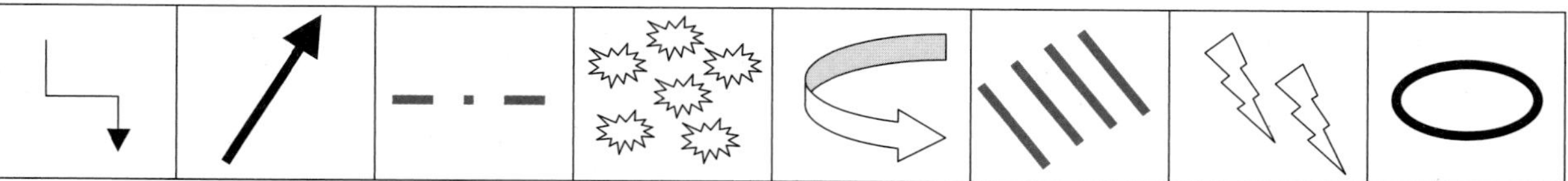

Hold up the cards and ask children to create a movement that relates to the image on the card. Repeat at different speeds and at different levels. Next, add music and move to the beat. For older children have them pair up and combine their two movements.

Creative movement and dance allows children to think with their bodies.

Studio Page

THE ELEMENTS OF DANCE

For each of the elements, give an example of an activity you could do with children that would reinforce the concept.

Movement

Space

Force

Time

Body

Studio Page

MEETING SPECIAL NEEDS

Creative movement activities can be challenging for children with special needs. Adapt each of these activities to meet the needs of the child described.

Child	Activity	Adjustments that might be made
A child who walks with crutches	Pretending to fly like birds	
A child who has limited vision	Crawling like worms	
A child with total hearing loss	Moving around the room and crossing a "river" made from tape on the floor	
A child with Down syndrome	Working with a partner mirroring each other's actions	

Studio Page

SELECTING APPROPRIATE CREATIVE MOVEMENT AND DANCE ACTIVITIES

Why are the following activities not appropriate for young children? Use what you know about children at different developmental ages.

1. Teaching toddlers to square dance.

____
____
____

2. Having preschoolers perform an elaborate ballet with many parts for their parents.

____
____
____

3. Presenting an activity to toddlers in which everyone has to move in exactly the same way, at the same time, over and over.

____
____
____

4. Putting on loud music and letting a group of preschoolers run all around the classroom.

____
____
____

Studio Page

OBSERVATION: CHILDREN MOVING CREATIVELY

Observe a group of children involved in a creative movement or dance activity.

Date of observation: ______________________ **Length of observation:** ______________________

Ages of children: ______________________ **Group Size:** ______________________

1. Do the children have control over their movements as expected for their developmental age?

2. Which movements come easily for them? Which types of movements give them difficulty?

3. How do individual children express themselves through their movement choices?

4. Suggest some other creative movement and dance activities that would be appropriate for this group of children.

5. What are the adults doing?

6. How are arts activities made available to the children?

7. How did the children participate in these arts activities? (Examples: tried once then left; engaged in nonverbal or verbal interaction with children and/or adults; worked alone; length of time at activity)

Chapter 12

Nurturing the Imagination

Questions Addressed in This Chapter:

- What are the dramatic arts?
- How do the dramatic arts help children grow?
- How are dramatic arts activities designed?

"*. . .the imagination is not just a faculty separate from the mind. It is the mind itself in its entirety. . .*"

—*Gianni Rodari (1996, p. 12)*

Young Artists at Work

"The puppet I'm making is going to be a spaceman."

"So's mine!"

"Let's pretend they are going to the moon."

"Okay, but what can we use for a rocket ship?"

"How about the tall drum?"

"That'll work. Hey, we can even drum on it to make it sound like the rocket is taking off!"

WHAT ARE THE DRAMATIC ARTS?

Drama and theater are highly integrative art forms. Visual art, music, and creative movement can all be incorporated into dramatic performances. In addition, communication skills, language usage, and storytelling play an essential role. This means that the dramatic arts are a vital way to foster literacy development in young children as well as offering a way to integrate learning across the disciplines.

Historically, theatrical drama has been used most often to entertain an audience. We are all familiar with the dramatic works of Shakespeare and the movie productions of Walt Disney. Both of these are examples of the dramatic arts. However, as we will see, the role of the dramatic arts is very different in the lives of young children.

The presentation of a theatrical production to an audience is the most formal form of the dramatic arts. This level of performance, however, is not developmentally appropriate for children under the age of eight (Edwards, 1993). It requires children to memorize lines and follow a director—skills beyond the ability of most young children. Instead, dramatic activities need to be built around children's own stages of play.

Drama and Play

For young children, drama is their natural form of play. Infants play with objects, discovering their properties and uses. Toddlers imitate what they see other people doing. By the age of four most children have entered the world of imaginative and symbolic play in which objects and actions can represent other things. A wooden spoon becomes a magic wand and an old shawl a king's robe. The ability to make-believe and create stories is the main characteristic of play in young children. As a result the pretend play of young children can be seen as the root of the dramatic arts (see Table 12-1).

Play and Cognitive Development

Vygotsky studied how children's play contributed to cognitive development. He thought that the object-focused play of infants at the sensorimotor or Piagetian practice level of play represented a stage of cognitive development in which the child was incapable of imaginative thought. The object and its meaning were

TABLE 12–1 Dramatic Elements of Children's Play

Dramatic Element	Children's Natural Play
Place: Setting and props	Explores the characteristics of objects and how they are used.
Characterization	Imitates and repeats behaviors of the people around them.
Language	Imitates vocalizations of people around them.
Movement	Imitates and invents movements.
Communication	Expresses ideas and feelings.
Imagination	Invents new uses for familiar objects. Creates pretend people, events, objects, and settings.
Narrative	Takes on roles. Creates sequences of events with beginning, middle, and end.

so fused together in the child's mind that the child could not think of it without actually seeing it. He saw the emergence of the ability of children to make believe as the beginning of abstract thought. Vygotsky also believed that play promoted learning by providing children the opportunity to practice social behaviors they had not yet mastered in a safe, accepting setting. Later researchers have supported this idea. Jerome Bruner (1990, 1996) and Brian Sutton-Smith (1998) see play as the way children learn how to adapt and be flexible in meeting future challenges in their lives. Bruner has also posited that play helps children learn how to think in logical sequence as they create story narratives.

The Power of Play

Through play, children learn about their world and how to interact with it. Children at play are active, intrinsically motivated, and integrating everything they know into a new creative form. In the act of playing children develop longer attention spans and pursue interests more deeply. They develop creatively, socially, emotionally, and cognitively. Most importantly, they are having fun.

The Dramatic Arts and Developmental Growth

Dramatic play affects a child's total development. Through dramatic arts activities children develop

- **Physically**—By moving the body to characterize the movements of real and fantasy people, behaviors, and objects. We see this when children pretend they are driving a car or flying like Superman. The skills and concepts of creative dance are also intimately connected to dramatization.
- **Socially**—By learning to make connections to others through facial and bodily behaviors, by trying out new roles, and cooperating with others to create meaning and narrative. Dramatic play allows children to connect to their own culture and to imagine that of others. We see this when a group of children, after learning about Mexico, pretends they are going to the store to buy tortillas.
- **Cognitively**—By developing the ability to think logically in narrative sequences. Play also lets children create and use symbolic thinking as they use one object or action to represent another. It is powerful because it allows children to repeat and analyze their behaviors. For example, a group of children, playing with puppets, may repeat their story several times, each time trying different ways for the puppets to act.
- **Language skills**—By using language to communicate ideas and feelings, and to tell stories. In playing a part children can explore the control they have over their voices and ways of speaking. Guided participation by the teacher in children's dramatic play has been shown to increase language and literacy skills (Copple & Bredekamp, 2009, p. 14; Bromley, 1998). Organizing play around a theme with materials, space, and time helps children develop more elaborate narrative skills. Dramatic arts activities are often the same as early literacy activities. Children build a sense of story from hearing books read aloud, and from telling and acting out their own stories, and those of others. Dramatic play increases children's comprehension and helps them become aware of narrative elements (Christie, Enz, & Vukelich, 2003; Wanerman, 2010).
- **Emotionally**—By giving children a sense of power and control and by reducing stress. In dramatic play children can take on the roles of the controlling adults in their lives, they can determine what will happen in their play, and they can take risks as they try out new ways of behaving. Dramatic

For children, drama is their natural form of play. As they imitate the activities of the adults in their lives they develop socially, emotionally, creatively, and intellectually.

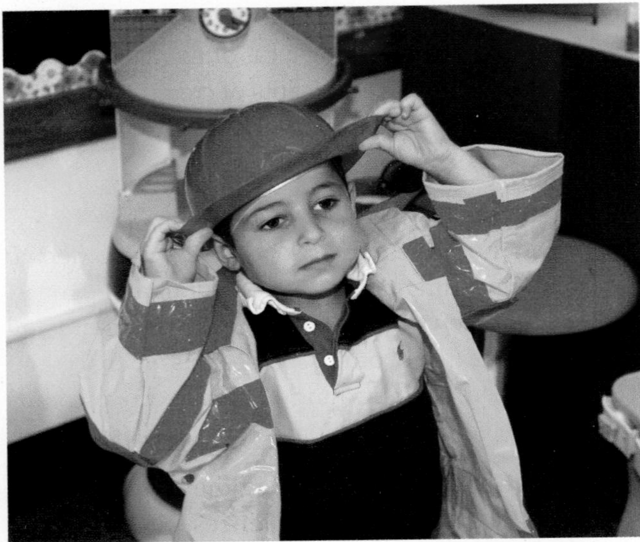

Through imagination stories come to life. Dressing up as a fireman allows a child to act out being brave, rescuing people, and putting out a fire.

play provides a setting in which children can develop independence and self-control as well as learn how to deal with conflict and diversity.

- **Drama concepts and skills**—By meeting the National Standards for the Dramatic Arts (Ponick, 2007, pp. 26–29).

National Standards in Theater

Based on the National Standards in Theater, by the end of the primary years children should be able to do the following:

Content Standard 1: Improvise dramatizations and write scripts/stories based on personal experience, cultural heritage, imagination, literature, and history.

Content Standard 2: Modulate voice, body movements, and behavior to create character roles and improvisations.

Content Standard 3: Create settings, select props, and choose costumes for dramatic play and performance.

Content Standard 4: Design and plan dramatizations.

Content Standard 5: Read about, research, and share information for use in dramatizations.

Content Standard 6: Compare, connect, and describe the visual, aural, oral, and kinesthetic elements found in a range of dramatic projects, such as pantomime, improvisation, plays, television, and films.

Content Standard 7: Explain preferences and create meaning from dramatic pieces.

HOW DO CHILDREN DEVELOP THROUGH THE DRAMATIC ARTS?

The elements of drama and dramatic play share much in common (see Table 12-1). First, to be successful as an actor a person must be able to imitate others. This requires proficiency in oral language and in controlling the body. The foundation for imitative behavior is established in early childhood as infants learn how to make themselves understood by parents, caregivers, and older children using gesture, words, and actions.

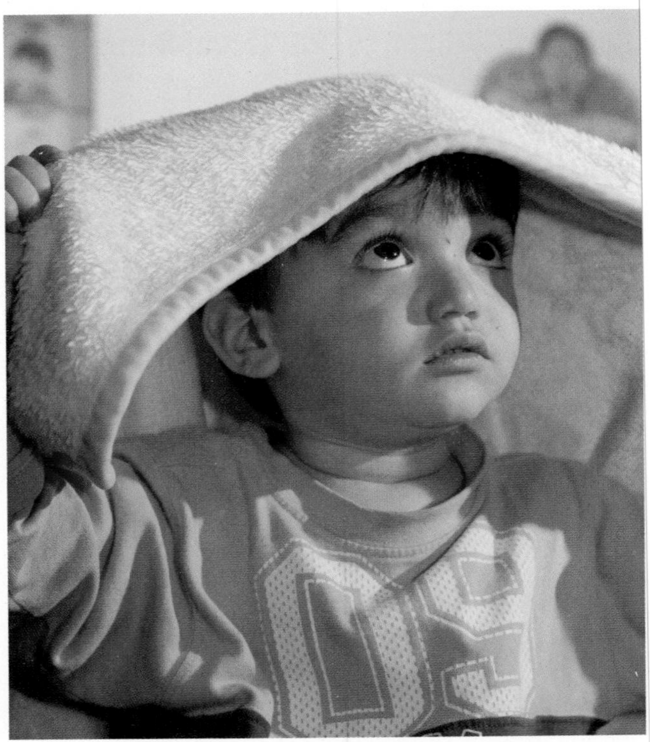

Playing peek-a-boo is the beginning of dramatic play. This child is learning to use a blanket as a prop to enhance the effect.

Second, actors also need to know how to use props, costumes, and settings as a way to enhance the meaning of their performance. Through play, the ten-month-old playing peek-a-boo with his father's hat, the toddler putting shoeboxes on her feet and pretending to skate, and the preschooler "cooking" a meal in the playhouse, are all learning how to use parts of their environment for dramatic effect.

Third, theater productions are formed around an aesthetically organized and creative presentation of a message or story. The development of narrative skills is a key feature of children's dramatic play. The toddler pantomiming falling in a puddle, the preschooler playing with an imaginary friend, kindergarteners acting out the story of *Goldilocks and the Three Bears*, and second graders writing and producing their own playlets about life in the rainforest are learning the principles of story creation and expression.

Dramatic skills develop rapidly in the early childhood years. By the age of five most children are capable of creating and performing complex stories, often sustaining them over an extended time period (see Table 12-2).

TABLE 12–2 Language Development and Dramatic Play

Stages of Play	Developmental Age	Language Skills
Based on Piaget & Vygotsky		Based on Allen & Marotz (2009) and Copple & Bredekamp (2009).
Practice Play	Infant: Birth to 4 months	Reacts to sounds Matches vocalizing Babbles when spoken to
	Infant: 4 to 8 months	Responds to name and to simple commands—eat, wave bye-bye Listens and imitates sounds Reads gestures and facial expressions Play back-and-forth games like peek-a-boo Expresses emotions "Talks" to toys
	Infant: 8 months to 12 months	Imitates noises Says da-da, ma-ma, nonsense syllables using all the consonants and vowels Recognizes name and some words Responds to simple gestures and "conversations"
Symbolic Play	Toddler	Uses gestures to get attention Repeats and uses one word, and then two-word phrases Talks to self Shows feelings in speech Speech grows from 25 to 70% understandable Responds to requests. Knows yes and no. Vocabulary grows to up to 100 words
	Preschooler	Speaks in full sentences, slowly adding adjectives, prepositions, and possessives and begins to use past tense. Changes tone to match feelings Answers questions and volunteers information Talks about things happening elsewhere Listens and makes requests in response Uses self-talk to control or direct behavior Recites nursery rhymes Vocabulary grows to up to 1000 words

(continued)

TABLE 12–2 Language Development and Dramatic Play (*continued*)

Stages of Play	Developmental Age	Language Skills
	Kindergartener	Listens and speaks with precision Tells stories Tells "jokes" Uses past tense consistently Vocabulary grows to up to 10,000 words
Game-Based Play	Primary age	Talks fluently Carries on adult-like conversations Uses mostly correct grammar Follows and gives instructions Makes up stories Tells jokes and riddles, verbal exaggerations Learns 10 to 15 new words a day with vocabularies growing to 20,000 words

**Remember: Age groups are approximate. Development is not uniform. Factors, such as previous experiences, cultural background, social relationships, as well as the child's current physical and psychological state, will determine a child's actual performance in one or more area.*

Using the Dramatic Arts to Assess Growth

Because dramatic play integrates so many of the growth areas, it provides an ideal situation in which to observe and evaluate children's learning.

Content knowledge. As children use what they have learned, teachers can observe the subject matter and concepts being used in children's play. For example, following a trip to the firehouse, a group of kindergartners playing in the housekeeping center might be observed play acting the safety practice of "Stop, Drop, and Roll" when pretending the food they are cooking is burning or children acting out the metamorphosis of a butterfly can be watched to see if they repeat the life stages in the correct order.

Critical and creative thinking. Decision making plays a key role in dramatic play. Teachers can observe the choices children make as they act out their ideas. For example, are the events in a logical order? Do the props and costume choices relate to the children's purpose? Are their choices unique and reflective of creative thinking?

Physical control. In order to play a role or imitate a behavior children must exhibit both gross and fine motor control. Pretend play provides a noncompetitive setting in which children can explore the extent of their body motion. A toddler wiggling around pretending to be a worm, or a first grader stretching as high as possible to reach imaginary apples on a tree are moving their bodies in ways not commonly found in ordinary events. Careful observation of how children handle props and move as they play can provide feedback on general physical development.

Language development. Teachers can also assess children's interest in stories and how well they have comprehended them by observing which stories are chosen for retelling and how they are reenacted. They can also observe vocabulary usage and sentence structure.

Meeting Special Needs

Dramatic activities, because they involve movement and language, require many of the same adaptations as creative movement and dance so that all children can participate fully.

Children with auditory needs. For consistency, use the same visual start, stop, listen, and relax signals developed for creative movement and dance activities. Select activities that do not rely exclusively on language. Use picture cue cards for preschoolers and word cue cards for those who can read. Visually mark the area of the performance space.

Children with visual needs. Start by making sure the children know the location of the props and the boundaries of the area to be used. Survey the area with them before beginning the activity. Give personal asides during dramatic play that let the child know where to find things. Provide a buddy and plan activities for pairs.

Joining children's pretend play is a wonderful way to enhance language skills.

Accepting differences. A large part of the dramatic arts is stretching the imagination. Challenge stereotypes by refusing to accept stereotypical responses. There is no reason that a girl cannot play the part of a boy or vice versa. With a little imagination a child in a wheelchair can fly like a butterfly.

HOW ARE DRAMATIC ARTS ACTIVITIES DESIGNED?

In the classroom dramatic play can be used to help children develop their language skills, experience the creative process, consider the visual aesthetics of settings and costumes, and much more. These kinds of dramatics activities should be designed in open-ended ways that allow children to use their imaginations to re-create and express ideas and feelings.

Informal Dramatic Play

Informal dramatic play is characteristically spontaneous, growing out of the natural inclinations of the children. It is child-initiated, but can be supported by teachers when they enter into children's ongoing play and provide facilitation, such as by joining a tea party and modeling the use of "please" and "thank you" as part of the play. Elaborating on children's pretend play scaffolds language usage and models positive ways to interact socially.

Facilitating with words. Close observation of children's play allows teachers to facilitate language skill development. For example, a caregiver might notice two toddlers playing with toy cars and making car sounds, but not using words. She might walk over to them and join in driving a car too, while asking them questions about where their cars are going.

Facilitating with props. Teachers can also enrich play by showing children how to create their own props. An observant teacher notices that a group of kindergarteners has built thrones and are pretending they are kings and queens. He puts out some paper strips, scissors, glue, and sparkly paper and invites them to make their own crowns.

Social facilitation. The flexibility of dramatic play, allows everyone to participate. Children, such as those with developmental delays or autism, may not know how to enter into group play situations. We need to be aware of potential social difficulties and be ready to step in. One way to do this is to model how to ask to join a playgroup. Another is to make suggestions that open up the play to more participants. If two children are imagining they are a shopper and a store clerk and another wants to join, the teacher could point out that there are usually many shoppers in a store. Another is to set up rules to make play fair. Vivian Paley (1992), for example, told her kindergarteners that they could not tell other children they could not play, and then enforced the rule through storytelling and ongoing discussions with her students.

Play Centers

The teacher can also set the stage for informal dramatic play by creating play centers that build on children's natural interests and everyday experiences, such as a housekeeping corner or a store. Other centers can help children learn about how things work or address concerns. For example, many children are fearful of doctor's visits. Creating a doctor's office in which to play can help children work out their fears. See Table 12-3 for other center ideas.

TABLE 12–3 Suggestions for Play Centers

Center Ideas	Suggested Age Group(s)	Suggested Props
Family (For infants, start with what is most familiar)	Infants	Baby dolls in variety of skin colors Blankets Photos of family members *Recordings of family members talking
House: giant box with door and window holes	Mobile infants, toddlers	Let children decide what to bring inside
Hats	Toddlers	Large shatterproof mirror Assorted hats, including those reflective of children's culture. *Pictures and paintings of diverse people wearing hats
Dress-up	Toddlers, preschoolers	Large shatterproof mirror Child-size clothing (cut down adult clothes so they do not drag or make movement unsafe): sleepwear, capes, scarves, suits, ties, jackets, hats, gloves, shoes Costumes: animals, prince/princess Ethnic wear: kimono, dashiki, serape, headscarf, etc.
Housekeeping (Be sure this center reflects the different cultural backgrounds of the children)	Toddlers, preschoolers	Child-size stove, sink Beautiful dishes Pots, utensils Plastic food, reflecting different cuisines Mirror Dolls, clothes, bedding, stroller Dress-up clothes, including those reflective of children's cultures *Telephone
Auto garage (Set up after a trip to the local gas station)	Toddlers, preschoolers, and kindergarteners	Toy cars and trucks Mat with roads marked on it or strips of laminated paper to be used to build roads *Road maps Toy tools Gas pump Oil can
Train or plane (Set up after a trip to a train station or airport)	Preschoolers, kindergarteners	Chairs in a line Clothing for engineer, conductor, or pilot and stewards Suitcases *Tickets *Travel brochures
Doctor's office or hospital (Set up to address children's fears)	Preschoolers, kindergarteners	Child-size table and chairs Toy medical kit and supplies Real stethoscope *Eye chart *Medical charts *Prescription forms, lab coats
Space station or rocket (Watch NASA video of life on board the space station)	Preschoolers, kindergarteners	Table and chairs for command center Computer Space suit costumes Telescope Helmets Heavy gloves *Ship log Star mural, pictures/mobiles of stars and planets

TABLE 12–3 Suggestions for Play Centers (*continued*)

Center Ideas	Suggested Age Group(s)	Suggested Props
Post Office (Set up after a trip to the post office)	Preschoolers, kindergarteners, primary	*Paper, envelopes, "stamps" "Mail box" Date stamp to cancel mail Cubbies for each child's letter Mail sack Hat, uniform
Submarine (Set up as part of *What is an ocean?* integrative unit)	Preschoolers, kindergarteners, primary	Refrigerator box with portholes Periscope Scuba equipment Flippers Fish mobiles Pictures of sea creatures Fish net Shells *Books on ocean and fish
Garden shed (Tie in with planting a real garden outside)	Preschoolers, kindergarteners	Plastic flower pots Plastic flowers Styrofoam packing material "dirt" Watering cans Spades and other garden tools Garden clothing Hoses *Empty seed packets *Garden catalogs
Store/business (supermarket, clothing store, shoe store, drug store, pet store, bank) (These centers provide a wonderful way for children to learn how to handle money and for primary students to practice making change)	Preschoolers, kindergarteners, and primary	Cash register Shelves Items to sell: empty food boxes for grocery store, stuffed animals for pet shop, medicine containers for drug store, etc. Play money White shirt for clerks *Receipt book *Paper and markers to make signs and labels Shopping basket or cart Bags for purchases Note: Primary students can set up a "factory" and make their own items to sell—writing paper, books they have written, badges, bookmarks, paper jewelry, etc.
Restaurant (This center provides a good place to model manners)	Preschoolers, kindergarteners	Table and chairs Dishes, play food or play dough, wooden spoons Toy stove, sink, refrigerator Placemats, napkins *Menu, order book Aprons, chef hat Cash register
Puppet Theater	Preschoolers, kindergarteners, primary	Put out puppets that relate to units being studied as well as materials for making puppets Puppet theater with curtains Props: kerchiefs, wands, small items *Paper and markers to make signs
Book-inspired (After reading a book with a distinctive setting, create a center that allows students to re-create the story)	Preschoolers, kindergarteners, primary	Props based on the story *Paper and pencils for script writing Arts materials and large paper to make scenery

**These items enrich the literacy potential of the center.*

Prop boxes. Prop boxes are similar to play centers in providing children with starting points for child-initiated dramatic play. They have the advantage of being easy to store and ready to use at the opportune moment.

A prop box consists of a collection of objects that will spark children's imaginations. The items can all relate to the same main idea, such as a butterfly net, a wide-brimmed hat, magnifying glass, "cages" made from berry baskets, plastic caterpillars, and butterflies. Other prop boxes can be based on an experience. Prop boxes can include child-safe objects, books, tapes of relevant music, and suggestions for use. Label the box clearly when putting it away for storage so it is immediately ready to use another time.

Prop boxes can be used individually or with small groups of children and are particularly effective when using emergent curriculum design and for the primary grades, where large play centers are less likely to be found. For example, a teacher might make up prop boxes to go with the children's literature used in the classroom as a way to provide opportunities to revisit the story through role-plays.

Addressing Diversity

Diversity and bias can be addressed through dramatic play activities by the careful selection of materials.

Play centers. Play centers can include items that recognize cultural and ethnic differences. In selecting materials, make sure that all the cultural backgrounds of the children in the class are represented. Families are usually quite happy to help out with suggestions and donations of items. Once there is representation of all family backgrounds, expand the offerings to include items from ethic groups and cultures not found in your classroom. These can become springboards for research and discussion.

Anti-bias props. In choosing culturally diverse props look for different eating utensils, ethnic foods, unisex materials for different kinds of work, realistic clothing from other cultures, and props for different disabilities, such as wheelchairs, crutches, canes, hearing aids, leg braces, and dark glasses.

Selecting dolls. Dolls for pretend play should be selected to show the different skin tones of the wide range of groups found in the United States. There should also be fair representation of male and female dolls and those with disabilities. Commercial dolls can be supplemented with "Persona Dolls" (Derman-Sparks & the A.B.C. Task Force, 1989). These are handmade dolls or large puppets that are given specific characters through the telling of their life story by the teacher. Persona dolls can be customized to represent children with disabilities, diverse ethnicities, or unique family experiences.

Having persona dolls in the class provides a way to bring up topics or feelings that would otherwise be difficult. Derman-Sparks recommends introducing the persona dolls that are most like the children in the class first. To allay first-day fears, for example, she suggests having three dolls talk about how they got to know each other and how they felt when they said goodbye to their parents. If there is a child with a disability in the class, a persona doll with that disability can offer opportunities to talk in a more relaxed way about the child's special needs and equipment.

Adding diversity to prop boxes. Prop boxes also make ideal ways to integrate multicultural materials into children's play (Boutte, Van Scoy, & Hendley, 1996). For example, seeing an interest among several girls in playing with each other's hair, a teacher could

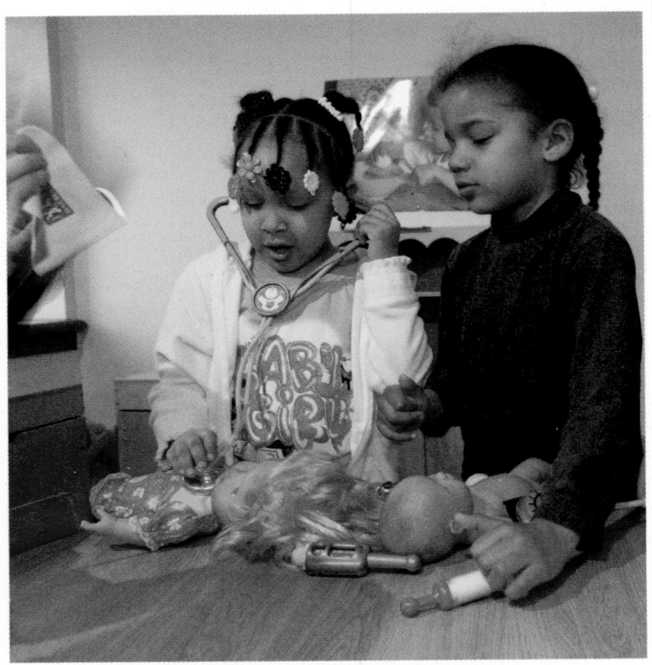

Props, such as these toy doctor instruments, increase children's engagement in dramatic play, and help children explore different occupations while at the same time helping them overcome any fears they may have about going to the doctor.

take out the hair dressing prop box. In the box are not only the typical hairbrushes, combs, empty containers of shampoos, and barrettes, but also empty containers of hair products used by other cultural groups. In addition, there could be books about hair, such as *Cornrows* (Yarborough, 1997) and *I Love My Hair!* (Tarpley, 2001) as well as photographs of men and women from different races and cultures wearing a wide variety of wonderful hairstyles.

Developing the Imagination

Mental imagery is at the core of all the arts. It is the ability to produce and act upon **sensory images** in one's mind. These images may involve one or more of the senses, such as visual, auditory, tactile, and olfactory. Although they are not real, these images can activate the same parts of the brain as do actual sensory experiences (Kosslyn, Gainis, & Thompson, 2006). The mind is able to combine, remember, and re-create such images to produce new thoughts. This is the realm of fantasy and imagination, and is the basis of literature, which relies on our ability to create mental images as we hear and read stories.

Mental imagery is used in the dramatic arts when authors visualize the characters and places in the stories and plays they write, and actors create mental images of the characters they are playing so they can become that person. In the visual arts artists plan their paintings in their minds before they begin. Dancers mentally rehearse their performance before they step on stage. Musicians and composers hear the music in their mind as they read the notes on a page.

Benefits of creating mental images. Creating mental images has been shown to be effective in improving skills, maintaining energy levels, and strengthening concentration. In one research study, first- and third-grade students who created mental images before reading a story had higher levels of comprehension (Rushall & Lippman, 1997).

Using our imaginations is also an important way to relax. When we are creating mental images, we can escape from everyday life into a world of our own creation. We can daydream ourselves into a favorite place, or do something we can only do in our dreams, such as swim deep under the sea with a mermaid. The relaxation aspect of imagery has been used to help people reduce stress, fear, and pain. Imagery has been shown to help cancer patients feel less stressed during chemotherapy, and to relieve tension during childbirth (Mandle, Jacobs, & Arcari, et al., 1996).

The power of imagery to affect our physical state has been elegantly presented in the well-known work of Ellen Langer (1989). She points out that it is our mental perceptions that influence how we see and understand the world, and not just the external stimuli around us. Langer, in particular, emphases the powerful link between mind and body. She gives the examples of the professor who felt no pain from his severe arthritis when lecturing, patients who tolerated surgical pain better when they imagined the injuries came from playing a football game or cutting themselves with a kitchen knife, and the proven ability of placebos to cure patients of disease.

Planning Guided Imagery Activities

With practice, mental images can become clearer and deeper. **Guided imagery** is one way to develop children's imaginations and get them ready for storytelling and other more active dramatic activities. It is most appropriate for children who have learned to fantasize and can remember what they have imagined, usually by the age of four or five. Start with simple visual imagery games and then proceed to more complex multisensory experiences.

Mind pictures. A good introductory activity is to have the children look at an interesting picture. It could be a photograph or famous artwork. Then have them close their eyes and describe the picture to you.

Memory pictures. Have the children close their eyes and imagine a place they have been. Then ask them to describe the place in words or make a drawing of it.

Imagining the familiar. After the children have become familiar with the classroom, have them lie on the floor or sit in a circle on a rug and close their eyes. Ask them to imagine they are walking around the room. Describe entering the room and some things you see as you walk around it, such as what is on the walls, on the desks, where the supplies are, and so on. Stop frequently and ask the children if you forgot anything. Accept all their additions to your description. When you have made a complete circuit of the room, have the children open their eyes and see if anything was missed.

Trips of the imagination. To begin an imaginary trip, have the children sit or lie down and close their eyes. Cue them to relax by saying: "Wiggle your toes. Now let them relax." Repeat for each body part moving up until you reach the head. Next, say: "Today we will be traveling to. . . . Or we will be imagining we are. . . ." Then in a slow, quiet voice describe the trip or characteristics of what is being imagined. Use many descriptive words that describe the sounds, colors, odors, and tastes you encounter. Add more complexity as the children become skilled at creating mental images.

Expressing mental images. Guided imagery is a good way to introduce arts activities. Follow up imagery experiences with opportunities to create freely such as having an open studio time during which the children can choose to express what they imagined by writing a story, acting it out, drawing a picture, or composing a musical work.

Here are some ideas for guided imagery experiences. Imagine you are:

- A cloud floating over the earth. Describe the different things you can see—birds, planes, forests, rivers, and houses below.
- Water flowing down a stream. Describe how it joins a creek, then a river, and finally reaches the sea.
- Traveling to another planet. Describe the blackness of space, the huge size of the planets as you get near to them, the stars, and the comets swooshing past.
- Traveling to a distant place. Describe all the different ways to travel. Start in a car, get on a train, then take off in an airplane, land, sail on a ship, and finally take local transportation depending on the place, such as a donkey or camel.

THE PANTOMIME EXPERIENCE

Pantomime is acting out an idea without using words, although it may include sound effects. This type of dramatic play can be child-initiated or teacher-guided and occurs when children are given cues either by the teacher as in guided pantomime, or are influenced by what has been taught, such as dramatizing a book the class read, or reenacting an event from history. One advantage of teacher-guided drama activities is that they help children explore ideas they might not think of otherwise and provide opportunity to practice dramatic arts skills. Participating in simple pantomimes prepares children for the more complex activities of role-plays and the dramatization of stories.

TEACHING IN ACTION

A Guided Imagery Experience: The Peaceful Cave

Step 1 Relaxation: Find a comfortable spot in the room and lie down. Gently close your eyes and breathe slowly and deeply. Inhale through your nose and exhale through your mouth. Now, little by little relax your body. Tighten your toes and release them. Tighten your legs and release them. Tighten your torso and release it. Tighten your hands and release them. Tighten your arms and release them. Tighten your shoulders and release them. Tighten your neck and release. Wrinkle up your face and release.

Step 2 The Journey: Now imagine you are walking into the mouth of a large cave. The floor and walls are very smooth and worn. As you walk it is slowly getting darker and darker. You turn on your lantern. The light makes the rock walls of the cave shine and shimmer. The rock is made up of bands of all different colors. As you get deeper in the cave you see on the ceiling what looks like dripping rocks. On the floor similar rocks rise up to meet the cone-shaped rocks above. You realize these are stalactites and stalagmites. Then you hear the sound of water running. You go deeper into the cave. The air is cool on your skin and you can smell dampness. You enter a giant cavern and see a beautiful lake with a waterfall at the end. The light from the lantern sparkles on the water and the colors of the rocks are reflected in the water. The waterfall makes a relaxing bubbling sound. You take a drink of the water. It is cool and refreshing. You sit down to rest. It is very peaceful and quiet. You fall asleep.

Step 3 The Return: When you wake up you are back in our classroom. Slowly open your eyes and take a minute to remember all the things you saw. End by having children share what they imagined with each other.

Descriptive pantomimes. In this form of pantomime the teacher or peer leader gives a series of descriptive statements, starting with a statement that cues them that they will be pretending, such as "Imagine you were. . . ." The children respond by inventing facial expressions and motions that reflect what is being described. Topics for descriptive pantomimes include sensory experiences, expression of emotions, characterization, and fantasy.

Begin with simple one-sentence descriptions (see Table 12-4). Be careful not to overwhelm the children by trying to do a whole string of them at once. It is better to do one activity a day, perhaps as a warm-up for a morning meeting.

More involved pantomimes can consist of extended descriptions that take the group on a journey or through a process. For example, the leader could think of a place and then guide the group around it. A trip through a castle might start by imagining crossing over the moat on a shaky drawbridge, stomping across a dusty courtyard, banging on the huge wooden doors, climbing the steps to the throne room, and bowing to the giant ogre king. Such pantomimes provide an ideal context, particularly in the primary grades, to review facts and concepts children have learned. If the children have been learning how grain becomes the cereal they eat, a pantomime might have them imagine they are a grain of wheat and go through the process of being harvested, milled, cooked and shaped into cereal, boxed, trucked to the supermarket, placed on the grocery shelf, and finally, bought and eaten.

TABLE 12–4 Ideas for Simple Descriptive Pantomimes

Topic	Activity
Senses	Imagine you were . . . Taste: Licking an ice-cream cone Eating a lemon Touch: Touching a spiny cactus Putting your hand in icy cold water Smell: Peeling an onion Meeting a skunk Sight: Peeking through a keyhole in a door Looking up at a skyscraper Hearing: In the middle of a thunderstorm Surrounded by millions of singing birds
Emotions	Imagine. . . How would you look if you were scared? How would you move if you were angry? How would you hold your head if you were sad?
Characters	Imagine you were. . . A giant dancing An ant climbing up a flower stalk A cowboy riding a horse

Planning Pantomimes

Brief pantomimes for young children can be spontaneous or even child-initiated; others will require a measure of preplanning. In planning pantomimes consider the following:

- Is the space adequate? Be sure there is enough room for the children to move actively. If necessary, outline the boundaries for movement or use a hula hoop or mark on the floor to keep the children in place.
- Do you know your audience? Be aware of the physical abilities and feelings of the children. Who is shy? Who tends to overreact physically? Adjust the activity to fit the needs of these children so everyone can be successful and potential discipline issues are avoided. Pantomime should be fun for all.
- Are there enough materials or **props** for everyone and are they safe? If a prop is part of the pantomime, such as a hat or flower, be sure to have one for every child. Make sure all surfaces are smooth and there are no sharp points. Avoid using sticks with active young children because even with care, accidents can happen.
- Can you see everyone? Pantomime has an element of spontaneity and can be adjusted as needed. By watching the children's reactions you can decide whether to expand the activity or stop it. You can also note any children having difficulty and simplify or clarify as needed.
- Can everyone see and hear you? Pantomime leaders should be active participants with the children. Use a loud and clear voice with plenty of enthusiasm.

Pantomime forces children to think of new ways to communicate concepts and ideas. What message do you think these two children are signaling each other?

- Do the pantomimes build on each other? Start simple. Build on the children's skills. When they can follow a one-sentence pantomime, add an extension as in this example: Imagine you are licking a delicious ice-cream cone in your favorite flavor (let them lick for a while)—suddenly a big dog jumps up and knocks it out of your hand. Show how you feel.
- Have you made the rules clear? Practice the start, listen, stop, and relax signals before beginning. Make sure the children know what is acceptable and what is not. Point out the boundaries in which they must stay.

The Pantomime Experience for Infants and Toddlers

Pantomime is strongly related to gesture, which is the earliest form of communication. We naturally use pantomime as we work with infants and young toddlers. We pantomime feeding ourselves when we want them to eat. We pantomime going to sleep, blowing kisses, being a pretend animal "eating" them up, and more. To make the experience more meaningful it is important to be aware of how we can use this most basic of the dramatic arts to reinforce learning and to develop creative thinking.

Doing things. Pantomiming familiar things helps children develop vocabulary and concepts. Together with the children act out ordinary actions, such as brushing teeth, eating soup, and shoveling snow. Add interest by exaggerating the movements and making silly sounds, such as slurping the soup.

Being things. Pantomiming objects in action helps children learn how things work. Together pretend to be inanimate objects. Be a clock using your arms as the hands. Be a pencil and write with your feet. Be a car steering the wheel with your hands as you drive around the room.

Being silly. Pantomiming with the total body helps develop physical control. Together act in exaggerated ways. Be a floppy rag doll or puppet that cannot stand up. Roll up into a ball and roll around the floor. Be a balloon blowing away in the wind. Be popcorn popping. Add music to enrich the experience.

Playing with props. Attach a short string to a piece of paper or a box and have the children interact with the dangling object as if it were a living thing. It can be anything the children imagine or make suggestions, such as a bird, kite, butterfly, or bee.

The Pantomime Experience for Preschoolers and Kindergarteners

For children between the age of three and six simple pantomimes that ask them to pretend to be something or do something fit well with their normal fantasy play. These experiences should be short and very open-ended. At the same time engage in pantomime often and encourage the children to contribute ideas for pantomime time.

How would? Ask the children how different things, with which they are familiar, might move or behave. How would a snowflake fall to the ground? How would a bird build a nest? How would a tall person fit under a low bridge?

Inside the picture. Have the children study a work of art and then pantomime what they would do if they were inside the picture, or select a piece of music and pantomime how it makes them feel.

Re-vision it. Take an ordinary object and pantomime using it in an unusual way. For example, use a

Making Plans

ONE-ON-ONE ACTIVITY PLAN: Faces

WHO? **Group composition age(s):** Older infant and toddler

Group size: One-on-one adult

WHEN? **Time frame:** 2 to 5 minutes

WHY? **Objectives:** Children will develop

- physically, by learning to control facial muscles. (Bodily-Kinesthetic)
- socially, by interacting with an adult. (Interpersonal)
- emotionally, by learning how to recognize emotional expression. (Intrapersonal)
- language skills, by learning how emotional expressions are described. (Linguistic)
- cognitively, by learning to match facial expression with an emotion. (Logical-Mathematical)
- dramatic skill and knowledge, by learning to control facial expression. (Content Standard 2)

WHERE? **Setup:** Child and adult sitting face-to-face.

WHAT? **Materials:** Large, shatterproof mirror

HOW? **Procedure:**

Warm-Up: Make faces at the child. Ask the child, "Can you make faces?"

What to Do: Make faces at the child and explain the emotions you are showing. Encourage the child to make faces back at you. Look in the mirror together and compare the expressions on your faces. Be patient if the child has trouble making expressions that match the emotion. This is a skill that takes practice. Do not be afraid to "clown around."

What to Say: Model what to do. "Here is my happy/sad/angry face. Can you make a happy/sad/angry face? Look at my mouth. Is your mouth doing the same thing? How do you think I look?" Express enthusiasm. "Wow, that's a happy face. What a big, big smile!"

Transition Out: When the child loses interest, move on to another activity. Play this game often. Being able to read facial expressions is an important social skill. To extend the game add hats, sunglasses, and other props to the play. Look at photographs of people and try to guess how they are feeling.

ASSESSMENT OF LEARNING

1. Does the child imitate your expression?
2. Can the child match the expression to the emotion?

Making Plans

GROUP ACTIVITY PLAN: Imagining It

WHO? **Group composition age(s):** Preschool and up

Group size: Preferably four to five preschoolers, but can be the whole group if the children are experienced at pantomiming.

WHEN? **Time frame:** 5 to 10 minutes

WHY? **Objectives:** Children will develop

- physically, by using their bodies to hold a position. (Bodily-Kinesthetic)
- socially, by working together to create a unified aesthetic event. (Interpersonal)
- emotionally, by gaining confidence to express ideas through pantomime. (Intrapersonal)
- language skills, by describing how the experience felt. (Linguistic)
- cognitively, by seeing that a whole is made up of parts. (Logical-Mathematical)
- dramatic skill and knowledge, by improvising a pantomime and modulating body movements to fit a role. (Content Standards 1 and 2)

WHERE? **Setup:** Large, open carpeted area

WHAT? **Materials:** Chart paper and markers

HOW? **Procedure:**

Warm-Up: Go outside and observe a car or truck. Look inside the hood when it is running. If possible, take a ride in it. If that is not possible, talk about how it feels to ride in it. (Option: This could be a fire truck and be done after a visit to the firehouse.)

What to Do: Have the children brainstorm a list of all the parts of the chosen vehicle. Have the children stand up and imagine they are that vehicle, and then have them pretend to drive it around the circle. Next, ask the children to work in a group. Assign each child in the group a role, such as being the engine, the wheels, the driver, the steering wheel, and so on. Have group members take turns being each of the parts. Have them add sound effects like an engine, horn, and so forth, if desired.

What to Say: Guide problem solving. "How do you think the _______ would move? How will the parts join together? Where should the driver, wheels, and so forth be?" Provide control. "Let's imagine we are driving. Go around in a circle until you are back in your starting spot." Give positive feedback. "You solved the problem of how to stay together in a workable way by holding hands."

Transition Out: Gather back on the rug and ask them: How did it feel when just you were the vehicle? Was it hard to get everyone to move together? What are some ways you used? Do you think it is hard to get all the parts of a real vehicle to work together? Follow up this pantomime with others that reinforce the idea that a whole is made up of parts, such as a computer (monitor, keyboard, mouse, plug) or cake (flour, sugar, milk, eggs). For primary students, try pantomiming systems being studied, such as the solar system, an ecosystem, or the human body.

ASSESSMENT OF LEARNING

1. Do the children work together cooperatively to make a working vehicle?
2. Can the children describe the differences in the two pantomimes?
3. Do the children understand the concept that the whole is made up of parts?

Making Plans

GROUP ACTIVITY PLAN: Communicating an Idea

WHO? **Group composition age(s):** Primary age

Group size: Whole class 20+

WHEN? **Time frame:** 2 days, about an hour a day

WHY? **Objectives:** Children will develop

- physically, by coordinating the movement of their bodies. (Bodily-Kinesthetic)
- socially, by taking a role and working cooperatively. (Interpersonal)
- emotionally, by working independently and evaluating their own work. (Intrapersonal)
- language skills, by describing and answering questions about their pantomime. (Linguistic)
- cognitively, by comparing and contrasting the pantomimes. (Logical-Mathematical)
- dramatic skill and knowledge, by designing, planning, and performing a pantomime. (Content Standards 1, 2, 3, 4, 5, and 6)

WHERE? **Setup:** Open area of classroom

WHAT? **Materials:** Materials for making props—paper, glue, scissors; chart paper and markers; 10–15 lengths of 3-foot-long ribbons or rope

HOW? **Procedure:**

Warm-Up: Review the rules for pantomimes and the cue signals. Ask the children to pretend they are any animal of their choice. Describe some ways for the animals to behave. For example: Imagine you are sleeping. Now you wake up. Look around for some food.

What to Do: *Day 1*—Follow up the practice pantomime by having the children share their animal. Make a list of the animals on chart paper. Next, introduce the terms *carnivore, herbivore,* and *omnivore.* Pass out picture books at their reading level about animals and have the children do research to find out whether the animals they chose were carnivores, herbivores, or omnivores. Return to the rug and on the chart label as many animals as possible. Add any additional animals they found in their research.

What to Say: *Day 1*—Why did you choose to have your animal move in that way? Have you ever seen this animal in a zoo or in the wild? Do all animals eat the same things? What do you think the animal you chose eats?

What to Do: *Day 2*—Gather on the rug. Referring to the chart paper, have pairs of children select one of the animals and invent a pantomime that will show whether the animal is a carnivore, herbivore, or omnivore. Put out the materials and explain that they can use these to make any props they need. Encourage them to add sound effects as well. Give them time to practice and then gather back on the rug. Have pairs name their animal and present their pantomime. When done, compare the different ways the pairs chose to show the concepts.

What to Say: *Day 2*—Give lots of positive feedback to each pair. Look at all the different ways our animals eat! Did everybody invent different ways to show what their animals eat? How did they move? How did they use the props?

Transition Out: On the rug have the students share how it felt to be the animal. Was it easier to show the animal eating after they learned the concept of herbivore, carnivore, and omnivore? Ask: How might they improve their characterization of their animal?

ASSESSMENT OF LEARNING

1. Do the children follow the rules and respond quickly to the signals?
2. Do the pairs work together cooperatively to create their pantomime?
3. Were the children able to identify differences in the pantomimes?

shoe for a telephone or a hairbrush for a toothbrush. Pass it around and have each think of a different thing to do with the prop.

Be someone. Have the children act out different jobs and sports activities.

Statues. Have the children move about as if they were animals, spaghetti, or made of gelatin. At a pre-established signal have them freeze and hold their positions. Walk around admiring their poses.

The Pantomime Experience for Primary Age

There is no question that pantomime offers a critical way to reinforce what is being taught across the disciplines. By first and second grade, children can create complex scenarios and can effectively take on the role of leader.

Messages. Put the children in pairs and ask them to imagine they cannot talk. Give each child a written message to communicate solely through gesture, movement, and facial expression.

Invisible objects. Have the children sit in a circle. Describe an object while acting as if you are holding it in your hands. Then pass the object to the child sitting next to you, who then passes it to the next and so on, each trying to hold it in a way that would be appropriate so that it retains its proper size, shape, and weight. For example, passing an invisible bowling ball will look very different from passing a slippery fish. Vary the activity by having the children change the object each time it is passed or do not say what the object is and have them try to guess it.

Who or what or where am I? Increase reading comprehension by having the children pantomime an object, character, or setting from a story that is familiar to everyone and then try to guess who, what, or where they are. Extend the activity by pantomiming a scene from the story.

Slow motion. Develop physical control by acting out familiar activities in slow motion. Challenge the children to line up, write their name, or eat their snack moving as slowly as they can. Vary the activity by asking them to move while shaking violently or bouncing up and down.

Tableaus. Another way to develop physical control is to study a work of art or an event in history and re-create the scene holding the pose for a minute without moving. Be sure to record the tableau on camera.

Verbs. Learn about action words by writing verbs, such as *swim, jump,* and *hop,* on index cards and giving each child a card. Have the children act out the verb.

THE IMPROVISATION EXPERIENCE

Like pantomime, **improvisation** is the representation of an idea through movements, but with the added attraction of using words as well. Like pantomime, improvisation has a spontaneous quality and calls on the creativity of the children to respond to the open-ended problems set by the teacher or peer leader. Role-playing is the most common form of improvisation, but most pantomime activities can also be extended with the addition of words.

Descriptive improvisation. As in descriptive pantomime, this form of improvisation begins with the leader describing a situation, event, character, or problem and then having the children act it out. Simple dramatic activities such as these give children a chance to try out different ways of communicating with language and help develop their ability to think on their feet (see Table 12-5).

Although for infants and toddlers one-on-one activities work best, in designing descriptive improvisations it is better to have older children perform in small groups or pairs because they will naturally be noisier than when pantomiming, which is done in relative silence. Alternatively, children can take turns performing their improvisation. Another effective method for some activities is to have the children form two concentric circles facing each other.

Role-plays. Role-plays are more involved than simple improvisations. They are most appropriate for kindergarteners and up who are able to work together in a small group.

Role-plays take more preparation than simple improvisation. In a role-play a pair or small group of children are assigned particular roles to play. For example, one child could be a current student and the other a new student to the school. Once roles are assigned the group is given a **scenario** or situation and each child acts how they think their character would. Role-plays can be used to help children develop dramatic skills, assist children in solving social problems, and help present concepts being studied in a fun and visible way (see Teacher Tip Box).

TABLE 12–5 Suggested Ideas for Descriptive Improvisations

Dramatic component	Suggested Age Group	Ideas
Voice control	All	Can you talk in a really. . . ? • High voice • Quiet voice • Low voice • Loud voice Can you make your voice sound like you. . .? • are underwater • are a robot • are out of breath • have a mouth full of food • are roaring like a lion • are chirping like a bird
Characterization	Preschool and up	Imagine you are a. . . . What would you say? How would you move? • Talking animal • Police officer (or any occupation) • Alien (or any fantasy creature) • Character from a book
Events	Preschool and up	Imagine you were. . . . Act out what you might do. • Meeting someone new • In the store (or any familiar place) • A king in a story (or any familiar character) • Driving in your car • Making the biggest sandwich in the world • Light as a feather

Teacher Tip

IDEAS FOR ROLE-PLAYS

Area	**Ideas to Try**
Dramatic Skills	Four children go for a walk in the woods and meet a friendly bear
	Two children are on a picnic and three large ants sneak in and eat their lunch while they are off playing
	Two space explorers are exploring a new planet and meet an alien
	Two workers are in a factory and the machine (played by two students) breaks down
	Two children are swimming in a lake and meet a talking sea serpent
Social Skills	A bully is bothering a child in a lower grade and two children come to help
	A family is eating dinner and a hungry person comes to the door
	A family is shopping in a huge store and one child gets lost
	Two children are on their way to school and one remembers a forgotten book bag
Content-Based	A family is traveling to Mexico (or any region or country being studied)
	A person is reading a book and several characters jump out and start talking to him or her

In designing role-plays try to make sure that the roles are equal in importance. When a role choice has to be made, a fair method is to write the roles on pieces of paper and have the children draw them out of a hat. This eliminates difficulties that can arise when children feel one part is more attractive than another. As children learn how to be more cooperative, they can be given the choice of roles.

Using Props for Improvisation and Role-Play

Props play an even more important role in improvisation than in pantomime. Children may feel more self-conscious when speaking a role than they did in pantomime in which they had to think only about what to do with their bodies. Props draw attention away from the performer and make the action clearer. For example, children who are asked to take the roles of different community workers will feel more confident if they can wear a piece of clothing or hat that reflects that occupation. Prop boxes can be an important resource for role-plays. In addition, children can use their imaginations and choose objects they find around the room to be props, such as substituting a yardstick for a cane. Art materials can be used to create masks, hats, paper costumes, and simple scenery as well.

Masks

Masks, like props, allow children to express themselves in ways that they might not otherwise. Behind a mask, children can feel like they are someone else; they may try acting in a new way or attempt things that might be too frightening barefaced.

Making their own masks and props allows children to express their creativity. Large eye openings, such as in this paper bag mask, not only make the mask safer, but also allow children to feel less enclosed.

Commercial masks have sanitary problems when used by more than one child, and often feel suffocating. Instead, encourage the children to make their own masks. Mask-making activities can be done with small groups working at a center, or by individual children who need to create masks to meet some particular requirement of their own self-selected dramatic play activities or for a role-play.

Materials for masks. Masks can be made from stiff construction paper, tag board, cardboard, or large paper bags in which eyeholes have already been cut. Chapter 9 explains how to make a papier-mâché mask. Paint, marker, and materials from the collage center, such as yarn for hair, can enhance the character.

Type of masks. Children can make three basic masks independently, requiring only a little assistance for the fitting.

1. **Stick mask.** Provide children with face-sized pieces of construction paper or tag board precut into circles, ovals, and other geometric shapes. Eyeholes (see following) should be precut. Create the character using crayon, marker, collage materials, or paint. Then glue the mask to a sturdy strip of cardboard or rolled up tube made from tag board. To use, the child holds the mask in front of his or her face. The tiger mask on the cover is an example of this type of mask.
2. **Paper bag mask.** Use large paper grocery bags with pre-cut eyeholes. Cut up the side slightly so the bag rests comfortably on the child's head. Tempera paint works well on the brown paper surface.
3. **Wrap-around mask.** Cut eyeholes in the center of a 12-inch-by-18-inch sheet of construction paper. After it is decorated, wrap it around the child's head, adding an extension strip of paper if needed, and staple it in place so that it rests on the child's shoulders and is loose enough for the child to lift off easily.

Eyeholes. Because few young children can manage to locate eyeholes in a safe, usable place, it is helpful to pre-cut the eyeholes in mask paper and bags. It is important that the eyeholes be large enough to provide safe visibility for children. Make eyeholes circle shaped, not eye shaped, and at least 2 inches in diameter, separated by half an inch. For primary students make a cardboard template they can use to trace eyes for a mask. Show them how to fold the paper and make a snip to start the hole. Note: Mouth and nose openings are unnecessary and can weaken the mask, making it more likely to tear.

Using the masks. Try to encourage the children not to take their masks home right away after making them. That way they will be able to develop richer dramatic play through interacting with the other children. By using their mask ideas, teachers can find related literature and themes to expand their play. For example, if several children have made animal masks, and others have made monsters, then an interesting zoo or circus could result. A group of robots could lead into dramatic play about outer space.

Ask questions that will help the children develop their characters. What character will you make? How will you show your character's special features? What will its eyes, ears, and so on be like? Think about how your character will talk and move. Practice being your character.

When several masks are finished, invite different characters to interact with each other. Have them role-play different situations. Which characters do you think have similar characteristics? Which ones are very different from each other? How would this character talk to that one? Do you think they would like each other? How do you think they would shake hands, sing together, go on a trip together, and so forth? How would these characters play together or how would they work together to build something? Talk about how they feel wearing the masks. Ask: "Does wearing a mask change how you act?"

The Improvisational Experience for Infants and Toddlers

Infants and toddlers will naturally add sounds and words to their dramatic play. The best approach is to enter into their play and model ways to change and control the voice while matching it to one's actions.

Faces and sounds. Together, explore making faces showing different emotions with matching sounds and words. For example, laugh for happy or whimper for sad.

Special Needs

• DEALING WITH A FEAR OF MASKS •

Adults or strangers wearing masks often frighten young children. Mask-making activities help them deal with this fear. To reassure children who are easily frightened, adults should

- make their own masks using the same materials available to the children.
- avoid masks that show gruesome features.
- always put the mask on and take it off in front of the children.
- play peek-a-boo games with simple masks.

Children may also be frightened or uncomfortable when masks tightly cover their own faces. Allow them to hold masks up to their faces. Tie them on only when requested. Always keep eyeholes very large. Some children may not want their full faces covered or may want to make goggles. Have available rectangular pieces, about 4 by 9 inches, with pre-cut eyeholes. These can be worn by fastening a paper strip around the back of the head.

Picture perfect. Clip interesting pictures of people and animals from magazines. Show a picture to a toddler and ask him or her to act the way that person or animal might act. These pictures can be made part of a dramatic play center.

Descriptive improvisation combines verbalization and action. Roaring like a ferocious lion helps children develop control over their facial expressions and vocal quality while at the same time providing emotional release.

Making Plans

GROUP ACTIVITY PLAN: News Show

WHO? **Group composition age(s):** Primary age

Group size: 20+ in groups of two to four

WHEN? **Time frame:** 2 days, about 40 minutes a day

WHY? **Objectives:** Children will develop

- physically, by controlling their bodies to create a character's movement. (Bodily-Kinesthetic)
- socially, by working together to improvise a role-play. (Interpersonal)
- emotionally, by working independently and developing personal pride in their work. (Intrapersonal)
- language skills, by developing skill in improvising dialogue. (Linguistic)
- cognitively, by developing skill in making plans. (Logical-Mathematical)
- dramatic skill and knowledge, by developing a character and improvising a role-play based on research about a topic they are studying. (Content Standards 1, 2, 3, 4, and 5)

WHERE? **Setup:** A large, open space for the role-plays and a well-supplied art center for prop making

WHAT? **Materials:** paper, scissors, glue, collage supplies; chart paper and markers; video of a local news broadcast

HOW? **Procedure:**

Warm-Up: Watch a short, recorded excerpt of a local news broadcast. Identify the different people involved in the show and list them on chart paper; for example, announcers, reporters, and people being interviewed.

What to Do: *Day 1*—Put the students into groups of two to four. Ask each group to invent a fantastic news event, such as a spaceship landing, or meeting a talking cow, and then create a newscast about it. Assign the children roles as announcer, reporter, and interviewee. Students then plan their part and figure out what props they need.

What to Say: *Day 1*—How do the people on the news program act? Do they move or talk in special ways?

What to Do: *Day 2*—At the art center students make any props they need, such as signs, hats, masks, and so forth. They can select music to play in the background and plan any special effects. Then they practice and present their parts to create a unified news broadcast. Videotape the resulting show.

What to Say: *Day 2*—Will you need a sign to introduce your part? Who will speak first? Where should you look when talking to someone on the show (in the audience)?

Transition Out: Watch the show and talk about how the show compared with the professional one they watched. What about the shows were similar? What is hard about making up a news show? How did the different parts fit together? Could we make news broadcasts about other things we study?

ASSESSMENT OF LEARNING

1. Do the children make their voices and actions fit the character of the role they are assigned?
2. Do the children plan a logical sequence of events in their news part?
3. Can the children find similarities between their work and the professional broadcast?

The Improvisational Experience for Preschoolers and Kindergarteners

Retain the spontaneous nature of children's play by adding improvisational experiences to play centers where the children have open-ended choices.

Sound effects. Add sound effects and motion to the reading of any book. If the book is about a duck, have the children quack and waddle in place every time you say "duck." This is a great way to develop listening skills.

Clown around. Make a collection of large, safe, colorful, and fun objects such as a hula hoop, bug net, plastic ladle, child's umbrella, pocketbook, silly sunglasses, and giant elastic tie, and keep them in a box labeled "Inspiration." Children can select an object and improvise a brief performance using words and movement. This box can be kept in a dramatic play center. Add a clown costume to the box for added fun.

The Improvisational Experience for Primary Age

As children mature, they are more capable of taking a role in a group improvisation. Role-plays provide a child-pleasing way to integrate subjects.

Card readers. Write a familiar word and action on index cards, such as *swim,* or *going in a door*. Pass the cards out at random and have the children say and do what the card says. Start by doing it normally. Then, after the children are familiar with what to do, challenge them to use funny voices, exaggerate motions, or do things backwards. Let them suggest other ways to act out the cards as well. This activity is a great way to practice reading skills, new vocabulary, and spelling words.

Do as i say. Have one child describe an action or character while another acts it out.

Talk back. Hand out index cards on which is written a character such as a reporter, clown, king, or troll and have the children pair up and take turns acting out their characters and trying to guess who the partner is. Characters can also be selected from stories being read.

THE STORY PLAY EXPERIENCE

Story play or **narrative drama** is based on children's own stories or on stories children have read or heard. Story play can be very simple. **Finger plays** and nursery rhymes are some of the first stories children learn. It can also be very complex. Primary age students can make up their own **story scripts,** assign roles, and act their story out using their developing reading and writing skills.

No matter what the level, narrative drama contains the following components:

- ***Characters***—There may be one or more people, animals, or fantastical characters.
- ***Verbal expression***—Stories may be told using words, sounds, or a combination of both as well as through mime.
- ***Use of the body***—The characters must act out their role through carefully planned movements.
- ***Plot***—The story is presented in a sequence, the simplest being beginning, middle, and end.
- ***Conflict***—Stories are most interesting when there is a problem or conflict that needs to be solved.
- ***Setting***—Stories usually occur in a particular time and place.
- ***Mood***—Throughout a story the characters may exhibit a variety of moods that relate to what is happening to them and around them.

Finger Plays

Finger plays are little stories acted out with the hands and fingers. These are usually accompanied by catchy rhymes. The words either give directions or suggest ways for the children to move their fingers, making the fingers the characters in the story. Because children can learn these when very young and because they involve both language and motion, finger plays are important ways to develop literacy skills. Here are some finger plays from my own childhood. Other finger plays can be found in books or learned from others.

Finger plays help children develop their language and fine motor skills.

Teacher Tip

SOME FINGERPLAYS

Open, shut them (open hands, close hands)
Open, shut them (open hands, close hands)
Give a little clap (clap)
Open, shut them (open hands, close hands)
Open, shut them (open hands, close hands)
Put them in your lap (hands rest in lap)

1 2 Tie my shoe (use finger to draw a bow on palm of hand)
3 4 Shut my door (clap hands)
5 6 Pick up sticks (hold fingers of one hand in other)
7 8 Lay them straight (straighten fingers)
9 10 A big fat hen (clasp hands together)
11 12 Dig and delve (make scooping motion with both hands)

Wiggle my fingers (shake fingers)
Wiggle my toes (shake toes)
Wiggle my ears (use hands to wiggle ears)
And wiggle my nose (wiggle nose)
That is where
My wiggles go. (wiggle whole body and then sit still)

More fingerplays can be found at http://www.songsforteaching.com/fingerplays/index.htm.

Storytelling

The next level of narrative drama is **storytelling.** Just like finger plays, storytelling is an ancient art form. Before there were printed books, it was the main way that history and culture were preserved and passed down to the next generation. Today storytelling remains an important practice in some cultures, but has been replaced by books, television, and movies in many others.

Vivian Paley (2004) has developed ways to inspire storytelling by young children. Her method begins with her own invented stories, which she shares daily with the children. In her stories she incorporates real events and problems that occur in the classroom in a fictional format. Next she sets up a storytelling center where her kindergarten children can come and dictate stories to her or another adult. At whole group time she reads the story while other children take the roles of the characters and act the story out in the middle of the circle. Paley finds that children who have participated in this process are likely to write more stories. She has also found that this is an excellent way to include children with special needs and second language learners in the group.

Storytelling and Literacy

Vivian Paley's model is an important one for teachers of young children to understand and incorporate into their classrooms. Dictation has been shown to be a powerful tool for early literacy development (Cooper, 1993). During the one-on-one time with the child the teacher can work on many aspects of literacy that best meet the needs of that child. The child gets to watch his or her words turn into letters that can be read back to others. The teacher can suggest words, model how a writer thinks, and ask questions that help the child develop the plot. The teacher can also assess the child's language development and comprehension of narrative elements. However, dictation is a time-consuming process. Elizabeth Kirk (1998) suggests limiting children to one page of dictation by gently saying to the child: "We are getting near the bottom of the page. How do you want to end your story?"

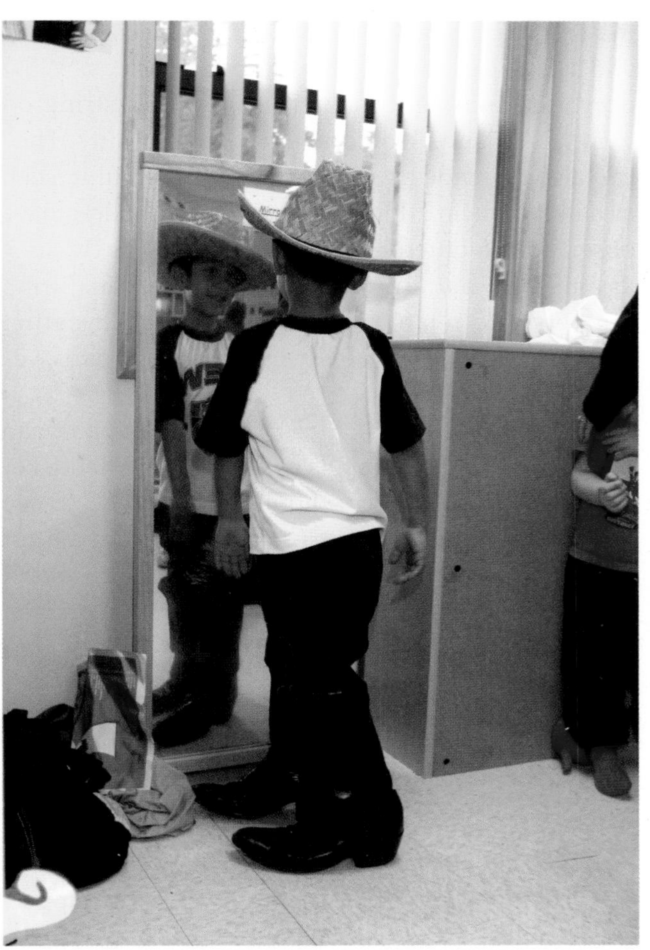

Dress-up clothes allow children to try out new roles, imagining they are characters in the books they have read.

That way everyone gets a turn at least once a week to dictate and act out a story.

Retelling Stories

Narrative drama features the physical retelling of familiar poems, fables, nursery rhymes, and stories. Enacting stories enriches children's language and develops reading comprehension (Bromley, 1998; Furman, 2000). Research by Brian Cambourne and Hazel Brown (1990) shows that retelling stories improved children's vocabulary, comprehension, and writing skills.

Children can create retell stories in a variety of ways. Toddlers often make up stories using toys or objects. Preschoolers dress up and become characters in the story, acting it out, and adding their own creative twists. Older children can write their own version of the story, creating scripts, props, costumes, and even scenery.

Puppetry

Using puppets is another way to retell or create stories. A puppet is really any inanimate object brought to life through the active manipulation of a child's hand. Most young children do not truly see the actual puppet, but rather the imaginary being it becomes through their play. Introduce children to the world of puppets by including purchased or adult-made puppets as regular visitors to the program. Puppets can share secrets, read stories, and play with the children. They allow the adult to enter the child's world. Many of the most successful early childhood television programs, such as ***Mr. Roger's Neighborhood*** and ***Sesame Street,*** depend heavily on the use of puppets.

Besides using commercial puppets, children can make their own. Making a puppet should not be a one-time activity but something the child will return to again and again in order to create a character or persona with which to face the world. After introducing puppet-making supplies at the art center, they should be available on a regular basis for whenever a child wants or needs to create a puppet. It is important, therefore, to keep the design of the puppets

Puppets come to life in children's minds. Wearing a glove turned into a puppet, a child discovers with his teacher's help, how to please an audience.

quite simple, and within children's ability to create independently, without step-by-step instruction.

Book Box

PUPPETRY RESOURCES

Almoznino, A. (2002). *The art of hand shadows.* Garden City, NY: Dover.
This book shows how to make characters from the shadows cast by your hand.

Bell, J. (2000). *Strings, hands, shadows: A modern puppet history.* Detroit, MI: Detroit Institute of the Arts.
Puppets from ancient to modern times and from around the world are shown in beautiful illustrations.

Engler, L., & Fjian, C. (1997). *Making puppets come alive.* Garden City, NY: Dover.
This book provides simple-to-follow directions for easy-to-make puppets. It also explains how to move puppets in ways that evoke feelings and ideas.

Ways to Make Hand Puppets

Stick puppets. A stick puppet consists of a shape mounted on a sturdy stick. It can be as simple as a face drawn on a paper circle or as elaborate as an animal complete with moving legs operated with supplementary sticks. For young children, use strips of cardboard or rolled-up tag board tubes for the sticks and paper shapes for the head. Children with well-developed fine motor skills can make smaller stick puppets using craft sticks as the support. Styrofoam balls can also be used for puppet heads. Show the children where the puppet supplies are, and invite them to make their own stick puppets any time they want. Suggest ways of using the collage materials to make hair and clothing. Be open to all of the children's versions of this activity. Even if it is just a scribble drawing attached to the end of the tube, in the child's mind, it is a persona. Interact with the children and their puppets to find out their intent.

String puppets. String puppets are made by attaching a string to a cut-out paper figure. Initiate making string puppets by showing a piece of string and asking carefully placed questions, such as,"What do you think might happen if you put a string on what you made? Would you like to find out?"They can also be made as part of an integrated unit, such as a unit on flying things, during which children have observed the different ways familiar things fly, such as a bee, fly, butterfly, kite, plane, and so on. String puppets also relate to topics such as the weather (wind), seasons (falling leaves, snowflakes), birds, vehicles, fish, and insects.

Shadow puppets. Stick and string puppets can be used as shadow puppets as can the bare hand. For toddlers and young preschoolers who prefer to see the effect they are creating, use an overhead projector or unshaded lamp to cast a light on a wall, in front of which they can play. Older children who understand that they can create an effect for others to see can use a shadow theater.

To make the theater place a piece of white paper over the regular puppet theatre opening or over an opening cut into a cardboard box. Use an overhead projector or a lamp to cast a light from the back. Moving parts can be attached with paper fasteners. Cloth can be wrapped around the stick to hide the puppeteer's hand.

Hand puppets. Hand puppets come in many different forms. Children love the action and reactions they get from manipulating these simple creations. Materials for hand puppets can be put out with those for stick puppets. Hand coverings can be a sock, lunch bag, short paper tube, cereal box, or juice can. The item should be able to fit over the child's hand or several fingers. Invite a puppeteer to visit, and put on a show. After the show, ask the puppeteer to show how the puppets work.

Finger puppets. Fold 3-inch-wide strips of felt in half lengthwise, and sew up along the outer edge. Cut the resulting tube into 3-inch sections. Children can slip these on their fingers. Use markers, small assorted felt shapes, or small collage items (yarn, buttons, etc.) to create the puppets' features. Cut an opening out of the bottom of a shoebox, and glue on fabric curtains to make a mini-theater.

Classroom Museum

SHADOW PUPPETRY

Shadow puppets originated in China and are commonly used in many Asian cultures today. The elaborately designed puppets are made from leather and usually have three rods to give them movement. An interactive presentation on Chinese shadow puppetry can be found at Artsedge http://artsedge.kennedy-center.org/shadowpuppets (Heathcott, 2010).

Storing Puppets

Provide a place for the children to keep their puppets, such as a box decorated as a house or bed. When it is time to transition to another activity, have the children put their puppets to sleep.

Storytelling Experiences for Infants and Toddlers

For children who are just beginning to talk, storytelling experiences should foster a love for story and a development of descriptive language.

Making Plans

ONE-ON-ONE: It's in the Book

WHO? **Group composition age(s):** Infant or Toddler

Group size: One child and one adult

WHEN? **Time frame:** 5 to 10 minutes

WHY? **Objectives:** Children will develop

- physically, by moving like the characters in a book. (Bodily-Kinesthetic)
- socially, by interacting with a caring adult. (Interpersonal)
- emotionally, by developing independence. (Intrapersonal)
- language skills, by learning vocabulary. (Linguistic)
- cognitively, by matching actions and words. (Logical-Mathematical)
- dramatic skill and knowledge, by learning how to control voice and action. (Content Standard 2)

WHERE? **Setup:** Child sitting in an adult's lap in a comfortable chair

WHAT? **Materials:** A favorite children's book with an easy to act out main character, for example the hen in *The Little Red Hen*

HOW? **Procedure:**

Warm-Up: Point to a picture of the character in the book and say: "Look at. . . What does a. . . do? "How would a. . . talk or sound?" Invite toddlers to help invent the character's motions and voice. Then act out something characteristic of that character. For example, if the character is a hen, cluck like a chicken, talk in a high-pitched voice, and flap arms.

What to Do: Read the story adding, the sound and movement and encourage the child to join in. Point to the character on the page or have the child try to find the character on the page. As you turn the pages ask the child to predict what the character might say or do next.

What to Say: "How would the . . . move? Can you do this too? Let's pretend to be the. . . . What do you think . . . will do next?"

Transition Out: At the end of the story say goodbye to the character. Next time the book is read, use the same actions or invent a new way to show that character.

ASSESSMENT OF LEARNING

1. Can the child find the character on the page?
2. Does the child join in acting out the character?

Making Plans

CENTER ACTIVITY PLAN: Story Writing

WHO? **Group composition age(s):** Preschool and kindergarten

Group size: One child and one adult

WHEN? **Time frame:** 10 minutes

WHY? **Objectives:** Children will develop

- physically, by using muscular control in acting out their stories. (Bodily-Kinesthetic)
- socially, by working with the teacher to write a story and interacting with others in telling their stories. (Interpersonal)
- emotionally, by expressing their feelings through voice and body. (Intrapersonal)
- language skills, by communicating their ideas in story form. (Linguistic)
- cognitively, by making decisions about their stories and who will act in them. (Logical-Mathematical)
- dramatic skill and knowledge, by writing a story, acting it out, and expressing preferences. (Content Standards 1, 2, and 7)

WHERE? **Setup:** A storytelling center, later on the rug. The storytelling center can be any table and chairs in a quiet area of the room or on a cozy spot on the rug.

WHAT? **Materials:** Writing supplies

HOW? **Procedure:**

Warm-Up: Model storytelling by telling stories regularly at group time.

What to Do: At the center invite the children one at a time to tell a story while you write it down. Later at group time, ask the children if they want to act out their stories. Choose children to be the characters in the story. Then read the story line by line, pausing as the children act out what the sentence says. Audiotape reading the story or videotape the performance.

What to Say: At the center ask: "How will your story begin?" If the child has trouble beginning, give some suggestions, such as "Once there was" or "One day." Encourage the child to continue by asking, "What happened next?" To help the child reach an ending, ask, "We are almost at the end of the page. How will it end?" Offer to read back what the child said.

On the Rug: Ask the child if he or she wants to act out the story. Have the child choose people to be the different characters.

Transition Out: Cheer and clap when the performance is done. Go around the circle and have the children share something they liked about the story. If a video is made, share it with the parents. An audiotape can be put in the listening center so the story can be enjoyed again.

ASSESSMENT OF LEARNING

1. Does the child tell the story fluidly or is prompting needed?
2. Which story elements does the child use? Which ones have not yet been mastered?
3. Check for growth by comparing the tape of the current performance to those done earlier and kept in the portfolio.

Family stories. Children's favorite stories are the ones families tell about events in their own lives—when the car broke down on the trip to Florida, getting caught in a thunderstorm while boating on the lake, or grandma's remembrance of her first day of school. Tell these family stories over and over. Caregivers can share stories about themselves and their families as well as learning some of the child's own stories. Tell stories about events in the life of the child too.

Making Plans

CENTER ACTIVITY PLAN: Acting Out a Story

WHO? **Group composition age(s):** Primary

Group size: Whole class

WHEN? **Time frame:** 3 days, an hour each day

WHY? **Objectives:** Children will develop

- physically, by practicing controlling the body to act like the character. (Bodily-Kinesthetic)
- socially, by making decisions in cooperation with others. (Interpersonal)
- emotionally, by developing self-control skills. (Intrapersonal)
- language skills, by reading from a script. (Linguistic)
- cognitively, by inventing new characters for a familiar story. (Logical-Mathematical)
- dramatic skill and knowledge, by writing and performing a story based on a piece of literature. (Content Standards 1, 2, 3, 4, and 5)

WHERE? **Setup:** On the rug and at tables

WHAT? **Materials:** Art center materials for making props and signs; large roll of paper to make backdrops

HOW? **Procedure:**

Warm-Up: Read a brief familiar story that lends itself to dramatization. Ask: "What would it be like if the characters were different? How would the story be different?" For example, "What if the bears in the story *Goldilocks and the Three Bears* had been aliens who did not speak English?"

What to Do: With the students identify the setting, characters, and basic plot. Assign students to groups of three to five with the task of writing and then performing a new version of the story. Demonstrate how to write each character's lines in script form. On the second day have the groups practice their new stories to learn their lines and make props. On the third day the groups will perform for the class. Videotape the performances for the children's portfolios.

What to Say: If the characters are different, do you think the plot should change too? Why or why not? How will the new characters sound and look? Will you need to make masks or puppets to help tell the story better? What is a fair way to decide who will play the different characters?

Transition Out: Cheer and clap for each performance. Go around the circle and describe the ways the retellings were the same or different from each other.

ASSESSMENT OF LEARNING

1. Do the students work cooperatively, assigning different tasks to everyone in the group in a fair way? Do they help and encourage each other?
2. Are props used to enhance the performance?
3. Do the students identify differences in the productions?

Read read read. Introduce the world of children's literature to infants from birth. It is never too early to read to a child. Read nursery rhymes, folktales, fairy tales, and traditional stories from the child's ethnic heritage. Based on oral traditions these simple stories provide an introduction to the basis of storytelling—character, setting, and plot.

Tell me. Encourage young children who are talking to tell about something they just did. Cue them with a "What happened when you. . . . ?"

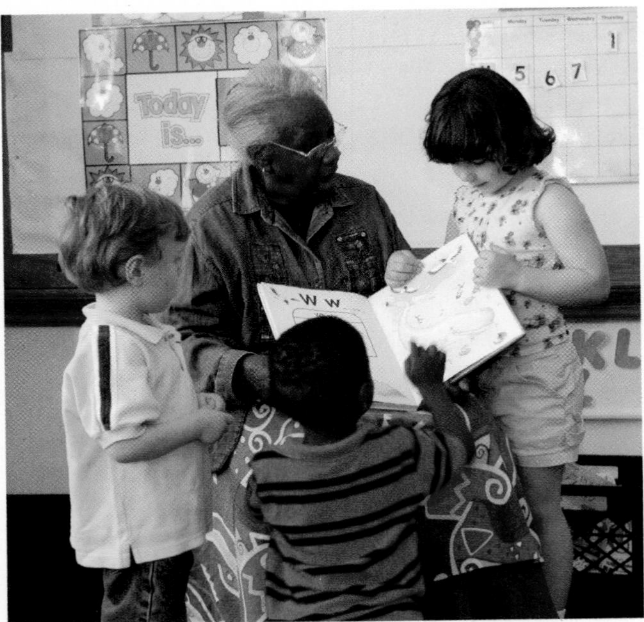

Instill a sense of story by reading to children every day.

Classroom Museum

Introduce the work of Alexander Calder, the inventor of the mobile. Children enjoy hearing about the miniature circus he made and then used to put on performances for his friends, and about how he made the world's largest mobiles by painting jet planes with original artwork. (Print available: *Fish Tail and Lobster Trap* [Take 5].)

Storytelling Experiences for Preschool and Up

Storytelling is so much a part of the play of young children that the list of possible activities is endless. Create daily opportunities for story making.

Family and school stories. Continue to tell and retell stories about events in the life of the children and their families. Add stories about happenings in school, such as "Remember the day when the paint spilled all over my pants?"

Retell. Model the art of storytelling by retelling familiar tales from memory. Add props, finger movements, and actions. Speak with intensity, using voices to match the characters. These things will help you remember the story and keep the focus of the children as well.

Puppets. Put out commercial theme-related puppets at the puppet theater. For example, animal puppets can be used when studying habitats.

Masks. Make masks to represent the different characters in a story and as you read the book hold up the mask at the appropriate time and speak in the character's special voice.

Take a role. Give each child a prop, mask, or puppet that goes with the story. As you tell the story have the child do something related to the tale using the prop, mask, or puppet. For example, give out bowls and spoons to go with a telling of Goldilocks. When the bears eat their porridge, the child with the appropriate size bowl stands up and mimics eating.

Draw it. As you tell a story illustrate it by drawing simple line drawings.

Storytelling Experiences for Primary Age

By the primary grades children are developing vocabulary at a rapid rate and learning how to read and write. These new skills can be reinforced and enhanced through dramatic activities.

Story jar. Place a number of small objects equal to the number of children in the group in a jar or box, such a toy figurines, jewelry, or pieces of cloth. Have the children sit in a circle and start off a story with an exciting sentence. Pass the jar around the circle and have each child remove the object and add a sentence to the story that includes that item.

Odd pairs. Select two words for things that are not usually associated together, like fish and tricycle, and invent a story that includes both things.

Everyone's story. Sit in a circle and start off a story with an exciting sentence. Each child adds on to the story in turn.

One word. Say a word, such as *dog,* and have the children think of other words that mean close to the same thing or go with it, such as puppy, collie, mutt, collar, leash, dog bone, and so forth. Make up a story using all the words.

"What would happen if. . . ." Develop imaginative stories by asking what would happen if . . . completed with a fantastical occurrence, such as the sky suddenly turned red, the school started to float, or all the fish in the sea started walking around on land. Let the students invent their own "what if" story starters, too. Make up cards with "what if" ideas for times when everyone needs a creative spark and keep them at a storytelling center.

Describe it. To introduce the use of descriptive language, have the children name different kinds of people, animals, or objects, such as a detective, panda, or pencil. Then on separate paper have them brainstorm a list of describing words, such as angry, sneaky, or broken. Put the lists together and have each child select a character and a descriptive word and then tell a story that includes that character. Try two or more of the descriptive words.

Setting easel. Make a class collection of settings. On large pieces of tag board, have children draw possible settings, such as a farmyard or an ocean. Then share the settings with the whole group. Ask, "How would you act if you were in one of these places?" Place the settings in turn on an easel and have pairs of children come forward and act out an appropriate event or animate a puppet in front of the scenes.

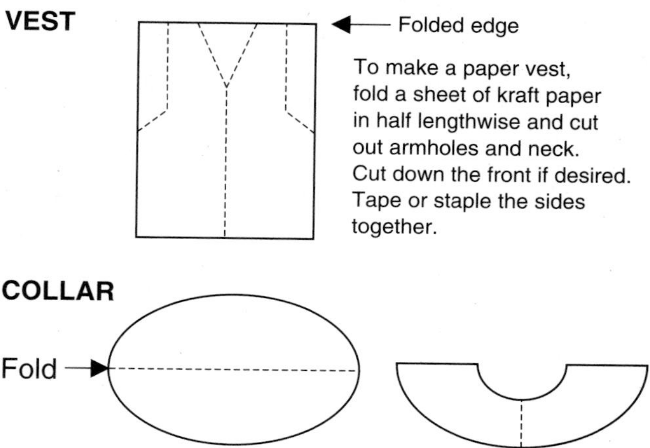

VEST
Folded edge
To make a paper vest, fold a sheet of kraft paper in half lengthwise and cut out armholes and neck. Cut down the front if desired. Tape or staple the sides together.
COLLAR
Fold
To make a paper collar, cut out an oval from a sheet of kraft paper or construction paper. Fold in half and cut out the neck hole. Add a slit for easy on and off.

FIGURE 12–1 Making paper costumes.

Costumes, Hats, and Jewelry

Making costumes, hats, jewelry, and other body decorations is another way that art and dramatic play interact. As with puppets and masks, body-wear items should be simple enough for children to make on their own.

Costumes. Simple costumes can be made from strips of cloth and brown kraft paper. Lengths of cloth about 3 to 4 feet long can be made into all kinds of capes, wraps, and cloaks. Provide an assortment in interesting colors and types of fabric. Filmy nylon can be a veil, heavy velour a king's robe. Kraft paper can be cut into simple clothing shapes, such as vests, collars, and wrap-around skirts, and painted or drawn on with markers and crayons (see Figure 12-1).

Hats. Hats can be used to enrich dramatic play and storytelling. Place premade hatbands and hat bases close to the art supply area, or set up a hat-making center by the dramatic play area. Display child-made hats in this center. Premade hatbands are 2-inch-wide strips of tag board glued into circles large enough to fit over the children's heads and rest on their ears. For a hat base, use paper plates, 14-inch diameter cardboard or tag board circles, or make paper cones. Bring the two corners of 12-by-18-inch paper rectangles together to form a cone-like shape; glue or tape them together. These hat forms can be decorated and worn in many ways. They may need to be tied on to keep them in place. Alternatively, use paper plates with string attached on opposite sides. With a little imagination children can make crowns, wizard's caps, bonnets, helmets, and more.

Jewelry. Jewelry can take many forms. Necklaces, bracelets, pins, and badges can all be simple enough for children to make independently. These activities provide an excellent way to work with the art element of pattern. Create a jewelry-making center near the dramatic play area. Put items to string in low trays. For easy access, notch a piece of cardboard, and place a pre-cut piece of knotted yarn in each notch. Try some of these things for stringing: cut cardboard tubes (1/2- to 1-inch sections), paper shapes with holes punched in them, small pieces of Styrofoam trays cut into shapes with punched holes in the center, straight macaroni,* child-made soda-clay beads (see Appendix D: Recipes). Children with more developed fine-motor control can string the larger sizes of pony beads sold commercially (see Appendix C: Supplies). These mix well with handmade soda beads. For safety, items for children under age three must pass the choke test (see Appendix A).

Strips of paper with the ends glued together can be used as bracelets, headbands, armbands, or watches. Encourage the children to draw patterns on their strips before gluing or to attach collage items after they are glued.

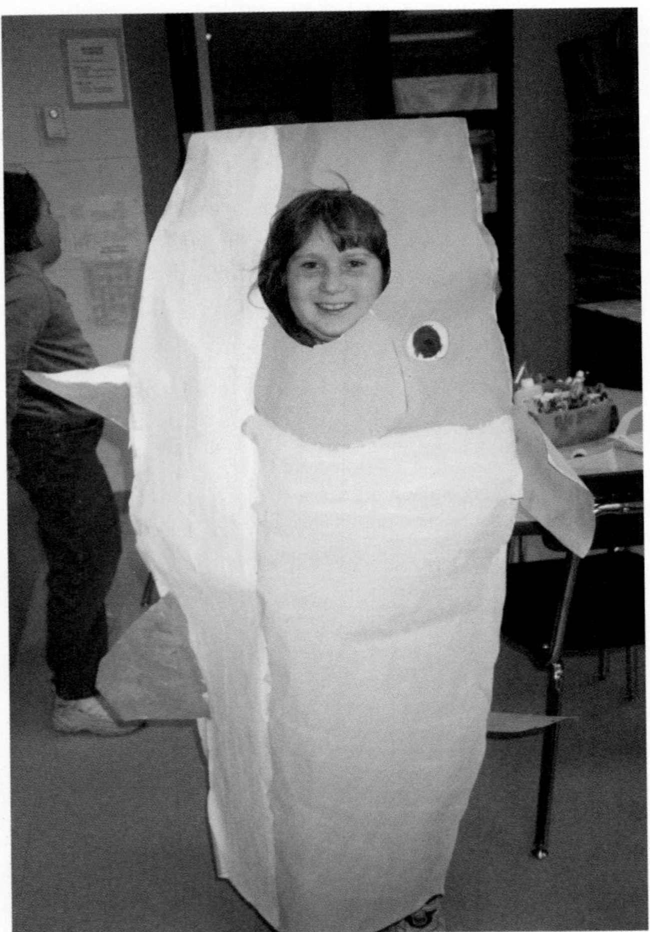

Stacy, age 8, models the fish costume she made from a folded piece of brown kraft paper stapled up the sides and painted with tempera paint. The large hole for her face makes the costume safer and allows her voice to be heard clearly during her skit.

CHILDREN'S THEATER

Besides creating their own dramatic play scenarios, young children should have the opportunity to attend drama performances done by older children and adults. Exposure to this level of dramatics will inspire children to expand their own dramatic play and narratives. A backstage tour will introduce children to the role of lighting, stage sets, and costuming in creating the illusion of reality. Being able to see actors first in their character roles and then as themselves helps them distinguish between fantasy and reality. They will also learn how to behave as an audience.

Finding performances. Children's theater is especially designed to meet the attention span and need for interaction that young children require. Often a local drama group or a high school dramatics club will be willing to perform a program especially for young children.

Local and state arts-in-education programs can often provide information, links to performers, and grants to school groups. More information on these programs can be found at the Arts Education Partnership http://www.aep-arts.org. Many states have Councils for the Arts, which provide grants to groups who perform for schools. Performances geared to children can also be found at street fairs and arts festivals such as the First Night events held in many cities on New Year's Eve.

Theater Experiences for Toddlers

For children who have only seen recorded performances, a live performance in which they can interact with the actors provides a wonderful model of what the dramatic arts can be. At the same time, we need to remember that young children believe that what they are seeing is real. If possible, have the actors talk to the children first and then put on their costumes. At the end actors can remove the costumes and answer children's questions about what they were wearing, why, and how the costumes were made.

For a positive experience we need to make sure the children are comfortable. Because of their short attention spans, initial theater experiences for toddlers should be no more than 20 to 30 minutes long. Performing in the classroom or another familiar place is helpful as chairs in an auditorium or theater may be too large and visibility difficult. Having children sit on the floor is one possible alternative. The ideal performance for this age has only one to three actors with minimal staging who carry out their show very close to the children.

Theater Experiences for Preschoolers

With their longer attentions spans, most preschool age children can attend longer performances about 60 minutes in length. They particularly enjoy stories and characters they are familiar with and will notice any changes that have been made in the narrative. Like toddlers, preschoolers may still be too small to sit comfortably in adult size seating. Before going to a performance make sure to ask about seating. Some theater groups let the children sit in a circle on the stage or on simple risers.

Puppet shows work well because small children can get a good view of the raised up puppet stage.

Theater Experiences for Kindergarteners and Primary Students

By the age of 5 or 6 children are ready for lengthier performances. They are better able to sit in adult-size theater seats and have a longer attention span. Most children by this age have heard many stories and will be aware of the story elements in the play they see. Wanting to know the ending of the story will motivate them to sit through the play to the end.

Theater Etiquette

Susan Fishman (2010) recommends that adults model how to be good audience members. This begins before the performance during which children are shown how to listen, when to participate, and how to show appreciation by clapping at appropriate times. These skills can first be practiced when viewing performances by peers. Later, when taking a group to a show, invite parents to accompany the group so there is a high adult to student ratio, and be sure to go over audience skills with both children and volunteers.

Advise children to watch an adult if they are not sure what to do.

If a child cannot sit still and pay attention, or is plainly uncomfortable during a performance, rather than disciplining the child and making the experience unpleasant, just quietly leave early with the child, and then try another performance when the child seems more ready.

With a little bit of effort the wonder of live theater can be shared with children.

CONCLUSION: IMAGINE IT!

> *I am enough of an artist to draw freely upon my imagination. Imagination is more important than knowledge. Knowledge is limited. Imagination encircles the world.*
>
> —*Albert Einstein*

The dramatic arts are the world of story and imagination with its roots in children's natural fantasy play. Through dramatic play, pantomime, improvisation, and storytelling children can learn to control their bodies and words to create personas. They can become anything and anybody. Literacy skills are nurtured and developed as children become enthusiastic storytellers and scriptwriters. Music, dance, and visual art play a role in children's dramatic work. The processes of pantomime, improvisation, and storytelling can be used to enhance everyday teaching and make facts and concepts more meaningful for students.

Teachers must also be performers. The skills of drama can also enhance how we teach. We can add flair to what we say, intensity to how we move, and story to what we tell.

FURTHER READING

To learn more about the dramatic arts read the following books:

Hamilton, M., & Weiss, M. (2005). *Children tell stories: Teaching and using storytelling in the classroom.* Katonah, NY: Richard C. Owen.

This book presents ways to use storytelling with children. It explains how storytelling develops language skills, and provides tips and resources as well as ways to tell a good story. A DVD of 25 stories to tell accompanies the book.

Hening, R. B. (1993). *Creative drama for the classroom teacher.* Englewood Cliffs, NJ: Prentice Hall.

Although geared to older children, this book provides excellent guidelines for designing and leading dramatic activities.

Langer, E. J. (1989). *Mindfulness.* Cambridge, MA: Perseus Books.

A fascinating look into how the mind and body are one, this classic work presents numerous examples of how to feel younger, be more creative, and feel less stress and pain through the use of imagery.

Rodari, G. (1996). *The grammar of fantasy.* (J. Zipes, Trans.) New York: Teachers & Writers Collaborative. (Original work published 1973.)

This book provides a rare insight into how children invent stories and pretend play.

For additional information on teaching the dramatic arts to young children visit our Web site at http://www.cengagebrain.com

TEACHING IN ACTION

Puppets: Transcript of a Student Observation

When I entered the three- and four-year-olds' room, I saw the teacher's aide working with a small group of children. They were sitting on a rug, and the aide was using a puppet made of a cardboard tube and a piece of round paper with a simple face on it. She was using a funny little voice and singing a song that described something about each child. When she said the child's name, she would lightly touch the child's hand with the puppet. The children seemed delighted. They giggled whenever the puppet touched them. Then she asked them if they would like to make a puppet, too. The children seemed very excited by the idea.

She had paper circles in a basket, and she let the children each choose a circle and gave them each some markers in a small tray. The children drew a face for their puppets. I noticed that some of them were already talking in little, high-pitched puppet voices as they drew. When they were done, they went to a table and glued a cardboard strip to the back of the face. The aide had moved to the table and assisted them by asking if they had put on enough glue and reminding them to hold the paper to the cardboard until it was stuck.

Next, the children began to have their puppets talk to each other. Two of them took them to the housekeeping area and fed them and pushed them in the carriage. Several others joined the aide in singing the song again, this time using their own puppet to touch a friend. When it was time to go home, the teacher asked the children to put their puppets to sleep in the puppet house [a decorated box that looked like a house]. I thought it would be hard to get them to leave the puppets, but the way she said, "Tomorrow you can wake them up to play again" seemed to fit with how the children thought about the puppets—like real playmates—so they all came over and carefully laid their puppets in the box to sleep. When their families picked them up, some children took family members over to see the puppets sleeping. They were so cute. They would say, "Shhh. . . . Don't wake them up."

Stick puppets are the easiest for very young children to make and to use. These children drew faces on shaped paper and then glued them to a piece of cardboard. Puppets are by Damon, age 3; Michael, age 4; and Emily, age 5.

Studio Page

THE IMPORTANCE OF PLAY

For each of the developmental growth areas, give an example of how dramatic play facilitates skill development.

Social

Physical

Language

Cognitive

Emotional

Studio Page

USING GUIDED IMAGERY

Select one of the guided imagery suggestions in this chapter or make up a scenario of your own. Write a script for this experience that you could use with young children.

Step 1: Relaxation

Step 2: The Journey

Step 3: The Return

Studio Page

DESIGNING A PLAY CENTER OR PROP BOX

Select a developmental age level, an appropriate topic, and learning objectives, and then write a plan of what you would include in a dramatic play center or prop box. Be sure to include a book or two, and multicultural and antibias materials.

Children's ages: ______________________________

Topic: ______________________________

Objectives: Using this center or prop box the children will develop

Physically ______________________________

Socially ______________________________

Emotionally ______________________________

Language skills ______________________________

Cognitively ______________________________

Dramatic skill and knowledge ______________________________

Describe what materials will be in the center or prop box.

____

____

____

____

____

Studio Page

TELLING A STORY

Prepare yourself for telling a simple story to a group of children.

1. Select a folktale, fairy tale, or create an original story. Write a brief summary of it.

2. List the props you will use to enhance your presentation.

3. Describe how the children will actively participate as you tell the story. For example, how will they move or what sounds will they make?

Appendix A

SAFETY GUIDELINES

The following guidelines provide the information needed to create the safest environment possible for young artists.

NOTE: The Art and Craft Materials Institute has a voluntary labeling program. The AP Seal stands for a product certified to contain insufficient quantities of any material that is toxic or injurious to humans or that will cause acute or chronic health problems. The CP Seal means that the product meets manufacturing standards. Always look for these seals on the arts supplies used. In addition, Material Safety Data Sheets (MSDS) should be obtained from the manufacturer or seller of materials and kept on file. These sheets contain the raw ingredients and how to treat ingestion or contamination with the product. Sheets for many products can also be found at the National MSDS repository: http://www.msdssearch.com/.

Material Safety Checklist

Examine the material and circle "yes" or "no" for each question:

1. Is there a high probability that it will be ingested?
   yes   no
2. Is dust produced?
   yes   no
3. Is it difficult to wash off skin and surfaces with water?
   yes   no
4. Will spray, vapor, smoke, or fumes be produced?
   yes   no
5. Are the ingredients unknown?
   yes   no
6. Is it intended for adult use?
   yes   no
7. Will it be difficult for children to handle safely?
   yes   no

Avoid any product that has one or more "yes" answers.

Guidelines for Safe Teacher Behavior

- Any room or space used by children must be totally free of hazardous materials.
- When there is a choice, buy the least hazardous arts materials that will meet personal needs. For example, choose the following:

  Water-based markers instead of permanent markers

  Liquid paint instead of spray paint

  White glue instead of rubber cement

  Tacky craft glue instead of epoxy
- Keep all hazardous materials in a locked metal cabinet.
- Do not use any hazardous arts supplies in front of children. For example, do not use rubber cement while the children use safe white glue.
- When working with dusty materials, wear a dust mask.
- When working with skin irritants, wear rubber gloves.
- When working with solvents or hazardous fumes, wear an approved face mask with the proper filters. This is essential when using fabric dyes or doing stained glass.

- Adequate ventilation means the outdoors. Unless there is a sealed glove box that is ventilated to the outside, never use hazardous materials at home or in the classroom, even if children are not present. An open window is not sufficient. Fumes and dusts can remain in the air or collect on surfaces and contaminate the children or teacher days later.
- Handle sharp, dangerous tools with care. Pass scissors to children in a safe way. Store the paper cutter where children cannot see or touch it.

Risk Factors

Factor	Risks to Children	Action to Take
Metabolism	Children absorb toxins more rapidly than adults	Do not use art supplies intended for adults
Body Size	Children's mouths and noses are closer to the work surfaces	Sit children at child-size tables and chairs
Muscular Control	Children have less developed fine motor control and hand-eye coordination	Provide child-size tools and ample workspace. Use safety scissors.
Behavior	Children have less self-control	Set clear limits, supervise closely, and remove dangerous items from the setting. Make sure that for children under age three small items pass the choke test.*
Health	Each child has unique health issues	Check for allergies, asthma, and other health issues that may be irritated by materials

**A simple device to check the size of objects can be purchased from most school supply catalogs and stores. A general rule is that objects shorter than 2 inches in length and less than 1 inch in diameter should not be used by children under age three.*

SAFE SUBSTITUTIONS

Category	Art Materials Found In	Safer Alternative
Solvents:	Oil paint, turpentine, and other thinners	Water-based paints
These are poisonous if swallowed, flammable, and cause brain damage if inhaled over time. They are usually labeled "Keep out of reach of children" and "Flammable"	Lacquer and thinners Shellac and alcohol thinners	Coat objects with water-based acrylic gels
	Permanent printing ink	Water-based printing ink
	Permanent markers	Water-based markers
	Rubber cement and thinners Superglue, airplane glue, and epoxy	White or gel glues, craft glue, school paste
Aerosol Sprays:	Spray glue	White or gel school glue
Inhaling these can cause bronchial irritation, asthma attacks, and increased susceptibility to respiratory infection	Spray paint	Use a brush
	Charcoal/chalk fixatives	Press a paper to finished picture to remove excess dust. Laminate finished work.

Category	Art Materials Found In	Safer Alternative
Toxic Pigments: Colors made from cadmium, lead, cobalt, chromium, and so forth are poisonous	Artist quality paints	Use AP seal paints intended for children
	Artist quality pastels	Use AP seal colored chalks intended for children
	Ceramic glazes	Paint clay with child-safe paints or have adult put on glaze away from areas where there are children
	Copper enameling	Make jewelry in other safe ways. See text.
Dusts: Inhaling these can cause bronchial irritation, asthma attacks, and increased susceptibility to respiratory infection. Clay dust may be contaminated with asbestos.	Firing clay	Use only wet clay. Make sure clay is labeled "talc free."
	Ceramic glazes	Paint clay with child-safe paints or have adult glaze the pieces away from children
	Plaster	Do not mix in the presence of children. Avoid carving dried plaster. Due to excessive heat do not make hand casts.
	Powdered tempera	Do not mix in the presence of children. Wear a filter mask. Avoid activities that use sprinkled powdered paint.
	Chalk	Use on a wet surface. Place newspaper under paper. Have children wash hands immediately after use.
Dyes: Commercial dyes may contain chemicals that cause bladder cancer and severe allergic reactions	Fabric dyes	Use natural dyes made from plants or unsweetened packaged drink mix
	Wax	Do not melt in the presence of children
Fumes and Toxic Gases: Strong lung irritants may be released when a material is heated	Crayons	Do not melt or iron in the presence of children
	Plastics	Do not melt or use glues, which contain solvent that melt the plastic. Attach with chenille stems, yarn, or wire.
Bacteria Contamination	Styrofoam trays and plastic food containers	Rinse containers and their lids in hot, soapy water. Soak for 1 minute in a disinfectant solution of three-quarters of a cup of chlorine bleach per gallon of water. A final rinse in warm water is necessary to remove the bleach solution. Cover clothing and protect hands from the bleach by wearing rubber gloves. Do not allow children to use this disinfectant solution.
	Play dough and other similar shared materials	Older children can be asked to wash their hands or use a tissue before use. For toddlers and young preschoolers, a good solution is to give the children their own pieces of modeling dough and their own storage containers or resealable bags
	Cardboard tubes	Substitute rolled paper tubes. A rolled half-sheet of 12-by-18-inch tag board makes a very sturdy tube. Regular construction paper can also be used.

Sample Letter to Families: Child Safety Information

Dear Family,

All of the arts materials used in our program have been carefully selected to be safe for young children. Some children, however, have special sensitivities. To help us select the safest arts materials for your child, please answer the following questions:

1. Is your child allergic to anything? yes no
   If yes, please list:
2. Does your child have any respiratory problems? yes no
   If yes, please explain:
3. Is your child's skin sensitive to anything? yes no
   If yes, please list:
4. Are there any art materials that your child should not use? yes no
   Please list and explain.

Thank you for taking the time to complete this form. Together we can make sure that your child will have a safe and fun time creating art.

Your child's teacher,

Appendix B

PLANNING ARTS ACTIVITIES

Whether a curriculum is planned around themes, projects, learning centers, or play areas, the individual components are the activities—the specific things the children and the educator will be doing. It is important to plan these activities carefully, to ensure that nothing is forgotten and to provide a measure against which we can assess our delivery.

Plans for individual arts activities need to take account of the factors that will affect the dynamics of a particular group of children and answer the following questions: who, why, where, when, what, and how? By planning answers to each of these questions ahead of time, teachers are better prepared to guide the arts activities they offer the children.

WHO? GROUP COMPOSITION

Every group of children is unique. The following three characteristics should be considered when making plans.

1. **What are the ages and number of children?** The ages and number of students will affect the amount of time, space, and supervision for which the teacher must plan. Planning an activity with 4 one-year-olds will require very different decisions than designing a program for 20 five-year-olds. If the children are of mixed ages, will all of them be able to work with the same amount of supervision and be successful?
2. **What are the children's previous experiences?** The less familiar children are with an arts medium or technique, the more exploration they need. If the children are competent with a material, then more responsive activities can be planned. If a group contains children of various ages, developmental phases, and experience, then care must be taken that the selected arts activities are open-ended having many possible ways for children to carry them out. This will allow children to work comfortably at their own developmental levels.
3. **Are there children with special needs?** Check that each activity will be able to be accomplished by individual children. Do the activities need adaptation so that a child with special needs can have success? Select arts activities that can be done by a wide range of children, and modify the materials, tools, and setup as necessary.

WHEN? TIME FRAME

Next, consider the amount of time that will be available for the children to work on their arts activities. Make sure that there will be sufficient time to complete an activity, whether on the same day or over a period of days. Will wet projects be able to dry? Will children be able to reach completion? Be sure to allow time for sharing and discussing as well.

WHY? GOALS AND OBJECTIVES

Good activities have clear educational goals. Goals are the long-term changes in behavior that the activities are meant to foster in children. They are why the activities are selected. These are not changes that will happen after one activity or even two. To reach set goals children need many opportunities in which to learn and to practice. Self-confidence, for example, comes after many successful experiences.

Writing Objectives

Short-term goals are called **objectives.** An objective is a statement describing a behavior that can be accomplished within the time frame of the activity.

Objectives are usually phrased in terms of observable skills and behaviors. One way to write effective objectives is to think of them as having two parts. The first describes the growth area and the skill or behavior to be practiced in the activity. The second describes how we will know that this growth is happening by describing what we should see or hear the children doing. For example, a skill objective for a cutting activity might be written as follows:

Part 1: In this activity the children will develop physically as they coordinate eye, hand, and finger movements while using a scissors.

Part 2: I will know that this is happening when I see the children freely cutting shapes out of the paper.

The first part of this objective focuses our attention on the behaviors we need to facilitate so that the child will be successful. The second part of the objective provides a way for us to immediately assess the child's progress. The following sample objectives show how objectives relate to the growth areas discussed in Chapter 1.

Here are the developmental areas, some suggested *specific* skills, and some examples of well-written objectives.

Social Objectives

These are behaviors or skills that help children get along better with others.

Examples of social skills:

being helpful

patiently waiting a turn

sharing

showing kindness

working cooperatively

taking a role

listening respectfully

following direction

Complete objective example. *Children will practice* patiently waiting a turn. I will know this objective is being met when I see the children sitting quietly in the circle and raising hands when they want to speak.

Physical Objectives

These are behaviors or skills that help children develop control over their bodies.

Examples of gross motor physical objectives:

throwing and catching

balancing

coordinating movement of arms and legs

being flexible

Examples of specific fine motor physical skills:

cutting and pasting

zipping and buttoning

using a writing or drawing tool

picking up small pieces

Complete objective example. *Children will practice* balancing. I will know this objective is being met when I see the children walk at least 3 feet on a plank laid flat on the floor.

Language Objectives

These are behaviors or skills that help children receive and communicate ideas through listening, speaking, reading, and writing.

Examples of language skills:

naming

telling or retelling

discussing

describing

defining

answering questions

matching letters and sounds

identifying words

listening to stories and so forth being read aloud

reading words

comprehending

using correct language forms (grammar)

writing stories, poems, and reports

using the writing process—drafting, editing, revising, and publishing

Cognitive Objectives

These are behaviors or skills that help children develop the ability to reason, think logically, organize information, and solve problems.

Examples of intellectual skills:

naming

observing

counting

calculating

measuring

comparing and contrasting

predicting

ordering

finding patterns

testing ideas

making a plan

graphing

using a graphic organizer (like a Venn diagram)

Complete objective example. *Children will practice* listening to and retelling a story. I will know this objective is being met when I see the children sitting quietly during the story and when they draw pictures of their favorite part in their journals.

Complete objective example. *Children will practice* measuring and comparing. I will know this objective is being met when they use a scale to measure some pumpkins and then use what they learn to decide which one is the heaviest.

Complete objective example. *Children will practice* combining things they know in a new way. I will know this objective is being met when I see the children taking roles of characters in the story and acting out something different from the story ending.

Perceptual Objectives

These are behaviors or skills that help children use their senses to perceive and make sense of the characteristics of the objects and environments that surround them.

Examples of visual perceptual or spatial skills:

Identifying visual elements, such as colors, shape, textures, and forms

Matching visual elements

Observing placement and relationships between objects

Looking from different viewpoints

Observing how parts form a whole or vice versa

Examples of auditory perception skills:

Identifying auditory elements, such as pitches, timbres, tempos, and dynamics

Matching auditory elements

Matching rhythms with movements

Complete objective example. *Children will practice* looking at three-dimensional forms from different viewpoints and describe what they see. I will know this objective is being met when I see the children turning their clay sculptures around and talking with each other about how they look.

Emotional Objectives

These are behaviors or skills that help children develop independence, self-knowledge, and confidence in their own abilities.

Examples of emotional skills:

working independently

evaluating their own work or behavior

using self-control

expressing their feelings or preferences

showing pride in their work

showing trust

Complete objective example. *Children will practice* evaluating their own work. I will know this objective is being met when they assess their growth in writing by comparing a journal entry they wrote in September to one they wrote in May and I hear the children saying things like, "Look how I used to make 'A.' Now I make it so much better!"

Arts Objectives

These are behaviors or skills that help children develop expertise in the particular art form. These objectives may be based on local or national arts standards. See the Exploring the Arts chapters for summaries of the standards for each of the art forms, or go to http://artsedge.kennedy-center.org/. Under Teach, click on Standards for a complete listing.

WHERE? SETUP

One way to foster children's disposition to create art is through how the environment is organized. The environment is everything that surrounds children when they create art. It is where the child works and learns. It is the room and any other space used for arts creation—hallways, play areas, and the outdoors. It is how orderly the supplies are and how appropriately sized the furniture is. It is the arrangement of the workspace and the other children in it. How this environment is planned and used will determine how much the child can concentrate on learning about and creating art.

This part of the plan describes where the children will be working. How should the furniture be arranged? Where should the supplies be located? What changes will have to be made so that this activity will run smoothly?

WHAT? MATERIALS

It is important to list the supplies needed for each activity. This will quickly indicate which items are on hand and what has to be found or bought. It is often possible, with a little creativity, to make substitutions, but the key to success is to keep the materials basic and safe. The more the children can handle the tools and supplies on their own, without constant supervision, the more they will grow artistically.

HOW? PROCEDURE

Once an activity is selected, it is necessary to plan how to present it. Every activity has three parts: an introduction or warm-up, what the children will do, and how you will interact with the children.

The Warm-Up or WOW

First, it is necessary to introduce the materials and procedures to the children. An activity can be started many ways, but the most effective ways are those that entice the children by awakening their natural curiosity. These introductory experiences or "wonderful opportunities to wonder" (WOW) must be rich in sensory and visual stimuli. They should be memorable—full of opportunities for asking questions and making observations. Most important, the experience should flow directly into the arts activities that are offered to the children.

Warm-ups for arts activities can range from something as simple as playing a beat on a drum to something as complex as a field trip to a museum. The type of introduction or warm-up will depend on the age of the children and their previous experiences.

Real object. For young children, who are only just beginning to think symbolically, warm-ups should always include a carefully selected real object and related questions that draw them into the activity. But even older children can be inspired by a wonderful object of wonder. Finding a real object takes extra time, but it is worth it. Presenting a real object that draws children's attention makes the difference between an ordinary experience and a wonderful one.

The real object should be something that the children can see, touch, and possibly use. In some cases, a new art material, tool, prop, or musical instrument can be the real object. For example, a teacher might show the children a large paintbrush at circle time and say: "Here is a new brush to try when you go to the easel today. What kind of line do you think it will make?" In other cases, the real object may be a nature object, such as a shell or a bird feather. Whatever it is, it should be presented with so much showmanship and enthusiasm that it elicits a "Wow!" from the children.

A book. A wonderful children's book is another way to introduce an arts activity. Many wonderful examples of books about the arts are given throughout this text. However, no matter how terrific the book is, try to accompany books with a real object as well. Just imagine the difference in the children's creative work between these two examples. In the first, a teacher reads a book about ladybugs and then suggests that the children make ladybug pictures at the drawing center. In the second, a teacher reads a book about ladybugs and then displays a jar of live ladybugs. After the children observe using hand lenses and share what they see, the ladybugs are placed in the drawing center. In the first warm-up, the children have just the memory of the pictures in the book when they go to the drawing center. Only the second warm-up draws children into the activity and sustains it as they go to the center and re-experience the ladybugs.

Works of art. Another way to start an arts activity is to display a reproduction of an artwork, listen to a work of music, or watch a recording of a play or dance. These can be done by adults or children. Talking about the work can model how the children can talk about their own work while they participate in the activity. However, these works should never be held up as models for the children to imitate or copy in their own work.

An experience. Going outside and touching trees, looking at trees, and laying beneath trees is a wonderful way to introduce a creative movement activity focused on trees. Activity-related experiences that take children out of the classroom can be an inspiring way to begin an activity. Field trips and walks in the neighborhood are rich in such possibilities.

Guided discovery. Guided discovery is a form of warm-up that is an ideal way to introduce children ages four and up to a new material, technique, or center. The purpose is to develop interest and excitement in the children while at the same time establishing guidelines for use. Guided discovery consists of three parts.

1. **Unveiling.** Wrap a small item related to the activity in wrapping paper, or put larger ones in an interesting basket, box, or bag. Centers can be covered with a cloth or blocked with a banner or screen. Ask the children to guess what the object is, or what the center might contain. Slowly give clues or unwrap it.
2. **Exploring**. Show the object or parts at the center. Ask questions about how it might be used. Focus on what would be careful, safe ways to handle the materials or to behave in the center.
3. **Rule setting**. Finally, summarize the children's positive suggestions into easy-to-understand words or pictures, and make a sign to post near the center or workspace. When behavior is inappropriate, refer to the sign as needed.

WHAT TO DO

Although flexibility must be an integral component of teaching, describing step by step what the children and you will be doing can provide guidance in making sure maximum learning takes place.

WHAT TO SAY

It is a good idea to plan ahead of time some of the questions and vocabulary words that will be asked during the activity. Often when busy dealing with active young artists it is easy to forget one's good intentions. Consider carefully the kinds of concept-based questions you will ask, vocabulary you will use, and responses you will give to the young artists at work. It is through teacher-student interaction that knowledge about the art form, skill in performance, the disposition to think as an artist, and feelings of self-confidence in the arts are acquired.

TRANSITION OUT

In the same way plan how to provide the children with closure at the end of each activity. The transition out should restate the basic concept of the activity while extending the learning in some way.

This could be a statement that summarizes what the children have been doing, or a question that makes them reflect on their learning and then invites them to carry what they learned to a new setting.

For example, a creative drama activity focused on pantomiming meeting someone new could end as follows: "Look at all the friendly ways we thought of to make a new friend! Let's try some of these ideas out the next time a new visitor comes to our class."

ASSESS THE LEARNING

An activity is not complete unless there is some way to know how the children have gained in knowledge and skill. In this section, prepare several questions you could ask or behaviors you could observe that will provide information on what has been learned. In writing these refer back to the objectives originally set for the activity.

WRITING AN ARTS ACTIVITY PLAN

The following is an example of one way to write an activity plan. It is the format used in this book. This or a similar form can be used whenever a new activity is being considered. The outline provides one way to organize the basic information needed to create successful activities.

ACTIVITY PLAN FORMAT

ACTIVITY:

WHO?	**Group composition age(s):**
	Group size:
WHEN?	**Time frame:**
WHY?	**Growth Objectives:** In this activity children will develop . . .
	Socially
	Physically
	Intellectually
	Linguistically
	Perceptively
	Emotionally
	Arts Objectives: In this activity the child will grow as an artist . . .
WHERE?	**Setup:**
WHAT?	**Materials:**
HOW?	**Procedure:**
	Warm-up:
	What to do:
	What to say:
	Transition out:
ASSESSMENT OF LEARNING:	

SAMPLE ACTIVITY PLAN: A Painting Exploration

WHO? **Group composition age(s):** Three- and four-year-olds

Group size: two or three at a time

WHEN? **Time frame:** 3-hour session

WHY? **Growth Objectives:** In this activity children will develop . . .

- Socially, by learning how to get along and talk with other artists. I will know that this is happening when I see them talking about their paintings to each other.
- Physically, by exercising hand-eye coordination. I will know that this is happening when I see them filling scoops, mixing paint with a spoon, and using different paintbrushes.
- Linguistically, by learning new art vocabulary. I will know this is happening when I hear them describe a texture and see them point to one of the textures.
- Cognitively, by observing and describing cause and effect. I will know that this is happening when I hear them making predictions about what will happen to the texture of the paint and then describing the result.
- Perceptively, by making their own choices of what textures and colors to mix together. I will know that this is happening when I see them select a color and texture to combine that is different from the others.
- Emotionally, by strengthening their self-confidence using paint. I will know that this is happening when I see them actively exploring the paint.
- Arts skills and knowledge: In this activity children will grow as visual artists by gaining skill in applying different textures of paint. They will identify the visual art element of texture.

WHERE? **Setup:** Warm-up activity on rug. Painting at the easel, table, or paint center.

WHAT? **Materials:**

Containers of tempera paint in a variety of colors

Labeled containers of different materials to add to paint: sand, salt, soap flakes

Small scoops, brushes, and paper at the easel or on newspaper-covered table

HOW? **Procedure:**

Warm-Up: Large group: (on rug) Pass around a piece of sandpaper, then a piece of fake fur. Ask the children to describe how it feels. Play the "Texture Search" game: Name a texture; each child then has to find something with that texture and touch it. Have the children take turns naming the textures they find.

What to Do:

1. Ask: "What is the texture of paint?"
   "How could we change the texture of paint?"
   "What do you think would happen if you added these things to the paint?"
   "Would you like to add one and see what happens?"

(Continued)

(Continued)

2. Demonstrate how to add one of the materials to the paint. Tell the children that they can add any of the materials to their paint when they come to the painting place.
3. As the children come to paint, supervise them as they add materials to the color of their choice, and then use it in their paintings.

What to Say:

Descriptive: "You are using the large brush." "You used the textured paint to____."

Questioning: "Which paint did you like using better?" "Which paint was hard to spread?"

Transition Out:

Say: "You had fun painting with the different textured paint. You can add a different texture the next time you paint. Let's put your painting over here to dry. What would you like to do now? I see your friend Ann is having fun with the blocks."

ASSESSMENT OF LEARNING

1. Do the children use descriptive words to talk about their textures?
2. Do the children gain more control and confidence in using brushes and paint?
3. Can the children see differences in the paint and identify what was added to change the texture?

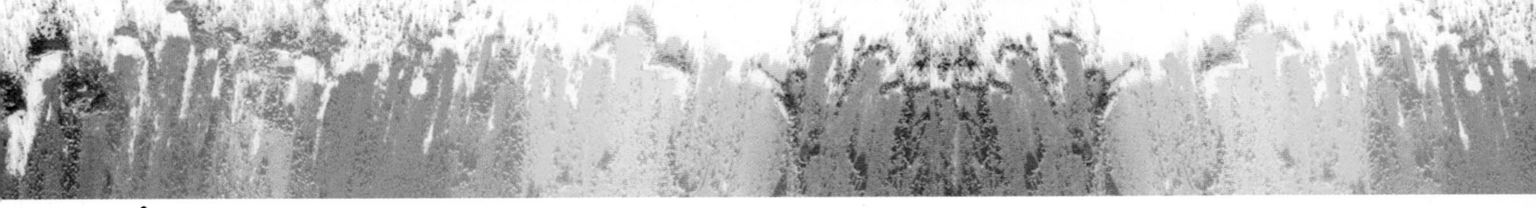

Appendix C

TEACHER RESOURCES

Arts Supplies

Boxes, for storing large prints, big books, and portfolios.

Available from:

Calloway House (cardboard storage boxes and units)
451 Richardson Dr.
Lancaster, PA 17603-4098
http://www.callowayhouse.com

Paint daubers (Chapter 9)

Paint markers, refillable (Chapter 9)

Paint scrapers and fingertip painters (Chapter 9)

Papier-mâché paste (Chapter 9)

Precut mats (Chapter 4)

Tempera blocks (Chapter 9)

Vertical floor loom (Chapter 9)

All these items are all available from many arts supply companies, including:

Dick Blick
P.O. Box 1267
Galesburg, IL 61402-1267
1-800-447-8192
http://www.dickblick.com

Lakeshore Learning Materials
2695 E. Dominguez St.
Carson, CA 90749
1-800-428-4414
http://www.lakeshorelearning.com

NASCO
901 Janesville Ave.
Fort Atkinson, WI 53538-0901
1-800-558-9595
http://www.enasco.com

Sax Arts and Crafts
P.O. Box 51710
New Berlin, WI 53151
1-800-558-6696
http://www.saxarts.com

Triarco
14650 28th Ave. No.
Plymouth, MN 55447
1-800-328-3360
http://www.triarcoarts.com

ARTIFACT SOURCES

Art Institute of Chicago
The Museum Shop
Michigan Avenue at Adams St.
Chicago, IL 60603
1-800-621-9337
http://www.artic.edu

Davis Publications
50 Portland St.
Worcester, MA 01608
1-800-533-2847
http://www.davis-art.com

Global Crafts
300 B Flagler Avenue
New Smyrna Beach, Florida 32169
1-866-468-3438
http://www.globalcrafts.org

Oxfam America
P.O. Box 821
Lewiston, ME 04240
http://www.oxfamamerica.org

Save the Children
P.O. Box 166
Peru, IN 46970
1-800-833-3154
http://www.savethechildren.org

Southwest Indian Foundation
P.O. Box 86
Gallup, NM 87302-0001
1-505-863-4037
http://www.southwestindian.com

Ten Thousand Villages
704 Main Street
PO Box 500
Akron, PA 17501-0500
1-887-883-8341
http://www.tenthousandvillages.com/

Unicef
P.O. Box 182233
Chattanooga, TN 37422
1-800-553-1200
http://www.unicef.org

SOURCES OF PRINTS AND POSTERS

All Posters
P.O. Box 60000
San Francisco, CA 94160
888-654-0143
http://www.allposter.com
Online source for reasonably priced posters of all kinds

Art Image Publications
P.O. Box 160
Derby Line, VT 05830
1-800-361-2598
http://www.artimagepublications.com
Online source for fine art prints and kits

Art.com
10700 World Trade Blvd.
Suite 100
Raleigh, NC 27617
800-952-5592
http://www.art.com
Online source of fine art prints

Art Institute of Chicago
The Museum Shop
Michigan Avenue at Adams St.
Chicago, IL 60603
1-800-621-9337
http://www.artic.edu
Prints and postcard reproductions from their collection

Art with Heart
Syracuse Cultural Workers
P.O. Box 6367
Syracuse, NY 13217
1-315-474-1132
Contemporary posters and postcards, many featuring African American and Native American artists

Crizmac
P.O. Box 65928
Tucson, AR 85728-5928
1-800-913-8555
http://www.crizmac.com
Individual and sets of prints, including Take 5, of Native American, Haitian, African, and other art from many times and places

Crystal Productions
1812 Johns Drive
Glenview, IL 60025-6159
1-800-255-8629
http://crystalproductions.com
Take 5 poster sets, DVDs, and art games

Davis Publications
50 Portland St.
Worcester, MA 01608
1-800-533-2847
http://www.davis-art.com
Sets of large, laminated reproductions on many topics, including the arts elements and multicultural art

Dover Publications
31 E. 2nd St.
Mineola, NY 11501
http://store.doverpublications.com
Postcards and inexpensive books that can be cut apart to use as prints: Native American, African, Asian, and Central and South American

Knowledge Unlimited
P.O. Box 52
Madison, WI 53707-0052
1-800-356-2303
http://thekustore.com
Posters featuring Ancient cultures, Native American, African American, women artists, and others

Metropolitan Museum of Art
255 Gracie Station
New York, NY 10028-9998
1-800-468-7386
http://www.metmuseum.org
Print and postcard reproductions of artwork in their collection

Museum of Fine Arts, Boston
P.O. Box 244
Avon, MA 02322-0244
http://www.mfa.org
Prints and postcard reproductions from their collection

Museum of Modern Art
11 W. 53rd St.
New York, NY 10019-5401
1-800-447-6662
http://www.moma.org
Prints and postcards from their collection

Nasco Arts and Crafts
901 Janesville Ave.
Fort Atkinson, WI 53538-0901
1-800-558-9595
http://www.enasco.com
Caraway book series on world art forms, Take 5 and many other print series, and famous artists' postcard sets

National Gallery of Art
2000B South Club Dr.
Landover, MD 20785
http://www.nga.gov
Postcards and medium-size prints of works in their collection

Sax Visual Arts Resources
P.O. Box 51710
New Berlin, WI 53151
1-800-558-6696
http://www.saxarts.com
Print sets reproducing African American, African, and Native American art and more

MUSIC SUPPLIES

Musical instruments are available from:

House of Musical Traditions
7040 Carroll Avenue
Takoma Park MD 20912
301-270-9090
http://www.hmtrad.com/catalog/
Traditional and folk instruments from around the world

Lakeshore Learning
2695 E. Dominguez St.
Carson, CA 90895
800-778-4456
http://www.lakeshorelearning.com
Safe rhythm instruments for infants, toddlers, and preschoolers

MusicKids
1175 Groveland Dr.
Chuoluota, FL 32766
407-446-6818
http://www.musickidsonline.com/
Instruments for infants and toddlers, including chimes and music mats

Production Associates
12 W. Collins Avenue
Orange, CA 92867
714-771-6519
http://www.wesign.com
We Sign music videos in American Sign Language

Two Little Hands Productions
P.O. Box 581037
Salt Lake City UT 84158
801-533-5151
http://www.signingtime.com/
Songs and stories in American Sign Language on video and CD

COMPUTER SUPPLIES AND SOFTWARE

Art Software

The following CD-ROM software is for both Macintosh and Windows platforms. Consult programs for specific computer requirements.

Disney's Magic Artist Deluxe by Disney Interactive MAC/WIN

Kid Pix Deluxe 4 by Broderbund MAC/WIN

Please note: Some of these programs contain coloring-book types of activities. These are not creative art. Use only the free draw sections that allow the child to start with a blank screen and draw lines and shapes.

Suppliers

Educational Resources
1550 Executive Dr.
Elgin, IL 60123
1-800-624-2926
http://www.edresources.com

Smart Kids Software
P.O. Box 590464
Houston, TX 77259
888-881-6001
http://www.smartkidssoftware.com

Input Devices

Adesso Cyber Drawing Tablet with wireless mouse and pen

Bamboo Pen Drawing Tablet by Wamcom

These devices attach to the computer and allow you to draw with a pen on the tablet. They come with Abode Photoshop.

Keyboard Protective Covers

Fellows Custom mail Order Keyguard Cover

Green Onions Universal Keyboard Cover

Safeskins Keyboard Cover

These are widely available at online electronics stores

Appendix D

RECIPES

Modeling Doughs

Cooked play dough

Ingredients:

4 cups flour
1 cup of salt
1 tablespoon cream of tartar
4 cups water
1 tablespoon oil
food coloring (optional)

Directions:

1. Combine the flour, salt, and cream of tartar.
2. Add the water, oil, and food coloring.
3. Cook over medium heat until thick.
4. Remove from heat and knead when cool.
5. Store in sealed plastic bag or airtight container.

Makes 4 cups

Note:

This is a pliant play dough that stays soft for a long time. Add cornmeal, sawdust, coffee grounds, sand, or other grainy items to change the texture.

Uncooked play dough

Ingredients:

4 cups of flour
1 cup salt
4 tablespoons cooking oil
1 and ½ cups water
Food coloring

Directions:

1. Mix together oil and food coloring and pour into water.
2. Mix together flour and salt.
3. Add water, oil, and coloring mixture to flour.
4. Then stir and knead till smooth and flexible.
5. Store in sealed plastic bag or air tight container.

Baking dough

Ingredients:

1 cup flour
½ cup salt
½ cup warm water
food coloring (optional)

Directions:

1. Combine all of the ingredients in a bowl.
2. Mix and then knead until smooth.
3. Add more flour if too sticky, more water if too dry.

Makes 1 cup

Note:

1. This dough does not keep. Use it in one day.
2. Add 1 teaspoon alum as a preservative if you want to use it longer.
3. This dough can be baked at 300°F until hard—approximately 20 to 60 minutes, depending on the thickness of the pieces.

Alum play dough

Ingredients:

2 cups of flour
2 tablespoons alum
1 cup salt
1 cup water
2 tablespoons cooking oil
Food coloring as desired

Recipe

Mix dry ingredients together. Add food coloring, oil, and water. Mix well. Then knead till smooth.

Soda Clay for Beads

Children can make bead shapes from dough made from the following recipe. They must be made a day or two before stringing.

Ingredients:

1 cup baking soda
½ cup cornstarch
⅔ cup warm water
food coloring or tempera paint (optional)

Directions:

1. Mix ingredients and heat until thick as mashed potatoes.
2. Pour on a cool surface, and knead when cool.
3. Add coloring, if desired, during kneading process.
4. Store in plastic bag until ready to use.
5. Shape beads.
6. Use a drinking straw to make holes (holes made with toothpicks are too small for young children to thread).

7. To speed drying, bake 10 minutes at lowest oven setting or 30 seconds in a microwave on medium setting.

Makes 1 cup

(Suggestion: Make several batches in different colors.)

Homemade Pastes

Flour paste: *Recipe*—Add water to flour until it reaches a thick but spreadable consistency.

Advantages: This is a quick and handy recipe. It is easily made from ingredients found in most kitchens in any amount needed. It works very well on most kinds of paper. It is safe and does not stain clothing. The texture is very different from school paste and provides an interesting change for children. This is one of the few pastes that children can make themselves.

Disadvantages: Flour paste cannot be stored and should be used when it is first made. It wrinkles thinner papers and provides a relatively weak bond so it cannot be used with collage objects. It washes off easily when wet but requires soaking and scrubbing if allowed to dry on surfaces.

Cornstarch paste: *Recipe*—Mix one part cornstarch to three parts cold water in a saucepan. Add 2 tablespoons sugar and 1 tablespoon vinegar for each part of cornstarch (¼ cup cornstarch and ¾ cups water will make about half a pint). Stirring constantly, slowly heat the mixture until it clears and thickens. Cool before using. Paste can be stored in the refrigerator several weeks if kept in a tightly sealed container.

Advantages: Cornstarch paste has a very pleasant texture and is not too sticky. It is a safe, almost colorless paste that dries clear and washes out of clothing. It forms a stronger bond than flour paste and can be used for lightweight items, such as fabric, yarn, ribbon, rice, and thin cardboard.

Disadvantages: This is probably one of the better homemade paste recipes in terms of strength, but because it must be cooked, it has to be prepared ahead of time. It is also hard to remove from surfaces when dry, requiring soaking and scrubbing.

Fingerpaint Recipes

Super Quick Recipe: Mix ¼ cup liquid starch with 1 tablespoon food coloring or tempera paint. Store in tightly closed container.

Sweet and Soapy: Heat 3 tablespoons of sugar and ½ cup cornstarch in 2 cups of water. Stir until mixture thickens. Add food coloring and a tablespoon of soap flakes or dish detergent. Put in closed container and let cool.

References

Allen, K. E., & Marotz, L. R. (2009). *Developmental profiles* (6th Ed.). Belmont, CA: Wadsworth.

Amabile, T. (1983). *The social psychology of creativity*. New York: Springer-Verlag.

Amabile, T., Hennessy, B. A., & Grossman, B. S. (1986). Social influences on creativity: Effects of contracted-for reward. *Journal of Personality and Social Psychology, 34,* 92–98.

Amabile, T. & Hennessy, B. A., (2002). The motivation for creativity in children. In A. K. Boggiaro, & T. S. Pittman (Eds.), *Achievement and Motivation* (pp. 54–74). New York: University of Cambridge.

Anvari, S. H., Trainor, L. J., Woodside, J., & Levy, B. A. (2001). Relations among musical skills, phonological processing, and early reading ability in preschool children. *Journal of Experimental Child Psychology, 83,* 111–113.

Arnheim, R. (1969). *Visual thinking.* Berkeley, CA: University of California Press.

Baker, P. M. (2005). The transformation of space into place. In L. Gandini, L. Hill, L. Cadwell, & C. Schwall (Eds.), *In the spirit of the studio: learning from the Atelier of Reggio Emilia* (pp. 107–113). New York: Teachers College Press.

Bandura, A. (1973). *Aggression: A social learning analysis.* Englewood Cliffs, NJ: Prentice-Hall.

Bandura, A. (1989). Social cognitive theory. In R. Vasta (Ed.), *Annals of child development.* Vol. 6. Six theories of child development (pp. 1–60). Greenwich, CT: JAI Press.

Barbe-Gall, F. (2002). *How to talk to children about art.* Chicago, IL: Chicago Review Press.

Bebko, J. M., Burke, L., Craven, J., & Sarlo, N. (1992). The importance of motor activity in sensorimotor development: A perspective from children with physical handicaps. *Human Development, 35,* 226–240.

Benari, N. (1995). *Inner rhythm: Dance training for the deaf.* New York: Taylor & Francis.

Bennett, C. (2010). *The confident creative. Drawing to free hand and mind.* Moray, UK: Findhorn.

Bisson, J. (2002). *Celebrate: An anti-bias guide to enjoying holidays in early childhood programs.* St. Paul, MN: Redleaf.

Boden, M. A. (1990). *The creative mind.* New York: Basic Books.

Boutte, G. S., Van Scoy, I., & Hendley, S. (1996). Multicultural and nonsexist prop boxes. *Young Children, 52*(1), 34–38.

Bower, B. (2002, July 6). The eyes have it. *Science News, 162,* 4.

Bower, B. (2003, May 24). Repeat after me. *Science News, 163,* 330–332.

Bradley, J. (2005). When to twinkle – Are children ever too young? *American Suzuki Journal, 33*(3), 53.

Brehm, M. A., & McNett, L. (2007). *Creative dance for learning.* New York: McGraw-Hill.

Bromley, K. (1998). *Language arts: Exploring connections* (3rd Ed.), Boston, MA: Allyn & Bacon.

Brouillette, L. (2010). How the arts help children to create healthy social scripts: Exploring the perceptions of elementary teachers. *Arts Education Policy Review 111,* 16–24.

Bruner, J. (1979). *On knowing: Essays for the left hand.* Cambridge: Harvard University Press.

Bruner, J. (1990). *Acts of meaning.* Cambridge, MA: Harvard University Press.

Bruner, J. (1996). *The culture of education.* Cambridge, MA: Harvard University Press.

Buck, P. S. (1967). *To my daughters with love.* NY: John Day.

Butzlaff, R. (2000). Can music be used to teach reading? *The Journal of Aesthetic Education, 34*(3), 167–178.

Cadwell, A. (2005). Pedagogical patterns. In L. Gandini, L. Hill, L. Cadwell, & C. Schawall (Eds.) In *The spirit of the studio* (pp. 175–194). New York: Teachers College Press.

Cambourne, B., & Brown, H. (1990). *Read and retell.* Portsmouth, NH: Heinemann.

Caine, R. N., & Caine, G. (1974). *Making connections. Teaching and the human brain.* Alexandria, VA: Association for Supervision and Curriculum Development.

Caine, R. N., Caine, G., McClintik, C. L., & Klimek, K. J. (2004). *12 Brain/Mind learning principles in action for making connections, teaching, and the human brain.* Thousand Oaks, CA: Corwin.

Cameron, J. (1992). *The artist's way: A spiritual path to higher creativity.* New York: G. P. Putnam's Sons.

Carey, J. (Ed.). (2002). *Brain facts* (4th Ed.). Washington, DC: Society for Neuroscience.

Cecil, N. L., & Lauritzen, P. (1995). *Literacy and the arts for the integrated classroom: Alternative ways of knowing.* White Plains, NY: Longman.

Cermak, S. (September 2009). Deprivation and sensory processing in institutionalized and postinstitutionalized children. *Sensory Integration Special Interest Section Quarterly*: American Occupational Therapy Association.

Chalufou, I., & Worth, K. (2004). *Building structures with children*. St. Paul, MN: Redleaf Press.

Chard, S. (1998a). *The project approach: Making the curriculum come alive.* New York: Scholastic.

Chard, S. (1998b). *The project approach: Managing successful projects.* New York: Scholastic.

Charney, R. (1992). *Teaching children to care.* Turners Falls, MA: Northeast Foundation for Children.

Chenfeld, M. B. (2000). *Teaching in the key of life.* Washington, DC: National Association for the Education of Young Children.

Cherry, C. (1990). *Creative art for the developing child.* Carthage, IL: Fearon Teacher Aids.

Cherry, C., Godwin, D., & Staples, J. (1989). *Is the left brain always right? A guide to whole child development.* Belmont, CA: David S. Lake.

Chin, C. (2003). The development of absolute pitch. *Psychology of Music, 31,* 155–171.

Christie, J. F., Enz, B., & Vukelich, C. (2003). *Teaching language and literacy: Preschool through the elementary grades* (2nd Ed.). Boston: Allyn & Bacon.

Church, E. B., & Miller, K. (1990). *Learning through play: Blocks.* New York: Scholastic.

Clayton, M. (2001). *Classroom spaces that work.* Turners Falls, MA: Northeast Foundation for Chidlren.

Cohen, E. P., & Gainer, R. S. (1995). *Art: Another language for learning.* Portsmouth, NH: Heinemann.

Cooper, P. (1993). *When stories come to school. Telling, writing, and performing stories in the early childhood classroom.* New York, NY: Teachers and Writers Collaborative.

Copple, C., & Bredekamp, S.(Eds.). (2009). *Developmentally appropriate practice in early childhood programs serving children from birth through age 8* (3rd ed).Washington, DC: National Association for the Education of Young Children.

Costa-Giomi, E. (1999). The effects of three years of piano instruction on children's cognitive development. *Journal of Research in Music Education, 47*(3), 198–212.

Cox, M.V. (1993). *Children's drawings of the human figure.* Hove, UK: Erlbaum.

Craft, A. (2002). *Creativity and the early years: A lifelong foundation.* New York: Continuum.

Craft, A. (2010). *Creativity and futures.* London: Trentham.

Csikszentmihalyi, M. (1996). *Creativity: Flow and the psychology of discovery and innovation.* New York: HarperCollins.

Csikszentmihalyi, M. (1997). *Finding flow: The psychology of engagement with everyday life.* New York: Basic Books.

Curtis, D., & Carter, M. (2003). *Designs for living and learning.* St. Paul, MN: Redleaf.

d'Amboise, J. (2006). In *Ballet Encyclopedia.* Retrieved December 2010, from http://www.the-ballet.com/damboise.php

Davis, J. H. (2008). *Why our schools need the arts.* New York: Teachers College.

Davis, M. D., Kilgo, J. L., & Gamel-McCormick, M. (1998). *Young children with special needs.* Needham Heights, MA: Allyn & Bacon.

Dedrick, D. (1996). Color language universality and evolution: On the explanation for basic color terms. *Philosophical Psychology, 9*(4), 497–524.

Dennis, W. (1966). Goodenough scores, art experience, and modernization. *Journal of Social Psychology, 68,* 213–215.

Derman-Sparks, L., & the A.B.C. Task Force. (1989). *Anti-bias curriculum: Tools for empowering young children.* Washington, DC: National Association for the Education of Young Children.

Derman-Sparks, L., & Ramsey, P. G. (2006). *What if all the kids are white?: Anti-bias multicultural education with young children and families.* New York: Teachers College Press.

Dewey, J. (1920). *How we think.* Boston: D.C. Heath.

Dewey, J. (1958). *Art as experience.* New York: Capricorn Books. (First published in 1934.)

Di Leo, J. H. (1970). *Young children and their drawings.* New York: Brunner/Mazel.

Di Leo, J. H. (1973). *Children's drawings as diagnostic aids.* New York: Brunner/Mazel.

Dissanayake, E. (1995). *Homo aestheticus: Where art comes from and why.* Seattle, WA: University of Washington Press.

Dodge, D. T. & Colker, L. J. (1995). *The creative curriculum.* Washington DC: Teaching Strategies.

Dodge, D.T., & Phinney, J. (1990). *A parent's guide to early childhood education.* Beltsville, MD: Gryphon.

Edwards, B. (1979). *Drawing on the right side of the brain.* Los Angeles: J. P. Tarcher.

Edwards, C., Gandini, L., & Forman, G. (1993). *The hundred languages of children: The Reggio Emilia approach to early childhood education.* Norwood, NJ: Ablex.

Edwards, L. C. (1990). *Affective development and the creative arts.* New York: Macmillan.

Edwards, L. C. (1993). The creative arts process: What it is and what it is not. *Young Children, 48*(3), 77–81.

Einon, D. (1985). *Play with a purpose.* New York: Pantheon Books.

Eisner, E. (1972). *Educating artistic vision.* New York: Macmillan.

Eisner, E. (1976). *The arts, human development, and education.* Berkeley, CA: McCutchen.

Eisner, E. (1983). *Beyond creating.* Los Angeles: Getty Center for Education in Art.

Eisner, E. (2002). *The arts and the creation of mind.* New Haven, CT: Yale University Press.

Elkind, D. (1974). *Children and adolescents.* New York: Oxford University Press.

Engel, B. S. (1995). *Considering children's art: Why and how to value their works.* Washington, DC: National Association for the Education of Young Children.

Engel, B. S. (1996). Learning to look: Appreciating children's art. *Young Children, 51*(2), 74–79.

Erikson, E. (1963). *Childhood and society.* New York: Norton.

FeinFein, S. (1993). *First drawings: Genesis of visual thinking.* Pleasant Hill, CA: Exelrod Press.

Feldman, E. B. (1970). *Becoming human through art.* Englewood Cliffs, NJ: Prentice Hall.

Fox, K. R. (1999). The influence of physical activity on mental health. *Public Health Nutrition, 2*(3A), 411–418.

Franklin, A., Bevis, L., & Ling, Y. (2010). Biological components of colour preferences in infancy. *Developmental Science, 13*(2), 346–354.

Franklin, A., Drivonikou, G. V., Bevis, L., Davies, I. R. L., Kay, P., & Regier, T. (2008). Categorical perception of color is lateralized to the right hemisphere in infants, but to the left hemisphere in adults. *Proceedings of the National Academy of Sciences, 105*(9), 3221–3225.

Fraser, D. L. (2000). *Danceplay: Creative movement for very young children.* Lincoln, NE: Author's Choice Press.

Friedman, S. (2010). Theater, live music, and dance. *Young Children 65*(2), 36–41.

Frost, J. (2005). Lessons from disasters: Play, work, and the creative arts. *Childhood Education, 82*(1), 2.

Furman, L. (2000). In support of drama in the early childhood education, again. *Early Childhood Education Journal, 27*(30), 173–178.

Gardner, H. (1973). *The arts and human development.* New York: John Wiley & Sons.

Gardner, H. (1983). *Frames of mind.* New York: Basic Books.

Gardner, H. (1991). *The unschooled mind.* New York: Basic Books.

Gardner, H. (1993). *Multiple intelligences: The theory in practice.* New York: Basic Books.

Gelfer, J. (1990). Discovering and learning art through blocks. *Day Care and Early Education, 17*(4), 21–24.

Genishi, C. (1993). Art, portfolios, and assessment, *Early Childhood Today, 8*(2), 67.

Goldman, E. (2004). *How others see us: Body movement and the art of communication.* London: Routledge.

Goetze, M., & Horii, Y. (1989). A comparison of the pitch accuracy of group and individual singing in young children. *Bulletin for the Council for Research in Music Education,* No. 99, 57–73.

Goleman, D. (2006). *Emotional intelligence.* New York: Bantam.

Goleman, D., Kaufman, P., & Ray, M. (1992). *The creative spirit.* New York: Dutton.

Golomb, C. (1981). Representation and reality. *Review of Visual Arts Education, 14,* 36–48.

Gonzalez-Mena, J. (1993). *Multicultural issues in child care.* Mountain View, CA: Mayfield.

Goodenough, F. L. (1926). *Children's drawings as measures of intellectual maturity.* New York: Harcourt Brace Jovanovich.

Graham, G. S., Holt-Hale, S., & Parker, M. (2001). *Children moving: A reflective approach to teaching physical education* (5th Ed.). Mountain View, CA: Mayfield.

Graziano, A. B., Peterson, M., & Shaw, G. L. (1999). Enhanced learning of proportional math through music training and spatial-temporal training. *Neurological Research, 21,* 139–152.

Greenberg, P. (Ed.). (1972). *Art education: Elementary.* Washington, DC: National Art Education Association.

Greenberg, P. (1992). Teaching about Native Americans? Or teaching about people including Native Americans? *Young Child, 47*(6), 27–30.

Greenman, J. (1988). *Caring spaces, learning places: Children's environments that work.* Redmond, WA: Exchange Press.

Gruhn, W. (2002). Phases and stages in early music learning. *Music Education Research, 4*(1), 51–71.

Guilford, J. P. (1977). *Way beyond IQ.* Buffalo, NY: The Creative Education Foundation.

Guilford, J. P. (1986). *Creative talents: Their nature, uses, development.* Buffalo, NY: Bearly.

Hamilton, M., & Weiss, M. (2005). *Children tell stories: Teaching and using storytelling in the classroom.* Katonah, NY: Richard C. Owen.

Harris, D., & Goodenough, F. L. (1963). *Children's drawings as measures of intellectual maturity.* New York: Harcourt, Brace & World.

Hart, B. & Risley, T. R. (1995). *Meaningful differences in the everyday life of young American children.* Baltimore: MD: Paul H. Brookes.

Harvard Health Letter. (2009 November). Using music to tune the heart. *Harvard Health Letter,* 4–5.

Heathcott, A. (2010). Playing with shadows. *Artsedge.* Retrieved December 2010, from http://artsedge.kennedy-center.org/multimedia/series/AEMicrosites/playing-with-shadows.aspx.

Helms, J. H., & Beneke, S. (Eds.). (2003). *The power of projects.* New York: Teachers College Press.

Hening, R. B. (1993). *Creative drama for the classroom teacher.* Englewood Cliffs, NJ: Prentice Hall.

Hetland, L. (2000). Learning to make music enhances spatial reasoning. *The Journal of Aesthetic Education, 34*(3–4), 179–238.

Heward, W. L. (2000). *Exceptional children* (6th Ed.). Upper Saddle River, NJ: Merrill.

Hildebrandt, C. (1998). Creativity in music and early childhood. *Young Children, 53*(9), 68–73.

Hirsch, E. S. (Ed.). (1974). *The block book.* Washington, DC: National Association for the Education of Young Children.

Honig, A. S. (2005). The language of lullabies. *Young Children, 60*(5), 30–36.

Hope, G. (2008). *Thinking and learning through drawing: In primary classrooms.* Thousand Oaks: Sage.

Hymes, J. L. (1989). *Teaching the child under six.* West Greenwich, RI: Consortium Press.

Ilari, B., & Polka, L. (2006). Music cognition in early infancy: Infants' preferences and long term memory for Ravel. *International Journal of Music Education, 24*(1), 7–20.

Ilari, B., Polka, L., & Costa-Giomi, E. (2002). *Babies can un-Ravel complex music.* Paper presented at the 143rd Annual Meeting of the Acoustical Society of America, Pittsburgh, PA.

Jenkins, P. J. (1995). *Nurturing spirituality in children.* Hillsboro, OR: Beyond Words.

Jensen, E. (1998). *Teaching with the brain in mind.* Alexandria, VA: Association for Supervision and Curriculum Development.

Jensen, E. P. (2000). *Music with the brain in mind.* Thousand Oaks, CA: Corwin.

Jensen, E. (2005). *Teaching with the brain in mind.* Alexandria, VA: Association for Supervision and Curriculum Development.

Jensen, E. (2005). *Arts with the brain in mind* (2nd Ed.). Alexandria, VA: Association for Supervision and Curriculum Development.

Jensen, E. (2008). *Enriching the brain.* Hoboken, NJ: Jossey-Bass.

Johnson, G. (1991). *In the palaces of memory: Explorations of thinking.* Albuquerque, NM: University of New Mexico Press.

Jones, E., & Nimmo, J. (1994). *Emergent curriculum.* Washington, DC: National Association for the Education of Young Children.

Juricevic, I. (2010). Translating visual art into tactile art to produce equivalent aesthetic experiences. *Psychology of Aesthetics, Creativity, and the Arts, 3*(1), 23–27.

Kamii, C., & DeVries, K. (1993). *Physical knowledge in preschool education: Implications of Piaget's theory.* New York: Teachers College Press.

Kantner, L. (1989). Beginnings: Children and their art. In S. Hoffman & L. L. Lamme (Eds.), *Learning from the inside out* (pp. 44–51). Wheaton, MD: Association for Childhood Education International.

Kariuki, P., & Honeycut, C. (1998). *An investigation into the effects of music on two emotionally disturbed students' writing motivations and writing skills.* Paper presented at the Annual Conference of the Mid-Atlantic Research Association, New Orleans, LA.

Katz, L. G., & Chard, S. C. (2000). *Engaging children's minds: The project approach.* (2nd Ed.). Norwood, NJ: Ablex.

Kaufman, K. A. (2006). *Inclusive creative movement and dance.* Champaign, IL: Human Kinetics.

Kellogg, R. (1969). *Analyzing children's art.* Palo Alto, CA: National Press Books.

Kellogg, R. (1979). *Children's drawings/children's minds.* New York: Avon Books.

Kelly, L., & Smith, B. S. (1987). A study of infant musical productivity. In J. C. Peery, I. W. Peery, & T. W. Draper (Eds.), *Music and child development* (pp. 35–53). NY: Springer-Verlag.

Kent, T., Murphy, H., & Stanton, R. (2010). Television and video viewing time among children aged 2 years. *Morbidity and Mortality Weekly Report 59*(27): 837–841.

Kindler, A. (Ed.). (1997). *Child development in art.* Reston, VA: National Art Education Association.

Kindler, A., & Darras, B. (1994). Artistic development in context: Emergence and development of pictorial imagery in the early childhood years. *Visual Art Research, 20,* 1–3.

Kirk, E. W. (1998). My favorite day is "story" day. *Young Children, 53*(6), 27–30.

Koff, S. (2000). Toward a definition of dance. *Childhood Education, 77*(1), 27–31.

Kohl, M. F. (1985). *Scribble cookies.* Bellingham, WA: Bright Ring.

Kohl, M. F. (1989). *Mudworks: Creative clay, dough, and modeling experiences.* Bellingham, WA: Bright Ring.

Kohn, A. (2006). Five reasons to stop saying good job. In B. A. Marlow & A. S. Canestrari (Eds.), *Educational psychology in context* (pp. 200–205). Thousand Oaks, CA: Sage.

Kosslyn, S. M., Ganis, G., & Thompson, W. L. (2006). Mental imagery and the brain. In Q. Jing, M. R. Rosenzweig, G. d'Ydewalle, H. Zhang, H. C. Cheng, & K. Zhang (Eds.), *Progress in psychological science around the world, vol. 1: Neurological, cognitive, and developmental issues* (pp. 195–206). New York: Psychology Press.

Krumhansl, C. L. (2002). Music: A link between cognition and emotion. *Current Directions in Psychological Science, 11*(2), 45–50.

Langer, E. J. (1989). *Mindfulness.* Cambridge, MA: Perseus Books.

Lay-Dopyera, M., & Dopyera, J. E. (1992). Strategies for teaching. In C. Seefeldt (Ed.), *The early childhood curriculum* (pp. 16–41). New York: Teacher's College Press.

LeeKeenan, D., & Nimmo, J. (1992). Connections: Using the project approach with 2- and 3-year-olds in a university lab school. In C. Edwards et al. (Eds.), *The hundred languages of children* (pp. 251–267). Norwood, NJ: Ablex.

Levick, M. (1986). *Mommy, daddy, look what I'm saying: What children are telling you through their art.* New York: Evans.

Light, A., & Smith, J. M. (Eds.) (2005). *The aesthetics of everyday life.* New York: Columbia University Press.

Lightfoot, C., Cole, M., & Cole, S. R. (2009). *The development of children.* New York: Worth.

Louv, R. (2008). *Last child in the woods.* Chapel Hill, NC: Algonquin.

Lowenfeld, V., & Brittain, W. L. (1987). *Creative and mental growth.* New York: Macmillan.

Luvmour, J., & Luvmour, S. (1993). *Natural learning rhythms.* Berkeley, CA: Celestial Arts.

Malchiodi, C. A. (2006). *Art therapy sourcebook.* NY: McGraw-Hill.

Mak, B., & Vera, A. (1999). The role of motion in children's categorization of objects. *Cognition, 71*(10), B11–B21.

Mandle, C. L., Jacobs, S. C., Arcari, P. M., et al. (1996). The efficacy of relaxation response interventions with adult patients: a review of the literature. *Journal of Cardiovascular Nursing, 10*(3), 4–26.

Marshall, H. H. (1995). Beyond "I like the way . . ." *Young Children, 50*(2), 25–28.

Mayesky, M., Nueman, D. & Wlodkowski, R. J. (1990). *Creative activities for young children* (4th Ed.). Clifton Park, NY: Thomson Delmar Learning.

Mayesky, M., Neuman, D., & Wlodkowski, R. J. (2002). *Creative activities for young children* (7th Ed.). Clifton Park, NY: Thomson Delmar Learning.

McCormick, L., & Feeney, S. (1995). Modifying and expanding activities for children with handicaps. *Young Children, 50*(4), 10–16.

McFee, J., & Degge, R. M. (1981). *Art, culture, and environment: A catalyst for teaching*. Dubuque, IA: Kendall/Hunt.

MacKinnon, D. W. (1962). The nature and nurture of creative talent. *American Psychologist,* 17, 484–495.

McWinnie, H. J. (1992). Art in early childhood education. In C. Seefeldt (Ed.), *The early childhood curriculum* (pp. 264–285). New York: Teachers College Press.

Merryman, R. (1991). *First impressions: Andrew Wyeth*. New York: Harry N. Abrams.

Mesrobian, J. (1992). Rediscovering the Ninja Turtles' namesakes. *Day Care and Early Education, 20*(1), 18–19.

Michalko, M. (2001). *Cracking creativity: The secrets of creative genius*. Berkeley, CA: Ten Speed Press.

Michalko, M. (2006). *Tinker toys* (2nd Ed.). Berkeley, CA: Ten Speed Press.

Miller, S. A. (1994). *Learning through play: Sand, water, clay, & wood*. New York: Scholastic.

Mitchell, L. C. (2004). Making the MOST of creativity in activities for young children with disabilities. *Young Children, 59*(4), 46–49.

Mithen, S. (2006). *The singing Neanderthals: the origins of music, language, mind, and body.* Cambridge, MA: Harvard University Press.

Montessori, M. (1967). *The absorbent mind*. New York: Holt, Rinehart & Winston.

Nachmanovitch, S. (1990). *Free play*. Los Angeles: Jeremy P. Tarcher.

Nakahara, H., Furuya, S., Obata, S., Masuko, T., & Kinoshita, H. (2009). Emotion-related changes in heart rate and its variability during performance and perception of music. *In The Neurosciences and Music III: Disorders and Plasticity: Annuals of the New York Academy of Sciences 1169*, 359–362.

Nakamura, K. (2009). The significance of Dewey's aesthetics in art education in the age of globalization. *Educational Theory 59*(4), 427–440.

National Association for the Education of Young Children. (2009). *Position statement on developmentally appropriate practice in early childhood programs serving children from birth through age 8*. Retrieved December 2010, from http://www.naeyc.org/files/naeyc/file/positions/PSDAP.pdf.

National Center for Health Statistics (2006). *Health, United States, 2006.* (DHHS Publication No. 2006–1232). Washington, DC: U.S. Government Printing Office.

New, R. S. (1990). Excellent early education: A city in Italy has it. *Young Children, 45*(6), 4–10.

Newcome, Z. (2002). *Head, shoulder, knees, and toes and other action rhymes.* Cambridge, MA: Candlewick.

Newell, F. N., Wallraven, C., & Huber, S. (2004). The role of characteristic motion in object categorization. *Journal of Vision, 4*(2), 118–129.

Noyce, R. M., & Christie, J. F. (1989). *Integrating reading and writing instruction*. New York: Allyn & Bacon.

Olson, J. L. (1992). *Envisioning writing.* Portsmouth, NH: Heinemann.

Ormrod, J. E. (2003). *Educational psychology: Developing learners* (4th Ed.). Upper Saddle River, NJ: Merrill.

Oster, G. D., & Crone, P. G. (2004). *Using drawings in assessment and therapy.* New York: Brunner-Routledge.

Paced, M., & Black, J. (1994). *Authentic assessment of the young child: Celebrating development and learning.* New York: Macmillan.

Paley, V. G. (1992). *You can't say you can't play.* Cambridge, MA: Harvard University Press.

Paley, V. (2004). *Wally's stories*. Cambridge, MA: Harvard University Press.

Pantev, C., Oostenveld, R., Engelien, Ross, B., Roberts, L. E., & Hoke, M. (1998). Increased auditory cortical representation in musicians. *Nature, 394*(6678), 434.

Parsons, M. J. (1987). *How we understand art*. New York: Cambridge University Press.

Parsons, M. J. (1994). Can children do aesthetics? A developmental account. *Journal of Aesthetic Education, 28*(1), 33–45.

Perret, P., & Fox, J. (2006). *The well-tempered mind: Using music to help children listen and learn.* Washington D.C.: Dana.

Piaget, J. (1959). *The child's conception of the world*. (J. Tomlinson & A. Tomlinson, Trans.). Savage, MD: Rowman & Littlefield. (Original work published 1929.)

Piaget, J. (1962). *Play, dreams and imitation in childhood*. New York: Norton. (Original work published 1945.)

Piaget, J. (1967). *Six psychological studies*. (A. Tenzer, Trans.). New York: Random House. (Original work published 1964.)

Pica, R. (2009). *Experiences in movement: Birth to age eight*. Belmont, CA: Wadsworth.

Piirto, J. (2004). *Understanding creativity.* Scottsdale, AZ: Great Potential Press.

Pinker, S. (1997). *How the mind works.* New York: Norton.

Ponick, F. S. (Ed.) (2007). *National standards for arts education*. New York: Rowman & Littlefield.

Putnam, J. W. (1998). *Cooperative learning and strategies for inclusion. Celebrating diversity in the classroom*. Baltimore, MD: Brooks Publishing.

Rauscher, F. H., & Hinton , S.C. (2003). *Type of music training selectively influences perceptual processing*. Proceedings of the European Society for the Cognitive Sciences of Music. Hannover, Germany: Hannover University Press.

Rauscher, F. H., Shaw, G. L., Levine, L. J., Wright, E. L., Dennis, W., & Newcomb, R. L. (1997). Music training causes long-term enhancement of preschool children's spatial-temporal reasoning. *Neurological Research 19*(1), 2–7.

Read, H. (1956). *Education through art*. New York: Pantheon Books.

Redleaf, R. (1983). *Open the door: Let's explore: Neighborhood field trips for young children*. Mt. Rainer, MD: Gryphon.

Ringgenberg, S. (2003). Music as a teaching tool: Creating story songs. *Young Children, 58*(5), 76–79.

Robinson, D. (1996). *World cultures through art activities*. Portsmouth, NH: Teacher Ideas Press.

Rodari, G. (1996). *The grammar of fantasy*. (J. Zipes, Trans.). New York: Teachers & Writers Collaborative. (Original work published 1973.)

Rodriquez, S. (1997). *The special artist's handbook*. Palo Alto, CA: Dale Seymour.

Rogers, C. (1976). Toward a theory of creativity. In A. Rothenberg & C. Hausman (Eds.), *The Creativity Question* (pp. 292–305). Durham, NC: Duke University Press.

Rogers, F. (1982). *Talking with families about creativity*. Pittsburg, PA: Family Communications.

Rowe, G. (1987). *Guiding young artists*. South Melbourne, Australia: Oxford University Press Australia.

Rushall, B. S., & Lippman, L. G. (1997). The role of imagery in physical performance. *International Journal for Sport Psychology, 29*, 57–72.

Sadker, M., & Sadker, D. (1995). *Failing at fairness: How our schools cheat girls*. New York: Touchstone.

Sanders, S. W. (2002). *Active for Life: Developmentally Appropriate Movement Programs for Young Children*. Washington, DC: National Association for the Education of Young Children.

Saracho, O. N., & Spodek, B. (Eds.). (1983). *Understanding the multicultural experience in early childhood education*. Washington, DC: National Association for the Education of Young Children.

Schaefer-Simmern, H. (1950). *The unfolding of artistic ability*. Berkeley: University of California Press.

Schellenberg, E. G., & Trehub, S. E. (1999). Culture-general and culture-specific factors in the discrimination of melodies. *Journal of Experimental Child Psychology, 74*, 107–127.

Schiller, M. (1995). An emergent art curriculum that fosters understanding. *Young Children, 50*(3), 33–38.

Schuman, J. M. (1981). *Art from many hands*. Worcester, MA: Davis.

Schwall, C. (2005). The atelier environment and materials. In L. Gandini, L. Hill, L. Cadwell, & C. Schwall (Eds.), *In the spirit of the studio: learning from the Atelier of Reggio Emilia* (pp. 16–31). New York: Teachers College Press.

Sciarra, D. J., & Dorsey, A. G. (2007). *Developing and administering a child care and education program* (6th Ed.). Clifton Park, NY: Thomson Delmar Learning.

Scripps, L. (2002). An overview of research on music and learning. In R. J. Deasy (Ed.), *Critical links: Learning in the arts and student academic and social development* (pp. 143–147). Washington, DC: Arts Education Partnership.

Seefeldt, C. (Ed.). (1992). *The early childhood curriculum*. New York: Teachers College Press.

Seefeldt, C. (1995). Art—Serious work. *Young Children, 50*(3), 39–45.

Seitz, A. J. (1989, August). *The development of bodily-kinesthetic intelligence in children: Implications for dance artistry*. Paper presented at the American Psychological Association Convention, New Orleans, LA.

Seitz, J. A. (2000). The bodily basis of thought. *New Ideas in Psychology, 18*, 23–40.

Seskin, S. (2008). *Sing my song: A kid's guide to songwriting*. Berkely, CA: Tricycle Press.

Shahin, A., Roberts, L. E., & Trainor, L. J. (2003). *Enhanced auditory envoked potentials in young children enrolled in musical training*. Paper presented at the Brain, Behavior, and Cognitive Society 13th Annual Meeting, McMaster University, Ontario, Canada.

Sheridan, S. R. (2010). *Handmade marks*. West Conshocken, PA: Infinity.

Shore, R., and Strasser, J. (2006). Music for their minds. *Young Children 61*(2), 62–74.

Silver, R. (2002). *Three art assessments*. New York: Brunner-Routledge.

Slavin, R. E. (1995). *Cooperative learning: Theory, research, and practice* (2nd Ed.). Boston: Allyn & Bacon.

Smith, N. R. (1979). How a picture means. *New Directions in Child Development*, (3), 59–72.

Smith, N. Ed. (1998). *Observation drawing with children*. New York: Teachers College.

Schifferstein, H.N.J., and Desmet, P.M.A. (2007). The effects of sensory impairments on product experience and personal well-being. *Ergonomics 50*: 2026–2048.

Sobol, E. S. (2008). *An attitude and approach to teaching music to special learners*. Savage, MD: Rowman & Littlefield.

Solomon, K. (1989). Bringing the outside in: Craftspeople share. *Day Care and Early Education, 16*(4), 26–27.

Sousa, D. A. (2001). *How the brain works* (2nd Ed.). Thousand Oaks, CA: Corwin.

Stacey, S. (2008). *Emergent curriculum in early childhood settings*. St. Paul, MN: Redleaf

Stallings, J. (1975). Implementation and child effects of teaching practices in follow-through classrooms. *Monographs of the Society for Research in Child Development, 40* (Serial No. 163).

Starko, A. J. (1995). *Creativity in the classroom*. White Plains, NY: Longman.

Stellaccio, C. K., & McCarthy, M. (1999). Research in early childhood music and movement education. In C. Seefeldt (Ed.), *The early childhood curriculum: Current findings in theory and practice*. New York: Teachers College Press.

Stone, J. G. (1969). *A guide to discipline*. Washington, DC: National Association for the Education of Young Children.

Stuckey, H. L., & Nobel, J. (2010). The connection between art, healing, and public health: A review of current literature. *Journal of Public Health 100*(20), 254–263.

Sutton-Smith, B. (1998). *The ambiguity of play*. Cambridge, MA: Harvard University Press.

Sylwester, R. (1998). *Student brains, school issues: A collection of articles.* Arlington Heights, IL: Skylight.

Szekely, G. (1991). *Play to art.* Portsmouth, NH: Heinemann.

The Task Force on Children's Learning and the Arts: Birth to Age 8. (1998). *Young Children and the Arts: Birth to Age 8.* Washington, D.C.: Arts Education Partnership.

Thompson, C. M. (1995). Transforming curriculum in the arts. In S. Bredekamp & T. Rosegrant (Eds.), *Reaching potentials: Transforming early childhood curriculum and assessment* (pp. 81–96). Washington, DC: National Association for the Education of Young Children.

Topal, C. W. (1992). *Children and painting.* Worcester, MA: Davis.

Topal, C. W. (1998). *Children, clay, and sculpture*. Worcester, MA: Davis.

Torrance, E. P. (1963). *Education of the creative potential.* Minneapolis: University of Minnesota Press.

Torrance, E. P. (1970). *Encouraging creativity in the classroom.* Dubuque, IA: William C. Brown.

Turner, T. (1990). *Whole language planning.* Transitions: SDE Sourcebook. Peterborough, NH: The Society for Developmental Education.

Tzu, Lao (1963). *Tao Te Ching.* (D. C. Lau, Trans.). New York: Viking Penguin.

Using music to tune the heart. *Harvard Heart Letter 20*(3): 4–5.

Van Ausdale, D., & Feagin, J. (2001). *The first R: How children learn race and racism.* Lanham, MD: Rowman & Littlefield.

Vongpaisal, T., Trehub, S. E., Schellenberg, E. G., & Papsin, B. (2004). Music recognition by children with cochlear implants. *International Congress Series 1273* (pp. 193–196). St, Louis, MO: Elsevier.

Vygotsky, L. (1976). Play and its role in the mental development of the child. In J. Bruner, A. Jolly, & K. Sylvia. (Eds.). *Play: Its role in development and evolution* (pp. 537–554). New York: Basic Books.

Vygotsky, L. S. (1978). *Mind in society*. Cambridge: Harvard University Press.

Wade, N. (2003, September 12). We got rhythm: The mystery of music and evolution. *New York Times Science*, F1, F4.

Wallas, G. (1926). *The art of thought.* New York: Harcourt Brace.

Walter, T. (1942). *Invitation to dance*. New York: Barnes.

Wanerman, T. (2010). Using story drama with preschoolers. *Young Children 65*(2), 20–29.

Webber, D., Corn, D. A., Harrod, E., Shropshire, S., & Norvell, D. (1998). *Travel the globe: Multicultural story times.* Englewood, CO: Libraries Unlimited.

Wein, C. G. (2008). *Emergent curriculum in the primary classroom: Interpreting the Reggio Emilia approach in schools.* New York: Teachers College.

Weinberger, N. M. (2004). Music and the brain. *Scientific American, 292*(2), 89–96.

Whitehead, A. N. (1929). *The aims of education*. New York: Macmillan.

Willard, C. (1972). *Frank Lloyd Wright.* New York: Macmillan.

Williams, R. A., Rockwell, R. E., & Sherwood, E. A. (1987). *Mudpies to magnets*. Mt. Rainer, MD: Gryphon.

Wilson, B., Hurwitz, A., & Wilson, M. (1987). *Teaching drawing from art.* Worcester, MA: Davis.

Winner, E. (1982). *Invented worlds: The psychology of the arts.* Cambridge, MA: Harvard University Press.

Winner, E. (1989). Children's perceptions of aesthetic properties in art. *British Journal of Developmental Psychology, 4,* 149–160.

Winner, E., Blank, P., Massey, C., & Gardner, H. (1983). Children's sensitivity to aesthetic properties in line drawings. In D. R. Rogers & J. A. Sloboda (Eds.), *The acquisition of symbolic skills* (pp. 86–96). London: Plenuum.

Wolf, A. D. (1984). *Mommy, it's a Renoir!* Altoona, PA: Parent Child Press.

Wolf, D. (1979). *Early symbolization*. San Francisco: New Directions for Child Development.

Wolf, D., & Perry, M. D. (1989). From endpoints to repertories. *Journal of Aesthetic Education, 22,* 17–34.

Wolf, J. (1994). Singing with children is a cinch! *Young Children 49*(4), 20–25.

Wolf, J. (2000). Sharing songs with children. *Young Children 55*(2), 28–30.

Wolfe, D. E., & Horn, C. (1993). Use of melodies as structural prompts for learning and retention of sequential verbal information by preschool students. *Journal of Music Therapy, 30*(2), 100–118.

Wolfe, D. E. & Stambaugh, S. (1993). Musical analysis of Sesame Street: Implications for music therapy practice and research. *Journal of Musical Therapy, 30*(4), 224–235.

Woodward, R. J., & Yun, J. (2001). The performance of fundamental gross motor skills by children enrolled in Headstart. *Early Child Development and Care, 169,* 57–67.

Wurm, J. P. (2005). *Working in the Reggio way.* St. Paul, MN: Redleaf.

York, S. (2005). *Roots & wings: Affirming culture in early childhood programs.* Englewood Cliffs, NJ: Prentice-Hall.

Glossary

A

abstract In art, a work that emphasizes formal elements over subject matter.

Abstract Expressionism Artistic style in which art has no recognizable subject and focuses on color and media, often applied in a kinesthetic way.

Abstraction Art that is based on real images but uses them as design elements.

acrylic A painting made from acrylic polymer paints.

acrylic paint A synthetic, resin-based paint that dries quickly and permanently. Not suitable for use by young children.

active listening A nonverbal way of responding to a child, which includes waiting, maintaining eye contact, and gesturing in response.

actual developmental level Skills or behaviors a child can do independently.

aesthetic Special characteristics that attract one's attention.

aesthetics The study and appreciation of the idea of beauty.

American Sign Language A system of hand, body, and facial gestures used by the deaf community in the United States. Similar systems exist in other countries as well.

anecdotal records Recorded detailed and objective descriptions of a child's behavior. Also known as *anecdotal notes*.

anti-bias Actively address discriminatory behavior and actions.

appliqué A design made by attaching pieces of cloth to a fabric background.

arch A curved structure supporting the weight of part of a building.

aria A song for a solo voice, usually found in an opera.

art A creative work, most often used to refer to visual art works.

art elements The basic visual components of artworks—line, shape, color, form, texture, value, and space.

art form One of the arts, such as dance, drama, music, or visual art.

art therapy The use of visual art to help children and adults express their feelings as they work through problems.

artifact A handmade, three-dimensional cultural art form.

the arts Expressing ideas and feelings in an expressive way through music, dance, drama, and visual art.

arts elements The basic components of an art form that are found in the particular creative work. In the visual arts these are line, shape, color, pattern, form, texture, and space. In music these are rhythm, pitch, dynamics, melody, harmony, timbre, and form. In creative dance these are space, effort, direction, and connection. In drama these are setting, characterization, language, movement, communication, and narrative.

auditory discrimination The ability to tell the difference between different sounds and notes.

auditory perception Being sensitive to the aesthetic qualities of sounds and music.

B

baker's dough A modeling compound made from flour, water, and salt, which can be baked in a household oven.

ballet A theatrical art form using dancing, music, and scenery to convey a story, theme, or atmosphere.

basket A container woven from twigs, reeds, or another sturdy fiber.

beam A long, straight piece of solid material, such as wood or metal, that supports the weight of some of the building.

bisque Unglazed clay that has been fired in a kiln.

bodily-kinesthetic intelligence In Howard Gardner's theory of multiple intelligences, the ability to use the body to solve problems or to make things.

bogus drawing paper A heavyweight (80 lb.) gray paper with a rough-textured surface that provides contrast to the smoothness of most other paper.

break A section of a song in which only instruments play.

bridge An optional part of a song, usually at the end, that harmonically joins two different sections.

C

calligrapher A person who writes beautiful lettering.

calligraphy The art of writing beautifully.

cannon A musical form in which a tune is repeated at regular intervals, like a round.

cantata A vocal work that can be religious or secular.

carding Brushing wool fibers to straighten them.

cellophane A thin, transparent film.

checklist An assessment method in which observed behaviors are recorded by checking predetermined categories.

chenille stems Fiber-covered wires, also called *pipe cleaners*.

choral A work performed by a chorus or group of singers.

chord Three of more notes played together at the same time.

chorus A melody line or group of lines that repeats at the end of every verse, emphasizing the theme of the song.

cityscape A representation of a city.

classroom The inside area of a location used by the children.

clay Any soft modeling compound, but especially that formed from earth.

clicking In computer use, pressing the button on the mouse to select an item on the screen.

cognitive development Growth in the ability to think logically.

coil A long rope of clay made by rolling it on a flat surface with the palms moving outward.

collage A picture containing glued-on objects or paper.

color The surface quality of an object or substance as revealed by the light that reflects off of it and is seen as a hue in the spectrum.

color-blind Being unable to distinguish some of the visible wavelengths of light.

column An upright support in a building.

compose Create an original piece of music or adapt a familiar piece.

composer A person who writes original pieces of music.

composition The arrangement of arts elements into a whole.

computer monitor A piece of electrical equipment that displays viewable images generated by a computer.

concerto A musical piece written for one instrument accompanied by an orchestra.

concrete operational The stage of cognitive development at which, according to Piagetian theory, children begin to think logically about events that they observe. This usually occurs at around the age of seven.

conformity Pressure to be the same as everyone else.

cognitive Pertaining to intellectual reasoning based on the use of judgment, logic, and memory.

connection In creative movement the way we use our bodies in relationship to all parts of our body, other objects, and the people around us.

construction paper A medium-weight paper that comes in a wide variety of colors.

contrast An unlikeness in quality.

cooperative play When children interact and communicate in meaningful ways during an activity.

copper enameling A process in which copper pieces are covered with melted glass. It is not a safe activity for young children.

craft Any art form that produces a usable product, such as a fabric, container, or puppet. Often based on traditional techniques, such as basket weaving, embroidery, glassmaking, quilting, pottery, tinwork, and weaving.

creative dance Creative expression based on the movement and positioning of the body in space in which participants can move in their own inventive ways to the music.

creative movement Movement activities in which each participant can respond in a multitude of ways.

creative process A combination of mental processes that will lead to the final creative product or action.

creativity Solving problems or expressing ideas and feelings in unique ways.

Cubism Artistic style in which art represents three-dimensional objects as if they were made of geometric shapes and forms.

cultural aesthetic When a group of people shares similar ideas and judgments about beauty.

cursor A blinking line or shape that indicates where the first mark will appear on a computer screen.

D

dance To move feet and body in a rhythmic pattern. Creative dance is the process of adding one's own unique interpretation to the movement.

descriptive statement A sentence that gives specific details about what is being discussed.

dictation The act of writing down a child's words or stories.

disposition The attitude or state of mind we have toward a particular behavior.

documentation Materials collected to show the process of creating an artwork or participating in an activity.

documentation panels A display of materials that share the process of arts creation with the public. Also called *presentation panels*.

drama Creative expression of ideas and feelings through voice, action, and body, such as pantomime, play-acting, and storytelling; a work of art that communicates an idea or story through language and action.

drama therapy The use of the dramatic arts to help people deal with emotional and physical stress.

dramatic play The acting out of roles and behaviors by children.

dramatics The act of participating in a creative work that communicates an idea or story through language and action.

drawing A picture made from any linear art material: pencil, marker, charcoal, ink, chalk, and so on.

duet A piece of music written for two instruments or singers.

dye Any substance that changes the color of a material.

dynamics Changes in volume from loud to soft or soft to loud and the accenting of certain tones.

E

effort How much time, force, and speed we use as we move our bodies.

elaboration The ability to improve ideas by adding on or expanding them.

embroidery A design made with thread on cloth.

emergent curriculum An open-ended curriculum design in which children's interests provide the springboard for the selection of topics and activities to be taught.

environment Everything that surrounds us—the setting. The physical environment usually refers to the classroom spaces and/or exterior spaces, and the way they are furnished.

ethnic folk art Artistic works reflecting a particular culture or heritage created by anonymous artists.

experience chart A written account of what children say about an event or experience they have had.

exploration Discovering how to use new materials and techniques.

Expressionism An artistic style focused on showing emotions.

extrinsic motivation Giving rewards and prizes.

F

fabric dye Any substance that permanently colors cloth. Not all dyes are safe for children to use.

fantasy The creation of imaginary worlds. It is where the mental images of the imagination are brought to life through story.

fiber A fine, threadlike material.

fiber art Art forms, such as weaving, appliqué, and embroidery, that use fibers or materials created from fiber.

fingerpaint A kind of paint intended to be applied with the fingers.

finger play A little story acted out with fingers.

firing Slowly heating clay in an insulated oven called a *kiln*.

firing clay A modeling compound formed from earth that dries out in the air and becomes hard when fired in a kiln.

fixative Any substance that affixes chalk permanently to paper. Fixatives are not safe to use around children.

flexibility Being able to see things from alternative viewpoints.

fluency Being able to generate a multitude of diverse ideas or solutions.

folk art Artworks created by people who have not had formal training in art, or who use nontraditional art media in ways that reflect their culture.

form The whole of a work of art; also, the three-dimensional equivalent of shape that has the qualities of mass and volume, or the structure that organizes the elements of music.

free-form An irregular shape.

fresco A painting made in wet plaster.

Fresnel lenses Thin-grooved lenses, available in large plastic formats, that magnify.

fugue Similar to a cannon, but has intervals of repeated passages and then free-form passages.

G

genre A type of music (e.g., gospel, jazz, lullaby, opera, rock and roll, and sonata).

geometric A shape that conforms to mathematical principles.

glaze A finely ground mixture of minerals that when fired at a high temperature forms a glassy coating on clay.

goal A statement of the kind of growth in a child's behavior that would be expected over a period of time and after many explorations.

Goodenough-Harris Draw-A-Person Test A test in which children's cognitive developmental levels are assessed by asking them to draw a person.

graphic Something that is pictorial or written.

greenware Clay that has air-dried.

Gregorian chant Voices in unison with no regular beat.

guided discovery A process in which a new activity or center is introduced in the context of establishing guidelines for safe, logical use.

guided imagery Creating sensory pictures in the mind based on prompts or stories provided by a leader.

guiding adult The person who selects and prepares the supplies, maps out the possible routes, and provides encouragement along the way.

H

hand spun Yarn that has been made by hand.

hand wedging Kneading clay to bend it and remove pockets of air.

hand-woven Cloth that has been created on a loom.

hardware Computer equipment, including a monitor, mouse, keyboard, system board, and hard drive.

harmony A sequence of tones that enrich a melody.

hue Color, such as red or yellow.

I

illustrator A person who makes pictures to go with a story in a book.

imagination Mental images, which are ideas of things that can be manipulated in the mind. These images can be visual, auditory, and sensory.

immersion Being intensely focused on creating something unique.

imposing statements Statement in which the viewer describes their feelings about a work or performance as if they were the same as the artist's.

Impressionism A style of art concerned with capturing the effect of light.

improvisation Inventing a dramatic action in immediate response to a cue or scenario; music created spontaneously as it is played.

incubation A period of time in which individuals think and process what they know and what they wish to do.

Individualized Education Plan (IEP) A document that details how a child with special needs will be taught and what special adjustments will be made so that child will be successful and make educational progress.

Individuals with Disabilities Act A U.S. federal law, updated in 2004, that guarantees children with special needs a free public education tailored to their needs and delivered in the least restrictive environment.

infant A child from birth to 18 months in age.

informal dramatic play Spontaneous, child-initiated play.

input device A hardware device that transforms and sends information to the computer.

integrated learning units A planned group of activities that are interconnected by a shared meaningful question.

intelligences (multiple intelligences theory) A conception of human cognition, proposed by Howard Gardner, that recognizes seven different realms of intellectual capability within each individual: linguistic, logical-mathematical, spatial, musical, bodily-kinesthetic, interpersonal, and intrapersonal.

intensity The brightness or dullness of a color.

interior In art, a representation of the inside of a building.

interpersonal intelligence In Howard Gardner's theory of multiple intelligences, the ability to understand and work with others.

intrapersonal intelligence In Howard Gardner's theory of multiple intelligences, the ability to understand oneself.

intrinsic motivation A natural curiosity and desire to explore.

J

jam session When two musicians improvise together.

joystick A handheld device with a stick that can be moved in different directions to control the movement of the cursor on a computer screen.

judgmental statements Comparison of a work or performance to another work or a standard.

K

key The tone or chord that is the focal point or center of a musical piece. It is often the notes on which the piece ends.

keyboard A set of typewriter-like keys that enable users to enter data into a computer.

kiln An oven made from firebrick in which clay can be fired to temperatures over 1000 °F.

kindergartener A child between the ages of five and six.

kinesthetic awareness The system of sensors found in our muscles, joints, and tendons, which provides information on posture, equilibrium, and the effort required for a motion to occur.

kinesthetic memory That part of mental processing which allows us to remember how to move in specific ways.

kinesthetic thinking The ability of the brain to order movement through motor logic.

kinetic art Art that moves or has moving parts.

knowledge The concepts, vocabulary, and understandings that individuals already know about what they are exploring.

Kraft paper Medium-weight brown paper similar to grocery bags, often sold in rolls. Sturdy enough for drawing and other arts activities.

L

landscape A representation of the outdoors.

leather hard Clay that is still damp but no longer flexible.

line A continuous stroke made with a moving tool. A boundary between or around shapes.

linguistic intelligence In Howard Gardner's theory of multiple intelligences, the ability to manipulate the symbols of language.

logical-mathematical intelligence In Howard Gardner's theory of multiple intelligences, the ability to manipulate numerical patterns and concepts.

loom A frame or machine on which yarn is stretched for weaving cloth.

low-fire Firing a kiln to a temperature no higher than 1500 °F.

lyrics The words of a song.

M

mandala A circular design with radiating straight lines.

manila paper A medium-weight, inexpensive, and durable paper in a pale golden beige with a slight texture.

march Music with a strong beat designed for marching.

mazurka A Polish dance in triple time.

medium Any art material. Plural: media.

medley A group of tunes played together.

melody A sequence of tones that changes or repeats.

mental imagery The ability to produce and act upon sensory images in one's mind.

menu A list of choices available in a computer program, from which the user can select options using the mouse or keyboard.

metronome A device that produces a regular beat that can be changed.

mixed media A piece of sculpture made from a combination of materials, such as paint, paper, wire, and fabric.

mobile Three-dimensional art that moves.

modeling Showing how to use a material or tool or perform a technique.

molas Textile art form worn on clothing.

monoprint A printing method that produces only one copy of the original.

mood The way a particular combination of music elements affects the listener.

mosaic A picture made from small pieces, such as stones, seeds, or paper bits.

motivation The inner drive to accomplish something.

mouse A handheld device, that when rolled in different directions along a surface, controls the movement of the cursor on the screen.

mouse pad A soft, foam pad on which a mouse is moved.

movement The positioning and changing stance of the body in space.

multicultural art Art relating to, reflecting, or adapted to diverse cultures.

mural A large piece of artwork, usually hung or painted on a wall. Also, a very large, two-dimensional piece of artwork created by a group of children.

music Organized sound.

music therapist A trained individual who uses music to help people deal with emotional difficulties.

musical intelligence In Howard Gardner's theory of multiple intelligences, the ability to manipulate rhythm and sound.

N

narrative drama Play or performances based on children's own stories or stories they have heard or read.

narrative play Dramatic activities based on stories. Also called *story play*.

natural dye A dye obtained from plant materials, such as flowers, leaves, or bark.

naturalistic-environmental intelligence In Howard Gardner's theory of multiple intelligences, the ability to sense and make use of the characteristics of the natural world.

newsprint A lightweight, inexpensive, slightly gray paper.

nonhardening clay Modeling compounds that never harden but stay soft and pliable.

nonobjective Art based on geometric and organic shapes and forms.

non-Western art Creative works produced by people living in Asia, Africa, and Australia.

normative development The level of skills and behaviors a child might be expected to have at a given age.

notation Writing down music using some kind of a symbol system. Staff notation in which notes are indicated on a five-line staff is the most common system used today.

note A single sound or tone.

O

objective A statement describing a behavior that can be accomplished within the time frame of the activity.

observation Taking particular care in watching something.

octave A musical interval of eight notes, such as C to C or D to D.

oil A painting done with oil-based pigments.

olfactory perception Being sensitive to the aesthetic quality of odors.

Op art Art based on visual illusions and perceptions.

open-ended Activities that have no right answer and a multitude of possible results and ways of getting there.

opera A play in which the actors sing accompanied by an orchestra.

orchestra A large group of musicians, grouped by instrument, and playing parts together.

organized play Games and sports in which there are set rules for everyone to follow.

originality Being able to think of ideas or solutions that have never been thought of before.

outdoor area A contiguous play area outside the classroom.

P

pantomime Acting out an idea without using words, although it may include sound effects.

papier-mâché A mixture of paper and paste that can be used to cover objects or formed into shapes and allowed to become dry and hard.

parallel play A form of interaction in very young children in which two children sit side by side and do similar things, but do not communicate or interact directly.

paraphrase To restate what has been said.

pastel A drawing made with chalk composed of ground pigments.

pattern A repeated, recognizable combination of art elements.

percussion The beating or striking of a musical instrument.

pitch How high or low a sound is.

Pointillism A painting style in which the painter uses small dots of different colors.

polka A lively originally Bohemian dance.

Pop art Art that is based on images from everyday life and popular culture.

portfolio A collection of the child's work and related materials made over a period.

portrait A representation of the outer and inner characteristics of a being.

positive feedback A praise statement that includes a description that gives specific reference to what was done.

post and lintel Two upright supports (posts) that hold up a horizontal piece of solid material (lintel), such as wood, stone, or metal, to create an opening such as a door or window.

potential developmental level Skills or behaviors a child can do with assistance.

potter A person who works with natural clay.

pottery clay Fired clay.

practice Developing control through repeated use of a material or technique.

practice play A level of play in which infants explore and interact with objects using repeated actions.

prekindergardener A child between the ages of 4 and 5. This classification is often used for children who have birthdays at or around the cut-off point for entrance into kindergarten. They may also be considered preschoolers.

preoperational According to Piagetian theory, the period during which children are focused on learning language and using symbols in imaginative ways, but cannot mentally manipulate information in concrete logical ways. They cannot yet imagine someone else's point of view. It occurs between the ages of 2 and 6.

preschooler A child between the ages of 3 and 5.

presentation panel A display of materials that shows the process of creating works of art.

prevention A form of behavior control in which misbehaviors are anticipated and activities, materials, and settings are adjusted to make the behavior less likely to occur.

primary age Children between the ages of 6 and 8 who are in first and second grade or its equivalent.

primary colors The three basic colors from which all other colors are derived, and which cannot be mixed from the other colors. In painting, these are red, yellow, and blue. In colored light, they are magenta, cyan, and yellow.

print A picture made using any technique that produces multiple copies, including woodcut, serigraph (silk screen), etching, and lithography.

printer A machine that produces a paper copy of what is visible on the screen.

production The tangible expression or product that is the end result of the creative process.

project approach An emergent curriculum design in which children pursue research on a topic of interest to them.

prop Anything used to assist with or enhance a dramatic performance.

Q

quartet A musical work designed to be played by four instruments.

quilt A fabric design created by piecing together smaller bits of fabric.

quilter A person who makes quilts.

quintet A musical work designed to be played by five instruments.

R

raga A musical form based on the classical melodies of India.

Realism An artistic style that focuses on representing what our eyes see.

recital A performance by one musician, who may or may not be accompanied.

redirection A form of behavior control in which the guidelines or rules are restated.

refrain In a song, two lines repeated between each verse.

removal A form of behavior control in which a child who is misbehaving is removed from the setting.

representation Communicating ideas and feelings through the arts.

responding Actively engaging with others.

responsive Able to express ideas and feelings using a particular arts material or technique.

rhapsody A free-form musical work that feels like it is spontaneous in design.

rhythm Time-based pattern that orders sound.

riff A repeating melody or refrain in jazz and contemporary pop music.

Romanticism An artistic style concerned with making things look more beautiful than they are.

S

scaffold To restate what was said while adding more description or vocabulary that is more complex.

scenario An outline or synopsis of a play.

score The complete work of music in written form.

scraffito Using a stick or pointed tool to scratch designs into the surface of clay.

sculpture A three-dimensional artwork. Sculpture can be made from a limitless variety of materials, including wood, stone, clay, metal, found objects, papier-mâché, fabric, plaster, wax, and resins.

seascape A representation of the sea.

secondary colors The colors created by mixing two of the primary colors.

senses There are five senses: auditory or hearing, visual or seeing, olfactory or sense of smell, taste, and tactile or touch.

sensorimotor level of development Based on Piagetian theory, this is the stage when children depend on their senses and actions in order to understand their world. It usually occurs from infancy to age 2.

sensory awareness To notice the characteristics of objects and environments using all of one's senses.

sensory images Images that may involve one or more of the senses, such as visual, auditory, tactile, and olfactory.

sensory integration The ability to combine information from all the senses into a meaningful whole.

sensory integration dysfunction (SID) The inability to make meaning from information acquired by the senses.

sensory mode Processing information using one or more of the senses.

shade A color darkened by the addition of black.

shape A two-dimensional area or image that has defined edges or borders.

skill The development of expertise in using tools and materials or in carrying out an action.

slab A flat piece of clay made by either pressing with the palms or using a rolling pin.

slip Liquid clay made by combining clay with water to form a thick, custard-like substance. It is used to join clay pieces.

software Computer programs, stored on disks, that enable a computer to perform tasks.

solitary play A form of activity in which a child entertains herself or himself independent of others.

solo A performance by one individual or instrument.

sonata A musical form composed for two instruments and having three or four movements played at different tempos.

space An open or empty area in an artwork.

spatial intelligence In Howard Gardner's theory of multiple intelligences, the ability to visualize the configuration of objects in space.

spindle A stick used to twist and hold yarn as it is spun.

spinner A person who turns fiber into yarn.

spinning The process of turning fiber into yarn.

spinning wheel A hand- or foot-powered machine used to turn fiber into yarn.

still life A representation of an arrangement of objects.

stitchery A design made with yarn or cloth.

story cloth Appliquéd and embroidered textile, made by the Hmong people of Southeast Asia, that record traditional folktales and personal life stories.

story play Drama activities that are based on children's own stories or on stories children have read. Also called *narrative play*.

story script A written version of a narrative drama.

storytelling Oral presentation of a traditional or original story.

style A particular way of doing something that is characteristic of an individual or group.

suite A musical work consisting of several shorter pieces.

Surrealism An artistic style concerned with fantasies or dreams.

symbolic play When a child pretends that one object is really something else, such as a large pot used as a helmet.

symmetrical The same on both sides of a dividing line or a mirror image.

symmetry Equilibrium or balance created by placing art elements equally on both sides of a central axis.

symphony A musical piece written for an orchestra. It usually has four parts, with the first part being a sonata.

T

table loom A loom small enough to be used on a table.

tactile defensiveness Having extreme sensitivity to touch.

tactile perception The awareness and appreciation of how things feel to the touch.

tagboard A stiff, smooth, bendable board, also called *poster board* or *oaktag*.

tempera Also known as *poster paint*, a water-based paint that is available in bright, washable colors and goes on smoothly.

tempo The rate of speed of a musical piece or passage.

textile A woven fabric.

texture The tactile or visual surface quality of an object or artwork.

thematic unit A form of integrated curriculum in which learning is focused on a teacher-selected theme.

three-dimensional Having height, width, and depth.

tie-dye A design made by tying parts of a cloth together and then dying the cloth.

timbre The unique quality of a sound that makes it recognizable.

tint A color lightened by the addition of white.

toddler A child between the ages of 18 months and 3 years.

tone The relative lightness or darkness of a color.

two-dimensional Having height and width, but no depth.

U

unconditional praise A general positive statement that conveys no information related to what is being praised. It typically uses words like good, nice, and great.

unglazed Fired clay that has not received a coating of glaze.

V

value The range of lights and darks of colors.

valuing Seeing the importance of a behavior or personal relationship.

verse In a song, groups of two or more lines that have the same melody, but different words.

vertical loom A loom on which the yarns for weaving (warp) are held vertically to the ground.

vestibular sense Keeps track of the motion and position of the head relative to the rest of the body.

visual arts Expression of ideas and feelings through visual and tactile elements.

visual perception The awareness of and appreciation for how things look.

W

weaver A person who weaves cloth.

weaving The process of creating a fabric by interlocking threads and yarns.

weaving frame loom A simple wooden frame on which yarn is wrapped at even intervals to allow the handweaving of cloth.

wedging Kneading and pressing clay to remove air pockets and to create an even texture.

Western art Creative works produced by people living in Europe, Canada, and the United States.

white drawing paper A sturdy paper with a smooth surface.

whorl A weight on the end of a hand spindle.

Y

young artist (child) A child between the ages of 18 months and 8 years.

Z

zone of proximal development The point between where a child needs total adult assistance and where a child can work independently. According to Vygotsky, this is where the best learning takes place.

Index

C

E

S

T